THE COLLECTED WRITINGS OF

W.E.VINE

VOLUME 5

THE COLLECTED WRITINGS OF

W.E.VINE

VOLUME 5

publishers since 1798

THOMAS NELSON PUBLISHERS

Nashville • Atlanta • London • Vancouver

Published in Nashville, Tennessee, by Thomas Nelson, Inc. and distributed in Canada by Nelson/Word, Inc.

Library of Congress Cataloging-in-Publication Data

Vine, W. E. (William Edwy), 1873–1949.
[Selections. 1996]
Collected writings of W. E. Vine.
p. cm.
ISBN 0-7852-1159-4 (5-volume set)
0-7852-1179-9 (Vol. 5)
1. Bible—Criticism, Interpretation, etc. 2. Theology.
I. Title.
BS511.2.V55 1996
220.6—dc20
96–8957
CIP

Printed in the United States of America.
1 2 3 4 5 — 00 99 98 97 96

CONTENTS

MISSIONS AND CHRISTIAN SERVICE

The Divine Plan of Missions

A Guide to Missionary Service

Approved of God

Service

THE SECOND COMING AND THE LAST DAYS

Touching the Coming of the Lord

Witnesses to the Second Advent

The Church and the Tribulation

The Rapture and the Great Tribulation

The Roman Empire in the Light of Prophecy

The Four Women of the Apocalypse

The Sealed Book of the Apocalypse

SPECIAL ISSUES

The Evolution Theory in the Light of Genesis

Spiritism Unmasked

NEW TESTAMENT GREEK GRAMMAR

Course of Self-Help for the Layman

INDICES

Missions and Christian Service

V

V

The Divine Plan of Missions

LIST OF ABBREVIATIONS

The undernoted abbreviations are used in the Notes.

A.V.	Authorized Version
chh.	chapters
ca., circa	about the year
cp.	compare
ct.	contrast
e.g.	for example
Eng.	English
et al.	and other passages
Gk.	Greek
Heb.	Hebrew
i.e.	that is
in orig.	in the original
lit.	literally
LXX.	the Septuagint, a translation of the Old Testament from Hebrew into Greek, made between 250 and 150 B.C.
marg.	margin
MS., MSS.	manuscript(s)
N.T.	New Testament
O.T.	Old Testament
R.V.	Revised Version
vv.	Verses
viz.	namely

|| at the end of a paragraph or note indicates that all the New Testament occurrences of the Greek word under consideration are mentioned in it.

CHAPTER ONE

The Times Determined

The steps taken by God in the carrying out of His plans have been eternally predetermined both as to time and mode of accomplishment. Nothing can change them, nothing can thwart them. His acts are the expressions of His character. His immutability shines out in the actings of His providence. God's designs are as unalterable as His nature; His modes of procedure vary, His plans never change.

Variation in His methods does not indicate inconsistency in His designs. If He is said to repent, that does not argue the nonachievement of His purposes, it simply signifies a necessary alteration of His attitude consequent upon a change in the attitude of His creatures toward Him. Any such alteration on His part is but consistent with, and is an exhibition of, the immutability of His attributes.

With Him the future is as assured as the past. He dwells in an eternal present. Hence, what is yet future is often spoken of in the past tense. This is strikingly illustrated, for instance, in the second Psalm. Nations may rage, peoples imagine a vain thing, kings may set themselves, and rulers take counsel together against the Lord and against His anointed. All is foredoomed to failure. The purposes of Jehovah are sure. He does not even say: "Yet *will* I set My King upon My holy hill of Zion." The predetermined act is as good as accomplished. In the climax of the predictions the language changes from the future tense to the past. He says, "Yet *have* I set My King."

What is thus true of all God's works receives a special testimony in Scripture concerning His redemptive acts, such as the incarnation of His Son as a preliminary step to the atoning sacrifice of the Cross, and again the sending forth of the gospel on its worldwide mission, and eventually the revelation of Christ in glory for the deliverance of Creation from its bondage.

The time of the Incarnation is indicated in various ways, and is signalized as "the fullness of the time," "the consummation of the ages," and "the end of the times." "When the fullness of the time came, God sent forth His Son, born of a woman, born under the Law, that He might redeem them which were under the Law, that we might receive the adoption of sons" (Gal. 4:4, 5). The phrase, "The fullness of the time," suggests that everything which the divine counsels had appointed in the course of the preceding ages had been fulfilled. Step after step had been taken according to God's predetermination, and exactly at the appointed time. The nation into which "the Seed of the woman" should be born, had been formed, developed, trained and preserved. We may trace in the book of Genesis the measures taken by God for the formation of Israel prior to its existence, and from the book of Exodus onward the whole design of the training and preservation of the nation works out in the Old Testament with a continuity of development which impresses the reader with the manifold wisdom of God and the inspiration of His Word. For the Jews the Law had done the work designed for it in shutting up all under sin. The affairs of the gentile world just prior to the birth of Christ give evidence that everything was ripe for that event.

The next phrase, "The consummation of the ages," presents the same fact in another aspect. That is the phrase used by the writer of the epistle to the Hebrews, and mistranslated in the Authorized Version by "the end of the world." "Now once at the consummation of the ages hath He been manifested to put away sin by the sacrifice of Himself" (Heb. 9:26). Here again the birth of Christ is in view, and the great object for which He came to earth. The Cross, for the suffering of which a body was prepared for Him (Heb. 10:5), was the climax of God's dealings with man. All preceding ages had led up to these crowning acts of divine grace. All succeeding ages will look back to them.

Again, "Christ . . . was manifested at the end of the times" (1 Pet. 1:20), i.e. at the close of those ages which had led up to this climax. Cp. Hebrews 1:2, R.V.

The time of the atoning sacrifice itself is similarly spoken of. With the Cross immediately in view the Lord said, "The hour is come, that the Son of man should be glorified" (John 12:23). It was the Father's glory that He had in view when He said, "Now is My soul troubled; and what shall I say? Father, save Me from this hour. But for this cause came I unto this hour." For what cause? Surely that by His death He might glorify the Father. His next words suggest it: "Father, glorify thy Name." At once the Father's answer comes, "I have both glorified it, and will glorify it again" (vv. 27, 28). The beginning of the next chapter speaks of the time as "His hour"; "before the feast of the Passover, Jesus, knowing that His hour was come that He should depart unto the Father, . . . riseth from supper" (13:1–4). Again, on the night of the betrayal, He begins His prayer with the statement, "Father, the hour is come." That was the hour for which He had come into the world, the hour of the consummating act of His obedience to the Father, the hour of the completion of the work the Father had given Him to do.

As with the incarnation and the atonement, so with the work of the gospel. The special time appointed for it is alluded to by Paul in his first epistle to Timothy: "Christ Jesus . . . gave Himself a ransom for all; the testimony to be borne in its own times" (1 Tim. 2:6, R.V.). As the statements concerning the incarnation pointed on to the cross as being the object in view, so this statement of the times appointed for the gospel points back to the cross as the basis of the testimony to be given.

The word rendered "times" might be more suitably translated "seasons." A season suggests that a particular feature characterizes the period indicated. The work of the gospel is that which signalizes the present era. The divine plan of this testimony was succinctly stated by James at the gathering of the apostles and elders in Jerusalem as recorded in Acts 15. God is visiting the Gentiles "to take out of them a people for His Name" (v. 14)—a people, that is, who should own His authority and represent His character.

"A people for His Name" is a description of the Church. The Church is eternally to exhibit, in union with Christ and under His headship, all that the name of the Lord signifies. The gospel, while provisionally universal in its scope, is not universal in its effects, nor is it destined to be so. It is the instrument of God's grace toward men, proclaiming salvation through the death of His Son, but its purpose is the formation of the Church, which will in itself eternally be the exhibition of "the exceeding riches of His grace" (Eph. 2:7). During the present era the Church is being taken out from among the nations, each individual who believes being given "out of the world" to the Son by the Father (John 17:6). At the second coming of Christ the Church will be taken physically out of the world in resurrection life, to its destined heavenly home and sphere, the dead in Christ being raised and the living transfigured (1 Thess. 4:15–17; Phil. 3:20, 21).

This design and scope of the gospel was embodied in the teaching of the Lord prior to His ascension. We behold Him amidst His disciples, His redeeming work accomplished, His heart's affection engaged on behalf of mankind for whom He had given up Himself. "Jesus came to them and spake unto them, saying, All authority hath been given unto Me in heaven and on earth. Go ye therefore, and make disciples of all the nations, baptizing them into the name of the Father and of the Son and of the Holy Ghost: teaching them to observe all things whatsoever I commanded you: and lo, I am with you alway, even unto the end of the age" (Matt. 28:18–20).

But this was not all. They could not go until the appointed time, a time to be marked by God by an act which would usher in the new era of the gospel. The evangel had been provided through the death and resurrection of His Son, the work itself must be carried on by the presence and power of the Spirit. Nothing could be done until He was sent. Before leading the disciples out to the place of the Ascension, the Lord, having opened their mind, that they might understand the Scriptures, said unto them, "Thus it is written, that the Christ should suffer, and rise again from the dead the third day; and that repentance and remission of sins should be preached in His Name unto all the nations, beginning from Jerusalem. Ye are witnesses of these things. And behold I send forth the promise of My Father upon you: but tarry ye in the city, until ye be clothed with power from on high."

The place and character of this mission of the Holy Spirit in the divine plan call for further consideration. Suffice it here to say that the discharge of our responsibilities in the work of the gospel depends, not upon our own efforts, but upon the power of the Spirit of God and our willing obedience in presenting ourselves to Him Who worketh in us "both to will and to work for His good pleasure" (R.V.).

▪ CHAPTER TWO ▪

The Sending of the Holy Spirit

We can discern the wisdom of God in planning that the work of the gospel should be carried on by the operations of the Holy Spirit. It is His office to glorify Christ, in receiving of His and giving it to His followers, that they, in the energy of the Spirit, may fulfill God's will in their ministry. In order for this it was essential that Christ should be exalted to that place which it was His prerogative to occupy, the glory which He had with the Father, "the right hand of the throne of the majesty in the heavens." Only after the exaltation of Christ could the Holy Spirit glorify Him, and, in applying to the hearts of men the effects of the atoning work of the Cross, accomplish that which the divine counsels had planned for this age. During the earthly ministry of the Lord, the Spirit was not given "because Jesus was not yet glorified" (John 7:39).

The Lord Himself made it clear to the disciples that apart from His ascension the Holy Spirit could not be given. They might have wondered why their Master could not stay with them and the "other Comforter" come too, but this could not be, nor would it have made for their highest advantage. "It is expedient for you," He says, "that I go away: for if I go not away, the Comforter will not come unto you, but if I go, I will send Him unto you" (John 16:7). While the coming of the Spirit was necessarily conditional upon the presence of Christ in glory at the Father's right hand, yet even so the Lord would not be absent from them spiritually. The removal of His bodily presence would be followed by His spiritual presence in the hearts of them all. The authority He had exercised in directing their service thus far while among them in the days of His flesh would still, indeed, be operative, but in a manner suited to the new era of worldwide gospel enterprise. His authority would now be exercised from the throne, and by the indwelling Spirit, His power and energy being the portion of each believer. The Spirit of God is the Spirit of Christ, the minister of the promised presence and power of the risen and ascended Lord. The Advent of the Spirit at pentecost was the fulfillment of the Lord's promise, "the promise of the Father which, said He, ye heard from Me" (Acts 1:4). For that reason He is called "the Holy Spirit of promise" (Eph. 1:13).

On the evening of His resurrection day the Lord gave the disciples a sign of the coming fulfillment of His promise. He breathed on them, and said, "Receive ye the Holy Ghost." The Lord's act was apparently a typical impartation of the Spirit, a foreshadowing of the sending of the Spirit at pentecost, and an indication of the gift of spiritual life in accordance with the power of His resurrection. In that power they were to bear testimony to His death and resurrection, and by means of their testimony sins would be remitted for the believer and retained for the rejector.

Only by the personal presence and power of the Holy Spirit could the Lord's will be carried out by His followers. His power, unhindered by human interference, was adequate for the fulfillment of the divine plan. Just as human efforts have attempted to reshape or modify the perfect design of the founder, so has there been either ineffectivity and failure, or the establishment of something opposed to the divine intention and impossible of the Lord's approval here or hereafter.

In sending the Spirit the Father signalized, in the sight of angels and men, the enthronement of His Son at His right hand. He thereby gave proof of the completeness and perfect efficacy of the atoning and redeeming work of the cross of Christ, and of His resurrection and exaltation. He showed, in a way conceivable only to the infinite wisdom of God, that the sacrifice of Calvary and the gift of the Spirit were associated as cause and effect. This is made abundantly clear in the line of teaching running through the latter half of the epistle to the Galatians. For instance, the apostle says, "Christ redeemed us from the curse of the Law, having become a curse for us . . . that we might receive the promise of the Spirit through faith" (Gal. 3:13, 14). Again, "God sent forth His Son . . . that He might redeem them which were under the Law, that we might receive the adoption of sons. And because ye are sons, God sent forth the Spirit of His Son into our hearts" (4:4–6, R.V.).

At the same time, the Holy Spirit was the gift of the Father in response to the prayer of Christ. He had told the disciples that He would "make request of the Father," and "He would give them another Comforter, that He might be with them forever" (John 14:16). Again, Christ would Himself send Him unto them (16:7)—a striking proof of the absolute oneness of the Father and Son in the Godhead, and a confirmation of His statement, "My Father worketh hitherto, and I work." To this, as the act of Christ Himself, Peter bore testimony when to the astonished crowd in Jerusalem at pentecost he said, "Being therefore by the right hand of God exalted, and having received of the Father the promise of the Holy Ghost, He [Jesus] hath poured forth this which ye see and hear" (Acts 2:33).

Pentecost was the birthday of the Church. The Holy Spirit then prospectively formed it into a spiritual unity. The local church established that day in Jerusalem was a miniature of the whole. It was also the first of all local churches. They were to be God's strongholds in a revolted world. In them the headship and authority of the risen Lord were to be acknowledged under the power of the indwelling Spirit. His power would be exercised to offer mercy, on divine terms of infinite grace and love, to the revolted. All who laid rebellion aside and turned in repentance and faith would receive admission into the Church. Entrance otherwise must be refused.

In order for the fulfillment of all that Christ had designed for and through the Church, the work should have been carried out under the unrestricted control of the Spirit. Who would have dared to interfere with the divine arrangements had Christ in visible person taken up residence on earth? The impertinence of tampering with His plan would have been patent. The impertinence is none the less impious in the interference on the part of ecclesiastical authorities with the order and arrangement permanently established by the Holy Spirit, Who, one with the Father and with the Son in the Godhead, was sent forth as the resident agent in the Church in the execution of the plan. The Spirit not only came Himself to operate, but in the Holy Scriptures, penned under His own infallible superintendence, He has presented the Church with its one and only code, an all-sufficient and permanent guide for the fulfillment of the divine will throughout this era. We say all-sufficient and permanent, for the Scriptures constitute "the faith once for all delivered to the saints" (Jude 3, R.V.). To alter the plan there laid down, to modify it either by addition or omission, is to be guilty of impugning the divine sufficiency of the Holy Spirit and to stand convicted of presumptuous impiety. It was incumbent upon all who professed the Christian faith to respect the plainly revealed intentions of the head of the Church, instead of burdening it with doctrines and regulations of human fabrication, after the traditions of men.

With the gift of the Spirit came the means of the endowment of all spiritual gifts for the work of the gospel and all that would be involved in its ministry. When Christ ascended on high, "He led captivity captive, and gave gifts unto men. And He gave some to be apostles, and some evangelists; and some pastors and teachers; for the perfecting of the saints, unto the work of ministering, unto the building up of the body of Christ" (Eph. 4:8–12). All these gifts were to be provided by the immediate operation of the Spirit, "dividing to each one severally according to His will" (1 Cor. 12:11).

All that was needful for the testimony to the world, and for taking out from the Gentiles a people for His name, and so for the formation of the Church, the body of Christ, was thus supplied by the coming of the Spirit. Despite satanic aggression and deception, despite human declension and self-will, the purposes of God will be accomplished by His Spirit without the possibility of frustration or failure. The Church will be seen in its completeness by all created beings in the day of its manifestation with Christ in resurrection glory. Then will the Lord's Prayer, prayed in the presence of the disciples, be seen to have been fully answered,

"Neither pray I for these alone, but for them also which shall believe on Me through their word; that they all may be one; as Thou, Father, art in Me, and I in Thee." Then will be realized the truth of His words of divine love and grace, "The glory which Thou hast given Me I have given unto them; that they may be one, even as We are one; I in them, and Thou in Me, that they may be perfected into one; that the world may know that Thou didst send Me, and lovedst them, even as Thou lovedst Me."

▪ CHAPTER THREE ▪

The Method and Its Permanency

The object of the Lord's commission to His disciples was that all men everywhere should receive the gospel. They were to be His witnesses "both in Jerusalem, and in all Judaea and Samaria, and unto the uttermost part of the earth" (Acts 1:8). The disciples seem to have been slow to apprehend the will of their master. Their tendency to cling to Jerusalem brought into requisition the divine instrument of adversity in order to compel the dissemination of the good tidings.

"The persecution that arose about Stephen" led to the scattering abroad of those who were unduly retaining the precious treasure, the benefits of which they alone could dispense. Even so they failed at first to carry out the terms of the commission. Instead of preaching the gospel to every creature, they that were scattered abroad preached to none save Jews (Acts 11:19). It is true that Philip was instrumental in the conversion of an Ethiopian official, and Peter in that of a Roman officer and his household, but each rendered his service as the outcome of the compelling power of a divine intervention, Philip in response to a command from an angel, Peter by force of a startling vision.

The more general ministry of the gospel to Gentiles began with those members of the dispersed Jerusalem church who were at the same time men of Cyprus and Cyrene (11:20). This took place at Antioch in Syria. Here "they spake unto the Greeks* also, preaching the Lord Jesus" (11:20, R.V.). This general testimony both to Jew and Gentile, given without divine interposition either by angel or vision, met with the Lord's signal approval. "The hand of the Lord was with them." A great number believed and turned to the Lord. The moment these dispersed gospel-bearers from Jerusalem entered into the spirit of the master's commission, the moment, in other words, they burst the bonds of their Jewish exclusiveness and realized that the work of the gospel was not a favored-nation enterprise but God's provision of grace for Jew and Gentile alike, that moment the Lord's loving favor smiled upon their efforts.

But mark how the work began! We might have expected Luke's record to tell of an apostolic mission from Jerusalem to this large city of the north, or of some prearranged visit of an apostle there, and of his preaching to vast crowds of people. How strikingly different are the facts! Here in the capital of an important Roman province, a busy center, in touch with both the Greek-speaking and the Syriac-speaking world, there arrives a band of fugitives, all of them earnest promulgators of the most glorious tidings ever given to men. They could not hire a building. They could not arrange and advertise meetings. Even had these facilities been possible, such methods would probably not have been as effective as these they adopted. They simply *"spake"* to people. The word is suggestive, not of congregational ministry, but of individual dealing, doubtless of house to house visitation, as well as of conversations in public places; and in this most casual and unostentatious way the work began to grow. The growth was rapid. A very large community of disciples—Christians, the townsfolk called them—came into existence.

Here, then, at the very outset of missionary activity, we learn that the work carried on was independent of human authority. No council at Jerusalem controlled the service. No organized society directed it. The Lord Himself exercised His authority and the Holy Spirit manifested His power. Dependence on the suf-

*Not "Grecians," as in A.V., but Gentiles.

ficiency of the exalted head in the glory will ever meet with His responding approval and blessing.

Let us note well this first method of gospel activity among Gentiles as well as Jews. This is the method successfully adopted today by propagandists of the numerous false teachings which, with such unremitting aggressiveness, are being spread abroad. It is, of course, the method necessarily pursued by pioneer missionaries in lands where Christ is not known, or again in those where the truth of Christ has been obscured by a paganized Christianity. Individual conversational testimony is, speaking generally, the only possible means there, at all events in the first period of the work. It should be continued. There is the formation and maintenance of churches to consider, but that may be called the second stage of mission work. The first continues in each locality, coincidental with, and subservient to, the second, where diligent aggressive work proceeds.

Our attention must not be confined, however, to Antioch. The book of the Acts gives other illustrations in this respect. The same kind of testimony was carried on, for instance, by Paul and Barnabas at Antioch in Pisidia after their initial ministry in the synagogue (13:43). At Iconium they tarried a long time "*speaking* boldly in the Lord" (14:3). In Athens Paul "*reasoned*" every day in the market place with them that met with him, not in formal meetings, but, as the word in the original makes clear, by way of conversational discourses with snatch audiences (17:17).

We should note, too, that in the more conventional kind of meeting, in synagogues and other places, the ministry frequently was more by way of a dialogue than that of a set formal address or sermon. In the synagogue at Thessalonica Paul *reasoned* (literally, "dialogued") with the Jews (17:2). So again in Corinth (18:4). In Ephesus for three months he spake boldly, "*reasoning* and *persuading* as to the things concerning the kingdom of God," and subsequently in the same city for two whole years in the school of Tyrannus he *reasoned* daily with the Jews and Gentiles (19:8–10). In Troas, at the meeting for the breaking of bread, he *discoursed** with the believers until midnight and afterwards talked with them until break of day. This method of discourse was probably carried on chiefly by means of question and answer. It is much more effectual than the set address. Difficulties are cleared up and misunderstandings removed which otherwise remain lingering in mystified obscurity.

The apostle's touching farewell to the elders of the church at Ephesus is very illuminating as to his missionary methods, both in the beginnings of his work there and subsequently. "Ye yourselves know," he says, "from the first day I set foot in Asia, after what manner I was with you all the time, serving the Lord with all lowliness of mind, and with tears, and with trials which befell me by the plots of the Jews; how that I shrank not from declaring unto you anything that was profitable, and teaching you publicly and from house to house . . . by the space of three years I ceased not to admonish every one night and day with tears" (20:18–20 and 31). With what earnestness and zeal, with what patient, lowly determination, this passionately devoted man served his Lord! Publicly, and from house to house, he labored. House to house visitation! That is what tells. Here lies a secret of effective gospel effort. It is not a flash-in-the-pan business. Unostentatious, difficult, exacting and laborious, and calling for divinely imparted tact, wisdom and patience, it is the thing that counts. More converts are obtained, more solid church building is done, by this means than by any other.

We surely have yet something to learn from all this. Advocates of religious cults, antagonistic to the Christian faith, albeit loudly claiming adherence to it, are adopting methods intimated for our guidance in the book of Acts. Whether they have learnt their methods directly from it or not, they are proving that in this way lies the path to success. The spiritual adversary knows the most effective means of accomplishing his work, and he frequently does it by the imitation of the divine plans.

Today the house-to-house visitation and conversation method is backed up by a constant and an abundant supply of literature. Let servants of God go from house to house sup-

*So the same word is here rendered in the R.V.

plied with something short and readable setting forth the various truths which are counteractive to error, and much good will be done. Many an assembly has found its beginnings from informal gatherings in private houses to which neighbors and others have been invited to hear the Word of God ministered.

CHAPTER FOUR

The Formation of Churches

In the last chapter we considered the way in which the gospel first came to be preached in a general manner to Gentiles as well as Jews, and how at Antioch the testimony was marked by God's direct approval, and a great number turned unto the Lord. We noted, too, that the mode of operation was not that of a formal mission nor was it organized under the control of the church in Jerusalem, nor even under apostolic authority.

Now Antioch is, in this connection, especially signalized in another way. For, after Jerusalem, this is the first place definitely mentioned as containing a church.* Churches were no doubt formed in other places meanwhile, but Antioch is the first to receive this mention, and the church here has the high honor of becoming the base from which distinctive missionary activity proceeds. Thus did the Lord manifest His pleasure at the first endeavor to communicate the gospel to Gentiles.

The events at Antioch necessarily drew the attention of the church in Jerusalem. What relation would there be between the two? That question will come for more general consideration later. Here we may notice that on receiving the news of the rapid development in the northern town, the church in Jerusalem sent Barnabas thither. For whatever reason the twelve apostles refrained from sending one of their number, the fact remains they did not even give the appearance of bringing the church at Antioch under their authority. The sending of Barnabas certainly has this significance, and at the same time the selection was in accordance with the proof he had given of his spiritual power, zeal and reliability. On his arrival there he saw what Luke describes as "the grace that was of God,"† a phrase which in the original lays stress upon the fact that the effect produced was manifestly the work of God and not of man. The rapid increase in the number of the disciples led him, so far from seeking to establish his personal authority or to enhance his prestige, to go to Tarsus in order to bring Saul to cooperate in the ministry. His experience of Saul in the past (9:26–28) convinced him of his suitability in every way for the growing responsibilities of the work. And now for a whole year "they were gathered together with the church at Antioch."

In this way it is that the community of believers there becomes recognized as a church. This and the subsequent history of the Acts, as well as the early part of the Apocalypse, make clear that in the divine intention those who were by grace saved through faith, though they were thereby incorporated into the one Church, the body of Christ, were not to remain isolated units in their Christian course in this life. The gregarious instinct belongs to man as a divinely created being, and there is a counterpart to this in the spiritual realm. This incorporation of believers into a community in Jerusalem by the operation of the Spirit of God on the day of pentecost was but the initial step in a line of action to be developed throughout this era everywhere where the gospel would be carried.

Sin has ever proved a disruptive element in the natural sphere, whether in the family or the state, an element tending to disintegrate that which God had made associative. Christianity was therefore essentially counteractive against this tendency. Faith was to unite where sin had worked for disunion. That which produced discord must be superseded by that

*In Acts 9:31, the R.V. rightly has, "So the church throughout Judaea and Galilee had peace," that is to say, the Jerusalem church in its scattered condition (compare 8:1 and 11:19), and not a number of churches described as a whole.

†This is the force of the repetition of the definite article in the Greek—"the grace the [i.e., which was] of God."

which creates harmony, a harmony and a union impossible to natural effort. Processes of decomposition were to yield place to the unifying power of the risen and ascended Lord acting through the Spirit. The binding energy would be inward and spiritual, not external and natural. There would be, not only in the whole but in the local as representing the whole, "one body and one Spirit . . . one hope . . . one Lord, one faith, one baptism, one God and Father of all."

That this incorporation of believers into local companies was part of the divine plan was made clear by the Lord Himself in the days of His flesh. Not only did He announce the coming formation of His whole Church, consisting of all believers, and the foundation testimony relating to Himself upon which He would build it (Matt. 16:18), but He indicated also the existence of companies, conditioned by local circumstances, indeed, but gathered together in His name, His presence being in their midst (Matt. 18:17–20).* These communities, or churches, would consist of those who had been "called out" (as the term *ekklesia* signifies) from the world into living spiritual union with Himself, just as Israel, "the church [*ekklesia*] in the wilderness" (Acts 7:38), had been called out of Egypt (Hos. 11:1).

The Church, the body of Christ, is a fixed entity, growing throughout the present age into an invisible but real spiritual unity, to be completed numerically and united actually at the time of the Rapture. Never is it described in Scripture as "the Church on earth." Heaven is its sphere and destiny. Nor again is it described by any partial or local appellation such as would justify the use of phrases like "the Indian church" or "the Chinese church." On the contrary, local churches, albeit in certain respects they each represent the whole, yet vary both in numbers and condition, these being determined largely by their obedience to the Lord in response to the direction and teaching of the Spirit of God, through the Scriptures, and their steadfastness in the faith.

The formation of these churches was, then, an essential part of the Lord's design in the work of the gospel. Their constitution, character, government, and service in relationship to missionary activity are dealt with in later chapters. Here we may note that they were designed to be themselves testimonies for God in the world and to maintain a testimony for His name. For this purpose did God "visit the Gentiles," not for the universal incorporation of all men into the church, but that He might take out from among the nations "a people for His Name" (Acts 15:14). And though that was said with reference to the whole company of the redeemed in the present era, yet it is equally applicable to the local companies constituted into churches.

They were to be seen "as lights [or rather "light-bearers"] in the world, holding forth the word of life" (Phil. 2:15). They were each one to be, in the locality where they were formed, "the house of God, the Church of the living God, the pillar and ground of the truth" (1 Tim. 3:15). Their testimony was to be distinct, definite and constant, its character in these respects being determined solely and permanently by the teaching of Christ and His apostles, as eventually and finally declared in the completed Scriptures. These were to form the guiding principles of all their corporate life and witness. Self-determined arrangements, ecclesiastical accretions or modifications, the establishment of church authority apart from that which is laid down in the New Testament, could only dishonor God, mar the testimony, stultify the divinely appointed position, and meet with the Lord's disfavor and disapproval at the Judgment Seat—all of which is borne out by His judicial pronouncement in favor of the church in Philadelphia, "Thou didst keep My word, and didst not deny My name" (Rev. 3:8).

It is significant that in connection with this commendation the Lord says, "Behold, I have set before thee a door opened," suggestive of an entrance for the gospel and the ministry of the Scriptures, as in Colossians 4:3, "that

*This has been regarded by some as spoken by the Lord with reference to Jewish communities existing at the time when He was engaged in His public ministry. This view is untenable. The Lord had been already predicting to His disciples the circumstances of His death and the character of the path they were subsequently to tread, as well as the formation of the Church (see Matt. 16:18, 19, 21–27), and His teaching in the 18th chapter is to be understood in the light of the instruction He had already given.

God may open unto us a door for the word" (R.V.).

The churches, gathered according to the simple yet profoundly significant plan laid down in the New Testament, were accordingly to be witnesses to the very existence of God, to His revelation in Christ and His redeeming work, to His living headship and lordship at the Father's right hand, to the indwelling presence, prerogatives and power of the Holy Spirit, and to the divine authority of the Word of God. Hence the importance of realizing that the ministry of the gospel is not merely evangelization, not merely the deliverance of men from perdition, but the establishment of local, corporate witness for God everywhere. Hence, too, for each believer, the importance of identification with such churches, or assemblies, as seek to conform to the divinely appointed pattern as revealed in the New Testament, apart from human traditions and deviations therefrom.

CHAPTER FIVE

The Call to the Work

The first gospel testimony at Antioch having received the signal marks of the divine approval in the adding of "much people unto the Lord" and the formation of a large church, a second token of His approbation was to be given in the call of missionaries to go to the regions beyond. "There were in the church that was at Antioch certain prophets and teachers" (Acts 13:1). Probably one or two of those mentioned were among the prophets that had come from Jerusalem (vv. 11, 27). But the Spirit of God had also raised up others to give instructions in the things of the Lord.

Five names are given, the first being that of Barnabas, the last that of Saul. Again, we notice that none of the twelve apostles seem to have been present. Contrary to what might have been expected, the extensive and important missionary service now to be initiated was to be carried on altogether apart from the authority and supervision of the apostles. The work was to be developed under the immediate guidance and direction of the Holy Spirit. To any who would have planned the enterprise according to natural designs and proposals, Jerusalem would have been the appropriate basis of operations, and apostolic jurisdiction would have been called into exercise; but such was not the mind of the Lord.

We are not necessarily to gather from this that the apostles had lost authority. The fact is that, had the missionary work been inaugurated under apostolic control or under a council at Jerusalem, the character of the work would have been permanently altered. The pattern set before us in the Acts and the epistles would have been very different from that which remains for our guidance. The freedom and elasticity of operation, which are conspicuous features of the New Testament plan, would have been circumscribed to a degree prejudicial to the development of the service of the gospel. There would then have been some justification for the establishment of other ecclesiastical organizations with central authority to control the movements and service of missionaries. New Testament history is a witness against this kind of thing.

We may here remark that Scripture history is not a mere narration of facts, it consists essentially of spiritual instruction. The historical records in the Bible can never be dissociated from those parts of it which constitute direct teaching. Both are welded together into one whole. The historical parts, with all their marvelous and significant economy of detail, are not only consistent with that which is purely doctrinal, they serve to illustrate it. This stamps the narratives of the Bible as radically different from secular history. The natural historian states facts and draws his conclusions from them. It is never so in the Scriptures. The teaching does not consist of deductions from the narratives, it is basic to them. We trace, therefore, the narratives of the Acts in relation to missionary work, not merely as so many incidents in an enterprise, but as a revelation of the mind of the Lord as to the principles upon which it is to be carried on. The history provides guidance which, if followed in dependence upon the Holy Spirit, makes for the greatest possible efficiency and for the most rapid and successful spread of the gospel in the world. To supersede the Scriptural pattern in any respect by arrangements of human devising, either depreciates or nullifies the value of the work in the divine estimate.

It was while the prophets and teachers referred to were ministering to the Lord and fasting, that the Holy Ghost said, "Separate Me Barnabas and Saul for the work whereunto I have called them" (Acts 13:2). Possibly the statement "as they ministered to the Lord and fasted" describes what was a constant feature of the service in which they were engaged. Yet there is an indication that the occasion mentioned was one of special exercise of heart, perhaps under the impression of an impending missionary development, it may even be under a divinely imparted desire for an extension of the sphere of gospel activity. During the year in which Barnabas and Saul had been assembling with and teaching the church, the feeling had doubtless been growing that the good tidings must be spread, that the will of the Lord as made known in His great commission must be carried out. There was the heathen world around and beyond, the object of the divine mercy, yet lying in the same benighted condition as had until lately been their lot. This was "a day of good tidings," and they must not hold their peace.

To whatever extent this was realized, the condition of the church was such that the Holy Ghost was pleased to respond thereto, and to show His approval by intervening in a manner which influenced all missionary labor as subsequently recorded in Scripture. Let us not fail to observe this clear intimation, that where a church is in a prosperous spiritual state, seeking devotedly to learn the mind of the Lord and carry out His will, the Spirit of God is ready to act where otherwise His power would be withheld. In a certain region the Lord Jesus Himself "could do no mighty works" because of the unbelief of the people (Matt. 13:5, 8).

It is not improbable that the revelation of the mind of the Spirit, in the command to separate Barnabas and Saul for the work in view, was communicated through the gift of prophecy in the church. The injunction stresses the prerogatives and authority of the Holy Ghost, and indicates His union with the Father and the Son in the triune Godhead. The missionaries were to be separated for Him personally, and for the work to which He had called them. They were to be under His authority and direction. As the Lord had said to His disciples, "Behold I send you forth," so now in the Acts, in regard to the work of the Spirit, we read, "So they being sent forth by the Holy Ghost" (v. 4).

The divine message came to the whole church. That is to say, it was made known to the assembly itself that missionaries were being called to go forth from its midst. Have we not here an intimation that, where an assembly is in true fellowship with the Lord, it may be made aware of what the Spirit of God is doing in this respect, before any mention on the part of the one who is chosen by the Lord for such work, of a conviction as to having received a call to go? It is true that at Antioch the message came by supernatural means, and that therefore the church could not help knowing. Yet the conclusion seems justified. Although the Spirit of God does not now, since the mind of God has been fully made known to us in the completed Scriptures, adopt the same means in conveying a divine communication, yet He is able to give to those who have the spiritual care over a church, powers of discretion to discern what He is doing in the case of one whom He is preparing for missionary service. It is incumbent upon them ever to be on the lookout for indications that the Lord is raising up such gift, just as in the case where there is evidence of the development of pastoral gift. It is not always necessary that one who is so being prepared should be the first to make known any conviction he may have that he has received a call from God. Indeed, we may search the New Testament in vain to find an instance in which that was the case. That does not mean, of course, that the Lord does not act in this way, but the general teaching of the Acts of the apostles in this respect is such as to impress upon assemblies and their overseers the weight of their responsibility in regard to such matters.

This leads us to a consideration of the next detail, namely, that "when they had fasted and prayed and laid their hands on them, they sent them away" (v. 3). There is a difference of judgment as to whether it was the prophets and teachers who fasted and prayed or the church itself. A careful perusal of the passage makes it difficult to regard what was done as other than the act of the whole church. We can scarcely dissociate the church in this respect from those who were in responsibility over it. It was the church which was appointed to set Barnabas and Saul apart, and it would be the church that would dismiss them with fasting and prayer and laying on of hands, even if the last act was performed by the elders as representatives of the whole company.

Accordingly the Holy Spirit made the assembly at Antioch His instrument in the setting apart of these servants of God for their missionary work in other lands. Later on Paul speaks of such as "the messengers [lit., the apostles] of the churches" (2 Cor. 8:23). We may compare his description of Epaphroditus, as the apostle of the church in Philippi (Phil. 2:25).

The realization by the assembly of the solemnity of the event is clear. They gave themselves to fasting and prayer, an example which we need to take to heart when such occasions arise today. The farewell meeting for Barnabas and Saul was a time, not of feasting, but of fasting—not necessarily of total abstinence from food, but a reduction to such a minimum as would be consistent with health, and as would encourage a spirit of humiliation before God, submission to His will, and an earnest response to His leading. The laying on of hands was of course not by way of ordination, for Barnabas and Saul had long before received their divine ordination. Nor did it involve the impartation of any spiritual gift or power, for of all this they were already in possession through the work of the Spirit of God. The act was an outward recognition of the fact of the divine call and an expression of the identification of the church with these laborers in the service which lay before them. Such an act was entirely consistent with the spirit of wholehearted fellowship with the purposes of God.

Much is conveyed, too, in the Word in the original rendered "they sent them away." It rather denotes "they let them go." This suggests that whereas, naturally speaking, they would have preferred that these men of God, whose ministry among them had been so valuable, should remain with them, yet in loyal response to the Spirit's call natural reluctance gave way to willing obedience. The release was wholehearted. In these four acts of the church are indicated respectively, firstly, their exercise of heart toward God; secondly, their dealings with God; thirdly, their recognition of the work of God; fourthly, their submissive obedience to His will; and they are recorded for our instruction concerning what is essential in the sight of God in similar circumstances today, and to impress upon all who have the responsibility of commending others for service in the gospel, their solemn duty in the matter, if the will of God is to be discerned.

To sum up, this narrative of the setting out of missionaries from a local church states three distinct acts of the Holy Spirit: (1) He had called them to the work abroad (v. 2); their going was not the result merely of their desire or impulse; (2) He Himself made it known to the church while they were in a fit spiritual condition to hear His voice (v. 2); (3) the two servants of God were "sent forth by the Holy Ghost" (v. 3).

▪ CHAPTER SIX ▪

Two and Two

Every detail of the Word of God has a significance demanding the earnest consideration of the reader. As regards the narrative of the missionary activity which developed from the church in Antioch, there is something to be learnt from the fact that two servants of God were called by the Holy Spirit to go forth to the regions beyond. The Spirit of God was continuing the method initiated by Christ Himself in the days of His flesh. He sent forth His twelve disciples "by two and two" (Mark 6:7), and later on, when appointing seventy others for similar work, He likewise "sent them two and two before His face into every city and place, whither He Himself was about to come" (Luke 10:1).* So now we read of two, Barnabas and Saul, called to leave their service in the church at Antioch, and to go forth with the Word of Life. It is true that John Mark accompanied them, but he did so as their "attendant" (Acts 13:5). When the two became separated, Barnabas chose Mark and Paul chose Silas. The circumstances which led to this were unhappy, but the continuance of the two-and-two arrangement was ordered of God.

We cannot but be struck with the Lord's wisdom in all this. "Two are better than one; because they have a good reward for their labor. For if they fall, the one will lift up his fellow; but woe to him that is alone when he falleth, and hath not another to lift him up" (Eccl. 4:9, 10). The companionship of two who are under the same divine control, energized by the same Spirit, and inspired by the same motives, is happy indeed.

There is a benefit in the exercise of submitting to another's judgment, and not being in a position where one has it all his own way. The discipline derived from being subject one to another provides an antidote to self-assertiveness; it is a counteractive against the domineering spirit, against "lording it over the charge allotted to us" (1 Pet. 5:3); to such a tendency a missionary laboring alone is especially liable.

Again, where two are working together they are able to render help one to another by way of comfort in sorrow, counsel in perplexity, and sympathetic advice and warning in times of temptation. An ear ready to receive wise counsel may mean deliverance from succumbing to temptation.

It has sometimes been remarked that the case of a married couple carries out the mind of the Lord in this respect. But this can scarcely be said to answer to the teaching of Scripture on the subject. It is true that much of what has been said applies to the circumstances of husband and wife together, but there is much in the joint service of two brethren, or two sisters, that cannot be fulfilled in the case of husband and wife. There are matters, for instance, in connection with church discipline where a missionary, in virtue of his pastoral capacity, has to act apart from the wife, and needs the cooperation of a similarly gifted brother.

We are not suggesting, of course, that single-handed missionary work is always contrary to the mind of the Lord. There are no regulations in Scripture in this respect. Many a servant of God has been called to tread a lonely path for a long period and to prove the entire sufficiency of the presence of the Lord

*There are numerous other instances in Scripture of this association. For example, when sending for the colt for His journey into Jerusalem He sent two of His disciples for the purpose (Mark 11:1). Similarly, it was two who were sent into the city to make arrangements for the Passover Feast (Mark 14:13). Two prophets, Moses and Elijah, were appointed to appear with Christ, in the glory of His transfiguration (Luke 9:30). Two witnesses are to bear testimony in Palestine at the time of the rule of the Beast (Rev. 11:3). These answer to the symbolism of the two olive trees, the two sons of oil, in Zechariah 4:13, 14; cp. Daniel 12:5.

and the power of the Spirit of God. Yet the instances given in the Word of God of the two-and-two arrangement, and the intimations they contain, are sufficient to cause servants of God to weigh the matter carefully before Him, and to seek His mind as to whether they should not be accompanied by a yoke-fellow in their service. This need not necessarily be one of the same nationality, or even race. How much such companionship may involve for the future welfare of the work! For to be constantly in the presence of a man of God is an education in itself, not only for the younger one, who has everything to learn, but for the elder one, too.

There is another side to this subject of joint service, namely, the harmony of mind and action which it is the Holy Spirit's will to maintain. The adversary is ever on the alert to disunite those who are serving together. Against this danger the Spirit of God has set up a warning signpost in the narrative of Acts 15:33–40, in the case of the very first two missionaries who were called to go as yoke-fellows to the regions beyond. The brief record of the separation of Paul and Barnabas and of the trouble that gave rise to it, is written for our admonition.

The apostle's subsequent teaching in 1 Corinthians 3 inculcates a spirit counteractive against the danger referred to. Speaking of another who was associated with him in the service of the gospel he says, we are "God's fellow-workers" (v. 9). Not "laborers together with God" (as in the A.V.), as if they were working in common with Him, but fellow-laborers who belong to Him and are associated together in doing His work. "God's fellow-workers"!—the thought is suggestive of fellowship in the same cause, and in the realization that each belongs to the same Lord. There is no room here for the spirit which says, "This is my work, and that is yours; you must leave me to mine and I will leave you yours." It is true that the Lord assigns to each His work, but the very recollection that this discrimination is His prerogative and His alone, conduces to harmony in service. The recognition that the association with a fellow-worker is the appointment of God, enables us to cherish true fellowship and to banish any tendency either to a lordly or dictatorial spirit on the one hand, or to that of in subjection on the other.

It is helpful to remember the character of the position we are occupying. This the apostle points out in the passage just referred to: "What then is Apollos?" he says, "and what is Paul? Ministers . . . and each as the Lord gave to him" (v. 5, R.V.). Servants! That is the position. Servants finding their one basis of action in devotion and implicit obedience to Him Who has appointed them to His service. As an anonymous writer said years ago, "Alas, either when servants want to make themselves masters, or when those among whom they labor want to make masters of them!"

The apostle goes further still. He says, "Neither is he that planteth anything, neither he that watereth" (v. 7). In other words, they are nothing. God is everything. There can be no contention between those who are nothing, for they have nothing for which to contend. Their only strife is "striving together for the faith of the gospel." There is no room here for pride or self-importance. On the contrary, such are possessed of the spirit of Him Who in His self-imposed humiliation said, "I am a worm and no man." To be nobody in our own estimation is to be somebody in God's. It is that spirit which will bring the highest reward in the day when each one gives to God an account of his service.

How happy, how effective, how sure of the divine blessing, is co-work carried on in the absence of selfish individualism in the spirit of mutual esteem, and in a constant recognition of what is involved in being "God's fellow-workers"! That was the character of the service engaged in by Paul and Timothy. Here was an association of maturity and youth. Such was their companionship and labor that the apostle could say of Timothy, after some eleven years of joint missionary toils, "I have no man like-minded, who will care truly for your state. For they all seek their own, not the things of Jesus Christ. But ye know the proof of him, that, as a child serveth a father, so he served with me in the furtherance of the gospel" (Phil. 2:20–23). The apostle does not even say "as a son." His use of the word "child" bespeaks his deep appreciation of Timothy's humility of spirit. The elder man was ever ready to encourage the younger. The younger on his part did not manifest independence of the elder.

The tranquillity of mind and the added strength derived from unity of heart and purpose, make not only for efficiency, but for comfort in the trials and afflictions inevitable to it. Above all, the labors of those who are truly "fellow-workers unto the Kingdom of God" are radiant with the smile of the Lord's favor. Such learn to be "of the same mind, having the same love, being of one accord, of one mind!"

▪ CHAPTER SEVEN ▪

Human Appeals or the Divine Call?

A striking feature of the mission work which originated from Antioch, as recorded in the Acts of the apostles, is the smallness of its beginnings and the limited character of its development. In view of the Lord's commission to His disciples to go into the whole world and preach the gospel to every creature, the work might, naturally speaking, have been expected to proceed on a much vaster scale than was actually the case. God is never in a hurry. To the human mind His mode of operation frequently seems surprisingly slow, and for this reason His children are sometimes tempted to hasten things forward according to their own consideration of what He might be likely to do. To endeavor to anticipate God is to court disaster. To act without the guidance of the Word of God and the leading of the Spirit, Who always acts in conformity thereto, is to open the way for Satan to take the advantage he ever seeks to obtain. Abraham and Sarah sought to hurry God by bringing about the fulfillment of His promise according to their natural counsels, with resulting trouble, strife and confusion, both in their home life and among their descendants, and with such long-lasting effect that even today the national animosity between Jew and Arab forms one of the most serious political problems in the Near East. God's apparent delays are but the fulfillment of His unfailing purposes. He ever works according to plan. His designs are carried out with such precision that the antagonism of His enemies and even the interference of His would-be followers can never frustrate the accomplishment of His counsels. Nay, He takes up the efforts of His foes to hinder, and uses them to bring about the ends He has in view.

How strange it seems to the natural mind, when considering the appalling spiritual needs of humanity in the first century of this era, that the countries, for instance, of Asia Minor and Greece should be reached with the gospel in such an entirely unassuming and apparently slow manner! A couple of missionaries, acting, indeed, upon the call and under the superintendence of the Holy Spirit, go forth from Antioch, first to Cyprus, and from thence to one or two provinces of Asia Minor. The gospel is preached, Jews and Gentiles are converted, churches are formed in certain centers, and after a comparatively brief period of such service, carried on amidst difficulties, opposition and persecution, consequent upon satanic hostility, Jewish prejudice and Gentile resistance, the laborers return to Antioch "from whence they had been committed to the grace of God." There they tarry "no little time with the disciples" (Acts 14:28). The first battle for the faith having been fought and won in Jerusalem, the missionaries prepare to go forth on another journey.

This time they separate, Barnabas taking Mark to Cyprus, Paul choosing Silas, and going through Syria and Cilicia, confirming the churches (15:41). With a third added to them, the latter two missionaries are led by the Spirit to cross to the continent of Europe. Again we are struck with the small beginnings made and the gradual development. Here is a whole continent lying in darkness, nations hitherto without heralds of the Cross to bear the message of light and life. Here are peoples, until lately possessed of a high degree of civilization, giving eloquent evidences of the fact that natural education and enlightenment, instead of effecting moral and spiritual amelioration, tended the rather to render man more skilled in the practice of vice, with the result of national and civil degradation and despair. Who would not naturally be inclined to think that the churches established in Asia might have been organized to conduct an aggressive evangelistic campaign to meet the urgent need, and reach across into Europe in a combined attack upon the strongholds of satanic power? How entirely different were the means adopted by the Holy Spirit! God's thoughts are not man's thoughts, neither are man's ways His ways! Only one laborer is now called from these churches. There is no addition from those in Syria and Judaea. The call of Timothy was the result of the definite leading of the Spirit of God. Through the gift of prophecy, exercised very probably on the part of the apostle himself while at Lystra, the young man was signalized as one whom the Lord had chosen for missionary work in the regions beyond (see 1 Tim. 1:18, R.V., *margin*). This was but the culmination, in his case, of an early and constant training in the Scriptures, and a godly and devoted life and service which gained the approval and commendation of the elder brethren of the assemblies in the district.

There was no appeal to the churches by the missionaries to send out laborers. There was no humanly arranged effort to meet the tremendous needs of other lands. Everything was done by the Spirit of God. There was an entire absence of sensationalism or human advertisement. The physical instruments were not mighty and attractive to the human view. The treasure was in earthen vessels "that the excellency of the power might be of God and not of man." The Saul's armor method ever appeals to the devisings of the flesh; it is unavailing to meet the spiritual forces of darkness. The divine arrangements are the most unexpected and unlikely to the carnal mind. It is the foolish things, the weak things of the world, that God has chosen, so as to put to shame the wise and the strong, "the base things of the world, and the things that are despised . . . yea, and the things that are not, that He might bring to nought the things that are: that no flesh should glory before God."

In that manner, under the distinct guidance of the Lord, was the gospel sent into Europe. The course of events recorded in Acts 16 bears much the same complexion as that which we have already noticed in the previous narratives. The cases of conversion are remarkable rather for their variety than for their number. At Philippi, however many were comprised in the phrase "the brethren" in verse 40, the number can have been only few compared with the population. A larger number turned to God in Thessalonica, and again in Berea. In Athens there were just one or two cases. Amidst the darkness and degradation of Corinth the grace of God met with a somewhat greater response. The Lord had much people there. Yet in every place Christ's description of His true followers as a "little flock" still applied.

In Greece, as in Asia, churches were formed, and developed under divinely appointed elders. From the southern province of Achaia, Paul, unable to fulfill an earnest longing to return to Thessalonica, writes two letters to the church there, the first of his epistles in the New Testament, save perhaps that to the Galatians. In these, as in all his other epistles, as we have noticed in the Acts, there is an absence of appeal to churches for missionaries to go forth to other lands. This in no way implies that the need did not weigh upon the apostle's heart. The spiritual condition both of Jew and Gentile pressed heavily upon him. He made himself "servant to all that he might gain the more." He became "all things to all men," that he might by all means save some (1 Cor. 9:22). No one could have been more diligent and earnest in his missionary work than this passionate-hearted, whole-souled, deeply devoted man. And in this he is an example to us all.

Nor again is there any suggestion that the churches were not stirred to a sense of their responsibilities relating to the gospel. The church at Thessalonica, doubtless inspired by the example and influence of the apostles, had sounded forth the word of life through the whole country. What was true of them should be true of all. The spread of the gospel is not to be left to a few individual missionaries who are specially called to pioneer work, it is the responsibility of the churches wherever these are formed. Again and again the apostle appealed to the churches which were the outcome of his missionary service, to pray for him and his fellow missionaries, when they had left them for the regions beyond. As those who were in partnership with the blessed enterprise, they were kept informed of what God was doing elsewhere, and they learned to take a definite part in praying for and helping on the work of the missionaries. This is the responsibility, nay, the privilege of us all. But the teaching of the New Testament is against an effort to call for men and women to go forth to the mission field by means of general appeals, accompanied by stirring accounts of the needs of the heathen. There is a danger in so doing.

It is likely to work simply upon the emotions, and to create an impression that the existence of a need constitutes a call to go. The call to go forth is today as much the work of the Holy Spirit in the hearts of those whom He chooses as it was in the first century. It is incumbent upon us to avoid adopting methods which would anticipate His work and be the means of hastening any to other lands under a misconception, or a failure to discern the will of God.

The argument that, because there are large numbers of believers and churches in a certain country or district, while other regions of earth are lying in heathen darkness, Christians in the former should go forth in numbers to meet the needs of the latter, has no Scriptural basis.

How careful we need to be to have the assurance that we are in the current of the Lord's will, and are in fellowship with Him in His counsels, before we make general statements or give statistics by way of stirring up Christians to go forth in the Lord's work!

The whole course of apostolic missionary enterprise confirms the statement in Acts 15:14, that the purpose of God in the present age is "to take out from among the Gentiles a people for His name." This goes far to explain the facts to which we have called attention regarding the character and effects of the work of the gospel as recorded in the New Testament. In the coming day it will be found that not one member of the Church, the body of Christ, will be missing. The course of procedure by which the whole company is being formed lies within the wisdom, counsels and actings of God. The work of raising up missionaries is His and His only. To this end our Lord enjoined upon us to pray the Lord of the harvest "that He may send forth laborers into His harvest."

The consequences of this kind of appeal for fresh workers may be serious indeed. For anyone to engage in missionary work as the result of anything not endorsed by the teaching of the Word of God, is, as has been well said, an intensely grave mistake, "not only for his or her own sake, but for the sake of those whom the Lord has thrust forth, for it involves much hindrance to the work, in hampering other laborers in their service, and ofttimes causing divisions and other difficulties."

▪ CHAPTER EIGHT ▪

Churches and Their Spiritual Guides

While the work of the gospel has for its ultimate object the taking out from the nations the one Church, the body of Christ, there is also an immediate design, which covers the present era, from pentecost till the Rapture; that is, the formation of local churches as the Lord's lamps of witness in the darkness of the world, the light of their testimony being maintained in direct dependence upon Himself, and by the power of the Holy Spirit. These churches, themselves temporary miniature representations of the whole corporate community, are each one the object of His love and care, for each one has been purchased by His blood (Acts 20:28). Each derives its spiritual nourishment from Him, and is sustained by Him, and comes under the exercise of His all-wise discipline (Col. 2:19, and Rev. 2 and 3). His holy presence is in the midst of them. Searching the reins and the hearts of all who constitute them, with eyes from which nothing is hid, He discerns their ways and actions, so as to give to each one hereafter according to his works (Rev. 1:13, 14; 2:23).

The historical records of Scripture, as, for instance, the narratives of missionary enterprise in the Acts, are as much matters of doctrine as the more purely doctrinal parts of the Word of God. Each consists of a revelation of the Lord. History and doctrine are inseparably interwoven in Scripture. They are mutually interpretive. Those who would carry out His will are under obligation to acquaint themselves with all the instructions given, lest their work be one-sided and defective. Just as the Old Testament histories were written for our admonition (1 Cor. 10:11), so the New Testament, alike with the Old, is not only God-breathed, but is written for our instruction so that we may be furnished completely unto every good work (2 Tim. 3:16).

There is another fact of the greatest importance in this connection, namely, that God's plan in regard to any particular subject as given in His Word for our guidance, is complete and final. He gave a perfect and perfectly sufficient revelation of His will when by the Spirit He committed the completed Scriptures to the churches, as a deposit to be guarded and valued by them as their safe and unerring guide through the whole of the present age. They constitute "the faith once for all delivered to the saints" (Jude 3, R.V.). "Once for all," be it noted. That obviously indicates finality. There are many other such indications, one of which we may note here, namely, the character of the apostle Paul's closing instructions to Timothy. Apostolic testimony as a whole was nearing its end, and Paul, now writing his last epistle with its final messages to his younger fellow worker, exhorts him not only to guard the good deposit himself, holding fast to the pattern of sound words which he had heard from the apostle, but also to commit that which he had received to faithful men, in order that they might in their turn teach others (2 Tim. 1:13; 2:12). Here is a fourfold succession in the maintenance of the faith. There is no intimation here, or anywhere else in the Scriptures, that further truth would be revealed after the apostles' days, or that under any changing circumstances of later times some modification of the instructions already given might be required. No! the faith would be final and must be received as such.

Now the divine plan of mission work, as given in the New Testament, whether in narrative or doctrinal form, essentially belongs to the faith, and accordingly the plan was intended to be permanent; it was neither to be tampered with by human device, nor to be modified to meet changing conditions. The plan is always up-to-date. It remains as workable in the twentieth century as in the first, and is as possible in the wilds of heathendom as in the midst of civilized communities. Its power and efficiency are being proved today, and adherence to the plan alone makes for true success in the mission field.

In considering the plan it is necessary to keep before us the whole scope of the instructions found in the later or pastoral epistles as well as in the earlier, and also in the narratives of the Acts. We may not press one part of the teaching at the expense of another, nor can we find anything incongruous or contradictory on comparing one with another. Details in one part are complementary to those of another.

The missionary narratives of the Acts record the continued formation of such local churches as are mentioned above, and their formation and the arrangements regarding them, do not differ from those already existent in Judaea and Syria. The souls of the disciples are confirmed. They are exhorted to continue in the faith amidst the tribulations which they must inevitably experience. Elders are "appointed" for them "in every church" and, matters having thus been arranged for the care of the assemblies, the missionaries commend them to the Lord on Whom they have believed (Acts 14:23, R.V.). Obviously the provision of elders was the immediate work of the Spirit of God. The apostles in appointing them were recognizing His previous ordination; for those whom He had already ordained and spiritually equipped were now to receive the recognition of their assemblies in each case.

On referring to Acts 20, we learn something more regarding those who, as a result of missionary work, were raised up to exercise spiritual care over the churches. At Miletus Paul sends for "the elders of the church" at Ephesus in order to bid farewell to them. He reminds them that the Holy Ghost has made them "bishops" (or overseers) to feed (or rather, to tend, that is to say, to act as shepherds or pastors over) the flock. That they are viewed not only as elders and bishops but also as pastors, is indicated by the fact that the apostle speaks of the church under their care as a flock. They are themselves represented in a threefold capacity. As elders they are men of mature experience in the things of God. As bishops they exercise spiritual oversight over the local church. As pastors they tend the flock. They have no single ecclesiastic over them. They are jointly responsible for the care of the church. This plurality of elders or bishops over each church is in evidence throughout the teaching of the New Testament on the subject.

The church at Philippi was under the care of "bishops" (*marg.*, overseers) when the apostle wrote his epistle to the saints there (Phil. 1:1). Later on Titus was left in Crete, that, setting in order the things that were wanting there, he might "appoint elders in every city" (Titus 1:5). That the elders were bishops is clear from the apostle's explanation as to what kind of man was to be appointed: "if any man is blameless, the husband of one wife, having children that believe, who are not accused of riot or unruly. For the bishop [i.e. one occupying a place among the elders, to whom he has just referred] must be blameless, as God's steward; not self-willed, not soon angry, no brawler, no striker, nor greedy of filthy lucre; but given to hospitality, a lover of good, sober-minded, just, holy, temperate, holding to the faithful word which is according to the teaching, that he may be able both to exhort in the sound doctrine, and to convict the gainsayers." To this corresponds the apostle's words to Timothy concerning the character and qualifications of a bishop, "Faithful is the saying, If a man seeketh the office of a bishop, he desireth a good work. The bishop therefore must be without reproach, the husband of one wife, temperate, sober-minded, orderly, given to hospitality, apt to teach; no brawler, no striker; but gentle, not contentious, no lover of money; one that ruleth well his own house, having his children in subjection with all gravity (but if a man knoweth not how to rule his own house, how shall he take care of the church of God?), not a novice, lest being puffed up he fall into condemnation of the devil. Moreover, he must have good testimony from them that are without; lest he fall into reproach and the snare of the Devil" (1 Tim. 3:1–6).

Such spiritual guides are obviously indicated in 1 Thessalonians 5:12 as acting over the church at Thessalonica, in writing to which Paul says, "But we beseech you, brethren, to know them that labor among you, and are over you in the Lord, and admonish you, and to esteem them exceeding highly in love for their work's sake." There is no record here of apostolic appointment, though it was probably the case. The omission of any reference to it suggests an intimation that the time would come when apostolic authority would no longer be present, and that inasmuch as the Holy Spirit would continue to raise up spiritual guides, they must receive the recognition of the churches as here enjoined. A further instance of the responsibility attaching to those who are divinely appointed to the care of churches is in the injunction given by Peter in his first epistle. He exhorts the elders to tend the flock of God, "exercising the oversight thereof" (1 Pet. 5:1).

In addition, therefore, to the responsibilities of the missionary to see that converts are baptized, and are taught the necessity and significance of assembling themselves together in church capacity, there is that of looking to the Lord for the raising up of elders from among them to exercise oversight and pastoral care over the churches. The missionary will encourage such to fulfill their responsibility in the fear of God and will teach the converts to recognize them and to submit themselves to them as those who have been appointed by the Spirit of God to discharge the functions of eldership.

That the recognition of elders is enjoined as in the passage in 1 Thessalonians 5 shows that the true development and progress of a church according to the Scriptures could not be maintained without them. The raising up of pastoral, spiritual gift from among the members can only be hindered by the permanent existence of a single pastor or "minister."

It is clear that the authority of divinely raised up elders or bishops had its basis, not in human appointment, whether by an ecclesiastical delegate or through an election by the congregation, but in the relation of all to the Lord.

CHAPTER NINE

The Missionary and His Care of Churches

As an introduction to this chapter, it will be well to restate briefly certain points already dealt with.

Firstly, missionary service in other lands as recorded in the New Testament was not a calling upon which anyone ever entered when setting forth. To become "a foreign missionary," as if entering upon a vocation in life, is not countenanced in Scripture. Those who received the call to labor in the regions beyond had for a considerable period been missionaries in their own localities.

Secondly, while missionaries encouraged churches to pray for them and otherwise to cooperate in their service, they never made appeals for fresh workers. The raising up and calling of such was regarded as the prerogative of the Holy Spirit.

Thirdly, a responsibility rested upon missionaries to see to it that elders (otherwise described as bishops or overseers), having been divinely appointed over every church, should receive recognition of such churches, and that their authority should be acknowledged by them.

A perusal of the later epistles shows that the responsibility just mentioned sometimes necessitated a prolonged stay on the part of the missionary in a district where he had been called to labor. Titus, for instance, was left in Crete that he might "set in order the things that were wanting and appoint elders in every city" (Titus 1:5), and evidently his task was even then by no means finished; he could leave to rejoin the apostle only when another laborer, either Artemas or Tychicus, had come to take over the work (3:12). Similarly with Timothy and the work in the province of Asia. He had been left there by Paul to carry on evangelistic and pastoral work in Ephesus, a work involving much difficulty and hardship owing to the conditions prevailing in that church, and indeed in the whole province. "As I exhorted thee," he says, "to tarry at Ephesus, when I was going into Macedonia . . . so do I now" (1 Tim. 1:3, 4, R.V.). This suggests that perhaps Timothy was inclined to move elsewhere, possibly under the pressure both of the needs of other districts and of the difficulties existing in Ephesus itself.

Evidently the growth and development of the work had resulted in increased responsibilities on the part of the missionary. It was needful for him to stay and guide the affairs of the church so that the object of its existence might be achieved, and that its testimony collectively and individually might be maintained. The purpose for which Paul wrote to him was that he might know "how men ought to behave in the house of God, which is the church of the living God, the pillar and ground of the truth" (3:15, R.V.). The apostle's motive in writing was not merely that Timothy might know how to behave himself, but that he might be able to instruct those who comprised the church as to their conduct and the testimony which they were called to give in the world. For the local church, being the house of God, is to be characterized by holiness (Ps. 93:5). The truth, of which each church is the pillar and ground, must be maintained by godliness of life. Local churches are God's witnesses in the earth, centers of light from which the truth of His Word is to radiate. But doctrine is of value only as the lives of those who teach it correspond to it.

The enforcement of this was the task devolving upon Timothy in his missionary service. He must see to it that "the men pray in every place, lifting up holy hands without wrath and disputing" (2:8); that "women adorn themselves in modest apparel with shamefastness and sobriety; not with broidered hair, or gold or pearls, or costly raiment, but (which becometh women professing godliness) through good works" (vv. 9, 10). The relative position of the woman was to be regulated according to God's plan in creation, and in view of the circumstances of the Fall (vv. 12–14). She would be "saved through childbearing," that is, by means of bringing children into the world, and training them in the fear of God, she would be preserved from failing to take her place in the service and testimony of the church, saved also from falling back into the snare of the heathen conditions from which she had been delivered at conversion.

Bishops were to be without reproach, exemplary in character, given to hospitality, apt to teach, ruling their own houses well and having a good testimony from the world. So also with the deacons. They were to act in that capacity on the condition that they had been found blameless. They were to hold the mystery of the faith in a pure conscience. Their family life, too, was to be without reproach. They were to order their own houses well, and their children were to be in subjection to them. The wives both of the overseers and deacons were to be "grave, not slanderers, temperate, faithful in all things."

It was needful for the missionary to put the brethren in mind of these things, and so to be "a good minister of Christ Jesus, nourished in the words of the faith" (4:6). He was to command and teach these things and be himself an ensample to the believers "in word, in manner of life, in love, in faith, in purity." He was to give heed to reading (that is, public reading), to exhortation, to teaching . . . to be diligent in these things and give himself wholly to them that his progress might be made manifest to all. He was to take heed to himself and to his teaching and to continue in these things, that he might save himself and those who heard him (vv. 12–18).

He was also to see to it that the various branches of service maintained by the church, such, for instance, as the maintenance of widows, were to be carried on according to the mind of God and worthily of His name; that the elders who ruled well were respected, and supported materially, especially those who labored in the Word and in teaching. He was to do nothing by prejudice and partiality, and was to be careful not to lay hands hastily on any man. He was to see to it that Christian servants so acted toward their masters that the name of God and the doctrine should not be blasphemed. The rich were to be warned to set their hope, not on riches, but on God from Whom they received them, and to do good and be rich in good works. The missionary himself was to be free from the love of money. He was to flee these things and to follow after "righteousness, godliness, faith, love, patience, meekness."

All this serves to show how weighty and solemn are the responsibilities attached to missionary service in any given locality as the work develops. While the second epistle makes clear that Timothy was not expected to settle in the district for the remainder of his service, but was to hold himself free as the servant of the Lord for further labors in other localities, yet it was necessary for him to exercise pastoral care for a considerable time over the church over which he had become responsible. This part of missionary work involves much exacting labor, with hardships and trials which constantly bring the servant of God down before Him in heaviness of heart. The difficulties experienced are often proportionate to the faithfulness of the laborer in fulfilling the Lord's will, yet in this faithfulness we are following in the steps of Christ Who suffered for His faithfulness far more than any of His followers ever could do. It is faithfulness, not success, which will be rewarded when we stand before the Judgment Seat of Him who now is watching over our service and weighing with unerring estimate its true value.

▪ CHAPTER TEN ▪

The Continuity of Testimony

At the opening of the narrative of the Acts of the apostles, Luke, summing up the contents of his gospel, says that he had written it "concerning all that Jesus began both to do and to teach until the day in which He was received up." The Lord's ministry on earth was therefore only a beginning of what He would continue during the present era. The Acts records the continuation, now wrought by Him through human instrumentality in the power of the indwelling Spirit. Missionary work so carried on, work that conforms to the will of God as revealed in Scripture, is but the extension of what Christ wrought in the days of His flesh. Of this He gave intimation when He said, "As the Father hath sent Me, even so send I you." For the Father Who sent Him was with Him, and in sending His followers into the world with the gospel, He says, "Lo, I am with you alway, even unto the end of the age."

For the maintenance of divine testimony in the world, the maintenance of the faith "once for all delivered to the saints" (Jude 3), spiritual gifts in the churches were required, and provision for this was made, and still continues to be made, by the ascended Lord. Before the completion of the canon of Scripture, the truth was ministered by the apostles and by prophetic gift in the churches, exercised in an *ex tempore* manner under the immediate control of the Spirit of God (see 1 Cor. 14:31). That, however, was a temporary provision, necessary to the divine purposes until the completion of the God-breathed written Word.

While the New Testament was in course of production, the apostles and others communicated doctrine orally, but they were not the Church. The churches were to maintain what they received whether by oral or written ministry. The apostles and elders in Jerusalem once settled a controversy regarding Judaism (Acts 15), but they were not constituted a permanent church authority for doctrine. The truth became permanently conveyed in the completed Scriptures. That the Church was originally the source of doctrine is a fallacy.

In the course of this early ministry elders were raised up in the churches, their appointment being first by the Spirit of God and then by human recognition. Amongst these elders, or bishops (always, as we have observed, more than one in every church, a fact consistently set forth in the New Testament and therefore essential and designedly permanent in the divine plan for the pastoral care of churches), there were those who, under the guidance of the Spirit, gave themselves to the ministry of the Word of God. It is clearly intimated that not all elders were so gifted. The apostle says, "Let the elders that rule well (involving bearing the brunt of every difficulty and sorrow) be counted worthy of double honor [i.e. regard or respect, including ample maintenance where necessary], especially those who labor in the Word and in teaching" (1 Tim. 5:17).

This laboring in the Word indicates something more than the *ex tempore* exercise of oral ministry. It involved constant and prayerful meditation in the Scriptures, as definite preparation for the edification of the saints. Strenuous work this! A veritable laboring! Not a reliance upon immediate guidance at the time of speaking, but preparatory meditation, diligent, persevering and prayerful.

While, then, the Scriptures comprising the New Testament were being formed, the way was being prepared for permanent instruction in the complete Word of God. Only so could believers be established in the truth, growing in the grace and in the knowledge of the Lord, and thus in conformity to Christ. Only so could they be safeguarded against the numerous forms of error which were springing up on every hand. The sowing of the tares followed rapidly on the sowing of the good seed. As a counteractive against dissemination of error the churches were each to be the "pillar and ground [or stay] of the truth" (1 Tim. 3:15). Men were therefore requisite who, like the missionary himself, would "handle aright the word of truth" (see 2 Tim. 2:15, R.V.).

The apostle has this need in view when he gives a charge to Timothy to commit the things which he had heard from him to faithful men who would be able to teach others also (2:2), a clear intimation that the time was approaching when fresh revelation of truth would cease. It was a charge concerning the handing on, not of authority or of so-called "holy orders," but of the truth. Timothy was to hand on what he had heard, that is, what he had himself been taught, not his authority or ordination. Authority is received, not heard; conferred, not taught. No one can pass on authority which he himself has received from the Lord. Nor again can the Church ever become an authority for the communication of fresh truth. The Church is never, in Scripture, the teacher, but the taught. The responsibility of the churches is to maintain the truth already received, as contained in the Scriptures.

Timothy's responsibility, therefore, was far more than to preach and teach the Word of God in His public ministry. There was the special duty of handing on the truth to men who were manifesting themselves as spiritually competent to do the same in their turn. This is the only kind of apostolic succession intimated in the Scriptures, a succession of men who would maintain and pass on the doctrines of the faith in their purity. There is not a hint of the impartation of an official right to preach. What the apostle is enjoining is the continuous propagation of the truth in successive generations of spiritual ministry, with a view to the perpetuation of the faith throughout the present age. The competency of the men who showed themselves fitted for such ministry was the work of the Spirit of God, ever the provider of spiritual gifts (1 Cor. 12:11).

This command was not a temporary expedient, designed simply for the locality where Timothy was laboring. The injunction was obviously intended to be of permanent and universal application in the churches. Had it been consistently carried out after Timothy's day they would have been safeguarded against many of the evils and abuses which marred their testimony and led to widespread declension from the faith.

So now in these latter times, when there has been a revival of adherence to the Scriptures in matters relating to the constitution and service of local churches, and of missionary activities as energized by the Holy Spirit, the question arises whether there has been sufficient regard at home and abroad to this necessary provision for the continuity of testimony. Has there been a diligent effort to seek out in each locality faithful men and commit the truth to them with a view to their doing the same to others after them? Is sufficient heed being paid today to the apostle's injunction? God be thanked for the diligent and faithful services of those who continue laboring in the Word in any church. There is room, however, for something more than the regular ministry of the edification of believers. The Spirit of God is ever waiting to provide spiritual gifts in the churches, and besides the constant teaching of the Word of God, there is scope for more definite instruction of those whom God is raising up and equipping by the Spirit to engage in such ministry, faithful men "who shall be able to teach others also."

It is the responsibility, therefore, of those who have the spiritual care of a church to seek God's guidance as to the recognition of such loyal, trusty and competent men, in order that the truth may be committed to them. In this way the maintenance, by those who have an understanding in the things of God, of the doctrines provided once for all in Holy Scripture, will continue when the missionary himself, or one of the elders, as the case may be, has moved elsewhere, or has been taken to be with the Lord.

There are indications in various countries today of a tendency to legislative restriction upon the public preaching of the Word of God. How needful, therefore, to seek help from God to fulfill the injunction we have been considering! And not only in the regions beyond, but in every church, adherence to the divine plan in this respect will meet with God's approval in the resulting provision for the future testimony until the Lord returns.

▪ CHAPTER ELEVEN ▪

The Relationship of the Churches

A conspicuous feature of the development of the missionary activity recorded in the New Testament is the independence of the churches one of another by way of ecclesiastical authority and constitution. While there was necessarily an interrelationship, there was no combination under human control whether local or general. The divine plan is characterized by an entire absence of any amalgamation of churches, determined by either geographical or racial or ecclesiastical organization. Each church was a self-contained unit, responsible alone to Christ, the risen and glorified Head. The New Testament phraseology itself marks the individuality of the churches.

Whenever, for example, they are referred to as in a district the plural is used, save in one instance, which is not an exception. There are "the churches of Galatia" (1 Cor. 16:1), "of Asia" (v. 19), "of Macedonia" (2 Cor. 8:1), "of Judaea" (Gal. 1:22), "which are in Judaea" (1 Thess. 2:14). In Acts 9:31, "the church throughout all Judaea and Galilee and Samaria" (see the R.V.) signifies the local church as just scattered from Jerusalem, and not a community of churches in that region.* Never do we meet with such expressions as "the Galatian Church," "the Macedonian Church." There was no such corporate union as "the Church of Judaea." So with the racial descriptions, we read of "the churches of the Gentiles" (Rom. 16:4), but never of "the Gentile Church." Such terms, therefore, as "the Chinese Church," "the Indian Church," the church of any country, are foreign to Scripture.

Nor, again, were the churches ecclesiastically organized under a council. The so-called council of Jerusalem (Acts 15) was an incidental gathering of the apostles and elders to consider a particular question. No permanent institution was established, nor is there a record in Scripture of the repetition of such a council. What was then decided came as the inspired instruction for the guidance of all churches, and the circumstances under which it was drawn up constituted a single occasion. The divine will was not again communicated from an apostolic convention, nor did any other locality become a center at which decisions were made and from which decrees were issued for the instruction of churches or the regulation of their affairs.

The fact that the churches are constituent parts of one great entity, the body of Christ, involves an essential similarity in the constitution of each and an intercommunion among all, as well as a certain interrelationship, such as the cultivation of hospitality, the assistance of the poor, and the commendation of a believer from one church to another. All such details serve to illustrate the sense of the unity of the whole church. So also does the fact that each single local assembly is called a temple, or sanctuary, of God, as is the whole church, each, as well as the whole, being indwelt by the Spirit of God (1 Cor. 3:16, with Eph. 2:21). But each one is represented in the teaching of Scripture as having a unity and a corporate life of its own. The local church is "the pillar and ground of the truth," sustaining indeed the truth common to all, but responsible in itself for the maintenance of a witness for God, and answerable only to Christ the Head.

---

*Only a brief interval had elapsed since the scattering of the members of the church in Jerusalem recorded in chapter 8:1. The church in Jerusalem is still called the church, though in a scattered state. Apparently there had not been time previous to the circumstances recorded in 9:31 for the fugitive saints to be formed into regularly constituted churches. It was only shortly after the scattering abroad as mentioned in verse 4, that Saul was converted and the church which had been dispersed through all Judaea and Galilee had peace. It is some time after the renewal of peaceful conditions that we read of "the churches of Judaea" (Gal. 1:22).

While, then, the apostles cultivated the friendliest intercourse and relations between the churches, they did not establish any formal connection between any or all of them. Each was dealt with on its own basis, as being responsible, not to any central authority, but to the Lord. What was taught in one church, in respect of the communication of the faith and the principles of Christian doctrine and practice, was taught in another. These principles were either the direct commandments of the Lord received by an apostle (see e.g., 1 Cor. 14:37), or were divinely communicated through him, whether orally or by inspired writings. When Paul, for example, says "and so ordain I in all the churches" (1 Cor. 1:18), he is not issuing decrees from a given center, but is simply informing the church at Corinth that the instructions he was giving them were what he gave in every church. He appeals either to traditions he had himself received and passed on to them and to others, or to his own divinely-given qualifications for judgment or edification.

There is no instance in which a particular circumstance or question, such as the exercise of discipline calling for decision in any given church, was put before the other churches for their consideration and judgment. The responsibility, for instance, of the excommunication of the guilty person in the church at Corinth rested with that church alone. An endorsement of the act was called for by another church only when the said person applied for fellowship there. As for the excommunication of a local church itself by any other church or churches, the divine plan lends no countenance to such an act, nor contains a hint of it. No organization of churches was formed which would admit of it.

The development of missionary work in any district had clearly defined limitations. To exceed these could only defeat the divine purposes, either bringing confusion and disintegration, or so altering the character of the work as to establish something different from the design of the founder. The apostolic missionaries preached the gospel and formed the converts into local churches with their bishops divinely qualified and appointed, and with deacons appointed by the church for attendance upon matters temporal. That was the extent to which the enterprise was carried in any locality. Never did one church become a center for the supervision or direction of others in the neighborhood. Never was a council established at which missionaries periodically met to hold jurisdiction over the churches in any particular area and decide matters relating to them. Nor did the apostles take steps for the establishment of any council to be attended by representatives in a district. The work of the gospel was facilitated in various ways, but with an entire absence of any institution or organization beyond the founding of churches.

The means by which disorders arising in a church were corrected, was not by modifying its constitution or its mode of service, nor by the establishment of some form of ecclesiastical court of jurisdiction, but by the maintenance of the divine principles according to the teaching of the Spirit of God and the recognition of His prerogatives. Again, there was scope for the expansion of a local church and of its activities in the service of the Lord, and for the spread of its testimony, leading to the formation of other assemblies according to the divine pattern, and without any control by such mother church. The seed sown produced plants similar to the parent plant but independent of it.

Again, there was no such thing as the founding of a mission with its branches and agencies. Nothing like this was required for the divine purposes. Only when the churches departed from the apostolic teaching and failed to recognize the prerogatives of the Spirit of God and His sufficiency for the continuance and maintenance of the work under the control of the head of the church, were such human expedients adopted, developing into ecclesiastical systems and organizations representing something different from, and contrary to, the divine intention.

If the question arises whether the apostolic methods were intended to be final, or whether they represented an enterprise in its infant stage with freedom of modification or adjustment to suit later times and circumstances, that question raises the other and vitally important one, whether the Scriptures are a sufficient guide, as giving a complete revelation of the will of God for His people. The teaching of the Acts and the epistles concerning these apostolic methods in the work of the gospel and the formation, constitution and life of the churches, forms part of "the faith once for all delivered to the saints" (Jude 3, R.V.). That word "once for all" gives, as do other passages, a clear intimation of the finality of Scripture as a divine revelation. Moreover, the simple unencumbered methods employed by the apostles, under the Lord's injunctions and the guidance and control of the Spirit of God, have never proved unsuitable in any nation or age. They are as workable today in every country as they were then. Nor could anything else be reasonably expected. For the churches were formed from amongst all sorts and conditions of men independently of national distinctions and of degrees of civilization, and were brought into being by a gospel and a teaching of universal application throughout the present era.

To adopt expedients of human devising in order to meet any contingency, is to tamper with the divine arrangements and mar God's handiwork.

CHAPTER TWELVE

Church Discipline

In our last chapter we sought to show that anything like an organization of churches under a local central authority in any district was conspicuous by its absence from the divine plan. We pointed out incidentally that no case of discipline in a particular church was made a test case for the decision of other churches in general. The subject of church discipline, and its importance in missionary enterprise, now calls for consideration.

The fellowship into which believers are called with one another is of a very blessed and at the same time an intensely solemn character. Being based upon the atoning and redemptive efficacy of the sacrifice of Christ, it is a fellowship possibly only to believers. Being a fellowship with the Father and the Son, and of the Holy Spirit, it is a fellowship consistent with the holiness of God. Being divinely formed and maintained, its recognition is dependent on divine principles, and not on regulations framed by human deductions with motives of safeguarding it. As it is expressed locally and collectively in partaking of the bread and the cup of the Lord's Supper, the privilege of partaking belongs to all believers unconditionally, save in such respects as are stated in the Word of God.

These are clearly laid down therein. The guilt of immorality is one ground upon which exclusion from fellowship is enjoined. Concerning the moral delinquent in the church at Corinth the apostle writes, "Put away the wicked man from among yourselves" (1 Cor. 5:13).

That this kind of sin is one of a larger class is shown by the preceding injunction upon which the immediate command is founded: "I write unto you not to keep company, if any man that is named a brother [i.e. in distinction from the world, v. 10] be a fornicator, or covetous, or an idolater, or a reviler, or a drunkard, or an extortioner; with such an one no, not to eat," (v. 11). And the underlying principle is that "a little leaven leaveneth the whole lump." The old leaven is therefore to be purged out (vv. 6, 7).

Again, concerning the adoption of basic error, apostolic instruction is equally clear. Anyone who brings not "the teaching of Christ" is neither to be received nor to be given greeting. To do so would be to have fellowship in his evil works (2 John 11). The apostle was obviously speaking not of uninstructed believers with defective knowledge of the truth, but of disseminators of error in fundamental doctrine. The context shows that one who brings not the true doctrine of Christ is regarded as a teacher of evil doctrine. It is noticeable that the same statement which the apostle Paul made to the church at Corinth, concerning the effect of immoral practice, he also made to the churches in Galatia concerning false doctrine: "A little leaven leaveneth the whole lump" (Gal. 5:9).

The apostle adopts a similar metaphor of the disastrous effects of evil doctrine, in the case of Hymenaeus and Philetus, who were guilty of error concerning the Resurrection. "Their word," he says, "will eat as cloth a gangrene" (2 Tim. 2:17). The subject there is not, indeed, church discipline in regard to such cases, but the line of conduct necessary for the individual believer so that he may be "a vessel unto honor." He is to purge himself from vain babblings, which, in the sense of the passage, involves dissociation from their exponents. The passage therefore does not countenance the retention in church fellowship of such men as Hymenaeus and Philetus. But there is no suggestion of the exclusion of fellow believers who are free from immoral practice or corrupt doctrine. The apostle is setting forth the qualifications essential, not for association with other believers, but for fitness for "the Master's use."

A further instance is given in the case of the church at Pergamos, with whom the Lord remonstrated for having in their midst those who held error (Rev. 2:14, 15). Such, then, were to be debarred from fellowship. The church at Ephesus was commended for having tried and detected the false apostles who had come among them (2:2).

Apart from the scriptural disqualifications referred to, the apostle's command holds good, "Receive ye one another, even as Christ also received you, to the glory of God" (Rom. 15:7). His "one another" has no limitations narrower than membership of the body of Christ. The fellowship of believers is not conditioned, for instance, by divergence of judgment upon cases of church discipline, where there is no actual partnership in the evil.

The solemn act of exclusion from the local church fellowship (a fellowship not confined to the breaking of bread) is not an end in itself, it is a means to the end of the spiritual welfare of the saint who is under discipline, and his restoration after self-judgment and confession (2 Cor. 2:6–11). But meanwhile the erring one is "put away," and this places a solemn restriction on social intercourse with him. The command is, "put away from among yourselves"; clearly that is more than exclusion from one particular gathering of the church, such as that for the breaking of bread. The love which ignores sin and maintains the same intercourse as if no discipline had been exercised is mere sentiment, devoid of the love of God and the fear of God, and is a breach of the divine principles of fellowship. True brotherliness is consistent both with the righteousness that demands discipline and with the self-abasing love which seeks restoration in the divinely appointed way, and this involves on the part of all who belong to the assembly that brokenness of spirit that knows the priestly service of "eating the sin-offering in the holy place." For how often a sinful course might have been averted had the assembly as a whole been in the right spiritual condition! Pastoral dealing might have at least so arrested the evil as to prevent the extreme measure of exclusion from fellowship.

The necessary measure having been taken, it calls for recognition on the part of the other assemblies who may be in any way affected. That would be the case where one who had been excommunicated applied for fellowship in another assembly. Reception by the church in Philippi after exclusion at Corinth would falsify the meaning of Scriptural fellowship. Hence the need of letters of commendation. That such were required among the churches is clearly intimated in the apostle's expostulations with the church at Corinth that, since they were themselves his credentials, they needed no letter commending him, as was necessary in other cases (2 Cor. 3:1–3). Compare the case of Apollos (Acts 18:27).

Such letters were not only safeguards helping to remove suspicion and distrust, nor did they simply provide a right to partake of the Lord's Supper; they were a commendation to the confidence and love of the saints, and to the privileges of their fellowship.

The idea of cutting off an assembly for failure to endorse the decision of another assembly, finds no support in Scripture, and is contrary to the principles relating to the character and constitution of local churches. For, as we have seen, there was in the divine plan no ecclesiastical organization or amalgamation of churches marked by geographical delimitations.

▪ CHAPTER THIRTEEN ▪

Baptism

The terms of our Lord's commission to the apostles were as follows: "Go ye, therefore, and make disciples of all the nations, baptizing them into the name of the Father and of the Son and of the Holy Ghost; teaching them to observe all things whatsoever I have commanded you: and lo, I am with you alway, even unto the end of the age"* (Matt. 28:19, 20). We have now before us those parts of the "all things" which relate to the two ordinances of baptism and the Lord's Supper, as instituted by Him. These cannot be dissociated from His moral precepts. The ordinances are not simply ceremonial rites, they are essentially doctrinal, and the doctrines involved are such as regulate the Christian life in conformity with the will of God. Each ordinance is associated with the death and resurrection of Christ, and their application to the Christian life.

First, with regard to baptism, the order in the Lord's injunctions is "make disciples . . . baptizing them . . . teaching them." This may not be taken to mean "make disciples by baptizing them." There is no support in Scripture for such an interpretation. Even regarding John's baptism, the order is first discipleship and then baptism: "Jesus made and baptized . . . disciples [though Jesus Himself baptized not, but His disciples]" (John 4:1-2); and as to baptism after pentecost, both the practice and the teaching are authoritative for the same order.

The rite of circumcision has been advanced as an argument for baptism as a means of prospective discipleship. But, with the Jew, circumcision was the outward sign of a covenant relationship with God, enjoyed by natural birth. Through the sacrifice of the Cross, however, Jew and Gentile alike were proved to be spiritually dead, and under the judgment of God, each requiring regeneration (2 Cor. 5:14, 15). The Cross did away with the carnal ordinances of Judaism. None of those finds any correspondence in baptism. Remission of sins comes with faith in Christ (Acts 10:43) and therewith the new birth, and baptism was ministered subsequent to that experience and on the ground of it. This is the case in all the instances in the Acts. "They that received the word were baptized" (2:41). "When they believed . . . they were baptized" (8:12). So with the Ethiopian eunuch (8:36–38), Saul of Tarsus (9:18), Cornelius and his household (10:47, 48), Lydia and hers (16:15), the jailer at Philippi and his (16:33). Again, "many of the Corinthians, hearing, believed and were baptized" (18:8). At Ephesus "certain disciples . . . were baptized"† (19:1, 5).

With regard to the conversion of Saul of Tarsus and the subsequent command given him by Ananias, "Arise, and be baptized, and wash away thy sins, calling on His name" (22:16), the context makes clear that this does not teach that baptism is the means of the washing away of sins. Saul was already a believer. Ananias addressed him as "Brother Saul" (v. 13). His voluntary submission to the act of baptism would be a testimony on his part that the change had taken place. Whereas he had hitherto been a bitter opponent of Christ and His gospel, in ignorant, albeit culpable, zeal, now, having been converted, he would in baptism confess Christ as his Lord, thereby giving public testimony that his past

---

*This is to be distinguished from the baptism of John unto repentance for the remission of sins, and from the baptism of the Spirit at pentecost (Matt. 3:11), and the baptism of fire, a baptism of judgment upon the Jewish nation in the future time of tribulation for their rejection of Christ.

†That these had already been baptized with John's baptism shows that the observance of a different form of baptism from that commanded by the Lord did not render baptism by immersion unnecessary. It also indicates the obligatory character of the ordinance.

had been wrong, and symbolically washing away his sins in rejecting the Son of God. His guilt itself had already been removed by justifying grace. Thus he would himself figuratively do what had actually already been done spiritually.*

Again, that this order, first regenerative faith and then baptism, is essential, is obvious from the very significance of baptism, by which the person who undergoes it gives testimony not only to the death, burial and resurrection of Christ, but to his identification with Him in these three respects. The baptism of an unbeliever, or of a child whose infancy makes faith impossible of realization, both contravenes the injunctions of the Word of God and renders nugatory the symbolic meaning underlying the ordinance. In baptism the believer acknowledges that in the death of Christ, he has died unto sin and is "alive unto God in Christ Jesus" (Rom. 6:11, with vv. 3, 4), an acknowledgement impossible in the cases just referred to. So in the Colossian epistle, the apostle, speaking of the meaning of baptism, says "Having been buried with Him in baptism, wherein ye were raised with Christ, through faith in the working of God, Who raised Him from the dead" (2:12), statements which not only show that faith is essential, but at the same time sufficiently indicate the mode of the ordinance, as involving immersion and emergence.

Again, the teaching of the Acts and the epistles shows the important significance of the order in the Lord's commission: "make disciples . . . baptizing them." For plainly baptism is a confession of discipleship. The very essence of discipleship is a practical apprehension of the truths inculcated by Him Whose disciples we are, and the practice of the Christian faith is summed up in the explicit identification with Christ conveyed in the apostle's commentary on baptism, "The death that He died, He died unto sin once: but the life that He liveth, He liveth unto God. Even so reckon ye also yourselves to be dead indeed unto sin, but alive unto God in Christ Jesus" (Rom. 6:10, 11).

The injunction given by the Lord that baptism was to be "in the name of the Father and of the Son and of the Holy Ghost" is clearly imperative. There is nothing contradictory to it in the records in the Acts. When Luke states that believers at Samaria were baptized "in the Name of Jesus Christ" (Acts 18:16), that Peter commanded Cornelius and his kinsmen and friends to be baptized "in the name of Jesus Christ" (10:48), that certain disciples at Ephesus were baptized "into the name of the Lord Jesus" (19:5), he is not recounting a formula used on the occasions of these baptisms, he is simply stating historical facts. There is no reason for supposing that the Lord's command in Matthew 27 was not carried out in each case—in other words, that those who baptized did not accompany the act as directed by the Lord. Nor would it have been suitable to the historian to repeat the form of words contained in the commission.

The apostle Peter declares that baptism is "not the putting away of the filth of the flesh, but the interrogation [or rather "appeal"†] of a good conscience toward God, through the resurrection of Jesus Christ" (1 Pet. 3:21). Baptism, then, does not remove the defilement of sin but, in its figurative setting forth of the death and resurrection of Christ, provides the believer, as one possessed of a good conscience, with an appeal to the death of Christ as the means of his freedom from condemnation, and likewise an appeal against the claims of sin, owing to his identification with Christ in His death and resurrection.

The practice of the baptism of households as such, including, that is to say, the baptism of infants or of unregenerate persons, has no warrant whatever in Scripture, either in historical fact or doctrine. In the cases where households were baptized, the only legitimate conclusion is that all persons were believers. All who belonged to the house of Cornelius, having heard the word, received the Holy Spirit, and so were baptized (Acts 10:24, 33, 43–48; 11:14). The simple statement concerning Lydia, that "she was baptized, and her household" (16:15), can rightly be understood

*This is confirmed by the use of the Middle Voice in each of the verbs "be baptized," "wash away," the precise and literal meaning being "get baptized," and "wash away for thyself thy sins."

†That the word *"eperōtēma,"* was a law court term denoting an appeal, has been established by the discovery of its use in the papyri documents of the same period as that in which the New Testament was written.

only in the light of the teaching of Scripture on the subject. In order to make it fit with the idea that infants were baptized, it is necessary to suppose that Lydia was married, and had children, and that her children were with her, or that members of the household had children—all of which is pure inference and in some respects highly improbable. Certainly her case affords no ground for a practice which contradicts the plain teaching of Scripture. Concerning the Philippian jailer, the word of the Lord was spoken to all that were in his house: "he rejoiced greatly, with all his house, having believed in God" (16:32, 33). The plain conclusion is that the joy realized by all was the outcome of the response of faith on the part of each to the spoken word. At Corinth Paul baptized the household of Stephanas (1 Cor. 1:16), but the apostle states that the house of Stephanas had "set themselves to minister to the saints" (16:15).

The views that the children of believers are brought into covenant relationship with God, or that baptism is introductory into the kingdom of God or into a sphere of temporal privilege, and so forth, are without a vestige of support from Scripture. Inferences are drawn from the Old Testament teaching concerning the households of Israel, and these are transferred literally over to the households of believers now, whereas the teaching conveys instead spiritual lessons for the household of faith.

If we press the New Testament teaching, the charge is raised of making everything of baptism, and the saying of the apostle in 1 Corinthians 1:14–17 is brought up as evidence that it is a matter of indifference. But when the apostle says to the Corinthians, "I baptized none of you but Crispus and Gaius . . . for Christ sent me not to baptize, but to preach the Gospel," there is no ground for the conclusion, either that some believers then were unbaptized, or that he did not attach importance to baptism. He plainly states that he did not himself perform the baptism in every case, lest he should be accused "of baptizing in his own name." Again, had he baptized unregenerate members of households, the place he gave to baptism would have been inconsistent with his statement as to the commission given him.

How important, then, is the Scriptural mode of baptism as an accompaniment of the proclamation of the gospel, often with a very imperfect knowledge of the language of the hearers! Not only is the ear addressed by the spoken word, but an appeal is made through the eye in setting forth the truth of the believer's burial and identification with Christ, in His death to sin and in His resurrection life. With what force would the ordinances of baptism and the Lord's Supper speak to the heart and conscience of those whose language might make it difficult to set forth clearly these great truths of Holy Scripture! The burial and putting out of sight of the man after the flesh could not be more vividly and plainly set forth than in the mystic grave of baptism; but it is robbed of all its meaning and can but solemnly mislead, when infants or unregenerate members of a household are counted fit subjects for Christian baptism; it becomes a thorough unreality, and the important truth conveyed by it, when submitted to by the believer, is lost. There is no difference between the household of an Israelite and that of an Egyptian naturally. It is the blood of the Lamb that makes the difference. These ordinances are for believers alone.

Accordingly an essential part of missionary service is the impartation of instruction from the Scriptures, to those who are truly born again, concerning the mode and meaning of the baptism of believers as taught therein. It may be an advantage, wherever possible, for the actual baptizing to be carried out not by the missionary, but by a native brother in the Lord who has the confidence of his brethren, as himself bearing a consistent testimony by his godliness.

CHAPTER FOURTEEN

The Lord's Supper

We have pointed out the great value attaching to baptism as an object lesson in missionary service in its earlier stages in lands where a language has to be acquired. The same is true of the Lord's Supper. Each of these ordinances reveals the manifold wisdom of the Lord in His counsels relating to the effects of the work of the gospel in the life and testimony of converts.

Like baptism, the loaf and the cup of the Lord's Supper, the visible emblems of His death, make their appeal through the eye to the heart. The very fact of the weekly observance of the feast, in the manner in which the Lord instituted it, is of the utmost importance in that part of mission work which consists of the building up of local churches and leading converts in "the ways that be in Christ." For the testimony of the observance is twofold. Outwardly the gathered saints "proclaim the Lord's death" (1 Cor. 10:26); they give witness, as to its fact, its meaning and its object, to unseen powers in the spiritual realm, to the world, and to any persons present who do not partake of the feast. There is also the inward witness, the reminder, to the individual participant, of Christ Himself and His work of redeeming grace on the Cross; and who can tell what this constant reawakening of our affections toward Himself must mean for a spiritual life?

Moreover, the keeping of the feast is a matter of personal devotion to Christ, a matter of love that responds to the love of His heart. For He says, "This do in remembrance of Me"—not merely in memory of what He once accomplished, but in occupation of the heart with the Lord Himself. The word in the original rendered "remembrance" suggests that.

The deep significance of the Lord's Supper is grasped only gradually, but the act of partaking, and the regular recurrence of the feast, when kept in all its simplicity, are of the greatest assistance in the impartation of such instruction by a missionary. The privilege of partaking is dependent, not on the degree of apprehension of what the Lord's Supper means, but on the facts that its institution was the Lord's act and that its observance is His will. Enlightenment thereon is a process dependent on an increasing understanding of the teaching of the Word of God. He whose part it is to instruct finds his ministry the easier by means of the very details and character of the ordinance.

This is illustrated by the circumstances of the apostle's relationships with the church at Corinth. A few years had elapsed between the founding of the church there as a result of his gospel work in the city, and his first epistle to that church. Yet in this epistle he has much to impart to them in addition to the instruction he had given when in their midst. Even if he had already taught them most of what he now writes to them, so little had they apprehended the nature and significance of the ordinance, that they were making it an occasion for selfishness and drunkenness, rendering it impossible for them to eat the Lord's Supper (v. 20, R.V.). He had taught them how the Lord Jesus had instituted the feast, bidding His disciples partake of the bread and of the cup in remembrance of Him, and telling them what each represented—the bread His body, the cup the new covenant in His blood. All this he reminds them that he himself had received from the Lord. Doubtless, too, he had informed them that on every occasion of their partaking they proclaimed the Lord's death "till He come." Their treatment of the ordinance necessitated still further instruction. How little had they entered into the meaning of the feast! How little had they apprehended its practical bearing upon their daily life as believers! How little have we, who have the responsibilities attaching to a fuller light and to greater privileges than they had been able to enjoy!

He had to point out to them that to eat the bread and drink the cup unworthily is to be "guilty of the body and blood of the Lord." He was doubtless referring immediately to their evil doings when they assembled for the purpose, doings which constituted a gross perversion of the feast. But their mode of partaking was clearly an indication of the general manner of their daily life. Their carnality and worldliness and self-importance are evident from the way the apostle has to write to them, and the greed and drunkenness of which they were guilty when they assembled cannot be supposed to have been confined to those occasions. The obvious conclusion is that it was an unworthy manner of life, and a lack of self-judgment concerning it, that led to partaking of the Lord's Supper unworthily. What pleasure could the Lord find in an outward observance of His ordinance if there was sin in the life? "To what purpose," the Lord had said to Israel, "is the multitude of your sacrifices unto Me? When ye come to appear before Me, who hath required this at your hand, to trample My courts? Bring no more vain oblations . . . I cannot away with iniquity and the solemn meeting . . . Wash you, make you clean; put away the evil of your doings from before Mine eyes; cease to do evil, learn to do well" (Is. 1:11-17). Are the words of the apostle any less solemn? On the contrary, they are even more so. For to practice that which is displeasing to God, and so to partake of the Lord's Supper unworthily, is, as already mentioned, to be guilty "of the body and blood of the Lord" (v. 27). That is to say, to act in such a way is a denial of the truth and value of His atoning sacrifice, and therefore constitutes identification with the world that crucified Him.

Accordingly the believer is to "prove," or test himself, and so to eat of the bread and drink of the cup. He is to prove himself, so that he may be conscious of being personally true and loyal to His rejected Lord, and thus of having His approval. In that condition alone can he rightly partake of the Lord's Supper, his thoughts being adjusted to the mind of the Lord in regard to the ordinance. "For he that eateth and drinketh, eateth and drinketh judgment unto himself if he discern not the body," that is, the Lord's body (v. 29).

The apostle's teaching, then, forcibly reminds us of the bearing of the Lord's Supper upon the work and testimony of believers individually. To partake of the feast worthily will preserve us from the poison of worldliness which is the cause of many a weakness and sickness, and the falling asleep prematurely of not a few, though those who are thus removed may not be themselves in default. Accordingly, mission work in which the ordinance is neglected, or given a less prominent place in the church than that assigned to it in the New Testament, both falls short of the divine plan, and fails to produce those abiding results in the separated lives of the converts which the Lord intended to be produced.

How intimately associated the ordinance is with the daily life of the believer, is taught by the apostle in the tenth chapter, which forms the background of what he sets forth in the eleventh. In the former he shows how utterly incongruous it is to partake of the Table of the Lord and yet to have association with what is controlled by the powers of darkness. Having illustrated his point from the history of Israel, with admonitory application to the present time (10:1-15), he draws a parallel between the provision made for the people of Israel from the altar of sacrifice, and the provision made for believers through the death of Christ, as represented by the cup and the loaf of the Lord's table, and sets in contrast those things of which the Gentiles partake. He enforces, too, the solemnity of the significance attaching to the acts of the memorial symbols: "The cup of blessing which we bless [i.e., for which we give thanks], is it not a communion of [i.e., participation in] the blood of Christ? The bread which we break, is it not a communion of [participation in] the body of Christ?" (v. 16). The cup is here put first, since the blood of Christ is the basis of the union enjoyed.

Now with Israel the altar supplied the table for those who partook: "Thou shalt offer thy burnt offerings, the flesh and the blood, upon the altar of the Lord thy God, and the blood of thy sacrifices shall be poured out upon the altar of the Lord thy God, and thou shalt eat the flesh" (Deut. 12:27). "Behold Israel after the flesh," says the apostle, "have not they which eat the sacrifices communion with the altar?" So with the Lord's table, that which is provided for the participants is provided for them as a result of the sacrifice of Christ. There is a third basis of communion, that which supplies the table of demons (to whom gentile sacrifices are actually offered), a communion prohibited to the believer: "Ye cannot drink the cup of the Lord and the cup of demons; ye cannot partake of the table of the Lord and of the table of demons" (v. 21).

While the apostle immediately speaks of idol sacrifices, the principle underlying his teaching is of that wider scope intimated in the remonstrances he makes in his second epistle, "What fellowship hath righteousness with iniquity? Or what communion hath light with darkness?" (2 Cor. 6:14). Since the whole world "lieth in the evil one" (1 John 5:19, R.V.), fellowship with it is incompatible with fellowship with God, and it follows that the apostle's words regarding the Lord's table apply equally in this respect. The believer cannot have fellowship with the world and likewise partake of the table of the Lord. There can be no bridging of the gulf between the two.

All this serves then to show the place the Lord's Supper has in missionary work, not merely as an ordinance appointed for the churches, but in its bearing upon the lives of those who constitute them.

Not one thing that the Lord has commanded can be dropped without loss to our souls and a dimming of the glory of Christ. Every detail of the divine instructions is essential. A missing pin would mean a slack cord and this would bring a curtain out of place in the tabernacle. Thus the whole structure would suffer and God's name be dishonored. The Lord expects implicit obedience, faithfully and effectually rendered with all our heart.

▪ CHAPTER FIFTEEN ▪

Financial Matters
Part I—The Care of the Poor

The particular feature of the subject of finance which comes before us first in the work of the earliest missionaries, is the care of the poor. In writing to the Galatians, the apostle Paul points out that upon the occasion of his visit with Barnabas to Jerusalem, when an understanding was arrived at that they should go to the Gentiles, they were urged to remember the poor, "which very thing," says the apostle, "I was also zealous to do." The poor especially referred to were the saints in Judaea, where, owing both to persecution and famine, poverty had become acute.

The scope of Scripture narrative is limited to that which is of permanent value in spiritual instruction for the Lord's people generally. Thus the facts relating to the offerings of the church for poor saints in Jerusalem are recorded in order to show what an essential part in missionary enterprise the care of the poor was intended to form. This is confirmed by the prominence given to the subject throughout the epistles.

At the time referred to in the epistle to the Galatians the church at Antioch, the first church formed by missionary work amongst Gentiles as well as Jews, had already been stirred to minister help to the brethren in Judaea, and had done so through Barnabas and Saul (Acts 11:29, 30). "The disciples, every man according to his ability, determined to send relief," literally, "to send for ministry." The whole church rose spontaneously to the occasion, each believer taking his part in the offering.

Probably this wholehearted expression of practical sympathy was largely the outcome of the spiritual instruction already given by Barnabas and Saul in that church. They had been there a whole year, and had "taught much people" (v. 26), and it is deeply significant that the narrative immediately proceeds to record the incident of this ministry to poor saints, suggesting that the instruction given had an issue in this practical manner. True "disciples" these! Followers of Him Who made the poor the special object of His care!

In such service, then, Paul and Barnabas had been engaged before they were called to the regions beyond as missionaries. That he also consistently carried it out in his missionary service is clear from other epistles. Concerning the same need he informs the church at Corinth that he had given order to the churches of Galatia, and writes, "Now concerning the collection for the saints . . . on the first day of the week let each one of you lay by him in store as he may prosper, that no collections be made when I come."

These instructions, arising from the immediate need, convey principles for the guidance of believers. Firstly, as to the *manner* of their giving, that it should be *regular,* the setting aside of money, not in a spasmodic, desultory manner, but definitely and constantly. Secondly, as to the *method,* that it should be *universal.* The whole assembly was to contribute. The poorer were not to rely upon the richer to do everything. "Each one of you," says the apostle. Thirdly, as to the *measure,* that it should be *proportionate.* No commandment concerning tithes was laid down, as under the Law. Even under the Law much more was contributed by the Israelite than the tenth. In the church, each one was to contribute according to the measure of his prosperity. The word rendered "prosper" literally denotes to have a good road. The path of each believer is one of God's goodness and mercy, and this will produce a practical response where the heart is rightly exercised. By means of such exercise of heart and by such methods as the apostle enjoined, sudden collections, under the impulse of the moment, would be avoided, with a resulting increase in the amount contributed.

The second epistle throws further light upon this. Speaking of the cooperation of the suffering churches in Macedonia in this matter, in which "in much proof of affliction [i.e. trial that had stood the test] the abundance of their joy and their deep poverty abounded unto the riches of their liberality," he describes their offering in various ways. It is a *grace* (8:4), that is, an expression of the grace of God acting in them; a *fellowship,* a having in common, regarding what was theirs as that which should be shared with others (v. 4; the same word is rendered "contribution" in 9:14); a *bounty* (8:20), a word suggesting fullness, "a fat contribution"; a *ministration* (10:1, 13), or service; a *blessing* (*eulogia,* rendered "bounty," 9:5). Such a variety of description serves to show not only how important this ministry to the poor is in God's sight, but with what satisfaction He looks upon it.

In the first epistle instruction was given particularly to the individual believer, though obviously the offering was made by the church. In the second epistle the collective aspect is predominant. While individually it was contributed according to the ability of each (cp. 2 Cor. 8:11), yet as that which was to be received by the saints in Judaea it was the practical expression of the fellowship of the church at Corinth. The Macedonian churches set a magnificent example in this respect. They gave "of their own accord"; that is, without an appeal on the apostle's part (8:3). They gave "out of their poverty," and the deeper the poverty the greater seems to have been their joy in giving. They gave "beyond their power," not of course failing in the discharge of their liabilities, but, apart from this, denying themselves in the matter of their necessities. They preceded their act of contributing their offering by "giving themselves to the Lord" (v. 5). That is to say, their giving sprang from a definite realization that they themselves belonged wholly to the Lord.

There are other principles which the apostle applies here. In stirring up the saints in Corinth to complete what they had been ready to do before, he makes clear that he had no idea of easing the situation in Jerusalem at the expense of placing a burden upon the church in Corinth. There would certainly be a reciprocal blessing. The overflow from Corinth to supply the want in Judaea would lead to an overflow from the saints in Judaea in spiritual benefit to the saints at Corinth. This he bases upon what is recorded in Exodus of the scattering of the manna. "He that gathered much had nothing over, and he that gathered little had no lack." Each man has a limited capacity for the satisfaction of his own requirements. To hoard beyond that brings trouble and anxiety. On the other hand, what is given to meet the needs of others brings a return in spiritual blessing.

A further principle is taken metaphorically from the circumstances of harvest, "He that soweth sparingly shall reap also sparingly, and he that soweth bountifully [lit., with blessings] shall reap also abundantly." That is why Paul wanted the gift from Corinth to be a matter of bounty and not of extortion, not, that is to say, as a kind of claim on their purse. More still, the bountiful giver is like God Himself: "Let each man do as he hath purposed in his heart; not grudgingly or of necessity, for God loveth a cheerful giver." In giving abundantly we give as God gives, and thus we delight His heart. "There is that scattereth, and increaseth yet more. And there is that withholdeth more than is meet, but it tendeth only to want. The liberal soul shall be made fat: and he that watereth shall be watered also himself" (Prov. 11:24, 25).

To act thus in fellowship with God brings His enabling power "to make all grace abound" unto us, so that "always having all sufficiency in everything," we on our part "may abound unto every good work." A good harvest is thus secured, and a permanent one. It is a harvest of righteousness in God's sight. Thus it is with the "blessed man" of Psalm 112, which the apostle here quotes: "he hath scattered abroad [i.e. the seed of bountiful giving], he hath given to the poor: his righteousness abideth forever." And now he assures them that God, Who supplies "seed to the sower and bread for food," will supply their seed for sowing and increase the fruits of their righteousness. That is how they will be "enriched in everything unto all bountifulness." This serves to illustrate the fact that righteousness is not merely strict integrity toward our fellowmen. Righteousness is being right with God, and this cannot be the case where there is a lack of practical sympathy with those who are in need. The apostle speaks again of the joint offering from Macedonia and Achaia as "fruit," when writing to the Romans (Rom. 15:28).

An important point in regard to the handling of money contributed by churches is the care required that everything should be free from the possibility of reproach. With this in view two brethren at least were appointed to take charge of the offering. Thus, taking the marginal rendering of 1 Corinthians 16:3, as correct, the apostle says, "When I arrive [i.e. at Corinth], whomsoever ye shall approve, them [note the plural] will I send with letters, to carry your bounty unto Jerusalem: and if it be meet for me to go also, they shall go with me." This committal of such matters to more than one brother obviates the danger that any should be able to find cause for a charge of misappropriation of the funds.

▪ CHAPTER SIXTEEN ▪

Financial Matters
Part II—The Methods of the Missionary

We have pointed out that those who are recorded in Scripture as having been called of God to go forth from the churches with the gospel to other lands did so apart from the authority or direction of a missionary organization or church council. We have further sought to show that the Scriptures which narrate these missionary methods were divinely intended to be for the permanent guidance of God's people throughout the present era, these records being not merely a narration of historical facts, but an essential part of the faith once delivered to the saints. Had missionaries been sent forth under the control of an ecclesiastical organization it would have been responsible both for their guidance and their maintenance. Such, however, was not the case. Being sent forth by the Holy Spirit, they went in dependence upon God for the supply of their needs.

They doubtless received material assistance from the churches with which they had been identified prior to their leaving. No doubt, too, further aid was ministered as far as possible. They also received help from the churches which were established as a result of their missionary service, though there were some who failed in this respect. Thus the apostle Paul says that in the beginning of his labors in Europe, when he departed from Macedonia, no church had fellowship with him, in the matter of giving and receiving, save that at Philippi. The saints there were diligent in this respect. While he was in Thessalonica they sent once and again to meet his need (Phil. 3:15, 16). Afterwards, while he was at Corinth, the brethren which came from Macedonia supplied the measure of his want (2 Cor. 11:9). They endeavored to continue communications with him after he had gone further afield, but seem to have lacked facilities for doing so until the time of his imprisonment at Rome, when Epaphroditus brought gifts from them. "I rejoice in the Lord greatly," he says, "that now at length you have revived your thought for me [the metaphor is that of the blossoming of a fruit tree]; wherein ye did indeed take thought, but ye lacked opportunity" (v. 10). The consciousness of his intimate relationship with the Lord, as His servant, led him to speak of these gifts as "an odor of a sweet smell, a sacrifice acceptable, well pleasing to God" (v. 18). What he received, therefore, was accepted, not as so much assistance afforded to a missionary, but as an offering directly presented to the Lord.

Apparently the Philippian church was not the only one which communicated with him when he was in Greece. "I robbed other churches," he says to the Corinthians, "taking wages of them that I might minister unto you" (2 Cor. 11:8). He might reasonably have expected to receive support from them, but he forbore. The supplies which came from the saints in Macedonia he willingly accepted, as there was no possibility of his being misunderstood by them in so doing. His "robbing" metaphor is a kindly protest against the spiritual state of the church at Corinth. There were conditions there which led him to render his service without in any way burdening the church. Had he received gifts from them, his antagonists, ever ready to seize an occasion of making a charge against him, would have put the worst possible construction upon his action.

There were other reasons, upon occasion, for which the apostle forbore to receive gifts from a church, as, for instance, in the case of Thessalonica. While Paul kept himself from being "burdensome" to the Corinthian church (lit., from the benumbing them—an ironical expression), preaching the gospel of God for nought in order not to play into the hands of his detractors, at Thessalonica it was different. There he and his fellow missionaries wrought night and day that they might not be burdensome to (lit., to put a weight upon) the saints. The best relationship existed between the missionaries and the Thessalonian converts, but the latter were poor and sorely persecuted (1 Thess. 2:6). As a nurse cherishing her own children (v. 7), then, they not only ministered the gospel to them freely but were ready to spend and be spent for them, imparting to them their own souls, that is, their very lives. Hence they earned their own living while among them, working night and day with labor and travail (v. 9)—expressive words, the former denoting toil resulting in weariness, the latter stressing difficulty and hardship involved in the work. In this they afford another example of how missionary work may be done in the will of God where financial help could not be taken.

All this, however, makes clear that a missionary is justified ordinarily in receiving gifts from those on whose behalf he is laboring. There would no doubt be frequently some hesitancy in mentioning matters of this sort, but in any case it is not a question of soliciting assistance. The apostle never did this; what he did was to seek to exercise the consciences of believers in regard to the fellowship in the gospel, and especially those converted through his ministry: and this he did, not, as he says, with a desire of receiving the gifts to supply his own needs, but with the aim of the spiritual welfare of the churches "that fruit might increase to their account." Ministration to a servant of God is ministration to the Lord Himself. So Christ had taught. "He that receiveth you," He said, "receiveth Me, and he that receiveth Me receiveth Him that sent Me" (Matt. 10:40). Thus the Lord identifies Himself with His servants, and on this ground they rightly regard what is done on their behalf as done for His sake. These early believers needed instruction in such matters, and today, with the apostolic pattern before us in the Word, the duty and privileges of converts in these respects need to be brought home to them.

In the Galatian epistle the apostle stresses the responsibility devolving upon those who receive instruction in the things of God to minister temporal supplies to those by whom the instruction is imparted. "Let him that is taught in the Word," he says, "communicate [or share] with him that teacheth in all good things" (Gal. 6:6). Spiritual benefit is the highest benefit. Ministry which produces increase in the knowledge of God and His will is of the utmost value. It pertains not only to the life which now is, but that which is to come. Accordingly those who are the subject of such ministry are called upon to recognize in a practical way the service rendered to them. Such ministry he speaks of as "sowing unto the Spirit." Sowing to the flesh is not confined to the grosser appetites and doings. He also sows to the flesh who takes thought merely for his own needs and disregards the claims of God concerning others. He sows to the Spirit who, recognizing the divine claims, wholeheartedly presents himself to the Lord to fulfill His will. Hence, in reference to doing good to others, the apostle proceeds to say, "Let us not be weary in well doing: for in due season we shall reap if we faint not" (v. 9).

CHAPTER SEVENTEEN

Financial Matters Part III—The Responsibility of Churches

Having considered apostolic methods in relation to financial help from the point of view of the laborers themselves, their dependence upon the Lord, their receipt and use, or their refusal of, gifts, we will now look at the subject with regard to the churches. The principles relating to the subject of giving for the assistance of the poor, as mentioned in the last chapter but one, apply equally to the practical assistance of those who are engaged in the work of the gospel.

The instruction given by Paul to the church at Corinth concerning his prospective labors in the regions beyond, shows that the carrying of the gospel further afield was in one respect contingent upon the practical fellowship of that church. Only when their faith increased—clearly a faith that was to find expression in works, active faith that renders aid—could he extend his service in the direction intended. "Having hope," he says, "that, as your faith groweth, we shall be magnified in you according to our province* unto further abundance, so as to preach the gospel even unto the parts beyond you" (2 Cor. 10:15, 16), that is to say, western Greece, probably also Italy and even Spain.

Not that the apostle was thinking merely of material assistance. His chief concern was their spiritual state, but from what he says elsewhere in the epistle, he evidently had in mind that the faith which betokened a healthy spiritual condition, and by reason of which he would be set free for work in the regions beyond, would inevitably produce practical results in wholehearted cooperation in these further efforts. Their progress in faith would enable him to break up new ground in the sphere allotted to him by the Lord.

We may learn from this that if our faith in God is such that we enter into His counsels concerning the perishing (for whom Christ died as much as for us), if we have the mind of Christ concerning the work of His servants and their labors in the gospel, we shall so further them by our practical support as to enable them to reach the hitherto unreached.

The church at Philippi seems to have been preeminent in the matter of giving for the support of the Lord's servants, and may be taken as a model in this respect. The saints there not only ministered to Paul's needs while he was present with them, they sought to maintain their practical fellowship as far as possible in his subsequent labors elsewhere. There was an interval of at least nine years between the time when he was first at Philippi and the time when he wrote the Philippian epistle. Of their earliest and ready fellowship with him he reminds them in tones of the deepest appreciation: "And ye yourselves also know, ye Philippians," he says, "that in the beginning of the gospel [i.e. in his pioneering work in that district], when I departed from Macedonia, no church had fellowship with me in the matter of giving and receiving [opened, as it were, an account with me, and entered into partnership], but ye only; for even in Thessalonica [as if to say, "when I had but recently left you"] ye sent once and again unto my need" (Phil. 4:15, 16). For, as we have seen, he could not there be chargeable to the converts (1 Thess. 2:9).

*The margin "limit" gives a clearer meaning than "province." The figure is that of a measuring rod; the apostle is referring to his avoidance of overlapping or interfering with the work of other men. Compare verse 13.

Again, during the first five years between his first and second visits, messengers were dispatched to Greece by the apostle (see, for instance, Acts 19:22), and as Philippi lay on the main road between Asia and Achaia, those who were sent to the latter province would often, if not always, stay on the way with the church in the Macedonian city. Opportunities for the transmission of gifts were, therefore, comparatively speaking, frequent.

A third visit by Paul himself is referred to in Acts 20:5, 6, the last before his imprisonment in Rome. After that visit they had sought opportunities for communicating, but had not been successful. Paul had become aware of this through the information received shortly before he wrote the epistle. While rejoicing in the renewal at length of their practical assistance, he says, "Wherein ye did indeed take thought, but ye lacked opportunity" (3:10).

As far as in them lay, therefore, they had constantly rendered assistance to him through all these years. Regarding this he says, at the outset of his epistle, "I thank my God upon all my remembrance of you, always in every supplication of mine on behalf of you all, making my supplication with joy for your fellowship in furtherance of the gospel from the first day until now" (1:3–5). It was God Who was working in them "both to will and to work for His good pleasure" (2:13).

They had heard of Paul's arrival in Rome and had now sent contributions to him by the hand of Epaphroditus, of whom he speaks as their "messenger" (literally, their "apostle"). Possibly Epaphroditus was a member of the church at Philippi, though it is by no means necessary to suppose that this was so. He was at all events a channel of communication between the church and the missionary.

All these things are written for our admonition. In its love, its diligence, its self-denial and zeal, the church at Philippi is an example to all churches. The churches which expressed practical fellowship in the spread of the gospel, did so on behalf of those who had labored in their own midst, but we should not be justified in drawing the conclusion that material assistance on the part of believers was intended to be limited to those servants of God who have personally labored on their behalf in the gospel. One of the reasons why the apostle John wrote his brief epistle to Gaius was to commend him for his liberal entertainment of missionary brethren who were strangers to him, and to exhort him to assist in their expenses. "Beloved, thou doest a faithful work," says the apostle, "in whatsoever thou doest toward them that are brethren and strangers withal; who bare witness to thy love before the church: whom thou wilt do well to set forward on their journey worthily of God: because that for the sake of the name they went forth, taking nothing of the Gentiles. We therefore ought to welcome such, that we may be fellow workers with the truth" (3 John 5–8). We are called then to follow the example both of the church at Philippi and Gaius.

The facilities for reaching missionaries with gifts were exceedingly circumscribed in early times. It was not easy, comparatively speaking, for an assembly in Greece to reach a missionary in Rome. Suitable occasions must have been rare despite the willingness. How different it is today! We have every possible facility for constant communication with the servants of God, no matter how far afield they have gone. International exchange and postal services have shortened time, bridged space, and bound the world into a comparatively small compass. The Epaphroditus type of ministry can, in one respect, be done without a long and difficult journey. There are also those who freely give their services to stimulate and maintain fellowship, by acting as channels of communication, providing information, giving advice, and adopting the most useful means of transmitting offerings. For some to render such assistance as will facilitate missionary enterprise, without compromising the principles of God's Word relating to the carrying on of the work seems to be the mind of God, as was the appointment of men in the earliest days of church history to see to the distribution amongst the poor, when difficulties arose in connection with the daily ministration (Acts 6). There is clearly Scriptural justification for the work of such "treasurers" (Neh. 13:13).

The message given by the apostle John to Gaius provides evidence that there were brethren engaged in carrying the gospel from place to place, in simple dependence on God for the supply of their needs, refusing to take money from the unconverted. Missionaries they were, men whose supreme object was the glory of "the name," men who, regardless of their own interests, were swayed, as the apostle Paul had been, by the desire "that Christ might be magnified."

The assistance of such is, in the inspired language of the epistle, "a faithful work." Those who render them help are "fellow workers with the truth." A holy partnership! A business paying excellent and permanent dividends! And what a standard the apostle sets before us! Our practical help is to be rendered "worthily of God." There can be no grander description. The very character of God is to be displayed in our giving. He gives liberally. So should we. He gives because He loves. "God so loved . . . that He gave." Love is to be the inspiring motive of our giving. What we minister is to be ministered "as of the strength which God supplieth: that in all things God may be glorified through Jesus Christ" (1 Pet. 4:11). "Worthily of God!" If our giving is consistent with His honor, the hands of His sent ones will be strengthened continually, and who can measure the effects of the work in which they are engaged?

CHAPTER EIGHTEEN

Marriage

There is no evidence to show that the missionaries who are recorded in the Acts of the apostles as having been called to leave the churches where they were first laboring, and to go to the regions beyond, were married men. In the case of Paul the evidence is to the contrary. In giving instructions to the church at Corinth he says, "But I say to the unmarried and the widows, it is good for them that they abide even as I" (1 Cor. 7:8). Scripture is silent upon this matter in regard to Barnabas and Silas, and Timothy. That does not afford a conclusion that they remained unmarried, or that their marriage would have been inconsistent with the will of the Lord. Indeed Paul says of himself and his fellow missionaries, "Have we no right to lead about a wife that is a believer, even as the rest of the apostles, and the brethren of the Lord, and Cephas?" (1 Cor. 9:5). This would suggest, however, that up to that time at least, Paul and the three missionaries mentioned forbore to enter upon the married state. His testimony elsewhere is significant. We may take it that when he says, "He that is unmarried is careful for the things of the Lord, how he may please the Lord" (7:32), he himself is an example in this respect.

Timothy, it would seem, remained unmarried during all the period of his missionary service in which he was associated with the apostle Paul. The suggestion is sometimes made that in countries where immorality is prevalent it is strongly advisable, if not practically necessary, for a young man to become married. We do well to bear in mind, however, that the countries in which Timothy was called to labor were characterized by the grossest forms of immorality. The associations of a younger man with a senior servant of God was in itself evidently a divinely appointed safeguard against the dangers referred to. So it proved to be in Timothy's case. Writing to the church at Corinth, after some six years of joint missionary service, Paul could speak of him as his "beloved and faithful child in the Lord" (1 Cor. 4:17), and again, four or five years later still, could say to the saints at Philippi, that he had no man like-minded who would genuinely care for their state, and that as a child serveth a father, so he had served with him in the furtherance of the gospel (Phil. 2:20–22). The deadly surroundings of heathendom had not proved too dangerous for the young unmarried man whom God had called and associated with a senior missionary in this way.

These facts afford intimations of the mind of the Lord on the question of marriage in the early period of service in the regions beyond. We will assume that the call given to a certain worker to go forth is clear, that is to say, the call to leave previous gospel service in the locality of the church with which a laborer has been identified (for such is the pattern set before us in the Acts) and to go to another land, and that the church is ready to commend the worker to the grace of God for the new service. Obviously, in response to the call, the life has been presented to the Lord, to be devoted to Him on behalf of the people and their spiritual needs in the country whither He is leading. The work will therefore be undertaken in entire freedom from self-interested motives, nothing being allowed which would distract the heart from devotion to the Lord and His cause, or detract from the efficiency of the work.

In order for this it is undeniably necessary for a worker who is new to a country to become thoroughly acquainted with the people, their manners and customs, their ideas and susceptibilities, and their interests. To this end, also, where a different language is spoken, one's energies have to be devoted diligently to acquire such fluency as will enable the worker to converse freely with the people and to impart instruction to them. Such a task, usually of a most exacting nature, if real efficiency is in view, has to be undertaken with due regard to the change of climate in a new country and its effect upon one's health. "The body is for the Lord," and needs to be maintained in efficiency for His service so far as in us lies.

If a young woman, freshly undertaking such service, with all that it demands in the respects just mentioned, becomes married before sufficient time has elapsed for her thorough acquaintance with the people and their language, and for her acclimatization, it is impossible for her work to be efficient. More than this, the twofold responsibility imposes an undue strain upon her. There are first the claims of home life, and, in the ordinary course of things, all that is involved in the birth and rearing of children. There remain also the claims of the people, for work among whom she gave herself to the Lord. The two distinct responsibilities, each of them fresh to her, cannot be discharged worthily of God. If her heart is still really burdened with the needs of the people, and she endeavors to fulfill her God-given desires toward them, her home life suffers, and, should a child or children come, the attention and care due in that respect cannot be adequately given. On the other hand, if the home and family duties are properly discharged, the work among the people suffers. Their language remains unacquired, and, even should language-learning be unnecessary, there cannot be that thorough acquaintance with them which the work of reaching them, and winning them with the gospel, demands. How can one who has the duties of family life to attend to, give, in the first year or two of her service, the time requisite for due intercourse with the natives, and for such acquaintance with them as will equip her for efficient missionary work among them? How often has the effort to undertake both duties in the early stage of her work produced a breakdown in health, and rendered continuance in the country impossible! To incur permanent detriment to health in this way, and the deleterious effects upon one's offspring, can scarcely be in the mind of the Lord for His servants.

Such considerations have led some missionary societies to lay down stringent regulations for those who are sent out under their control, prohibiting marriage for a certain number of years, until there has been time for acclimatization and for acquaintance with the people and their language. If, notwithstanding this, there is a readiness on the part of many to be subject to such human regulations, should those who go out in acknowledged dependence on the Lord, have a lower standard of devotion, and by contracting early marriages use their liberty in acting contrary to the experience of godly men in societies? Nay, surely it behoves them, consistently with their professed adherence to the principles of Scripture, the more to abide by the example, intimations and teaching of the Word of God.

Faith in God will ever lead us to act for His glory in a spirit of genuine disinterestedness. Faith not only produces the inquiry, "Lord, what wilt Thou have me do?" but leads us to discern His will from the Scriptures. Thus we are saved from acting by the mere impulse of the flesh, and from following some intuition which lacks the guidance of the Word of God.

The first years of such arduous toil as missionary labor entails should be free from distractions, and we may well question whether those who give themselves to the service are not called to impose upon themselves the self-denial of refraining even from the absorbing correspondence contingent upon a matrimonial engagement. In the ordinary course of things in the so-called homelands a considerable period of industrious toil is required before a young man can marry. Should not the very claims of Christ lead one to give a full measure of time to undistracted energy in becoming efficient in the high and holy calling of missionary service? Should we not seek to avoid even the appearance of making such service a shortcut to the joys of married life? The actual attempt would be such a travesty of real dependence upon the guidance of the Spirit of God as to involve serious consequences for those who so acted.*

*"A young man who believes that he is called of God to the service of the gospel may well ask himself if he is prepared for some self-denial in the matter of marriage, as well as in other ways: not because of rules, but in simple devotedness to the Lord. Treading the difficult path of service in a foreign land with a wife and family is very different from doing so alone (i.e., unmarried, or in conjunction with a senior missionary). We call special attention to this, because it is a fact that, while men who follow a business or profession often have to spend a good while in attaining a position in which they can marry, some who go out as missionaries are not prepared to give a few years to the work before marriage, and, indeed, some think they must be engaged before they begin."—The late Mr. W. H. Bennet, in "Principles of Missionary Work," p. 24.

For the argument that since the Lord sent out His apostles two and two, the going forth of two who are married is an adherence to His plan, see chapter six.

Again it has been advocated that a woman married to a missionary might in certain cases be simply a missionary's wife, without herself being regarded as acting in the capacity of a missionary. But how can such a distinction be consistent with marriage in the Lord? Such a marriage involves a union of hearts, of motives and aims. A missionary needs one to be his partner in life who will sympathetically share his burdens, face difficult situations, and enter into his counsels—one who, in other words, will be a true helpmeet for him, and this involves missionary service on her part of a very real nature. To attempt to establish such a distinction is to contravene the divine principles which are intended to govern the married state. A missionary's wife is one who is appointed to such a share in her husband's service that his call to the work means her identification with it. Hence the need of qualifications in her case giving evidence that she, too, has been called and appointed by the Spirit of God for the service.

We would urge upon overseeing brethren in the churches the prayerful consideration of these important matters, so that, insofar as what we have pointed out carries conviction as being according to the divine plan, they may be helped thereby to give godly counsel to those in whose cases they discern a call to the regions beyond and such qualifications as are confirmatory of the call, so that the high standard of the Lord's work in the mission field may be maintained.

CHAPTER NINETEEN

The Relationship of the Gospel of Matthew

In giving the apostles His parting commission, our Lord declared that all authority had been given unto Him in heaven and on earth. In view of this they were to go and "make disciples of all nations" (literally, "disciple all nations") the idea being to impart instruction with a view to discipleship. They were to baptize them "into the name of the Father, and of the Son and of the Holy Ghost," and were to teach them to observe all things whatsoever He had commanded them. "And lo," He says, "I am with you alway [literally, all the days], even unto the end of the age" (Matt. 28:20). His "lo" carries with it the assurance of a circumstance which naturally would have been contrary to expectation. There was nothing beyond what they would ordinarily expect in the command to go and preach the gospel and impart their Master's instructions, but to have His continuous presence with them all the time from the beginning to the very end was something far exceeding human anticipation.

The Lord's design, therefore, in gospel service was not merely evangelization; instruction was likewise to be given in all the divine will. Conversion was to be followed by discipleship, with consequent conformity to the mind of the Lord. The will of God is at once the directing aim and the molding power of discipleship. All that Christ has enjoined and taught must be passed on by the preachers of the gospel if converts were to be brought into harmony with the purposes and ways of God. There was to be no selection of the Lord's instructions according to human ideas of what might be appropriate or convenient. His "all things" is clear, and compulsory.

There is no justification for the supposition that His commission, as recorded in these closing words of the Gospel of Matthew, was not designed for fulfillment in the present era. The apostles, being those to whom the instructions were personally given, were themselves intended to carry them out, though actually they would be required to wait until they had received "power from on high." There is not a hint here or anywhere else in Scripture that the fulfillment was to take place in a period subsequent to the present era of the formation and testimony of the Church. Clearly, too, the same duties were to be discharged by their successors throughout the present age. This lies in His promise, "and lo, I am with you alway, even into the end [or consummation] of the age." By "the age" the Lord plainly intended the period to be introduced subsequent to His ascension and the sending of the Spirit, and to be consummated at His Second Coming.

The pledge of His abiding presence would be fulfilled throughout the whole era, until the gospel had completed its mission among the nations, in other words, until "the consummation of the age," the time when everything will have headed up to the climax of events destined to transpire at the end. A distinction is to be made between the consummation of the age and its actual termination. The Rapture of the Church is to take place previously to the actual termination of the age. The Lord's presence has never been removed from His followers. The Holy Spirit, given at pentecost, the enabling power for the witness of the gospel, still remains, and today, while everything is rapidly reaching the appointed consummation, the terms of the Lord's commission continue obligatory.

The idea that the Gospel of Matthew is simply Jewish, in the sense that its contents apply directly and chiefly to the nation of the Jews, and contain but a remote application to the saints of this age, is void of Scriptural foundation. There are, indeed, many indications to the contrary to give full details of which would be beyond the scope of the present chapter. We may mention a few. The teaching of the so-called "Sermon on the Mount," cannot have been intended to apply merely to the "dispensation" of the Law, as if the Lord's precepts belonged simply to that era and the doctrines of grace are to be sought for in the epistles. That assumption is not supported by Scripture evidence. The apostle Peter spoke of the Law as being "a yoke which neither our fathers nor we were able to bear" (Acts 15:10). How different are the commandments of Christ! He Who spoke "the Sermon on the Mount" says, "My yoke is easy and My burden is light" (Matt. 11:30). And was not His gracious invitation, "Come unto Me, all ye that labor and are heavy laden, and I will give you rest," intended for all, Jew and Gentile, throughout this day of grace?*

Practically all the commandments and exhortations in the Sermon on the Mount are to be found in one form or another in the eistles. The injunctions regarding loving our enemies, blessing those who curse us, praying for persecutors, are, to all intents and purposes, the same in Matthew 5, 6, 7 and in the epistles. It is difficult to conceive how the Sermon on the Mount can be intended to apply to the millennial earthly kingdom promised to Israel. Persecution for righteousness' sake is hardly likely to take place then. That will not be a period when men "reproach" and "persecute" the saints, and say all manner of evil against them falsely for Christ's sake. Nor is it likely that conditions at that time will render necessary the command, "Resist not him that is evil: but whosoever smiteth thee on the right cheek, turn to him the other also; and if any man would go to law with thee, and take away thy coat, let him have thy cloak also." Nor again can it be imagined that there will be false prophets going about in sheep's clothing, though actually in the character of ravening wolves (Matt. 7:15). Compare, on the other hand, Paul's warning to the elders of the church at Ephesus concerning such men (Acts 20:29).

Again, to those who are reproached and persecuted for Christ's sake the Lord promises a "reward in heaven" (vv. 11, 12). Rewards in heaven do not appertain to Israel's millennial condition. The whole tenor of the Lord's teaching in these chapters is characteristic of the time of Christ's rejection and His absence from the world. Everything goes to show that in thus addressing His disciples His instructions were intended to apply as much to this period of gospel service and Church testimony as to the time of His presence with them prior to the Cross. That He was accustomed to repeat some of the precepts He had given in the Sermon on the Mount, seems clear from their occurrences in the Gospel of Luke. His words, though actually addressed to them, have been left on record for the admonition and instruction of all His saints throughout this age, and it is necessary for all, who, engaging in the service of the gospel, make and instruct disciples to inculcate those same principles.

The teachings of Matthew 5, 6, 7, then, are among the "all things" that the Lord commanded. Conformity to His will therein revealed is not legality, it is the permanent design contemplated in the preaching of the gospel of the grace of God. We can hear the echo of the Lord's behest to go and make disciples of "all nations" in Paul's statement that he and his fellow apostles had received grace and apostleship from the Lord, "unto obedience of faith among all nations, for His Name's sake" (Rom. 1:5), and again, that the preaching of Jesus Christ "is made known unto all the nations unto obedience of faith" (16:26).

The great condition laid down in the gospel is the confession of "Jesus as Lord" (Rom. 10:9), and this involves obedience to His commands. "Why call ye Me, Lord, Lord," He says, "and do not the things which I say?" Obedience to His commands is the evidence,

*Further, when we consider the Lord's teachings in the parables in Matthew 13 it becomes clear how largely they refer to conditions existing in this present age of gospel testimony. The idea that this and other parts of the Gospel of Matthew have to do with the proclamation of the earthly kingdom of the Jews immediately after pentecost, and the postponement of the kingdom consequent upon their rejection of the proclamation, is pure inference. We need to be on our guard against hyper-dispensationalizing of the Scriptures.

not of bondage to the inexorable claims of the Law, but of response to the love of God in Christ: "And hereby we do know that we know Him, if we keep His commandments. He that saith, I know Him, and keepeth not His commandments, is a liar, and the truth is not in Him. But whoso keepeth His word, in Him verily is the love of God perfected: hereby know we that we are in Him" (1 John 2:3–5). Obedience to the precepts of Christ is exhibited both in love to God and to one another: "By this we know that we love the children of God, when we love God, and keep His commandments. For this is the love of God, that we keep His commandments, and His commandments are not grievous" (1 John 5:2, 3).

▪ CHAPTER TWENTY ▪

The Great Design

In the mind of God the grand ultimate object of missionary activity is the formation of His Church, the corporate company of those who by means of the gospel are brought into vital and permanent union with Christ. It is described as "His body, the fullness of Him Who filleth all in all" (Eph. 1:23). Spiritual ministry of whatever character, as provided by the Lord, and directed by the Spirit of God, has as its aim the building up of this body (Eph. 4:12). Membership of it is effected, apart from all national and social distinctions, immediately upon reception of Christ by faith.

The truth relating to the constitution of the church in this respect is succinctly set forth by the apostle Paul as "the mystery of Christ, to wit, that the Gentiles are fellow heirs, and fellow members of the body, and fellow partakers of the promise in Christ Jesus through the gospel" (Eph. 3:4–6). Concerning the mystery, he had received both a revelation and a stewardship. The effect of the revelation was to give him an understanding in the mystery (v. 4); the purpose of the stewardship was that he might "fulfill the Word of God" (Col. 1:25), suggesting that this great truth was, so to speak, the keystone of the edifice of the doctrines of the faith. Here the divine designs and creations reach their height. The trust imposed upon him met with a zeal comparable to, and indeed surpassing, even that which characterized his former antagonism. "Now I rejoice," he says, "in my sufferings, for your sake, and fill up on my part that which is lacking of the afflictions of Christ in my flesh for His body's sake, which is the Church." Christ Himself endured the Cross, bearing sin and suffering in expiation thereof. Subsequently, as He Himself had foretold, His followers would suffer, not expiatory sufferings indeed, but manifold afflictions inseparable from their faithful testimony to His name and to the saving efficacy of His atoning sufferings. These afflictions the apostle did not shirk. His missionary enthusiasm for this sublime object never flagged. Writing now from prison after many years of service he adds, "Whom we proclaim, admonishing every man in all wisdom, that we may present every man perfect in Christ; whereunto I labor also, striving according to His working which worketh in me mightily."

By means of the formation, constitution and position of the church, God has determined to make known even now "unto the principalities and the powers in the heavenly places" His manifold [lit., "much varied"] wisdom, "according to the eternal purpose which He purposed in Christ Jesus our Lord" (Eph. 3:10, 11). To engage in the work of the gospel is therefore to have part in providing instruction to angelic beings in the mysteries of divine grace.

The formation of this great corporate monument to the grace of God in Christ was designed, in the divine intention, to produce local churches throughout this era in every place where the gospel bears fruit, each church being so constituted as to represent in many respects a miniature of the whole. For each is described as a temple, as is the whole (1 Cor. 2:16; Eph. 2:21), and each, as well as the whole, is designated as a body (1 Cor. 12:27; Eph. 4:8–16). While the whole church is the body as distinct from the head, for Christ is Himself the Head (Eph. 4), yet, in the local use of the metaphor, individual members are viewed as parts of the head, e.g., the eye and the ear, as well as other members of the body, and Christ acts, as Lord, throughout the whole of the body (1 Cor. 12).* We are speaking of

*Such terms as "body" and "temple," which are applied both to the whole Church and to each local company, serve to indicate the scope of the word "church" itself. A body represents something integral, an entity; so does a temple. Since then a local church is a body, with members discharging their several functions, to apply the term

the churches as described in the plan and pattern in the New Testament, and not of those modifications of it existing in what is called Christendom. As we have pointed out, the New Testament design for churches was not a temporary arrangement requiring modification to fit changing conditions.

In the Ephesian epistle the apostle shows very fully how the parts of the whole are related to one another. "There is one body . . . one Spirit . . . one hope . . . one Lord, one faith, one baptism, one God and Father of all, Who is over all and through all and in all" (4:6).* This expresses a unity of origin, design and destiny. The Church owes its existence to the counsels and the power of the triune God. Its formation and unity are established by the working of the Holy Spirit, are maintained under the headship and authority of Christ as Lord, and, each member being related to God as Father, the whole is derived from Him and under His control—He is "over all"; it is pervaded by His presence as its energizing power—He is "through all"; and in all its parts it is indwelt by Him —He is "in all." As its source, its sustenance and its service are all dependent upon Him, it bears the impress of His character and attributes.

In this passage the unity of the body and the unity of the hope are directly associated with the Holy Spirit: "there is one body, and one Spirit, even as also ye were called in one hope of your calling." The unity of the faith and the "one baptism" are associated with the "one Lord." The "one faith" brings the members into union with Him, and builds them up in Him. The one baptism constitutes the outward recognition and confession of this inward union with Him and of His Lordship. The whole is the "habitation of God." This is the one true and holy catholic Church, not established on earth, nor visible yet on earth. Its members are "not of this world," even as Christ is "not of this world" (John 17:14). This Church Christ Himself began to build at pentecost, in fulfillment of His word to Simon Peter on the occasion of his testimony to the facts relating to His Person: "And I also say unto thee, that thou art Peter: [*Petros*], and upon this rock [*petra,* "Myself thus witnessed to"] I will build My Church; and the gates of Hades shall not prevail against it" (Matt. 16:16–18). The great truth revealed to and uttered by Peter is indissociable from Christ Himself; He Himself is the immovable foundation. The building has been in process ever since pentecost, as one and another have become united to Him by faith, through the gospel, and the structure will ere long be completed. Then by His word of transforming and resurrection power the whole will be brought into complete conformity to Himself, made perfect through His comeliness, and seen to be worthy of Himself and of His work of redeeming grace.

This glorious act, crowning the work in which He is now engaged, is intimated in the "one hope" of Ephesians 4:3. The Church will be raptured into His own presence, to stand before His Judgment Seat and to be presented to Himself, thereafter to become His partner in the exercise of His authority over His universal kingdom. At His Second Advent in manifested glory, when He intervenes in the world's affairs, to overthrow the foes of God and hurl the great adversary to his doom, He will come "to be glorified in His saints, and to be marveled at in all them that believed." Then will all that is intimated in those grand metaphorical descriptions of the church in the epistle to the Ephesians be exhibited in their fullness. In perfect holiness of character, and perfect harmony of activity, His redeemed will then entirely satisfy the heart of Him Who "loved the Church and gave Himself up for it, that He might sanctify it, having cleansed it by the washing of water with the Word, that He might present the Church to Himself a glorious Church, not having spot or wrinkle, or

"church" to the believers living in a country, or to a group of churches in any locality, is inconsistent with the teaching of Scripture. They could not be a body, for they do not represent that which functions in the local sense, according to the teaching of 1 Corinthians 12:27, and they form only a fraction of the whole Church, the Body of Christ as set forth in the epistle to the Ephesians.

*In these respects there is an interrelationship of churches. Nowhere, however, does Scripture countenance the establishment of anything like an ecclesiastical amalgamation or federation of churches. Those in any given locality are never found associated under a central authority.

any such thing; but that it should be holy and without blemish" (Eph. 5:25–27). Thus have we been called by the Gospel "to the obtaining of the glory of our Lord Jesus Christ" (2 Thess. 2:14). As we contemplate the greatness of this transcendent scheme of divine grace, which the apostle sums up in the phrase, "the unsearchable riches of Christ," we are constrained to say, in the words of his ascription of praise to God, "Unto Him be the glory in the Church and in Christ Jesus, unto all generations forever and ever. Amen."

CHAPTER TWENTY-ONE

Present-Day Problems and Opportunities

Since the war came to an end, we have entered upon a period in which, if the Lord does not come, there are likely to be untold possibilities of missionary activity for the salvation of the perishing, and the Scriptural instruction of converts. It may be that God has been preparing for this during the great world conflict. The operation of His Spirit in this work is neither furthered by mere social schemes, nor hindered by antagonistic circumstances, if God has determined that the work shall be accomplished, and if His people are ready to rise to their responsibilities. It is our high privilege to take our part, every one of us, in promoting the service of the gospel, both in this and other lands. Whether we are called to go forth to regions beyond, or to remain in our own locality, no believer is exempt from this God-given work. Indeed, how can any adequate sense of God's mercy toward us in Christ, and the fact that we ourselves are on our way to the glory, instead of going down to the pit of eternal doom, and all this through the redeeming work of the Cross, fail to meet with a devoted response in presenting ourselves to the Lord for this purpose?

Let us then be awake to the realization of the fast-fleeting opportunities granted us. The fields are "white unto harvest." The possibilities are immense. The Holy Spirit is still calling and preparing the hearts of young men and women to be willing to go forth with the word of life, either to fill gaps in the ranks or to evangelize places where Christ has not been named.

There is also a renewed call for elder brethren to encourage and instruct those who give evidence of being raised up to go forth to other lands as messengers of Christ.

Effective ministry of the gospel requires men who have received definite training under the guidance of the Holy Spirit, and who have sought and obtained counsel and help from men of God. Suitable courses of training can be obtained and are important, not only for efficient work, but in view of the ever-increasing number of propagandists of error throughout the world. False teachers, who themselves have been trained for their work, and, while professing to teach the truth, are skilled in so handling the Scriptures as to use them to teach erroneous doctrines. The evil one has his sowers of tares where the good seed is being scattered.

The training of servants of God should therefore embrace instruction as to how to meet from the Word of God the heresies promulgated. Only by a knowledge of the Scriptures and power to use them against error can converts be guarded against the intrigues of those who would come in among them and beguile them from adherence to the truth.

There have been useful courses of training conducted in certain localities by competent teachers resident in the districts who have voluntarily rendered help to men and women who, having been commended by the elder brethren of their assemblies, were expecting to engage in missionary service abroad. These courses included some medical tuition. Developments along these lines would be very advantageous.

Those who will be working with fellow missionaries in the land where they expect to go, will find that the experience of being associated with others during their period of preparation has been of great advantage (see also chapter six of this volume). There are evidences in the Gospels of the wisdom and grace of the Lord in this very respect in regard to the disciples whom He had gathered out to receive from Himself a preparation for their subsequent ministry as His apostles. A striking example of this is given upon the occasion in the Upper Room, when, after they had been striving among themselves as to which of them was the greatest, He rose from His couch at the table, girded Himself with a towel, and went round washing their feet. He made this the ground of exhortation as to the need of doing to one another as He had done to them, and the apostle Peter evidently recalls this in his first epistle when he says, "Likewise, ye younger, be subject unto the elder. Yea, all of you gird yourselves with humility to serve one another" (5:5, R.V.).

Reference has been made in preceding pages to the undesirability of appeals for young men and women to go forth as missionaries. This is indeed to be deprecated. The absence of any such thing in the New Testament is significant. The needs in every land were as great in those days as they are now, yet the apostles never made appeals in this respect. To stress the opportunities and privileges at the expense of faithful representations of the hardships and responsibilities is not helpful.

The great essential in preparation is that of being "approved of God" (1 Thess. 2:4, R.V.), and this is a matter not of a few months but of years. It is important to observe in the New Testament the considerable length of time during which those who were called to go to regions beyond were gaining experience in the localities from whence eventually they went forth. During this preliminary period they gave evidence of their qualifications, and approved themselves both to God and to their brethren in the churches. Much is to be learnt in these matters from the records concerning Saul of Tarsus, Barnabas and Silas, and the details regarding the history of Timothy are especially illustrative. After all, the assembly is ever the principal sphere of training.

The influence of the rush and haste of these times tends to prove detrimental to the thoroughness and efficiency of missionary service. To endeavor to hasten matters in the energy of human zeal can result only in calamity and confusion in the work abroad.

We may mention here some of the qualifications which should be in evidence before any are commended to go forth. Chief among these are (1) godliness of life through years of fellowship with God; (2) a knowledge of His will and of the mind of Christ as a result of meditation on the Scriptures; (3) a self-sacrificing compassion for the perishing; (4) an aptitude for setting forth the gospel in its fullness and simplicity, and for teaching converts to observe all things the Lord has commanded (Matt. 28:20), instructing them in the ways of the Lord and in matters relating to church fellowship and testimony; (5) a manifest ability to work with other servants of Christ in humble and happy cooperation; (6) an ability to learn the language where such is necessary, and a willingness to devote oneself to language study in a spirit of energetic and continuous application; (7) a knowledge of first aid, and at least some knowledge of medicine and of nursing.

Great possibilities of a more widespread evangelization in other lands lie in the present rapid developments of means of transit. Good roads have been, and are being, constructed in many countries, and facilities for traveling by motor car and motor van are increasing. It is easy now for a missionary to go the rounds of the villages and townships in the district where work has been extending. The use of the car to attend conferences of workers is giving greater opportunities than ever for consultation with fellow missionaries and native workers.

Another factor conducing to these ends is the means of travel by air. Visits to missionaries and their districts are being undertaken in this way, and some brethren are giving themselves to more permanent and systematic cooperation by the use of the airplane.

All this calls for prayer for guidance from the Lord for those whose hearts are exercised about rendering assistance to already existing work, and seeking to facilitate work of a pioneering character.

While all that is taking place in the world today points to the nearness of the Lord's return, the expectation of which should be constant in our hearts, yet the very realization that the time is short should impel us all to devote ourselves the more earnestly to the furtherance of the cause of Christ and His gospel and the great object of gathering out from among the nations a people for His Name for the formation of His great spiritual body, the Church.

V

A Guide to Missionary Service

CHAPTER ONE

The Divine Authority

The mind of God concerning the carrying of the gospel to all nations is made known to us in the New Testament Scriptures. The record in the thirteenth chapter of the Acts reveals the operation of the Holy Spirit in what would appear to man an irregular way, but only so because He would show His sovereignty in working where, how, and by whom He would. It was not from Jerusalem that special work of the Holy Spirit in the evangelization of other lands proceeded, but from Antioch. Nor did it partake of the character of a commission from a church or even a council. It was not human ordination to a mission at all. What took place was the separation of men by the Holy Spirit for the express purpose of carrying the gospel to regions beyond. It was He Who set apart from among those who were already accredited in the assembly at Antioch, and that assembly a comparatively recently planted one, certain individuals by name, and these probably those pillars in the church who could least be spared. We gather this from the word used in verse 3, which really signifies, "They let them go."

The Prerogatives of the Spirit of God

Here, then, we see the authority of the Holy Spirit maintained. Missionaries were not sent forth by an assembly or a group of assemblies to evangelize any given locality, but were entirely in the hands of the Holy Spirit, He Himself directing their movements from city to city and the duration of their stay in each. They were in simple dependence on the energy of the Spirit and acted under His leading.

This is the plan which is according to God. The effect of mere human order and arrangement, on the contrary, is invariably to interfere with this dependence upon the Spirit of God and personal responsibility to the Lord Jesus Christ. There is ever a tendency to forget this. In any attempt to remedy self-will in fellow servants of Christ, and to exercise some control in their service, there must be ever present the danger of limiting the Spirit of God.

Proving and Approval by God

Paul speaks of himself and his fellow missionaries as having been "approved of God to be entrusted with the gospel" (not "allowed," as the A.V. renders it), 1 Thessalonians 2:4. Approval is the result of being proved, of having stood the test. "To be entrusted" implies a proved trustworthiness.

All those whom the Spirit sent forth, as recorded in the Acts and the epistles, had been engaged in gospel work in their own localities first. They did not become missionaries either when, or because, they went from the churches to other lands. Missionary service is not a sort of career upon which one enters when setting forth, from which time one will be regarded as a "missionary."

The inquiry sometimes made by a young person as to how to "become a missionary" may be the outcome of a genuine desire, but it gives evidence of a need of searching the Scriptures as to what a call from God means.

A noticeable fact in the New Testament records is the absence of any intimation about an application on the part of anyone for permission to render service in the gospel. The possession of gift is the authority to use it. This is not to suggest in any way that it is unscriptural to make known to elder brethren in one's assembly the conviction as to the leading of the Lord in the matter of engaging in other lands in the work of the gospel in which one has already been engaging in one's own locality, and to seek their prayerful counsel; but there is a deep significance attaching to the silence of Scripture as to any application to be sent as by human appointment.

Scripture Narratives Are for Our Guidance

Certain facts stand out conspicuously in Paul's circumstances after his conversion before he was sent forth to service abroad: *(a)* his testimony began as soon as he was converted (Acts 9:18-20); *(b)* he spent a considerable time in practical fellowship in the assembly in Antioch (Acts 11, 12, 13); *(c)* his spiritual fitness became so evident that the assembly there sent him with Barnabas on a special mission to Jerusalem (11:29, 30); *(d)* he gained the esteem and appreciation of one who had been in the Lord's work some time before him (11:25); *(e)* he became known as a servant of God by the saints in three places—Damascus, Jerusalem and Antioch; *(f)* he was so valued at Antioch that at the time of the call the assembly would gladly have retained him, as is implied in the verb *apoluō,* to set free, to let go, unhappily rendered "sent away"; the sending was by the Holy Spirit (Acts 13:3, 4).

All this is not mere narrative. These facts testify to the mind and will of God regarding the life and labor of any person before being called to go forth to another land. They are part of the Holy Scriptures given for our instruction, guidance and fulfillment. Departure from them, or neglect of them through eagerness and haste, the result of appeals or our own views of needs abroad, can result only in the frustration of God's purposes and in consequent detriment and loss.

These facts, and all that is said similarly concerning Silas and subsequently Timothy, form a needful introduction to the consideration of such matters as qualifications and preparation. Our departed missionary brother C. F. Hogg well advocated that more vigorous tests should be applied to all who seek to go forth along the lines laid down in the New Testament. "Possibly there would be fewer workers, but possibly compensation in power, and those who are called and fitted would be better furnished."

God's ways are surprising to the natural mind. His methods are not in accordance with merely human ideas, though motives may be good and zealous. It was a surprisingly small company, but thoroughly efficient, that went in the earliest times into dark Asia Minor and the "dark continent" of Europe. Nevertheless, God's ways are always right, and any deviation from them prejudices the cause of His gospel.

▪ CHAPTER TWO ▪

Qualifications

The qualifications requisite for missionary service are spiritual, practical, and physical.

(a) Spiritual Qualifications

1. Those who are going forth in the Lord's work should give evidences of true conversion to God, manifested in spiritual mindedness, in a life of service and devotion to Christ.

2. They should have a good knowledge of the doctrines of Scripture, that they may be able to "hold the pattern of sound words" (2 Tim. 1:13), handling aright the Word of truth (2:15, R.V.). Timothy had known from his childhood the holy Scriptures (3:14).

There should be an aptitude for setting forth the gospel in its fullness and simplicity, and for instructing believers, ever working with the aim of leading them to become witnesses of Christ to their fellow countrymen. If a person is uninstructed in Scripture truth and is inefficient in making the gospel known intelligently in this country, how can he or she be commended to go and minister it amidst the difficult and exacting conditions abroad? How can the truth be rightly handled when confronted by the skeptic, or the propagandist of error, or even the genuine inquirer? There may be zeal, but, if it is not "according to knowledge," it serves only to create more difficulty. There are certain sound courses of training, but those of an institutional character tend to be too exhaustive. It is useful to go through a Correspondence Course of Bible Study. Great value attaches to the work of a brother in an assembly who opens his house to help in the study of the Scriptures a small number of those who are commended by assemblies in the district for eventual service in this country or abroad.

"And He appointed twelve, that they might be with Him, and that He might send them forth to preach" (Mark 3:14). "With Him!" What a Doctor of Divinity! What a training school for missionary work! The Great Example ever before them, and they sitting at His feet and learning of Him, catching something of His look, His manner, His Spirit, knowing Him, not by an occasional visit but by years of closest intimacy and daily and hourly intercourse! They were trained, not in isolation from fellow men, in colleges and seminaries, but, as doctors are trained in actual contact with disease, so they witnessed His treatment of the good and sinful, the wise and foolish, the haughty Pharisee and the hated publican, the scornful scribe and the outcast sinner, the frivolous and the sad. Yet, though called, commissioned, authorized and ordained by the Lord Himself, with all these advantages and qualifications, their training motive, method and authority were nothing without the power of the Holy Spirit. Everything depended upon their being full of the Spirit of God.

3. They should have been in the practice of seeking to win souls for Christ. If a person has not been a soul winner in his or her own locality, he or she is unlikely to be successful in doing so abroad, and particularly in view of the appalling conditions, the temptations, and trying circumstances of regions lying in even a far grosser darkness than in this country. As a well-known servant of God who has labored long in such a region has said: "Some workers have had, on entering the darkness and sin of paganism, such a revelation of the terrible and almost overwhelming power of the satanic forces of evil around them, and of the flesh within, that they have become bewildered, depressed, and afraid."

4. They should themselves have submitted to believer's baptism and be able to teach converts the necessity for, and the significance of, the ordinance.

5. They should be able to give instructions concerning assembly fellowship, the Scriptural mode of united worship and of partaking of

the Lord's Supper, and the prerogatives of the Holy Spirit in these matters. This is to be obtained by careful study of the Word of God and by receiving help from well-taught brethren. Workers should have such a grasp of the principles relating to a Scriptural Assembly that they may intelligently answer questions asked by native converts.

6. They should be of such a definitely Christlike character and disposition that their attitude should be loving and sympathetic toward natives, so as to win their confidence, avoiding any such thing as an air or conduct of superiority.

7. They should have a good report from those for whom and with whom they have been working in their avocation, not only as to high moral character but of application and capability in their occupation. Much more is needed than the fact that a person has engaged in spiritual work in connection with the assembly and even has enjoyed some success. That Timothy had "a good report" meant more than a good testimony as to his capabilities in gospel work.

If incapacity has been manifested in one's employment, going out as a missionary will not alter matters. What will not do for the ordinary business of this world's affairs must surely prove a disqualification for the stringent and exacting and even weightier labor of the mission field.

8. Elder brethren should have discerned in them a spirit of humility and willingness to take advice, according to the exhortation: "Likewise ye younger, be subject unto the elder; yea, all of you gird yourselves with humility to serve one another" (1 Pet. 5:5).

9. hey should be characterized by such chastity of heart and life that will stand the test of the immoral conditions which prevail in other lands. Any evidence of laxity or carelessness in relationships with the opposite sex disqualifies for service for God. It is sometimes suggested that a young man should marry and thus be possessed of a counteractive influence against the danger. There is, however, no hint of this in the New Testament in regard to the lives of missionaries. The case of Timothy is significant and suggestive, working as he did in lands where vice stalked in all its nakedness. The preventive lay not only in his own character but in his association with an older worker, Paul.

(b) Practical Qualifications

1. There should be an adaptability to work harmoniously in cooperation with others, especially in view of the likelihood that a younger worker may for some time be called to cooperate with a senior missionary. There should be a readiness to take the advice of such, and act as a true yokefellow. After a few years of joint service Paul could say of Timothy to an assembly, "Ye know the proof of him that, as a child serveth a father, so he served with me in furtherance of the gospel" (Phil. 2:22). One who is difficult to get on with in the mission field is a great hindrance to the work. There was no awkwardness in the walk Timothy maintained—he was willing to listen to counsel. He did not act independently of Paul, and Paul recognized all that was of God in him. Of others Paul had to say that they sought not "the things that are Jesus Christ's." The contrary was the case with this young missionary.

2. It is important to have an ability to learn a language (where it will be necessary), and a willingness to devote a strenuous, self-denying and unremitting application to it, with regular self-discipline in the use of time. One who has had insufficient education can scarcely apprehend the difficulty of learning a foreign language. Yet how can anyone adequately understand the mentality of people without learning to speak their language?

In the case of certain countries it is necessary to postpone the learning of the language until reaching the country. Even so, a course of training in language-learning is useful before going out, and there are means of doing so in this country. Speaking generally, such habits of study should be formed, in the years of preparation, as will be of help in giving oneself to assiduous acquirement of the language immediately upon reaching the country abroad. To do so when there in a desultory manner can only mean inefficiency in the work. Let one who is exercised about the Lord's work abroad test at home his or her ability in language-learning. Even if the ability is possessed, time may well be spent in further education. To attempt to speak freely in a language before sufficient knowledge of it has been gained, tends to produce ridicule from the unconverted and to harass the feelings of native believers.

In some countries—as, for instance, in a French-speaking colony—a good knowledge of French is requisite for the fulfillment of obligations to the governmental authorities and their representatives.

For this purpose a period spent in Belgium, France or Switzerland is advisable, and particular attention should be paid to the phonetics of the language.

We recommend the taking of a course at the School of Oriental and African Language Studies at the University of London, Clarence House, Matthew Parker Street, London, SW1, before going to such countries as India and the Far East and Central Africa.

In New Testament times the preaching of the gospel was facilitated by the fact that everywhere the Greek common language was spoken and understood in the countries of the Middle East and the lands round the Mediterranean, and this invalidates any argument that the learning of a language was not considered necessary. Let it be borne in mind that language-learning is not so easy after the age, of, say, thirty or thirty-five, as before.

3. There are various things of a practical nature to which a young man finds it necessary to turn his hand after arriving at his sphere of service abroad. It will be all to the advantage of his service if he has acquired a knowledge of carpentry, gardening, brickmaking, clothes-mending and other forms of constructive work. If he has had some experience as to cooking a dinner, it will be all to the good. Missionary work is not all preaching and teaching; it involves manual labor. A young man who remonstrates that he "came to preach, not to sweep floors," is not only an objectionable type, but has mistaken his calling, and would be better back in the country from which he came and occupied in earning his living there.

Some knowledge of medicine, dispensing and first aid is practically essential. A man is sorely handicapped if he knows nothing in these respects. By all means let part of his preparation consist of receiving such instruction.

For a young woman a knowledge of nursing is most desirable. Apart from the fact that many sisters go out as qualified nurses to render help in missionary hospital work and in dispensaries, some amount of training is invaluable.

(c) Physical Qualifications

It is well to consider the fact that earnest missionary service involves much physical strain. Some are prone to worry, and many a person, with a keen desire to do the utmost to further the work of the gospel, overtaxes the strength by doing really more than is needful. We need the guidance of the Spirit of God both as to what we should do and what we should refrain from doing, so as to keep the whole being fit for "the Master's use."

In this respect it is noticeable how the Lord called the disciples to come "apart into a desert place and rest awhile. For there were many coming and going" (Mark 6:31). "Mountaintop" experience is important. We quote the following from Mr. J. Griffith's booklet entitled *Counting the Cost*.

"Experience has shown that in some cases where the young worker has made a very great and self-denying effort to keep pace with the strenuous life and activities of the mission center, he discovers, suddenly or gradually it may be, that the love for prayer and reading of the Word of God is lost or greatly diminished. This may be due, in some instances perhaps, to the failure of other workers in not wisely discerning the extent of such mental and physical strain. There is no longer the interest or joy in service. Everything seems wrong, and often is so, owing to this condition of things, and serious misunderstandings may be created.

"In Dr. Schofield's delightful little book, *The Radiant Morn,* which every tired and depressed worker ought to read, he says, 'There is this great and radical difference between a healthy mind and a healthy body; the latter may be diseased, yet the person may be full of brightness and joy, but if the mind be worn out or diseased the joy all goes. Work, steady work, is an essential, but must not be carried on to the point of exhaustion.'

"Extreme monotony of mental occupation is also very bad for the mind; the rigid, narrow grooves or ruts in which the lives of some of the best Christian workers seem fixed, are almost as conducive to an unhealthy mind as the lives of the monks of old. It is not so much the amount of work as the manner in which it is done that breaks us down. Warning signs of mental trouble are seen in changes for the worse in the temper, in affection, in a total loss of the sense of humor (that most sane and healthy of qualities), and in the occurrence of constant mistakes; coupled with these are found some morbid fancies or feelings. All should be regarded as symptoms of exhaustion. One of the earliest signs of overwork is staleness. The occupation becomes wearisome, little worries upset, little mistakes are made, little things are forgotten, lassitude and depression ensue. It does not amount to much, but it is significant. Most mental and nervous breakdowns can be distinctly traced to some perfectly preventable violation of the laws of health and common sense. We have no warrant to believe that if we persistently set the laws of nature at defiance, God will save us from the results of our own folly. The work should be stopped, a sufficient change taken with congenial friends, and the routine should not be resumed until one feels vigorous and anxious to get to work again."

Before coming to any decision as to going in the Lord's work to another land, where, usually speaking, the climate will be very different from that of this country, it will not be a departure from the path of faith to consult a Christian doctor as to one's physical condition. There are Christian doctors who are glad to devote their service in examining and giving advice in such cases.

▪ CHAPTER THREE ▪

The Responsibility of Elders

In connection with those mentioned in the New Testament who were called of God to go forth from churches to serve the Lord in other regions, the part taken by the elder brethren receives significant notice. It was those who were exercising spiritual responsibility in the church at Antioch to whom the Holy Spirit said: "Separate Me Barnabas and Saul for the work whereunto I have called them" (Acts 13:1, 2). They it was who "committed them to the grace of God for the work" (14:26, R.V.). And when Silas went forth with Paul, they were "commended by the brethren to the grace of the Lord" (15:40). The commendation, be it noted, was to the Lord.

Commendation and Identification

So again in the case of Timothy, he was "well reported of by the brethren that were at Lystra and Iconium" (16:2). The "presbytery," i.e., the elder brethren, laid their hands on him, thus identifying themselves with him as one chosen and called of God (1 Tim. 4:14), (for the term "presbytery" compare Acts 20:17, R.V., margin, "presbyters," a number acting in, and for, the single church at Ephesus).

The circumstances in each case give evidence of deep exercise of heart before God on the part of the elders, and of the great importance which the local churches attached to the going forth of missionaries from their midst. The fasting, in addition to prayer, suggests, not a mere formal rite, but a spirit of self-humbling before God under the weight of their responsibility in the matter. The laying on of hands was not an ordination to the ministry; Paul and Barnabas had received their divine ordination before. It betokened the identification of the assembly with the servants of God, acting through the elder brethren.

Consultation with Other Missionaries

In view of the fact that new workers will mostly be joining those engaged in existing spheres of service, brethren so working abroad already should be consulted by, or on behalf of, those who are coming out to their district. They will be helped considerably by the judgment and commendation of the elder brethren of the assemblies from whence the fresh laborers are going forth. Assurances that experience of them has proved that they are such as will work harmoniously and readily receive counsel, will lead to a joyous welcome. Moreover, it must be a happy anticipation and an encouragement to one who is going out for the first time to have the approval of those with whom he or she will be associated.

The fellowship of the assembly with the missionaries did not cease with their departure. They returned to it after their first period of service, "gathered the church together and rehearsed all that God had done with them" (Acts 14:27). So again between the second and third periods, and from the same assembly Paul set out for the third time. All this indicates a continued relationship.

Continued Fellowship

When a laborer goes forth in simple dependence upon God for his maintenance, the commendation of the assembly, or assemblies (there was more than one in Timothy's case), from which he or she departs carries with it a responsibility for the continuance of fellowship as God may enable. The work of a missionary is work in which the assembly is engaged. He or she was working in their midst before leaving on service abroad. The change of sphere does not involve a cessation of practical cooperation. Nay, the work of the assembly has been extended. These are some of the principles underlying the teaching of the facts recorded in the New Testament, and their joyous realization is practicable in a very extended way and measure in these times.

The Ground of Commendation

Commendation cannot rightly be given unless there is a unanimous conviction and assurance on the part of elder brethren of the fact that a brother or sister is one chosen and called of the Lord to go forth in His service. Such conviction must needs be based on their experience of the entire fitness of such an one for the serious and exacting work about to be undertaken.

What has been said as to the qualifications necessary to be in evidence may be of help in this respect. Without some years of the personal experience of the character and work of one who professes to be exercised about going forth in the Lord's service, commendation should be withheld. We are warned "to lay hands suddenly on no one."

Some words written in *The Witness* for December 1925, by an esteemed brother who gave himself to the furtherance of missionary work in the British Isles and abroad, are still cogent and weighty:

"Young men ought to be warned of the danger which has . . . become intensified by the lack of employment and the irksome conditions of many employments in the present day—that is, to escape these unpleasant experiences by going out to be evangelists or missionaries.

"Some undercurrent of thought like this may be running deep in the heart all unconsciously to the individual, and nothing but the searchlight of the Word of God, applied by the Holy Spirit, can detect it.

"Wherever missionary work offers the prospect of material and social *advantages,* instead of the *sacrifice* of those advantages, there danger lurks, and young people should be faithfully warned of it by the elders of their Assemblies."

Certain Tendencies and Their Dangers

Surely this calls for prayerful consideration in the present times, marked as they are by a haste and by a zeal not according to knowledge, which things are obviously contrary to the Lord's methods and operations as revealed in Scripture. Is quality keeping pace with quantity? Everyone sent of God will be confronted with difficulties, and by His power will surmount them. Anyone sent as the result of mere human encouragement, and furthered simply by the assistance of fellow believers, cannot really help in the work and is likely to become a hindrance.

In this connection the following words of sound admonition written several years ago still carry weight: "There is an air of romance about going abroad to work amongst the heathen, or there is a spirit of adventure. A volunteer will spring from insignificance into prominence and be regarded as a kind of spiritual hero for his spirit of self-sacrifice. The greatest danger to those who believe they have heard the call lies in mixed motives and the subtle workings of the human heart. . . . The new volunteer is congratulated and made much of, receives a lot of nice things as necessary (and sometimes unnecessary) outfit, and feels a kind of halo round his head. After some months in the field the elements of romance fade away, realities have to be faced, and the halo disappears."

There is no less claim upon elder brethren for prayer and fasting than in apostolic times, if God calls someone to go forth from their midst in the Lord's service. The call is as divine and the work as important.

▪ CHAPTER FOUR ▪

Appeals for Fresh Laborers and Intercessory Prayer

Urgent appeals are sometimes made for young men and women to go out to the mission field. No such appeals are to be found in Scripture. The Lord said: "Pray ye the Lord of the harvest that He would thrust forth laborers into His harvest." Prayer is one thing, stirring calls for fresh workers are another. It has been remarked that some appear to read the text as it is said: "Pray ye the laborers to go forth into the harvest."

Urgent calls for volunteers make a strong appeal to earnest-minded young people, and there is a danger in a missionary address which recounts successes and spiritual results but omits to record the difficulties and temptations, the hardships, disappointments and trials.

To encourage prayer for more workers is good. The Lord Himself said: "The harvest truly is plenteous and the laborers are few." Let us beware, however, of using methods of appeal which lack the endorsement of the Word of God. To press young people to go forth into the mission field is unwise and unscriptural. Let such as have any inward feeling that they may have a call from God and should respond to an appeal, wait patiently upon the Lord, and abide in the calling which they have been following, until they receive the clearest guidance from Him that they should serve Him abroad. Let them be willing to be tested by Him, and seek to give such evidence to the elder brethren of their assembly in the matter that they will be able to lay hands upon them unhesitatingly. This takes time and involves much exercise of heart.

Prayer is one of the mightiest weapons that can be used for the furtherance of the Lord's work. Let appeals then be made for intercessors whose spiritual condition of heart and life enables them to have power with God. It is prayer in the Holy Spirit, the prayer of faith, that prevails.

"The principalities and the powers," "the world rulers of this darkness," "the spiritual hosts of wickedness in the heavenly places" (Eph. 6:12, R.V.) seem to be mustering their forces against all truly evangelistic work, in the realization that their time is short. Our wrestling is against these, and for this reason we need to be "strong [to be made powerful] in the Lord and the strength of His might"; we need to put on the whole armor of God, that we may be "able to stand against the wiles [lit., the methods] of the Devil," and that we may be "able to stand in the evil day, and, having done all, to stand." The present time is certainly an "evil day." Lawlessness abounds, and the falling away, foretold in 2 Thessalonians 2, as that which will precede the rise of "the man of sin" (or rather, of lawlessness, i.e. the rejection of all the will and claims of God) has manifestly set in.

Special prayer is therefore called for on the part of the Lord's people, confronted as we are with a world situation of a special character. It would be advisable for appeals to be made for the appointing of constant and definite times for collective prayer that the guidance and help of God may be given regarding all preparations for the extension of missionary service along Scriptural lines.

Different forms of antagonism are in evidence in different countries where missionary labors have been carried on with extending activities for a century or more by servants of God who have gone forth, as called and directed by the Holy Spirit, from the British Isles, a few other countries of Europe, from North America, Australia and New Zealand. Governmental and religious pressure is being exerted in increasing measure to expel such missionaries and in other ways to cause evangelical activity to cease.

It is true that evangelists, pastors and teachers, native to the countries where early pioneers and their successors have carried on their gospel ministry, are being raised up to continue and extend the work, and earnest prayer is needed continually that divine guidance and blessing may be granted to such, and that their numbers may be rapidly increased. But it is not sufficient to intercede for this. Is the number of qualified laborers who go forth from the countries named above to be decreased, because of the manifold opposition of the adversary? The work done by such in the past illustrates what the apostle said to the church of God at Corinth, "a great door and effectual is opened unto me, and there are many adversaries" (1 Cor. 16:9), and what was said by the Lord to the church in Philadelphia, "Behold, I have set before thee a door opened, which none can shut" (Rev. 3:8).

What is needed, therefore, is prayer that assemblies may be characterized by the same spiritual state as that in Philadelphia, and may see the Lord's hand still holding the door opened, so that, in spite of changing and adverse political and religious circumstances in the world, men and women may be called of God to go forth. While doors in certain countries are closed, the door of access to the throne of God ever remains open.

CHAPTER FIVE

Marriage

Real devotedness to the Lord and His work in the mission field demands and is marked by a spirit of self-sacrifice. Whatever would tend to lessen efficiency, particularly in the first few years of such service, will be avoided. To give one's being and energies to the Lord for missionary service involves the necessity of acquiring a working knowledge of the language (there are very few regions where a foreign language is not spoken). A person who does not learn to speak to natives in their own tongue, but is content to speak by interpretation or to engage in a desultory study and practice, is not equipping himself or herself sufficiently as one who is called of God to win souls and bring on converts in His ways. This cannot in general be done efficaciously where the learning of their language is abandoned or inadequately undertaken. No occupation or condition which prevents or hinders this all-important matter should be engaged in.

Paramount Considerations

For young people to look upon marriage as essential before beginning missionary service abroad is not conducive to that efficiency which such service demands for the sake of Christ and His gospel. The responsibilities of husband toward wife and of wife toward husband—the maintenance of home life, with the possibility of having a child to care for—cannot but detract from the prime and paramount duty of winning souls and teaching converts. For these purposes not only is there the requirement of language-learning, there is the need of becoming thoroughly familiar with the ways and condition, character and disposition of the people. This latter requirement is important even where, as in parts of the West Indies, a new language is not necessary. In other parts there is scope for a married couple of maturity, just as there is in the villages of this land.

To involve oneself in the affairs of married life in heathen lands at the very outset or during the first period of service is, in most countries, a hindrance to the twofold responsibility of language-learning and familiar acquaintance with the people and their ideas. There is a third exigency which demands prior consideration to that of marriage, and that is acclimatization. In many countries, especially in the tropics, the climatic conditions impose no small physical strain. The circumstances of married life, with its home cares and the possible rearing of a child, render it advisable to become accustomed to the climate before marriage, or there will be the risk of an early breakdown in health, demanding either the care and attention of senior workers or even the leaving of the field of service.

In view of these things most missionary societies, in the exercise of their control over the missionaries employed by them, impose a restriction prohibiting marriage until a fixed time has elapsed. This insistence is the effect of the experience of the above-mentioned disadvantages to the work. In this connection the following is quoted from the booklet, *Principles of Missionary Work:*

> The Highest Motive
>
> "Should those who are not under such rules come short of this? Are there not good reasons for adding to the fixed time rather than diminishing it? A young man who believes that he is called of God to the service of the gospel may well ask himself if he is prepared for some self-denial in the matter of marriage as well as in other ways, not because of rules, but from simple devotedness to the Lord. Treading the difficult path of service in a foreign land with a wife and family is very different from doing so alone. We call special attention to this because it is a fact that, while men

who follow a business or profession often have to spend a good while in attaining a position in which they can marry, some who go out as missionaries are not prepared to give a few years to the work before marriage; and, indeed, some think they must be engaged before they begin."

We ought to guard against the word "alone" (used above) being misunderstood, as if we would encourage a brother to go alone to any place. In sending His disciples "two and two" the Lord declared His mind as to fellowship in service. It is not good for even a married couple to be alone at any station, nor wise for such to be accompanied by only one single brother or single sister, and the tendency to open new stations without experience of things in general and sufficient knowledge of a language is also to be deprecated.

▪ CHAPTER SIX ▪

Financial Considerations

(a) The Privilege of All Believers

Those who set a true value upon the gospel of Christ which has wrought its saving work in their own case will surely give evidence of their estimate not only by seeking to win others for Him but by helping other servants of God to go forth with the message of life to the perishing in regions beyond. The love of Christ will constrain us to further this soul-saving work by doing all within our power for the practical assistance of those who are called and sent of God for this purpose, and who engage in this service in simple dependence upon the Lord for the supply of their need.

There are, of course, other Scriptural demands upon our purse than those we are now considering, but all require that exercise of heart which, delighting in the understanding and the fulfillment of the Lord's will, leaves nothing undone which His Word reveals should be done. To disregard the matter of practical fellowship with the Lord's missionary servants abroad because of other claims for our support, cannot be pleasing to Christ. It is our responsibility and high privilege to take our part, every one of us, in promoting the work of the gospel both in this and other lands. Whether we are called to go forth to regions beyond or to remain in our own locality, we are none of us exempt from this God-given service. Indeed, how can any adequate sense of the mercy of God toward us in Christ, and the fact that we ourselves are speeding on our way to the glory, instead of going down to the pit of destruction, and all this through the redeeming work of the Cross, fail to meet with a devoted response in presenting ourselves unto God for this purpose?

What the apostle Paul said to the church at Philippi was written for our instruction. His commendation given to the saints there because of their practical assistance to him is an unfolding of the mind of the Lord for all of us. He says: "I rejoice in the Lord greatly that now at length ye have revived your thought for me . . . ye did well that ye had fellowship with my affliction. . . . In the beginning of the gospel, when I departed from Macedonia, no church had fellowship with me in the matter of giving and receiving, but ye only; for . . . ye sent once and again unto my need. Not that I seek for the gift; but I seek for the fruit that increaseth to your account" (Phil. 4:16–18).

(b) The Lord's Estimate

Let us note that phrase "the fruit that increaseth to your account." That lifts the giving for the work of the gospel above even the matter of fellowship, it at once presents the Lord's view, it is something in which He finds pleasure, and in which the Holy Spirit operates for the present blessing of those who give. Moreover, the phrase carries us from the present to the future. The Lord puts down our gifts "to our account," which points to the coming time of reward for whatever has been done for Him.

What deep significance attaches to His remarks concerning the poverty-stricken widow who "out of her want cast in all that she had"! His comment on her act reveals at once the glory of His divine knowledge of her circumstances, His unerring estimate of her motives, and the grace of His kindly attitude toward her. Man takes account of what a person owns, the Lord takes account of how he uses it.

She might reasonably have given one of the mites to the temple treasury (it was well supplied) and used the other for her own needs. Her faith made her lose sight of those and seek only the glory of God. Her devotion took its practical effect in connection with the earthly temple. Those who devote their offerings to the work of the gospel do so in connection with the building of a spiritual and eternal temple. The world uses money to gratify its own desires. Those who are not of the world seek to gratify the desires of Him Who gave Himself to redeem them and make them His own. And His desires are toward the perishing multitudes for whom He died.

(c) The Continued Assembly Fellowship

When an assembly is assured that one of their number has been called and qualified by the Lord to go from their midst in missionary service, thus sharing the conviction in the person's heart that this is His will, they commend such an one to the Lord Himself and show their fellowship in a practical way. The fact that they concur with the person's decision to depend in faith upon God for His supply of their need, according to the teaching of Scripture, does not remove the responsibility of expressing fellowship by continuing to send financial assistance according to their ability. That they do not guarantee maintenance does not involve abstention from rendering help toward it.

Prayer and practical fellowship go together, and there will be prayer not only for the spiritual prosperity of the one who goes, but that additional channels may be used of God for the supply of the needs both of the daily life and of the work.

(d) Various Missionary Requirements

In this latter respect there are various details requiring consideration. In uncivilized parts there is the need of suitable house accommodation and upkeep. What is set forth in the New Testament does not afford ground for the idea that a missionary must always be moving from place to place. Timothy and Titus both received instructions to remain in certain localities to help toward the spiritual development of assemblies. Yet Timothy was not left at Ephesus to continue his work there indefinitely. Paul says: "As I exhorted thee to tarry at Ephesus, when I was going into Macedonia . . . so do I now" (1 Tim. 1:3, 4, R.V.). But he was "to do his diligence" to rejoin the apostle later (2 Tim. 4:9). Titus was left in Crete that he might set in order the things that were wanting and appoint elders in every city. In certain countries very considerable periods of residence in one district are necessary, with certain forms of service, such as the translation of the Scriptures, and teaching the believers to read, both of which take a considerable time, but are requisite for well-founded work; hospitals (both general and special, such as those for lepers), dispensaries, and schools and orphanages, make a still greater demand in this respect. Accordingly, not only ordinary housing accommodation but these other adjuncts to the work where the Lord guides His servants to establish such, provide opportunities for the practical cooperation of assemblies. Medical work involves the purchase of instruments, drugs, bandages and other commodities.

Then again, missionary service involves a considerable amount of journeying, involving constant expenses. Traveling incurs the provision and upkeep of a variety of means of itinerating, such as motor cars, motor Bible coaches, launches set apart for gospel work. There is also the cost of railway, bus and boat fares. In regions like Central Africa itinerating often involves the payment of carriers.

Some missionaries undertake the printing and publishing of the Scriptures and Scriptural literature, which involves considerable expense. Others purchase copies of the Scriptures for distribution.

In addition to all that has been mentioned, the widows and orphans of those who have labored in the gospel, and the support of retired missionaries, provide opportunities for practical cooperation.

All these and other expenses necessarily involved in missionary service need to be borne in mind by those who would seek intelligently and wholeheartedly to support the work for the Lord's sake; yet never in such a way as to diminish or divert the gifts from the needs of the worker's everyday life. Moreover, many a missionary, seeking to fulfill the divine intimations of Scripture, realizes that when the Spirit of God has raised up native elders to care for an assembly (as was the case, e.g. in Crete), the way is opened of the Lord to go to a fresh district with the gospel, trusting that not only souls may be saved but assemblies on Scriptural lines may likewise be formed there. That involves all that such moving means, and the building of fresh housing accommodation.

In passing, the need of moving to another part of a region as soon as local spiritual gifts have been developed and appointed by the Holy Spirit, has ever to be considered. Where this is done the paying of visits to the assemblies so formed and provided for by the Lord, means traveling expenses. There are large regions still lying without a Scriptural testimony, and the methods indicated in the New Testament must be adopted more fully if these localities are to be reached.

Family considerations have likewise to be taken into account. The moving and housing of a family means no small expense. And as the children grow up their education has to be provided for. To send children to a suitable school means no small cost. Even where education is free there are the expenses of traveling, clothing, and other items.

Since those who look to God for the supply of their needs do not make appeals for financial help, there is all the greater need of exercise of heart on the part of assemblies as to rendering financial assistance to such servants of the Lord. Need, too, of looking to Him to grant a realization of the varied conditions, needs and exigencies, some of which have just been mentioned.

(e) Voluntary Cooperating Agencies

"In the last days perilous times shall come." The word rendered "perilous" more frequently has the meaning "difficult." Certainly the times in which we are living are such. As a result of world wars governmental legislation and restrictions have of necessity been imposed and have involved unprecedented difficulties in financial matters.

It seems clear, therefore, to large numbers of the Lord's people that He has raised up voluntary agencies, e.g., in Britain, Australia, New Zealand and America, to seek to facilitate communications with His servants in other lands. These channels of communication do not constitute a departure from the principles of Scripture. On the contrary, they are developments of the principles embodied therein. Such agencies are not constituted into societies or organizations, controlling the going forth, the movements and the work of servants of God, or providing them with salaries. They are ready to give advice, provided that a person who seeks it has received the unanimous commendation of an assembly through its elder brethren. They are ready to render help in the forwarding of gifts when those commended have reached their destination.

In many cases these agencies have been the means of sending gifts when direct transmission has been impossible, and this has been especially the case amidst the difficulties of recent times, but they have never sought to hinder or restrain the sending of gifts direct.

Those who engage in such work do not appeal for money or for workers. There is no example of either kind of appeal in Scripture. To appeal for workers would involve the risk of encroaching upon the rights and prerogative of the Spirit of God Who Himself is the power for raising up and sending forth laborers into the great harvest field. To appeal for money would be compromising the principles upon which those on whose behalf they act have professed to go forth; that is to say, in dependence upon God for the supply of their needs.

The fact that gifts are sent through them or that money is entrusted to them, whether by living donors or by bequests from those who have gone to be with Christ, does not involve a departure from the path of faith on the part of those who have gone forth from assemblies. That a servant of God is aware that he may be receiving a gift from time to time from such channels does not mean that he ceases thereby to look to the Lord for his supplies. He simply has reason to thank God for such help. It does not constitute his stipend, nor does it modify or alter his relationship with the Lord Who has sent him.

Elijah was possessed of the knowledge of where his supplies would come from all the time that, by God's ordering, he dwelt by the brook Cherith. For the Lord informed him that He had commanded the ravens to feed him there. He did not cease to walk by faith and in simple dependence upon God, in spite of the fact that he knew by what instruments he would be maintained morning by morning and evening by evening. When the brook dried he was told how his needs would be met in another way.

Just so in regard to those who have been guided by the Spirit of God to go forth in His service in dependence upon Him and His providential dealings as to their needs; the fact that they are cognizant of the existence of certain channels through which some supplies may probably reach them does not cause them to cease trusting Him and to look merely to human aid.

The forwarding of gifts in this way is in accordance with the principle underlying what is recorded in Philippians 4:18. It was necessary in the early days of this era for long and hazardous journeys to be taken in order to convey gifts to a servant of God. Epaphroditus took a journey from Philippi to Rome in order to take the gifts of the assembly to Paul. There were no such postal facilities and means of transmission as, under the providential dealings of God, exist today. That money can be forwarded with far less difficulty now, and that there are brethren who devote time and labor to see by what means it can best be transmitted so as to save time and loss, is not a departure from the fulfillment of the mind and purpose of God as made known in His Word.

Those who give themselves to engage in this service of giving counsel when sought, providing information and forwarding gifts, have satisfied themselves that they are carrying on the work in accordance with the teaching of Scripture and that by cooperating in this service they are not compromising any of the principles of the Word of God.

Many engaged in earning their living give all their spare time available to the work of the gospel. Such are certainly occupied in rendering missionary service and are to be regarded as missionaries. Many servants of God have taken up posts in other lands to earn their daily bread, but primarily to be witnesses there for the Lord and to help forward the work of the gospel. Even those who go out in whole-time service must be prepared at times to earn their living. Hence the importance of becoming qualified in some earthly occupation before going out. The very first laborers who were sent of the Lord to other lands, as recorded in the Acts, are themselves examples of this. The apostle Paul and one of those who wrought with him maintained themselves upon occasion by tentmaking (Acts 18:3; cp. 2 Cor. 12:13).

What the apostle Paul says in 2 Corinthians, Philippians and 1 Thessalonians about his receiving gifts, shows that there was no question of soliciting financial assistance. The apostle never did this; what he did was to seek to exercise the consciences of believers concerning fellowship in the gospel, and especially those converted through his ministry:and this he did, not, as he says, with a desire of receiving the gifts to supply his own needs, but with the aim of the spiritual welfare of the churches, "that fruit might increase to their account." Ministration to a servant of God is ministration to the Lord Himself. So Christ taught (Matt. 10:40).

▪ CHAPTER SEVEN ▪

The Service of Sisters in the Mission Field

When we consider the testimony of the New Testament concerning the service rendered by women in connection with the work of the Lord, and what the Scriptures teach in regard to their services, the importance which He attaches to it is obvious.

It has been well said that "It is clear from Scripture and from experience, that a sister has a work to do which a brother cannot do. It is not at all a case of the brother having the monopoly of the gift of utterance, or of knowledge. After all, there are far more women and children in the world than there are men, and a sphere of service is open to her in this connection, which in point of numbers, at least, offers her as wide a sphere as any other, and one which will call for all her spiritual energies."

Again, "Euodia and Syntyche had labored with [had striven along with, had fought at the side of] the apostle in the gospel, and along with Clement and the rest (Phil. 4:2, 3). Such labor seems clearly not to have been confined to material and domestic ministry alone, but had involved a share in the spiritual furtherance of the message. This did not involve pioneer work on their own account, but they worked in association with brethren, and their service would be subject to the limitations elsewhere laid down, and would be confined, when rendered publicly, to their own sex and amongst the young. We are told, according to Clement of Alexandria, that Peter's wife acted as his coadjutor, ministering to women in their own homes—by which means the gospel of Christ penetrated, without scandal, the privacy of women's apartments. Whether Clement's testimony is to be relied upon or not, it is what we might expect of Peter's wife; and how many sisters since have found in such all-important service their life work for the Lord!"

The injunctions as to the silence of women in the church gatherings are clear and specific (1 Cor. 14:24), and the meaning of 1 Timothy 2:8–15 is unmistakable, but there is no Scripture which even discountenances the going forth of women to render service in missionary work abroad. Indeed, the Scriptures to which reference has been made above teach the contrary. Apart from the need of the help of sisters in medical, nursing and school work where such is carried on in the furtherance of gospel activity, the cooperation of sisters in dealing with women and girls and visiting homes is invaluable. They need the commendation of their home assemblies just as much as brethren.

The following, written by a servant of God some years ago, is worth repeating here: "We cannot urge too strongly absolute loyalty to the Scriptures. There is too much talk about the times having changed, as if the Scriptures on the point are not binding now. The Scriptures are for all time. . . . Let Christian women rise from their study of Scripture determined to carry out its instructions as to their relation to man; to illustrate by their conduct the truth of Christ and the Church; to be individually a protest against the lawless spirit of the age; to glory in the unique place which is theirs. Then will God be glorified. Then will their true usefulness be available to the full. Then will Christian men profoundly respect them, and be helped and influenced by them, and find what the description 'help meet'—which alone belongs to women—means."

Conclusion

The following advice is on the lines suggested by an experienced brother now with the Lord to any who might be exercised as engaging in the work of the gospel in other lands: (1) *do not go unsent;* (2) *do not go prematurely;* (3) *do not act from doubtful motives;* (4) *do not go without good credentials;* (5) *do not rely upon impressions;* (6) *see that you have the full fellowship of your brethren.*

The great need of all concerned is the deepening of the Holy Spirit's work through self-humbling before God, that Christ may be revealed and magnified in the life. Further, considering the character of the present times and the manifold antagonism of Satan and all the powers of darkness, there is a clamant need of individual and collective prayer, of earnest and constant laying hold of God in regard to all matters relating to the work of the gospel both existent and prospective, both in the so-called home countries and abroad. Prayer is needed for the raising up of men and women qualified by, and filled with, the Holy Spirit; for a revival among the assemblies of God's people; for a realization of the mind and heart of the Lord, who still has compassion on the multitudes for whom He died and that lie in darkness, and Who enjoins us to pray for the thrusting forth of laborers; for unity based upon adherence to the Word of God; for Spirit-guided zeal and energy in the fulfillment of His will in a self-denial and devotion that responds to the Lord's love and mercy.

"Go now, and 'work,' believers!
But work at peace and free!
Of grace the glad receivers—
Its true exponents be.
Ye toil for glory guerdons,
'Exceeding great reward':
Then down with Egypt's burdens,
Ye ransomed of the Lord!"

V

Approved of God

Qualifications for Service at Home and Abroad

"Approved of God to be entrusted with the gospel" (1 Thess. 2:4, R.V.). "Approved" is the word. Its significance is far more comprehensive than that of being allowed. Not permission but approval is the meaning of the expression used by the apostle; approval, too, as the result of being proved.

Tested men, men approved as having stood the test, that is the missionary type in the New Testament. That provides the standard. Let us not lower it. Loyalty to the Word of God demands that we maintain it.

"Approved of God": the application of this to the men whom God called to go to other lands with the gospel is confirmed by the Scripture narratives about them. As to the apostle Paul the biographical details of the period of about fourteen years from his conversion till, being called by the Holy Spirit, he was separated by the brethren in the church at Antioch to go abroad in the work, are full of instructive facts as to probation. So with Barnabas, of whom we first read in Acts 4:36. The earliest mention of Silas records him as already one of the leading* men among the brethren (15:22).

Conspicuous features of the probation time in Timothy's case are his early knowledge of the Scriptures, his unfeigned faith (2 Tim. 1:5), and his sterling character and spiritual fitness, attested by the brethren in at least two assemblies (Acts 16:2). All this provided the ground of the commendation given by them, and of Paul's choice of him.

Such, then, were the men who were "approved of God" to go with the Word of Life. Nor must we fail to observe the significance of the word "entrusted." It implies a proved trustworthiness. Every one of them had been engaged in local gospel service, and had been proved and approved therein before being sent forth by the Holy Spirit to regions beyond. All these things were written for our instruction and as guidance for our following. Failure to do so brings dishonor upon the name of the Lord and the work of the gospel.

The men thus set before us did not become missionaries either when, or because, they went from their assemblies to other lands. Going to another country in the work of the gospel does not make a servant of the Lord a missionary. This may sound elementary; and yet the tendency is far from being nonexistent of regarding such service as a sort of career upon which one enters as an alternative to an ordinary avocation. We do well to avoid technicalities which conduce to unscriptural methods.

Another fact which stands out conspicuously in New Testament instruction on the subject is that the local assembly is the divinely appointed training ground for service, first in the immediate vicinity, and then further afield if the Lord so leads. Additional means may be, and often are, found useful, but they should not become substitutes. A period of collaboration with a senior brother in gospel work in the home country is valuable. Such association should be based on the goodwill of the elder brethren of the prospective worker's assembly. This affords a probation with a view to the extended approbation they hope to give.

It would be a great advantage, too, if the elder brethren of the assembly invited a young man who had gained their confidence regarding his working in regions beyond, to attend their periodic deliberations concerning the affairs of the church under their care. The experience gained thereby should serve him well in the similar responsibilities he will most probably have to shoulder early after arrival. Grave mistakes in judgment are, alas! made at times through lack of such experience.

"Approved of God!" Let us see further what is involved in this, what those who commend a worker to the Lord for service in another land will require to see as a result of their intimate acquaintance with, and experience of,

*The usual meaning of the verb rendered "chief."

him, before the step is taken. Zeal and energy and earnest desire are not sufficient. They may of themselves lead to disastrous mistakes.

Has the prospective worker evinced the tactful civility, the politeness, the Christian courtesy, which indeed are requisite in the home country, and still more when face to face with the pride and prejudice of people in foreign lands? Anything lacking in this respect will fail of the divine purpose, that the human instrument should himself commend the message of the gospel. Is he prepared rigidly to avoid acting as though he were racially superior to those amongst whom he has come?

Has he a good report in the calling he has been following? Has he shown capability and diligence therein? There must be "a good testimony from them that are without." What will not do in this world's business will certainly not do in the Lord's work.

Is he known as one whose disposition will make him a true yokefellow with those who have been laboring in the country before him? Incompatibility of temperament will but mar the work, scandalize the gospel, and undo much of what has been accomplished. How could elder brethren lay hands on a young man without having discerned in him such a spirit of humility as makes him willing to take advice from others? Will he go forth as one in whom they have confidence that he will fulfill the command, "Likewise, ye younger, be subject unto the elder"?

Is he free from that self-assurance which will make him a critic of his senior workers and lead him to seek almost at once to introduce methods which he himself regards as superior to theirs? Meekness and a readiness to be subject under trying and disadvantageous conditions are all-important qualifications in cooperating with others. The mind and character of the Master should be expressed in His servant. He should therefore be known as one whose temperament tallies with the love depicted in 1 Corinthians 13:9, the paramount quality, requisite indeed in all who are Christ's and likely to be tested especially in the conditions of fellow service in other lands. Moreover, service in the gospel involves hardship (2 Tim. 1:8, R.V.). Such endurance should have been evinced in gospel work long before engaging in it in regions beyond. In order that the genuineness of the desire may be proved in such cases, some years of intimate acquaintance on the part of the elder brethren may be required, and this period of testing will enhance the value of their ultimate commendation, if their approval has been gained.

Is there evidence of freedom from mixed motives, such as the desire to avoid the arduous character of a somewhat unremunerative occupation in the home country, or the desire to arrange a marriage earlier than could be the case at home? Where there is lack of employment, or where employment tends to become irksome, there is sometimes a temptation to escape these difficulties by "becoming a missionary," especially if going forth in this capacity appears to hold out advantages, whether material or social. These dangers, by no means imaginary, require faithful dealing on the part of elder brethren. Without it, missionary service will become increasingly scandalized, a reproach on the testimony and a dishonor to the name of the Lord.

It is not a very infrequent occurrence today that two who express exercise of heart about work abroad desire to become married even before setting out, indicating ignorance of the ill effects upon a woman of assuming the double occupation of household duties and missionary work, while unacclimatized and among strange people (often with a language to be learnt), with whose ways and manners and prejudices a worker needs to become familiar if effective work is to be done.

If souls are to be won for Christ, the new worker should surely devote his time undistractedly to becoming thoroughly familiar with the character and ways, the prejudices and susceptibilities of the people, and to the efficient acquisition of their language. To this an early matrimonial engagement can scarcely but be detrimental.

Has he such knowledge of the Scriptures as has already made him known as one capable of handling them rightly and preaching the gospel effectively? In addition to the all-important factor of his private, constant and systematic study of the

Scriptures, well is it for him if he has had the benefit of a weekly meeting for the teaching of Scripture, whether by a well-conducted "Bible reading" or by invited speakers. If a man is inefficient in making known the gospel scripturally and intelligently in his native land, how can he be called of God to preach it elsewhere? If he has not been proved as one who is capable of "handling aright the Word of truth" (2 Tim. 2:15, R.V.), how can he be commended to go and minister it amidst the still more difficult and exacting conditions abroad? How can he use it aright when confronted by the skeptic, the propagandist of error, the genuine inquirer? He may have zeal, but if it is not "according to knowledge," knowledge of the mind and ways of God as revealed in His Word, his very zeal will only plunge him into difficulty, mar his testimony and serve the more to confirm people in darkness and error.

Is he possessed of ability to learn a language, where such is necessary? Attempts to speak it before sufficiently acquiring it will produce ridicule from the unconverted and harass the feelings of native believers. Even if he is known to be possessed of this important qualification, he will do well to seek still further to improve his education during such time as is available to him before going abroad.

Is he known to be possessed of that godliness and moral fiber which will strengthen him against succumbing to the grossly immoral influences which exist among peoples abroad? Any evidence of laxity or carelessness in regard to the other sex is sufficient to disqualify for service for God. Marriage is sometimes advocated as a counteractive. What the Spirit of God has set before us, however, in Timothy's case is strikingly different. Firstly, his known purity of life inspired confidence in him on the part both of the elder brethren and of Paul. Secondly, the Holy Spirit's safeguard was not marriage but association with his fellow senior worker. The glib tongue of scandal is counteracted by the association of two men like this. Such was the case with this younger missionary, that he could eventually be trusted to remain for a prolonged stay at Ephesus, where vice stalked in all its nakedness, as it does in many a place abroad today.

Without the knowledge that the prospective laborer possesses the above qualities, let elder brethren faithfully refrain from the commendation he seeks. In any case their requisite personal acquaintance with him will mean no inconsiderable period of probation. Only so can they prevent that undue haste, so characteristic of these times, and assure themselves that he is one "approved of God." Only so will they be able to communicate, with a confidence and joy imparted by the Spirit of God, with brethren who are already working in the district which the new worker has before him, before he prepares to set out. Such a previous communication is, of course, always important, both for the sake of the Lord's servants out there and for the satisfaction of the one who is going forth in realizing that he has their approval and that they can anticipate with pleasure his addition to their ranks. No one should go abroad to join other workers without their full fellowship. Paul chose his helpers, Timothy and Silas.

As elder brethren consider these weighty matters in the presence of God, they will the more readily commend to the work of the Lord one whom God commends.

V

Service

▪ PREFACE ▪

The following chapters on "SERVICE" have been republished from leading articles in *Echoes of Service* in booklet form by special request. Their former publication at intervals in that magazine, and the association of some of the subjects contained in them, have resulted in a certain amount of repetition of theme in some parts. For this the writer must ask the reader's kind forbearance. The papers were written with a view to provide some little help in gospel work in this and in other lands, and some of the later chapters have more especial reference to such work. The first chapter or two direct the attention *to* the character and the service of the Lord Jesus Christ, and in considering such a subject it is important that He should be first before our minds. The articles are now set forth in their present form in the earnest desire that they may be owned of God for His glory, and for the help of many whose privilege it is to engage in His service.

W.E.V.

▪ CHAPTER ONE ▪

The Lord's Servant

The portion of the prophecies of Isaiah which commences at chapter forty contains a series of promises of blessing to Israel. These promises center in the Messiah; they are based upon His atoning sacrifice, and their fulfillment will be consummated in His reign of righteousness upon the earth. In the forty-second chapter, and onward to the fifty-third, the Messiah is depicted as the Servant of Jehovah, and it is through Him in this capacity that His purposes are to be accomplished. The first declaration, "Behold My Servant" (42:1), stands in significant contrast to what has preceded. In the forty-first chapter the Lord addresses Israel as His servant and speaks words of comfort to the nation, but rebukes the sin of idolatry, the sin which was accountable for their failure and punishment; if blessing is to come it must come through one who will adequately represent God's interests and perfectly fulfill His will. In this capacity, therefore, the Messiah is now revealed: "Behold My Servant, whom I uphold; Mine elect, in whom my soul delighteth; I have put My Spirit upon Him; He shall bring forth judgment to the Gentiles." He it is also who by His redemptive work will restore Israel to its position as God's servant; this is brought out later on in the forty-third to the forty-ninth chapters, in which the Lord again addresses the nation as His servant whom He has redeemed, so that eventually they can say, "The Lord hath said unto me, Thou art My servant, O Israel, in whom I will be glorified" (49:1–3, with 43:1, 10; 44:1, 21, and 48:20).

But now in chapter forty-two, after a prediction of the work of grace which Jehovah's Servant will accomplish, and the manner in which He will effect it, His character is depicted by a remarkable paradox. This is introduced by a sharp rebuke to the people, who by reason of their trust in molten images had become deaf to the voice of God and blind to His revelations. The remonstrance makes the paradox the more striking. "Hear, ye deaf," He says, "and look, ye blind, that ye may see. Who is blind but My servant? or deaf, as My Messenger that I send? Who is blind as He that is at peace with Me, and blind as the Lord's Servant? Thou seest many things, but Thou observest not; His ears are open, but He heareth not. It pleased the Lord, for His righteousness' sake, to magnify the Law, and make it honorable" (vv. 18–21, R.V.).

To read this description of Jehovah's servant as if it referred to Israel is to misunderstand the passage. The Servant in verse 19 is none other than the One so described in the first four verses of the chapter. Israel had failed to receive the instruction of God's law; their ears were closed to His admonitions; their sins had blinded them to the light of His truth. Let us never fail to remember that in these things they have become a warning to us, and that it is possible for us to drift into a Laodicean condition, a condition requiring that we obtain eyesalve from the Lord, to anoint our eyes with, that we may see. Inasmuch as Israel, deaf and blind through their apostasy, had incurred God's displeasure and rendered themselves unfit to act as His servant, He shows them that there is a deafness and a blindness which are pleasing to Him and which, indeed, should characterize those who render service to Him. When the nation has been purged from its sins and has turned in repentance to its Messiah, then will the decree be issued, "Bring forth the blind people that have eyes, and the deaf that have ears . . . ye are My witnesses, saith the Lord, and My servant whom I have chosen" (43:8, 10).

We will now consider the character of Christ as thus predicted, "Who is blind but My servant? or deaf as My messenger that I sent? Who is blind as He that is at peace with me, and blind as the Lord's Servant?" The word rendered "He that is at peace with Me" (in A.V., "He that is perfect") gives the point of the whole description; it indicates that condition of peace which accompanies complete submission to God, and so the word has the meaning "the devoted or submissive one." As a proper name, Meshullam, it occurs in Nehemiah 3:4, 6, 20, and elsewhere. The great object for which the Son of God came to the earth and spent His life here was to do the will of the Father. "I came down from heaven," He said, "not to do Mine own will, but the will of Him that sent me" (John 6:33). In complete submission to His will he passed through the experience of obedience and the suffering which it involved, consequent upon the alienation of man and the hostility of the powers of darkness. "He learned obedience by the things which He suffered." To every voice that would allure Him from the path of devotion to the Father He was deaf. To every sight that would attract Him from the fulfillment of His will He was blind.

This is strikingly borne out in the temptations to which He became subject at the outset of His public ministry. The Devil's persuasions that He should satisfy hunger by turning stones into bread, and test the power at His disposal by casting Himself down from the pinnacle of the temple, fell upon deaf ears. The vision of the power and glory of the kingdoms of the world, as possible for His immediate possession on one condition, was presented to eyes that were blind to aught but the honor of the Father. This attitude of the perfect Servant is again evidenced in His reply to Peter when his lips became Satan's instrument to tempt the Lord from His path to the Cross, "Get thee behind Me, Satan; thou art an offense unto Me, for thou savorest not the things that be of God, but those that be of men" (Matt. 16:23). A later chapter in Isaiah gives us the secret of this attitude of unswerving devotion, when of Messiah he writes, "The Lord hath given Me the tongue of them that are taught [R.V.], that I should know how to speak a word in season to them that are weary: He wakeneth morning by morning, He wakeneth mine ear to hear as they that are taught: the Lord God hath opened mine ear, and I was not rebellious, neither turned away back" (50:4, 5). The words which follow show whither the path was leading, the path He trod undeterred by all opposition; "I gave My back to the smilers, and My cheeks to them that plucked off the hair: I hid not My face from shame and spitting."

"Who is blind as he that is at peace with Me?" How entirely true of the Lord! Peace is, as we have seen, that which characterizes—and it did so perfectly in His case—one who lives in devoted submission to God. That adds a special meaning to His words, "Peace I leave with you, My peace I give unto you." There was no peace like His peace, because it was the outcome of a heart entirely and unceasingly at rest in the Father's will. Only in the measure in which we are delighting in the will of God can we enjoy His peace. It is as the God of peace that He makes us "perfect in every good work to do His will, working in us that which is well pleasing in His sight." Thus and thus alone can we, as servants of God, walk in the footsteps of His perfect Servant. Oh, for grace to be blind continually to whatever would obscure our vision of the Lord and the things which are eternal, and would hinder us from "enduring as seeing Him who is invisible"! So shall we behold with open face the glory of the Lord and be changed "into the same image from glory to glory." Thus alone shall we who have received any ministry be enabled to say with the apostle, "We faint not . . . we commend ourselves to every man's conscience in the sight of God" (2 Cor. 3:18; 4:1, 2). Oh, to be deaf to every sound that mars communion with the Lord, to every voice that would woo our affections from Him and rob Him of the glory due to Him from our lives!

There is no difficulty in seeing the connection of Isaiah 42:21 with the preceding verses. When it says, "It pleased the Lord for His righteousness' sake, to magnify the Law, and make it honorable," we discern at once the divine commentary on the life and service of the perfect Servant. Every requirement of the Law was carried out by Him, and so, fulfilling all righteousness, He magnified the Law and made it honorable. That the servant-character of Christ was constantly in the minds of His followers in the early days of the Church is evident from their prayer as recorded in Acts 4. The adversaries were gathered together, they said, "against Thy holy Servant Jesus." They prayed that wonders might be done, "by the name of Thy holy Servant Jesus" (vv. 27, 30).

There is much more in Isaiah's prophecies about the servant-character of Christ, but we must now notice the closing mention. This is given at the beginning and the end of the fifty-third chapter, that is to say, taking, as we should do, the last three verses of the fifty-second as the opening words of the fifty-third. There Jehovah says, "Behold, My Servant shall deal prudently"—that speaks of His service in the days of His flesh—"He shall be exalted and extolled, and be very high"—that speaks of His resurrection, ascension, and session at the right hand of the Father, of His High Priestly service and His kingly power. Then follows the prophecy of his humiliation, sufferings, and atoning death. All is to be read in the light of the opening pronouncement, "Behold, My Servant." At the close of the passage He is described as "My righteous Servant." As such He will make many righteous, for "He shall bear their iniquities." And, finally, as to His reward! "Therefore," says Jehovah, "will I divide Him a portion with the great." Even here, too, this Blessed Servant delights to show His grace in sharing the fruits of His victory: "He shall divide the spoil with the strong." May it be ours to serve as He served, and so to share His reward hereafter.

CHAPTER TWO

The Will of God in Our Service

In the book of Psalms, the will of God is directly mentioned twice only. The first expresses a delight in doing His will (Ps. 40:8). The second is a prayer to be taught to do it (Ps. 143:10). In each case the Psalmist addresses the Lord as "My God," suggesting his joy in the Almighty power of Him whose will is the law of his life. The language of the fortieth Psalm tells prophetically of the perfect obedience of the Son of God to His Father in the days of His flesh. Never did He deviate from the path of delighted subjection to His will. Of Him alone the words were absolutely true, "Lo, I come; in the volume of the Book it is written of Me, I delight to do Thy will, O My God; yea, Thy law is within My heart." His joy in the Law of the Lord found its expression in the constant fulfillment of His Father's will. In this the Father publicly manifested His infinite pleasure, when, on the occasion of the baptism of Christ, He said, "Thou art My Beloved Son; in Thee I am well pleased," and again, on the Mount of Transfiguration, when He said, "This is My beloved Son: hear Him."

Three times, as recorded in the Gospel of John, the Lord Jesus referred to His fulfillment of the will of His Father. On the first occasion, addressing His disciples, He spoke of His satisfaction therein. He said, "My meat is to do the will of Him that sent Me" (John 4:34). On the second occasion, addressing the hostile Jews, He stated that the will of the Father was His purpose in life: "I seek not Mine own will but the will of the Father who sent Me" (v. 30). On the third occasion, addressing the multitude, He specified the great object for which He came to carry out that will: "I came down from Heaven," He said, "not to do Mine Own will, but the will of Him that sent Me. And this is the Father's will which hath sent Me, that of all which He hath given Me I should lose nothing, but should raise it up again at the last day. For this is the will of Him that sent Me, that every one which seeth the Son, and believeth on Him, may have everlasting life: and I will raise him up at the last day" (6:39, 40).

To the natural mind it might cause surprise that for the first thirty years of His life He remained in seclusion in His Jewish home, and that even subsequently, in spite of the fact that there were vast regions lying in darkness outside Palestine, His public ministry was confined to that small tract of country. Yet we know that in this matter, as in everything else, He acted, not by the guidance of circumstances, but in unbroken communion with the Father, and in accordance with His will. Nor has anyone ever been able to impute to Him failure either in the plan of His work or in its method or in its effects. His Cross and its results will prove to be a sufficient answer to any such charge. With His perfect example before us we may learn not to allow even the best natural considerations to turn us aside from what we know to be the will of God. If we so walk as He walked, we shall neither run in advance of God's leading, nor lag behind in neglect of it. It is almost as easy to be carried away by our zeal and to be overengrossed in our service and its possibilities instead of making the will of God our guide, as it is to fail to do His will through carelessness. Well may we take up the language of Psalm 143 and say, "Teach me to do Thy will."

The Word of God is full of instruction for us in this respect. Firstly, we are *to be filled with the knowledge of His will* "in all spiritual wisdom and understanding" (Col. 1:9, R.V.). The will of God is thus to engage our whole being. This is far more than a mere mental apprehension of it. We are to be led by it to walk "worthily of the Lord unto all pleasing, being fruitful in every good work, and increasing in the knowledge of God." These mighty effects in our Christian life are possible only according as we are enabled to discern the will of God "in all spiritual wisdom and understanding."

The three results referred to will follow: (1) a worthy walk, (2) fruitful service, (3) the knowledge of God Himself. No one can have a higher knowledge than this. It comes by diligent and prayerful meditation in the Word of God, and by the practical fulfillment of it in our Christian life and conduct.

Secondly, we are *to understand what the will of the Lord is* (Eph. 5:17). This is set in antithesis to the foolishness of not walking circumspectly; just as being filled with the Spirit is contrasted with drunkenness. An understanding of His will leads us to a careful walk, and a careful walk leads us to redeem the time. For all this we need the filling of the Spirit, and then, just as the drunkard is given up to the power of drink, so shall we be given up to the Spirit for power to do the will of God.

Thirdly, we are *to prove what the will of God is*. "I beseech you therefore, brethren," says the apostle, "that ye present your bodies a living sacrifice, holy, acceptable unto God, which is your reasonable service. And be ye not conformed to this world: but be ye transformed by the renewing of your mind, that ye may prove what is that good, and acceptable and perfect, will of God" (Rom. 12:1, 2). This exhortation may be summed up in the three words, *consecration, separation, transformation*. For the carrying out of God's will there must be first the consecration of our body to Him as a living sacrifice. Then we must walk in separation from that which would interfere with our wholehearted service. The process of transformation will inevitably follow. A life consecrated to the Lord leads to conformity to His character.

Fourthly, we are *to stand perfect and complete in all the will of Cod* (Col. 4:12). The word "complete" is rightly rendered in the R.V. "fully assured." Our adversary, who in the wilderness endeavored to tempt the Lord to depart from His Father's will, is ever busy seeking to lead us to do the same. "He only consults to cast us down from our excellency," as He consulted against Christ. What is our excellency but pleasing God? Oh! for steadfastness in the faith! These are times of declension, perilous times. Let us, like Epaphras, wrestle in prayer for one another, that we may stand "perfect and fully assured in all the will of God."

Fifthly, we are *to live to the will of God* (1 Pet. 4:2). This the apostle Peter sets in contrast to our former manner of life when we followed carnal desires. If standing in the will of God denotes unwavering adherence to it, living to it suggests constant and wholehearted occupation in it. This the apostle tells us is only possible as we arm ourselves with the same mind which characterized Christ. He suffered in the flesh, we are to do the same. "He that hath suffered in the flesh hath ceased from sin." We shall not in this life become sinless. Yet death to sin means a life lived to the will of God.

Sixthly, we are *to do the will of God from the heart* (Eph. 6:6). The apostle is giving instruction in this passage directly to servants, but His words are applicable to all believers, inasmuch as all are servants of Christ. Literally the phrase is "from the soul," and the immediate explanation of this is, "with good will doing service as to the Lord." "As to the Lord"—that is the first great motive. Another follows, namely, the prospect of reward, "knowing that whatsoever good thing each one doeth, the same shall he receive again from the Lord, whether he be bond or free" (R.V.). The realization of the Lordship of Christ will prevent our service from becoming drudgery. The prospect of reward will enable us so to toil for Him as to anticipate eagerly the time when, having received our reward, we shall use it in perfect service for Him in His eternal kingdom.

Seventhly, we are *to delight to do the will of God*. The words of Psalm 40, which we have already referred to, express the ideal in this. Happy are we if in any measure we can say, "I delight to do Thy will." The path of willing obedience is the path of prosperity and happiness. Such delight can only be enjoyed in the realization of the smile of our God and Father upon us. Be it ours, then, to cultivate that condition of soul day by day in which we can enjoy the presence of the Lord, and constant communion with Him.

In the first epistle to the Thessalonians there are two passages in which the will of God for us is definitely stated. Firstly, the will of God is our sanctification (2:3). This is immediately defined as purity of life. In whatever way the passage may be understood, whether of married life, or of the body of the believer,

God's will is that we should be set apart for Him, free from all that would contaminate us and hinder us from enjoying the peace and happiness of a life of holiness. The second mention in the epistle has reference to joy, prayer and thanksgiving. "Rejoice alway," says the apostle, "pray without ceasing; in everything give thanks; for this is the will of God in Christ Jesus to you-ward" (vv. 16–18). If we are fulfilling the first condition as to sanctification, we shall then, and only then, be able to fulfill the second. May we be led more and more to realize that constant prayer, and thankfulness in everything, are the commandments of God for us, the commandments of One who has our best interests in view!

▪ CHAPTER THREE ▪

Service that Glorifies God

The great aim of all Christian life and service is summed up by the apostle Peter in the following words, "that God in all things may be glorified through Jesus Christ" (1 Pet. 4:11). This was indeed fulfilled perfectly by the Lord Himself in the days of His flesh. At the close of His earthly life He said, "I have glorified Thee on the earth." Never for a moment, in thought, word, or deed, did He abandon that perfect submission to His Father's will by which He glorified Him. The fulfillment of His will was His constant delight. He described it to His disciples as His very sustenance (John 5:34). His testimony to the Jews was, "I am come down from heaven not to do Mine own will, but the will of Him that sent Me" (6:38, R.V.).

The passage in Peter's epistle shows us that Christ is still glorifying the Father on the earth, but now through the lives of His saints. If they are to glorify God it must be "through Jesus Christ." It is possible to attempt to render service to God by mere self-impulse and self-effort, to seek to do right things in our own way and not according to His plan and direction. We must learn what God's will is before we attempt to serve Him. Otherwise we shall act in the energy of the flesh. It is possible to do this without going so far as to act in rebellion to, and disregard of, His known will. The teaching of the Lord on the latter subject is intensely solemn. "Not every one," He says, "that saith unto Me, Lord, Lord, shall enter into the kingdom of heaven; but he that doeth the will of My Father which is in heaven. Many will say to Me in that day, Lord, Lord, have we not prophesied in Thy Name, and in Thy Name have cast out demons, and in Thy Name done many wonderful works? And then will I profess unto them, I never knew you; depart from Me, ye that work iniquity" (Matt. 7:21–23). The word rendered "iniquity" would be better translated "lawlessness"—that is the literal meaning of the original. Lawlessness is disregard of the will of God. While referring to this passage it seems necessary to remark that the language of verse 23 can never apply to one who is a child of God. To none of His redeemed will the Lord ever say, "I never knew you; depart from Me." God's children can never be disinherited. The life that is given to them is eternal, and will never be extinguished. But it is possible for a mere professor, one who is not really born again, one whom the Lord here describes as "a corrupt tree," to attempt to do His work, and it is to these that the Lord addresses such solemn words. The teaching of the passage is, however, of the greatest importance for all who are genuinely the Lord's servants. It shows that only what is done according to the will of God will obtain His recognition and approval.

Now the will of God centers in Christ. None can fulfill it, apart from Him. "Apart from Me," He says, "ye can do nothing." We must first say, "Teach me to do Thy will"; then we may be able to say, as He did, "I delight to do Thy will." Christ must be the motive power for all valid service to God. To the question, "What is the duty of man?" the Shorter Catechism rightly answers, "To glorify God and enjoy Him forever." We learn from Peter the secret of the power to do so. It is "through Jesus Christ."

Similarly the writer of the epistle to the Hebrews, at the close of his exhortations, expresses the desire that God would "make the saints perfect in every good work to do His will, working in them that which is well pleasing in His sight *through Jesus Christ*" (Heb. 13:21). God works all things by Christ. How necessary that our hearts should be in unison with His before we undertake any service for Him! The cultivation of heart communion with the Lord ensures that what we do is what

He works in us. Our service will not be the outcome of leaning to our own understanding, and of self-effort, when we take His yoke upon us and learn of Him. When we cease from our own works we obtain the rest which He gives, and find that this rest accompanies the activity of our service for Him. We learn, too, that "it is God which worketh in us both to will and to work for His good pleasure" (Phil. 2:13, R.V.). The fruits of righteousness are through Jesus Christ, and in order to be filled with these it is necessary that our love should abound in knowledge and in all judgment (Phil. 1:9–11). When our love abounds toward Him, His power abounds through us. Love to Christ is the secret of fruitful service. It is a love, however, which works, not by mere emotion and enthusiasm, but by a knowledge of His mind and a discernment of His will. Thus is God glorified in our lives through Jesus Christ. If, like George Muller of Bristol, we make it our aim first and foremost each day to be in the happy enjoyment of the Lord's presence and love, our lives will constantly bring glory to God. However humble our service may be, however much of routine there may be in it, we shall "serve the Lord with gladness." Then, too, our Lord will not have to say to us, as He did to the church in Sardis, "I have found no works of thine fulfilled before My God," for He will Himself be working in and through us.

The passage at the close of the epistle to the Hebrews is strikingly parallel to that in 1 Peter 4. In each case the words "through Jesus Christ" are followed by a doxology, ascribing the glory to Him by whose power alone what has been enjoined can be carried out. Inasmuch as the fulfillment of God's will through us, and His being glorified by us, are due to Christ, all self-gratulation is precluded, all self-satisfaction is ruled out. His alone will be the glory. And the one who is delighting to do His will will ever be led to attribute all to Him.

Not to ourselves we owe
That aught by us is done
To glorify Thine Holy Name;
Christ's is the power alone.

The words in 1 Peter 4, "that God in all things may be glorified through Jesus Christ," express the great purpose of all the exhortations that precede from verse 7 onwards. This is dearly brought out in the revised translation, which rightly links all the injunctions together. It is observable that the first concerns prayer, indicating that the soul must be right with God if the rest are to be fulfilled. Then follow exhortations to love, to hospitality, to the unselfish use of whatever God has given us, "as good stewards of the manifest grace of God"; those who speak are to speak as the oracles of God. Those who do service ("ministry" is not here confined to ministry of God's Word; it comprehends any form of service for God) are to render it as of the ability, or strength, which God gives. We may do less than He would have us do. In that case we are missing the blessing in this life, and the reward in the next, that come from power received from God, and from service rendered to Him by means of it. We may do more than God wills for us to do. In that case we must be adding our own strength to what God supplies. This makes for weakness, and may hinder others from the service God has for them. It must not be forgotten, on the other hand, that more than his share may devolve upon one servant of God through the failure of others to undertake their responsibility. Paul's "I can do all things" is qualified by "through Christ which strengtheneth me." If we are to be strengthened with might, it must be "by the Spirit of God in the inner man," and by the indwelling of Christ in the heart by faith. Thus through Him we shall "glorify God in all things." Thus and only thus shall we be able to say, "I live; and yet no longer I, but Christ liveth in me: and that life which I now live in the flesh I live in faith, the faith which is in the Son of God, who loved me and gave Himself up for me."

▪ CHAPTER FOUR ▪

The Priestly Character of Service

Under the dispensation of law, the distinction between priests and people was of God's appointment. Only one tribe was set apart in Israel for priestly service. None other than those of the tribe of Levi were permitted to engage in that work. With the introduction of the dispensation of grace, and the formation of the Church, a new order of priesthood was constituted. From pentecost onward no such distinction as had existed formerly was in the divine intention. There is not a hint in the New Testament that any single man or set of men was appointed of God to act in a priestly capacity for the other members of the church. The distinction between clergy and laity is foreign to the New Testament. That there are divinely-appointed elders, overseers or pastors, is quite another matter. As to the service of priesthood, the apostle Peter shows clearly that in the Church, priests are numerically coextensive with the Christians who constitute it. He describes all believers as first, "a holy priesthood" and then, "a royal priesthood." Addressing all saints, he says, "Ye also as living stones are built up a spiritual house, to be a holy priesthood, to offer up spiritual sacrifices acceptable to God through Jesus Christ . . . Ye are an elect race, a royal priesthood, an holy nation, a people for God's own possession; that ye may show forth the excellencies of Him who called you out of darkness into His marvelous light" (1 Pet. 2:5 and 9, R.V.). Any humanly ordained or select priesthood in the Church is contrary to the mind of God and dishonoring to the High-Priestly service of God. And for this reason especially, that for any man to stand as a priest between his fellowmen and God is to usurp the position and function of Christ. He alone is our means of access to God. "There is one mediator between God and men, Himself Man, Christ Jesus" (1 Tim. 2:5). Having a High Priest over the House of God we can draw near to Him. We have boldness to enter into the holiest by His blood (Heb. 10:19, 22). Any other supposed means of approach is a delusion and a snare. "Will a man rob God?" Yet that is what those do who, with their ecclesiastical assumption, endeavor to act as priests between God and man, and thus presume to stand in the place only possible to His Son. He is the one mediatorial High Priest. The only other priesthood embraces every believer, and is quite distinct from His. Thus the apostle John says in the opening doxology of the Apocalypse: "Unto Him that loveth us, and loosed us from our sins by His blood; and He made us to be a kingdom, to be priests unto His God and Father; to Him be the glory and the dominion forever and ever. Amen" (R.V.). That doxology is the praise of all saints.

Characterized as *holy,* our priesthood is Godward; we are to offer up spiritual sacrifices to Him. Characterized as *royal,* our priesthood is manward; we are to display to the world the excellencies of Christ. In each case, whether Godward or manward, our service is rendered to God. Let us consider first the service of our holy priesthood. "Ye also as living stones are built up a spiritual house, to be a holy priesthood." Accordingly believers are both a temple and priests in the temple. As holy priests we are appointed to offer up spiritual sacrifices. These are varied in character. In the Old Testament they frequently stand out in contrast to the sacrifices on the altar. Spiritual sacrifices are constantly mentioned in the Psalms. There are the sacrifices of righteousness (4:5; 51:19), the sacrifices of joy (27:6), the sacrifice of thanksgiving (50:14, R.V.; 107:22), the sacrifice of a broken spirit and a contrite heart (51:17). Hosea exhorts apostate Israel to return to God, acknowledge their iniquity, and "render as bullocks the offering of their lips" (14:2, R.V.).

In the epistle to the Hebrews we are exhorted to offer up a sacrifice of praise to God continually, "that is, the fruit of the lips which make confession to His name." We are also not to forget to do good and to communicate: "for with such sacrifices God is well pleased" (13:15, 16). In this the church at Philippi set a good example. Paul speaks of the gifts they sent to him through Epaphroditus as "the odor of a sweet smell, a sacrifice acceptable, well pleasing to God."

Behind all these must come the presentation of our bodies "a living sacrifice, holy, acceptable to God, which is our reasonable service" (Rom. 12:1). This we are to do constantly. If we ourselves are not devoted to God, our other sacrifices are valueless. When the churches of Macedonia sent a gift of help to their poor brethren in Judaea, they first gave their own selves to the Lord (2 Cor. 8:5). The spirit of the giver determines the character of the gift.*

The saints are also constituted, as we have observed, a royal priesthood. Shortly after the people of Israel had been brought out of Egypt, the Lord declared to them through Moses, that if they obeyed His voice and kept His covenant they would be a peculiar treasure to Him, a kingdom of priests, an holy nation (Ex. 19:5, 6). Their failure to fulfill the conditions has resulted in their temporary rejection. They will yet become an earthly kingdom of priests to God, but meanwhile the kingdom has been taken from them and given to a nation bringing forth the fruits thereof. That nation is the Church, the holy nation of which the apostle Peter speaks. As we have already noticed, Christ has made us to be a kingdom, to be priests unto His God and Father (Rev. 1:6).

The sovereign power of that kingdom is not yet in exercise by the Church. Paul charges the saints in Corinth with attempting to reign before the time. He says: "Ye have reigned without us: yea, and I would that ye did reign, that we also might reign with you" (1 Cor. 4:8, R.V.). In the coming age kingship and priesthood will be perfectly combined. They are already combined in the priesthood of Christ. His priesthood is after the order of Melchizedek, who was both king of Salem and priest of the Most High God. So, when God sets His king upon His holy hill of Zion, and the world that still rejects Him bows beneath His sway, "He shall be a priest upon His throne: and the counsel of peace shall be between them both" (Zech. 6:13). That is to say, kingship and priesthood will be joined in complete harmony. (Cp. Rev. 20:6).

Rulers of nations have again and again endeavored to combine in themselves the imperial and priestly functions and so to control both the affairs of men and their consciences. Were it an absolutely certain attainment the combination would be the strongest possible. But in every case failure has resulted. Men have constantly sought to establish a state church, and so to unite political and religious power, but instead of the counsel of peace being between them, the history of nations in this respect has been one of constant friction or open warfare. The Son of God alone will harmonize the two. His throne will be that of a King-Priest in the perfect exercise of the double function. His servants, associated with Him, whether Israel on the earth, or the Church in the heavenlies, will be a kingdom of priests. In the present age we are a royal priesthood, not for the wielding of governmental power, but to show forth the excellencies

*There are two words in the original which with their associated forms, describe priestly service (though their use is not entirely confined to that meaning), *latreia* (with its verb *latreuō*, I serve) and *leitourgeō* (with its forms *leitourgos*, a minister, and *leitourgeō*, I serve). Of these two the latter was used especially to denote priestly service. Thus in Luke 1:23, Hebrews 9:21; 10:11, it refers to the service of the tabernacle. In Hebrews 8:2 and 6 it is used of the High-Priestly work of Christ. Then in the broader view of the various forms of service which believers render as priests, it is used of the ministry of prophets and teachers in the Church, Acts 13:2; of gospel ministry, Romans 15:16; of fellowship in the gospel, Philippians 2:25 and 30. *Latreia* originally signified the work of a hired servant, as distinguished from the compulsory service of a slave, but in the course of time it largely lost that significance, and in its usage in Scripture there was added to free obedience the thought of adoration. From the spiritual standpoint, used of service to God, it thus received the idea of a service characterized by worship; see, for example, Philippians 3:3; Hebrews 8:5; 9:1, 6, 9; 13:10. Thus in Hebrews 9:14 it refers to the priestly service of all believers; see also Revelation 7:15 and 22:3.

of Christ. As a holy priesthood we are called to render service unmarred by defilement. As a royal priesthood we are in our service worthily to represent Him to the world. Thus it is that we shall be prepared for the day when, in the full display of the powers of His kingdom, we shall reign with Him as kings and serve Him as priests.

▪ CHAPTER FIVE ▪

A Guiding Principle for Service

One of the characteristics of the writings of the apostle Paul which strikes the reader is the way in which he passes from particular instances to broad principles. In the seventh chapter of 1 Corinthians, for instance, where, in dealing with the subject of marriage, he is replying to questions concerning the giving away of marriageable daughters, he turns for a moment from the special subject to make a statement of general application: "But this I say, brethren, the time is shortened, that henceforth both those that have wives may be as though they had none: and those that weep, as though they wept not; and those that rejoice, as though they rejoiced not; and those that buy, as though they possessed not; and those that use the world, as not abusing it: for the fashion of this world passeth away" (1 Cor. 7:29–31, R.V.). Two corrections in the Revised translation in verse 29 are important. Firstly, the apostle states that the time is shortened (not merely that it is short). Secondly, what follows is given as a purpose. That is to say, the time is shortened, in order that Christians may take a wise view of their circumstances here below.

God gives two views of the present dispensation, one in regard to the unsaved, the other in regard to the saints. For the unsaved the period is lengthened. God is long-suffering, "not willing that any should perish, but that all should come to repentance" (2 Pet. 3:9). For the saints the period is shortened, and this fact is to govern their lives. The apostle has been charged with a mistaken notion in thus regarding the return of the Lord as near at hand, whereas this age has lasted for nearly two millenniums and the Lord's Second Advent, which terminates it, has not yet taken place. The mistake lies with those who make the charge. Under the inspiration of God, Paul was writing for others than for the saints of his own day. His message was intended for those of each generation throughout this age. The purpose of God was that the expectation of the Lord's return should characterize Christians at all times. The attitude of the church of the Thessalonians should have been that of the saints from their day to ours. They turned to God from idols to serve Him, and "to wait for His Son from heaven." For them the time was short. Their serving was characterized by expectancy; their expectancy was compatible only with wholehearted service. Expectation of the return of the Lord was the constant attitude of the apostle himself, as is evidenced throughout his epistles. In his epistle to Titus, chronologically his last but one, he still teaches the same thing. We are to look for "the blessed hope and appearing of the glory of our great God and Savior Jesus Christ" (Titus 2:13).

The message to the saints in Corinth, then, is a message for us all. The providential extension of the age to its present limits does not weaken the apostle's argument. The Word of God is not to be interpreted by historical facts. Facts of history are to be observed in the light of Scripture.

Again, we must not miss the meaning of the passage by supposing that when Paul says that those that have wives are to be as those that have none, his words are directed toward a lower view of the marital relationship than that which is given elsewhere in his or any other teaching of the New Testament. Nor, when he says, "Those that weep, as though they wept not; and those that rejoice as though they rejoiced not," that he is inculcating a stoical view of sorrow and joy. His records of his own tears and rejoicing are a repudiation of that. What he does teach is that the Christian is never to abandon himself to the interests of this life. Nothing earthly is to be paramount in our lives. Sorrow and joy are not to engross our minds to the detriment of our devotion to

Christ and of our expectation of His return. Deep and real as are our joys and sorrows, they are to be tempered by the power of that hope. Mere earthly interests pale into insignificance in the light of His Coming and all that it means. Everything is to be carried on by the believer as one who has had notice to quit. Just imagine the Israelite, aware of the impending Exodus of the nation from Egypt, entering into partnership with an Egyptian!

The prospect of our speedy removal from this scene is calculated to keep alive within us a due sense of disengagedness with regard to the affairs of this life. That does not mean a lack of diligence in the conduct of our business. Some of the saints at Thessalonica became forgetful of that; and hence the exhortation of the apostle that they were to do their own business and work with their hands, that they might walk honestly toward them that were without. The hope of the Lord's return was to be not only a comfort in sorrow, but a counteractive against indolence. There is a use of this world which is quite consistent with our relations to the other. The danger lies in the abuse, or perhaps, as the margin reads, in using it to the full. There is an abuse which consists of an overuse. The real value of all our actions is determined by our attitude to Christ. If we are not to be "slothful in business," it is because we are to be "serving the Lord." To the saints at Corinth the apostle puts it as their main purpose, that they "may attend upon the Lord without distraction." Let all our occupations center in Christ, and we shall live as those for whom the next thing is His appearing. Serving the living God we shall wait for His Son from heaven. He who estimates at their true value the things which are not seen, the eternal things, will keep himself from entanglement in the things that are seen, that are temporal. He who realizes that "the time is shortened," and that "the fashion of this world passeth away," will use this world only as he may thereby serve the Lord and wait for His return. A loose hold on the things of this life enables us to lay hold on eternal life. At the same time, laying hold on eternal life makes us "rich in good works, ready to distribute, willing to communicate," "ready to every good work" and to do good to all men. The attachment to Christ which produces detachment from the world enables us to live in it as He did, who "went about doing good."

The teaching inculcated by the apostle stood in marked contrast to the general notions of that time. To the man of the world there was nothing beyond this life. His great resource was to throw himself into such pleasure or business as the world offered. If earth's joys were obtainable they were voluptuously pursued. If sorrow came, its blow was irretrievable and led to hopeless despair. That was where materialism drove society then. Is it not where materialism is driving men today? The New Testament was written during one of the darkest periods of ancient history. Politically and morally things were at the lowest ebb. Disaster followed disaster, kindling gloomy forebodings. There seemed no end to the misery. There was a general apprehension that a crisis was approaching. The message that was needed for the Lord's people was just that which the apostle gives. "The fashion of the world," he says, "is passing away." The phrase used is that of the change of scene in a drama, where, while one scene is going on, another is being prepared. It was in view of another scene that the lives of the saints were to be lived. The Lord's return was so important and engrossing that it forbad their being absorbed in the transient events of the time.

That is just how we stand today. Indeed there is a striking parallel between the circumstances of those times, as briefly described above, and the condition of things that prevails in the world today. The nations have been passing through terrible judgments of late, but these have apparently left the masses, comparatively speaking, unmoved. There is, however, a general expectation of some impending crisis. How applicable, therefore, are the words of the apostle to us! How needful that we should heed his exhortations, and view the things of this life in the light of the near return of the Lord! To say that, as the saints in days gone by have been mistaken in their expectations of the nearness of His Coming, so we are likely to be mistaken now, is tantamount to saying, "My Lord delayeth His coming." Rather let us realize that the time of our redemption draweth nigh, and lift up our heads in joyful anticipation of the great event. Let the return of our Lord be such a reality that it will regulate our views, direct our energies, and mold our lives. Then, in the apprehension of the shortness of the time for service and of the eternal rewards for faithfulness, we shall make the best use of our talents and opportunities, and spend and be spent for the glory of our Redeemer.

No, not from earth our expectation is;
Within the veil it blooms beneath the eyes
Of God, a tree of life, and nourished in
The garden of our glad, blood-ransomed
 souls.
By the sweet, living, ever-flowing brook
Of His firm, steadfast and eternal truth,
And fragrant in the sunshine of His love,
It fills the heart with everlasting joy.
Nor can it wither till He come, for whom
We wait with patience; then our hope
 shall give
Place to possession.

▪ CHAPTER SIX ▪

Readiness for Service

Effectual service for God demands the consecration of the life to Him for the purpose. He whose members are to be "instruments of righteousness" must present himself to God. If the vessel is to be "meet for the Master's use and prepared unto every good work," it must first be sanctified. We are called to present our bodies to the Lord as a living sacrifice; and in this definite yielding of the life to Him—in itself "our reasonable service"—we shall be in readiness for a call for any special service He may have in store for us.

Much is involved in this preparation. It necessitates two things at least; one, a spirit of self-judgment, and the other, a heart in sympathy with the thoughts and purposes of the Lord. We must learn to pass sentence upon everything in our lives which is inconsistent with the will of God. For this we need the help of His Word. It is the great heart-searcher. It is "quick to discern the thoughts and intents of the heart." Its holy light reveals all that meets with the displeasure of its Author. It teaches us to pray, "Search me, O God, and know my heart: try me, and know my thoughts; and see if there be any way of wickedness in me, and lead me in the way everlasting" (Ps. 139:23, 24). The judgment of self under the power of the Word is not calculated to drag the soul into despondency. Self-judgment does not mean gloomy introspection. He who is poor and of a contrite spirit, and trembles at God's Word, is the object of His special regard (Is. 66:2). Such a one He can use for the carrying out of His purposes. "He that walketh in a perfect way, he shall serve Me," saith the Lord (Ps. 101:6). We need to keep short accounts with God. We must suffer nothing to remain that may have come in to mar our enjoyment of the Lord's presence and communion with Him. Full provision, too, has been made for us. For the soul that is humbled before God there is the efficacy of the blood that cleanseth from all sin, and the ministry of our Advocate with the Father. For the rectification of the life and the cleansing of the way, there is the guidance and separating power of the Word of God, and the help of the Holy Spirit. Should we not ever seek to have "A mind at perfect peace with God"?

To be ready for service we need, too, a heart in unison with His counsels. We must know our God if we are to "be strong and do exploits." To know Him is to understand His will and His ways. We may form many plans for rendering service to Him, but they may not be His plans. To serve Him rightly, His thoughts must be our thoughts, and His ways our ways. Now oneness with the Lord's thoughts and purposes depends upon the cultivation of habits of private prayer and meditation in the Scriptures—not the former without the latter, nor the latter without the former. Prayer without meditation in the Scriptures cannot enable us to know the Lord; meditation in the Scriptures without prayer will make us mere students and not disciples.

These conditions by which we may be in readiness for God to use us are strikingly illustrated in the case of Isaiah, in the circumstances narrated at the commencement of the sixth chapter of his prophecies. When the vision of the Lord sitting upon His lofty throne, His train filling the temple, and hosts of worshiping seraphim in attendance, was given him (a vision in purposive contrast with King Uzziah's presumption in the earthly temple, and his consequent leprosy and death), Isaiah was not aware that God had the particular service in view in which he was about to be engaged. The vision, however, brought about the spirit of self-judgment which was an essential preparation for it. The revelation of the glory of the Lord drew from his heart the contrite confession, "Woe is me! for I am undone; because I am a man of unclean lips: for mine eyes have seen the King, the Lord of Hosts." The confession was real and full of meaning. Uzziah's fatal error of seeking religious ends in his own way, and ignoring God's way, was the characteristic sin of the nation, and with this national sin Isaiah identified himself, and judged himself for it. His confession and immediate forgiveness reestablished that communion with God which was necessary for what was to follow.

That the prophet had a heart to will according to the will of the Lord, while manifest throughout his writings, is at once evident in the circumstances under consideration. And here we must notice that, in the first instance, the call to the special service God required to be rendered did not come to him personally. Yet he was so in touch with God, so fully in the current of the divine thought and purpose, that immediately on hearing the voice of the Lord saying "Whom shall I send, and who will go for us?" he offered himself for the task. In his "Here am I; send me," there was no pondering over possible difficulties. Such a man, self-judged and devoted, was, in God's estimate, entirely suited to the work. He at once says "Go." There was no romance about the errand. The message he had to deliver would be anything but popular. But no difficulty could daunt the man who was out and out for God. He who stands in the counsels of the Lord, shrinks not from hardships. He is proof against any degree of discouragement. He knows that God's mountains are wont to become His ways. Can we wonder that Paul witnesses of him, "Isaiah is very bold."

Isaiah's call was not a case of compulsion, nor of half-reluctant submission. There was no struggle to decide upon a path which conscience made it impossible for him to refuse. Nor, on the other hand, were there any ulterior motives of self-interest, such as the prospect of notoriety or some other advantage as likely to accrue from entrance upon the service. He was moved neither by pressure without, nor by selfish ambition within. He heard the voice of God declaring a divine requirement, and, being in the necessary readiness of mind and heart, he spontanously offered himself.

What an example for us! Where such are the conditions of preparation, the worker is not likely to stop short of the fulfillment of the service, not likely to abandon the appointed path, through the attractiveness of some other course, nor through a gradual declension first into flagging of interest, and then into heartlessness for the work. Self-abasement before God, self-consecration to His service, and the self-obliteration of a will that is lost in His will, are safeguards against that state of which the Lord has to say, "I have found no works of thine fulfilled before My God" (Rev. 3:2).

How great are the claims upon us to devote ourselves entirely to Him! When we consider the awful doom that awaited us, and that His was the love and grace that endured the unutterable suffering and judgment of the Cross to deliver us, when we think of our mercies which are the outcome of His death, mercies innumerable, inestimable, unutterable, unmerited, we surely cannot but be moved to consecrate our all to our Redeemer. "I beseech you," says the apostle, "by the mercies of God, that ye present your bodies a living sacrifice" (Rom. 12:1). "The mercies of God" would form a fitting title for the first eleven chapters of the epistle to the Romans, and those mercies may be summed up in the words which close the eighth chapter, "the love of God which is in Christ Jesus our Lord." David's appeal to His people, "Who then is willing to consecrate his service this day unto the Lord?" drew forth a loyal response, "With perfect heart they offered willingly to the Lord" (1 Chr. 29:5, 9). Shall ours be less wholehearted who have upon us the claims of a Redeemer's love? The churches of Macedonia are examples to us. The secret of the devotion of their service lay in this, that "they first gave their own selves to the Lord" (2 Cor. 8:5). His love it was that stirred theirs.

A further incentive is the desire of Christ toward the perishing. Discipleship of Christ involves identity of our desires with His. Have we fully entered into His thoughts concerning the lost whom He came to seek and to save? Is there a danger lest we should unconsciously get into a way of thinking, that we to whom the gospel has been brought, and who have experienced its saving power, are a kind of privileged caste?

Not so if we know the meaning and purpose of the Cross, and the deep yearning of the

Savior who hung and suffered there. He still bids us look on the fields. He calls us to share His compassion for those who sit in darkness and the shadow of death, and for whom the light that shines from Calvary was intended to shine as much as for us.

Shall we, whose souls are lighted
  With wisdom from on high,
Shall we to man benighted
  The lamp of life deny?

We may not be called to go to other lands, but we are called to take such part as He will assign to us in fulfilling His purposes toward the souls for whom He died. For this we need to be in readiness. Let us, therefore, fervently breathe afresh the prayer:

Take my life, and let it be
Consecrated, Lord, to Thee;
Take my moments and my days;
Let them flow in ceaseless praise.

CHAPTER SEVEN

The Field of Service

To make known Christ through the gospel is the purpose of God for us in the world. The parting words of the Lord on the day of His ascension were, "Ye shall be witnesses unto Me." This witness is the great object of service for God. Gospel testimony is not confined to preaching, nor is this testimony the service of a particular section of the Lord's people. Christ is to be made known constantly by all the life and work of His followers. Paul's desire should characterize us all, that "Christ may be magnified in our body whether by life or death." Scripture knows no division of our work into the secular and the religious. Whether we follow an avocation in order to earn the bread that perisheth, or whether we engage in spiritual work, each form of occupation may equally have the glory of Christ as its aim. All is to be done "as unto the Lord." What is mistermed a secular calling will, if the Lord has called us to it, be in itself the means He has appointed for us to make known His name and His salvation. And not only may we thus be a savor of Christ in our immediate sphere of service, but as the Lord prospers us, we have the opportunity of assisting our fellow servants who, whether in this or other lands, go with the gospel where we cannot go. So shall we be His witnesses "unto the uttermost part of the earth."

In His interpretation of the parable of the wheat and the tares, the Lord speaks of Himself as the sower of the wheat; of the field as the world; and of the good seed as the sons of the kingdom. This surely finds an application in the details mentioned above in relationship to ourselves and our witness for Christ. "The field is the world." The Lord was thus anticipating His final commission, "Go ye into all the world and preach the gospel to every creature." In the preceding parable the seed is the Word of God and the field is the human heart. In the parable of the tares the good seed represents the testimony and influence of the lives of Christ's followers in the world. Thus, in a single view of the seed, as presented in both parables, the saints of God are identified with the Word of truth which they proclaim (vv. 20 and 38, R.V.). For the seed of the first parable is sown through them. This is illustrated by the statements in the Acts, "The Word of God increased," "the Word of God grew and multiplied" (6:7; 12:24). So also in Colossians 1:6 the apostle speaks of the Word of the truth of the gospel bearing fruit and increasing in the saints, and thereby in the world.

The world is a field—not a garden, not a paradise of mere enjoyment. It is a place into which the Lord sends *laborers*, a scene of diligent and difficult toil, not of ease and luxury. Nor was it intended that some parts of the field should be crowded with workers while others are vacant. How grievously have we failed to apprehend the simple meaning of those words, "Go ye into all the world"!

Our Master had a plan. His was the sole right to have it. He still has the same plan. From it He has never swerved. According to it each of those who own His lordship has his work assigned below, and thereby will receive his reward above. And the plan is that all the world might have the gospel. How have we viewed that plan? How far have we shared His view as made known in His own words? Part of His plan was that we ourselves should be saved. Well and good, and therein we rejoice and praise His blest name, and so we should. But that was not all. There is the other part of the plan, that we should be sown in the field and bring forth fruit, that we should have our part in the carrying out of His designs of grace toward the rest of the world. Had we our view broadened to be commensurate with His, not one of us could rest content for a day, that parts of the world should be lying in dark ignorance of the salvation we are enjoying, that parts of the field should be without the presence of a son of the kingdom. Oh! for a heart that shares the sympathies of His! We hear Him say, "Pray ye the Lord of the harvest, that He will send forth laborers into His harvest." But what lay behind this injunction was a heart deeply stirred by the spiritual needs of the people. "When He saw the multitudes, He was moved with compassion . . . Then saith He unto His disciples, The harvest truly is plenteous, but the laborers are few; pray ye therefore the Lord of the harvest that He will send forth laborers into His harvest" (Matt. 9:35–38). A sense of our own needs drives us to prayer. Equally so should the sense of the needs of others. We are surely in the mind of the Lord when we pray that prayer.

He was Himself the answerer in the case of His disciples, and those whom He taught to pray were the ones He chose to send. He called them to Him, gave them authority, and sent them forth. How solemn it is that His "Pray ye" and His "Go ye" were uttered nearly two thousand years ago and yet there still are places in the harvest field without a laborer. Two-thirds of the people in the world remain in ignorance about the Christ who died for them, and still under the sway of him from whose bondage He came to deliver them. These two-thirds consist, roughly speaking, of a billion souls.

To us, Thy people, whom Thou hast
 redeemed,
To us belong the sin, the humbling shame;
We have not reaped, we have but slept
 and dreamed,
Nor called with holy ardor on Thy name.
 Lord, send the laborers forth.

We must think, not only of the unreached regions, but of the scarcity of laborers in many districts where gospel work has been and is being carried on. In many a place there are workers for whom the growing responsibilities consequent upon the development of the work are proving too great a tax. We speak sometimes perhaps of the advisability that a missionary should abstain from undertaking more than his strength will permit. But when we remember how extremely difficult it is for one who, in devotion to Christ, has a passion for rescuing souls, and who sees around him abounding needs and abounding opportunities, to refrain from endeavoring to meet the needs and seize the opportunities, we shall do well to consider whether we have fulfilled our responsibilities; whether we have fervently prayed the Lord of the harvest to send forth laborers to cooperate with these tried and tired servants in the field. And there is something more. Intelligent and constant prayer concerning the needs of the harvest field is sure to lead to exercise of heart as to how we may share in the work in other ways. Were it not that there is one who is equal to the need, we might be tempted to despair. But Christ is in the place of authority. To Him all power is given. Yet has He committed to His saints the solution of the difficulty under the ready guidance of the Holy Spirit.

The voice that bade the disciples "look on the fields" still speaks to us. This is one great step in the solution—a careful contemplation of the condition of the fields. "Pray ye." That is another step. These we are all called to take. There are others. But which of us shall say the one for the other what he or she is to do in addition? How to follow up the contemplation and the prayer lies in the realm of the individual conscience and its exercise in the presence of the Master who has a definite part for each one to take. "The night is far spent; the day is at hand," the day when sower and reaper shall rejoice together and all that was done for the Lord of the harvest will receive its eternal reward.

CHAPTER EIGHT

An Essential Factor in Training for Service

One of the outstanding features of Timothy's premissionary life was the instruction he had received in the Word of God. The apostle says, "From a child thou hast known the Scriptures." We may read that in the light of 2 Timothy 1:5, where mention is made of his mother and his grandmother, and we are not far out in inferring that in his earliest days instruction in the Word of God had been given to him by each of these godly women. He had not only been taught by them, but he had evidently been helped to meditate in the Word of Truth. It had made him what Paul describes him, "a man of God" and "a minister of God." By these Scriptures (i.e., the Old Testament Scriptures, which constituted Timothy's Bible) he had "learned to war a good warfare." What we read further of the apostle's testimony to this younger fellow laborer, who had been commended by the elder brethren and whom the apostle had taken with him as a companion in missionary enterprise, is traceable, no doubt, to his knowledge of the Word of God.

The testimony concerning him in Philippians 2 is very striking. Three things are there said of Timothy:

1. "I have no man likeminded, who will naturally [i.e., genuinely] care for your state" (v. 20). Timothy had a real pastor's heart, and sought the welfare of the saints. He was no hireling. Our brethren who come from other lands, and those who have similar work in this land, know what trial and difficulty are involved in caring for converts, and how greatly this service casts one upon God.

2. The second statement, though negative in character, provides a positive testimony concerning him. For when the apostle says of others, "All seek their own, not the things that are Jesus Christ's," he clearly implies that it was otherwise in Timothy's case, and that he sought not his own things but Christ's. The Lord's glory was paramount in all his ministry. His service was rendered not for its own sake, but for the sake of the Lord Jesus. What a grand testimony to have!

The Holy Spirit, who is the author of the Scriptures, uses them not merely to equip us for our work, but in order that by the Word of God we may learn to use our energies for the glory of Christ, and that our whole heart's devotion may be set upon Him. That is the message to us from this witness to Timothy. The Scriptures that he had been taught exercised, as they should do in our lives who are privileged to have a more extended Bible, a marked influence, drawing his heart toward the one center, Jesus Christ. Just according as our service is rendered to Him and for His glory, so is it acceptable to God. This younger man, no doubt, drank deeply of the spirit of his senior partner in toil, whose aim it was "that Christ should be magnified in His body, whether by life or by death."

3. "As a son with the father, he hath served with me in the gospel" (v. 22). He knew what it was to be a true yokefellow, knew how to "keep in step." Two men walking together out of step are apt occasionally to give each other an inconvenient bump. There was no such awkwardness in Timothy's walk. He served as a son with a father. There was willingness to listen to counsel. There was a manifestation of subjection. Timothy did not act independently of Paul, and Paul recognized all that was of God in Timothy. This very passage is evidence of that. Thus sharing the apostle's toils and dangers, which were many, he learned to enjoy the peace and comfort derived from the Scriptures. How often must he have rested on the promises of the Old Testament! How often do we derive such comfort! How real it is in these difficult days! It is the Word of God that becomes the strength and solace of our souls,

and that strength is all the greater if our memories have been stored with the Scriptures in early days.

Paul's threefold testimony of Timothy, then, may be summed up thus: devotion to welfare of the saints; devotion to his fellow worker; and devotion to Christ; these three, but the greatest of these is devotion to Christ. Let us now revert to the early cause of all this. "From a child thou hast known the Scriptures." There is an urgent claim today upon us for the training of the young minds over which we have charge, that we may do for them what was done for Timothy. The effects of higher criticism and new theology are widespread today. The dangers for our young people are greatly increased. The devil has done his work persistently, systematically, thoroughly, especially in the past fifty years. What diligence we need in forearming the young mind against the insidious attacks of infidelity and skepticism! There is a widespread tendency today to call into question the validity of the Word of God and to explain away the miraculous in it. Against this a beginning must be made in the home. There is a great power in the cumulative effect of the constant daily reading of the Word of God, and that not in a haphazard, helter-skelter fashion, but in regular course. Of Timothy it was said, "Thou hast known the Holy Scriptures." That does not mean "part of the Scriptures." Thank God for any homes where the Scripture is read and instruction is given therefrom daily.

Much is gained by systematic, regular reading straight through the book. Young people also need to be helped to read for themselves, daily and prayerfully. Doubtless Timothy had favorite portions, as we all have, but there had been no neglect of the Word of God as a whole. "The Law, the Psalms and the Prophets," all had their effect upon him. So in the young potential missionaries of today, the Scriptures are to become a power which will enable them to render effectual service. It is in the home, in the church, in the Sunday school, in the Missionary Study Class, that the armor-plate should be forged which shall be proof against the batteries of skepticism and infidelity. In view of the aggression of the enemy, necessity is laid upon us to get our young people thoroughly established in the truth of the divine origin and inspiration, and claims of the entire Scriptures. Thus will they become a bulwark to the abounding errors of the day.

CHAPTER NINE

Yokefellows in Gospel Service

The frequent occurrence in the New Testament records of the association of two laborers in gospel service gives evidence that such partnership was intended to have a considerable place in the divine plans for the carrying on of the work. This method was adopted by the Lord both when He sent the twelve disciples forth to preach and heal, and again subsequently when He sent seventy others into the cities and districts whither He Himself was about to come (Mark 6:7; Luke 10:1). Immediately after pentecost the two apostles, Peter and John, are found associated in the service in Jerusalem, in the healing of the lame man, in preaching in the temple, in consequent imprisonment, and in testimony before the Sanhedrin (Acts 3:6–11; 4:1, 13, 19). The history of mission work among the Gentiles as narrated in the Acts and epistles abounds in instruction regarding the subject before us. We will consider first the case of Barnabas and Saul, the men selected for the earliest pioneering tour. We must not fail to observe the conditions of their appointment. The Holy Spirit made the choice and gave the call. These were, and ever remain, His prerogatives. No change either in the character of the times or in the conditions and circumstances of nations affords ground for the supposition that the Holy Spirit has relinquished these prerogatives or has relegated them to others as successors to the apostles. To disregard His claims and to set up human machinery for the ordination of men for gospel ministry is to deny one of the first principles of the work of God in the testimony committed to the Church. The fact that in apostolic times supernatural guidance was miraculously provided, and that this mode of direction ceased with the completion of the Word of God and with the passing away of the apostles, is no reason for thinking that the Spirit of God no longer, by His direct operation in the heart, makes the choice and gives the call but commits the selection and ordination to human authority. Lack of recognition of His power to act in these matters apart from human instrumentality is dishonoring to God.

Again, His choice involves His preparation of workers for the service which lies before them. Such preparation is evidenced in the work and testimony in which prospective laborers engage before they actually go forth. This preliminary period of service provides an evidence of their fitness when the fact of their call is made known to the church. It then becomes the responsibility of the church to recognize the call and to engage in practical cooperation with them in their new service. Barnabas and Saul were occupied as prophets and teachers in the church at Antioch for some time before the Spirit of God commanded their separation to Himself for the work whereunto He had called them.

That the church laid hands upon them was no act of ordination; they had received divine ordination long before this. What the church did was to express identification with them in the service upon which they were about to enter. The church is said to have "sent them away." The point of the original is perhaps missed in this translation. A closer rendering would be "they let them go," suggesting that while there was complete acquiescence in the will of the Spirit of God, there was also regret at parting from those who had been their spiritual helpers. The statement which follows, to the effect that they were sent forth by the Holy Ghost, enforces further the fact of His operation in the matter, and the word rendered "sent forth" is quite different from that used just previously in regard to the action of the church. The church parted with them, the Holy Ghost sent them. At the same time it seems to be clearly implied, indeed the circumstances make it obvious, that the church assisted them practically. We must not forget, too, the further description of the part the saints took in their going forth, in the statement at the close of chapter 14, that they were "committed to the grace of God for the work" (v. 26, R.V.).

Under these conditions, then, the two men set out on their momentous journey to the dark regions beyond. The companionship had been prepared of the Lord. Barnabas, "the son of consolation," had come to the help of Saul just after his conversion, to relieve the difficult situation arising from the fear of him entertained by the disciples in Jerusalem, and, by his explanation of the circumstances, had opened the hearts of all to receive him (Acts 9:27). The friendship thus formed was to be cemented later.

When the work at Antioch extended, and Barnabas, on coming from Jerusalem, saw the rapid increase in the church there and the need of additional spiritual help, he took a journey to Tarsus to seek out Saul, and after finding him brought him to Antioch, with the result that the two were united in service there for a whole year. Thus the Lord prepared for their association in the difficult pioneering work that He had in store for them.

That they were prevented from a continuance of their labors together in the matter of a second journey, by their division of heart concerning John Mark, is recorded not for our criticism of either, but that we may receive admonition concerning our service with others, lest work in which we are jointly engaged should be marred by the energy of the flesh. The adversary, after being unsuccessful in his efforts in various ways, often accomplishes his ends by bringing in contention and severance of heart from heart, and life from life, in the very cases of those who have been yoked together by the guidance and power of the Spirit of God.

But though such cases should humble us and exercise us deeply, the Devil is never victorious in the end. God overrules all for the carrying out of His plans. He has another yokefellow ready. Silas becomes the associate of Paul, and they, again, are "commended by the brethren to the grace of the Lord" (15:40). Here the action of the Holy Spirit is not mentioned, though His guidance and power were at work. "Paul chose Silas," a man whose life and service had been proved. He had been one of the chief men among the brethren in Jerusalem (15:22), "and a prophet" (v. 32). Shortly after, we learn of Paul's choice of Timothy as another companion in service. He had been well taught and trained in the Scriptures from his earliest days, had gained the esteem and commendation of brethren in his district (Acts 16:2), and the gift which had been divinely imparted to him had been formally recognized by the elders (1 Tim. 4:14). The apostle therefore was not associating with himself one who was a novice, though Timothy was still a young man. Here, then, was an instructive example of the association of youth with maturity, and the references in the Acts and epistles to the joint service show how harmoniously it was rendered. The younger did not act in a spirit of independence of the elder. Paul could speak of Timothy, after a year or two of companionship in gospel labors, as "my beloved and faithful child in the Lord" (1 Cor. 4:17, R.V.), and after twelve years of such service he could say, "Ye know the proof of him, that, as a child serveth a father, so he served with me in furtherance of the gospel" (Phil. 2:22). It is no wonder that, serving the Lord in such a spirit of humility and harmony with his senior fellow worker, he truly cared at the same time for the state of the saints (v. 20). But while the younger wrought in happy subjection to the elder, the latter did not lord it over the younger. We read on one occasion of Paul's beseeching Timothy to remain at Ephesus instead of accompanying him into Macedonia, whereas he might have used his apostolic authority to charge him to remain (1 Tim. 1:3).*

As a result of this unity of heart the apostle, when he is writing to the church at Thessalonica, is able to associate his younger fellow workers with him in regard to all he has to say of their coming among them, their work on their behalf, and their conduct while in their midst. How striking is the testimony of the epistles to the Thessalonians as to the oneness of both motive and action on the part of

*The A.V. "besought" is perhaps right here; the word is so rendered in the R.V. of 1 Corinthians 16:12, in the similar case of Apollos, as well as frequency elsewhere.

the missionaries who had brought them the gospel (see especially 1 Thess. 1:5, 6; 2:1–12; 3:1–10; 2 Thess. 3:7–9)! This association of his fellow workers with himself was not a matter of style of writing or of mere courtesy, it was the outcome of the grace of God, devotion to Christ and subjection to the Spirit, working in each heart and binding these fellow servants together in mutual love and appreciation.

Noble work has been done by many a lonely pioneer laboring without human companionship. But when two are brought together in service there are the joys of friendship and intercourse, of counsel and support, and all that is involved in a community of purpose and work in serving the same Lord. "Two are better than one," said the preacher, "because they have a good reward for their labor. For if they fall, the one will lift up his fellow" (Eccl. 4:9, 10). There are, however, dangers in this connection, consequent upon difference of temperament and of judgment. "Can two walk together except they be agreed?" In order that agreement may be maintained, any evidence of divergence of opinion or difference of disposition calls for constant and united waiting upon the Lord, for mutual patience and forbearance, for the exercise of that love which "suffereth long, and is kind . . . envieth not . . . vaunteth not itself, is not puffed up, doth not behave itself unseemly, seeketh not its own, is not provoked, taketh not account of evil . . . beareth all things, believeth all things, hopeth all things, endureth all things" (1 Cor. 13:4–7). When these graces are in us and abound, we shall have joy in one another, joy in service and its results, joy in present trial, and, above all, joy in Him whom we unitedly call Master and Lord.

▪ CHAPTER TEN ▪

Commendation for Service

The records in the New Testament of the relationship between churches and the servants of God who went forth from them in gospel service, indicate sufficiently the mind of the Lord in these matters. He might have sent His servants apart from church relationship, but this was not His will. While the first missionaries went forth in simple dependence upon Him for guidance and support, that is to say, without being under the control or direction of a human society, yet there remained a definite connection between them and the churches with which they had been associated.

Of Barnabas and Saul we are told that the church at Antioch "committed them to the grace of God for the work" (Acts 14:26). The circumstances under which this took place are narrated in the thirteenth chapter. The prospective missionaries had for some time been ministering to the Lord in the church, when the call of the Holy Spirit came, "Separate me Barnabas and Saul for the work whereunto I have called them." In response to this, after a time of fasting and prayer, the elders, representing the church, "laid hands on them, and sent them away" (or rather, "let them go").

This gives evidence both of deep exercise of heart before God and of the great importance which the local church attached to the going forth of the missionaries from their midst. The question might have been raised whether there was a need to fast as well as pray concerning the matter, when the will of God and the guidance of the Spirit were so clear. Was there anything more required than merely to obey the command, to separate those who had received the call, to hold a farewell meeting and speed them on their way? Certainly more was felt to be necessary for the fulfillment of the will of the Lord. That there was fasting demands our careful consideration. The fasting was not a perfunctory rite, nor an act of formal asceticism; it was a spontaneous expression of self-humiliation before God, under a sense of the great responsibility attaching to the ministry to which He was calling His servants. The exercise of heart concerning it found a fitting accompaniment in either partial or complete abstinence from food for a time. The church took no superficial view of the sending forth of missionaries. The fact of a call from God forbade that; it laid a weight of responsibility upon the hearts of His people which demanded more even than prayer.

The call of God summoning fresh laborers to the field still makes itself evident in the assemblies of His people. Have they become accustomed to take a lower view of it than did the assembly at Antioch? Is missionary service regarded today with a less serious sense of responsibility than in the earliest times? Is the call less divine, or the work of less importance, because of the absence of the apostolic element? Is there less claim upon us for prayer and fasting now than there was in the times of the apostles? Surely the contrary is the case. Do not these questions deserve the serious attention of all who genuinely have the cause of Christ at heart?

We must not omit to notice the significance of the laying on of hands as recorded in the passage. This was not a matter of ordination to the ministry. Barnabas and Saul had already received their divine ordination. They had for some time been prophets and teachers in the church from which they were now setting out. The act of the laying on of hands bears directly upon the subject under consideration upon the relationship between the church and those who were proceeding from it with the gospel to the regions beyond. The church, in recognition of the call and appointment by the Holy Spirit, thus gave through its elders a public expression of its identification with the missionaries in the service that lay before them.

The association of the laborers with the church in Antioch did not cease with their departure. This is clear from the fact that, upon the fulfillment of their service, they returned thither, "gathered the church together, and rehearsed all that God had done with them" (14:27). By the same assembly Paul and Silas were commended at the outset of the second missionary journey, and thither again they returned at its close. The interval between the second and third journey was spent in the same church, and from it Paul set out for the third time. Thus throughout the greater part of his missionary activities there existed a close relationship between the servant of God and the church from which he went.

The Lord has called all His saints to take a definite part in helping forward the gospel. His command, "Go ye . . . and make disciples of all the nations, baptizing them in the name of the Father and of the Son and of the Holy Ghost, teaching them to observe all things whatsoever I have commanded you" (Matt. 28:19, R.V.), was not limited to those to whom He was immediately speaking; for He said, "And lo, I am with you alway, even unto the end of the age." Obviously His word holds good for all His followers until the age reaches its close. The commission could not imply that all were to go in person to other lands; it does, however, indicate that all have a part to fulfill in the great work. An assembly in which God calls an individual to go forth in missionary work, and gives to the saints an evidence of the call, may well rejoice in the privilege afforded of taking part in this way in the furtherance of the gospel in addition to the regular testimony in the immediate vicinity. Other assemblies in the same locality, who have had experience of the life and service of the worker now called to go forth, likewise have the claim upon them of this fellowship. Thus it was that Timothy was commended. He was "well reported of," not only by the brethren in his own assembly in Lystra, but also by those at Iconium in the same district.

The privilege of an assembly in being instrumental in sending the gospel by a representative to a remote country is no small one. At the same time, the responsibility involved in commending a worker is very great. When a laborer goes forth in simple dependence upon God for his maintenance, the assembly which commends him thereby associates itself with his conviction that God is so leading him. A commendation therefore carries with it the responsibility, first of assistance in any necessary preparations, and then of the continuance of fellowship, as God may enable, throughout the period of the service in which the worker is occupied. For the missionary, though at his work in another land, is still identified with the assembly from which he went forth. The work carried out is not merely that of the laborer abroad, it is work in which the assembly is collectively engaged. The missionary is not the servant of the assembly; all are fellow servants of God. Was there not partnership between him and his fellow saints in service before the call came for the laborer to go? Had he not been ministering to the Lord in the assembly? The change of his sphere has not broken the bond of church fellowship in service. On the contrary, the sphere of the assembly has only been enlarged. Let not distance and time diminish the apprehension of the association. The fellowship should be abiding not only in fact but in realization.

The commendation of an assembly should mean more than that an interest will be taken in the work of the one commended. Taking an interest in the work is a poor way of regarding it. The true view is that of fellowship and cooperation. The work may be on the other side of the world; it is nevertheless work undertaken by the assembly with which the laborer is identified. A recognition of this will prevent the elder brethren of an assembly from laying hands hastily on a candidate. Commendation cannot rightly be given unless there is an absolute conviction on the part of elders, as well as of the prospective worker, that the Lord has called the latter to go; and the conviction should be based not only upon a verbal statement as to the call but also on the proof of the candidate's fitness, consequent upon the character of the work in which he or she has already been engaged. But behind this there is the necessary qualification of "a good report" both in the home life and in such avocation as the candidate may have been following. If incapacity has been displayed in the latter, how can it be expected that anything different will be shown in the spiritual work of the gospel? What will not do for the ordinary business of this world's affairs, cannot surely be suitable for the work of the mission field. Timothy had a good report. This meant more than a good testimony as to his capacities in gospel service. There was the character of his life behind his oral testimony. Then again, one who is going forth, with the prospect of serving with fellow laborers who have been in the country before him, should be expected to have given evidence of his ability to work harmoniously with others, and of a readiness to act in a spirit of subjection to senior workers, and to listen to their counsel. These are some of the considerations which will weigh with elder brethren, who, acting on behalf of an assembly, have before them the question of the commendation of a worker. Where such a one has been both proved and approved, how happily can the saints commend their fellow laborer to the Lord for His guidance and blessing, conscious of the smile of His approval and assured of the manifestation of His power in the life and work of His servant in the regions beyond!

▪ CHAPTER ELEVEN ▪

Hindrances in Service

The Lord's work makes progress not only in spite of difficulties but frequently by means of them. Service to God is rendered in a world where the enemy has power and uses it in untiring and varied aggression against all that is done for God. This ceaseless opposition, directed against the glory of Christ, has beneficial effects. It reminds His servants of their inability to do anything in their own strength and of their dependence on the Lord, and casts them upon Him for His everready help. It thereby proves the means of strengthening them to continue their arduous labor with joy of heart, and to face and go through every difficulty, strong in the Lord and the power of His might, and undeterred by any obstacle however formidable.

The way in which God turns to good account the adversary's opposition to His servants is frequently illustrated in the Scriptures. One of the most striking cases is the result of the hindrance placed by Satan against the return of the apostle Paul to the church at Thessalonica. He would fain have come to them, he says, once and again, but Satan hindered (1 Thess. 2:18). Whatever the actual hindrance was—not improbably it lay in the fact that pledges against the renewal of trouble had been extracted by the city authorities from Jason and the other converts (Acts 17:9)—nevertheless resulted in the apostle's writing to them instead. Accordingly the effect of the Devil's opposition is that we are in possession of the priceless treasures of the two epistles to the Thessalonians. In a similar manner we might trace the circumstances which produced the later epistles written during Paul's confinement in Rome. Again, in recording the events connected with the penning of one of these very epistles, he says that the things which had happened to him there had proved to be for the progress of the gospel; for his bonds had become manifest in Christ "throughout the whole Praetorian Guard, and to all the rest." This suggests that the soldiers of this famous regiment, as well as others, had heard the gospel from his lips. A further result of his difficulties he speaks of as follows: "Most of the brethren in the Lord, being confident through my bonds, are more abundantly bold to speak the Word of God without fear" (Phil. 1:12–14, R.V.).

Here, then, was a missionary, hampered in his work, restricted in his activity, and circumscribed in the sphere of his service, the object of Satan's ceaseless and varied hostility. To all appearances the efforts of the enemy had resulted in a serious setback to the spread of the gospel. One is inclined perhaps to conceive that greater advances might have been made, had this servant of God been at liberty to continue his journeys, founding new churches, visiting those already established, and otherwise furthering the cause of Christ. Not so in the thoughts and purposes of the Lord. God is not thwarted by the work of His foes. "None can stay His hand." How little we are able to calculate the far-reaching effects of the apostle's testimony in Rome, or the full extent of the meaning of his inspired statement, "The things which have happened unto me have fallen out rather unto the progress of the gospel"! And after all, was he not following in the steps of his Master whose faithful and devoted servant he was, and whose own claims and authority had seemed to the world absolutely invalidated by the overwhelming degradation and shameful humiliation of the Cross? The death of Christ was but a seeming defeat. The enemy who sought to accomplish it met his doom in his apparent success. The secret of the glorious victory over that effort of the evil one was made known in Eden, at his first attempt to thwart the divine will. The bruising of the heel of the seed of the woman, would mean the bruising of the head of the foe himself. The death of the Son of God was the destruction of His adversary.

We similarly see God's wonder-working way in the matter of physical weakness. How many a worker who is tried in health feels that much more effective service could be rendered if only he were free from the malady! Here again the lesson of Paul's life has been recorded for our comfort. Doubtless he felt that his loved ministry was much impeded by his "thorn in the flesh." He besought the Lord thrice that it might depart from him. Though his request was not granted, the Lord saw to it, not only that he should be comforted, but that all that was needed by way of explanation should be made known to him. There was both the preventive side of the trouble and the empowering side. Not only did he learn that it was inflicted lest he should be exalted overmuch through the greatness of the revelations he had received, but he also learned gladly to glory in his weaknesses, that the power of Christ might rest upon him. Let us note, too, the abiding effect which the gracious word of the Lord had upon him. He records it not as a mere historical incident, but as something the comfort of which he had felt ever since, and was still enjoying. "He *hath said* [not "He said"] unto me, My grace is sufficient for thee; for My strength is made perfect in weakness" (2 Cor. 12:9). The consequence was that he could say, "When I am weak, then am I strong." That was the outcome of Satan's buffeting. The hindrance became a help. Satan's messenger became the Lord's minister. Many and many a servant of God has been similarly tried. How blessed the comfort of this record of Paul's experience! And how wonderful will be the revelation, in the coming day, of God's dealings with us in our service here below!

We learn from the apostle of other ways in which his service was hampered. His heart must have been sorely tried by the constant activity of those who traduced him, imputing things to him of which he was not guilty, and seeking to undo his work by misrepresentation and insinuation. This he particularly mentions in the second epistle to the Corinthians. The gospel had proved fruitful in Corinth, both among Jew and Gentile. During the initial difficulties the Lord had revealed to him that He had "much people in that city." We are therefore not surprised to find that the opposition of the adversary was vigorous and varied. The character of his ministry was disparaged by influential opponents. He was accused of changing his opinion and of fickleness (2 Cor. 1:17, 18); of walking according to the flesh (10:2); of inferior capacities in his ministry (10:10); of acting toward the saints by guile and taking advantage of them for his own ends (12:16, 17). Unfavorable comparisons were made between him and other apostles (11:5, 6), and the service he had rendered in such disinterestedness and genuine love was in other ways defamed. All this must have been exceedingly burdensome. Moreover these matters required firm handling, not in the spirit of mere self-defense, but for the sake of the Lord's work and the profit of the church. We can understand something of the stress under which this epistle was written.

There can be scarcely anything more trying for the servant of the Lord than misrepresentation of his motives and methods, and especially when he might have expected that those who act thus would seek an opportunity of an interview with him, and of becoming acquainted with facts. Sometimes it pleases God thus to test faith. Yet even these obstacles are under His control and become His instruments for the carrying out of His purposes. Difficulties are intended to draw us nearer to the Lord. Thus, learning that all our resources lie in Him, we derive from Him the power to enable us, if our private interests are at stake, to manifest the spirit of Christ toward our detractors. If, on the other hand, the honor of His name and the blessing of His people require that the matter be taken up in any way, the Lord is ready to impart the wisdom and strength to do so, and from Him alone can we derive it. In each respect the apostle, who so closely followed the Lord, has set us an example.

Hindrances in service come from within as well as from without. Against these we ever need to be on the watch. There is always a tendency for our service to become merely mechanical, in other words, void of that spiritual power which must ever be present if we are to be used of God. Only the help of the Holy Spirit is sufficient for the maintenance of that power. It is His gracious ministry to lead us constantly into communion with God, that is to say, into the realization of fellowship with the Father and with the Son, and this He does through the Word of God. Times of communion, alone with the Lord, undistracted by earthly circumstances, are essential for spiritual vitality in service. We must be first occupied with Christ if we are to be occupied for Him. Indeed, the presentation of our bodies "a living sacrifice, holy, acceptable unto Him" is described as our reasonable (or intelligent) service (Rom. 12:1). The word in this passage denotes that form of service which is itself an act of worship.

Then, again, the influence of the world without is apt to find a ready entrance into our inner life. Contact with the world, inevitable in our work for the Lord, tends to deaden our sensitiveness to sin. For the isolated missionary, surrounded continually by the grossness of heathenism, the conditions are acknowledged to be unspeakably testing in this respect; but nowhere can we afford to be negligent in watching against the gradual encroachment of the power of the world upon our spiritual life, and the consequent diminution of spiritual vigor.

How perfect is the provision made for us, by which the hindrances arising from the flesh within may be counteracted and removed! The unremitting ministry of our Great High Priest, the efficacy of His precious blood, the work of the Holy Spirit in our hearts, and the rectifying and guiding power of the Word of God, these are our unfailing resources.

CHAPTER TWELVE

Rewards of Service

To the devoted servant of Christ the service He appoints carries its own reward. The love that has liberated him from the bondage of sin has captivated his soul. For one who appreciates, even in a small measure, what his Redeemer has done for him, it suffices that he should be the bondservant of Jesus Christ. Grace it is that provides us with service to render. "I was made a minister [or servant]," the apostle says, "according to the grace of God which was given me" (Eph. 3:7). The unutterable love of Christ is enough to preclude our looking upon any reward of our service as the motive of that service. Still less as the outcome of merit on the servant's part. He Himself taught His disciples to say, after they had fulfilled their service, "We are unprofitable servants; we have done that which was our duty to do."

There is, however, another side to this, and the Lord constantly directed the hearts of His followers for their encouragement to the reward which would eventually be theirs. Thus, concerning deeds of kindness He said, "He that receiveth a prophet in the name of a prophet shall receive a prophet's reward; and he that receiveth a righteous man in the name of a righteous man shall receive a righteous man's reward, and whosoever shall give to drink unto one of these little ones a cup of cold water only, in the name of a disciple, verily I say unto you, he shall in no wise lose his reward" (Matt. 10:41, 42, R.V.).

Concerning rejection and reproach for His sake, He said, "Blessed are ye when men shall hate you, and when they shall separate you from their company, and shall reproach you, and cast out your name as evil, for the Son of man's sake. Rejoice ye in that day and leap for joy: for behold your reward is great in heaven" (Luke 6:22, 23).

Again, concerning self-sacrifice for His sake, "There is no man that hath left house, or parents, or brethren, or wife, or children, for the kingdom of God's sake, who shall not receive manifold more in this present time, and in the world to come life everlasting" (Luke 18:29, 30).

Faithful stewardship would result in the reward of authority hereafter (Luke 12:44), and similarly the Lord's explanation of the parable of the nobleman and his servants who were left to trade with his money, was "Unto every one that hath, to him shall be given; but from him that hath not, even that which he hath shall be taken away from him" (Luke 19:26).*

So elsewhere in the Word of God, the Holy Spirit constantly directs us to have regard to the reward, and warns us of the possibility of losing it. Moses is brought before us as a pattern for our faith in this respect. The reason assigned to his decision to be "evil entreated with the people of God," instead of enjoying pleasures of sin for a season, was that, "accounting the reproach of Christ greater riches than the treasures of Egypt, he had respect unto the recompense of the reward." Reproach for Christ was his present riches. The reward would come after. That is ever to be the order. Christ Himself, first; the reward He gives, second. Loyalty to Christ will never fail of present blessing and future recompense. Never did a saint suffer spiritually by accumulated wealth accruing from endurance of reproaches for Christ.

The manner in which the apostle Paul had respect unto the recompense of reward is strikingly brought out in his first epistle to the Corinthians. Speaking of his service in the gospel, he tells of his efforts to gain both Jew and Gentile; he says, "I am become all things to all men, that I may by all means save some.

*With these teachings of the Lord as to rewards we cannot but associate His promises to the overcomers in the seven letters to the churches (Rev. 2 and 3).

And I do all things for the gospel's sake, that I may be a joint partaker thereof" (1 Cor. 9:22, 23, R.V.). How thoroughly the messenger was identified with his message! The blessing wrought by the gospel was his own blessing. There could be no half-heartedness about work carried on like that. He then applies to his service the metaphors of the racecourse and the boxing match, "I therefore so run," he says, "as not uncertainly; so fight I [the Greek word means "box"; see R.V., margin] as not beating the air: but I buffet my body and bring it into bondage: lest by any means after that I have preached to others, I myself should be rejected."* There was no false step in the running, no random blow in the buffeting. We miss his meaning if we take him to indicate the actual beating of the body in outwardly imposed, ascetic discipline. On the contrary, he kept his natural inclinations and propensities in severe check, in order that his members might be in entire subjection to the will of God for His service. He mortified the deeds of the body. But while he does this for the Lord's sake, as His servant, his eye is on the Judgment Seat. It is possible to be eternally saved by grace as a believer and yet to be disapproved at the time of reward-giving there. In the Olympian games in Greece, a competitor who had infringed the regulations was pronounced *adokimos* at the *bēma*. But the matter did not end there. He was required to place at his own expense a bronze image of Jupiter at the entrance of the arena, as the lasting memorial of his disqualification. The intense solemnity of the possibility of disqualification at the Judgment Seat of Christ, led the apostle to undergo the rigid discipline mentioned above. Stretching forward to the things that are before, he pressed on "toward the goal unto the prize of the high calling of God in Christ Jesus."

There is a solemn passage in the same epistle regarding reward, and loss of reward, in connection with gospel work and subsequent service in building up assemblies. First, there is the metaphor drawn from agriculture. One laborer plants and another waters. Both are one, as God's fellow workers. Their rewards are to differ according to the labor of each. Then there is the metaphor of the builder. "If any man buildeth on the foundation gold, silver, precious stones, wood, hay, stubble, each man's work shall be made manifest: for the day shall declare it because it is revealed in fire; and the fire itself shall prove each man's work of what sort it is" (1 Cor. 3:8–13). It is possible to engage in service in connection with the gospel according to methods which may appear attractive and successful, but which are not in conformity to the will of God. The Lord gauges our service, not by its success, but by our faithfulness to Him. Apparent success may after all be the outcome of building wood, hay and stubble on the foundation. "If any man's work shall abide which he hath built thereon, he shall receive a reward. If any man's work shall be burned he shall suffer loss: but he himself shall be saved, but so as by fire." The fire will consume, not purify. Not the man himself is to be burned but his work, work which, figuratively, consists of wood, hay or stubble, work that has been done in the energy of the natural will, rather than by faithful adherence to the instruction of God's Word under the guidance of the Spirit. How important it is to do all things "according to the pattern that has been shown us"! The theme is continued in the next chapter, where Paul speaks of himself and his fellow workers as "servants of Christ." In this respect we are not to judge one another before the time. When the Lord comes he "will both bring to light the hidden things of darkness, and make manifest the counsels of the hearts; and then shall each man have his praise from God" (4:1–5). We must not act toward our fellow servants as if we were on the Judgment Seat. The Judge Himself, by whom actions are weighed, will in that day bestow upon each one the praise that is due.

How faithfully the apostle wrought in building up the saints! How true to the pattern was his work! Consequently he is able to say with confidence to the Thessalonian saints, "For what is our hope, or joy, or crown of glorying?

*The rendering "castaway" in the Authorized Version of 1 Corinthians 9:27 is misleading. The word *adokimos* means "disapproved through failure to stand the test." It is the negative of *dakimos*, "approved," as, for instance, in James 1:12, "Blessed is the man that endureth temptation: for when he hath been approved, he shall receive the crown of life, which the Lord promised to them that love Him."

Are not even ye before our Lord Jesus at His coming?"—lit., "in His Parousia" (1 Thess. 2:19). Similarly the saints at Philippi are his "joy and crown" (Phil. 4:1). Here are rewards open to all, rewards for winning and caring for souls. Then, a special reward is to be given for faithfulness in pastoral work. The under-shepherds who have themselves been examples to the flock the while they have shepherded them, will receive from the Chief Shepherd a crown of glory at His appearing (1 Pet. 5:3, 4).

Let all our service be characterized by two things especially. Firstly, let it be rendered "heartily as to the Lord." For "of the Lord we are to receive the reward of the inheritance." Secondly, let our heart's affections be set upon His return. The crown of righteousness is to be given to all them that have loved His appearing. Loving His appearing is something very practical. With the apostle it meant fighting the good fight, finishing the course, and keeping the faith (2 Tim. 4:7, 8). To the day of reward the Lord Himself looks forward, and almost His last word to His servants is, "Behold I come quickly; and My reward is with Me [suggesting His pleasure in bestowing it], to give every man according as his work shall be."

The Second Coming and the Last Days

V

Touching the Coming of the Lord

with

C. F. Hogg

▪ INTRODUCTION ▪

Little is necessary by way of introduction to the pages that follow. The writers proceed on the assumption, which seems to them well-founded, and as fully confirmed by the record of fulfilled prophecy, that the "apocalyptic," or "eschatological," or, in more popular, if less exact, language, the "prophetic," element in Scripture is as authentic as the rest of the revelation of the mind of God. It is not unreasonable to suppose that if God has spoken concerning the past and the present He should speak concerning the future also.

It has been contended, in opposition to the main proposition of this book, that God moves slowly to His appointed ends, and that His Kingdom comes not with observation. This is true. Nevertheless God is not to be denied the right to vary His methods at different stages of His work. One day is with the Lord as a thousand years, indeed; but also a thousand years is as one day. He speaks in the still small voice—and also in the thunder. The grass grows noiselessly; the pestilence-laden air is scattered by the fury of the tempest. God is long-suffering now, as He was when men were equally heedless in the days of Noah. And in the days of Noah the Flood came. Is it so certain that God will never stretch out His arm again, to act directly in the affairs of men?

If it is conceivable that God should send His Son into the world once, it is not incredible that He should do so again. If it was consistent with the character of God to display His moral glory in the walk and conversation of His Son in lowly guise upon earth, it cannot be unworthy of Him to display the complement of that glory in the majesty of heaven.

The dogmatic spirit is peculiarly inappropriate to the exposition of the "word of prophecy." We may not adopt the same tone when we speak of the future as when we speak of the past. Prophecy is something more than history written in advance. It is a means the Lord has chosen whereby we may be brought into closer fellowship with Him in His purposes. The writers hope they have written nothing inconsistent with this end of the Lord. They will be profoundly grateful if it please Him to use their testimony, and this attempt to open the Scriptures, to the growth of their readers in the true grace of God. The purpose of prophecy is as practical as that of any other part of the Bible. It is hoped that this is made plain throughout the book, and not merely in chapter nine.

The writers would in all sincerity remind their readers of the exhortation of the apostle to a church as yet in its infancy, "Prove all things; hold fast that which is good," words which they would venture to paraphrase, "Test all teachings; hold fast to that which accords with what is written" (1 Thess. 5:21).

References are to the Revised Version throughout. January, 1919.

▪ CHAPTER ONE ▪

The Expectancy of Christ

"God loves to be longed for, He longs to be sought,
For He sought us Himself with such longing and love:
He died for desire of us, marvelous thought!
And He yearns for us now to be with Him above."

When men permit themselves to contemplate the future, when they project their thoughts beyond the grave, the natural tendency of the mind is to become overcast by fear. Fear draws its strength from the unknown, and is accentuated by the consciousness of failure and the sense of accountability. Fear demoralizes men, robs them of courage and of hope, and drives them to new depths of evil. Fear, anticipating the adverse verdict of the Day of Judgment, causes suffering even here and now; "fear hath punishment." There is but one way of dealing with fear, this natural tenant of the human mind; fear must be cast out. But how? Love alone is equal to the task. "There is no fear in love; but perfect love casteth out fear." "Perfect love," that is the love manifested in the death of the Lord Jesus Christ. It is only in the knowledge of the purpose of His death that the believer is able to think without fear of the Day of Judgment, for "as He is, even so are we in this world" (1 John 4:17, 18).

The tenses must be closely followed here. The apostle does not say as He is so we shall be, nor that as He was so we are, but quite plainly, and by the addition of the unmistakable phrase "in this world," as He is now at the right hand of the Majesty on High, so are we here and at this present time. What, then, is His place or condition there to which our present state here corresponds? Surely this, that He, after He had borne our sins in His body on the tree, experiencing there that separation from God which is the consequence of sin, was raised from among the dead and exalted to the throne of God. He is thus on the other side of the Judgment, so to speak; having suffered in the flesh for sin He has now passed out of any relation with sin, i.e., He is no longer a sin-bearer (1 Pet. 4:1).

And as He is, so are all they that have put their trust in Him. The Christian is not a man who contemplates the Day of Judgment with mingled feelings, hoping that it will see him exculpated on the ground of the death of Christ, and yet fearing lest it should not. Rather he is one who shall not come into the Judgment of that Day at all ("shall never stand in the dock," John 5:24), since he knows himself to be already justified by Christ and accepted in Christ, seated with and in Him in the heavenlies (Eph. 2:6). This the perfect love of God has accomplished for him, and the assurance of this has set him free from fear.

The Promise to the Son

John's statement is a particular instance of a general principle; the principle itself is capable of wide application. Thus if it is asked why the Scriptures insist so much on the waiting attitude of the believer, that he is ever to be on his watch for the coming of the Lord, the answer assuredly is that that is the attitude of the Lord Himself toward the future, and that as He is in this respect, so also are we. Or, to express the same thing in another way, God has called us "into the fellowship of His Son Jesus Christ our Lord" (1 Cor. 1:9). But fellowship at the least means this, that those in fellowship with one another share each other's hopes, they have a common outlook, their hearts are set on the same ends. If it is true, as John declares, that "our fellowship is with the Father and with His Son Jesus Christ," then this fellowship must extend to the purpose of the Father for the Son and to the expectation of the Son Himself (1 John 1:3). It is not conceivable that the hope of the believer could be of any potency, that it could have any actuality, that it could even exist, were it not primarily the hope of the Lord Himself.

Now this plain deduction from the known facts is fully confirmed by the testimony of Scripture. The Father's purpose for the Son is declared in such words as those of Psalm 110:1, 2:

> "The Lord saith unto my Lord,
> Sit Thou at My right hand,
> Until I make Thine enemies thy footstool.
> The Lord shall send forth the rod of Thy
> strength out of Zion:
> Rule Thou in the midst of thine
> enemies."

In the second Psalm the Father addresses the Son:

> "Ask of Me and I will give Thee the
> nations for Thine inheritance,
> And the uttermost parts of the earth for
> Thy possession."

In complete correspondence with these words the writer of the epistle to the Hebrews says concerning Christ, that "He, when He had offered one sacrifice for sins forever, sat down on the right hand of God; from henceforth expecting till His enemies be made the footstool of His feet" (Heb. 10:12, 13). (H-J, p. 179).

To have the mind set upon that consummation, to refuse the world's plans for permanent government in favor of God's plan for the universal and eternal Kingdom of Christ, is to be to that extent in fellowship "with the Father and with His Son Jesus Christ." To ignore the declared purpose of God is to put oneself outside that fellowship, insofar as this purpose is concerned, and, as an inevitable consequence, to fail to appreciate the ways of God with men alike in the past, the present, and the future.

The Constituents of Hope

The attitude of Christ toward the future is here described as one of expectancy, and the objective before His mind is His triumph over everything that opposes the will of God by the establishment of the Kingdom of God upon the earth. And he who among men is in fellowship with Christ will have his heart set upon that consummation also.

Toward the end of his letter, written to the believers at Thessalonica to correct some misconceptions concerning his teaching about the coming of the Lord, the apostle prayed for them, "The Lord direct your hearts into the love of God, and into the patience of Christ" (2 Thess. 3:5). That is, that lifted above the level of merely natural love, the love of affinity of aim and taste, they should learn to love each other, and all men, after the pattern and measure of the love of God. Similarly, that they might learn to be patient in their hope, even as Christ is patient until the fullness of the time for His return comes in. That it is the patience of the risen Lord in His present session in the heavens of which the apostle is thinking seems clear. For one reason, because the language suggests a present condition of mind rather than a past experience, and for another because the title "Christ" is appropriate to Him in His exaltation to the throne of God, whereas the name "Jesus" brings to mind the years preceding the Cross, as in Hebrews 12:2, "Looking unto Jesus . . . Who . . . endured." "This Jesus" has, in His resurrection, been made "Christ" (Acts 2:36).

The Word of My Patience

The apostle John speaks of the share that he and those to whom he wrote had "in the tribulation and kingdom and patience which are in Jesus" (Rev. 1:9). This arresting sentence suggests how deeply "the disciple whom Jesus loved" had been impressed by the patience of his Master in the days when his own slowness to believe, and that of his companions, and their consequent slowness to understand, made constant and heavy demand upon it. But the Lord's patience was not a virtue that had served its end and passed with the occasions that life among fallen men provided. It is in exercise still as He beholds the afflictions of His people in the world, and the reign of iniquity that can be brought to an end only when His Kingdom is established in the earth.

His sympathy with His own, whose sorrows touch Him with a poignancy beyond our experience, and His compassion for the masses of men, "distressed and scattered as sheep not having a shepherd" (Matt. 9:36), are still what they ever were, burdens upon His heart. And if He charges us to "let patience have its perfect work" that is because patience is working perfectly in Him. If we are to await the hour of our deliverance that is because He, too, is awaiting "the fullness of the time" that will bring Him from heaven again to be our Savior and the Deliverer of the whole Creation (Phil. 3:20; Rom. 8:21).

The Lord is quick to mark the response of the soul to His message. "Because thou didst keep the word of My patience, I also will keep thee from the hour of trial, that hour which is to come upon the whole inhabited earth, to try them that dwell upon the earth" (Rev. 3:10). "My patience," says the Lord, for His is the source of ours, and ours can only be because it is His first, and we share it by the ministry of the Spirit. "For of His fullness we all received, and grace for grace."* The grace of our patience is evoked by, and answers to, the grace of His.

> "On the earth the broken arcs;
> In the Heaven, a perfect round."

The two words translated "wait" in 1 Thessalonians 1:10 and Hebrews 9:28 are carefully chosen to meet the spiritual condition of the readers in each case. In the first passage the word used suggests the thought of abiding quietly, for the Thessalonians needed sobering and to be reminded that so they had been taught from the outset.† The ebbing faith, the waning hope of the Hebrews, on the other hand, are stimulated by the word which suggests the tiptoe, the outstretched neck, of intent expectancy.‡ The ideas are combined at Romans 8:25, "if we hope . . . then do we with patience [expectantly] wait."§

The Safeguards of Hope

Patient expectancy is thus the characteristic element in the Christian hope. The suggestion of uncertainty, inseparable from the word in its ordinary use of human affairs, is eliminated from it in those New Testament passages which speak of the coming of the Lord. In this hope there is no faintest trace of the possibility of an unforeseen contingency, or of an insuperable obstacle, or of a changed plan, such as disturb the calculations of the most farsighted among men. We may say, indeed, that the Lord Himself shares this hope, or rather that His purpose is our hope; and as the first is guaranteed by His power to bring the universe into subjection to Himself, so the second "putteth not to shame" those who cherish it in fellowship with Him (Phil. 3:20; Rom. 5:5).

Hope is liable to abuse; with eagerness there is a tendency to relaxation of discipline and to neglect of duty, as at Thessalonica, for this condition is reflected in both the epistles to the church there, and particularly in the second. Or patience may degenerate into lethargy and indifference, as seems to have been the case with those to whom the apostle Peter addressed his second epistle. The Christian hope is the happy mien; it is an expectant patience, a patient expectancy. The Christian lifts up his head to look for his approaching salvation. He looks toward heaven "as with outstretched neck" for his Lord's return. But not less does he "trade" diligently with that Lord's "pound" until He be pleased to return (Luke 19:13; 21:28). This is the paradox of the Christian life; working he waits, and waiting he works.

"In the night in which He was betrayed" the Lord Jesus spoke, for the first time so far as the records show, of His purpose to return in person for "His own that are in the world." Of their resurrection in response to His voice they had already heard from Him, and of His

*So far as the utterances of the Lord Jesus are recorded He did not Himself use the word "hope" save in Luke 6:34, "If ye lend to them of whom ye hope to receive," and John 5:45, "Moses, on whom ye have set your hope." Neither of these passages is concerned with the Christian hope. Nor do any of the New Testament writers speak of the Lord's "hope," what He expects to happen, but of His purpose, what He "shall" or "will" do.

†*anti* = "answering to," John 1:16.

‡*anamenō*.

§*apekdechomai*.

coming in the glories of heaven to put His enemies to confusion they had heard Him speak publicly again and again (John 6:39; Matt. 16:27; 24:30). But now, in the holy privacy of the Upper Room, and on the eve of His departure from them, with the cold shadow of the Cross already fallen into His heart, He addresses Himself to the comfort of men who must soon know the desolating sorrow of a bereavement the possibility of which had not heretofore entered their minds. But the separation from those who had "continued with Him in His trials," and whose sympathy in them was to Him unpriced, meant something to His own heart also.

The Secret of the Lord

For His sympathy with men is the complement of His desire for their sympathy with Him. God created man with social instincts; he was not made for solitude; companionship is the law of his life. Therefore in this as in all things "it behoved Him . . . to be made like unto His brethren," and for this reason, that, first of all, they were made like unto Him (Heb. 2:17; Gen. 1:26, 27). Hence it is that the desire of the redeemed to be with the Redeemer is the reflection, and the fruit, of His desire for their presence with Him.

Now this personal feeling seems audible in the words He spoke for their comfort, as though He found in them a comfort of His own. "I go to prepare a place for you," He said, "and if I go and prepare a place for you, I come again, and will receive you unto Myself; that where I am, there ye may be also" (John 14:2, 3). Never before had He used the first personal pronoun when He spoke of His return—in the wider circle of His public ministry and to His opponents he usually spoke of the coming of the Son of man. In this speech there is an arresting directness, the sense of intimacy and immediate personal concern. It is "the secret of the Lord," and it is for "them that fear Him." It was His secret, now it is theirs also, for He shares it with them, because He loves them "unto the uttermost." How shall the world that knows neither Him nor them know their secret? (1 John 3:1). And, again, how shall their joy in that secret exceed His own? If it is to make their hearts glad, that can only be because it has first gladdened His.

The language of the apostle Paul suggests the same desire of the Lord for the presence with Him of His redeemed. "Christ . . . loved the Church and gave Himself up for it . . . that He might present the Church to Himself a glorious Church, not having spot or wrinkle or any such thing; but that it should be holy and without blemish before Him." It is to this end, and because of His own interest in its completion and perfection, that He is said to "nourish and cherish it." At the appointed time He is to have the joy of receiving the Church to His Father's house, of causing it to stand with Himself, partaker of His holiness and meet companion in, and instrument of, His universal reign (Eph. 5:25–29). (F, p. 179).

The comfort and glory of the Church in that day is not the primary thought in the passage, however, but rather what that day will bring to Him in the accomplishment of a purpose which involved such costly sacrifice, and in the attainment of which His love sustained Him to the end of His toil.

The Lord's Memory

In the last of the series of five impressions of the glory and the sufferings of Christ—in this order—which occupy Isaiah 52:13–53:12, the prophet declares of the Messiah that "He shall see of the travail of His soul, and shall be satisfied" (v. 11). The perfection of the manhood of the Lord Jesus consists in the perfection of all the elements essential to manhood, and among these memory has its place as well as sympathy. Memory is the power of the mind to reproduce the past in its original form and color, to recall into the present the experiences of the past without loss of reality. With men memory fails; impressions can never be renewed to their full value; the heights of an old joy can never be attained again; into the depths of an old sorrow we can never again be plunged. Thus the defects of memory mean loss indeed, but not loss without compensation. Were our griefs to be continued, or could they be renewed in their first acuteness, the heart of man would fail, life become intolerable. Time by weakening memory assuages grief under the merciful hand of God.

But we may not conceive it to be so with the Lord. To Him the past can have lost nothing. No pang endured is forgotten. The price paid has not lost its value because it is so long since it was paid.

> ". . . Mine affliction and My outcast state, the wormwood and the gall, My soul hath them still in remembrance . . ." (Lam. 3:19, 20).

And on that day when He shall say "Behold, I and the children which God hath given Me," there will be no regret. Looking back over the past, realizing to the full all our redemption cost, He yet declares it to have been worthwhile!

Compensation

When certain Hebrew Christians showed signs of relaxing confidence under the attacks of their multiplying adversaries, attacks now fierce, now subtle, they were reminded of the hidden power that had sustained the heroes of their race under the sorest afflictions and that had impelled them to fine achievements. They had endured as seeing the unseen God; they had put their trust in Him that in His own time He would recompense them in the city for which He had taught them to look, and of which He is both architect and builder. And yet, brilliant examples of the power of faith though these were, even their greatest had failed, and failed in that very thing of which they, in the general tenor of their lives, and at so many critical junctures in their lives, were shining examples. Always men fail at their strong points; there is something at work that forbids perfection to the children of Adam. These witnesses to the faithfulness of God are to be remembered, indeed, but beyond all things else must the Christian run his race "looking unto Jesus, the author and perfecter of faith."* They were leaders of the faithful; He is leader-in-chief. They were illustrations of the way and power of faith; He is its consummator. He trusted God from His birth; He lived in the fear of God; He died with the words of faith upon His lips (Ps. 22:9; Is. 11:3; Luke 23:46). And throughout His sustaining thought is of "the joy that was set before Him"; because of that "He endured the Cross, despising shame" (Heb. 12:1, 2).

Thus the prophetic vision is reproduced historically; but the point of view is necessarily different. Here the price has still to be paid; the rough and thorny way is as yet untrodden; the agony of the Cross is still in the future; the cup awaits Him. And the joy that is to be the issue sustains Him "to the uttermost." Whereas in Isaiah's vision the journey is already accomplished; the goal has been reached; the shame and the agony are exhausted; the cup has been drained. The retrospect confirms the prospect: the joy realized does not fall short of the joy anticipated. The prize in possession is no less than it seemed in prospect. The compensation for the sorrow of the lonely death is the gladness of the fellowship in resurrection.

This joy, moreover, is not merely the joy of the Son; no less is it the joy of the Father also, and of the Holy Spirit. The joy of the shepherd over the found sheep, of the woman over the recovered coin, is boldly declared to be the reflection of the joy in heaven over a sinner restored to God. It is noteworthy that this joy in heaven is not said to be the joy of the angels, but "joy in the presence of the angels." The words seem to be chosen to suggest the joy of God. For just as the angels are in His presence so is He in the presence of the angels. And this joy over the repentant soul even here and now, becomes an "exceeding joy" in that day when the Son presents the hosts of the redeemed to His Father, saying, "Behold, I and the children which God hath given me" (Luke 15:7, 10, 22–24; Heb. 2:13).

At the Gate of Nain

An incident in the life of the Lord Jesus, recorded in Luke 7, provides a picture in which

*There is neither article nor pronoun in the original. The reference is not to "the faith once for all delivered to the saints," nor yet to any operation within the believer whereby faith is begotten and strengthened, but, as the context demands, to the life of realized dependence and uninterrupted faith of the Lord in the days of His flesh.

may be discerned the joys of that day. As He approached the gate of Nain there met Him a funeral procession, a widow's only son carried out to burial. Moved with compassion for the sorrowing woman He bade her dry her tears. But more than words is needed to stay the flood of grief. The astounded crowd heard Him address the figure upon the bier: "Young man, I say unto thee, Arise." The writ of the Prince of Life runs in the realm of the dead! The lad sat up and began to speak. But the Lord does not only snatch the prey from the mighty. He binds up broken hearts and wipes tears away from all faces. So "He delivered him to his mother," and made effective His command "Weep not." Her son is not only brought back from the gates of the tomb, he is restored to her as a gift from the Lord.

So, that eventide, was sorrow turned into joy. They who witnessed the scene rejoiced that God had visited His people. The lad was glad to see the light of the sun again and to be with his widowed mother. The mother was glad—how much more glad!—to receive her son alive from the dead. And surely gladdest of all was the Lord Himself thus to taste beforehand the victory of the Cross.

There are degrees of gladness, heart differs from heart in power to enjoy. It is experience of sorrow that gives capacity for joy. The spectators were not involved in the tragedy; however its unexpected issue may have touched them, it was not to them a vital thing. The lad, whatever sorrows he had known, was young, and grief does not strike its roots deeply in the heart of youth. Small, therefore, was his capacity for joy in comparison with those whose span had been longer upon the earth, but such as it was the Lord met and satisfied it. But the mother—the years had brought to her more of bitter than of sweet. In sorrow and anguish she had travailed for her son (John 16:21) and now she had closed his eyes in death. Husband, family, all were gone; what an experience of sorrow hers had been; what capacity for joy it had given to her heart! This, too, the Lord satisfied to the full. And what of the Lord Himself? "A Man of sorrows and acquainted with grief," what experiences of sorrow, actual and in anticipation, were His! Outside the gate of Nain that day we may be sure that the gladdest heart was His own.

So shall it be in that other day within the gates of heaven. The little graves shall be opened and they that sleep therein shall be made glad to the measure of their capacity for joy. And those who lived longer and sorrowed more will be made glad also, each after his measure. But the "exceeding joy" is the joy of God. It is the joy of the Father Who gave His Son to death that that day might be brought about. It is the joy of the Son Who "Himself took our infirmities and bare our diseases," "Who His own self bare our sins in His body upon the tree" that He might have with Him forever those for whom He died, and to Whom it is said,

> "Thy God hath anointed Thee
> With the oil of gladness above Thy
> fellows." Hebrews 1:9

It is the joy of the Holy Spirit Who led Him to the Cross and through Whom He "offered Himself without blemish unto God" (Heb. 9:14) and Whose present ministry enables the Christian to "rejoice in hope of the glory of God."

▪ CHAPTER TWO ▪

The Resurrection and the Rapture

The Teaching of the Lord

When the Lord Jesus appeared among the Jews as a public teacher they had long been divided into two main religious parties, Sadducees and Pharisees. The former though smaller in numbers were the more wealthy, and socially and politically the more powerful, the latter were the more popular party. The doctrinal difference between them is thus defined by Luke—"The Sadducees say that there is no resurrection, neither angel nor spirit: but the Pharisees confess both" (Acts 23:8). To the Sadducees the resurrection was an irrational fancy; to the Pharisees it was a hope. The Sadducees did not reject the Old Testament Scriptures, but they did not discover there the hope of resurrection as the Pharisees did.

Whether or no the dead would be raised was thus an open question among the Jews. It is true there is little in the Old Testament concerning resurrection or a future life, still the doctrine is present. Hence the Lord in His reply to a Sadducean interlocutor declared that the error of his school arose out of ignorance of the Scriptures and of the power of God, thus justifying the Pharisees in their hope (Luke 20:27–40).

Reasoning from the Scriptures

On this occasion the Lord deduced from the words of Moses in Exodus 3:15, "the God of Abraham, the God of Isaac, and the God of Jacob," that inasmuch as God was still their God though they had died, they were in fact living persons still; for if to die means to cease to exist, then He would be the God of the nonexistent, plainly an absurd conclusion. Therefore the dead, i.e., those whose bodies have seen corruption, continue to live, for their spirits still hold fellowship with God. And to this the inevitable corollary is that they will one day be raised.

The other recorded references of the Lord to the resurrection, and particularly to the resurrection of those who believe on Him, are the subject of this chapter. His utterances will be taken in the order in which they were spoken, so far as that can be ascertained. We shall endeavor to learn His mind as He Himself unfolded it to those who, while they believed that the dead would ultimately be raised, had no certain knowledge of the extent of the resurrection, whether all men, Jews and Gentiles, were to partake in it, or Jews only; or how, or when, that resurrection would take place. We are to forget, for the moment, all that was subsequently revealed on the subject, and, as far as may be possible, to put ourselves in the place of those to whom the Lord originally spoke.

Subsequent communications of the Holy Spirit, made through the apostles, to supplement the words of the Lord and to complete the revelation, will form the subject of other chapters.

The Inner Sanctuary—His Body

The first passage with which we are here concerned is John 2:19–22, where He referred, under a figure, to His own resurrection. "Destroy this temple," He said, "and after three days I will raise it up." It was to His own body He alluded, though at the time no one of His hearers perceived His meaning. Hence the words provided His enemies with one of the accusations upon which they ultimately secured His death, and John records that the disciples themselves understood their significance only after His resurrection from among the dead (Matt. 26:61).

After John the Baptist had been thrown into prison, and the Lord Jesus had begun to attract general attention, the disciples of the former came to inquire about the purposes and claims of the latter. The Lord drew their attention to the works in which He was engaged, in which power was at the service of beneficence, and in His recapitulation of these works He included the raising of the dead. The two evangelists who recorded the words do not set the incident in the same relation to the events of the Lord's ministry. Luke inserts the visit of these disciples in his narrative between the raising of the widow's son at Nain and the raising of Jairus's daughter. Matthew, who does not include the incident at Nain, places it after the raising of the girl. (See Luke 7:11–17, 22; 8:49–56 and Matt. 9:23–26; 11:5.) It seems probable, that, here at least, Matthew's is the chronological order. Certainly the words "the dead are raised" seem to suggest that more than one person had, at that time, been restored to life.

All this was intended to familiarize the minds of the disciples, and of His hearers generally, with the idea of resurrection, and to show them the possibility of the return of dead persons to life. It is the way of God to lead the believing mind into the light by easy stages, and to furnish it with aids to an understanding faith. These were first steps toward that larger thought which He was about to begin to unfold to them.

The next passage that calls for notice is the paragraph on hospitality, Luke 14:12–14, with its concluding words, "thou shalt be recompensed in the resurrection of the just."* The reference to resurrection here is incidental only; the Lord is not expounding the doctrine, nor is He adding anything by way of new revelation. He alludes to it as something His hearers would understand without further explanation. (See Acts 24:15.) Two things are clear from this statement; that there is to be a resurrection of a class of people described as "the just," and that they are thereafter to be rewarded for kindness shown in this life to the needy.

The rest of the Lord's teaching on this subject is found in the Gospel of John, which simplifies matters from the chronological point of view. We have now only to take the words He spoke in their order as there recorded, and of these the earliest is found in chapter 5, verses 28 and 29.†

The Son, Creator and Quickener

The Lord had healed a long-standing case of physical weakness; to the scandal of the Jews He had done this on the Sabbath day. To their expostulations He replied in words that involved a claim to equality with God. This deepened their hatred, and strengthened their determination to put Him to death. Not only did He not repudiate the construction they had put upon His words, He confirmed it, and enlarged it into an assertion of a unique relation with God, Whom He called not "our" but "My Father." And that this might be made unmistakable, the Father, He declared, had committed to Him the dispensation of all judgment, so that to refuse to the Son the honor due to the Father, whether as Savior or as judge, is to dishonor God.

Moreover, as the Father is the source of life, so also is the Son; the honor due to God the Creator is His also. Hence it is that all who believe on Him themselves become partakers of life, here and now. And not only so, those who will to hear His voice now are quickened, the rest remain untouched, they continue in their natural state of "alienation from the life of God" (Eph. 4:16). But "the hour cometh in which all that are in the tombs shall hear His voice and shall come forth; they that have done good unto the resurrection of life; they that have practiced [so marg.] ill, unto the resurrection of judgment." So absolute is the jurisdiction of the Son over the destinies of all men, in life and in death, in time and in eternity, so immediate is His control, so imperative His word.

This declaration of the Lord enlarges the scope of the resurrection, and confirms the Pharisees in their reading of the Scriptures (Acts 24:15); for whereas Luke 14:14 speaks

---

*It is not possible in every case to settle the order of occurrence of the Gospel incidents, or to fix with precision the time at which certain words were spoken. It is impossible to say that Luke 14:14 is actually the first reference to resurrection in the teaching of the Lord. Whether it is placed before or after the discourse of John 5 is, however, not material in this connection.

†See Appendix, Note A.

only of "the resurrection of the just," this present passage speaks of the resurrection of all men. The class there described as to their character, "the just," are here described as to their conduct, they "have done good." There the dead are said to be raised to reward, for their works are in question. Here they are said to be raised to life, for the purpose of the Lord is to declare that His claim to deity will ultimately be vindicated in this act of quickening.

The next utterance of the Lord which deals with this subject is found in John 6, where those who are to be raised are further described. That the same persons are intended is to be presumed, each separate description presenting a characteristic common to all who are to share in "the resurrection of life." It may be convenient to tabulate these descriptions here. They are:

The Just	Luke 14:14
Those who have done good	John 5:29
Those who are given by the Father to the Son	John 6:39
Those who behold the Son and believe on Him	John 6:40
Those who are drawn by the Father to the Son	John 6:44
Those who eat the Flesh and drink the Blood of the Son of man	John 6:54

"These are they that are accounted worthy to attain to that age, and the resurrection from [lit., out of] the dead . . . and are sons of God, being sons of the resurrection" (Luke 20:35, 36).

The time of the resurrection is now declared. It is to take place "at the Last Day," a phrase which occurs but once again in the recorded teaching of the Lord.*

Death and Resurrection at Bethany

Lazarus had been dead four days at Bethany, and the Lord had made no sign. He had not come to him in response to the message that His friend was sick, nor had any message from Him reached the sisters to relieve their anxiety; or if one had come, it could have been only: "This sickness is not unto death, but for the glory of God, that the Son of God may be glorified thereby" (John 11:4). And these words could only mean to them that Lazarus would not die of the sickness that had brought him low. Yet he had succumbed to it. Thus was their faith most sorely tried.

The sisters had hoped for help; now they longed for comfort. "If He had been here, Lazarus had not died," was the regretful refrain as they reviewed their sorrow while the silence of the Lord remained unbroken. At least this was the thought uppermost in the mind of each when they saw the Lord. To Martha, who met Him first, He replied: "Thy brother shall rise again." Martha, busy woman though she was, and somewhat burdened with the care of the home and its guests (Luke 10:40), is nevertheless in touch with the teacher; she has fresh in her mind the last thing He had said about resurrection. She could, moreover, identify her brother as one of those whom the Lord described when He spoke of His purpose to raise certain from the dead. Accordingly she replies in the true disciple spirit: "I know that he shall rise again in the resurrection at the last day." But the Lord had not said anything about the last day when He spoke of the raising of Lazarus. There was an immediate boon for the home at Bethany. Nevertheless the new and nearer promise did not abrogate the older and more remote. It remains true that Lazarus will be raised again at the last day. This is a significant illustration of the Lord's ways. Ultimate and final blessings are often promised first; subsequent promises may have previous fulfillment but they do not cancel those given earlier. Neither do earlier assurances of ultimate blessing prevent the Lord from revealing His purposes to do yet other things while these still wait.

The Faith of Martha

To return to Martha; it was to this busy woman of domestic affairs He chose to carry the revelation of His purpose a long step in advance. He said to her, "I am the resurrec-

*John 12:48. See Appendix, Note B.

tion and the life: he that believeth on Me, though he die yet shall he live: and whosoever liveth and believeth on Me shall never die. Believest thou this?" The words are apparently inconsistent; the second clause seems to be an absolute statement admitting of no exception, whereas the first clause provides for an exception. Martha did not understand them, and she was too honest to pretend she did. But not only was hers an intelligent apprehension of the teaching of the Lord; to spiritual knowledge she added spiritual understanding. "The word of the Lord tried" her, as it tried Joseph when he lay forgotten in the prison (Ps. 105:19), and as it tries every faithful soul that submits itself to be exercised under it. Faith triumphs. Martha appeals from the word, the meaning of which she did not perceive, to the Lord Who spoke it and Whom she had learned to trust. "Yea, Lord," she answered, "I have believed that Thou art the Christ, the Son of God." No remonstrance falls from His lips. Why should it? He speaks as we are able to bear His word, and this saying had to lie unexplained for many years, twenty at least, until the time came for the discovery of its hidden meaning.

It is necessary now to notice one feature common to all the passages so far quoted in this chapter. In no one of them is the presence of the Lord indispensable to the accomplishment of His purpose. It is not necessary that the Lord should return to this earth in order to raise the dead. All that He has undertaken to do He could do from heaven. The power of the voice of the Son of God is not diminished by distance. He Who at Cana could heal the son of the nobleman at Capernaum, twenty miles of hill and vale notwithstanding, could if He chose to do so, empty the graves of earth without leaving His Father's throne, (John 4:46–54).

Soon after the raising of Lazarus came the Lord's last meal with His disciples. During the conversation that followed He said to them, "I come again, and will receive you unto Myself," and in these words intimated for the first time His purpose to come in person for His own. But these words do not themselves suggest whether His promise to receive His people is to be redeemed before that glorious appearing of which He had spoken in public (Matt. 24:30, e.g.), or simultaneously with it, or subsequently to it. All this He left for a later day.

▪ CHAPTER THREE ▪

The Resurrection and the Rapture

The Teaching of the Apostles (i)

The Lord's own teaching concerning resurrection, briefly sketched in the preceding chapter, may be summarized thus. Those who refuse to acknowledge His claims to paramount authority over the lives and destinies of all men, and particularly over their own, who neglect His teaching concerning the way of life and the way of living, who pursue mean and worthless ends,* who refuse their rights to God and to men, these are to be raised to the judgment of the Great White Throne† (John 12:48; 5:29; Rev. 20:11–15).

Those who, being the gift of the Father, and having been drawn by the Father to the Son, live because they commit themselves to Him and depend upon Him, who seek to render what is due to God and to men, who do the things that are good, these are to be raised to life and reward (John 6:39, 40, 44, 54; Luke 14:14; John 5:29).

It is to be observed that in neither case are these descriptions of different classes of men. The characteristics mentioned are complementary one of the other, and mark all who belong to that particular class. For those who are drawn to Christ and believe on Him, learn of Him what the Christian life is, and receive from Him power to live it. Whereas those who refuse Christ refuse with Him His counsel and His strength, and thus, by their own choice, are left to their own resources. The Christian man is so one with Christ that the Son of God has become to him at once a living Savior and a living hope.

Moreover, the Lord is Himself to come to gather His redeemed to Himself when the hour for the accomplishment of His purpose arrives. All this is to be learned from the Lord's own words, but so far as the records go, He Himself carried the revelation no further, not even after His resurrection, though His presence among the disciples under such conditions must have illuminated the word for them, as, indeed, it does for us.

The words to Martha are not included in this summary. They seem to have been left by the Lord in designed obscurity until the time became ripe to display the counsel of God that lay hidden in them.

Acts and the Epistle of James

After the ascension of the Lord and the descent of the Holy Spirit, the apostles and the disciples carried the gospel far and wide. A selective record of their activities is provided in the "Acts of the apostles," but such references to resurrection as are found therein are either apostolic testimonies to the resurrection of Christ (4:33) addressed to the Jews (13:34) or to the Gentiles (17:31), or are restatements of the beliefs of the Pharisees (23:6), beliefs in which, as we have seen, the Lord confirmed them. But neither by Luke himself, nor by any one of the speakers whose words he reports, is the doctrine carried forward a step beyond the point at which it had been left by the Lord Jesus.

The epistle of James calls for notice next, as it may very well be the earliest of the New Testament writings. It need not detain us, however, for it does not contain any specific reference to resurrection at all, and only one to the coming of the Lord (5:7, 8) where the reader is exhorted to be patient in view of the imminence of the Parousia of the Lord, which is said to be "at hand." But neither does James supplement what had already been revealed.

**Phaulos*, "ill"; the same word is used in John 3:20.

†Judgment is not equivalent to trial here; this is the ratification of the condemnation under which men lived while upon earth and from which they refused to escape when God provided a way through the Cross. See John 3:18.

The Epistles of Paul

Next in order of time are the epistles of Paul, and of these the earliest is either that to the Galatians or those to the Thessalonians. In the former, however, there are but two references to the coming of the Lord, or perhaps three (1:4; 5:5, 21), and these are rather allusions to matters of knowledge common to the writer and to his readers, than statements of doctrine. Hence neither do they contribute anything to the end now in view.

Paul's Teaching at Thessalonica

The epistles to the Thessalonians offer a mine of wealth to the student of prophecy, and, as we shall find, carry the revelation of the manner of the fulfillment of the purpose of the Lord a considerable stage further than any utterance that preceded them. From the opening part of the first epistle we learn that during his brief stay at Thessalonica the apostle had taught the converts, "to wait for His [God's] Son from Heaven, Whom He raised from the dead, even Jesus, which delivereth us from the wrath to come" (1:10).

" 'The wrath to come' is to be understood of the calamities wherewith God will visit men upon the earth when the present period of grace is closed."* (H-J, p. 179). The wording of the A.V., "which delivered," seems to make the reference to be to the deliverance of the believer from condemnation which Christ accomplished at the Cross. The tense is present, however, indeed the word is a title, "our Deliverer"; but the deliverance contemplated is not past but future; and it is a deliverance which can be accomplished only by one who has been raised from among the dead.

How this deliverance is to be effected the apostle does not seem to have declared, indeed there is no evidence that he himself had up to this time received any revelation on the subject. His stay among these new converts had been but brief, and in the interval between his sudden departure from their city and the writing of this letter, he had heard that some of their number had died. Not only had these losses plunged them into sorrow; they were perplexed by them, uncertain as to the consequences to their fulfillment of the promise of the Lord to come to deliver them from the threatened calamity. And this perplexity would be the greater if, as is possible, the deaths were the result of persecution. Might not that mean that they had been the victims of the very catastrophe—the Day of the Lord—from which they had been promised deliverance?

Paul's Letter to Thessalonica

Hence this letter, and particularly that section of it which begins at chapter 4, verse 13. The apostle first declares that "them also that are fallen asleep through [marg.] Jesus will God bring with Him." That is, when God "again bringeth the Firstborn into the world" (Heb. 1:6), He will also, and by the instrumentality of the person who died for them, bring with Him those who had fallen asleep. The reference is to the event to which the Lord Himself first referred at Caesarea Philippi, "the Son of God shall come in the glory of His Father with His angels" (Matt. 16:27), and of which He spoke many times thereafter. For up to the time of the writing of the epistle nothing earlier than this appearing of the Lord had been revealed. (H-J, p. 179).

But how? They were dead; their bodies given over to corruption. How then can they come with the Lord when He appears in His glory? Verse 15 meets this difficulty. There is a word from the Lord to reassure them. Now this "word" is plainly not a quotation from the Old Testament; nothing like it is to be found there. Neither is it an utterance of the Lord Jesus during His ministry upon earth. Nothing resembling these words is on record in the Gospels. What the apostle is about to write to them is a freshly given revelation. The Spirit of God through him is fulfilling the promise of the Lord Jesus to His disciples, "when He, the Spirit of truth, is come, . . . He shall declare unto you the things that are to come" (John 16:13). The things that the Lord Himself refrained from saying, because the time was not ripe, nor were hearts prepared, the Holy Spirit would reveal. And in particular the words of the Lord to Martha (John 11:25, 26) that

*From a note on the passage in *The Epistles to the Thessalonians, With Notes Exegetical and Espository.* By the same Writers.

had so long waited explanation, are now made plain. When the Lord comes as described in these words, those who have believed upon Him will be divided into two classes, "we that are alive," and, "the dead in Christ." There is no statement elsewhere in Scripture that any are to be removed from the earth prior to this time. And of these two classes all are accounted for in the words "shall rise" and "shall . . . be caught away." There is no room in such an inclusive statement for another class, living or dead, to be left behind when these are taken.* (G-F, p. 179).

The words of the Lord correspond to those of the apostle, and the meaning of the earlier utterance is made clear by the latter. "He that believeth on Me, though he die [lit., even if he were to die] yet shall he live," stand over against "the dead in Christ shall rise first." "Whosoever liveth and believeth on Me shall never die," is explained by, "We that are alive that are left unto the Presence [marg.] of the Lord." The two classes had their typical representatives at Bethany. Lazarus, who had died, and Martha and Mary, who waited for the Lord in life. So it has been always, so must it be unto the end. And inasmuch as the time of the Lord's descent is unknown, because unrevealed, living believers describe themselves as "we that are alive, that are left."† Not that they are thereby guilty of the folly of asserting that the Lord will assuredly return in the lifetime of any particular believer, but because the proper attitude of Christian people is enjoined upon them by the word of the Lord: "What I say unto you I say unto all, Watch" (Mark 13:37).

The Rapture

The second epistle to the Thessalonians does not advance the doctrine we are now considering. But before we leave these epistles we may notice two things. That which in the Old Testament and in the Gospels is the hope of resurrection, becomes, from the writing of the letter to the church of the Thessalonians, the hope of resurrection and rapture. This later word, which is defined as "the act of conveying a person from one place to another," is the translation of a Greek word which is rendered "snatch" in John 10:12, 28, 29, and "caught away" in Acts 8:39. Thus the rapture of the saints, or "of the church," is an entirely Scriptural expression, and describes vividly the instantaneous removal of those who are in Christ, whether living or dead, at the word of the Returning Lord.‡

The other matter that calls for notice is that, so far as the revelation has been carried up to this point, there is nothing to indicate that any change will pass on the bodies whether of the dead in Christ or of living believers.

*See Appendix, Note C.
†See Appendix, Note D.
‡See Appendix, Note E.

▪ CHAPTER FOUR ▪

The Resurrection and the Rapture

The Teaching of the Apostles (ii)

Next in chronological order is the first epistle to the Corinthians, in which the doctrine of the indwelling of the Holy Spirit in the body of the believer is enunciated for the first time in the words: "Know ye not that your body is a temple of the Holy Spirit which is in you, which ye have from God?" (6:19). This indwelling has a very important bearing on the rapture of those in whom He has taken up His abode, as we shall see a little later on.

In chapter fifteen the apostle deals with the resurrection at some length. Now whereas it is quite true that the words "resurrection of the body" do not occur in Scripture, it is also true that in Scripture the word resurrection is used exclusively of the body, never of the soul or spirit.*

Hence when the apostle speaks of "the resurrection of the dead," verse 42, he has in mind the bodies of the dead, for this is the subject with which he is dealing, and of course only the body dies.† The "it" which follows can, therefore, refer only to the body. But there is to be a change, and this is suggested in a general way in the series of contrasts that follow. This change is to be accomplished by the quickening power of "the last Adam," and its effect will be to transform the body of the believer from conformity with an earthly into conformity with a heavenly type; that is, his new, or resurrection, body will be congruous with, and fitted for, the heavenly environment to which he is destined.

Change there must be, however, for, the apostle affirms, "flesh and blood," that is, "we that are alive, that are left unto the presence of the Lord," while in that condition, "cannot inherit the Kingdom of God." And as for the dead in Christ, "neither doth corruption inherit incorruption" (v. 51). Now this is the first intimation of the necessity for such a change; no earlier word, spoken or written, suggests it. The revelation concerning the rapture and the resurrection had exercised the minds of Christians who felt the difficulty of forming a mental picture corresponding to the apostle's words. This difficulty found expression in the question of verse 35, "How are the dead raised? With what manner of body do they come?" Nature, indeed, pointed the way to a solution of their perplexity; as far as nature could take them, therefore, they must go with nature. But nature unaided is not enough. When nature fails, God speaks.

"Behold," proceeds the apostle, "I tell you a mystery," that is, a secret, something that could not be discovered, or otherwise learned, save as God Himself is pleased to reveal it. And this mystery is, not that "we shall not all sleep," for that had already been made known in the letter to the Thessalonians, but that "we shall all be changed, in a moment, in the twinkling of an eye, at the last trump;‡ for the trumpet shall sound, and the dead shall be raised incorruptible, and we shall be changed. For this corruptible must put on incorruption, and this mortal must put on immortality.§ But when this corruptible shall have put on incorruption, and this mortal shall have put on immortality, then shall come to pass the saying that is written, Death is swallowed up in victory." (G-F, p. 179).

---

*Philippians 3:11 is not really an exception to this rule. An exceptional form of the word is there used, *exanastasis*, and the intention of the apostle seems to be to assert his desire to walk "in newness of life" (Rom. 6:4). *Anastasis* has also another range of meaning in the New Testament; the statement of the text refers, of course, only to those passages in which resurrection is in view. See further at chapter 6.

†See Appendix, Note F.

‡See Appendix, Note G.

§See Appendix, Note H.

"Then," but not until then, when the Lord comes, for this victory complete and final, is "through our Lord Jesus Christ," the "Life-giving Spirit," "the Son," Who "quickeneth whom He will" (v. 45; John 5:21).

The Christian and Death

In this second letter to the Corinthians the apostle, laboring under a sense of physical weakness and of the hardships he had endured for the gospel's sake, contemplates the possibility that his bodily frame might prove unequal to the strain. That the "earthly house of this tabernacle," a temporary dwelling in any case, "should be dissolved" does not dismay one the assurance of resurrection; "knowing that he who raised up the Lord Jesus shall raise up us also with Jesus, and shall present us with you" (2 Cor. 4:14; 5:1).

In contrast with 1 Thessalonians 4:15, where he associates himself with those who are to be alive and upon the earth when the Lord descends to meet them in the air, he here associates himself with those who will have already fallen asleep, and who will, therefore, be no longer among the mortal but among the corruptible, before that event takes place. That he is not in either place forecasting what he believes to be in store for himself or for his contemporaries seems sufficiently clear. Nowhere in his writings does the apostle commit himself to the belief that the Lord would return in his lifetime.* He does not foreclose the possibility however; rather he is ready for it, and hails it with joy, and would have all Christians rejoice with him. He who a few sentences earlier had spoken of his confident hope of resurrection, here declares that in this body "we groan, longing to be clothed upon with our habitation which is from heaven . . . that what is mortal may be swallowed up of life" (5:2–4).† That is, as he had already expressed it, that "this mortal" might "put on immortality" (1 Cor. 15:53).

However deeply he may have been impressed by the possibility of death bringing his service to an end, his ardent desire was that the Lord might come to call him to the meeting in the air. Not that he feared death; should that be the will of God for him, he can look death steadily in the face, for he had learned to say "O death, where is thy victory? O death, where is thy sting?" So now he declares that he is "always of good courage" in view of the possibility of the separation of the spirit from the body; and reiterates it with emphasis; "we" (it is normal Christian privilege and should be normal Christian experience) "we are of good courage, I say, and are willing rather to be absent from the body, and to be at home with the Lord." For death itself, enemy as it most surely is, but ushers the Christian into the presence of his Lord.

The Resurrection and the Eternal House

The fifteenth chapter of the first epistle to the Corinthians, and the earlier part of the fifth chapter of the second, are not contradictory but complementary the one of the other. The first establishes the continuity of the spiritual with the natural body, "it is sown . . . it is raised." The second establishes the suitability of the changed body to the new conditions for which it is destined, "a building from God, a house not made with hands, eternal, in the heavens." The words change and resurrection imply this continuity, indeed, but that does not mean that the body which is to be is identical, as to the particles of matter of which it composed, with the body that is now. "That which thou sowest, thou sowest not the body that shall be . . . so also is the resurrection of the dead" (1 Cor. 15:37, 42).

And yet when wheat is sown so also is that which is reaped wheat; but not that particular grain of wheat which was dropped into the earth. In this characteristic of nature the apos-

*See Appendix, Note D.

†Second Corinthians 5:1 cannot mean that a body is provided for the spirit between death and resurrection. Nowhere else is such a body mentioned. This "building from God" is itself "the habitation which is from Heaven," for which the Christian longs. Now he does not long for death, verse 4, and consequently not for any temporary body which could only be necessary in case of death. Moreover, the apostle has a distaste for what he calls the "naked," the "unclothed" state, that is, the interval during which the spirit is absent from the body. But how could he speak of that as an unclothed or naked state for which a body is expressly prepared?

tle finds an analogy with the body in death and resurrection. The illustration must not be pressed too far. From one grain of wheat an abundance is raised. That is the glory of the grain; it died and, because it dies, does not abide alone. The glory of the resurrection body is different; sown in corruption, dishonor, and weakness, it is raised in incorruption, glory, and power.

"What Manner of Body?"

It is easy to go beyond what is written here. The apostle John warns us that it is not yet made manifest what we shall be (1 John 3:2), and the language of Paul implies as much. Where Scripture is reticent we may not attempt to be explicit. The identity of the body does not depend at all on the identity of the particles that compose it, for these come and go from moment to moment. So long as the body lives it is in a state of flux, receiving new supplies of material from food and air to replace what has become effete and waste. The body of the man is the body of the child developed; throughout life it is looked upon as the same body, and is called without qualification "my body." Nevertheless there is no particle of matter that has remained in that body during its growth from childhood to manhood.

The scar remains in the body through all the years of a man's life, though the actual particles of matter that sustained the injury have long since passed away from it. So with the resurrection of the dead. "With what manner of body do they come?" Each in his own, given him by God, though no particle therein should have had a place in that which clothed the spirit here. The body is not less the same on that account, any more than the body of the man is a different body from that of the child because of the exchange of matter particles in the process of nutrition, growth and repair.

The Indwelling Spirit

It has been noticed already that the earliest mention of the indwelling of the body of the believer by the Holy Spirit is found in the epistle that deals at length with the resurrection of that body. In 2 Corinthians there are two references to this indwelling, one in chapter 2, verse 22 ". . . God; Who also sealed us, and gave us the earnest of the Spirit in our hearts," the other in chapter 5, verse 5, "Now He that wrought us for this very thing [the change from mortality to immortality] is God, Who gave unto us the earnest of the Spirit." This it is, the apostle proceeds, that gives the believer courage in the face of death, for the indwelling of the Spirit is also God's pledge, or earnest, that they who die and whose bodies see corruption shall be raised from death in bodies incorruptible.

At the close of the argument of the seventh chapter of the epistle to the Romans, which follows 2 Corinthians in order of time, the apostle described the present habitation of the spirit of the believer as "the body of this death," words which by themselves might be taken to countenance the pagan doctrine of the inherent evil of matter, verse 24. Against this misconception, however, he shortly provides. In chapter 8, verse 11, he calls it, as in the letter to the Corinthians, the mortal body or body capable of, and liable to, death. And in harmony with the teaching of his earlier letters he declares that this mortal body is to be quickened,* it is to be "swallowed up of life." The quickener is God, "Him that raised up Jesus from the dead," and the ground on which it is to be quickened is that here and now it is already the dwelling place of the Holy Spirit, "because of His Spirit that dwelleth in you," according to the well supported reading of the margin.†

In 1 Corinthians chapter 6, verse 19, the mention of the indwelling of the Holy Spirit has an immediately practical end in view. The body in which He has taken up His abode must itself be kept holy. But has the body that is thus honored no other future than to be discarded as an irreclaimably evil thing? This wrong deduction is promptly repudiated; since it is a temple of the Spirit of God it also has a glorious future, "body of death" though it be.

*See Appendix, Note J.

†The Holy Spirit is not said to have raised the Lord Jesus. Neither is He elsewhere said to raise the believer. It is unlikely that this passage is an exception to the rule.

Redemption, Past and Future

The argument is repeated in verse 23. "We which have the firstfruits of the Spirit, even we ourselves groan within ourselves, waiting for our adoption, to wit, the redemption of our body." Redemption has a double use in the New Testament. In one series of passages it refers to the Cross, where the price was paid, as in Ephesians chapter 1, verse 7; in the other it refers to the coming of the Lord when He will take possession of that which He purchased. (E-G, p. 179). "This body of death" has been redeemed from its bondage, and when He comes it will be delivered into the glorious liberty, which is the inheritance secured for it by the offering of the body of Jesus Christ once for all, and which is assured to us by the grace of the Spirit in taking up His abode therein (Heb. 10:10).

In one of his later letters the apostle again brings the two things into the same relationship. "Having . . . believed, ye were sealed with the Holy Spirit of promise, which is an earnest of our inheritance, unto the redemption of God's own possession" (Eph. 1:14; see also 4:30). When the man turned to God in Christ, then He was sealed for God (the mark of finality and security) to be His forever, and the Spirit came to make His abode in the body of the man, to be an earnest of the purpose of God that that body, being the peculiar property of God in virtue of the redemptive act of the Cross, should, at the coming of the Lord, be to the praise of the glory of God, exhibiting His power to redeem what is mortal and corruptible from the power of death and the grave. Thus the body in which the power of sin, both in life and in death, is now so abundantly manifested, that it is even called "this body of death," becomes "God's own possession." In it the salvation of God is made evident, both in life and in death, whereof the Holy Spirit who dwells therein is the power and the pledge.

Conformity to the Type, Christ

Reverting to Romans 8, in a verse intermediate between those on which we have already dwelt, verses 11 and 23, namely, verse 19, a hint is given of the climax of the revelation concerning the resurrection and rapture of the Christian. "The earnest expectation of the creation waiteth for the revealing of the sons of God." The reference to "the sons of God," where "the Son of God" might have been expected, is somewhat surprising. Later the apostle explains, "whom He foreknew, He also foreordained to be conformed to the image of His Son, that He might be the Firstborn among many brethren," verse 29. In 1 Corinthians chapter fifteen, verses 47–49, there is a similar hint, but, as might be anticipated from the analogy of the progressive method of the revelation, a slighter hint. And in what was probably his last communication to any church, so far as these have been preserved, the purpose of God in this regard is categorically stated. "Our citizenship is in heaven; from whence also we wait for a Savior, the Lord Jesus Christ; Who shall fashion anew the body of our humiliation, that it may be conformed to the body of His glory" (Phil. 3:20, 21). Thus the inevitable question is answered. To be changed—but into what likeness? Into the likeness of our Lord, and this not morally only; the body spiritual which is to replace the body natural, is to bear the image of that in which He showed Himself in the Mount of Transfiguration, and in which He appeared to John in Patmos, and in which He will yet appear when He comes to establish the rule of God upon the earth.

And by whom and by what power is this to be accomplished? The words of the Lord were "I will raise him up at the Last Day"; "all that are in the tombs shall hear His voice [the voice of the Son of God] and shall come forth"; and "I come again and will receive you unto Myself." It is both "by means of Jesus" and "with Him" that God will bring the dead in Christ, when He comes to reign. Christ Himself it is, then, Who is to "fashion anew" this body of sin and of pain "according to the working whereby He is able to subject all things unto Himself."*

*Such power is essentially divine. No higher power is conceivable. Nor is it conceivable that He Who wields this power should Himself be other than God.

The Limits of Revelation

So far Scripture carries us. Not every question is answered. There remain many things impossible to say or to hear now. Impossible for God to say, for earth has no language wherein to describe these heavenly things. Impossible for us to hear, for as yet we have had no experience to enable us to bridge the gulf, to pierce the veil, that separates the material from the spiritual world. And this the apostle John asserts when he writes that "it is not yet made manifest what we shall be." But if, in the meantime, satisfaction is denied to the intellect, there remains at least comfort for the heart, for, "we know that, if He shall be manifested, we shall be like Him" (1 John 3:2). It is enough for the disciple that he be as his teacher, for the servant that he be as his Lord. Than this he cherishes no higher ambition. And this ambition will be realized to the full "when we shall see Him even as He is."

▪ CHAPTER FIVE ▪

The Parousia of the Lord

"The midnight is past, the bright Star of the Morn
Soon shall appear;
Soon the last briar, soon the last thorn,
Soon the last tear.
Heavenly Lover, come quickly! O come!
No longer Thy blood-bought this desert would roam;
The soul-stirring shout that shall gather them home
They are waiting to hear."
From *"The Story of the Glory"*—BOYD

Our Lord's discourse to His disciples on the night of His betrayal was calculated not only to comfort them in the sorrows they would experience after His departure, and to strengthen them to endure trial and opposition, but also, while conforming their faith in Himself during His absence from them, to direct their hearts to the prospect of His return. Spiritually present with all His followers throughout the age then about to commence, He would eventually return, but not merely in the spiritual sense. "I go," He said, "to prepare a place for you. And If I go and prepare a place for you, I come again, and will receive you unto Myself; that where I am, there ye may be also"; and further, "A little while and ye behold Me no more, and again a little while, and ye shall see me" (John 14:2, 3; 16:16). Such language could not indicate a spiritual coming. His words were unequivocal; their directness and simplicity forbid their being explained away by a spiritualizing interpretation. He was going from them in bodily presence; in bodily presence He would return and receive them to Himself. In His resurrection body "He showed Himself alive after His passion . . . appearing unto them . . . and assembling with them." No phantom form rose from their midst at His ascension. With that same tangible body "He was taken up," and thereupon His promise was renewed by the assurance given by the heavenly messengers, "This Jesus, which was received up from you into heaven, shall so come in like manner as ye beheld Him going into heaven" (Acts 1:3, 11). (H-J, p. 179).

An Event Yet Future

Albeit nineteen centuries have elapsed, His promised advent has not yet taken place. The end of the age throughout which He assured His followers of His spiritual presence with them has not yet come. The descent of the Holy Spirit at pentecost was not the "Second Advent," nor has the promise of His return been fulfilled either in the spiritual experiences of believers or at their departure to be with Him at their decease. All such ideas are precluded at once by the words of the apostle Paul, that "the Lord Himself shall descend from heaven with a shout, with the voice of the archangel, and with the trump of God: and the dead in Christ shall rise first: then we that are alive, that are left, shall together with them be caught up in the clouds, to meet the Lord in the air: and so shall we ever be with the Lord" (1 Thess. 4:16, 17). Clearly no spiritual advent is signified here. Nor has this prediction had its fulfillment on any occasion in past history. For the object of the descent herein stated is nothing less than the instantaneous removal of the completed Church by the Lord in person. Christians still fall asleep and await resurrection, and thousands await the day of rapture. (E-G, p. 179).

Equally clear is the statement of the apostle in his first epistle to the Corinthians: "We shall not all sleep, but we shall all be changed, in a moment, in the twinkling of an eye, at the last trump: for the trumpet shall sound, and the dead shall be raised incorruptible, and we shall be changed. For this corruptible must put on incorruption, and this mortal must put on immortality" (1 Cor. 15:51–53). The same event is described as in 1 Thessalonians 4, the effect of the resurrection being, however, chiefly in view here, while there the action of the Lord is prominent.

The Meaning of "Parousia"

The resurrection and rapture of the saints foretold in these passages constitute the initial event of what the New Testament calls "the Parousia of the Lord." Paul uses the word in the passage in 1 Thessalonians just referred to. "For if," he says, "we believe that Jesus died and rose again, even so them also that are fallen asleep in [marg. through] Jesus will God bring with Him. For this we say unto you by the word of the Lord, that we that are alive, that are left unto the coming [the parousia] of the Lord, shall in no wise precede them that are fallen asleep" (1 Thess. 4:14, 15). (F-H, p. 179).

Now the word "parousia" is a transliteration of the Greek word which is frequently rendered "coming," a rendering which, however, is quite inadequate. "Coming" is, indeed, misleading, and responsible for considerable misunderstanding and variety of judgment. There is indeed no single English term which exactly fits the meaning. Hence the value of the addition to our vocabulary of the transliterated word. "Parousia" literally signifies "a being with," "a presence." Not infrequently it is so rendered. It thus denotes a state, not an action. We never read of a parousia *to,* always of a parousia *with.* Paul tells the Philippian converts of his confidence that he will be with them "for their progress and joy in the faith, that their glorying may abound in Christ Jesus in him through his presence, his parousia, with them again." Further, he exhorts them as they have been obedient during his presence, his parousia, so much more in his absence, his apousia, to work out their own salvation with fear and trembling (Phil. 1:26; 2:12). In a Greek document of almost the same period as that in which the New Testament was written, a person states that attention to her property necessitates her parousia in a certain city. These examples suffice to show that, while of course the initial act of arrival is essential to a parousia, the word signifies the more or less prolonged period following the arrival.*

We take a further example from the New Testament to show that several passages where the word is rendered "coming" receive their true explanation only when the extended period just pointed out has its due consideration. Thus when Peter says, "We made known unto you the power and coming [parousia] of the Lord Jesus Christ . . . we were eyewitnesses of His Majesty" (2 Pet. 1:16), he is referring, not to a sudden and momentary manifestation of the Lord, nor to His future advent, but to the period of His transfiguration before the disciples. "For," says the apostle, "He received from God the Father honor and glory, when there came such a voice to Him from the excellent glory, This is My beloved Son, in whom I am well pleased; and this voice we ourselves heard come out of heaven, when

*Cramer, *Biblico-Theological Lexicon of New Testament Greek,* p. 238, says, "It is only . . . without giving the word its full force, that we can apply the name of *parousia* to the second advent. It is not easy to explain how the term came to be used in this sense." The difficulty is removed when it is recognized that *parousia* is always in Scripture used in its primary sense ("a being present, presence," Liddell & Scott), and that it is never an alternative name for what ordinarily is called the Second Advent, that is, "the Appearing of the Glory of our great God and Savior Jesus Christ." In each case of its occurrence with reference to the Lord the margin of the Revised Version has "Gk., presence." This is not an alternative rendering to that given in the text, but the literal meaning of the word. It is to be regretted that "presence" does not appear in the text in its twenty-four occurrences.

Cramer quotes some suggestive words from Ewald to the effect that the Parousia of Christ corresponds perfectly with the Shekinah of God in the Old Testament. For him also the doctrine of the Coming of Christ is obscured because he attaches a meaning to *parousia* which does not in fact belong to it. It seems too obvious to say that the usage of the word should regulate the theology, and not the theology prescribe the meaning of the word. Yet the neglect of the simple law of exegesis is responsible for some at least of the confusion into which the Hope of the Gospel has been thrown in the minds of many Christians.

we were with Him in the holy mount" (vv. 17, 18). The power and glory of the Lord's Parousia in the Mount of Transfiguration were no doubt anticipative of His future Parousia with His saints, but the passage refers directly to the past, not to the future. The importance of the word in this passage, however, lies not only in the illustration it gives of the meaning "presence" rather than "coming," but in its indication of a set period of time marked by well defined limits. This has a special bearing upon an aspect of the Lord's Second Coming, which calls for subsequent consideration.

The Teaching of 1 Thessalonians

In writing to the Thessalonians Paul makes constant use of the term in a way which makes it impossible to view it as applicable merely to the moment of the Lord's descent into the air. Speaking regretfully of his enforced absence from them, and looking forward joyfully to the certainty of reunion, when Satan's hindrances will be things of the past, and the Lord shall have gathered His people to Himself, he says, "For what is our hope, or joy, or crown of glorying? Are not even ye, before our Lord Jesus at [lit. in] His parousia? For ye are our glory and our joy" (1 Thess. 2:19, 20). Obviously the apostle is thinking of the time and circumstances immediately following upon the rapture of the saints rather than the moment of the rapture itself. The fruit of his service on behalf of the converts would then be seen, both in their presence before the Lord and in the praise and reward they would receive from Him at His Judgment Seat. That would provide abundant compensation for all the trials and afflictions experienced in his labors in the gospel. The converts themselves constituted his hope, which would attain its realization at the time of review; they were also his joy, a present joy, to be consummated at that time; they were his crown of glorying, ample reward to him for the fulfillment of the work committed to him, apart from the crown he would himself receive at the hands of the prize-giver. (F-H, p. 179).

Referring again to the same period, he says, "The Lord make you to increase and abound in love one toward another, and toward all men, even as we also do toward you; to the end He may stablish your hearts unblameable in holiness before our God and Father, at [lit., in] the coming [the parousia] of our Lord Jesus with all His Saints" (3:13). The word "coming" is clearly unsuitable here. It makes the verse appear to indicate the Advent of the Lord with His saints. That will take place at the close of the Parousia; at its commencement He will come for them, and it is to the circumstances of that intervening period itself that the apostle directs our thought in this passage.

His desire for the converts was that their Christian character might be so developed and perfected in this life that at the Judgment Seat in the Lord's Parousia they might stand clear of every possible charge against them. The substitution of "Parousia" for "coming" sets the passage in its true light, and is appropriate to the words which follow. We may observe here that the Parousia is to be with "all the saints"; no saint will be absent, none will have been left behind at the Rapture.

The Parousia period is again in view at the end of this first epistle, where the apostle, as a climax to a series of closing exhortations, expresses wishes for the converts similar to that which we have just been considering, and desires "that the God of peace Himself may sanctify them wholly, and that their whole spirit and soul and body may be preserved entire without blame at [lit., in] the Parousia of our Lord Jesus Christ" (v. 23). They were saints, or sanctified ones, by virtue of their calling. To this he desired that their daily life might correspond, so that, practically devoted to God and kept by His power in every part of their being, they might be found free of blame in the presence of the Lord when their works would be reviewed by Him.

The Teaching of the Apostle John

In anticipation of that time, the apostle John manifests the same jealous care of the spiritual well-being of the subjects of his past labors. "And now, my little children," he says, "abide in Him; that, if He shall be manifested, we may have boldness, and not be ashamed before Him at [or rather in] His parousia" (1 John 2:28). Again the issues of the present life are in view as they will be seen at the Judgment Seat of Christ. That in the words "if He shall be manifested" the apostle is referring to the Lord's coming for His Church is obvious from the succeeding context, where, using the same phrase, he says, "We know that if He shall be manifested, we shall be like Him; for we shall see Him even as He is." The hypothesis is no expression of doubt as to whether the Lord will be manifested; it conveys a warning to the saints to keep in prospect the possibility of the event at any time. The manifestation of the Lord to His saints, and their rapture by Him will be simultaneous. (E-G, p. 179).

The aspirations expressed in the close of the verse go beyond that initial event of the Parousia to the circumstances of the Judgment Seat of Christ. He desires that at that time both he who has cared for the converts to whom he was writing, and they who have been the objects of his care, may have boldness and not be ashamed before the Lord. That would depend upon their present spiritual condition. Would they abide in Christ, and "let that abide in them which they had heard from the beginning"? Or would they backslide and give heed to those who were seeking to lead them astray? By this would be determined their gain or loss of reward in the Parousia. Nor would the issue affect them alone; John who himself had shepherded them was interested in the consequences. The fruit of pastoral care seen in the steadfastness of the believers would lead to joy and boldness in that solemn scene; on their part in the reward bestowed upon them, on the apostle's part in the realization that his labor had not been in vain. On the other hand, faithlessness would lead to shame, through their failure to obtain a reward.

Thus the apostle is not cautioning them against a possibility that when the Lord comes they will shrink back from Him in shame on account of failure, and be left to remain on earth while others who have been faithful are taken away. The scene is heavenly, and the circumstances are those of the Judgment Seat of Christ. The teaching of John is in entire harmony with that of Paul in the passages considered above.

The apostle Peter also, in exhorting elders to a faithful discharge of their pastoral responsibilities toward the flock of God, similarly refers to the manifestation of Christ as the terminus of such service, and points them to the immediately succeeding time of reward for it. "Tend," he says, "the flock of God which is among you, exercising the oversight, not of constraint, but willingly, according unto God; nor yet for filthy lucre, but of a ready mind; neither as lording it over the charge allotted to you, but making yourselves ensamples to the flock. And when the Chief Shepherd shall be manifested, ye shall receive the crown of glory that fadeth not away" (1 Pet. 5:2–4). The manifestation of Christ for the removal of His saints from the earth is thus, in this passage also, shown to be the preliminary to His review of their earthly service when they stand before his Judgment Seat.

Other Descriptions of the Same Period

The Parousia, then, is not a momentary event, but a period during which Christ will be present with His saints after coming into the air to receive them to Himself, and will test their works as His servants with a view to rewarding them. The period is otherwise described by the following expressions, "the day of Christ" (Phil. 1:10; 2:16), "the day of Jesus Christ" (Phil. 1:6), "the day of the Lord Jesus" (1 Cor. 5:5; 2 Cor. 1:14), and "the day of our Lord Jesus Christ" (1 Cor. 1:8). It will be observed that in each of these designations one or both of the titles "Jesus" and "Christ" is used, and an examination of the passages will show that the reference is in each case to the time of the Parousia, and that this group of expressions is to be distinguished from "the day of the Lord," which latter refers to a period of an entirely different character. We will take the passages in the epistle to the Philippians first.

In recording his joy in the constant fellowship of the Philippian converts in the furtherance of the gospel, Paul asserts his confidence that "God who began a good work in them would perfect it until the day of Jesus Christ" (Phil. 1:6). That is to say, that through the power of God their steadfastness would continue throughout the time of their earthly service so that all would be estimated at its true value by Christ in the day when they would appear before Him at His Judgment Seat. Again, as he had prayed for the Thessalonian converts in view of the Parousia, that they might walk in love and be found blameless at that time, so now he prays for those at Philippi, "that their love may abound yet more and more in knowledge and all discernment; so that they may approve the things that are excellent; and be sincere and void of offense, until the day of Christ" (1:9, 10), a clear identification of that period with the Parousia. Similarly, as he regarded the Thessalonians as his hope and joy and crown of glorying before the Lord in His Parousia, seeing that their faithfulness and steadfastness were the fruit of his labor, so now he exhorts the Philippians "that they may be blameless and harmless and shine as lights in the world, holding forth the Word of life; that he may have whereof to glory in the day of Christ, that he did not run in vain, nor labor in vain" (2:15, 16). Thus, once more, the thought and language concerning that day are identical with those concerning the Parousia.

So at the outset of his epistle to the church at Corinth he expresses the assurance that the Lord will confirm them unto the end, that is, the end of their course on earth, so that they may be "unreproveable in the day of our Lord Jesus Christ," and reminds them of the faithfulness of God to undertake this confirmation, since He had called them into the fellowship of His Son (1 Cor. 1:8, 9). Parallel, again, with the sentiments in the other epistles above referred to is the expression, in the second epistle to the Corinthians, of his joy in the converts in prospect of that day. "We are your glorying," he says, "even as ye also are ours, in the day of our Lord Jesus" (2 Cor. 1:14).

The addition of the first clause of this verse is an appeal against the efforts and influence of the enemies who were seeking to depreciate the apostle's character and service in the eyes of the Corinthian church, and thus to undermine his work. Had he not brought the gospel to them? Were not the blessings they had received due to his ministry? Not only would they be his joy in the coming day as the fruit of his toil, but they would then rejoice in seeing him rewarded for his faithful service and testimony on their behalf.

Again, in giving instruction as to the discipline of one who was guilty of moral obliquity the apostle views the circumstances in the light of the same period of judgment. Discipline was necessary not only for the present welfare of the church, but for the ultimate benefit of the erring individual. He was "to be delivered unto Satan for the destruction of the flesh, that the spirit might be saved in the day of the Lord Jesus" (1 Cor. 5:5). The word "day" is constantly associated with judgment, inasmuch as the day, in contrast with the night, reveals things in their true character. Thus Paul says concerning his own service, "With me it is a very small thing that I should be judged of you, or of man's judgment [lit. man's day]: yea, I judge not mine own self. For I know nothing against myself; yet I am not hereby justified: but he that judgeth me is the Lord. Wherefore judge nothing before, until the Lord come, who will both bring to light the hidden things of darkness, and make manifest the counsels of the hearts; and then shall each man have his praise from God" (1 Cor. 4:3–5).

Man's day is the time when man passes judgment on things. The day of our Lord Jesus Christ will be the time when He will pass judgment on the service of His saints. "Each man's work shall be made manifest; for, the day shall declare it [i.e., the day in which Christ judges the work will manifest its real character] because it is revealed in fire; and the fire itself shall prove each man's work of what sort it is. If any man's work shall abide which he built thereon, he shall receive a reward. If any man's work shall be burned, he shall suffer loss; but he himself shall be saved; yet so as through fire" (3:13–15).

The Day of the Lord—A Distinction

Clearly, all these passages refer to the time and circumstances of the Parousia of Christ with His saints. On the other hand, "the Day of the Lord" is never used in reference to these events; it relates always to the Lord's judgment on the world and His personal intervention in its affairs, a subject which calls for more detailed consideration in another chapter.

In this connection, however, it is important to observe the correct reading of 2 Thessalonians 2:2, where the Revised Version rightly gives "the Day of the Lord" instead of "the Day of Christ" as in the Authorized Version. As the passage is connected with the Parousia we must consider it somewhat closely.

In the first chapter Paul had spoken of the future revelation of the Lord Jesus from heaven, "with the angels of His power in flaming fire, rendering vengeance to them that know not God, and to them that obey not the gospel of our Lord Jesus." At that time His saints, having been with Him in His Parousia, will accompany Him in manifested glory; "He shall come to be glorified in His saints, and to be marveled at in all them that believed" (2 Thess. 1:7–10). "When Christ . . . shall be manifested, then shall ye also with Him be manifested in glory" (Col. 3:4). The divine vengeance then rendered will usher in the Day of the Lord, and the apostle speaks of it in order to prepare for correcting a wrong impression entertained by the Thessalonian converts concerning that day. They were being told that the Day of the Lord had begun already, and their minds were consequently disturbed in relation to the Rapture and the Parousia. Paul had himself written to them that Christ would come and gather to Himself in resurrection power both their departed who had fallen asleep and the living together with them, and that certain events were destined to take place in the world prior to the beginning of the Day of the Lord. If, then, the latter had already set in, they might well be perplexed and troubled concerning His promised coming to receive them unto Himself.

Accordingly he must write again to correct their ideas concerning both events, and show the distinction between the Parousia and the Day of the Lord. In reminding them of the conditions which were inevitably to exist in the world ere that day begins, he would at the same time be regulating their view regarding the Parousia. This he does at the commencement of chapter two, as follows:

"Now we beseech you, brethren, touching [the Greek preposition, *huper,* is, lit., on behalf of, i.e., with a view to correcting your thoughts about] the coming [the parousia] of our Lord Jesus Christ, and our gathering together unto Him [i.e., at the rapture of the saints, as mentioned in 1 Thess. 4:17]; to the end that ye be not quickly shaken from your mind [i.e., become unsettled in your convictions and the steadfast purposes consequent upon them], nor yet be troubled, either by spirit, or by word, or by epistle as from us [i.e., a letter purporting to be from Paul], as that the Day of the Lord is now present [i.e., has already commenced]: let no man beguile you in any wise: for it will not be [i.e., the Day of the Lord will not set in] except the falling away [the apostasy from God and His truth] come first, and the man of sin be revealed."

Thus an understanding of the conditions which must necessarily precede the Day of the Lord would set their mind at rest concerning the Parousia. The apostle shows them that the man of sin is to be overthrown by the Lord "at the manifestation of His coming" (v. 8). Literally the phrase is "at the epiphany of His Parousia" or "the shining forth of His Presence." This event coincides with "the revelation of the Lord Jesus" mentioned in 1:7, and marks the close of the Parousia. (H-J, p. 179).

The Parousia Reviewed

Briefly summing up, the Parousia is a period which will commence with the coming of Christ into the air to raise the dead saints, change the living, and receive all together to Himself. They will render an account of their stewardship at His Judgment Seat, receiving rewards or suffering loss according to the measure of their faithfulness. The time of the duration of the Parousia is not definitely intimated in Scripture. Heavenly in its character it stands in contrast to circumstances in the world, which, after the removal of the church, will come under the judgments of God. At the conclusion of the Parousia the Lord will come with His angels and with His saints in manifested glory for the overthrow of His foes, an event which is described as "the manifestation of His Parousia."*

*The beginning of the Parousia of Christ is prominent in 1 Corinthians 15:23; 1 Thessalonians 4:15; 5:23; 2 Thessalonians 2:1; James 5:7, 8; and 2 Peter 3:4; its course in 1 Thessalonians 2:19; 3:13; Matthew 24:3, 37, 39; and 1 John 2:28; its conclusion in Matthew 24:27; and 2 Thessalonians 2:8. From the Writers' *Notes on the Thessalonians*.

▪ CHAPTER SIX ▪

The Judgment Seat of Christ

The period F-H, page 179, described in the New Testament as the Parousia, and the day of Christ, are of peculiar interest to the Christian, for in it his course of life is to be reviewed in order that he may be rewarded for all that he has done and suffered during the time of his responsibility in the world. Now this judgment is to be distinguished sharply from the judgment of the nations described in Matthew 25:31–46, for that is to take place after the appearing of the Lord in glory (H-J, p. 179), and its venue is the earth, whereas the judgment of which we now speak takes place "in the air" and between the Rapture and the Second Advent. At the former some are pronounced accursed and dismissed to eternal punishment, whereas at the latter no such condemnation is possible, as the conditions under which it is to be held plainly show. On the other hand, it is to be distinguished with equal clearness from the judgment of the Great White Throne, which takes place after the final catastrophe has overtaken Satan and his hosts at the close of the Millennium (Rev. 20:11–15). The terms in which these three judgments are described preclude any possibility of confusing them. It is essential, however, that the different writers must be allowed to know what they meant to say, and to have said what they meant. It is too readily assumed that meaning one thing they said another, or that, however differently they describe it, yet they all, and always, refer to the same general judgment. The Scriptures certainly cannot be made to mean that the world is rushing on to a final conflagration, to be followed by a universal assize. The words in which the Holy Spirit has spoken are not responsible for the widespread confusion of mind on the subject. Rather is that the result of careless reading, or of failure to credit the writers of Scripture with ordinary intelligence and honesty.

There are several passages in which the Judgment Seat of Christ is described; the principle of these now fall to be considered.

The word, translated, Judgment Seat is *bēma,* whereas the word used in each of the other cases (Matt. 25:31; Rev. 20:11) is *thronos,* the English word throne. This latter word is reserved in the New Testament for the symbol of authority in the heavenlies, whether good or evil, including that of God Himself. The only exception to this rule is the throne of David (Luke 1:32), which is referred to, significantly enough, only in a prophecy concerning the rule over Israel of "great David's greater Son." Even the throne of Imperial Caesar is called a *bēma,* as is that before which the Lord Jesus was condemned to death by Pilate (Acts 18:12; John 19:13). It will be seen, therefore, that the word lacks nothing in dignity as a symbol of competent authority. Its associations are of the most impressive character. Solemn, indeed, must be the issues involved for all who stand before a tribunal so entitled.

The time of the Judgment Seat of Christ is to be learned from the language of the Lord, recorded in Luke 14:14, "thou shalt be recompensed in the resurrection of the just." But this point need not be elaborated here in view of what has been written in an earlier chapter.*

This Judgment Seat is twice named, once as "of God," and once as "of Christ" (Rom. 14:10; 2 Cor. 5:10). These are not two but one, however, for "neither doth the Father judge any man, but He hath given all judgment unto the Son; that all may honor the Son even as they honor the Father. . . . And He gave Him authority to execute judgment because He is [the] Son of Man" (John 5:22, 23, 27). That there is but one judge is also plain from 1 Corinthians 4:5, "judge nothing before the time, until the Lord come, Who will both bring

*See chapter 5; see also chapter 10.

to light the hidden things of darkness, and make manifest the counsels of the hearts; and then shall each man have his praise from God." The reference to His coming makes it evident that by Lord the apostle here means the Lord Jesus, while the praise is said to come from God. The words of the apostle are thus in harmony with those of the Lord Himself.

Christians Alone to Stand Thereat

As to the persons who are to come before this Judgment Seat many Scriptures testify. The passage in the first epistle to the Corinthians (3:10—4:5) contemplates the Christians at Corinth: "ye are Christ's," says the apostle, "ye are a temple of God." They had been built upon, and were themselves builders upon, the foundation, the Lord Jesus Christ. The passage in Romans 14:1–12 is equally explicit. A man might be weak in faith, indeed, but that is a description which can be true only of one who is in Christ. God has received him; he is the servant of God. These are brethren sinning against brethren, but still they "are the Lord's." The other leading Scripture (2 Cor. 5:1–10), also contemplates Christians, and like the others, Christians alone. "The Church of God . . . with all the saints" is addressed (1:1). Sometimes the apostle speaks to them directly, "you," "your," as in 4:14, 15, for example; sometimes he associates them with himself, as in each of the verses from 1 to 9 of chapter 5. The conclusion is hardly to be resisted that in verse 10 also, "we" refers to Christians, and to Christians alone. There is no hint that the writer enlarges the scope of his address as he passes from one statement to another. The "we" who walk by faith, not by sight, who make it their ambition to be well-pleasing to God, who have received God's Spirit, who hope for the coming of the Lord, and who are yet of good courage in the face of death, are the "we" who "must all be made manifest before the Judgment Seat of Christ."

This follows also from the fact that this judgment takes place during the Parousia, and there is nothing said concerning others than Christians in connection with that. None save those who belong to Christ, living or dead, share in the Rapture that will usher us into the presence of the Lord when He descends into the air.

One other thing, already mentioned in a former chapter, must here be remembered. When Christians are taken away to be with the Lord Jesus they will be changed, "the body of our humiliation" will be "conformed to the body of His glory" (Phil. 3:20). It is clear, then, that the judgment with which we are now dealing is not concerned with the innocence or guilt of those who appear thereat. The matter of sin and salvation was, for them, settled long ago.* At the Judgment Seat of Christ no question is raised of their right to share in the salvation which brings them into the Parousia. They are there because they had become the children of God through faith in Christ Jesus; because they had been redeemed through His blood, and had received the forgiveness of their sins. The purpose of this judgment is in another direction altogether. What that purpose is we may learn from a brief consideration of the Scriptures already mentioned.

Salvation and Judgment

The broad principle underlying all God's dealings with men is, that salvation is always by grace, that judgment is always according to works. To this rule there is no exception. No one ever was saved, no one ever will be saved, because he deserves salvation. No one ever will be condemned save because the character of his ways demanded that he should be punished. No one will ever be rewarded save as in his ways and acts the reward has been earned. These are the right ways of God; their justice is beyond dispute.†

The apostle had heard tidings from Corinth that called for firm yet affectionate dealing with those whom he rightly regarded as his children in the gospel. He had laid the foundation of the church there and that foundation was Christ. Now they were building upon that foun-

*See chapter 1.

†*Misthos,* usually rendered reward, is rendered "wages" in Romans 6:23, and "hire" in 1 Timothy 5:18. That is, it refers to something earned, not merely bestowed.

dation. What manner of building would it be? He does not seem to be addressing any particular class in the church. All are builders, each in his measure is adding something to the structure; it might be "gold, silver, costly stones," but then it might be "wood, hay, stubble." One or the other they must be building into it. No person can be a member of a church without modifying its character, in a good way or in a bad; without adding to its fabric either noble and worthy things or things mean and worthless. Let each person (not the men only, for no noun is expressed) "take heed how he buildeth." Why? Because "each man's [person's] work shall be made manifest: for the day shall declare it." That is, the day of Christ, as we have already seen. For worthy work there is a reward, for He has said, "Behold, I come quickly; and My reward is with Me, to render to each man [person] according as his work is" (Rev. 22:12). If, on the other hand, the building has been of a mean, unworthy character, then that person shall "suffer loss," though "he himself shall be saved [shall be caught away at the Rapture] yet so as through fire." The possibility is thus presented to the Christian that at that judgment he may be without the word of praise and the crown which it is the joy of God to give to every faithful soul.

The Christian and the Church

It is in immediate connection with the life of the church that the apostle is speaking. The church in view here, however, is not "the Church which is His [Christ's body]," but the gathering in any place of those who name the Name of Christ, and in whose midst He is. The whole passage is intended to raise our conception of the responsibility of membership in such a church, and to teach us that each is expected by the Lord of the church to contribute his share to its corporate life, in view of the day when each must give account to Him. The thoughts of God concerning such churches are readily learned from the language he uses concerning this at Corinth: "Know ye not that ye are a sanctuary [marg.] of God, and that the Spirit of God dwelleth in [among] you?" What follows, then, if God dwells not in a house made with hands, but in the midst of His redeemed people? This, that what a man does to the church, that will God do to Him. "If any man destroyeth the sanctuary of God, him shall God destroy." And, conversely, if any man builds up, cheers, encourages, strengthens, by word or by example, the sanctuary of God, him will God assuredly reward (1 Cor. 3:10–17).

In the second epistle the apostle approaches the subject along a different line. Here the church is not directly before his mind, but the Christian in the whole round of his life. Of course the result is the same, for men do not live their lives in watertight compartments, and what a man is in his daily walk and conversation affects the church of which he is a member. He will be the same man, not a different one, on Sundays as on each of the other days of the week. The apostle is thinking of the certainty, and indeed of the near approach, of the end of opportunity for service. But whether it be by way of death, or by way of the immediate clothing upon with the new and heavenly body, this at least was assured, they would, one and all, "be made manifest before the Judgment Seat of Christ" (2 Cor. 5:10). The word "make manifest" suggests an open display. It is the summation of those other words in 1 Corinthians 4:5, "the Lord . . . will both bring to light the hidden things of darkness, and make manifest the counsels of the hearts."

The purpose of the words is plain. It is that we should neither do nor allow now that of which we know we would be ashamed then. The thought of the Judgment Seat of Christ is a deterrent from word and act inconsistent with the Name of the Lord, and a stimulus to the ambition to manifest every grace He manifested in His ways when He dwelt among men. It is true that our consciousness of sinfulness ("conscience of sins," Heb. 10:2), makes us shrink from the revelations of that day. But we need to correct our thoughts by at least two considerations. Then, with sin eliminated, we shall hate sin as sin, and as we ought to hate it now. We shall rejoice in the completeness of the Lord's victory over sin in us. Love of what is true will become so real that we shall have no desire to appear other than we are, as men have endeavored to appear ever since the day in which Adam and

Eve attempted to hide themselves in the thicket from the eye of God.

We should not dread anything that to the Lord seems wise and right; otherwise the question might well be asked, Where is your faith? Moreover, do not our delinquencies and failures, in a word, our sins, bring the Name of the Lord into disrepute, causing it to be blasphemed? At that day His name will be cleared. What belongs to Him in us, the fruit of His Spirit, will remain to His praise and glory and honor (1 Pet. 1:7). The rest will pass; that will be to our loss, indeed, but would we have it otherwise? The loss will not be of the worthless material built into life, the "burning" of that will be deliverance, and insofar gain, not loss. The loss will be of the glory to God and of the reward to us that might have been ours had we lived in accordance with His Word.

"Knowing, therefore, the fear of the Lord," the apostle proceeds. Not "terror," as in the Authorized Version, as though he had the judgment of God upon the ungodly before his mind, warning them to flee from wrath to come. Rather he is thinking of the character of the Lord, His holiness and righteousness; of what is due to Him and what He requires of, and inspires in, us. He is thinking also of his responsibility to answer from his own life and service, and urging upon the Christians at Corinth, and upon us in our day also, to hold our walk and conversation, and to fulfill our appointed service, as those who must give account thereof to such a Lord.

Sowing and Reaping

It is "the Lord, the righteous Judge" (2 Tim. 4:8), before Whom we are to be made manifest. And the principle on which He judges is declared, "whatsoever a man soweth, that shall he also reap" (Gal. 6:7). Hence the repetition of the word "destroy" in 1 Corinthians 3:17, to which attention has already been drawn. Hence, too, the words of 2 Corinthians 5:10, "that each one may receive the things done by means of [marg.] the body, according to what he hath done [lit., practiced], whether it be good or bad." The present body is the implement by which the will of the man is carried out; in the resurrection body the reward of his conduct will be received; if good, in some happy recognition as the wisdom of the Lord shall prescribe; if ill, in the loss of that which it would have rejoiced the Lord to give.

The words of Colossians 3:23–25 are in harmony with this principle also. "Whatsoever ye do, work from the soul, as unto the Lord, and not unto men; knowing that from the Lord ye shall receive the recompense of the inheritance: ye serve the Lord Christ. For he that doeth wrong shall receive again the wrong that he hath done [marg.]: and there is no respect of persons." The significance of the words is heightened by their context; they occur in the midst of a series of exhortations addressed to wives, husbands, children, servants and masters. Thus, and not otherwise, is life to be lived by all those, of whatever station in life, who hold the Name and the Word of the Lord in reverence.

"Shall receive again the wrong done." It may be difficult for us to conceive how God will fulfill this word to those who are already in bodies of glory, partakers of the joy of the redeemed in salvation consummated in spirit, soul and body. Yet may we be assured that the operation of this law is not to be suspended even in their case. He that "knoweth how to deliver the godly out of temptation, and to keep the unrighteous under punishment unto the day of judgment" (2 Pet. 2:9), knows also how to direct and to use the working of His law of sowing and reaping in the case of His children also. The attempt to alleviate the text of some of its weight by suggesting that the law operates only in this life, fails, for there is nothing in the text or context to lead the reader to think other than that while the sowing is here, the reaping is hereafter. It is clear that if it were not for this supposed difficulty of referring the words to the Christian in the condition in which, as we know from other Scriptures, he will appear at the Judgment Seat of Christ, the question whether that time and place were intended would not be raised.

The parallel passage in Ephesians 6:8 is varied in a direction that carries comfort, and gives courage to the Christian to be "zealous of good works." It runs thus, "knowing that whatsoever good thing each one doeth, the same shall he receive again from the Lord."

Concerning Crowns

The reward is assured, equally so the loss; nevertheless it is also written concerning the crownless at that day that they themselves shall be saved, yet so as through the fire (1 Cor. 3:15). For the crowns of which the Scripture speaks are rewards that must be earned; they are not the common heritage of the saints, falling to them by the operation of grace and without regard to works. A crown is not the equivalent of salvation; it is an inducement offered to those who have trusted the Lord to manifest their faith in obedience. It is the reward of the race and the fight for them that strive, and that strive lawfully, that they may attain. In his words to the Corinthian believers the apostle is not concerned about his salvation, whether or no he will be taken away with all those "that are Christ's" at His Parousia. For him that is a matter settled when he was delivered out of the power of darkness into the Kingdom of the Son of His [God's] love, for from that moment he was reckoned among the redeemed, among those who had obtained the forgiveness of their sins "through the Blood of His [Christ's] Cross"(Col. 1:13). What did concern him was lest having urged others to run with purpose he himself should, through relaxed vigilance and effort, fail to win the Amaranthine Crown.*

Years afterward, when the end of his service seemed very near indeed, the apostle wrote to the Philippians that he had but one ambition, that he might "gain Christ," that he might "know Him, and the power of His Resurrection, and the fellowship of His sufferings," that so he might become "conformed unto His Death." "If by any means," he continues, "I may attain unto the resurrection from the dead" (3:8–13). The word *(exanastasis)* is not elsewhere used in the New Testament. Is he now uncertain whether he will have any part in the resurrection and rapture of those that belong to Christ, the assurance of which it had pleased God to give to him many years before (1 Thess. 4:17) and to so many others through his voice and pen? Once more he is not concerned here about his salvation, for of that he had long been assured, and in it he had long rejoiced; whereas of this which now occupies him he declares that he is not yet in possession. Obviously not, if he is thinking of the resurrection of which he wrote in 1 Corinthians 15. Why should he pause to assert twice what was so evident? Moreover, a few sentences further on he declares himself to be among those who are waiting for the Lord from heaven (v. 20).

Is it possible that he has in mind an earlier resurrection than that of which he had previously written? To this solution there are at least two objections. He does not elsewhere refer to any such event.† Moreover, the desire for resurrection would include the desire for death, and the apostle never elsewhere expressed himself in this sense. Of death, as we have seen in an earlier chapter, he has no fear; but he does not desire it. He looks, even longs for, the coming of the Lord. And if, earlier in this letter to the Philippians (1:23) he speaks of the prospect of death as a happy one, that is only in comparison with his toils and sufferings here, and in the assurance that to depart is to be with Christ, "to have died is gain."‡

*Crowns, in the New Testament, are promised to the Christian as rewards for patient endurance or for faithful service. Cp.:

"An incorruptible crown," a general description applicable to all rewards promised to those who stand approved before the Judgment Seat of Christ (1 Cor. 9:25).

"The crown of righteousness," describing the character of the reward corresponding to the character of the giver (2 Tim. 4:8).

"The crown of life," describing the permanent nature of the reward, in contrast to the transient experience of trial in which it is won, and corresponding to the nature of the Living God Who gives it (James 1:12; Rev. 2:10).

"The crown of unfading glory, describing the reward of those who give themselves without ostentation, and without hope of gain, to the care of the flock in the absence of the Chief Shepherd (1 Pet. 5:4).

—From *Notes on the Thessalonians.*

†See chapter 5.

‡Philippians 1:21. "The tense denotes not the act of dying but the consequence of dying, the state after death," *Lightfoot.* And so what the apostle contemplates after the spirit leaves the body is not quiescence, sleep, oblivion, but a nearer sense of the presence of Christ and a more intimate communion with Him than is possible now. See Appendix, Note F.

The "out-resurrection from among the dead," toward which the apostle aspires so warmly here, is that which he describes in Romans 6:4 as the "walk in newness of life." He had urged others to reckon themselves "to be dead unto sin, but alive unto God in Christ Jesus" (v. 11), and these words to the Philippians reveal the same ambition in his own soul. Having preached to others he did not wish himself to fail of the prize that awaits those who live as baptized persons should. The difference in the form of expression is accounted for by the different purpose and method of the two epistles. In Romans, a more or less formal treatise, written to a church with which he had had no direct personal relationship, he is expounding and enforcing a doctrine. In Philippians, a letter breathing in every sentence the warmth of personal interest and feeling, because it is written to people whom he knew and loved as his children in the faith, he reveals the ambition of his own heart. In the one he is the teacher, propounding with authority the doctrines of the gospel. In the other he is the living example of the things he teaches. The "prize of the high calling of God in Christ Jesus" (Phil. 3:14) is the "incorruptible crown," "the crown of righteousness," of 1 Corinthians 9:25 and 2 Timothy 4:8.* It is probable that these rewards should be conceived of as suggested in the parable of the talents, "His Lord said unto him, Well done, good and faithful servant: thou hast been faithful over a few things, I will set thee over many things" (Matt. 25:21). For heaven is not a place of happy inactivity, of "ease with dignity," as though eternal youth could be happy, or even content, in idleness! Nor yet will that state be one in which energy is expended selfishly or aimlessly. For it is written that "His servants shall do Him service" there (Rev. 22:3).

**Ano*, here rendered "above" appears again in Colossians 3:1, 2. This seems to fix the meaning of the word here. The apostle who urges the Colossians to "seek the things that are above, where Christ is, seated on the right hand of God," and to set their minds "on the things that are above, not on things that are upon the earth," declares that this also is his own aim. "The prize of the high calling" and "the things that are above" seem to be alternative expressions of the same idea.

▪ CHAPTER SEVEN ▪

The Epiphany of the Parousia

"The vision is nearing,
The Judge and the Throne!
The voice of the Angel
Proclaims "It is done."
On the whirl of the tempest
Its Ruler shall come
And the blaze of His glory
Flash out from its gloom."

We are to be occupied in this chapter with what Scripture states concerning the closing scenes of the present dispensation. The testimony of the sacred page at once discourages any hope that the deliverance of mankind in general from its miseries and sorrows is to be achieved by human effort, or by some evolutionary process of amelioration, or even by the preaching of the gospel. Not that the Word of God holds out no hope of the future deliverance of the human race. The belief that the golden age, sung by poets and depicted by idealists, will one day dawn, is confirmed in all parts of the book. For the introduction of this millennial era God has His own plans. Concerning these the writers of Scripture are in complete agreement. The agencies of civilization find no place in the divine scheme for the redemption of the world. The wisest and most powerful enterprises on the part of man cannot banish the cause of the evil which stands in the way of deliverance.

Let it be clearly understood that we are not disparaging humanitarian efforts for the alleviation of suffering and misery. It would ill become those who profess to be followers of Christ to do so. He Himself ever had a heart of compassion for the afflicted and woebegone, and expects those who acknowledge Him as Master and Lord to share His sympathies and to be ready to every good work. Did He not send His disciples out, not only to preach the gospel, but to heal the sick? We seek to show in another chapter that the expectation of the Lord's return, so far from being incompatible with such practical Christianity, is calculated to stimulate Christians to engage in it. Failure to do so, on the part of any who profess to look for His appearing, is only to their shame. We each have our part to do in seeking to diminish the sum of human wretchedness. Let not a word be uttered to underestimate or discourage schemes of improvement, philanthropic, social, economic, political! Yet we must not fail to point out that the root of social and national evils lies too deep for these agencies to eradicate.

Sin does not come merely by ignorance; therefore it cannot be removed by knowledge. Sin does not come merely by environment; therefore it cannot be expelled by improved circumstances. Sin does not come merely by poverty; therefore it cannot be annihilated by economic changes. The redemption of the race from the cause of the evils which divide it, and work mischief and misery in it, must come about by the direct intervention of the Son of God, Who has already laid the basis of this redemption in His atoning sacrifice at Calvary. He Himself will introduce millennial blessing into the world, not by coming into a realm made ready for Him by human instrumentality, but by the sudden overthrow of the mighty forces of evil, human and superhuman, which will continue their opposition unabated till the end of this dispensation.

The End of the Age

The Word of God gives a dark picture of the condition of the world at the close of the present age. The apostle Paul says, "In the last days grievous times shall come. For men shall be lovers of self, lovers of money, boastful, haughty, railers, disobedient to parents, unthankful, unholy, without natural affection, implacable, slanderers, without self-control, fierce, no lovers of good, traitors, headstrong, puffed up, lovers of pleasure rather than lovers of God; holding a form of godliness, but having denied the power thereof" (2 Tim. 3:1–5). There is certainly nothing to indicate in present-day conditions that the apostle's predictions will be stultified, nor yet his further forecast, that "evil men and impostors shall wax worse and worse, deceiving and being deceived" (v. 13).

Again, the Lord paralleled the state of humanity at the close of this era with that prevailing in the days of Noah immediately prior to the Flood, and, further, with that of the cities of the plain in the time of Lot. He says, "And as it came to pass in the days of Noah, even so shall it be in the days of the Son of man. They ate, they drank, they married, they were given in marriage, until the day that Noah entered into the ark, and the flood came, and destroyed them all. Likewise even as it came to pass in the days of Lot; they ate, they drank, they bought, they sold, they planted, they builded; but in the day that Lot went out from Sodom it rained fire and brimstone from heaven, and destroyed them all; after the same manner shall it be in the day that the Son of man is revealed" (Luke 17:26–30). Not that these pursuits were in either case evil in themselves. The sin lay in excluding God from their thoughts, the while they engaged in lawful occupations. This condition the Lord signalizes as characteristic of mankind at the end of the present era. The moral result of "refusing to have God in knowledge" is recorded in the Old Testament history of the times of Noah and Lot, and in the first chapter of Paul's epistle to the Romans.

A League of Nations

Again, men hope for universal peace and safety by the eventual abolition of militarism as the weapon of lust for conquest and supremacy, and by the establishment of international and democratic unity. Christ, Who has proved accurate in His prediction that during this dispensation "nation would rise against nation, and kingdom against kingdom, and that there would be great earthquakes, and in divers places famines and pestilences," also stated at the same time that, instead of the prevalence of rest and security at the end of the age, "there shall be signs in the sun and moon and stars; and upon the earth distress of nations in perplexity for the roaring of the sea and billows; men fainting for fear, and for expectation of the things which are coming on the world: for the powers of the heavens shall be shaken" (Luke 21:10, 11, 25, 26). In proof that the time of the end is here in view He immediately after said, "And then shall they see the Son of man coming in a cloud with power and great glory," an event which will introduce the next age. It must be clear therefore that human statescraft cannot achieve universal success.

Such a League of Nations, for instance, as is proposed today as a panacea for national wrongs, not only has been foretold in Scripture as the last resource of international politics, but its failure has likewise been predicted. The various Gentile empires which were to hold dominions of a more or less worldwide character were made known to the prophet Daniel. These were symbolized as beasts. The fourth and last beast, i.e., the final form of Gentile rule, was seen to have ten horns. The interpretation of the vision is as follows: "The fourth beast shall be diverse from all the kingdoms . . . and as for the ten horns, out of this kingdom shall ten kings arise" (Dan. 7:23, 24). In the preceding part of the chapter the beast is personified (v. 17) and the symbol stands both for the imperial head and for his dominion. A corresponding vision was given to the apostle John. He also saw a beast with ten horns, and the symbolism is again explained, but in greater detail: "The ten horns that thou sawest are ten kings, which have received no kingdom as yet; but they receive authority as kings, with the beast, for one hour [i.e., for a brief time]. These have one mind, and they give their power and authority unto the beast" (Rev. 17:12, 13). Obviously these ten kingdoms are contemporaneous. The potentates ruling over them agree to a certain policy in handing over their authority to a superior ruler. No such league has existed in human history as yet.

It is manifest, too, from this Scripture that the existence of the league will provide the opportunity for a man sufficiently strong to dominate the situation. Of this man, and of the way in which he and his confederacy and power will come to their end by the revelation of the Son of God in judgment upon them, more presently. Their overthrow is sufficiently clear from the words which follow: "These [i.e., the beast and his confederate kings] shall make war against the Lamb, and the Lamb shall overcome them; and they also shall overcome that are with Him, called and chosen and faithful" (v. 14).

This personal intervention of Christ in the affairs of the world marks the close of His Parousia with His saints in the air, which formed the subject of a preceding chapter. It thereby also constitutes, as we shall see, the introductory event of the Day of the Lord, Paul describes it as "the manifestation [lit., the epiphany, i.e., the shining forth] of His parousia" (2 Thess. 2:8); and the Lord Himself spoke of it as follows: "For as the lightning cometh forth from the east, and is seen even unto the west; so shall be the Parousia of the Son of man" (Matt. 24:27). The Parousia of the Son of man is the Parousia viewed from the earthly standpoint. His Parousia with His saints in the heavenlies will be made known to men only when it is revealed. From its purely heavenly standpoint, as synchronizing with "the Day of Christ," or the period of His Judgment Seat for the review of the service of His saints, the Parousia then terminates. He then will come forth with them in manifested glory, and the Day of the Lord will begin.

Things That Differ

Certain events, such as the Great Tribulation, signs and judgments from heaven, and great distress in the earth, are destined to precede the Day of the Lord, and thus are to be distinguished from it. This is clear from a comparison of the prophecy of Joel, quoted by the apostle Peter, with the words of the Lord concerning the time of the Great Tribulation. Joel's prophecy is, "And I will show wonders in the heavens and in the earth, blood, and fire, and pillars of smoke. The sun shall be turned into darkness, and the moon into blood, before the great and terrible day of the Lord come" (Joel 2:30, 31). Peter speaks of it as "the day of the Lord . . . that great and notable day" (Acts 2:20).

The Lord Himself, speaking of the Tribulation, says, "Immediately after the tribulation of those days, the sun shall be darkened, and the moon shall not give her light, and the stars shall fall from heaven, and the powers of the heavens shall be shaken: and then shall appear the sign of the Son of man in heaven: and then shall all the tribes of the earth mourn, and they shall see the Son of man coming on the clouds of heaven with power and great glory" (Matt. 24:29, 30).

The Great Tribulation is "the time of Jacob's trouble," i.e., the fierce persecution of the Jews by the Antichrist. (G-J, p. 179). The Day of the Lord is the time of the personal exercise of Christ's authority in the world, and will be ushered in by His appearing in glory. (J-B, p. 179). The Day of the Lord is never spoken of in Scripture as referring to the Great Tribulation. The latter is also to be distinguished from the divine judgments to be manifested immediately before the Day of the Lord, the signs in the heavens and earth mentioned in the passage just quoted from Joel.

We have, then, a fixed order foretold. First, the Great Tribulation; second, signs in the sun, moon, and stars (Luke adds "distress of nations, men fainting for fear and for expectation of the things which are coming on the world, and the shaking of the powers of the heavens," Luke 21:25, 26); and, third, the revelation of the Son of man. Joel and Peter show that the signs in the heavens immediately precede the Day of the Lord; Christ showed that they immediately succeed the Great Tribulation, and immediately precede His manifestation as the Son of man. Accordingly His revelation in power and great glory, will be coincidental with the inception of the Day of the Lord. (H-J, p. 179).

That the Jewish people are to be the sufferers in the Great Tribulation is clear from the following Scriptures. Jeremiah prophesied that no period of tribulation will equal that of "Jacob's trouble," i.e., of the Jewish nation (Jer. 30:7). To Daniel it was foretold concerning his people, the Jews, that there would be a time of trouble "such as never was since there was a nation even to that time" (Dan. 12:1). The Lord said of the Great Tribulation that it will be "such as hath not been from the beginning of the world until now, no nor ever shall be" (Matt. 24:21). Wherever there are Jews at that time they will suffer in this worldwide pogrom. For, while prior to this they are to be nationally reinstated in Palestine, they will not all be resident there; considerable numbers will still be living in other countries. Accordingly, those who have been put to death in the Tribulation and are seen in the apocalyptic vision standing "before the Throne and before the Lamb," are said to have come "out of every nation, and of all tribes and peoples and tongues" (Rev. 7:9 and 14).

"The sign of the Son of man," is probably to be understood subjectively. There are to be preceding signs in the heavens, immediately after the Great Tribulation, but the sign of the Son of man is not to be classed with those. He will be His own sign. That is to say, the words may be understood as equivalent to "the sign which is the Son of man," and not as indicating a sign heralding His appearance. This is confirmed, perhaps, by the order of events given in Revelation 6, which correspond to that in Matthew 24. First there are preliminary judgments, war and famine and pestilence (vv. 1–8), then the signs in heaven (vv. 12, 13), and finally the appearance of the Lord in person, at the "shining out of His Parousia." That is the sign of the Son of man. The effect of this is that "the kings of the earth, and the princes, and the chief captains, and the rich, and the strong, and every bondman, and freeman, hide themselves in the caves, and in the rocks of the mountains: and they say to the mountains and to the rocks, Fall on us and hide us from the face of Him that sitteth on the Throne, and from the wrath of the Lamb: for the great day of their wrath is come; and who is able to stand?" (vv. 15–17).

The Man of Sin

The Scriptures not only speak in a general way, as in the passages already quoted, of the conditions which will characterize the world at the close of the age; specific details are also given. Some of these now call for consideration, as leading up to the Day of the Lord.

We have seen, in the chapter on the Parousia, that in the second epistle to the Thessalonians Paul was correcting the notion that the Day of the Lord had already set in. In contradistinction to his teaching concerning the coming of the Lord for His saints, as ever the next thing to be expected, he now showed that certain events must precede the Day of the Lord. "That Day will not be," he says, "except the falling away [lit., the apostasy] come first, and the Man of Sin be revealed, the Son of Perdition, he that opposeth and exalteth himself against all that is called God, or that is worshiped; so that he sitteth in the temple of God, setting himself forth as God" (2 Thess. 2:3–5). Two clearly defined events are here foretold as destined to precede the Day of the Lord (1) the apostasy, the turning away from, and repudiation of, divine truth formerly adhered to, and (2) the revelation of the Man of Sin, called in verse 8 "the Lawless One."

Again, this latter revelation is to be preceded by another event. Lawlessness, the apostle says, was already at work in the first century, as a mystery, i.e., as something not recognized in its true character by the world at large, but made known by revelation. A certain principle was, however, at work, hindering the manifestation of the Lawless One until the time appointed for him. This principle is described as "that which restraineth" (v. 6). It found concrete expression in a person representatively described as "one that restraineth" (v. 7). This restraint against lawlessness will be exercised until the restrainer is "taken out of the way."* When this takes place the man himself, the embodiment of lawlessness, will be revealed.

But what as to the power and policy of this world-ruler? These are detailed in other Scriptures. In 2 Thessalonians Paul, who is pointing on to the Day of the Lord, passes over the interval of the government of the Man of Sin, save for a brief mention of his satanic power and deceitful influence, and speaks at once of

*A more literal, and not improbable, rendering is, "when it, i.e., lawlessness, becomes out of the midst," i.e., becomes fully and manifestly developed. See *Notes on Thessalonians*.

his doom, declaring that "the Lord Jesus shall slay him with the breath of His mouth, and bring him to nought by the manifestation of His Parousia" (v. 8). The word rendered "manifestation" is literally "epiphany," i.e., a shining forth. This epiphany marks the close of the Parousia, the saints having been with the Lord hidden from the world since the Rapture. (F-H, p. 179).

The world itself will by this time have reached its climax of iniquity, men having only hardened their hearts against God by reason of the judgments premonitory of impending doom. "The rest of mankind, which were not killed with these plagues, repented not of the works of their hands . . . and they repented not of their murders, nor of their sorceries, nor of their fornication, nor of their thefts" (Rev. 9:20, 21). "They blasphemed the Name of the God which hath the power over these plagues; and they repented not to give Him glory . . . and they blasphemed the God of heaven because of their pains and their sores; and they repented not of their works" (16:9, 11). What a picture of the antagonism of the natural heart against God! What a witness to the helplessness of man to eradicate evil, to remove the curse from the earth! The testimony of Scripture is plain enough as to the darkness and evil which are to prevail at the close of this dispensation of "man's day." Nor can it be otherwise, since we are shown that mankind at large will still refuse to view sin according to the divine estimate, and to accept God's proffered pardon and grace through the sacrifice of His Son.

At length, human rebellion having reached its consummation under the Man of Sin, the Son of man appears in person to execute wrath upon him and upon all who own allegiance to him. He is "revealed from heaven with the angels of His power in flaming fire, rendering vengeance to them that know not God, and to them that obey not the gospel of our Lord Jesus" (2 Thess. 1:7, 8). One of the most ancient prophecies recorded in the Word of God foretold this solemn event, the past tense being used with prophetic significance, as is frequent in Scripture: "Enoch, the seventh from Adam, prophesied, saying, Behold, the Lord came with His holy myriads, to execute judgment upon all, and to convict all the ungodly of all their works of ungodliness which they have ungodly wrought, and of all the hard things which ungodly sinners have spoken against Him" (Jude 14, 15). Man's day will be over, the Day of the Lord will begin. (J-B, p. 179).

Closing Events

We may now briefly enumerate some of the events in the world which will lead up to this divine intervention.* The Word of God foretells that the Man of Sin will obtain world dominion as the result of a confederacy of nations, the rulers of which will, with one consent, commit their power and authority to him (Rev. 17:13 with 13:8); that, having first supported, and then overthrown the combined religious systems of the world with the aid of these potentates (Rev. 17:7, 16), he will "exalt himself against all that is called God or that is worshiped," and thus claiming deity, will demand, and receive, universal worship (2 Thess. 2:4 with Rev. 13:8); that he will be supported in this by another potentate described firstly as "another beast," and secondly as "the false prophet" (Rev. 13:11–15 with 19:20); and that they will establish a worldwide commercial system, prohibiting buying and selling save on the part of those who use the special mark officially appointed (13:16, 17). With the Jews, who will have been reestablished nationally in Palestine, he will at first enter into a covenant, but will subsequently break it, turning upon the nation with a view to its annihilation (Dan. 9:27). Thus will begin "the time of Jacob's trouble." "But he shall be saved out of it" (Jer. 30:7). Temporarily successful in his other enterprises, the Man of Sin will fail in this anti-Semitic campaign—fail through the intervention of the Lord Jesus, by Whom he will be destroyed. (H-J, p. 179).

The prophetic Scriptures to which reference has been made serve, perhaps, to throw light upon some of the world movements which are taking place at the present time. Certainly the trend of current events is not in a direction

*For a more detailed account, see "The Roman Empire in the Light of Prophecy," by W. E. Vine, M.A.

contrary to what the Scriptures have predicted.

Har-Magedon

We must dwell more fully upon the manner in which the Jews will be delivered, since their deliverance coincides with the manifestation of the Parousia and with the commencement of the Day of the Lord. (H-J, p. 179).

The attempt to destroy the Jewish nation will form the climax of the aggression of the Antichrist against God, and will constitute a war waged against the Son of God, the Messiah of the Jews. The armies of the Gentile powers, placed at the disposal of their great leader, will be gathered together "against the Lord, and against His Anointed." Having by mutual consent given their power and authority unto "the beast," these kings of the earth, with their supreme warlord, "will war against the Lamb" (Rev. 17:13, 14). "I saw," says the inspired seer, "the beast, and the kings of the earth, and their armies, gathered together to make war against His army" (Rev. 19:19). It had been permitted to the arch-oppressor to prevail against the Jews in the Great Tribulation of which he was the instrument; he will not prevail against the Son of God; his success is only "until the Ancient of days came" (Dan. 7:21, 22).

The issues at stake will differentiate this war from all that have preceded; they have been waged for dynastic or territorial or commercial supremacy, this contest will be fought to decide whether world dominion is to rest in the hands of Satan or of Christ. This is the battle of Har-Magedon, "the war of the great day of God, the Almighty," which will introduce the Day of the Lord. Satan it is whose utmost power will energize his human instruments to force a decision: "And I saw coming out of the mouth of the Dragon, and out of the mouth of the beast, and out of the mouth of the false prophet [a trinity of evil], three unclean spirits, as it were frogs: for they are the spirits of demons, working signs; which go forth unto the kings of the whole world, to gather them together unto the war of the great day of God, the Almighty . . . and they gathered them together into the place which is called in the Hebrew, Har-Magedon" (Rev. 16:13–16).

The Forces of the Victor

This, then, on the one hand, is the description of the massed forces of evil, of humanity in alienation from God, combined in impious rebellion against the Most High, and satanically deceived by the "power and signs and lying wonders" of the Man of Sin; deceived "because they received not the love of the truth, that they might be saved," duped into believing the lie, because "they believed not the truth, but had pleasure in unrighteousness" (2 Thess. 2:9–12).

Now as to the forces of righteousness, the armies of the King of kings, Who comes to establish peace by the overthrow of militarism, Who

> "Comes to break oppression
> To set the captive free;
> To take away transgression,
> And rule in equity."

Terrible in its grandeur is the apostle's vivid description of the Lord and His hosts: "And I saw the heaven opened: and behold, a white horse, and He that sat thereon, called Faithful and True; and in righteousness he doth judge and make war. And His eyes are a flame of fire, and upon His head are many diadems: and He hath a name written, which no one knoweth, but he Himself. And He is arrayed in a garment sprinkled with blood: and His name is called The Word of God. And the armies which are in heaven followed Him upon white horses, clothed in fine linen, white and pure. And out of His mouth proceedeth a sharp sword, that with it he should smite the nations: and He shall rule them with a rod of iron; and He treadeth the winepress of the fierceness of the wrath of Almighty God. And He hath on His garment and on His thigh a name written, King of Kings, and Lord of Lords. And I saw an angel standing in the sun; and he cried with a loud voice, saying to all the birds that fly in mid heaven, Come and be gathered together unto the great supper of God; that ye may eat the flesh of kings, and the flesh of captains and the flesh of mighty men, and the flesh of horses and of them that sit thereon, and the flesh of all men, both free and bond, and small and great. . . . And the beast was taken, and with him the false prophet, that wrought the signs in his sight, wherewith he deceived them that had received the mark of the beast, and them that worshiped his image: they twain were cast alive into the lake of fire that burneth with brimstone: and the rest were killed with the sword of Him that sat upon the horse, even the sword which came forth out of His mouth: and all the birds were filled with their flesh."

Thus it is that the Man of Sin is to be brought to naught by the manifestation of the Parousia of the Lord Jesus. Thus will the Son of man, coming on the clouds of heaven with power and great glory, usher in the Day of the Lord, a day terrible in its inception, blessed in its continuance, when to the outpouring of righteous wrath shall succeed a righteous peace, under the sovereignty of the King of kings. We may compare the prophecy of Joel: "The Lord uttereth His voice before His army [a striking association with Paul's words, "the breath of His mouth," 2 Thessalonians 2:8, and with John's vision of the sword proceeding from the mouth of the Lord]; for His camp is very great; for He is strong that executeth His word; for the Day of the Lord is very terrible; and who can abide it?" (Joel 2:10, 11).

Comparing the two passages above mentioned, viz., Revelation 19:19–21 and 2 Thessalonians 2:8, which each refer in different ways to the overthrow of the Man of Sin and his forces, the Thessalonians passage gives the effect, and the Revelation passage the process; the process is short and sharp, as the effect is decisive. Further light is thrown on the two by the prophecy of Zechariah: "Then shall the Lord go forth, and fight against those nations, as when He fought in the day of battle. And His feet shall stand in that day upon the Mount of Olives. . . . And the Lord my God shall come and all the holy angels with thee" (Zech. 14:3–5).

The Day of the Lord, which will reveal the Church in the heavenlies, glorious with the glory of Christ, will at the same time bring deliverance to His earthly people the Jews. The scene is predicted in the last chapter of Joel as follows: "Proclaim ye this among the nations; prepare war; stir up the mighty men; let all the men of war draw near, let them come up. Beat your plowshares into swords, and your pruninghooks into spears; let the weak say, I am strong. Haste ye, and come, all ye nations round about, and gather yourselves together; thither cause thy mighty ones come down, O Lord. Let the nations bestir themselves, and come up to the valley of Jehoshaphat; for there will I sit to judge all the nations round about. Put ye in the sickle for the harvest is ripe; come, tread ye; for the winepress is full, the fats overflow; for their wickedness is great. Multitudes, multitudes in the valley of decision! for the day of the Lord is near in the valley of decision. The sun and the moon are darkened, and the stars withdraw their shining. And the Lord shall roar from Zion, and utter His voice from Jerusalem; and the heavens and the earth shall shake; but the Lord will be a refuge unto His people, and a stronghold to the children of Israel. So shall ye know that I am the Lord your God dwelling in Zion my holy mountain; then shall Jerusalem be holy, and there shall no strangers pass through her any more."

The manifestation of the Parousia and the introduction of the Day of the Lord thus constitute the closing stage of the Lord's Second Coming. (H-J, p. 179).

CHAPTER EIGHT

The Final Gentile World-Ruler and His Dominion

The influence of "the Prince that shall come" (Dan. 9:26) upon the destiny of the human race is of such a determining character that more is demanded than the brief reference to his power and his policy included in the last chapter. His is to be the final attempt to monopolize world power, and his dominion is to be different in character from all that preceded it. Happily the Word of God provides us with a sufficiently clear revelation concerning the closing drama of Gentile power to enable us both to form a broad view of the trend and destiny of national affairs, and to understand the manner in which His Kingdom of righteousness will be universally established in the earth. (H-J, p. 179).

In order to ascertain the character of the final Gentile world dominion and its Imperial head, we must first refer to those Scriptures which indicate the course of Gentile government over the land of Palestine. It is necessary to remember that the prophetic Scriptures relating to national governments bear directly and always on the land of the Jews. Palestine is the center of divine dealings with nations, the pivot upon which those dealings turn. "When the Most High gave to the nations their inheritance, when He separated the children of men, He set the bounds of the peoples according to the number of the children of Israel" (Deut. 32:8). With that statement all Scripture history regarding Gentile power is entirely consistent. The land was foreordained of God as the eventual seat of Messiah's kingdom.

The Vision of the Image

The second chapter of Daniel describes a vision of a great image seen by Nebuchadnezzar, the Chaldean monarch, the first Gentile potentate to hold dominion over the whole of Palestine after that country had been given to Israel to possess. His subjugation of the land began the long period afterwards called by the Lord "the times of the Gentiles" (Luke 21:24), that is, the period during which Gentile nations govern the country. Almost immediately after Nebuchadnezzar had annexed the land and carried the people into captivity, a divine revelation was given of the program of Gentile government over them and of the character of the various forms of that government. The vision just referred to was the means of this revelation in the first instance.

The image was divided into four parts which were interpreted as symbolical of four kingdoms. Nebuchadnezzar's was immediately identified as the first. "Thou, O King," said the prophet, "art king of kings, unto whom the God of heaven hath given the kingdom . . . thou art the head of gold" (vv. 37, 38). The second and third, corresponding respectively to the breast and arms, of silver, and the belly and thighs, of brass, are subsequently shown to be the Medo-Persian and the Grecian, or Macedonian, kingdoms. Thus the prophet's prediction to Nebuchadnezzar, "after thee shall arise another kingdom" (v. 39), finds fulfillment in the historic record, "In that night Belshazzar the Chaldean king was slain, and Darius the Mede received the kingdom" (vv. 30, 31). The interpretation of a later vision, seen by Daniel, of a conflict between a ram and an he-goat, identifies the third kingdom with that of Greece: "The ram which thou sawest that had the two horns, they are the kings of Media and Persia. And the rough he-goat [which was seen to destroy the ram, v. 8] is the King of Greece" (8:20, 21; cp. 10:20).

The Fourth Kingdom

The fourth kingdom was symbolized by the legs of iron and the feet partly of iron and partly of clay, or, rather, earthenware (2:33). That kingdom would be strong as iron, but inasmuch as the feet and toes of the image were part of iron and part of earthenware, the kingdom would exist in a divided condition. Further, while it would always contain the strength of iron, yet the admixture of the earthenware would eventually render the kingdom partly strong and partly brittle (vv. 40–42) (not "broken," but liable to break). This characteristic is especially mentioned of the period corresponding to the toes (v. 42). Thus the form of government of the fourth kingdom would pass through certain stages.

This fourth kingdom is not specifically mentioned in the book of Daniel, but its identification is not difficult. The history of the overthrow of the Grecian Empire by the Romans is well-known. The Roman power is, moreover, indicated in the ninth chapter of Daniel where, following the prophecy that the Messiah would be cut off, is the prediction that "the people of the prince that shall come" would destroy the city and the sanctuary" (v. 26). This the Romans carried out in A.D. 70.

The Vision of the Four Beasts

A further revelation of the course of Gentile government over the Jews, given to Daniel himself, is recorded in the seventh chapter. Four powers were represented in that vision as wild beasts, symbols appropriate for a revelation to a Jew, in contrast to those of the Gentile monarch's vision, and indicative of the treatment Daniel's people would receive from Gentile rulers.

The similarity of the description of the fourth beast to that of the fourth part of the image makes clear that the same power is in view in each case. "The fourth beast would be a fourth kingdom, differing from all others; it would devour the earth, tread it down and break it in pieces" (7:23)—an accurate representation of the Roman power.

It is to be noticed that in each interpretation the fourth kingdom is predicted as the last Gentile power, and that it receives its overthrow at the hand of God, Who will thereupon establish an everlasting Kingdom. "In the days of those kings [i.e., of the potentates represented by the toes of the image] shall the God of heaven set up a kingdom, which shall never be destroyed, nor shall the sovereignty thereof be left to another people; but it shall break in pieces and consume all these kingdoms, and it shall stand forever" (2:44). So of the final head of the empire, represented by the fourth beast, it is said, "The judgment shall sit, and they shall take away his dominion, to consume and to destroy it unto the end, and the kingdom and the dominion, and the greatness of the kingdoms under the whole heaven, shall be given to the people of the saints of the Most High: His kingdom is an everlasting kingdom, and all dominions shall serve and obey Him" (7:26, 27). Clearly, then, no worldwide imperial power is to rule between the Roman kingdom, in its final stage, and the Kingdom of Christ. (H-J, p. 179).

Is the Last the Roman?

The inquiry may be raised as to how the Roman power can be the last of the Gentile empires which rule over the Jews as a nation, considering that the Roman Empire was overthrown in the fifth and succeeding centuries of the present era. Moreover, what of the Turkish dominion?

The book of the Revelation gives us light as to the first question. Here we are carried much farther in detail, just as the eighth chapter of Daniel gives fuller information than the second. This is in accordance with the progressive character of prophecy. We are shown, in the seventeenth chapter of the Apocalypse, that the power symbolized by the beast would, after a temporary lapse, be resuscitated. The apostle John received a vision of a beast with seven heads and ten horns, and carrying a woman. The identification of this beast with the fourth of Daniel's vision is established by the facts that each had ten horns, and that each becomes the object of divine judgment at the manifestation of the Son of God for the setting up of His Kingdom. (H-J, p. 179). The three periods relating to the power of the beast are thus indicated: "The beast that thou sawest was, and is not; and is about to come up out of the abyss"; and again, "he was, and is not, and shall come" (Rev. 17:8). This does not mean that it existed prior to John's time and was then nonexistent. The language is prophetic rather than historic, and simply implies (1) an existence, (2) a discontinuance, (3) a reappearance.

A Twofold Application

We must notice that the symbol of a beast represents both the kingdom and its final ruler. This is the case in both the 7th of Daniel and the 17th of Revelation. In the former chapter the interpretation is as follows: "These great beasts which are four are four *kings*. . . . The fourth beast shall be a fourth *kingdom*" (Dan. 7:17, 23). In the Revelation the beast is seen with seven heads and ten horns (v. 3). Here the whole animal is termed a beast. In verses 9–11, however, the beast is symbolically identified, not with the whole animal, but with one of the heads. Moreover, the seven heads are described first topographically and then personally. "The seven heads are seven mountains . . . and they are seven kings; . . . and the beast . . . is himself also an eighth, and is of the seven." Clearly the beast again represents two distinct yet closely associated things. In the first eight verses of the chapter the language is indicative of dominion. Then the scope of the symbol is narrowed and the individual ruler comes into view. Thus the entire animal represents, not merely the ruler, but his kingdom, as in Daniel 7:23.

The fourth, or Roman, Empire, as a matter of history, existed in the closing part of the past dispensation and in the first few centuries of the present one, that is, before and after the point C in the diagram. For many centuries it has not existed as an empire, that is to say, it is now in the "is not" stage.

The Turks

The Turks, who overthrew the eastern part of the Empire in the fifteenth century, occupied Palestine until 1917, but never ruled over the Jews as a nation, i.e., as the nationally recognized possessor of Palestine. Their relationship with the Jewish people differs fundamentally from that of the Chaldeans, Medo-Persians, Greeks, and Romans. The Jews had been scattered from their land before the Turks took possession. Turkish domination is therefore not noticed in the Scriptures we have considered.

The Final Form

Intimation is given in Scripture as to the form in which the fourth kingdom will be resuscitated, possibly during the period represented by G-J (p. 179) on the diagram. Of the ten horns on the fourth beast in Daniel's vision it was said, "As for the ten horns, out of this kingdom shall ten kings arise" (Dan. 7:24). And of the ten horns of the beast of Revelation, "The ten horns . . . are ten kings, which have received no kingdom as yet" (Rev. 17:12). That they will be contemporaneous and confederate is obvious, from the statement that they have one mind and agree to hand their kingdom over to a federal head (vv. 13, 17). Moreover, the countries over which they rule are spoken of not as kingdoms, but as a kingdom, indicating community of interest as well as territorial unity.

Clearly, therefore, a league of nations is in view, and this is apparently to be the new form of the old empire. Its reformed condition will render it "diverse from all the kingdoms," i.e., from the three preceding empires (Dan. 7:23).

Territorial Considerations

As to the territories of this reconstructed fourth empire, we have no definite intimation in Scripture, though there are indications that they will embrace at least the area occupied by all the four powers, the Chaldean, Medo-Persian, Grecian, and Roman. When in the vision the stone smote the image on its feet the whole image was broken in pieces (Dan. 2:34, 35). (H-J, p. 179). When the fourth beast was destroyed the dominion of the rest of the beasts was taken away (7:12). Probably there will be an expansion of territory beyond the ancient limits. Certainly the whole world will acknowledge the authority of the final head of the empire (Rev. 13:7).

Several territorial changes which have taken place during recent centuries—i.e., in the "is not" period—and especially of late, have shown a remarkable return toward the configuration of the ancient Roman dominions. All the territory of North Africa which was within the ancient empire, but which was subdued later by Turkey, has gradually come under the government of countries which belonged to the Roman kingdom. Spain governs Morocco; France governs Algeria and Tunis; Italy, Tripoli; and Britain, Egypt. Again, Alsace and Lorraine and other territory west of the Rhine, formerly in the Roman province of Gallia, are now reverting to France. The Trentino, which formerly belonged to Italy, has been regained by it. Austrian territory, which in the Roman Empire was confined to the district west and south of the Danube, is again reduced to that limit. Syria, Palestine, and Mesopotamia have been recovered from the Turk and are now under the influence of nations which belonged to the Roman world.* Moreover, those countries which have been freed from Turkish control have resumed the Western civil institutions and organizations, which have all along been Roman in character. Other territorial changes in Europe seem probable, which will render the approximation to the ancient delineations the closer.

We are not justified, however, in concluding that the territories of the League of Nations, indicated by the passages relating to the ten horns of the beast, will necessarily be confined to the area which has just been under consideration. Whatever the arrangement may be, the fact of the League will prepare the way for the government of the final and all-controlling despot.

This is foretold in Scripture as follows: "Out of this kingdom shall ten kings arise: and another shall arise after them; and he shall be diverse from the former" (Dan. 7:24). "[The] ten kings . . . receive authority as kings with the beast, for one hour [i.e., for a brief period]. These have one mind, and they give their power and authority unto the beast" (Rev. 17:12, 13, 17).

The Iron and Clay

Now the character of the power of the ten kings is indicated by the constitution of the toes of the image seen in the vision by Nebuchadnezzar. These were formed of a mixture of iron and earthenware (Dan. 2:42). As the different metals of the image obviously represent the character of the respective governments, the iron most appropriately symbolizes militarism. The earthenware is brittle—the fourth kingdom, in this form, was predicted to be "partly strong and partly brittle" (see marg.). This suggests an unstable form of government. That democracy is in view is extremely improbable. Many a republic has evidenced striking stability. On the other hand, such revolutionary forces as those of Communism, Anarchy, Bolshevism, etc., have always been liable to speedy disintegration. Moreover, revolutions instigated by such forces have almost always given rise to despotism, as in the case of the French Revolution.

Again, militarism is essentially so different in character from the associations referred to that, as the prophecy says, they could not cleave together, any more than iron and earthenware do. That they might mingle for a time is possible, especially if the will of the people lay behind the combination. This is perhaps indicated in the words "they shall mingle themselves by [marg.—i.e., by means of] the seed of men" (v. 43). We can conceive, therefore, of the outbreak of such widespread revolution in the confederate kingdom of the ten potentates,† coupled with a condition of impoverishment consequent upon war, that they would willingly commit their power into the hands of a man of consummate ability who might be ready for the occasion.‡

The Final Emperor

Concerning this final Gentile emperor Scripture has much to say, more than we can refer to in the present volume.§

The apostle Paul speaks of him as "the Man of Sin, the Son of Perdition," and "the Lawless One" (2 Thess. 2:3, 8). He is to have a parousia (v. 9) (see pp. 58–61 and 152), a

*See the writer's *The Roman Empire in Prophecy,* written in 1915.

†The word rendered "king" does not necessarily denote a constitutional monarch; rather it represents the head of any state, of whatever type.

‡See *The Roman Empire in Prophecy.*

§For a brief outline of his career, see *The Roman Empire in Prophecy,* chapter 6. See also *The Mystery of Iniquity,* by C. F. Hogg.

period commencing with his manifestation, and during which his power will be in exercise over the whole world. His parousia, apparently an imitation of the Parousia of Christ, will be "according to the working of Satan with all power and signs and lying wonders, and with all deceit of unrighteousness." In the language of the Apocalypse, "the Dragon gave him his power, and his throne, and great authority" (Rev. 13:2). Hence the rapidity of his rise to power and of the universal acknowledgment of his rule. "His stupendous power and brilliant abilities, the evidence of his superhuman origin, his phenomenal capacity for organization, and the consolidation of the empire under his absolute control, will cause the whole world to marvel at him."*

His Overthrow

Exalting himself in impious pride and blasphemy against all that is called God, and claiming and receiving universal worship, he and his supporters will make war against the Son of God. "These shall war against the Lamb, and the Lamb shall overcome them" (Rev. 17:14). That victory, synchronizing with the Second Advent, the ushering in of the Day of the Lord (H-J, p. 179), is variously described in the Word of God. The overthrow of the Beast is the falling of the stone upon the feet of the image of Nebuchadnezzar's vision, the annihilation of all Gentile government. He who in the days of His flesh refused to accept the kingdoms of the world at the hands of Satan, and to evade the sufferings of Calvary, will then by virtue of those sufferings, and of His victory over His arch-adversary, come to deliver the earth from its oppressors and from unrighteous government in all its forms.

The two contrasting circumstances of the Cross and the Glory are vividly depicted by Isaiah: "Like as many were astonied at Thee (His visage was so marred more than any man, and His form more than the sons of men), so shall He startle [marg., which seems accurate] many nations; kings shall shut their mouths at Him; for that which had not been told them shall they see; and that which they had not heard shall they understand" (Is. 52:14, 15). The astonishment of men who gazed upon His sufferings will have its counterpart in the astonishment with which His Second Advent will overturn the existing order of things and introduce the glory of His Kingdom.

The Kingdom of the King of Kings

Then will be fulfilled the saying that is written, "The kingdom of the world is become the kingdom of our Lord, and of His Christ; and He shall reign forever and ever." Then will ascend the song of praise in heaven. "We give Thee thanks, O Lord God, the Almighty, which art and which wast; because Thou hast taken Thy great power, and didst reign. And the nations were wroth, and Thy wrath came, and the time of the dead to be judged, and the time to give their reward to Thy servants the prophets, and to the saints, and to them that fear Thy Name, the small and the great; and to destroy them that destroy the earth" (Rev. 11:15–18).

"The stone that smote the image became a great mountain, and filled the whole earth." The interpretation of this is to be found, not in the imagined universality of the success of the gospel in the present dispensation, but in such prophecies as those of Isaiah when he says that "out of Zion shall go forth the law and the word of the Lord from Jerusalem. And He shall judge between the nations and shall reprove many peoples: and they shall beat their swords into plowshares and their spears into pruninghooks; nation shall not lift up sword against nation, neither shall they learn war any more. . . . The loftiness of man shall be bowed down, and the haughtiness of men shall be brought low; and the Lord alone shall be exalted in that day" (Is. 2:3, 4, 17). Jehovah's Servant, Israel's Messiah, "shall bring forth judgment to the Gentiles. . . . He shall not fail nor be discouraged, till He have set judgment in the earth; and the isles shall wait for His law" (62:1, 4). "The earth shall be full of the knowledge of the Lord as the waters cover the sea" (11:9).

**The Roman Empire in Prophecy.*

"All the kingdoms shall become
His whose imperial brow with crown of
thorn
The men of war in mockery did adorn.
Peace shall prevail, and every land shall
own
His rightful sway, and low before His
throne
Shall bow and worship; angels there shall
kneel.
The soul of the vast universe shall feel
The quickening touch of its life-giving
Head,
And shall break forth in song. The
heavens shall shed
Into the lap of earth immortal joys,
And every living thing, with thankful voice,
Shall sweetly raise the universal psalm
Of glory unto God and to the Lamb."

—BOYD

▪ CHAPTER NINE ▪

The Effect of the Hope

"O keep us, Jesus, Lord, until that day,
Walking with girded loins, apart from all
That savors of this world that Thee refused,
Until Thou come with shout and trump, and we
Behold Thee as Thou art and like Thee be."
From *"The Story of The Glory"*—Boyd

The Christian's hope of the Lord's return is a certain hope, "an anchor of the soul, both sure and steadfast," a hope "laid up in the heavens": "He that cometh shall come, and shall not tarry." But more than this, it is a practical hope, influencing every part of the life, energizing and purifying it. It forms, indeed, an essential part of that new life imparted by the Spirit of God to the believer. One who is born of the Spirit is by Him directed to the constant expectation of the return of the Christ Who died for him and rose again. With other believers he "waits for a Savior from heaven, the Lord Jesus Christ" (Phil. 3:20). It is as much a spiritual instinct for the regenerate being to lay hold on the hope set before him as it is a natural instinct for the infant to cling to something material. No one is living up to his privileges, no one is living in the full light and power of gospel truth, whose heart is not enjoying the prospect of the Lord's Second Coming. Nor can a preacher of the gospel be faithful to his ministry if he omits therefrom that which constitutes the hope of the gospel.

It will perhaps be helpful if we consider some of the effects of this hope upon the Christian life.

An Incentive to Diligence in Service

Anticipation of the Second Coming of the Lord is not indulgence in a mere spiritual luxury, nor does expectation of His return tend to make Christians unpractical. The expectation may be perverted into unscriptural theorizing and speculation; but the perversion of what is good neither disproves its essential goodness, nor provides an argument against its proper use. One of the most aggressively evangelical communities of the first century was the church of the Thessalonians. "From you," says the apostle, "hath sounded forth the Word of the Lord, not only in Macedonia and Achaia, but in every place your faith to God-ward is gone forth" (1 Thess. 1:8). Yet it is of these Christians that he also writes that they had turned to God from idols, not only to serve Him, but "to wait for His Son from heaven" (vv. 9, 10). They evidently did not find waiting for the Lord incompatible with service to God. Their expectancy neither damped their ardor nor repressed their zeal in the spread of the gospel and in other forms of practical Christianity. They were not stargazers. Paul speaks of their "work of faith and labor of love"; and these were only stimulated by their "patience of hope" (v. 3). The church at Corinth, likewise, both "came behind in no gift," and at the same time "waited for the revelation of our Lord Jesus Christ" (1 Cor. 1:7).

Paul himself, who certainly could never be accused of effortless Christianity, testified to the constantly practical effect the prospect had upon his life. In his defense before the governor Felix he boldly declared his hope toward God that there shall be a resurrection, and stated that "therein he exercised himself to have a conscience void of offense toward God and men alway" (Acts 24:16). It has been imputed to him that toward the end of his life his expectation of the Lord's Second Advent diminished. Yet in his letter to Titus, the last but one of those under his name in the New

Testament, and written shortly before his death, he speaks of "looking for the blessed hope and appearing of the glory of our great God and Savior Jesus Christ," and regards the hope as part and parcel of a sober, righteous and godly life (Titus 2:12, 13).

How could the knowledge that Christ is coming hinder the work of the church, or paralyze its effort? Those who, like the Thessalonians of old, wait for God's Son from heaven, find the expectation of the event an incentive to greater devotion to the service of their Master. The nobleman in the Lord's parable, who entrusted his servants with his money, commanded them, "Trade ye herewith, till I come" (Luke 19:12, 13). He who spake the parable thus set His coming again as the goal toward which the energies of His servants were to be directed.

The churches were certainly not more aggressive in Christian activity during those centuries of the present era in which the hope of the Lord's return was well-nigh lost, than they have been since the hope was resuscitated as it has been now for over a century. Simultaneous with the revival of interest in His Second Advent, and with an increased intelligent apprehension of the testimony of Scripture concerning it, has been the revival of zealous effort for the spread of the gospel, and for the evangelization of nations lying in heathen darkness.

A Strength for Endurance

The apostle Peter speaks of the Second Advent as "a salvation ready to be revealed in the last time," and then describes the joy-inspiring power of the prospect for the believer in the midst of trial. In this salvation, he says, "ye greatly rejoice, though now for a little while, if need be, ye have been put to grief in manifold trials, that the proof of your faith, being more precious than gold that perisheth though it is proved by fire, might be found unto praise and glory and honor at the revelation of Jesus Christ" (1 Pet. 1:5–8). Two points may be observed here.

Firstly, the trials are for "a little while." The phrase is suggestive of expectancy of the Lord's return. It was frequently on the lips of Christ Himself: "A little while, and ye behold Me no more; and again a little while, and ye shall see Me" (John 16:16, 17, 19; see also 7:33; 12:35; 13:33; 14:19). The words remained with Peter, and find an echo in his epistle, both in the passage above quoted, and later on when he says, "And the God of all grace, who called you unto His eternal glory in Christ, after that ye have suffered a little while, shall Himself perfect, stablish, strengthen you" (v. 10). Nineteen centuries have rolled away and the Lord has not yet returned. Albeit the prospect is ever near to the Christian. It is still "a little while." The writer to the Hebrews views the time even more briefly: "yet a very little while (lit., yet a little while, how little! how little!), He that cometh shall come, and shall not tarry" (Heb. 10:37). Paul's way of putting it in the second epistle to the Corinthians, "Our light affliction, which is for the moment," is briefest of all (2 Cor. 5:17).

Secondly, there is a "needs be." Why exactly it should be so may remain a mystery here. But the faith, which itself is undergoing the testing, can rest in the assurance of a loving heart and an unerring wisdom which planned the trial, and in the prospect of the day of Christ, when the Lord will make fully known the value He sets upon the patient endurance of trial, and show how all has redounded to His "praise, honor and glory."

Suffering for Christ's sake is lustered by the glory beyond. "We are," says Paul, "Joint heirs with Christ; if so be that we suffer with Him, that we may be also glorified with Him. For I reckon that the sufferings of this present time are not worthy to be compared with the glory which shall be revealed to usward" (Rom. 8:17,18). The apostle is here looking on to the manifestation of the Parousia, when the Lord "shall come to be glorified in His saints" (2 Thess. 1:10). The glory is not merely that which will be revealed to them: "to usward" conveys the more comprehensive idea of the revelation of His glory first to, and then in and through, them. Of this he speaks as "the liberty of the glory of the children of God" (Rom. 8:21).

Of the effects of the prospect upon sufferings resulting from Christian testimony Peter has more to say. Those on whose behalf he was writing were the objects of fierce persecution; "a fiery trial," he calls it. They were not, however, to count that kind of thing strange. Three incentives were given them to rejoice therein, past, future and present. As to the past, they were to rejoice because they were partakers of Christ's sufferings: that looked back to Calvary. As to the future, there lay before them "the revelation of His glory"; then they would rejoice "with exceeding joy." As to the present, "if ye are reproached," he says, "for the name of Christ, blessed are ye; because the Spirit of glory and the Spirit of God resteth upon you" (1 Pet. 4:12–14). The power to endure reproach for Christ's sake comes from the Holy Spirit. He is "the Spirit of glory" because He is Himself the pledge of coming glory. The present blessedness of reproach for the name of Christ is an earnest of the reward to be bestowed hereafter for such suffering. "If we endure, we shall also reign with Him."

This patient endurance in view of resurrection glory was what characterized the faithful of the former age. They saw the promises and greeted them from afar, and, confessing that they were strangers and pilgrims on the earth, they sought after a heavenly country. Some "were tortured, not accepting their deliverance; that they might obtain a better resurrection"—not a different kind of actual resurrection from that of other saints, but a resurrection which would bring with it a reward proportionate to their faithfulness in enduring hardship and suffering instead of seeking to escape it by compromise of the truth and dalliance with evil (Heb. 11:13, 35). They anticipated the inspired estimate given in a later age by one like-minded with themselves, counting light their affliction which was for a moment, reckoning that it was working for them more and more exceedingly an eternal weight of glory, and looking, not at the things which are seen, the temporal things, but at the things which are not seen, the eternal.

Accordingly the writer to the Hebrews, turning from these faithful ones to the author and perfecter of faith, and reminding them how for the joy set before Him He endured the Cross, and, further, how and why He "suffered without the gate," exhorts them to go forth unto Him, bearing His reproach (Heb. 12:2 and 13:12, 13). And the inducement? The Lord Himself. "Unto Him!" He must ever be the great attraction. Nothing signifies apart from Him. But with Him there is a further inducement, namely, the future glories, of which He will be the center. With those in view the apostle speaks of the heavenly Jerusalem. "For we have not here an abiding city, but we seek after the city which is to come." The glory of that city takes its light from the Cross, and reflects it, in all its spirit-strengthening radiance, upon the sufferings of this little while.

"The Cross is all thy splendor,
  The Crucified thy praise;
His laud and benediction
  Thy ransomed people raise.
Upon the Rock of Ages
  They raise thy holy tower;
Thine is the victor's laurel,
  And shine the golden dower."

An Encouragement in Conflict

When Paul exhorts Timothy to "endure hardship as a good soldier of Christ Jesus," warning him against entangling himself in the affairs of this life, he points him to the reward hereafter, adding the metaphor of the crown received by the victor in the games. To be crowned he must contend lawfully. The reference to the second coming of Christ is indirect, yet real, for it is only when the Lord comes that the crowning day will come. The illustration of abiding by the laws of a game imparts the lessons of faithfulness and obedience to Christ in view of the reward, despite the efforts of spiritual foes to oppose and to defeat, and despite every inducement to desist from the struggle with sin within and with the hosts of spiritual wickedness without. Anticipation of the crown begets strength for the conflict.

And Paul not only exhorts, he presents the example of his own life. "I have fought the good fight, I have finished the course, I have kept the faith: henceforth there is laid up for me the crown of righteousness, which the Lord, the righteous judge, shall give to me at that day; and not only to me, but also to all them that have loved His appearing" (2 Tim. 4:7, 8).

True, the apostle realized that he might be near the end of his earthly course: "The time of my departure is come," he says. But that did not lessen for him the power of the hope. Clearly, too, he implies that, looking back through his Christian life, he has joy in being of the number of those who love the Lord's appearing. This love is more than a longing for the great event to take place. Paul evidently implies that it involves fighting the good fight, finishing the course, and keeping the faith. This had all been done in his case with the Lord's coming and the crown of righteousness in view. The love of His appearing imparted courage in the conflict, steadfastness in the race, and faithfulness in adherence to the truth. His own example, then, was calculated to be an encouragement to every believer similarly to set the heart's affection on the Lord's appearing. No more striking evidence could be given of the power of the hope to affect the Christian life. The perfect tense looks back from the Judgment Seat of Christ where the past conduct of each believer will be reviewed. According as each will there be seen to have lived his life and finished his course under the stimulating influence of the Lord's return, so will be his reward.

That the Lord watches constantly, and with a view to their reward, the spiritual conflict in which His servants are engaged is evidenced in a special manner in the letters to the seven churches in Asia, in each of which He addresses the overcomer, reminding him of the time when faithfulness will receive its recompense at His hands. The present opposition is subtle, unremitting, and varied, but the promises are sure: "To him that overcometh will I give. . . ." What seems to be the greatest reward is for the overcomer in the church in Laodicea, the low spiritual condition of which calls forth His most solemn rebuke; the church that was lukewarm, rich in this world, but wretched and miserable and poor and blind and naked spiritually. In this church "He that overcometh," says the Lord, "I will give to him to sit down with Me in My throne, as I also overcame, and sat down with My Father in His Throne" (Rev. 3:21). This is a special identification with Himself as the Great Overcomer, and the reward is that of highest authority in the future glories of His kingdom.

But what is it to be an overcomer? The term implies the existence of obstacles to the exercise of faith and difficulties in the path of faithfulness. In each letter the obstacles and difficulties are clearly indicated in the mention of the various evils in the churches, and the trials to which some are subjected. The overcomer is he who in loyalty to His Lord and reliance upon His power surmounts the difficulty, triumphs over the obstacle, and remains steadfast amidst declension.

The prospect of the Lord's speedy return is definitely given to the church in Philadelphia: "I come quickly: hold fast that which thou hast, that no one take thy crown." But what to the overcomer? Here, again, we are directed to the glory of the city that is to be. "He that overcometh, I will make him a pillar in the temple of My God, and He shall go out thence no more: and I will write upon him the name of My God, and the name of the city of My God, the New Jerusalem, which cometh down out of heaven from My God, and Mine own new Name" (3:12).

"There is the Throne of David
  And there, from care released,
The song of them that triumph,
  The shout of them that feast;
And they who with their leader
  Have conquered in the fight,
Forever and forever
  Are clad in robes of white."

A Comfort in Sorrow

This is distinctly laid down by Paul both at the beginning and at the close of the passage relating to the subject in the fourth chapter of 1 Thessalonians. He prefaces his divinely given assurance of the fact that those who have fallen asleep will have part in the resurrection and rapture at the Lord's return, by stating that his object is to prevent needless sorrow. "We would not have you ignorant, brethren, concerning them that fall asleep; that ye sorrow not, even as the rest, which have no hope." Then, having shown how all are to be together again when the promised event takes place, and how all will be caught up to meet the Lord, he says, "Wherefore comfort one another with these words."

This hope is given us, then, not to preclude sorrow, but to mitigate it.

"Grief for the loss of friends is common to all, and is not inconsistent with acceptance of the will of God, neither does it deny the hope of the Christian. The Lord Jesus Himself wept in sympathy with the mourners at the grave of Lazarus (John 11:33–35). Paul, too, was apprehensive of the sorrow into which he would have been plunged had the sickness of Epaphroditus resulted in death (Phil. 2:27). The converts at Thessalonica grieved not merely for their own loss, they grieved also for the loss sustained, as the survivors supposed, by those of their number who had fallen asleep. It was to save them from grief on this account that the apostle wrote showing them that their fears were groundless. . . . Since, for the believer, to live is Christ, to die not loss but gain (Phil. 1:21), sorrow on behalf of departed saints is precluded entirely. For our loss we mourn, for their gain we rejoice."*

The knowledge that our loved ones who have fallen asleep are "at home with the Lord" should be sufficient to satisfy us completely as to their present felicity. To be at home with Him who loved us and gave Himself for us, is to be in the enjoyment of happiness which can be exceeded only by that of reunion in the resurrection and rapture with all the redeemed, and participation in the glories that are to follow. For those who mourn the loss of loved ones, the Lord both lusters the dews of sorrow by His love, and wills that the glory of His promised return should shed its comforting light into the darkness of our bereavements, and that the joy of that day should temper the sorrows of separation.

"Haste, thou glorious morning! welcome shadeless day,
Chasing with thy sunlight all our tears away;
Haste, O wondrous moment, when 'midst radiant skies
Sleeping saints and living at His word arise."

A Means of Molding Character

Men become like the objects of their worship. The character of the idolater receives an impress from the nature of his idol. "They that make them are like unto them." "If you think of Buddha and pray to Buddha," says the Eastern proverb, "you will become like Buddha." He whose heart's affection is set on Christ, inevitably becomes conformed to His character. "We all, with unveiled face, beholding as in a mirror the glory of the Lord, are [being] transformed into the same image from glory to glory, even as from the Lord the Spirit" (2 Cor. 3:18, marg.). There is first the unobscured vision, indicating heart occupation with Christ; then the transformation into His likeness. The more we learn of the Lord by means of the mirror of the Scriptures, the more we let the vision of His glory operate within us, the more conformed to His likeness we become.

But such devotion to the Lord is in Scripture associated with the prospect of His return, and this is definitely stated to be a means of conformity to His character. "Beloved, now are we children of God, and it is not yet made manifest what we shall be. We know that, if He shall be manifested, we shall be like Him; for we shall see Him even as He is." There will be no defect in the image when the resurrection shout has accomplished its work. Meanwhile the transformation of character is gradual: "Every one that hath this hope set on Him purifieth himself, even as He is pure" (1 John 3:2, 3). The Authorized Version "in him" is ambiguous and lends itself readily to the idea that the hope is within the believer. This of course is true, but it is not in the verse. Christ is the attraction. The hope is not merely that the event will take place, it is a hope set on Him. The immediate outgoing of the heart to Him is coupled with the joyful anticipation of what we shall find ourselves to be when we see Him even as He is, and share in His resurrection glory. "We shall be satisfied, when we awake, with His likeness" (Ps. 17:8).

The realization of what is to take place in His Parousia is an incentive to purity of heart and life. When we remember that according as we have purified ourselves, abstaining from, or discarding, all that displeases Him, so will be our capacity to serve Him in the ages to come. We have enough to inspire us to eschew every form of evil and to devote our lives and

*From *Notes on the Epistles to the Thessalonians*.

energies to Him in loyal obedience. And the standard of purity is His own unsullied character—"even as He is pure." The more effectively the power of the hope works within us, the more like our Lord we become.

Peter likewise gives testimony to the power of the hope to mold character. "Gird up," he says, "the loins of your mind, be sober and set your hope perfectly on the grace that is to be brought unto you at the revelation of Jesus Christ" (1 Pet. 1:13). The tense he employs is the vivid present—"is being brought unto you"—as if to make the future event immediately real. Then, presenting the same standard of holiness as John does, he continues, "as children of obedience"—suggesting the likeness of child to parent—"not fashioning yourselves according to your former lusts in the time of your ignorance, but like as He who called you is holy, be ye yourselves also holy in all manner of living; because it is written, Ye shall be holy, for I am holy." To set one's hope perfectly on the Lord's Second Coming thus produces conformity to His holiness in a life of obedience, with the consequent shaping of a character which is the reflection of His own.

In the second epistle, too, he points to the Day of the Lord and the passing away therein of the heavens, the dissolution of the elements, the destruction of the earth and its works by fire, and exhorts us, in view of that day, to live in all holiness and godliness, and to look for and earnestly desire "the Parousia of the Day of God." With this prospect before us we are to "give diligence that we may be found in peace, without spot, and blameless in His sight" (2 Pet. 3:10–14).

In writing to Titus Paul speaks of two appearings, one past, the appearing of grace, which has brought salvation to all men, the other future, the appearing of glory, "the glory of our great God and Savior Jesus Christ." Grace instructs us to deny ungodliness and worldly desires, and to live soberly and righteously and godly in this present world, but ever with our eye upon the glory that is to be revealed at the Lord's Second Advent. That hope is, then, to influence us in all the conditions and relationships of life, producing sobriety in our individual experience, righteousness toward our fellows, and godliness toward God (Titus 2:11–13).

And when the Lord Himself, in the closing declaration of Holy Writ, predicts His speedy return, He gives solemn admonition as to the effects of His Advent upon character, and points to the recompense which He will administer in person: "He that is unrighteous, let him do unrighteousness still: and he that is filthy, let him be made filthy still: and he that is righteous, let him do righteousness still: and he that is holy, let him be made holy still: Behold, I come quickly; and My reward is with Me, to render to each man according as his work is. I am the Alpha and the Omega, the first and the last, the beginning and the end. Blessed are they that wash their robes, that they may have the right to come to the tree of life, and may enter by the gates into the city" (Rev. 22:11–14).

▪ CHAPTER TEN ▪

A Synopsis of the Bible Doctrine of the Second Advent

The diagram is intended to present to the mind, through the eye, the way of the Lord Jesus from His ascension until His feet stand again upon the Mount of Olives, as foretold through Zechariah, see chapter 14, verse 4.

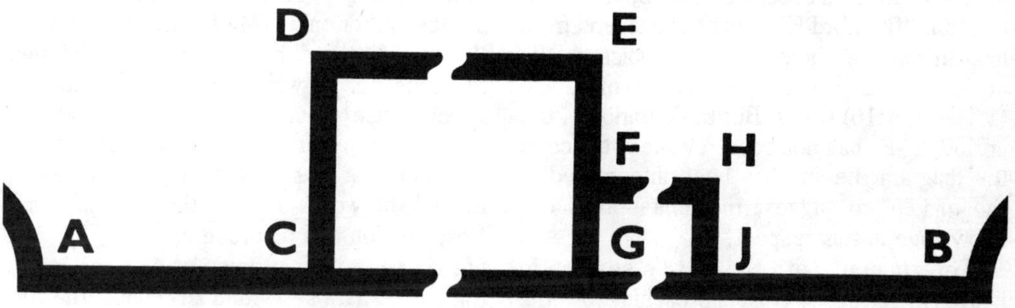

A – B = The World, the human race in time and upon the earth.
C – D = The Ascension of the Lord Jesus Christ.
D – E = The Session of the Lord on His Father's Throne.
C – G = The concurrent period upon the earth.
E – F = The Descent of the Lord into the air.
G – F = The Rapture of the Redeemed.
F – H = The Parousia of the Lord with His Redeemed.
H – J = The Manifestation of the Parousia to the World, the Second Advent.

The base line A-B represents the World, or Time, or the History of the Human Race on the one and in the other. The first event marked thereon, C, is the Ascension of the Lord, which is described in the New Testament in such terms as these: "He was taken up; and a cloud received Him out of their sight"; he "was carried up into Heaven"; He "passed through the Heavens"; He "ascended far above all the Heavens"; He "entered . . . into Heaven itself," where He is seated "far above all rule and authority and power and dominion, and every name that is named, not only in this age, but also in that which is to come"; "With His Father in His Throne"; "On the right Hand of the Throne of the Majesty in the Heavens" (Acts 1:9; Luke 24:51; Heb. 4:14; Eph. 4:10; Heb. 9:24; Eph. 1:21; Rev. 3:21; Heb. 8:1).

It is significant, however, that when the apostle has occasion to speak of the ascension of Christ, without previous reference to His heavenly origin, he is careful to add that before He ascended He descended; that is, he takes pains to guard against a wrong deduction from his words, as that the Lord had His beginning here. He was, indeed, born in Bethlehem of Judaea, but "His goings forth are from of old, from everlasting"; He "came forth from God" (Mic. 5:2; John 17:8).

Christ in Heaven

The occupation of Christ during His present session in heaven, D-E, is variously described.

"Whither as a forerunner Jesus entered for us"; "to appear before the face of God for us"; "to prepare a place for us" (Heb. 6:20; 9:24; John 14:2). He is "Great Priest over the House of God," "Whose House are we, if we hold fast our boldness and the glorying of our hope firm unto the end"; he "maketh intercession for us"; and "if any man sin," He is our "Advocate with the Father," and, as already noticed in an earlier chapter, He is also "expecting till His enemies be made the footstool of His feet" (Heb. 10:21; 3:6; Rom. 8:34; 1 John 2:1; Heb. 10:13).

The end of this session of the Lord on His Father's throne is described thus by the apostle Paul: "the Lord Himself shall descend from heaven, with a shout, with the voice of the archangel, and with the trump of God" (1 Thess. 4:16) (E-F). But the duration of the period, D-E, has not been revealed; hence in the diagram the line has been interrupted in the middle, to suggest the limitation of our knowledge in this respect.

Coterminous with the Lord's session in heaven is this age of Gospel preaching, of "the ministration of the Spirit" (2 Cor. 2:8). It began with the outpouring of the Holy Spirit, the gift of the Father and the Son (Acts 2:33). It is the age during which "the Church which is His [Christ's] Body" is being formed (Eph. 1:22, 23). The manner of its ending has been revealed in these words of the apostle: "the Lord Himself shall descend from heaven . . . and the dead in Christ shall rise first: then we that are alive, that are left, shall together with them be caught up in the clouds, to meet the Lord in the air" (1 Thess. 4:17) (G-F). But concerning the duration of the age of the Church, C-G, nothing has been revealed, hence this line also has been interrupted.

The Fixing of Dates Forbidden

Attempts have again and again been made to supply this lack of revelation by calculations based upon biblical and other data, astronomical phenomena and what not, or by deductions drawn from analogies assumed to be discernible therein. That such attempts are vain is abundantly evident from the failure that has invariably attended them. The only fruit they have had has been to discredit prophecy and to bring its study into disrepute. These attempts, moreover, are not merely vain; they are wrong, inasmuch as they are forbidden in the Scriptures which themselves provide the material on which such calculations are supposed to be based.

The principle underlying all communications of the divine will was thus enunciated by Moses, "The secret things belong unto the Lord our God: but the things that are revealed belong unto us and to our children" (Deut. 29:29). The Lord Jesus said to His disciples, "Of that day and hour knoweth no one, not even the angels of heaven, neither the Son, but the Father only" (Matt. 24:36). The words "day" and "hour" here seem to be equivalent to "time" in its wider, as well as in its narrower, sense. That is, the time was unknown, whether the year or the month, the day or the hour. Nor was it ever afterward revealed. Indeed the words used by the Lord after His Resurrection and recorded in Acts 1:7, "It is not for you to know times or seasons, which the Father hath set within His own authority," seem to be intended to declare that the withholding from His children of this knowledge is designed and for a purpose, and is intended to remain in force until the event takes place. The prohibition is plain enough; to attempt that which He has thus forbidden is disobedience, neither less nor more, however speciously it may be disguised or excused.

The Condition of Watchfulness

The words of 1 Thessalonians, chapter 5, verses 1 and 2: "But concerning the times and the seasons, brethren, ye have no need that aught be written unto you. For yourselves know perfectly that the Day of the Lord so cometh as a thief in the night," may be paraphrased thus, "you well know that nothing more can be known about the date of the Advent than that it will come when least expected." True the apostle went on to say, "When they [i.e., the ungodly] are saying, Peace and safety, then sudden destruction cometh upon them. . . . But ye, brethren, are not in darkness that that day should overtake you as a thief." The difference between the

No one is close enough To God to Know This Secret.
No Gift Of / Spirit Enables One " "

Christian and the ungodly, however, is not that the former knows the time of the Advent, for he does not, but that he is watchful for it at all times. It is with him as with the master of the house in the parable, who, had he known the hour of the night at which the thief was coming, would have been on the alert about that hour. But the Christian being assured that his Lord is coming, and knowing not the time of His coming, is to be on the alert all the while the night lasts. In every age His ever appropriate word to all His people is, "Be ye also ready; for in an hour that ye think not He will come" (Luke 12:37–40).

Two reasons may be suggested for this silence as to the date of the Advent. In the first place it is left unrevealed in order to induce in the Christian an ever-watchful spirit. Were the day of his Lord's appearing known this incentive to instant readiness would be lost. True it is the Christian ought to need no such aid to loyalty, but that is not to the point here. God has been pleased, in His wisdom, to provide the incentive, and what He gives we need. "Take ye heed, watch and pray; for ye know not when the time is. . . . Watch therefore: for ye know not when . . . and what I say unto you I say unto all, Watch" (Mark 13:33–37). All such language, and there is much of it in the New Testament, presupposes our ignorance of the time of the Lord's return. That known the sanctifying power of the hope would disappear. Moreover, had that time been revealed subsequently to the use of these words and others of a similar tenor, then the force of the oft-repeated exhortation to watch would have been dissipated.

It was not, then, a temporary expedient that this hour should be unknown for a season; neither was it left hidden in such a way that the diligent, or the ingenious, might discover it. From our point of view it has been left unrevealed that we might be "like unto men that wait for their Lord" (Luke 12:36). And yet there may be a deeper reason still.

The Sovereignty of the Living God

We must beware of the entirely unwarranted assumption underlying much of what is said upon this point, that the acts of God are fixed upon human almanacs, that His purposes are measurable by human calendars. Not the striking of a clock but the maturity of the conditions moves the hand of God. We must resist the tendency to think of Him as though He were limited to a merely mechanical activity; as if, like the Medo-Persian monarchs, He were the slave of His own laws. The state of the crops prescribes the time of the harvest. He waited for the iniquity of the Amorites to be filled to the full (Gen. 15:10). Nineveh repented, so the fortieth day did not see the destruction of the city albeit that was proclaimed by Jonah at His command. For the elect's sake the days of calamity are shortened, whereas the long-suffering of God lengthens the day of salvation. Yet these days are not two but one (Matt. 24:22; 2 Pet. 3:9). The same patience of God that wrings from the saint the cry, "O Lord, how long," puts the new songs of praise for salvation into the mouth of many a sinner.

It is difficult, rather it is impossible, for us to conceive of the full yet harmonious exercise of all the attributes of God. There seems to us some necessary antagonism between omniscience, which must know the end from the beginning, as well as all the steps of the way thither, and the dependence of any action of God upon the course and conduct of men. So also we ask how it is possible for God to be resisted if He is omnipotent? We must remember the inevitable limitations of our power to apprehend what it is to be God. God is omniscient and omnipotent; we cannot conceive of Him as anything less. But God is also a living and free person, and it is the prerogative of all living and free persons to adapt themselves to the changing conditions with which they have to deal. Are we to deny that to Him which we claim for ourselves? It is vain for us to reason that God cannot be this if He is that, cannot be the one if He is the other, when the very conditions of our being make it inevitable that we must ascribe that to God which, because of realized inconsistency or antagonism, would be inconceivable in ourselves. Moreover, the coming of the Lord is a proper subject for prayer. The Lord taught His disciples to say

"Thy Kingdom come."* To John He said, "Yea, I come quickly"; and to Him John responded, "Amen: come, Lord Jesus." "The Spirit and the bride say, Come. And he that heareth, let him say, Come" (Matt. 6:10; Rev. 22:17, 20). Thus the Spirit prompts the Christian, and even utters Himself, the very petition the Lord Jesus taught His disciples to present to God. And if the coming of the Lord is a proper subject for prayer, it is not possible for us to conceive of its hour as already fixed. It is noticeable, too, that when the Lord declared that that hour did not lie within His knowledge, He said, not that though it had been fixed by the Father it had not been revealed by Him, but that the Father had reserved the matter within His own authority. Does not this suggest, at least, that the fixing of the hour is for the Father when, in His wisdom, He sees that the time is ripe?

Our apprehension of the perfection of deity is feeble as yet. Our knowledge of God is but partial, and being partial may present insoluble problems to our minds. We must be content to await the larger capacity and the increased knowledge that are to be made ours when the Lord comes.

The Meeting in the Air

To return: at a time unrevealed and hence undiscoverable, "they that are Christ's" are to be caught away "to meet the Lord in the air"; or as the words run literally "to a meeting with" (F, p. 179). The word used is *apantēsis,* which occurs elsewhere only in Matthew 25:1, 6; Acts 28:15. The brethren who met the apostle at the Three Taverns returned with him to Rome; in the parable the virgins returned with the bridegroom to the place whence they set out. After this analogy those who are caught up to this meeting with the Lord in the air, are to return with Him to the earth, for we know that the earth is the appointed terminus toward which He is journeying when that meeting takes place.

There is nothing in the Word, neither is there anything in the context, to indicate that the return to the earth must follow immediately upon the meeting in the air. Or, to express the same thing from another point of view, the Lord's descent from heaven to earth is not of necessity continuous. Indeed there are cogent reasons for the conclusion that that descent will be interrupted for a measurable interval at the point of meeting with His redeemed people.

The Parousia

When the Lord Jesus descends from heaven with the quickening word which is to work in the bodies of all His own, the living and the dead, the change to the new and heavenly condition, they are to be carried together to meet Him at His parousia (F). It is unfortunate that the English Versions should have adopted, or retained, "coming" as a translation of the Greek word *parousia;* it would have been clear gain had they done with it as with the Greek word *baptisma,* that is had they transliterated instead of translating it. "Coming" does not at all convey the meaning of the original word.† The difference is that whereas "coming" is the name of an act and is equivalent to "arrival," "advent," *parousia* is the name of a state and is equivalent to "presence," which is, indeed, its literal meaning, as the margin of the Revised Version indicates. "Coming" is properly represented by a perpendicular line thus|; *parousia* by a horizontal line thus—. "Coming" is the act of arriving and hence does not denote duration, as *parousia* invariably does. It will be easy to test these statements by reference to the New Testament occurrences of the word. The effect of this confusion is evident in 1 Thessalonians 3:12, 13, for example, "the Lord . . . stablish your hearts unblameable in holiness before our God

*This word "come" is sometimes taken to mean "grow," "increase," "spread," as though the kingdom were to be established by the preaching of the gospel. The kingdom of God comes when its king comes; not before and not otherwise. The stone in Nebuchadnezzar's dream only began to grow after it had destroyed the image (Dan. 2:35). Rightly understood the prayer is most appropriate to the time now present and to the heart and lip of the Christian. To pray "Thy kingdom come," is to pray "Amen: come, Lord Jesus." To pray for the coming of the king is to pray for the coming of the kingdom.

†See Chapter 5.

and Father, at the coming [*parousia*] of our Lord Jesus with all His saints." This seems to refer to the Second Advent, "the appearing of the glory of our great God and Savior Jesus Christ," "with ten thousands of His holy ones" (Titus 2:11; Jude 14). And so the classic commentators understand it, see Alford, Ellicott, Lightfoot, among others. But this conclusion is only possible, as Cremer somewhat artlessly remarks, when *parousia* is made to mean what, in fact, it does not mean.* It is essential to an apprehension of the mind of the Spirit, and of the apostle, that the characteristic meaning of the word be preserved. To come with, and to be present with, are obviously different ideas, and would never be confounded in the pages of any secular writer. Why should it be supposed that they are synonymous in the Scriptures?

The Judgment Seat of Christ

The word used in this connection, then, demands that we conceive of an interruption in the descent of the Lord Jesus to the earth for an appreciable period of time, during which His redeemed people will be with Him at the place of meeting. How long the Parousia will occupy has not been revealed, hence the line F-H (p. 179), which represents this session of the Lord with His redeemed at their place of meeting, has also been interrupted. Apparently it is during this session that the Judgment Seat of God—or of Christ, both terms are used—takes place (Rom. 14:10; 2 Cor. 5:10). This seems the inevitable deduction from a number of passages. The resurrection of the just is the time of reward for faithful service (Luke 14:14). And this resurrection of the just takes place at the opening of the Parousia (1 Cor. 15:23, etc.). At (*en,* in) the Parousia of the Lord Jesus the apostle hoped to meet his converts who would then be his glory. And those converts would themselves be presented there, for the appraisement of life and service (1 Thess. 2:19; 3:13).

The apostle John also expected to meet at the Parousia those to whom he wrote, and his language suggests that that would be a time of the reviewing of life alike for himself and for them (1 John 2:28).†

The End of Gentile Times

Concurrent with the Parousia of the Lord with His redeemed in the air is the period represented by the line G-J on the diagram. It also is of an unrevealed duration, and hence has been interrupted. This period sees the rise and development of the final form of Gentile government as described in Revelation 13 and other passages. It includes the Great Tribulation, "the time of Jacob's trouble," under the persecuting power of the Antichristian monarch, whether he be called king or president, or whether another title be evolved for him more in keeping with the tendencies of the age.

The "times of the Gentiles" end only when a Jew assumes the sovereign power in Jerusalem. That is to say, when the Lord Jesus Himself appears to overthrow the world monarch and his empire. This catastrophe will be the effect of the manifestation of the Parousia; the veil that hides the host in the air is suddenly withdrawn, the presence of the Lord with His redeemed is manifested, "the kingdom of the world," becomes that of "our Lord and of His Christ, and He shall reign forever and ever" (Rev. 11:15).‡ This is represented by H-J.

During the period G-J, as in every preceding age, there will be a testimony for God in the world, a gospel preached whereby men may be saved, albeit the "Church which is His [Christ's] Body" having already been completed and caught away to meet Him, the salvation of those who then respond to the gospel does not carry with it membership in that body. (See Rev. 7; 11; 14:15; 15:1, 2; 20:4.) The gospel then, as now, will have for its center the once slain, now living, Lamb, and it

*See Note, Chapter 5.

†This passage and 1 Thessalonians 2:19 intimate plainly enough that the apostles expected to recognize those with whom they had been in contact in this life, and to be recognized by them.

‡See Chapter 7. The overthrow of the Turk in Palestine has not relieved the land from Gentile domination. The British also are Gentiles. Doubtless the change from the iron yoke of the Turk to the milder rule of the British is altogether for the better. But that does not alter the fact as stated.

will be made effective by the Holy Spirit, among both Jews and Gentiles.*

How this testimony for God may be carried over into the new circumstances when all who belong to Christ have been caught away, is not difficult to conceive. Sufficient to mention the multitudes to whom the gospel facts at least will be known, and the Bible and Christian literature generally, to suggest the possibilities of the situation. That persons are to be saved, and in large numbers, during the period between the rapture of the Church and the Day of the Lord, G-J (p. 179), is clear from the passages in the Apocalypse referred to above. Moreover, in Joel's foreview of the time when "the great and notable Day of the Lord" is imminent, he concludes with these words, "And it shall come to pass that whosoever shall call upon the Name of the Lord shall be delivered." It is worthy of note that "whosoever" is the characteristic word which describes the scope of the gospel of the grace of God in this present age. It will be no less so in that which is to follow. The line of demarcation between the day of grace and the Day of Judgment is clearly drawn. When the Lord Jesus is revealed in fire, "rendering vengeance [just retribution is the meaning of the word] to them that know not God, and to them that obey not the gospel of our Lord Jesus," then it is that "the Master of the House has risen up, and shut to the door" (2 Thess. 1:8; Luke 13:25). Until that hour (H-J, p. 179) grace reigns, and "whosoever shall call upon the Name of the Lord shall be saved."

The conditions during the period G-J (p. 179), however, will not be more but less favorable for naming the Name of the Lord than in this. The spirit of satisfaction with the progress of humanity and hope for its acceleration will increase. There will be no toleration for the godly, while for those who refuse the truth there will be a strong delusion, and a consequent ready belief in the lie that the antichristian ruler, the first beast of Revelation 13, is the man of destiny, his dominion the universal empire, the guarantee of settled peace and uninterrupted prosperity. (See 2 Thess. 2:8–12.)

After the Advent

With events after the Second Advent (H-J, p. 179) of the Lord Jesus the diagram is not concerned. The judgment of the nations then existent upon the earth will not long be delayed, for the scene is introduced in a way that fixes its relation in time with the Advent. "When the Son of man shall come in His glory, and all the angels with Him, then shall He sit on the throne of His glory: and before Him shall be gathered all the nations" (Matt. 25:31 ff.). This takes place, apparently, at the opening of the millennial reign. The characteristic of that reign may be learned from the symbol "a rod of iron" used to describe it (Rev. 12:5). That is to say the rule of the Prince of Peace and King of righteousness will be guaranteed by adequate force, for no other rule over unregenerate men is possible in any age.

This is to be man's final probation. As in all previous ages, so also in this. Immune from temptation from without, for during this period Satan is confined in the abyss, men will submit to force, now happily at the disposal of righteousness; but when the archenemy is free again to practice his deceits, they will readily respond to his approaches and once more assert themselves against God and the Anointed of God. The event is the final defeat of Satan and his doom.

Thereupon follows the resurrection of "the rest of the dead" and their judgment at the Great White Throne, where the Judge is the rejected Savior (Rev. 20:11 ff.; John 5:22 and 27). "From [His] Face the earth and the heaven fled away; and there was found no place for them." They make way for "new heavens and a new earth, wherein dwelleth righteousness" (2 Pet. 3:13).

*There does not appear to be adequate ground for identifying "the restrainer" of 2 Thessalonians 2:7, with the Holy Spirit, or for the statement that He is to leave the earth with the completed Church. It is in these "last days," indeed, that God is to pour forth His Spirit upon all flesh (Joel 2:28–30). See *Notes on Thessalonians*.

▪ APPENDIX ▪

Note A

John 5:29 and Acts 24:15 are the only places in the New Testament in which there is specific reference to the resurrection of others than those who have trusted in Christ. In John 12:48, and a few other passages, their resurrection is implied.

That "the Last Day" is a period covering more than a thousand years, is clear from Revelation 20:4–12. Neither in John 5:29, nor in the passages in which the phrase occurs, is there any indication of this interval. "The Last Day" opens with the resurrection and rapture of believers, G-F (p. 179), and closes with the resurrection and judgment of those who have not accepted Christ, and includes the millennium which intervenes, J-B (p. 179). It is not "the end of the world," vulgarly so called, but the last day, or period, of man's accountability to God in his condition as a fallen being.

The "hour" of John 5:24, "The hour cometh, and now is, when the dead shall hear the voice of the Son of God and they that hear shall live," has already extended to nearly two thousand years, C-G (p. 179). The "hour" of verse 28, "the hour cometh in which all that are in the tombs shall hear His voice, and shall come forth; they that have done good, unto the resurrection of life; they that have practiced ill, unto the resurrection of judgment," must be understood in the same way, G-B (p. 179). "Day" and "hour," both used in an extended sense, are interchanged in John 16:25, 26.

Intervals between events are not always marked in the predictions of Scripture. Things that are foretold in the same sentence may yet be separated by long periods of time in the fulfillment. In Genesis 3:15, for example, three distinct things are predicted. Enmity between the woman and the serpent sprang up immediately; the serpent bruised the heel of the woman's Seed at the Cross, four thousand years later; after six thousand years the bruising of the serpent's head is still awaited.

Of the prophecy of Isaiah 11, verses 1–3 were fulfilled at the First Advent of Christ; the rest of the chapter refers to the effects of the Second Advent. "The acceptable year of the Lord" was ushered in when He came the first time, and continues unto this day. "The day of vengeance of our God" arrives when the Lord Jesus is revealed "from heaven with the angels of His power in naming fire," H-J (p. 179). No interval is suggested in the words as they are recorded in Isaiah 61:2, yet the Lord ceased His reading at the end of the former phrase, and said, "Today hath this Scripture been fulfilled in your ears." The rest awaits. (See Luke 4:21; 2 Thess 1:7, 8.) The words of the Lord in John 5:29 present the same feature.

Note B

That John 5:25 does not refer to the resurrection but to the spiritual quickening, which is a present experience of each believer, seems plain enough. First, the addition of the words "and now is" which are absent from verse 28, is to be noted. Second, the Lord speaks of "all that are in the tombs" to describe those whose bodies have ceased to discharge the functions of life and passed into corruption, reserving the word "dead" for the spiritual condition of all men in virtue of their descent from Adam. (See Eph. 2:1.) Third, these words are explanatory of verse 24, where those who believe are said to have passed out of death into life, obviously not an event to happen to the body in the future, but a present experience of the believing soul.

Note C

A different deduction is sometimes drawn from certain Scriptures, such as Revelation

14:4, which speaks of "firstfruits unto God and unto the Lamb." The firstfruits of the harvest is that portion which is earliest garnered. The word is used in the Old Testament only in a literal sense, in the New Testament only in a figurative. Believers of the apostolic age were "a kind of firstfruits of His [God's] creatures," that is, the beginning of the great and varied harvest of the Cross (James 1:18).

The Thessalonian converts had been chosen of God "as firstfruits unto salvation" (2 Thess. 2:13, marg.), which is probably the correct reading. Salvation is defined in the following verse as "the obtaining of the glory of our Lord Jesus Christ." Many among them had deserved the apostle's censure, but exclusion of such is not suggested by the apostle. Not some of the believers at Thessalonica, but the whole of them, are thus described as "firstfruits unto salvation."

This principle must be borne in mind throughout. Epaenetus did not differ from the converts that followed him in Asia Minor (Rom. 16:5). The household of Stephanus were not more faithful than those in Achaia who were converted later (1 Cor. 16:15).

In 1 Corinthians 15:20, 23 Christ is said to be "the firstfruits of them that are asleep." That is Christ personal, not Christ mystical, as though any of those who believe on Him were contemplated as included with Him. This is clear from verse 20, for it was Christ alone who was raised from the dead. Moreover the word firstfruits is a singular noun, notwithstanding the final s. In the general statement of Romans 11:16 "firstfruit" is used, but the Greek word is singular throughout.

The only remaining occurrence of the word is Revelation 14:4, where it is applied to a company of 144,000 persons (possibly the number is symbolic), who are seen with the Lamb on Mount Zion. An exposition of the passage would be beyond the limits prescribed for these chapters. The following suggestions may, however, be offered. The preceding chapter describes the condition of the world under the first beast, the false prince of peace, who attempts, by mingled fraud and force, by diabolic and by human power, to establish a universal empire. Chapter fourteen presents the contrast. Here is the true universal monarch, set by God on His holy hill. With Him are associated a host who are described as "purchased out of the earth." This is the sole ground of their presence with the Lamb. There is no suggestion that by peculiar faithfulness or watchfulness they had earned the right to be there. It is possible they may be those who refused the mark of the beast. But there is no warrant for identifying them with an hypothetical company of faithful Christians who are to be caught away before the Great Tribulation, while the mass of then living members of the body of Christ pass through it. It is from the epistles of Paul that we learn of "the Church which is His Body," and of the resurrection and rapture of its members at the beginning of the Parousia, G-F (p. 179). These epistles know nothing of a rapture earlier than that of 1 Thessalonians 4:13–17, which is to include all who belong to Christ (1 Cor. 15:23). Nor do they know anything of a firstfruits from the Church, though they do of a firstfruits from the world, as we have seen.

Anti Christ Wants To Give You A Number
Christ " " " Name

144 K – Firstfruits Of An Age Or Dispensation.

Note D

The words "we that are alive, that are left unto the Parousia of the Lord," do not commit the apostle to the belief that the Lord Jesus would return during his lifetime. Shortly afterward we find him using the same language concerning resurrection (2 Cor. 4:14), "shall raise up us also"; but that did not commit him to the belief that he would die before the Lord had come.

When the Lord Jesus returns, believers will be as they are now, and indeed as they were at Thessalonica, divided into two classes, the living and the dead. But the time of that return has not been revealed, it is among the secret things concerning which God has kept His own counsel. (See Deut. 29:29; Mark 13:32; Acts 1:7.) Consequently, in speaking of the return of the Lord Jesus, the apostle sometimes associates himself with the one class, looking forward to resurrection, as in 2 Corinthians 4:14, sometimes with the other, looking forward to change, as in 1 Thessalonians 4:13–17, and 1 Corinthians 15:51. His sympathy with those who were anxious about their dead leads him to associate himself with the mourners at Thessalonica; his sense of failing physical powers leads him to associate himself with those who had died at Corinth.

The Hope Of - Resurrection Coincides w/ Rapture (Appearance)

The second epistle to the Corinthians, moreover, in which he associates himself with those lying asleep, was written at no greater interval than three or four years after that to the Thessalonians, in which he associates himself with the living, at the Parousia.

It contains a passage, 5:1–10, expressing his own attitude toward the alternative possibilities, death and the coming of the Lord, and in it also he uses "we." In verses 2–4 he expresses his longing for that which cannot take place until the Lord comes, to be clothed with "our habitation which is from heaven," the "building from God," the "house not made with hands." In verse 6 he asserts that he is of good courage in the face of death, and in verse 8 repeats the assertion, adding that he is "willing rather to be absent from the body and to be at home with the Lord," i.e., to die. Longing for the Parousia of Christ, which is certain to come, yet not afraid of death, which may possibly come first, is, then, the characteristic attitude of each generation of Christians.

Two Hopes

In the epistle to the Philippians, written perhaps seven years later still, while he describes his own attitude toward death, 1:21–24, in language akin to that used to the Corinthians, and suggests that it is no very remote contingency, 2:17, he yet uses "we" and "our" in describing the characteristic attitude of Christians to the coming of the Lord. His advancing years and the threatening nature of his circumstances, while they brought before his mind increasingly the possibility that he might die before the Parousia, did not prevent his saying, "heaven, from whence also we wait for a Savior" (Phil. 3:20).

And in the pastoral epistles, latest of all, whereas he uses language only explicable on the suggestion that he knew his own death to be imminent, he still speaks of the reward awaiting those who have loved the appearing of Christ (2 Tim. 4:6–8), and of the grace of God "instructing us, to the intent that . . . we should live . . . looking for the blessed hope" (Titus 2: 11–13). Indeed, before he closes the epistle in which he says, "I am already being offered," he urges Timothy to come to him "before winter," a season presumably still some distance away, and to bring with him Mark as well as some articles of which he anticipated he would be in need. As always, so now when there seemed to be no escape from death, the apostle stood ready either for suffering or for service, or for the rapture of the saints that would deliver him from the one and bring the other to an end.

It seems clear, therefore, that no conclusion can be drawn from the apostle's language as to his personal expectations. He shared in what should be the attitude of each generation of Christians, the desire for, and the expectation of, the Parousia of the Lord, but there is no reason to suppose that he knew more on the subject than he taught (cp. 1 Cor. 13:12). Neither is there any evidence that the statements of the later epistles are intended to correct those written earlier. On the contrary, as we have seen, they supplement, but in no case do they contradict, previous declarations. Moreover, these words to the Thessalonians claim to be a revelation from the Lord Himself, and, while they might be expanded or explained by later revelation, they would not be set aside, much less could they be attributed to a mistaken apprehension on the part of the apostle. Throughout his life, as it is reflected in his epistles, he maintains the same attitude toward the great alternatives. There is no inconsistency. His example and his words alike teach us to be prepared to meet death with unflinching courage, but, above all things, to look for the Parousia of the Lord.

Hosea 12:4; Romans 13:13; Hebrews 12:25 may be compared for examples of this use of "us" and "we."

It is true of each man at all times, as it was true of David pursued by Saul, "there is but a step between [us] and death." And yet true as the apostle knew this to be of himself, he knew also that the Lord might come first. Experience has taught men that death is the one thing which can be really reckoned upon as an ever-present possibility. In the gospel it is revealed that to the Christian the Lord may possibly come first. If wise men thus reckon with death, how much more should the believer count upon the Parousia of the Lord!

Note E

Too often, it is to be feared, the word "rapture" is taken to refer to the peculiar joy of the redeemed when they meet the Lord. But the idea of ecstasy which arises from the conception of being carried out of oneself with joy, is entirely absent from the New Testament use of the word *harpazō*. Nor is the word "secret" ever attached to it there. In view of unhappy controversies it is well to confine ourselves to Scriptural phraseology as far as possible. As to the fact, this much may be said, that what is to happen "in the twinkling of an eye," cannot be witnessed and therefore must, insofar, be secret. But the removal of even a "little flock" from among men could not long remain a secret, if it was ever a secret at all. See *Notes on Thessalonians*.

Note F

Neither soul nor spirit is said to sleep at death; the word of 1 Thessalonians 4:13 *(koimaomai)* is used only of the body of the believer. This is clear from such a passage as Acts 13:36, for example: "David fell on sleep . . . and saw corruption." That part of David which fell on sleep was the part that saw corruption. At death the unclothed spirit (a condition in itself distasteful to the apostle, as may be seen from a comparison of 2 Cor. 5, v. 3 with v. 8) is "at home with the Lord." It is in view of this that he is ready even to die, for, he writes elsewhere, "to die is gain . . . to depart and to be with Christ . . . is very far better" (Phil. 1:21–23). To suggest that the otiose state, quiescence, if not unconsciousness, of spirit would commend itself to the apostle as preferable to his life of activity in service here betrays a curious misconception of his character.

Moreover, the preposition translated "with" *(pros)* in 2 Corinthians 5:8, denotes not merely to be in the same place with another, it means to be in communication with, to be receiving impressions from and imparting impressions to, another. The preposition would be inappropriate were the souls or spirits of the dead in Christ to be conceived of as in a state of unconsciousness.

Note G

"The Last Trump." It is hardly possible that the reference is to the last of the seven trumpets of the Apocalypse. These are figures, not actual trumpets; like the seals and the bowls they are part of the symbology under which the future was unfolded to John. To suppose that Paul refers to the seventh of John's series is to mistake the character of the Revelation, and to assume that what John saw and heard were the actual things that are yet to be seen and heard when the fulfillment comes, and not symbols, or figures, of those things. Moreover, there is no hint in his writings that Paul had any knowledge of the form under which the developments of human history were revealed to John, or, indeed, that he was acquainted with the Apocalypse at all. Moreover, he is not describing a vision; he is imparting information, describing things that are to occur. All the rest of the passage is to be understood literally; so also must this according to any sound canon of interpretation. The figure is that of any army receiving the signal to march; the "shout" of 1 Thessalonians 4:16 is also a military word with a like significance. It is possible the apostle may have in mind the trumpets by which the Israelites were summoned. The first and second blasts gathered them, the third was the signal to march (Num. 10:2–6).

Note H

Like "resurrection," "mortal" is applicable only to the body, and, indeed, only to the bodies of the living. The word immortality of necessity follows it; that is, it also is applicable only to the bodies of living believers as these will be affected by the change which is to take place in them at the Parousia of the Lord. "The immortality of the soul" is a purely pagan conception, arising out of the mistaken notion that evil is inherent in matter, and that, therefore, the body is the seat of sin and the source of all the ills of life. The only other New Testament occurrence of the word *(athanasia)* is 1 Timothy 6:16. The common use of immortal as equivalent to continuously existing is not found in the Bible at all. Immortality is not used of the unregenerate there, but neither is countenance given to the notion that any man will ever cease to be.

Note J

Zōopoieō, "to make alive," in the New Testament invariably means to impart life to what is dead. God raises the dead, that is, the bodies of the dead, and imparts life to them; so also does the Son (John 5:24; 1 Cor. 15:22). Romans 8:11 is to be understood in the same way; God will impart life to this mortal body; it shall put on immortality. There is no other passage of Scripture in which *zōopoieō* means a reinforcement of vigor, spiritual, mental or physical. There is no reason for the introduction of this idea here, since it is unwarranted either by the usage of the word or by the context.

Witnesses to the Second Advent

Witnesses to the Second Advent

Psalm 2 (R.V.)

1. Why do the nations rage, and the peoples imagine a vain thing?

2. The kings of the earth set themselves, and the rulers take counsel together, against the Lord, and against His anointed, saying,

3. Let us break their bands asunder, and cast away their cords from us.

4. He that sitteth in the heavens shall laugh: the Lord shall have them in derision.

5. Then shall He speak unto them in His wrath, and vex them in His sore displeasure:

6. Yet I have set My King upon My holy hill of Zion.

7. I will tell of the decree: The Lord said unto Me, Thou art My Son: this day have I begotten Thee.

8. Ask of Me, and I will give Thee the nations for Thine inheritance, and the uttermost parts of the earth for Thy possession.

9. Thou shalt break them with a rod of iron; Thou shalt dash them in pieces like a potter's vessel.

10. Now therefore be wise, O ye Kings: be instructed, ye judges of the earth.

11. Serve the Lord with fear, and rejoice with trembling.

12. Kiss the Son, lest He be angry, and ye perish in the way, for His wrath will soon be kindled. Blessed are all they that put their trust in Him.

Revelation 19:11–21 (R.V.)

"And I saw the heaven opened; and behold, a white horse, and He that sat thereon, called Faithful and True; and in righteousness He doth judge and make war. And His eyes are a flame of fire, and upon His head are many diadems; and He hath a name written, which no one knoweth but He Himself. And He is arrayed in a garment sprinkled with blood: and His name is called the Word of God. And the armies which are in heaven followed Him upon white horses, clothed in fine linen, white and pure. And out of His mouth proceedeth a sharp sword, that with it He should smite the nations: and He shall rule them with a rod of iron: And He treadeth the winepress of the fierceness of the wrath of Almighty God. And He hath on His garment and on His thigh a name written, KING OF KINGS AND LORD OF LORDS.

"And I saw an angel standing in the sun; and he cried with a loud voice, saying to all the birds that fly in midheaven, Come and be gathered together unto the great supper of God; that ye may eat the flesh of kings, and the flesh of captains, and the flesh of mighty men, and the flesh of horses, and of them that sit thereon, and the flesh of all men, both free and bond, and small and great.

"And I saw the beast, and the kings of the earth, and their armies, gathered together to make war against Him that sat upon the horse, and against His army. And the beast was taken, and with him the false prophet, that wrought the signs in his sight, wherewith he deceived them that had received the mark of the beast, and them that worshiped his image: they twain were cast alive into the lake of fire that burneth with brimstone: and the rest were killed with the sword which came forth out of his mouth: and all the birds were filled with their flesh."

Revelation 11:15–18 (R.V.)

"And the seventh angel sounded; and there followed great voices in heaven, and they said, The Kingdom of the world is become the Kingdom of our Lord, and of His Christ: and He shall reign forever and ever. And the four and twenty elders, which sit before God on their thrones, fell upon their faces, and worshiped God, saying, We give Thee thanks, O Lord God, the Almighty, which art and which wast; because Thou hast taken Thy great power, and didst reign. And the nations were wroth, and thy wrath came, and the time of the dead to be judged, and the time to give their reward, to Thy servants the prophets, and to the saints, and to them that fear Thy name, the small and the great; and to destroy them that destroy the earth."

Witnesses to the Second Advent

The Second Coming of Christ is shown in Scripture to consist of two distinct events, namely, (1) the rapture of the Church to meet the Lord in the air (1 Thess. 4:13–17), followed by a period of divine retribution upon the rebellious condition of humanity; (2) the appearing of the Lord Jesus in His glory with the Church and with His angels, at the consummation of this period, for the destruction of the Antichrist and those who are associated with him, for the deliverance of the Jewish nation from their oppressors, and for the establishment of the Kingdom of righteousness and peace (2 Thess. 2:7–10; Rev. 19:11–21). To these events there has been a long line of witnesses, and the number is not yet complete.

The First Announcement

We must go back to the very beginnings of human history for the initial announcement of the Second Advent. No sooner had sin come into the world than God pronounced the doom of the Tempter whose malignant craft had effected man's moral collapse. The Seed of the woman should bruise his head. That judicial sentence embodies the first prophecy of the Second Advent. The crushing defeat which the Evil One sustained at Calvary by the Virgin-born Redeemer carried with it the inevitable doom by which that foe of God and man will, when Christ comes in glory, be bound by Him and cast into the abyss and shut up and sealed therein for a thousand years, thereafter to be cast into the Lake of Fire (Rev. 20:1–3, 10).

Enoch's Prophecy

The next testimony, chronologically, is to be found in the epistle of Jude in a statement of fact not recorded in the Old Testament. Speaking of the ultimate doom of ungodly men, he says: "And to these also Enoch, the seventh from Adam, prophesied, saying, Behold, the Lord came with ten thousands of His holy ones, to execute judgment upon all, and to convict all the ungodly of all their works of ungodliness which they have ungodly wrought, and of all the hard things which ungodly sinners have spoken against Him" (Jude 14, 15). The word "came" is in the past tense, because by Hebrew usage the past tense was idiomatically employed in predicting the future, a testimony indeed to the certainty of the events foretold. Here, then, was a witness among the antediluvians to the fact that Christ would come to judge the world in righteousness.

Job's Assurance

We now pass to the patriarchal age. The weight of evidence points to the likelihood that Job lived about the time of Abraham. We learn from the twenty-second chapter of Genesis that Uz was Abraham's nephew (v. 21, R.V.), and there is good reason for the supposition that this Uz gave his name to the land in which Job dwelt (Job 1:1). There is a remarkable passage in Job's sixth discourse in which his complaints give place for the moment to confident assurance of resurrection. Several of the great foundation truths of the gospel are packed into this brief utterance. He says, "I know that my Redeemer liveth, and that He shall stand up ["stand triumphantly" is the thought conveyed by the word] at the last over my dust (see R.V. marg.); and after my skin hath been destroyed, yet from my flesh shall I see God: Whom I shall see for myself, and mine eyes shall behold, and not another" (marg., not as a stranger) (Job 19:25–27).

The word "earth" here is the same as that rendered "dust" in Genesis 2:7; 3:19. It is true that Christ will stand on the Mount of Olives, when He comes to deliver Zion (Zech. 14:4), but Job is here speaking of the resurrection power of His Redeemer and how it will affect his mortal remains. He vividly describes the Lord as taking up a position as a mighty One over his dust, with the result that though his body has gone to disintegration yet in his flesh he will see God. Job's prediction then constitutes a striking testimony to the fact of the Second Advent.

Jacob's Prediction

Almost two centuries later, Jacob, on his deathbed, in pronouncing prophetic blessings upon his sons, declares that "The scepter shall not depart from Judah, nor the ruler's staff from between his feet, until Shiloh come; and unto Him shall the obedience of the peoples be" (Gen. 49:10). Shiloh means the Peacemaker, and the context shows that not the place but the person, the Messiah, is in view. Abraham rejoiced to see His day (John 8:56), and the same anticipation is here expressed by his grandson. Whatever partial fulfillment of Jacob's prophecy there may have been in the past, the complete antitypical fulfillment cannot take place until Christ comes to reign. Then, and not till then, the willing obedience of the peoples will be offered to Him.

Balaam's Prophecy

The next testimony to the Second Advent is Balaam's prophecy: it takes up and expands that of Jacob. That it relates to the time under consideration is made clear in Balaam's introductory words to Balak, "I will advertise thee what this people shall do to thy people in the latter days" (Num. 24:14). The time indicated is literally "the end of the days," a phrase which is found in other eschatological passages, e.g., Isaiah 2:7; Daniel 10:14; Micah 4:1. The phrase signifies the time when the promises of salvation made to Israel will have their fulfillment. It points, as has been well said, to the accomplishment of a prophetic announcement.

The prophecy is as follows: "I see Him, but not now: I behold Him, but not nigh: there shall come forth a star out of Jacob, and a scepter shall rise out of Israel, and shall smite through the corners of Moab, and break down all the sons of tumult. And Edom shall be a possession, Seir also shall be a possession, which were his enemies; while Israel doeth valiantly. And out of Jacob shall one have dominion, and shall destroy the remnant from the city" (Num. 24:17–19).

This prophecy cannot be rightly applied to the first advent. The details do not relate to the humiliation and sufferings of Christ, but to the glories which are yet to be. The mention of "the sons of tumult" has reference to the gathering of the nations at the end of this age in their effort to crush the Jews. The prophecy clearly relates to the time when Christ will come for their deliverance and establish the government of Israel in the earth.

We next come to

The Song of Moses

a prophecy uttered just before his death. It is recorded in Deuteronomy 32, which gives a concise history of Israel from the time prior to their actual existence, when the divine providence was arranging the geographical distribution of the various nations in view of the future settlement of Israel in their land (v. 8), until the final overthrow of their adversaries at the Second Advent (vv. 40–43). The history thus covers the long period from the dispersion from Babel to the issue of the warfare of Armageddon.

The main part of the song is devoted to a record of the waywardness of Israel in spite of the mercies of God, and to a prediction of the inevitable judgments which must consequently come upon the nation. They must be delivered over to their adversaries, until the divine vengeance has done its necessary work. Yet final deliverance will come, "The Lord shall judge His people, and repent Himself for His servants, when He seeth that their power is gone." Their foes, at whose hands they have suffered the woes of the Great Tribulation, will themselves be visited with the wrath of God.

The close of the prophecy, as correctly rendered in the Revised Version, makes a striking allusion to the doom of Antichrist and to the kings of the nations allied under him, the passage thus being remarkably coincidental with Revelation 17:12–14, and other passages relating to Armageddon. The foe is overthrown by the Son of God Himself, and the nations of the world, delivered from the tyranny and misrule of their despots, are invited to rejoice with liberated Israel. God's people and their land shall be blessed with peace and rest. With this prediction of the glorious intervention of Messiah the song terminates. From verse 39 to verse 42 the speaker is Jehovah.

We will quote in full the closing utterances

relating to the Second Advent: "If I whet My glittering sword (see Is. 34:5–8 and 66:16; and Rev. 19:15, 21), and My hand take hold on judgment; I will render vengeance (see 2 Thess. 1:8, R.V.) to Mine adversaries, and will recompense them that hate Me. I will make Mine arrows drunk with blood (see Is. 34:3, 7; 63:4; Ezek. 39:17–20; Hab. 3:11; Rev. 14:20), and My sword shall devour flesh; with the blood of the slain and the captives, from the head of the leaders of the enemy ('the head' is prophetic of Antichrist; 'the leaders' indicates the potentates gathered under him; see especially Ps. 110:6; Rev. 17:12–14, 17; 19:19–21; Dan. 7:24–27; and Hab. 3:13). Rejoice, O ye nations [Gentile peoples who are to be blessed in the Millennium] with His people [Israel]; for He will avenge the blood of His servants (see Rev. 6:10; 11:17; 13:7; 19:2), and will render vengeance to His adversaries, and will make expiation for His land, for His people" (see Is. 34:8; 63:4; Ezek. 39:20–22; Joel 3:16; Hab. 3:16; and the Psalms, *passim*).

The Septuagint inserts, "and let all the angels of God worship Him" after "Rejoice, O ye nations, with His people," and this Septuagint version is quoted in Hebrews 1:6, which is a Second Advent prophecy, and should read, as in the Revised Version, "And when He again bringeth the Firstborn into the world, He saith, And let all the angels of God worship Him." The Father brought His Firstborn into the world at His Incarnation; He will do so again when He comes in glory.

Hannah's Song

Passing now to the time of the birth of Samuel the prophet, whose ministry inaugurated the line of Israel's kings, we come to the prophetic Psalm prayed by his mother when she brought her child to Eli in the house of the Lord for his lifelong service therein. As with many other Spirit-controlled utterances, the theme passes from the immediate circumstances, in this case relating to the birth of the child, to events which have to do with the judgments of the Lord in the earth and the establishment of His Kingdom. The closing words of her song thus testify to the Second Advent: "They that strive with the Lord shall be broken in pieces; against them shall He thunder in Heaven. The Lord shall judge the ends of the earth; and He shall give strength unto His king, and exalt the horn of His Anointed" (1 Sam. 2:10).

The last two sentences are clearly prophetic of millennial blessing, and inasmuch as the Scripture teaches that the millennium will be preceded by the overthrow of the combined foes of Israel, the preceding clauses can only be rightly taken in their fullest meaning as applicable to that time. We may compare, for instance, the breaking in pieces of those who strive against God with Daniel 2:35, 44, and the prediction concerning God's thundering upon them with Revelation 16:18. Whatever may have been in Hannah's mind as to her own circumstances, she was speaking as a prophetess, and her words, inspired of God, were doubtless of wider significance than she herself realized.

This then is the list of the outstanding testimonies to the Second Advent from the time of Adam until Israel's entrance into the land of Canaan. It consists of God's declaration to Satan, and the prophecies of Enoch, Job, Jacob, Balaam, Moses and Hannah. There are other intimations, but those which have been mentioned are the definite utterances. The occasions are separated at comparatively lengthy intervals, the details, however, becoming increasingly distinct and the prophecy expanding as history proceeds.

The Time of the Kings

We now come to a period when the witness is more constant; it begins with the establishment of the kingdom under David and extends throughout the time of the kings of Judah and Israel, on through the captivity and the restoration, until the close of prophetic testimony in the nation under the era of the Law.

It is not our purpose here to consider in detail the wonderful series of predictions in the Psalms and the prophets relating to the Lord's Return in glory. The Psalms contain a large number of references to it. It may indeed be said to form one of the main subjects of their prophecies.

The Psalms

In the second Psalm, for instance, which together with the first, forms an introduction to the whole book, the intervention of the Lord in Person in the affairs of the world is foretold. The gathering of the kings of the earth and the rulers together against Messiah, as mentioned in the opening words, had only a partial fulfillment at the time of the death of Christ. The statement that the Lord shall speak unto the nations in His wrath and vex them in His sore displeasure has not yet received accomplishment, but will be fulfilled immediately prior to the setting of God's king upon His "holy hill of Zion" at the beginning of the Millennium (vv. 5, 6).

The Psalms are largely occupied with the sufferings and prayers and preservation of the godly remnant of the Jews in the time of the Great Tribulation. The experiences of David form an historical basis for the prophetic and divinely inspired utterances which relate to the experiences of God-fearing Jews who will at the close of this age suffer at the hands of the Antichrist. These Psalms are not merely the history of past events. They are the utterances of the Spirit of Christ, Who, through the Psalmists beforehand, was sympathetically identifying Himself with His oppressed people, the Jews. "The testimony of Jesus is the spirit of prophecy." The facts that the Antichrist is to be Satan's human instrument in his final effort to crush the nation of Israel, and that Christ will Himself come to their deliverance and hurl the tyrant to his doom, accounts for the character of the language of what have been called the imprecatory Psalms. That God's vengeance would eventually be dealt out upon the adversaries of Israel had long been foretold, as we have seen.

So-Called Imprecatory Psalms

The Psalms which breathe the spirit of vengeance were penned, not for the use of the Church, but for the Jewish people, and in fellowship with God and His counsels. Complaints against these denunciatory psalms, on account of their vindictive character, are the outcome of a misunderstanding both of their spirit and purpose. They were not written for an age when the Church is bearing witness in the gospel and is taught to pray for her enemies and persecutors, nor in regard to Israel were they written in the spirit of mere human spite and vengeance. Israel's treatment of their enemies is not a matter of mere human revenge. It is always primarily a vindication of the claims of God. That the Antichrist and those associated with him in their rebellion against the Most High should be denounced and overthrown is only consistent with the divine counsels.

The Spirit of God, knowing beforehand the solemn events that will characterize the close of this age, and the intense suffering through which the Jews must pass at that time at the instigation of the devil, caused the Psalms to be written for the use of God-fearing Jews at this future period. The cry for vengeance is a cry which God has determined to answer at the Second Advent. Only as we grasp this divinely foretold situation can we understand the full meaning and scope of the book of the Psalms. If the Psalms denounce rebellious nations, they also contain long-suffering warnings as to the need of repentance, and if they frequently foretell the doom of the foes of God and His people, there are also predictions of final mercy and blessing for the world, and this bright theme, which likewise characterizes the whole, provides the grand subject of the final series of songs. The wrath of God upon the Antichrist and the gathered foes of God will be a necessary step preliminary to the establishment of peace on the earth, and this can be brought about only in the way indicated, at the hands of the Messiah Himself.

The Psalms and Isaiah

These themes which run through the Psalms likewise constitute a large part of the testimony of the prophets. Isaiah's testimony is largely parallel to that of the book of Psalms. Let the reader compare the words of the second Psalm, "Thou art My Son," and "Yet have I set My King upon My holy hill," and "I will give Thee the nations," with Isaiah 9:6, 7, "Unto us a Son is given; and the government shall be upon His shoulders . . . of the increase of His government and of peace there shall be no end, upon the throne of David, and upon

His Kingdom, to establish it." Compare, as further examples, the sufferings and glories of Messiah in Psalm 22 and other Psalms with the similar themes in Isaiah 52:13–15 and 53; Psalm 137 and its denunciation of Babylon with Isaiah 47; Psalm 46:6, and similar passages foretelling the doom of rebellious nations, with Isaiah 63:1–6, etc.; the cries for deliverance in the so-called imprecatory Psalms, with such passages as Isaiah 64; the numerous Psalms of praise for deliverance, e.g., Psalms 46 and 47, with Isaiah 63:7, etc.; and, finally, the closing Psalms of millennial prosperity with the close of Isaiah's prophecies, 66:10 to end. Joel's prophecy predicts the circumstances of the warfare of Armageddon, and describes the intervention of Messiah as the treading of the winepress of God's wrath, amplifying the prophecy of Isaiah 53:3, and foreshadowing that at the close of Revelation 14.

The Witness During the Captivity

The prophets of the time of the Captivity, Ezekiel and Daniel, provide a testimony of a special character. The events connected with the Second Advent are foretold in these prophecies more precisely than in any that preceded. The general outline given in previous records is here largely filled in, many details, however, being reserved for the New Testament. In Ezekiel the subject bears more especially on Israel as a whole. In Daniel the range of prophecy is narrower; it has to do with the Jews in relation to the times of the Gentiles and the way in which the Second Advent will bring them to a close.

Post-Captivity Testimony

The prophets of the time subsequent to the return from captivity continue the theme, Zechariah giving details not previously supplied, as to the effects of the war upon Jerusalem, and the way in which the Lord will appear for deliverance.

The witness of the Old Testament prophets closes with the testimony of Malachi, "The Lord, Whom ye seek, shall suddenly come to His Temple: and the Messenger of the covenant, Whom ye delight in, behold, He cometh, saith the Lord of Hosts. But who may abide the day of His coming? and who shall stand when He appeareth? for He is like fuller's soap; and He shall sit as a refiner and purifier of silver, and He shall purify the sons of Levi, and purge them as gold and silver; and they shall offer unto the Lord offerings in righteousness. Then shall the offering of Judah and Jerusalem be pleasant unto the Lord, as in the days of old, and as in ancient years" (Mal. 3:1–4). The prophecy closes with the promise that Elijah shall be sent to the nation before "the great and terrible Day of the Lord" come. Here the voice of prophecy ceases until the appearance of Christ in the days of His flesh.

The Witness of Christ

The witness to the Second Advent, resumed by the Lord, was continued by His apostles until the cycle of revelation was completed. This period is characterized by a greater continuity of testimony and a greater fullness of revelation than during the preceding ages. Our Lord begins His testimony at the very outset of His public ministry. Just after His baptism He makes known to His disciples that they will see "the Heaven opened, and the angels of God ascending and descending upon the Son of man," obviously a Second Advent scene (John 1:50). His teaching on the subject is given both publicly and privately.

Each of the four Gospel writers records it, the details being appropriate to the general scope and design of his Gospel. Matthew, Mark and Luke devote whole sections to the prediction of the events and the circumstances attending it. The Gospels of Matthew and Mark view it especially in relation to the Jewish nation (the fig tree, Matt. 24:32; Mark 13:28); Luke's Gospel views it as it will affect both the Jews and the Gentile nations (the fig tree and all the trees, Luke 21:28). The Gospel of John gives the Lord's predictions as to the resurrection. This has a special bearing on Christ's testimony to His deity (John 5:28, 29; see the whole passage from v. 17). In this Gospel, too, the Lord unlocks further secrets to His disciples respecting His return, which are not disclosed in the Synoptists.

Apostolic Testimony

The apostles were thus prepared for their post-pentecostal witness, the last item in their instruction being given immediately after the Ascension, in the words of the two men who stood by them in white apparel and confirmed the Lord's own promise, by declaring that He Who had just been received up into heaven would so come in like manner as they had beheld Him going (Acts 1:10, 11).

As to the apostolic testimony, a perusal of the New Testament reveals the striking fact that only two of its writings, and these the brief and intimately personal epistle to Philemon and third epistle of John, do not contain a reference to the Lord's Second Coming. It has a prominent place in each of the four groups of

Paul's Epistles

In the first group, consisting of Galatians and 1 and 2 Thessalonians, the subject finds an incidental mention in Galatians, in chapter 6:9, and perhaps also in chapter 1:4; in 1 Thessalonians the Lord's return is the prominent theme; in 2 Thessalonians the apostle shows that the Rapture of the Church, the Parousia of Christ and His coming in glory with the Church for the destruction of the Man of Sin, formed regular subjects of his oral instruction in the churches (see 2 Thess. 2:5).

Of the second group Romans abounds in references to the subject. 1 Corinthians makes frequent mention of it, from the first chapter onward, and devotes the greater part of a whole chapter to it. The second epistle does not contain as many references to it as the first, yet it receives prominence in the fifth chapter.

In the third group, the epistle to the Philippians and Colossians all give prominence to it. Paul did not lose the power of the hope, or become slack in his testimony concerning it, as his years advanced. His imprisonment in Rome certainly did not damp his ardor regarding it.

This is clear, too, in the pastoral epistles. He keeps the Lord's return before Timothy and Titus as the consummation of their service and testimony. Timothy is to keep the commandment "without spot, without reproach, until the appearing of our Lord Jesus Christ" (1 Tim. 6:14). To suffer here will be to reign with Him hereafter; to deny Him will meet with His denial of a reward at His Judgment Seat (2 Tim. 2:12). Paul charges him "in the sight of God, and of Jesus Christ, who shall judge the quick and the dead, and by His appearing and His kingdom," to "preach the Word, be instant in season, out of season" (2 Tim. 4:1, 2). The Lord will in that day give the crown of righteousness to all them that have loved His appearing (4:8). Titus is reminded that the grace of God instructs us to be "looking for the blessed hope and appearing of the glory of our great God and Savior Jesus Christ" (2:13).

The subject is constantly before us in the epistle to the Hebrews, from the sixth verse of the first chapter onward (see remarks above in connection with Deut. 32). It is presented to us especially as the believer's hope (6:18, 20; 10:23, R.V.; 11:10); his desire (11:16); his expectation (9:28; 11:10); and his power for patience and faith in doing the will of God (10:36–38).

The Epistle of James

James, in his epistle, exhorts us to be patient, and establish our hearts, since the coming of the Lord is at hand. If we are not to murmur one against another it is that we may not be judged, for the Judge standeth before the doors, that is to say, He is ready to enter the tribunal, a figurative way of expressing that the Second Coming is near at hand.

The Apostle Peter

Peter points to the coming of Jesus Christ as that which will bring the recompense of the trial of our faith here (1:7). We are to set our hope perfectly on the grace that is then to be brought to us (1:13). He presents Christ as the One who is ready to punish the quick and the dead (4:5), and warns us that the end of all things is at hand (that is, the end of all present affairs). If we are to rejoice in suffering for Christ here, it is because ours will be exceeding joy at the revelation of His glory (4:13).

The Lord's Second Coming is still more prominent in his second epistle. It is viewed there as the time of our entrance into the eternal kingdom of the Lord (1:11). It is compared to the dawn of the day and the rising of the day star (1:19). In the last days mockers will scoff at the idea of the Lord's coming (3:4). Yet the Second Advent will introduce the Day of the Lord (3:10), which will be a day of judgment and the destruction of ungodly men. We are to be looking for and earnestly desiring this great event, and in view of it are to live in all holiness and godliness (3:11, 12), so that we may be found in peace without spot and blameless (3:14).

The First and Second Epistles of John

The apostle John earnestly pleads with his spiritual children that they may so abide in Christ that neither he nor they may be ashamed before Him in His Parousia (1 John 2:28). While it is not yet made manifest what we shall be, we shall certainly be like Him, and this hope is to be a purifying power within us (3:2, 3). God's love is made perfect with us, that we may have boldness in the Day of Judgment (4:17).

There are two references to the subject in his second epistle. Firstly, he says that "many deceivers have gone forth into the world, even they that confess not that Jesus Christ cometh in the flesh. This is the deceiver and the Antichrist" (v. 7). The original has the present participle here, "coming," so that the Authorized Version "has come" is wrong. That rendering seems to have been due to the idea that John was necessarily referring to the Incarnation.

The Antichrist will deny, not the well-established fact that a person known as Jesus Christ lived in the first century, but that He has been raised from the dead, and lives and is "coming in the flesh." How significant is the blasphemous teaching of the International Bible Students' Association, otherwise known as Millennial Dawnism, which declares that Christ is only a Spirit, and that His coming took place as a Spirit in 1914! This is a plain anti-Christian denial that "Christ cometh in the flesh."

The second reference is in the next verse, where the apostle desires that the converts may look to themselves that they may not lose the things which have been wrought on their behalf, but that they may receive a full reward (v. 8), that is to say, at the Judgment Seat of Christ, after He has come to receive the Church to Himself (see 1 Cor. 4:5).

The Epistle of Jude

To Jude's quotation of Enoch's prophecy of the judgment which is to be executed on the ungodly at the Second Advent, we have made reference before. His closing doxology is uttered in view of the time when we shall be set before the presence of Christ's glory without blemish with exceeding joy.

The Apocalypse

As to the Apocalypse, the Second Advent is practically its entire theme. In its three parts Christ is seen as the Judge, first in His own person (ch. 1), then of His saints (chh. 2, 3), then of the world (ch. 4:20); all culminating in the establishment of His kingdom upon earth.

In reviewing the testimony recorded in Scripture one cannot but be struck with the regular increase in the volume of witness given in the various periods. We have noticed this increase as we passed in our review from the Antediluvian, Patriarchal and Mosaic times to the period of the kings of Judah and Israel, and thence to the Captivity and the Restoration. Light on the subject shines with still greater intensity of brightness in the testimony of our Lord and His apostles, the climax being reached in the Apocalypse.

The Post-Apostolic Witness of the Church

The New Testament shows what prominence was given in all apostolic testimony to the subject of the Lord's Second Coming. Nor could it be otherwise, for being the hope of the gospel it forms an essential element therein. Imagine gospel ministry being carried on year after year with the hope of the gospel ignored.

The post-apostolic writings of early Church history make clear that the subject continued to engage the hearts of Christians universally for a considerable time. The hope was kept bright amongst them by the persecutions they experienced. Subsequently when prosperity replaced tribulation, and the Church, succumbing to the patronage of the world and its rulers, attained to affluence and political prestige, the Lord's return was lost sight of. Departure from the teachings and principles inculcated by Christ and His apostles blighted the hope which they had inspired. The rise of popery quenched the testimony. The humanly-devised, flesh-gratifying scheme of establishing the Church as a political power over the nations was radically inconsistent with the expectation of the Rapture and the Second Advent.

The Last Century

The light of the Reformation which shone in upon this medieval darkness lacked that element which was necessary to renew the hope, and only in isolated instances was it held with any degree of Scripturally instructed intelligence. Not until a little over a century ago was there anything like a revival of the witness. The early part of last century saw the beginning of a series of conferences of believers, convened with the one object of the consideration of Scripture relating to the Lord's return. The history of these conventions and of the testimony given therein provides interesting reading. A return to the Scriptures was bound to lead to a breaking away from human tradition and to a revival of the hope.

Lack of the prayerful study of the Scriptures bearing on the subject has been largely responsible for failure to apprehend the facts relating to the Second Advent. The Church has been supplied plentifully with sermons on texts, at the expense of the opening up of the Word of God. Let the Scriptures be unfolded book by book, passage by passage, and the Second Advent will inevitably obtain a large measure of attention, for the subject occupies, as we have seen, a place of great prominence in the whole volume. Where, however, a Church is persuaded that the golden age is to be introduced by statescraft, and that political schemes will eventually bring in the millennium, the Scripture view of the Second Advent is generally found to have little or no place.

Of late years the volume of testimony on the part of those who know and love the truth relating to this subject has greatly increased. Societies have been formed with the sole object of investigating it, and a considerable amount of literature upon it has been published. Views upon certain details differ, but the fact of the pre-millennial advent of the Lord remains dominant, and there is a general expectation of its proximity.

Miss Christabel Pankhurst

As a result of this many have had their eyes opened to see the truth. A striking case is that of Miss Christabel Pankhurst, formerly well-known as an ardent suffragette. In a book recently written by her, entitled "The Lord Cometh: The World Crisis Explained," she relates how the fact of the Second Advent dawned upon her in 1918, when, having lived before "in an atmosphere of illusion," thinking that once certain obstacles were removed, especially the disfranchisement of women, it would be "full steam ahead for the ideal social and international order," she came across writings on prophecy which directed her attention to the study of prophetic Scriptures in the Bible, and this provided the solution to her difficulties. Giving herself thus to the study of the Word of God, she learned to observe from a new vantage point the world events that every day are moving more rapidly toward the fulfillment of prophecy. "Above all," she says, "as I studied more profoundly what the Bible has to say my faith reached all its completeness."

It is ever so. "The opening of God's Word giveth light." The hiding of it keeps men in darkness. She found, what multitudes of others have found before her, that "only the return of the Lord in the way clearly foretold in Scripture would bring about the needed alterations in the circumstances of humanity," and that "the divine program is absolutely the only one that can solve the international, social, and political or moral, problems of the world."

To continue her words: "The only trouble was, that it seemed too good to be true. As yet I believed not for very joy. The mourning disciples could not for their joy believe they saw their risen Lord, and I for the same cause feared to believe that 'this same Jesus' will really come to break the vicious circle of history, put an end to human failure, and begin an entirely new dispensation."

The closing paragraph of her book is as follows: "Yes, He is coming! History is now rushing, racing on to the fulfillment of the great prophecy. The Bible's final message is from Him: 'Behold, I come quickly.' 'Surely I come quickly.' We who love His appearing make the apostle's prayer ours, 'EVEN SO, COME, LORD JESUS.'"

The Two Witnesses of Revelation 11

The Apocalypse shows that the world having been given over to delusion under the power of the Antichrist, with the apostate Jewish nation politically restored and in covenant treaty with Him, the Lord will send two witnesses to Jerusalem, the object of whose ministry will be to turn the hearts of the Jews to God and to expectation of the Advent of their Messiah. Their testimony will last for 1260 days, or three and a half years (Rev. 11:3).

Their names are not given. That Elijah will be one of them is likely. For this passage in Revelation 11 would seem to be connected with the prophecy in Malachi, "Behold, I will send you Elijah the prophet before the great and terrible day of the Lord come. And he shall turn the heart of the fathers to the children, and the heart of the children to their fathers" (Mal. 4:5, 6). Christ also, while showing that John the Baptist fulfilled the prophecy in a preliminary way, predicted that Elijah would eventually come and restore all things (Matt. 17:11).

The statement that the two witnesses are "the two olive trees and the two candlesticks [or rather, lampstands], standing before the Lord of the earth" is undoubtedly an allusion to Zechariah 4, the symbolism being appropriate to the giving of testimony. They will be sent to maintain the rights of God and to vindicate His sovereignty over the earth, in view of the satanic denial of those rights by the Antichrist. The ratification of their testimony will be the establishment of the Lordship of Christ over the earth at His appearing. That the two witnesses will be actual persons seems abundantly clear from the context.

The Jewish Remnant

Whether through their instrumentality, or by other means, a large number of witnesses will be raised up to take part in bearing testimony to Christ and His approaching Advent. A large proportion of these will consist of the godly company of Jews called in the Psalms and other Old Testament prophecies "the remnant." As in the case of the two witnesses, a considerable number of these will be slaughtered by the Beast and his agents (Rev. 6:9). Against them Satan will manifest his fiercest fury, but without permanent success, for "they overcame him because of the blood of the Lamb, and because of the Word of their testimony; and they loved not their lives even unto death" (12:11). Multitudes of the Jews are, however, to be preserved from death, and will form the nucleus of the nation in its regenerated condition after Christ has come to deliver it (12:14–16).

There is also to be the proclamation of

"The Everlasting Gospel"

which will have a worldwide effect in turning men from allegiance to the Antichrist to await the Second Advent. The words of this gospel are told us: the message is, "Fear God, and give Him glory; for the hour of His judgment is come: and worship Him that made the heaven, and the earth, and sea, and fountains of waters" (14:6, 7). "Worship God" is an eternal gospel. It suits all periods. At the time when it will be proclaimed throughout the earth the world at large will be worshiping the Man of Sin. Hence the command to worship God.

Thus the world will be divided, not as it is now into three divisions, the Jews, the Gentiles, and the Church of God, but into those, on the one hand, who worship God and are waiting for the appearing of Christ in glory as the Son of man, and those, on the other hand, who worship the Beast, and who must suffer punishment in consequence. The Gentile nations will, it would seem, be greatly affected by the witness of the multitudes of godly Jews who will have been converted from the apostasy of the nation.

The Great Fulfillment

Thus the long line of witnesses from the divine prediction in the Garden of Eden to the multitude who will stand for the truth at the end of this age, all bearing testimony to the great event which is to bring deliverance to the world from the antagonism and deception of Satan, will be completed.

The Lord Jesus Christ, who has in His own person already fulfilled so much of Scripture prophecy, will suddenly and completely ratify all its testimony as to His glorious and triumphant appearing. The wheels of divinely appointed destiny turn with unerring movement and with undeviating course. All the combined hostility of the powers of darkness, all the anti-God and anti-Christian amalgamations of humanity, can never frustrate the accomplishment of God's purposes.

He who has issued His irrevocable and unalterable decree on behalf of His Son, "I will give the nations for Thine inheritance, and the uttermost parts of the earth for Thy possession," will fulfill His Word and confirm the witness He has raised up, when "He sets His King upon His holy hill of Zion"; and in the grand inauguration of the kingdom, and the exercise of His sovereign power, His saints who have borne their testimony will have their part.

For the flight of ancient specters,
That had shaded with their gloom
Both the castle and the cottage,
Both the cradle and the tomb;
For the hope of holy triumphs,
In the eras yet to be;
For the pledge to captive millions,
Of release and jubilee—
Blessed be God, our God, alone,
Our God, the Everlasting One,
Who spake the Word, and it was done!

For the watchword of the prophets,
That "the just shall live by faith";

For the Church's ancient symbol
Of the life that comes through death;
For the standard of apostles,
Raised aloft and full unfurled,
Glad deliverance proclaiming
To a crushed and trampled world—
Blessed be God, our God, alone,
Our God, the Everlasting One,
Who spake the Word, and it was done!

For the martyr's song of triumph,
On the wheel or scorching pyre;
For his strength of meek endurance,
On the rack or torturing fire;
For the noble witness-bearing
To the Christ the Lamb of God,
To the One unchanging Priesthood,
To the One atoning blood—
Blessed be God, our God, alone,
Our God, the Everlasting One,
Who spake the Word, and it was done!

For the everlasting gospel,
Which in splendor has gone forth,
Like a torch upon the mountains,
Of a reillumined earth;
For the temple flung wide open,
At whose gates the goodly train
Of the nations had been knocking,
But in vain, so long in vain—
Blessed be God, our God, alone,
Our God, the Everlasting One,
Who spake the Word, and it was done.

DR. HORATIUS BONAR

The Church and the Tribulation

with

C. F. Hogg

PREFACE

The writers of the following pages collaborated some years ago in producing three books, two of them consisting of notes on the epistles to the Thessalonians and the epistle to the Galatians, the third being entitled "Touching the Coming of the Lord." Insofar as the subject matter of these volumes relates to the circumstances of the Rapture and the Second Advent, the author of a recently issued volume entitled "The Approaching Advent of Christ" classes the writers among those whom he sees fit to call Darbyists. In doing so, he imputes to them (p. 148, etc.), with characteristic dogmatism and assurance of the accuracy of his statements, the delinquency (from his point of view), of simply following in certain passages the teachings of Darby and Kelly. Delinquency or no delinquency, the imputation is unjustifiable. There is not a shred of evidence to confirm it. Not a single reference is made in any of their three volumes to the writings or teachings of any other author or expositor. If there is found, on the part of the present writers, some measure of agreement with what had been set forth by those servants of Christ, or any of the so-called Darbyists, such agreement is the result, not of our adherence to any particular set of teachers, but of an independent approach to the Scriptures of truth.

Our continued consideration of the subjects during the years since the books were published ("Touching the Coming of the Lord" was written nineteen years ago), has not led us to a change of view in the matter of exegesis as therein set forth, nor do we now find ourselves under the necessity, for the sake of the truth, of altering our views as a result of the recent publication of the volume, "The Approaching Advent of Christ."

In regard to that work, the conclusion just expressed has rather been strengthened than otherwise by the line of argument and the methods of interpretation adopted by the author, and this altogether apart from the fact that, had he evinced a happier spirit in his references to those upon whom he passes condemnatory judgment, his views concerning prophecy, though unconvincing, might have carried more weight. Scornful phraseology adopted toward sober and earnest servants of God who have, in freedom from fundamental error, sought to set forth what they believe to be the truth, is, to say the least, not the happiest way of treating a subject.

In this connection, it may not be out of place to quote a few lines from the introduction to the book "Touching the Coming of the Lord." The quotation may serve to indicate the facts relating to its production in contrast to the imputations made against the writers by Mr. Reese: "The dogmatic spirit is peculiarly inappropriate to the exposition of the 'word of prophecy.' We may not adopt the same tone when we speak of the future as when we speak of the past. Prophecy is something more than history written in advance. It is a means the Lord has chosen whereby we may be brought into closer fellowship with Him in His purposes. The writers hope they have written nothing inconsistent with this end of the Lord. They will be profoundly grateful if it please Him to use their testimony and this attempt to open the Scriptures, to the growth of their readers in the true grace of God. The purpose of prophecy is as practical as that of any other part of the Bible. . . . The writers would in all sincerity remind their readers of the exhortation of the apostle to a church as yet in its infancy, 'Prove all things; hold fast that which is good,' words which they would venture to paraphrase, 'Test all teachings; hold fast to that which accords with what is written'" (1 Thess. 5:21).

In the following pages the writer of the first

The Testimony Of Jesus Is The Spirit Of Prophecy.

chapter deals more especially with certain points raised in Mr. Reese's book. The second writer has added further subject matter to show that the teaching of Scripture is contrary to the view that the Church will be on earth during the Great Tribulation.

Bath, 1938 W.E.V.

CHAPTER ONE

A Review of a Book Entitled "The Approaching Advent of Christ"

This is a considerable book, extending to 328 pages. The writer is described on the title page as "The Rev. Alexander Reese," and from internal evidence we gather that he is a New Zealander, a missionary in Brazil. We learn also that almost a quarter of a century intervened between the completion of the draft manuscript and the publication of the work. The author has not spared pains to attain his end, which is to show that the teaching that the Lord's promised return is presented in Scripture as imminent is without authority in Scripture. This teaching, he alleges, had its origin with John Nelson Darby, an expositor of the last century. For some reason it is peculiarly obnoxious to Mr. Reese, but as we have often heard that it originated with Edward Irving, with the Jesuits, with a Jew named Ben Ezra, and ultimately with the Devil, Mr. Reese's conclusion is something of a relief, even though he should prove to be mistaken. Indeed he tells us himself that Mr. Darby got it from "a godly clergyman," a Mr. Tweedy, from the West Indies. Did he, in turn, get it from the Bible? After all, that is the sole question, as Mr. Reese recognizes.

The book, issued by Marshall, Morgan & Scott, London, 1937, owes its bulk not to the variety or abundance of its matter, nor to the necessities of its argument. If its attacks upon the character and competence of teachers, all of them God-fearing men, who sought to live honestly and to write sincerely, and many of whom were at least as competent and as well furnished as Mr. Reese himself, were eliminated, the size of the volume would have been considerably reduced and its general atmosphere sweetened. Erudite-seeming, lengthy, and irrelevant quotations could have been omitted with the same advantage. Citations from lexicons abound, but without any attempt to discriminate between the lexicographer's definition of words and his interpretation of Scripture. He gives large space to modern translations of the New Testament, ignoring the fact that their authors, for the most part, assume that the divine inspiration of the New Testament, if it exists, is general, not plenary. But where the Lord's claim for His language, in John 12:49, and Paul's for his in 1 Corinthians 2:13, are not accepted, the translator will not attempt to do more than give what he considers a general sense to the text he handles. The paraphrasists become not translators but interpreters of Scripture. Their readers should always bear this in mind. Wade, for example, page 128, paraphrases Titus 2:13 thus: "Looking forward to the hope [so fraught with happiness] of witnessing the Manifestation." Mr. Reese calls this a "translation," which it assuredly is not. It may be "idiomatic," but it is not what Paul said. The Christian does not look forward to being a spectator of "the appearing of the glory," but to being a sharer in it, according to Romans 8:19, 29 and Colossians 3:3, 4. Moffatt makes Paul speak in 2 Thessalonians 2:8, of the Lord's "appearing and arrival," whereas his words are "manifestation *of* His *parousia*," which not even Moffatt could render "manifestation of His arrival."

I have just been reading, in a secular review, of "the courtesies of debate" observed in the world, but these have escaped the notice of Mr. Reese, notwithstanding the example of Michael the Archangel, who did not dare to bring a railing accusation even against such a notorious evildoer as the Devil (Jude 9). Mr. Reese does not seem to have made up his mind whether those whom he attacks so trenchantly are fools, or only knaves; his language, indeed, frequently suggests that they are both! Here are some things he says about them, taken at random as the pages are turned: They are guilty of "aggressive sophistry and fantastic exegesis," and of "paltry reasoning." They prefer "any rubbish to the true and obvious explanation" of a passage, and they "wrest the Scriptures." Their preference for the line of teaching they favor is "no longer a question of exegesis . . . It is simply a question of ethics. . . . Have we the right moral disposition toward the truth, or will we still cling to error . . . shall we act against the truth or for the truth?" (This, on p. 244 causes the balance to dip rather toward the knave theory!) They are not God-fearing readers of the Bible, but "theorists," "showing little acquaintance with great exegesis." Their teaching is "consistent and ludicrous" in its "absurdity." Its effect is to blight "Bible study and Christian fellowship all over the world." "It has cursed the [Brethren] movement from the beginning." "They wrote their errors on their broad phylacteries." (For the significance of this grave judgment reference must be made to Matt. 23:5 and its context.) They "are misguided and misleading teachers." And, indeed, "Paul informs us that they were *false* teachers who taught thus" (p. 176). The list is not exhausted, but let this suffice. Mr. Reese has invented a term for those he opposes which most of them would repudiate with emphasis; while they may hold Mr. Darby in esteem as a teacher, they would strenuously object to be called "Darbyists." But see how the character of one great servant of Christ, and of many lesser, is outraged in such a collocation as "Sadducees and Darbyists." He brings his work to a climax in the words (p. 272), "the time has now come to say that the Lord Himself taught the founders of His Church (in a private discourse . . .) to beware of men who taught" four things alleged to be taught by Darbyists. He declares that "even if the apostle had mentioned a rapture at 2 Thessalonians 1:7, Darbyists would arrange three shifts to get rid of it. This is not cruel or churlish but the plain fact" (p. 211). And yet on page 222 he charges one of those whom he attacks with "contortions of exegesis . . . put forth with studied offensiveness." Conversely Mr. Reese describes himself and those who share his views as "we who accept Christ's teaching." Mr. Reese should have recollected the parable of the mote and the beam!

It is not pleasant to reproduce words in which it is impossible to discern the accents of Christ, nor to see that fruit of the Spirit which, to quote Mr. Reese's favorite translator, Moffatt, is "good temper, kindliness, generosity" (Gal. 5:22).

There is much in the book with which the present writer is in agreement. The postponement of the Gospel according to Matthew, the Sermon on the Mount, and the Great Commission, to a future age, for example, seems to me to be altogether wrong. The words of the late George Muller (p. 27) are acceptable. But to claim that because of Mr. Muller's prayerfulness, and his care of orphan children, his interest in missions and in Bible circulation, his views on prophecy should be accepted, is surely a strange argument (p. 116). Rather should we give heed to the exhortation to young believers (within a year the Thessalonian Christians had not heard of the gospel, apparently) which we may take the liberty of rendering, "test all teaching; hold fast that which is good" (1 Thess. 5:21). And this should be kept in mind by all readers of the book, for in it we read much of "the great exegetes," and find many appeals to authority, but little or no attempt to open up the Scripture.

Mr. Reese plays much with the phrase "secret rapture," which he says (p. 148) "is worked to death" by "every theorist," but which, in fact, is rarely used by those whom he criticizes. (Personally I might complain that in making a quotation from "Touching the Coming of the Lord," Mr. Reese omits an essential part of a statement, which was made, indeed, in the interests of peace and a good understanding, and holds up the fragment to ridicule:) This, however, is consistent with his putting words into the mouth of those whom he attacks, words, which, we may be sure, were never either spoken or written by those to whom they are credited. See pages 141, 177, 313.

The general impression is given throughout the book that the very foundations of the faith are in danger; certainly in that case it would be difficult to find stronger language in which to describe the perpetrators. Yet Mr. Reese acknowledges more than once that if the teaching he denounces were true it would minister to the comfort of the Christian; nor does it require argument that if he were persuaded of the immediacy—the imminence—of the

Lord's Parousia, that could not but constrain him to "live soberly and righteously and godly in this present age."

It is not unnatural for the afflicted, and for those whose minds are filled with apprehension of the things that are coming upon the earth, to long for their own deliverance and that of others. And undoubtedly much of a merely sentimental character has been unwisely written, with the effect of diverting the minds of believers from the appearing of the glory of the Lord to the Rapture, its necessary preliminary. But in so doing we become self-centered instead of Christ-centered. "The joy that was set before Him" (Heb. 12:2) was not merely that of having His redeemed around Him, but also that of vindicating the Throne of God, of establishing His Kingdom and of hushing the groans of creation. The Rapture, which is to precede the opening of the Seventieth Week, is the first step to this consummation, but it is not the consummation itself. And if it be argued that the appearing of the glory cannot be a sanctifying hope if we expect the Rapture, or the Seventieth Week, first, Peter supplies the answer, when he asks, "Seeing that these things are thus all to be dissolved, what manner of persons ought ye to be in all holy living and godliness, looking for and earnestly desiring the presence [R.V. marg., *parousia*] of the day of God, by reason of which the heavens being on fire shall be dissolved, and the elements shall melt with fervent heat?" And yet that day of God may be as far beyond our ken as is the fulfillment of 1 Corinthians 15:28, with which it may correspond.

On page 128 Mr. Reese quotes five translations of Titus 2:13 which he describes as "new." He omits an older and more accurate one, that of R.V., 1881, "Looking for the blessed hope and appearing of the glory of our great God and Savior Jesus Christ." He is quite right in saying, as he does on page 129, that "according to Paul the blessed hope of Christians *is none other than the glorious appearing itself*" (Mr. Reese's italics). What contribution "modern scholarship," of which he is enamored, has made to an understanding of the verse is not clear; and without confessing to being "half asleep" it is equally obscure to me, why the R.V. translation "spells the ruin, the irretrievable ruin" of the interpretation of Scripture he opposes with so much acrimony. Acknowledgedly it is not without its difficulties, and yet, perhaps, these are neither so many nor so great as those that attend upon the other interpretation. If there were a little more good will, less argument, and more chastened inquiry, how much we might learn together! Let us consider the implications of Ephesians 3:18.

It is puzzling, with reference to the quotation from an earlier writing of the present reviewer, that Mr. Reese should credit him with conveying the idea that "the blessed hope" of the glorious appearing is not strictly for the Church, since it occurs some years after the more glorious hope of the Rapture of 1 Thessalonians 4:17 (p. 130). This is just the contrary of what the extract expressly states. The object of our calling is that we may "obtain the glory of our Lord Jesus Christ" (2 Thess. 2:14), and assuredly we cannot be glorified without Him! "The creation waiteth for the revealing of the *sons* of God," that hour in which He shall be manifested, not alone, but as "the Firstborn among many brethren." "When Christ, Who is our life, shall be manifested, then shall ye also with Him be manifested in glory" (Rom. 8:19, 29; Col. 3:4). Nor does the reviewer believe that Paul "confused" the Rapture of the saints and the appearing of Christ; but, with respect, he does believe that Mr. Reese and his school fail to discriminate between them.

The evidence that we are waiting for a Savior from heaven (Phil. 3:20) lies not in the view we take of the order of future events, but in whether the hope is affecting our lives, constraining us to love of the brethren, whatever divergence of judgment there may be between us (1 John 2:14). Neither the school of Mr. Reese, nor that which he opposes, has a monopoly of godliness, and in that we may rejoice, and we do rejoice, for the very grace that teaches us to look for "the blessed hope" puts us under discipline "to the intent that, denying ungodliness and worldly lusts, we should live soberly and righteously and godly in this present age" (Titus 2:12). The essential thing, beside which all else is secondary and subsidiary, is that the Lord Himself should be the object of our hope, and that in our manner of living we might purify ourselves "even as He is pure" (1 John 3:3).

What then is the essential difference between the two schools of interpretation, that represented by Mr. Reese and that attacked by him? It might be urged with more than a little truth that the difference is not great: certainly in no sense could it be called vital. Chillingworth said (I quote from memory) that in Scripture what is vital is clear; and what is not clear is not vital. It would be disingenuous to claim that the teaching of Scripture is so clear on the matter under consideration that there can be no mistaking it, for he and the writer of this review differ in judgment of the intention of Scripture; nor does this writer doubt Mr. Reese's good faith in taking the view he has espoused with such fervor. But before attempting to define the difference between us, it may be as well to devote a little space to a principle of prophecy interpretation not ordinarily recognized, and that should induce in all of us a measure of humility of mind. To this end some words written elsewhere may be reproduced here.

"In 2 Kings 7 it is recorded that Elisha foretold two things, namely, that in a besieged city already reduced to cannabalism, food would be plentiful and cheap within twenty-four hours; and that a certain prominent official of the court would see, but would not partake of it. And so it fell out, but in a way that could not be mistaken, yet could not have been foreseen.

"It seems safe to draw two deductions from this narrative. The first that it is never possible to foresee how God will fulfill His word. The second, that when it is fulfilled the correspondence between the prophecy and the event will be abundantly evident, demonstration will not be necessary. A survey of fulfilled prophecy justifies these conclusions. Has it ever been possible for those to whom the prophecies came to foresee the manner in which God would accomplish His Word? Has it ever been possible to question the correspondence between the Word and its fulfillment? These questions must be answered in the negative, I judge, and if so, may we not conclude that what was true in the past will be true in what lies before us? However confident in the soundness of his forevision the interpreter of prophecy may be, he must not forget the plain lesson of the prophecies that have already passed into history. Caution becomes us; dogmatism here is out of place. May we not expect that once more God will surprise us all? He only doeth wonderful things, and His ways are past tracing out. But this, of course, does not absolve us from responsibility to consider with meticulous care all it has pleased the Lord to say to His children in His Word, and to do this with due respect to the grammar and the lexicon, indeed, but remembering that the Spirit Who gave the Word is its indispensable interpreter. James tells us to receive with meekness the implanted Word; Paul, that we are to test all teaching and to hold fast that which is good. So whether it be Darby or Newton or Reese, we must remember that "the law and the testimony" are the final court of appeal.

"For this reason it may be well for us to consider that as no one foresaw the circumstances in which Messiah would come into the world to suffer, so no one can foresee the circumstances of His coming to reign."

As against postmillenarians, both Mr. Reese and those he criticizes are premillenarians. As against the historicists and the amillenarians both are futurists. As against those who teach that the Rapture, whenever it may take place, will be partial, both hold that it will be complete. Both believe that the Seventieth Week of Daniel 9, or half of it, during which Antichrist will arise, is yet future and will precede the Advent. Unhappily this very large area of agreement is seldom surveyed, and the impression is left, and encouraged by writers of both schools, that the differences between them are fundamental. Nor, it must be acknowledged, is the truculence that so deeply marks this book to be found only in the writings of one school, as some of Mr. Reese's quotations testify. How much more "good and pleasant" it would have been had he made Erdman his model rather than Kelly! Two evils, however, do not make one good. Mutual recrimination gets us no further, either in the understanding of the Word of God, or in the brotherly love which, on the authority of the Lord, is the characteristic of those who belong to Him.

Happily there is full agreement between us that every word of the Lord will be adequately fulfilled, and the difference is reduced to this, that Mr. Reese and his school expect the *parousia* of the Lord to coincide with His Second Advent "in power and great glory" at the close of the Seventieth Week, whereas the other school believes that the *parousia* of the Lord will precede the Second Advent by the period of the Seventieth Week at least. The area of disagreement is thus of small dimensions. It is inexplicable that so much heat should be generated in its discussion. Certainly the children of God show themselves in an unlovely light when they quarrel, and "set at naught" their brethren, concerning the manner in which their Father will fulfill to all of them His "precious and exceeding great promises." After all is said, must we not wait and see?

On what grounds then do these who so highly displease Mr. Reese look for the Rapture of the regenerated before the opening of the Seventieth Week, during which, it is common ground, the Great Tribulation takes place? Much depends on the meaning of the Greek word *parousia,* which occurs twenty-four times in the New Testament, eighteen of these in an eschatological connection. Mr. Reese evidently feels this, for he devotes a whole chapter to the consideration of it. In dealing with it here the present writer does not represent any school, nor does he speak "officially," as Mr. Reese suggests on page 28. He speaks solely for himself. The reader must judge whether what he offers is "freak exegesis" (p. 146), and whether Mr. Vine, in chapter five of *Touching the Coming,* is guilty of "a complete mix-statement," and whether he is incompetent to read a lexicon, as Mr. Reese implies on pages 149, 150.

Here is Mr. Reese's definition of the *parousia* (p. 152): "far from being a prolonged period [it] is a single crisis breaking with the utmost suddenness." He insists that "arrival" is the sense of the word as against "presence," though in one place (p. 143) he adds "or the visit following," whereas my contention is that it always and only refers to the visit. Mr. Reese, speaks of a "rabbinical attempt to make it mean presence" on page 70. He quotes the R.V. in this connection, but fails to observe that wherever that version has "coming" in the text it has in the margin *"Gk. presence."* This, it is to be noticed, is not even an alternative rendering to "arrival," but an indication that "presence" is the meaning of the word. The reason the Revisers did not replace "coming" by "presence" in their text they themselves tell us in their preface, where they describe such marginal notes as "indicating the exact meaning of words to which, for the sake of the English idiom, we were obliged to give a less exact rendering in the text." He mentions several lexicons, but without exception these all give the primary meaning of the word as "presence," adding "arrival" and "coming" as secondary significances. Yet he says that "the new New Testament lexicons of Soutter, Abbott-Smith, . . . Milligan and Moulton . . . all give *arrival* or *coming* as one of the fundamental meanings of the word." Abbott-Smith has "1. usually in cl (assics) a being present, presence." Then "2. a coming, arrival, advent." But all the entries under 2 are just those under dispute, each must be considered on its merits. Mr. Reese himself says that Liddell and Scott's Lexicon "gives the senses *presence, arrival, occasion, visit,* and then says, 'In the New Testament the Advent.'" Yet in this, as in all lexicons, "presence" comes first, as the primary meaning of *parousia*. We would be justified here in turning Mr. Reese's question back on himself—"When teachers misread the lexicon, how can we trust their reading of the New Testament which it explains?" (p. 150).

Parousia is the present participle of *eimi,* to be, with the prefix *para* which means "beside." *Pareimi* is defined by Abbott-Smith, "to be by, at hand, or present," and hence to have arrived. The etymological structure of the word shows that it cannot refer to an action or an event, but that it refers to a condition or state. That is, not to "an arrival" but to "a visit." *Parousia* is related to *apousia* exactly as presence is related to absence. Moreover, in Philippians 1:26 and 2:12, R.V. has "presence" in the text, and Moffatt has "when I was present" in the latter. This the apostle sets in contrast with his *apousia,* which assuredly no one would think of translating, here or elsewhere, by "departure."

What is said above concerning Abbott-Smith's treatment of *parousia* in his Lexicon is true also of Cremer. Here are Mr. Reese's own words, "He [Cremer] gives the first meaning of *Parousia* as *presence,* with 2 Corinthians 10:10, and Philippians 2:12 as his examples of this sense. He then gives *arrival* as the second sense of the word. . . . He then goes on: "with this meaning is most probably connected the application of the word to *the second coming of Christ*." Mr. Reese says further (p. 150) that Cremer raises "a doubt about the rightness of using *Parousia* in the sense of *arrival*. But he is not quarreling with modern translators for translating the word *coming* or *arrival*. *His doubt is over the apostles themselves:* they used it undoubtedly in the sense of *arrival:* how did they do that when the original sense was *presence?* That is Cremer's argument." The true explanation is probably different. Following the conventional idea that the eschatological words of the New Testament are used indiscriminately, Cremer is puzzled to account for the use of *parousia* in the sense of *arrival,* when etymologically it means, and can only mean, *presence*. The answer we suggested, and still maintain, is that everywhere in the New Testament *parousia* retains its proper significance; that the meaning of *arrival* has been imposed upon it. It is not at all beyond the powers of an intelligent reader of the English R.V. (in an edition with the Revisers' Marginal Notes) to test what Mr. Reese, and his reviewer, say. He will be competent to decide whether the words on page 149, *"this is a complete misstatement of Cremer's position,"* are justified, or whether Mr. Reese has not once more misread the lexicon, or, to use his own not very elegant expression, read it "on the skew." (The italics throughout are Mr. Reese's.)

As Mr. Reese rightly says, we owe much to the labors of Deissmann and others for the light cast upon the New Testament vocabulary by papyri fragments, discovered in Egypt in comparatively recent years. But the light cast upon *parousia* in them is not a discovery of Mr. Reese, as might be gathered from his book. It may be pointed out that considerable use was made of the material of the papyri in a volume, *Notes on the Epistles to the Thessalonians,* by Mr. W. E. Vine and the present writer, published in 1914 (Pickering & Inglis, Second Edition, 1929), and in *Touching the Coming of the Lord,* by the same, in 1919 (Oliphants, Second Edition, 1932). Mr. Reese's conclusion from these sources is that *parousia,* "far from being a prolonged period is a single crisis breaking with the utmost suddenness" (p. 158). Now the conclusion we draw, and which we still maintain is, bar the word "prolonged," diametrically the opposite of this. Moreover, the evidence Mr. Reese himself provides amply justifies it.

Deissmann defines *parousia* as *"a technical expression for the arrival or the visit of the king or the emperor."* A little later he speaks of *epiphaneia* as the equivalent of *parousia,* which it never is in the New Testament, where we read of the *epiphaneia* of the *parousia* (2 Thess. 2:8). It is of importance that in dealing not with "words which man's wisdom teacheth, but which the Spirit teacheth" (1 Cor. 2:13), we should not follow translators, and others, who obliterate differences, but rather should seek the commendation of the apostle, who prayed that the love of the saints at Philippi might "abound yet more and more in knowledge and all discernment; so that [they might] prove the things that differ," literally, that they might become "distinguishers of differences" (a D.D. degree open to all!) (Phil. 1:10, R.V., *m.*).

We may look at a few of Deissmann's illustrations, and from them draw our own conclusions, without showing disrespect to his where we differ. First, however, let me quote, from *Notes on Thessalonians,* page 87, an example drawn from Milligan: "In a papyrus document . . . a person states that the care of her property demands her *parousia* in a certain city." Clearly she means not her arrival, but her *presence* there. One of Deissmann's illustrations is of that of the *parousia* of King Ptolemy for which a requisition of corn was made. Was this to be used on his arrival or during his stay? Another is that of a man healed in the temple of Asclepius (the Greek god of medicine), "and Asclepius manifested his *parousia*." Not that he there and then arrived at his temple, it was his alleged dwelling place, but that at that moment he made his presence known, for it was he who, invisible to the eyes of those present, had healed the man.

The striking parallel between this illustration and the words of 2 Thessalonians 2:8 will not be lost on the reader. Not the Lord's *parousia* but the manifestation of it is to bring the lawless man to nought, a distinction that Mr. Reese and the writer he quotes on page 175, like Deissmann, fail to make.

Deissman writes: "There is something peculiarly touching in the fact that toward the end of the second century, at the very time when the Christians were beginning to distinguish the 'first' *parousia* of Christ from the 'second,' an inscription at Tegea was dated 'in the year of the second *parousia* of the god Hadrian in Greece.'" The arrival of Christ was, of course, His birth in Bethlehem, but was it that event, or the thirty odd years that followed upon it, that could be described as His "first" *parousia?* One might ask what Deissmann himself would say, merely in the interests of exact scholarship, had he been asked whether *presence* were not the better, or the only appropriate, rendering of *parousia* here?

As Mr. Reese selects 2 Corinthians 7:6, 7 (p. 151) for special mention among the noneschatological passages in which *parousia* occurs, it may be well to point out that it was not the arrival of Titus, but his presence with the apostle that comforted him, as the word "while" (R.V.; A.V. has "when") makes clear. But he does not say that the "conjecture" he quotes, that "Titus walked in as Paul was writing," is not worth the ink with which it is written.

One other passage, not eschatological, that calls for notice is 2 Peter 1:16–18, "We made known unto you the power and *parousia* of our Lord Jesus Christ, . . . we were eyewitnesses of His majesty, . . . when there came such a voice to Him from the excellent glory . . . when we were with Him in the Holy Mount." It was not on their arrival there, however, but toward the end of the time they spent there that the voice came. Nor was it on their arrival that He was transfigured before them. Once more "presence" is the only appropriate translation, and so R.V. *m.* Moffatt, with characteristic disrespect for accuracy, translates by "advent" a word in common use for the birth of the Lord, to which it certainly does not refer here. Mr. Reese says (p. 146), "In 2 Peter 1:16 it is associated with the coming and kingdom of *the Son of man* in the Gospels." It is not clear what this means, but nothing can obscure the fact that Peter refers to the Transfiguration (see *Thessalonians,* p. 87).

It may be well to consider 2 Thessalonians 2:8–10, here, before we look at passages in which the *Parousia* of the Lord is concerned. "The Lawless One . . . whose *parousia* is according to the working of Satan with all power and signs and lying wonders, and with all deceit of unrighteousness for them that are perishing." Let the reader judge whether these words can refer to an arrival, "a single crisis breaking with the utmost suddenness," a "dazzling *parousia*" (pp. 152, 271), or whether they do not describe a continuous period during which the Lawless One comes to power? For it is surely inconceivable that he will suddenly appear on the scene; rather he will arise, as the dictators have always arisen, out of the despair or the tumult of the people. Not arrival, then, but presence is the meaning here.

Concerning 2 Thessalonians 2:8, on page 21, Mr. Reese quotes some excellent words of Trotter, to which he should have done well to give heed. They are, "the apostle . . . distinguishes between the *parousia* of our Lord Jesus Christ," and "the brightness [*epiphaneia;* R.V., "manifestation"] of His coming [*parousia*]." Throughout, Mr. Reese persists in ignoring this difference. On page 175, he has, "Antichrist is to be slain by Christ at His . . . *Parousia,*" and quotes approvingly, "the words *'epiphaneia'* and *'parousia'* are ultimately synonymous," thus obliterating a very obvious difference. For how can this be when the apostle speaks of the *epiphaneia* of His *parousia,* "the manifestation of His presence"? (R.V., *m.*). If Mr. Reese is correct, the words would be the equivalent of the "arrival of His arrival." But if the *Parousia* of the Lord is actually in being, where the Lord has met His redeemed "in the air" (1 Thess. 4:17), then the drawing aside of the veil *(apokaluptō)* that hides Him and them from the world, will result in the manifestation *(epiphaneia)* of what is so hidden. Hence it is that we read in Luke 17:30, "after the same manner shall it be in the day that the Son of man shall be 'revealed.'" "Revealed" represents *apokaluptō,* literally, to uncover, to make evident, and so to reveal. Cp. The Apocalypse, the Unveiling, the Revelation, as in our English Bibles. In a note on page 271, Mr. Reese says that "the . . . *parousia* of the Son of man (Matt. 24:39) and the day of the Son of man (Luke 17:30) coincide." It would be correct to say that the latter corresponds with the manifestation of the *parousia,* for it is then that the destruction of Antichrist is effected, and with him all that have believed "the lie." See also 2 Thessalonians 1:7, 8.

The first appearance of *parousia* in the New

Testament is in Matthew 24:3, where the disciples ask the Lord, "What shall be the sign of Thy *parousia?*" Not surely "the sign of Thy arrival," for that would be its own sign, no other would be required, and this is probably the meaning of Matthew 24:30, "Then shall appear the sign of the Son of man in heaven: and then shall all the tribes of the earth mourn, and they shall see the Son of man coming [*erchomai*] on the clouds of heaven with power and great glory." This is apparently the event that effects the destruction of the Antichrist (2 Thess. 2:9), a sudden crisis indeed, described in verse 27, "as the lightning cometh forth from the east, and is seen even unto the west; so shall be the *parousia* of the Son of man." It does not seem to require further demonstration that what is in view is the "manifestation of His *Parousia*."

What earlier teaching the Lord had given the disciples on the subject is not recorded, but it can hardly be assumed that this use of the word originated with them. However that may be, His answer to their question is recorded. The comparison between the *parousia* and "the days of Noah . . . those days that were before the flood," is a comparison drawn not between a period and an event, an arrival, but between two periods.

When in Luke 17:26–31 the Lord spoke of "the days of the Son of man," and compared them with "the days of Noah," He can hardly be understood to refer to the days after the Flood came or to the days after His Advent "in power and great glory," but to the days immediately preceding these events, for at His Advent in glory the careless, like the rebellious, are to be destroyed. When the veil is drawn aside, and His Presence, hitherto unsuspected by men on the earth is manifested, then judgment falls, that "wrath" from which He is to deliver those who wait for Him (1 Thess. 1:10).

We must now devote a little space to 2 Thessalonians 2:1, which runs, "Now beseech you, brethren, touching the *parousia* of our Lord Jesus Christ, and our gathering together unto Him." "Gathering together" represents *episunagōgē,* which is defined by Abbott-Smith as "a gathering together, an assembly." (Its only other New Testament occurrence is in Heb. 10:25.) That is, it refers not to the act of assembling, but to the condition of being assembled. The parallel between the two words demands that they be understood in the same way, for the one is the complement of the other. It seems clear, however, that since *episunagōgē* can only mean an assembly, not an assembling, so *parousia* here also means not an arrival but a period during which those who are assembled are in the immediate presence of the Lord.

But enough of this word, which, as Mr. Reese recognizes, is a key to the understanding of the end times. Let that be my apology for devoting so much space to it. I think it may be claimed that his witnesses, under cross-examination, fail to support him in his contention that "the humblest in the first century knew that the word meant the triumphant arrival of Messiah to put down all authority, and then to reign." And Mr. Reese himself makes no better showing. He seeks to impress his uncritical readers with a mass of undigested quotations, many of them from doubtful sources, calculated to confuse the mind of those who are not in a position to estimate the true value of the formidable array of "authorities" who, for the most part, have only opinions to offer, not facts.

As already indicated, failure to distinguish things that differ is characteristic of the book throughout. Mr. Reese assumes that the Day of the Lord and the Day of Christ are identical. Let us see. The matter is somewhat simplified for us by some words on page 271: "At this time in our inquiry it is assumed as proved . . . that the Coming [*parousia*] of Christ [Messiah] 26–28 according to 1 Corinthians 15:23, coincides with the day of Christ (Phil. 1:10, etc.) and the Coming [*parousia*] of our Lord Jesus Christ (2 Thess. 2:1), with the day of our Lord Jesus Christ (1 Cor. 1:8). "With this I agree as completely as I completely disagree with the preceding and succeeding statements of the note. He goes on, "Most emphatically, therefore, the Coming [*parousia*] of the Lord (1 Thess. 4:17; James 5:7, 8) coincides with the Day of the Lord (1 Thess. 5:2; 2 Thess. 2:2, R.V.). Remembering that emphasis is not proof, we may compare Scripture with Scripture, the only path to the discovery of truth.

The Day of the Lord is a subject of Old Testament prophecy. It is first mentioned by Amos (5:18) and Isaiah (2:12. See R.V., margin), who were contemporaries. From the former it seems clear that the phrase had been in use to describe the victories Israel had won over their enemies, who were Jehovah's enemies also. The day of victory therefore was the Day of the Lord. But defeat and exile awaited an inveterately disobedient people. Nevertheless a "great and terrible Day of the Lord" would surely come, a day of the vengeance of God upon the oppressors of Israel. See such passages as Ezekiel 30:1–5; Jeremiah 46:10; Joel 2:31; Malachi 4:5; Isaiah 13:9–11; 34:8; Obadiah 15. The day that sees the overthrow of Gentile power shall see also the setting up of "a kingdom which shall never be destroyed . . . it shall break in pieces and consume all these kingdoms, and it shall stand forever" (Dan. 2:44). It is not recorded that the Lord Himself ever used the words, yet it is evident that the Day of the Lord was before His mind when He spoke of the future of the nation in Matthew 24:30, and equally evident that it will be a "day of joy for the redeemed, of wrath for the impenitent" (p. 164), "of the Jew first and also of the Greek."

In the New Testament, the Day of the Lord is mentioned in Acts 2:20; 1 Thessalonians 5:2; 2 Thessalonians 2:2; 2 Peter 3:10. Cp. Revelation 6:17. At pentecost, Peter rebuked the Jews for charging the disciples with drunkenness by reminding them that in Joel's prophecy of the Day of the Lord certain features were mentioned similar to those they had witnessed. Other signs also were to mark its approach, but these were absent at pentecost. In his second epistle Peter describes the final cataclysm that will overtake the earth. This, however, cannot be understood to coincide with the opening of that day in which the Lord is to "reign until He hath put all His enemies under His feet." Hence we conclude that in his speech the apostle had the opening, in his epistle the close of the Day of the Lord in mind.

On page 173, Mr. Reese objects to the statement that at 1 Thessalonians 5:1 "the apostle proceeds to describe the effect of that revelation [that is "the appearing of the glory"] upon the world," and says "what is exact is that in 1 Thessalonians 4;14–18, the dead in Christ are in view; in 5:1–6 the living." A strange statement, for in the former passage both "the dead in Christ" and those "that are alive and remain," are mentioned. Thus the whole of the redeemed are in view there, and with these are set in contrast "they" that "are saying, Peace and safety," when "sudden destruction cometh upon them, as travail upon a woman with child; and they shall in no wise escape." So far from being identified with "the Day of the Lord," as I read the passage, the *parousia* is sharply distinguished from it. From the Day of the Lord believers are to be delivered, saved; in the *parousia* they are to meet the Lord and to be with Him. The scene of the Day of the Lord is the earth; the scene of the *parousia* is the aerial heavens. Moreover the circumstances of the two are different, as the reader can see if he will compare the passages.

There does not seem to be any doubt that 2 Thessalonians 2:2 should read as in R.V., "as that the Day of the Lord is now present." Reasons follow why this was a misunderstanding, arising from persecution to which the Christians had been subjected, as may be gathered from the epistle, although no account of it is given in Acts. Plainly their mistake arose from the fact that suffering of this character was associated with that day, and they feared that they had entered upon it, notwithstanding the assurance of the first epistle that "Jesus . . . delivereth us from the wrath to come" (1 Thess. 1:10). The translation of a present participle by a past tense in A.V. here is misleading. R.V. might very well have given "the Deliverer," as they did in Romans 11:26, the only other place of its occurrence in the New Testament. But Paul had not, when he was with them, told them how they would be delivered, for so far the means whereby God would accomplish His sure Word had not been revealed.

Mr. Reese insists that the Day of the Lord and the Day of Christ are alternative terms for the same period. The latter phrase, with some modifications, occurs six times in the New Testament, namely, 1 Corinthians 1:8; 5:5 (where R.V. *m.* omits "Jesus"); 2 Corinthians 1:14; Philippians 1:6, 10; 2:16. In no one of these is there any reference to the unbelieving world, but only to Christians. In each case accountability to the Lord is expressed or clearly implied. From this we conclude that the Judgment Seat of Christ falls within this period. Since the language used in each comparable text is similar we conclude also that the Day of Christ corresponds with the *parousia*. Compare, for example, 1 Thessalonians 2:19, where Paul looks forward to the *parousia* for the vindication of his labors as an evangelist, with Philippians 2:16, where he looks for the vindication of his labors as a teacher and pastor, as does John in his first epistle (2:28).

Philippians 1:6 and 10 are complementary. In the former Paul expresses his confidence that God, having begun His work in the saints, will not fail to carry it on until, as He will perfect it in, the Day of Jesus Christ. On the other hand, their responsibility is to be sincere, and to be vigilant against giving offense, with the Day of Christ before them. (In this paraphrase I have attempted to bring out the force of the two prepositions used, *achri* in the former, *eis* in the latter verse.) Here again we seem justified in concluding that the Judgment Seat is in view. Second Corinthians 1:14 lends confirmation to this deduction, which, considering the similarity of the language, does not call for modification on account of the variety in the titles.

First Corinthians 1:7, 8, presents no difficulty. I understand the revelation of our Lord Jesus Christ to refer to that which is, according to Romans 5:2; Titus 2:13, and other Scriptures, the proper hope of the Christian, the appearing of His glory, when He shall be crowned where once He was rejected, when the crown of thorns will be replaced by the many diadems (Rev. 19:12). Here Mr. Reese assumes that the "day" of verse 8 refers to the "revelation" of verse 7, but this is not a necessary deduction, whereas to understand the "day" to refer to the *parousia* here, as elsewhere, yields an excellent sense, with the advantage of consistency with the other places in which the phrase occurs.

Insistence on the meaning of "arrival" for *parousia* has led to misapprehension of the meaning of 1 Thessalonians 3:13, making it the warrant for the oft-repeated antithesis between the "coming for" and the "coming with" the saints. But 1 Thessalonians 4:16, 17 does not show the Lord as returning to the earth at all. Here are the words for all to read: "The Lord Himself shall descend from Heaven . . . then we . . . with them . . . meet the Lord in the air." Why put into the verse something that not only is not there, but which is excluded by what the verse does contain? Allowing *parousia* to retain its otherwise unvarying meaning of "presence," 1 Thessalonians 3:13 is in harmony with the rest of Scripture; the saints are to be seen established unblameable in holiness, "in [*en*, which is the appropriate preposition for "during," as in John 11:9, 10, for example] the Parousia of the Lord Jesus with all His saints." That is, during the *parousia*, at the Judgment Seat, their true state will be seen, the result of grace in their lives on earth.

Notwithstanding the charge of "exegetical looseness" brought by Mr. Reese on page 141, I still judge that in the language of 1 Thessalonians 4:15 a fresh revelation is implied. The article is absent before "word"; had it been present, attention would have been directed to some Old Testament Scripture. Its absence seems to indicate that what was about to be written was a message from God for the occasion, a new encouragement to tried faith. Moreover, when we ask where this "word of the Lord" regarding the removal of the living and the dead is to be found in the earlier writings, there is no answer; neither is there anything like it in the recorded words of the Lord. Mr. Reese says it was "given by the Lord Jesus Christ twenty years earlier." He does not give a reference, but if John 14:1-3 is in his mind, there is nothing there beyond a simple statement that the Lord will return for "His own." But of how and when He said nothing. Nor does he say anything of "the dead." It is possible, indeed that the Rapture* is adumbrated in His words to Martha, recorded in John 11:25, 26, where "though he were dead" (A.V.) is replaced in R.V. by "though he were to die." Here certainly two classes are in view; those who die, to them He is the Resurrection; those who are living and believing on Him, to them He is the life. But when and how? Answers to these questions had to await the appropriate time.

*From the Greek word translated "caught away" the English word "rapture" comes. It has nothing to do with "rapture" in the sense of "ecstasy," but, as in John 10:12, where it is translated "snatched," means to remove suddenly from one place to another.

Revelation is progressive, and prophecy should be studied in chronological order, insofar as that can be ascertained. First there is the broad outline, then details are added, it may be at long intervals. Had Mr. Reese observed this important, and even obvious, principle of interpretation, he would have found ample room in the earlier prophecies for the *Parousia,* the presence of the Lord with His people "in the air," before "the Day of the Lord come, that great and notable Day."

Discussing the words of the Lord concerning "the last day" (John 6), Mr. Reese assumes, as he does elsewhere, that by "day" a period of hours is intended. True he acknowledged that "something might be said" for the view that it may refer to "the last period of God's dealing with men in time" (p. 55). But this admission does not go nearly far enough. The phrase is not found anywhere save in the words of the Lord, and in what is apparently a quotation of them by Martha in John 11:24. Mr. Reese says it is significant that nothing is said of resurrection in the context of John 12:48, and that the Lord there refers to "the generation of unbelievers who survive to the advent, which is viewed as near" (p. 53). Leaving his usual method, he does not adduce the testimony of "the great exegetes" in their "scientific commentaries" for this surprising limitation of the words of the Lord, which, on the surface, seems to be a comprehensive statement of the consequence of unbelief until the end. It is not possible to exclude the implication of resurrection from the words. The purpose of the remark becomes evident when, immediately afterwards, we read, "It is worthy of note that in every case in the above text [i.e., excluding 12:48] the resurrection referred to is clearly that of the faithful dead. It is the resurrection of 'life' (John 5:29). . . . Here is a very definite point of time; does it differ from that marked for the resurrection by Isaiah 26:19, etc.? It does not." But this assumes that the "last day" is one of twenty-four hours, in the interests of which assumption it is necessary to remove the idea of resurrection from 12:48. But even if, which I take to be impossible, resurrection were eliminated from the verse, it still remains that John 5:29 includes "the resurrection of judgment." And we know from Revelation 20:1–6 that a period of one thousand years elapses between these resurrections. If in these passages, and many others, "day" is understood of an undefined period, the difficulty disappears, and with it many of the "arguments" of this book.

One feature of the prophetic word that must be borne in mind is that almost invariably the time element is excluded. Events separated by long intervals are mentioned together in many passages, Isaiah 11:1–9; 61:2, for example. This Mr. Reese recognizes, for he speaks of "the well-known characteristic of prophecy to unite events on a near and a distant horizon" (p. 45). The enmity of Genesis 3:15 began there and then; the bruising of Messiah's heel took place at Calvary; the bruising of Satan's head is not yet (Rom. 16:20).

Not only do we concede to Mr. Reese the "right to postulate that we may be quite sure that there is nothing in the epistles that is contradictory to the teaching given by the Lord of Glory about His return" (p. 103), we would insist upon it uncompromisingly. But we would also insist that the words of the apostles were necessary, else wherefore were they given? And just as the Old Testament must be read in the light of the New Testament—and as the New Testament, while it sets aside nothing in the Old Testament, supplements and develops the earlier revelation, so does the teaching of the apostles fill up and complete the words of the Lord. Thus John 11:25, 26 and 14:1–3, must be read in the light of 1 Thessalonians 4:13–16; Matthew 24:27 in the light of 2 Thessalonians 2:8.

One more question must be examined before we part company with this unhappy volume. Does "the Time of Jacob's Trouble," "the Tribulation, the Great One," fall without or within the Day of the Lord? (Jer. 30:4–11; Rev. 7:14, with Dan. 12:1; Matt. 24:21, 22). On page 212 Mr. Reese says that "it never seems to occur to writers of this school [i.e., those to whose teaching he is opposed] that immediately before the wrath of the Day of the Lord falls, God can call His saints to Himself" without a Rapture and a *Parousia*. I confess it had not occurred to me to doubt that God can do all that God wills to do. There is nothing inherently impossible in the conception that the Lord's purpose might have been to call "His own" away and to return with them immediately. The sole question is, is this what is to be learned from Scripture? Without arrogance, or unseemly dogmatism, I judge there is to be an interval, represented by that *parousia* which Mr. Reese, entirely without lexicon justification, and, indeed, against the testimony of every lexicon to which he himself appeals, persists in robbing of its distinctive meaning "presence."*

A little later he says: "On the authority of our Lord we learn that it happened thus in the days of the Flood: 'They did eat, they drank, they married wives, they were given in marriage, *until the day* that Noah entered into the ark, and the flood came and destroyed them all'" (Luke 17:27). (Mr. Reese's italics.) But considering that we are told in Genesis 7:1, 4, 10, that seven days elapsed after Noah entered into the ark before the Flood came, it is clear that the Lord's words are not to be understood as stating that the Flood came on the day that Noah entered it. Lot's case is different, for, in conformity with the narrative in Genesis, the Lord's words are "in the day that Lot went out from Sodom," the catastrophe befell the city. "After the same manner," said the Lord, "shall it be in the day that the Son of man is revealed," i.e., at the manifestation of His *Parousia*. Another significant factor in this problem is, that in verse 26 the Lord compares the "days" of Noah with the "days" of the Son of man. But in His reference to Lot the word is "day" in both cases. Comparison with Matthew's record, too, is illuminating. As already noticed the "days" of Noah are compared with the *parousia,* but how could this be if *parousia* is not a period, as "days" certainly are? Noah's contemporaries continued their customary manner of life "until the day that Noah entered into the ark, and they knew not until the flood came and took them all away; so shall also be the *parousia* of the Son of man" (Matt. 24:37-39). Here again the language of the Lord is elastic enough to admit of the seven days' interval which the history in Genesis 7 demands.

Let there be no misunderstanding here. Our calling is to suffer for righteousness' sake, for Christ's sake. The Lord made this perfectly plain on many occasions. And many have so suffered, up to the limit of human endurance, even when these powers of endurance were reinforced by the strength the Holy Spirit gives. The greatness of the Tribulation seems to lie in its extent rather than in its intensity. Sentimental consideration should be firmly set aside as being of no account here or elsewhere. If so be that Mr. Reese is right, that those of this present calling are to pass through that experience, the grace of the Lord will assuredly sustain us, as it will sustain all those faithful souls who are called upon to endure it, notwithstanding that we were mistaken in our expectation. If, on the other hand, Mr. Reese has misread the Scriptures, will he and his school not be penalized? Grace reigns! Hence I suggest that what he calls the "trump card" (p. 281) of those he opposes does not exist for the sober student of the Word.

It seems clear to me that the Tribulation precedes the appearing of the glory; that it falls within the Seventieth Week, and after the *Parousia* begins. It is the experience of the people of God who will be on the earth after the Rapture, and during the *parousia* of the Lord with "the Church which is His [Christ's] body" "in the air." When the Seventh Angel sounds (Rev. 11:15–18) "the Kingdom of the world" becomes "the Kingdom of our Lord, and of His Christ." Thereafter the four and twenty elders review the steps that led to this consummation in the words, "the nations were wroth, and Thy wrath came." Here, if I mistake not, the Tribulation, "the nations were wroth," is distinguished from the Day of the Lord, "Thy wrath came."

In Jeremiah 30:4–7 the wrath of the nations upon Jacob is described; in 8–11 their deliverance and the destruction of their adversaries.

In Zechariah 12:14, Jerusalem is besieged by the nations, but the hour of her deliverance has come in the destruction of these nations. Then it is that the feet of the Lord stand upon the Mount of Olives. "And it shall come to pass in that day . . . known unto the Lord; not day, and not night: but it shall come to pass,

*Since the body of this review was written the writer has been able to consult an early edition of Liddell and Scott, where *parousia* is defined as 1, "a being present"; 2, "arrival," as in later editions. Thayer's Grimm gives, 1, "presence" . . . opposed to *apousia,* absence; 2, "the presence of one coming, hence arrival, advent." Here, while the meaning of the word is confirmed, we see Grimm involved in the same difficulty that beset Cremer, and which no one that gives *parousia* the meaning "arrival" can escape.

that at evening time there shall be light" (Zech. 12:6, 7).

It is not claimed that the view here maintained is without its difficulties. The warning of 2 Kings 7 has not been forgotten. Yet we remember the words of Butler, quoted approvingly on page 225, "a truth being established, objections are nothing; the one is founded upon our knowledge, the other upon our ignorance." So if the reader has received light upon any passage of Scripture, let him wait for that further light in which all will be harmonized. Let not what we do not know loosen our hold upon what we do know—and the Lord give us understanding in all things.

This review is already long enough. It would take a considerable volume to trace out all the fallacies which Mr. Reese presents with an air of finality and authority calculated to impress those with whom assertion carries the weight of reason; "careless readers and others who believe what pleases their fancy," and who "are misled by specious reasoning, since they do not stop to examine it and test its validity" (p. 282). And if anyone desires an apt illustration of the words of Salmon, recorded on the same page, he will find it in Mr. Reese himself!

The title of the book raises hopes of a goodly and pleasant land, flowing with milk and honey, providing bread for the eater and seed for the sower. We have found it an arid country, abounding in bitter fruit, barren of aught either to comfort or encourage the heritage of God. The pity of it! As though misrepresentation and reviling of the children of God could be other than grieving to Him, and detrimental to the spiritual life of the reader. Mr. Reese acknowledges that when his *bēte noir,* J. N. Darby, wrote on prophecy his "courtesy and urbane spirit have been admirable." He adds: "Of course Darby could use another blade." Once more Mr. Reese fails to distinguish. Darby, contending "earnestly for the faith once for all delivered to the saints," could smite trenchantly the enemies of the Cross of Christ. Writing on prophecy for the household of the faith, he did not forget the Lord's words, "All ye are brethren." But Mr. Reese beats his fellow servants, sparing them as little as Darby spared those who, as he judged, opposed or betrayed the faith.

In conclusion, let me remind my readers of the words of the apostle, "Let all that ye do be done in love," that is, not for any other motive than the well-being of those with whom we may be dealing either by tongue or by pen, or in act. No authority inheres in pamphlets or addresses save that which is to be found in the Scriptures of Truth. What is spoken or written stands or falls by that. What is "school" or "theory" compared with the knowledge of the mind of the Lord, Who speaks again to us His words of long ago, saying, "Learn of Me; for I am meek and lowly in heart"?

Postscript

Throughout his book Mr. Reese gives the impression that what he so frequently calls "the new theories" are to be condemned because they are, or are alleged to be, new; indeed this is a favorite argument of the school to which he belongs, and many are impressed by it. Yet on page 29 he says that novelty is not itself a sufficient reason for rejecting any teaching, and utters a salutary warning against the real danger of closing the mind to what is new to us, lest, so doing we should be found resisting the Spirit of God. On page 316 he says further that "Darby had his place in causing fresh light to break forth from God's Word . . . and the great work goes on: fresh light always breaking forth from God's word." Is it not possible that the place of the Rapture and the *Parousia* in the end time, as understood by Darby and others, and which Mr. Reese stigmatizes as a "stupid obsession" (p. 266), may prove such new light as Robinson, two hundred years before Darby was born, exhorted the Pilgrim Fathers to expect. In 1736 Butler drew a striking analogy, to the same effect, between the two Books of the same Author, Nature and Scripture. Here are his words: "As, it is owned, the whole scheme of Scripture is not yet understood; so if it ever comes to be understood before the 'restitution of all things,' and without miraculous interpositions, it must be in the same way as natural knowledge is come at: by particular persons attending to, comparing and pursuing intimations scattered up and down it, which are overlooked and disregarded by the generality of the world. Nor is it at all incredible, that a book that has been so long in the possession of mankind should contain many truths as yet undiscovered. For all the same phenomena, and the same faculties of investigation, from which great discoveries in natural knowledge have been made in the present and last age, were equally in the possession of mankind several thousand years before."—Butler, *Analogy*, Part 2, chapter 3.

Notwithstanding that the Holy Spirit has been in and with the children of God from the beginning, their history shows that much revealed truth was lost, and that much has since been recovered. But we may not assume that this generation has nothing further to learn from what we all acknowledge to be the living oracles of the living God (Acts 7:38; Rom. 3:1). It is dangerous to shut out the possibility of the further recovery of truth in them, of further light shining out from them, as it is unwarranted to stereotype an exposition of any part of the book.

On the other hand, we may be assured that no new discovery of old truth will prejudice "the truth that is with us" (2 Pet. 2:12) and in which we are established. That the Rapture is to precede, and the *parousia* to run concurrently with, the whole or part of the Seventieth Week, does not disturb the harmony of what is taught by Mr. Reese's school in common with that he opposes. As it seems to me, the "new" teaching, or, as I should prefer to call it, the old truth recovered, is its complement. The broad outline has not been altered; details have been supplied that had not been discerned even by those who saw so much. Nothing is added to Holy Writ, nor aught advanced for the consideration of the children of God without adequate warrant therein. Finality belongs to the Scriptures alone, not to any interpretation of them.

C. F. Hogg

Part 1: The Significance of the Word "Church"

The question is frequently asked: "Will the Church go through the Great Tribulation?" This at once raises the prior question as to the use and significance of the word Church in Scripture. A widely held idea of the word is that it stands for the whole company of believers living on the earth at any given time. Such an interpretation is, however, nowhere endorsed in the New Testament.

Twofold Application of the Term

Apart from an application to the community of Israel, Acts 7:38 and Hebrews 2:12, the term *ekklesia* (church) is used in two respects. One denotes the complete corporate company of saints spoken of as the "Body" of Christ, comprising all the redeemed from among Jew and Gentile during the present era or age. Of that Body Christ is the Head, Ephesians 1:22, 23; 4:15; 5:23, 25; Colossians 1:18, 24. That is the company of which the Lord spoke in Matthew 16:18: "I will build My Church." It consists both of those who have fallen asleep in Christ, 1 Corinthians 15:18, and of saints who are living in the world, and of those who may yet be added through the gospel before the Rapture. What is said of this company in the epistles to the Ephesians and Colossians is comprehensive of all. The saints in heaven are still of "the body of Christ" and of "the household of God." They are not dismembered, because they are for the time being in the spirit state. When the Body is complete, the Lord will "descend from heaven with a shout, with the voice of the archangel, and with the trump of God; and the dead in Christ shall rise first; then we that are alive, that are left, shall together with them be caught up in the clouds, to meet the Lord in the air" (1 Thess. 4:16, 17, R.V.). Such figurative expressions as nourishing, cherishing and building up, as used in Ephesians, take in their scope the complete company which the Lord will ultimately present to Himself.

The view that the term "the Church" is also used to comprise all the saints in the world at any given time is not borne out by the teaching of Christ and His apostles. Such believers could not be spoken of as either "a body" or "the body" of Christ. At the inception of the present period only a small fraction of the Church, the Body of Christ, was actually in existence; since then those who have fallen asleep do not cease to form part of the complete corporate company. The use of the phrase "the Church on earth" is a contravention of the teaching of Scripture on this subject.

A Church of God

The other respect in which *ekklesia* is used is that of a local church; that is, a company of believers acting together in local capacity and responsibility. Of such a community the Lord spoke in Matthew 18:17. Each company is described as a church of God, or as the church of God in a given place, e.g., 1 Corinthians 1:2. In the plural such companies are similarly termed "churches of God," 1 Corinthians 11:16; 1 Thessalonians 2:14; 2 Thessalonians 1:4.

The passages which are regarded by some as supporting the view that the term "church" can be interpreted to consist of believers living in all parts of the world really teach the contrary when considered in the light of the immediate context or of the teaching of the epistle in which the word occurs. For instance, the passages in which the apostle Paul speaks of his persecuting the church, viz., 1 Corinthians 15:9; Galatians 1:13; Philippians 3:6, do not refer to all the believers in Palestine and elsewhere at the time, but to the local church in Jerusalem. That was the assembly of which it is said in Acts 8:3, "but Saul laid waste the church, entering into every house, and hailing men and women, committed them to prison." The next verse shows that many from that assembly were scattered abroad and went about preaching the Word. For some time their work would consist of testifying, and there is no evidence of the immediate formation of other churches, though that took place ere long. Some of those who were scattered had gone as far as Damascus, and Saul in his zeal went there, with the determination to bring them to Jerusalem for imprisonment. It is significant, by the way, that instead of the mention of an assembly at Damascus, Saul stayed with "certain disciples." That the persecuted belonged to Jerusalem is confirmed by the question asked in Acts 9:29: "Is not this he that destroyed them which called on this name in Jerusalem?"

It is true that in the passages referred to the apostle does not mention the city of Jerusalem, but that is no indication that he was using the term in any but the local sense. There was no need for him to mention the locality. In 1 Corinthians 15:9, he had just been speaking of Jerusalem, and the Lord's appearances there after He was risen. In Galatians 1:13 it would be evident to his readers that he was referring to the church in Jerusalem; moreover, it is significant that in verse 22, with reference to those who were not known to him by face, he speaks of "the churches [not "the church"] of Judaea." In Philippians 3:6 the description he gives of the circumstances of his preconversion days centers in Jerusalem.

In Acts 9:31, R.V., where the singular is used, the context indicates that the word still bears the local sense. The saints had been scattered from Jerusalem throughout Judaea and Samaria and Galilee. It was they who had comprised the church at Jerusalem, from the time of pentecost until the persecution arose. The formation of other churches does not up to that time receive mention.

The Church on Earth—an Unscriptural Phrase

Moreover, neither here nor in the other passages could they have been said to constitute "the Church on earth." These persecuted and scattered saints were not the only believers alive at the time, as is clear from the mention of some in Damascus.

It is true that when Saul was making havoc of the church the Lord in His divine interposition said: "Why persecutest thou Me?" But this affords no ground for the inference that there was such an entity as "the Church on earth." This identification of Himself with His persecuted saints could apply to any company of believers at any time who were suffering in this way, or to any single Christian; it does not betoken what is conceived of as "the Church on earth."

Neither can such an idea be derived from any use of the term "church" in the first epistle to the Corinthians. In 1 Corinthians 12:28 the context shows that the reference is to the local church at Corinth and not to a wider application of the term. In the preceding verse the apostle speaks of it as "a body of Christ" (there is no definite article in the original), a corporate company the members of which are to have the same care one for another (v. 25). This could not be said of believers constituting an assembly inclusive of those living in another land. What is here inculcated is the realization on the part of each member of a local church of the need of seeking the welfare of the fellow members of that church. How could that apply to those in a distant region?

The spiritual gifts mentioned in verse 28 all existed in the church at Corinth (the word "apostles" is used in its wider sense, as in 1 Thess. 2:6; Rom. 16:7; 2 Cor. 8:23). Yet whatever view is taken of the meaning of this verse, it could not apply to what is called "the Church on earth," a phrase unscriptural in its use and subversive in its import; for the position, establishment and destiny of the Church are heavenly. It constitutes "the Church of the firstborn who are enrolled in heaven" (Heb. 12:23, R.V.).

In 1 Timothy 3:16 it is the local church at Ephesus that is spoken of as "the house of God, which is the church of the living God, the pillar and ground of the truth," and not all the churches in the world as an amalgamated entity. The distinctly local application is evident throughout the epistle, the object of which is to give instruction "how men ought to behave themselves [the A.V. gives a wrong rendering here] in the house of God." The local application is again clear, for instance, in verse 16. Each assembly is "a house of God, a church of the living God." There is no definite article in the phrases in the original. The passage has no reference to such a company as "the Church on earth."

An Impossible Event

To speak, then, of the Church as destined to go through the Great Tribulation, is to use phraseology which receives no support from Scripture, and betokens a misunderstanding of the significance of the term. Some might say that their use of the word in this respect is simply a convenient mode of expression to comprehend all true believers who will be living during the time of the Great Tribulation, and that to regard one who uses the term in this way as holding an erroneous view, is simply making a person an offender for a word.

Yet to speak of the Church's going through the Great Tribulation involves the impossibility that those who are already with the Lord (who still form part of the Church) would come down from heaven to suffer with their fellow saints on earth the Great Tribulation woes.

If those who hold the view referred to, adopted Scripture phraseology and taught that individual believers or believers gathered as local churches or assemblies, would experience the sufferings of the period so described, we could understand their meaning. Even so there is this to be considered, that individual Christians and local companies could not endure more horrible afflictions than have from time to time been meted out to fellow Christians in times of persecution in the past, and that not even the woes of the Great Tribulation will exceed the tortures and privations, with their vast variety, which have been the lot of believers during past centuries. The question remains whether living members of the Church are destined to share with the Jewish people their unprecedented tribulation.

▪ CHAPTER THREE ▪

Part 2: The Great Tribulation and the Wrath of God

Let us see, then, what Scripture has to say with regard to the circumstances of that time. In the Lord's discourse to His disciples recorded in Matthew 24, He foretold that there would be "great tribulation, such as hath not been from the beginning of the world until now, no nor ever shall be" (v. 21). He indicated both the time of its occurrence and that of its termination.

Time Indications as to the Tribulation

It would take place when the "abomination of desolation spoken of by Daniel the prophet" would be seen standing "in the holy place" (v. 15). Immediately after the Tribulation "The sun shall be darkened, and the moon shall not give her light, and the stars shall fall from heaven, and the powers of heaven shall be shaken; and then shall appear the sign of the Son of man in heaven: and then shall all the tribes of the earth mourn, and they shall see the Son of man coming in the clouds of heaven with power and great glory" (vv. 29, 30). Obviously these events have not yet taken place.

The Prophecies in Daniel and Matthew

The same period and circumstances are foretold in Daniel 12:1, 2: "And at that time shall Michael stand up, the great prince which standeth for the children of thy people: and there shall be a time of trouble, such as never was since there was a nation even to that same time: and at that time thy people shall be delivered, every one that shall be found written in the book. And many of them that sleep in the dust of the earth shall awake, some to everlasting life, and some to shame and everlasting contempt" (Dan. 12:1, 2). The phrase "at that time," refers to what has just been related in the eleventh chapter, which predicts a war as destined to take place in Palestine. The unprecedented tribulation cannot therefore be regarded as extending through the present era since A.D.70.

In Matthew 24 fuller details are given: "When therefore ye see the abomination of desolation, which was spoken of by Daniel the prophet, standing in the holy place (let him that readeth understand), then let them that are in Judaea flee into the mountains: let him that is in the housetop not go down to take out the things that are in his house; and let him that is in the field not return back to take his cloak. But woe unto them that are with child and to them that give suck in those days! And pray ye that your flight be not in the winter, neither on a Sabbath: for then shall be great tribulation, such as hath not been from the beginning of the world until now, no, nor ever shall be. And except those days had been shortened, no flesh would have been saved: but for the elect's sake those days shall be shortened" (vv. 15–22).

Three passages in the book of Daniel speak of this "abomination of desolation," the context making clear that the time referred to is yet future and will immediately precede the personal intervention of Christ for the overthrow of the desolator and the setting up of the millennial kingdom, "to bring in everlasting righteousness." The first passage indicates that the Antichrist will make a covenant with the Jews for a period spoken of as "one week" (or *hebdomad*), that in the middle of this period, he will break the covenant and mark the reversal of his attitude toward the Jewish people by the installation of the abomination that maketh desolate: "he shall make a firm covenant with many for one week: and for the half of the week he shall cause the sacrifice and the oblation to cease; and upon the wing [or pinnacle] of abominations shall come one that maketh desolate; and even unto the consummation, and that determined, shall wrath be poured out upon the desolator" (9:27).

The R.V. word "desolator" (correcting the A.V., "desolate") should be noted, for it is upon him and his associates that the divine wrath is to be executed. The Jews themselves, that is, the godly remnant, the objects of the fury of the Antichrist are, as a nation, to be the subjects of divine deliverance (Jer. 30:7); those of the nation who remain apostate and worship the image of the Beast will be subject to the wrath of God alike with all others who do so (Rev. 14:9).

The second passage similarly predicts the breach of the treaty by the Antichrist: "he shall . . . have indignation against the holy covenant, and shall do his pleasure: he shall even return, and have regard unto them that forsake the holy covenant. And arms shall stand on his part, and they shall profane the sanctuary, even the fortress, and shall take away the continual burnt offering, and they shall set up the abomination that maketh desolate" (11:30, 31). The last passage is 12:11, which states the length of the period of tribulation as a thousand two hundred and ninety days, from the time that the burnt offering is taken away and the abomination that maketh desolate set up.

"The Time of Jacob's Trouble"

Jeremiah 30:7 defines the character of the period as relating to the nation: "It is even the time of Jacob's trouble." Then follows the assurance that the nation, as a nation (that is obviously the significance of the name Jacob, the name being put by metonymy for his descendants) will be "saved out of it." The subsequent context shows that the deliverance will introduce the millennial period of peace and rest. Strangers will no more serve themselves of the people, and judgment will be meted out to the nations who have oppressed them (v. 11). This very passage states that while the Lord will save His own earthly people, He will "make a full end of all the nations whither they have been scattered."

The efforts of the combined Gentile powers under the Man of Sin to destroy the Jews from being a nation, to cut off their very existence from the earth (for this is to be the object of their fierce hostility in the period of desolation consequent upon the breaking of the covenant previously agreed upon by the Man of Sin), will be immediately met by a series of retributive judgments, not merely punitive or remedial, but retributive, by which the wrath of God will be poured out upon the foe, and upon all those (including persistently apostate Jews) who own allegiance to the Man of Sin.

This divine wrath, in its manifold judgments, which will be God's answer to the utter rejection of His claims and the denial of His very existence, His answer to men's allegiance to, and worship of, the Beast (Rev. 13:3–8), and to their unprecedented maltreatment of His earthly people, will affect the world, that is, "them that dwell on the earth" (Rev. 8:13; 12:12; 13:8, 14, e.g.).

The Divine Wrath Extending Through a Period

That the wrath of God will extend over a period instead of being confined to one final judgment at the revelation of Christ with the angels of His power, is made clear in Revelation, chapters 6 to 19. In chapter 15:1, concerning the seven last plagues, it is said that "in them is finished the wrath of God" (R.V.) The verb in the original signifies to bring to an end, to complete, to finish, not to fill up (as in the A.V.). The same word is used, for instance, in 10:7 ("finished") and in 11:7. It corresponds to the noun *telos,* an end. The word "finished" makes clear that the judgments poured out in connection with the seven vials or bowls do not constitute the whole of the divine wrath to be exercised. The successive events which form the consummating acts of this divine wrath, are given in detail in chapter 16, and these are all preliminary to the personal advent of Christ in judgment as described in 19:11 to 21. Moreover, that these seven judgments themselves cover a certain period, is clear from what is said, for instance, of the sixth, in which the kings of the whole world are instigated by the powers of darkness to gather together "unto the war of the Great Day of God, the Almighty" (16:14).

As the events which take place in the execution of the wrath of God under the pouring out of the seven last plagues out of what are figuratively described as "seven bowls," constitute the finishing of His wrath, it follows that the preceding similar events described in the earlier chapters are likewise to be recognized as belonging to this same period.

An Important Distinction

This series of judgments in connection with the wrath of God, the immediate retribution by God upon the nations, is not to be identified with "Jacob's trouble," though the events will be concurrent. The judgment upon the Jewish nation as such, for their rejection of their Messiah and their persistent refusal to accept His claims, has consisted and will consist of bitter persecution at the hands of Gentile powers, reaching its culmination in the satanically instigated onslaught inflicted by the Beast (Rev. 12:13). At the time when the apostle wrote to the church of the Thessalonians the wrath had already begun to come upon the Jews and would proceed "to the uttermost" (1 Thess. 2:16). They were already a scattered people. Their land was under tyrants, their temple and city were about to be destroyed; heavier sorrows would come upon them, and, as the Lord Himself foretold, will do so, before final deliverance comes, Matthew 24:15–28. But God's wrath upon His earthly people, reaching its climax in the acts of the Man of Sin in "the time of Jacob's trouble" is one thing; the wrath of God to be poured out simultaneously upon that despot and his kingdom and all who associate with him, Jew or Gentile, is another. The two circumstances coincide but are to be distinguished.

Two Contemporaneous Events

This is made clear in the Apocalypse, as well as in other Scriptures. The time of "Jacob's trouble" and the judgments of the wrath of God begin when "the abomination that maketh desolate" is set up. The judgments meted out to the worshipers of the Beast are not withheld until the Great Tribulation is over. God no longer will maintain His attitude of long-suffering, waiting for men to come to repentance. The retributive hardness of heart which will characterize the adherents of the Man of Sin, will determine their irretrievable doom. The "coming" of that "lawless one" (his *parousia,* obviously his presence in the world and not his mere arising to prominence) will be "according to the working of Satan with all power and signs and lying wonders, and with all deceit of unrighteousness for them that are perishing; because they received not the love of the truth, that they might be saved. And for this cause God sendeth them a working of error, that they should believe a lie that they all might be judged who believed not the truth, but had pleasure in unrighteousness" (2 Thess. 2:9–12).

One great distinction between "Jacob's trouble" and the wrath of God upon the Beast and his kingdom, lies in this, that there is to be no deliverance for the Beast and all who acknowledge him; the wrath of God upon them will issue in their entire removal from the earth to their appointed doom (Rev. 14:9–11). Deliverance, on the contrary, is assured to the God-fearing Jews as a nation, for the tribulation which they experience at the hands of man will not see their extermination, but the preservation of this converted and faithful "remnant," the nucleus of the leading nation of the earth in the Millennium. "Two parts . . . shall be cut off and die; but the third shall be left therein. And I will bring the third part through the fire, and will refine them as silver is refined, and try them as gold is tried: they shall call on my name, and I will hear them: I will say, 'It is my people'; and they shall say, 'The Lord is my God.' Behold, a day of the Lord cometh, when thy spoil shall be divided in the midst of thee. For I will gather all nations against Jerusalem to battle; and the city shall be taken, and the houses rifled, and the women ravished; and half of the city shall go forth into captivity, and the residue of the people shall not be cut off from the city. Then shall the Lord go forth, and fight against those nations, as when He fought in the day of battle. And His feet shall stand in that day upon the Mount of Olives, which is before Jerusalem on the east, and the Mount of Olives shall cleave in the midst thereof toward the east and toward the west, and there shall be a very great valley; and half of the mountain shall remove toward the north, and half of it toward the south. And ye shall flee by the valley of my mountains; for the valley of the mountains shall reach unto Azel: yea, ye shall flee, like as ye fled from before the earthquake in the days of Uzziah king of Judah: and the Lord my God shall come and all the holy ones with Thee. And it shall come to pass in that day, that the light shall not be with the brightness and with gloom: but it shall be one day which is known unto the Lord; not day, and not night: but it shall come to pass, that at evening time there shall be light. And it shall come to pass in that day, that living waters shall go out from Jerusalem; half of them toward the eastern sea, and half of them toward the western sea: in summer and in winter shall it be. And the Lord shall be King over all the earth: in that day shall the Lord be one, and His Name one" (Zech. 13:8 to 14:9). Man breaks and will break his covenants, but God's covenant with Abraham will ever abide.

Revelation, Chapters 6 to 19

Before we return to this point of the subject, it is necessary to continue the consideration of the divine operations of judgment in the coming period, which constitute it as a time of the wrath of God upon the world, as well as a time of Israel's woe. For there is one fundamental truth connected with this, which has a direct bearing upon the question as to whether any of the saints who belong to the church, the body of Christ, are destined to pass through this period.

Previously to the pouring out of the seven vials or bowls there is a series of judgments to be executed under the sounding of seven trumpets. The events which are described as taking place in connection with these are obviously such as constitute measures of divine wrath upon "them that dwell on the earth" (see chapter 8, verse 7, to chapter 11, end). Nature itself is visited with disaster, as well as the circumstances and doings of men. After the sounding of the fourth trumpet a voice is heard pronouncing a threefold woe, "for them that dwell on the earth, by reason of the other voices of the trumpet of the three angels who are yet to sound" (8:13). Chapter 9 is descriptive of these further divine visitations, which, while they rise to a climax of retribution, meet with a refusal on the part of men to repent of their evil doings. After the sounding of the seventh trumpet, there is first an anticipative declaration in heaven as to the setting up of the kingdom of Christ upon the earth, and a retrospective statement looking back upon what has taken place as to the fury of the nations and the visitation of divine wrath upon them: "the nations were wroth, and Thy wrath came" (11:18, R.V.).

Tracing the events backward further, as characterized by wrath, we observe that previously to the sounding of the seven trumpets there are judgments carried out under the opening of the seals. These are described in chapter 6, and have the same features of divine retribution as those foretold in the subsequent chapters with reference to the sounding of the trumpets and the pouring of the contents of the seven bowls. The whole period covered by chapters 6 to 19 is thus seen to be one of the wrath of God upon the confederate nations and all associated with them, for their rejection of God and His Christ and their antagonism to His earthly people.

An Essential Difference

Without now considering, what to many seems obvious, that this closing period will on this very account be essentially contrary in character to that of the present time of the long-suffering of God and the preaching of the gospel of His grace, and that the latter will not continue into the period of wrath, yet the very fact that the wrath of God is to be poured out in the manner so clearly indicated in these chapters, must be regarded in the light of specific statements concerning the previous deliverance of believers who form part of the Church, the body of Christ (not, we say again, the Church on earth).

In 1 Thessalonians 5:9, the Scripture declares that "God appointed us not unto wrath, but unto the obtaining of salvation through our Lord Jesus Christ." The preceding verse makes clear that the salvation referred to is not deliverance from the perdition of hell (quite a different subject of salvation), but that which is to be brought unto us at the Lord's return to receive us unto Himself. With that event the passage from 4:13 to 5:11 deals. The wrath, then, from which we are to be delivered is that which is to descend upon "them that dwell on the earth," under the misrule of the Man of Sin.

This assurance in 5:9 throws light upon the statement in the 10th verse of the first chapter of this epistle, where the Lord Jesus is described, firstly, as the object of the expectancy of the saints, and, secondly, as "our Deliverer from the coming wrath." This is the plain meaning of the original. The R.V. has rightly used the present tense of the verb ("delivereth"). The A.V., "which delivered," is a mistranslation and is misleading; it has been responsible for giving a wrong impression as to the deliverance referred to. The construction is that of the definite article with the present participle of the verb, literally, "the delivering [One],"a construction commonly used as a title; for example, in Romans 11:26 the same phrase is actually translated "the Deliverer."

Ek and Apo

It has been urged that, since the preposition translated "from," *ek,* frequently means "out of" or "from the midst of," therefore this deliverance is destined to come while the wrath is being exercised, and that believers are to be delivered from the midst of its judgments. It is further argued that if the deliverance was destined to take place before the wrath descended, the preposition *apo,* away from, would have been used. As against such a view, in the first place, the preposition *ek* has a wider range of meaning than that which has just been represented. It is not always used in the way indicated. In 2 Corinthians 1:10 it is used in the statement, "who delivered us out of so great a death, and will deliver us." Here *ek* is plainly equivalent to *apo,* from, for death was not actually experienced, but was impending. In Matthew 17:9 it is used of descending *from* a mountain, not out of the midst of the mountain, for, as A. T. Robertson says, "we are not to suppose that they had been in a cave"; moreover, in the parallel passage in Luke 9:37, the equivalent preposition is *apo. Ek* is similarly used in Acts 12:7, "his chains fell off from his hands." Cp. *ek* in Acts 28:4, of the serpent hanging from his hand. Illustrations of the elastic use of this preposition in regard to circumstances of place, condition, or state, can be obtained from any comprehensive dictionary.

When, therefore, it is necessary to decide whether this preposition, in its use in 1 Thessalonians 1:10, signifies "out of the midst of," or "from that which is impending," the question is to be determined by a Scripture statement upon the subject concerning which no ambiguity is possible, and, as we have pointed out, such a statement is provided in the 9th verse of the 5th chapter, that "God hath appointed us not unto wrath, but to obtain salvation." This being so, believers who belong to the Church cannot be here to endure it, for the negative is followed by a positive assurance of salvation, the mode of which the context explains.

Appeal is made to Revelation 3:11, "I also will keep thee from the hour of trial, that hour which is to come upon the whole world, to try them that dwell upon the earth." Here, again, it is precarious to insist that *ek* means *out of* ("the hour"); moreover, the verb used in the promise is that of *keeping from,* not rescuing or even delivering, but guarding from it. It is not a promise of being kept through it, but of exemption from it. Even if the inference that this message, given to the assembly in Philadelphia, is of future and general fulfillment, no ground is afforded for the supposition that any members of the Church are doomed to pass through it.

A Specific Declaration as to Deliverance

The statement in 1 Thessalonians 5:9 is so definitely set in connection with the Lord's return to receive us to Himself, as a deliverance from the impending calamities to be suffered by the world under the righteous wrath of God at the close of the age, that we should regard this assurance as a fundamental part of the doctrines of the gospel relative to the return of Christ. To obtain salvation from this wrath and yet to endure it are clearly incompatible. And as the "wrath" and the "tribulation" are contemporaneous, to be exempt from the wrath of God carries with it exemption from "Jacob's trouble."

A Recapitulation

Recapitulating the subject as thus far treated, we have endeavored to show, firstly, that to speak of the Church as going through the Tribulation is to use unscriptural terminology and to convey the idea of what is actually an impossibility; secondly, that the time of the Great Tribulation is plainly indicated as immediately preceding the Second Advent, i.e., the manifestation of the Lord for the overthrow of His foes, the deliverance of Israel, and the setting up of His kingdom; thirdly, that the special characteristics of that Tribulation will be the unprecedented sufferings endured by the Jewish people at the hands of confederate nations under the human despots spoken of as the Beast and the False Prophet, following upon the setting up of "the abomination of desolation"; fourthly, that while the sufferings of the Jews at the hands of man will be the culmination of divine wrath upon His earthly people in punishment for their rejection of Christ, such wrath having come upon them "to the uttermost," this remedial punishment is to be distinguished from the retributive wrath of God poured upon Gentile nations, and upon Jews who remain in apostasy, a divine retribution because of their worship of the Beast, and their acceptance of his claims.

It is important to make this distinction quite clear even at the expense of a certain amount of repetition. The divine displeasure against the nation will be punitive and purgative; that against the Gentile powers will be purely retributive. The wrath of God upon His earthly people, exercised through the instrumentality of the Gentiles, under the Man of Sin, will thereby be mediate; the wrath poured out upon the Gentile powers and apostate Jews will be immediate.

Scripture also makes clear that these two sets of circumstances will synchronize. For, as we have seen, the series of judgments against the Gentile nations, otherwise spoken of as "them that dwell on the earth" (judgments which constitute the wrath of God), cover a considerable period, unfolded from chapters 6 to 19, culminating in the smiting of the nations by the personal intervention of Christ; at the same time the fury of the Gentiles is expended upon Israel (see especially ch. 12:13–17). This is in accordance with Scriptures in the Old Testament, e.g., Psalm 2; Isaiah 42:13, with verse 45, and 43:2; Joel 3.

Inasmuch, then, as "the time of Jacob's trouble," inflicted upon Israel through the human instrumentality of the nations under the Man of Sin, will be at the same time a period in which the wrath of God is poured out directly upon the Gentile powers themselves, it is to be a period from which, according to the specific statements of 1 Thessalonians 1:10 and 5:9, believers living up to the time of the Rapture, members of the Church, the body of Christ, are to be delivered.

The Mode of Deliverance

The way in which the deliverance is to come is foretold in the fourth chapter of 1 Thessalonians, verses 16, 17, which describe what has been rightly called the Rapture, a catching away, a word expressive of the statement, "We that are alive, that are left, shall together with them be caught up in the clouds, to meet the Lord in the air." It is not spoken of as a secret Rapture. There is no such word describing its character. It does, however, give a plain statement of facts. The inference drawn by some, that this Rapture is to take place at precisely the time when the Lord is manifested in the culmination of divine judgment to destroy the Beast, to deliver Israel and set up the kingdom, is not only a deduction unsupported by Scripture, but is directly opposed to what Scripture states most explicitly.

To deduce further from such an inference, that the solemn and august tribunal of the Judgment Seat of Christ is to take place simultaneously with the Rapture and the Lord's personal intervention in judgment upon the world, is utterly incompatible with the doctrines of Scripture both concerning the Rapture itself, the *Parousia* of the Lord with the saints, and with what Scripture testifies as to the character of the Judgment Seat of Christ.

Brittle Earthenware—a Distinction

With regard to the nation of Israel, while the many, or the mass, make a league with Antichrist, and, as "the clay" (the brittle earthenware), will be ground to powder when "the Stone" pulverizes the Gentile powers, a considerable remnant of the nation will refuse allegiance to the Beast, and, being preserved through the protecting care of the Lord amidst the Great Tribulation, will constitute God's earthly people, when the kingdom is set up. For that deliverance numbers of the Jews will be prepared through the special witness given by the prophet Elijah and other agencies, by means of which they will be converted from their apostate state, and will turn to the Lord in repentance (Mark 9:12, with Mal. 4:6; cp. Rev. 11:3).

As to the preservation of the godly Jews, see Matthew 24:16; Revelation 12:14–16; and Daniel 12:2. "At that time thy people [Daniel's] shall be delivered, everyone that shall be found written in the Book." The Lord has ever had a remnant of faithful ones among His earthly people. As it was in Elijah's day, and as it came to pass in the time of the Lord's first Advent, so in still greater measure will it be at the time of the end. On the contrary, those Jews who remain apostate, are destined to share the wrath of God meted out to the Gentile nations, but that wrath, as we have sought to show, is to be distinguished, in its inescapable retribution, from that which is ministered by God through human agency, constituting "the time of Jacob's trouble," the fiery furnace through which, and from which, the remnant of the Jewish people, converted to their Messiah, will be delivered at His Second Advent.

The Second Advent

The circumstances of that Second Advent (quite distinct in character and time from the Rapture of the Church) are described in many parts of the Scriptures.* The Lord Jesus will be revealed "from Heaven with the angels of His power in flaming fire, rendering vengeance to them that know not God, and to them that obey not the gospel of our Lord Jesus: who shall suffer punishment, even eternal destruction from the face of the Lord and from the glory of His might" (2 Thess. 1:7–9). That revelation of Christ constitutes the Epiphany (or shining forth) of His *Parousia* (v. 8), which previously will take its inception at the Rapture (1 Thess. 4:15–17).

May the foregoing papers be used of God both to counteract error and to stimulate the Scriptural and intelligent expectation of the return of the Lord for His Church.

W. E. Vine

*Many of them are enumerated in the writer's book, *"The Roman Empire, Its Revival and End,"* chapter 8.

The Rapture and the Great Tribulation

CHAPTER ONE

The Rapture and the Great Tribulation

In his discourse to the disciples, as recorded in Matthew 24, the Lord foretold that at a certain time there would be "great tribulation, such as hath not been from the beginning of the world until now, no nor ever shall be" (v. 21). He indicated both the time of its occurrence and that of its termination. It would take place when the "abomination of desolation spoken of by Daniel the prophet" would be seen standing "in the holy place" (v. 15); and immediately after it, He said, "The sun shall be darkened, and the moon shall not give her light, and the stars shall fall from heaven, and the powers of the heavens shall be shaken; and then shall appear the sign of the Son of man in heaven: and then shall all the tribes of the earth mourn, and they shall see the Son of man coming on the clouds of heaven with power and great glory" (vv. 29, 30). That these latter events have never yet been fulfilled is clear.

Turning now to the book of Daniel we find a prediction of the same period, with similar time indications. The closing chapter, the matter of which runs consecutively on from the eleventh, begins with the statement: "And at that time shall Michael stand up, the great prince which standeth for the children of Thy people: and there shall be a time of trouble such as never was since there was a nation even to that same time." As to the termination of the period, the prophecy declares, "at that time thy people shall be delivered, every one that shall be found written in the book. And many of them that sleep in the dust of the earth shall awake, some to [more literally, these shall be for] everlasting life, and some to [those shall be for] shame and everlasting contempt." The latter are set in contrast to the former. "These" are the "many," who are to be raised at that time; "those" are others who do not share in that resurrection, but await a different destiny. The time is to be one of deliverance for the Jewish people, and the intimation is that resurrection will be the portion of many. This deliverance has not yet taken place.

As to the circumstances which are to transpire when this great tribulation takes place, the opening words of the chapter, "At that time," point to what has just been related in the eleventh chapter, which predicts a warfare to take place in Palestine. The unprecedented tribulation cannot therefore be viewed as extending over the long centuries of the present era since A.D. 70. As the time of trouble is connected with a great war and the overthrow of a tyrant, on the one hand, and ends with deliverance and resurrection, on the other, the period must be still future. Again, in the passage in the Gospel of Matthew, the similar time indication, which speaks of the abomination of desolation as standing in the holy place, does not refer to anything which took place in A.D. 70. No warfare has continued all through the centuries. No abomination, or image, or anything of the sort, was set up in the holy place when the Roman armies under Titus besieged Jerusalem and destroyed the temple.

The prophecy in the book of Daniel, concerning the abomination to which Christ referred, is as follows: "and upon the wing [or "pinnacle"] of abomination shall come [or "be"] one that maketh desolate; and even unto the consummation, and that determined, shall wrath be poured out upon the desolator" (9:27; the R.V. rendering is undoubtedly accurate here). Nothing that is mentioned in that passage, as to a covenant with the Jews and the pouring out of divine wrath upon the desolator, was fulfilled in the case of the Roman power in the first century.

That the prediction uttered by the Lord, "when therefore ye see the abomination which was spoken of by Daniel the prophet standing in the holy place," had reference to others than the apostles, is indicated by Matthew's parenthesis, "let him that readeth understand." In similar phraseology Christ said shortly afterwards to Caiaphas and the scribes and elders, "Ye shall see the Son of man sitting at the right hand of power and coming on the clouds of heaven" (26:65). Caiaphas and his fellows personally will not be there to see the event. The Lord's words had reference to the Jewish people who will see it, and who were represented by the high priest and the others on the night of the betrayal. The disciples were not necessarily to be there in person to see the abomination or to flee to the mountains, nor is there any evidence that they were in Jerusalem in A.D. 70, and that they fled therefrom. There have been times of great tribulation in past history, but that to which the prophecies of the book of Daniel and those uttered by the Lord refer was clearly a well defined period, unprecedented in its severity, and of comparatively short duration. Jeremiah speaks of the same time when he says: "Alas! for that day is great, so that none is like it, it is even the time of Jacob's trouble; but he shall be saved out of it" (Jer. 30:7). The whole world will indeed be involved in the Great Tribulation, but what Jeremiah states marks an outstanding feature of it.

Two things stand out clearly, therefore, namely, that the Great Tribulation is destined to take place at the end of the present age, and that it will be terminated by the manifestation of Christ in glory for the deliverance of His earthly people the Jews.

Simultaneous Events

A Period of Divine Wrath

The closing period of the age is also marked in Scripture as a time of the wrath of God upon the world. Judgments of God have been remedial, and have brought men to repentance; but the Scriptures show that the judgments meted out in the period referred to will be purely retributive, and will culminate in "the revelation of the Lord Jesus from heaven, with the angels of His power in flaming fire, rendering vengeance to them that know not God, and to them that obey not the gospel of our Lord Jesus" (2 Thess. 1:7, 8).*

That the divine retribution will extend over a period, and that the period is to be distinct from the present time of God's longsuffering grace and mercy is unmistakably demonstrated as follows. The nineteenth chapter of Revelation describes the culminating act of this closing period, namely, the coming of Christ from heaven in judgment upon the foes of God (vv. 11–21), an event otherwise mentioned in the passage in 2 Thessalonians 1, already referred to. The fifteenth and sixteenth chapters of Revelation describe seven judgments which will precede that event, and the opening statement concerning these is, that "in them is *finished* the wrath of God" (15:1, R.V.). These judgments themselves extend over a period, including the execution of God's retribution upon "Babylon the great," which receives "the cup of the wine of the fierceness of His wrath" (16:19).

Clearly the series of judgments mentioned in chapter sixteen is to fall upon the world before the Second Advent, which is described in chapter 19:11 to 20:3. For under the fifth in that series the kingdom of the Beast is yet in existence (v. 10); under the sixth, the Beast and the False Prophet are still active and are engaged in preparations for "the war of the great day of God Almighty" (v. 14). These passages show, therefore, that this period of wrath will precede the appearing of Christ in glory at His Second Advent, for then it is that the Antichrist will be destroyed by the Lord Himself (2 Thess. 2:8).

That the calamities which will be inflicted in this period are not confined to the Beast and his confederates, is indicated in preceding chapters, for the woes are pronounced upon "them that dwell on the earth" (8:13).

Preceding chapters also describe similar circumstances of divine retribution upon the world (cp. for example, 14:9, 10). In chapter 11:18 the correct rendering is, "the nations were wrath, and Thy wrath came [not "is come"]." The circumstances in these chapters are not those of the display of God's

*That this passage refers to a premillennial event is indicated by the fact that vengeance is rendered to those who obey not *"the gospel of our Lord Jesus."* A fuller description of the circumstances is given in Revelation 19:11–21, where the Lord is seen coming with the armies of heaven to smite the nations and to tread "the winepress of the fierceness of the wrath of Almighty God" (v. 15.)

mercy. A distinct period is marked as characterized by the wrath of God.*

A Distinctive Assurance

The Scriptures we have considered indicate, then, firstly, that the Great Tribulation will occupy the closing period of this age, and secondly, that the world also is at that time to come under the wrath of God. The two are to be simultaneous.

Deliverance from Coming Wrath

In writing to the church at Thessalonica, the apostle Paul reminds them how "they turned unto God from idols to serve the living and true God, and to wait for His Son from Heaven, even Jesus, which delivereth us from the wrath to come" (lit. "the coming wrath") (1 Thess. 1:10). The phrase rendered "which delivereth" consists, in the original, of the article with the present participle. It has been wrongly rendered in the Authorized Version by the past tense. The phrase is, literally, "the One delivering," and is equivalent to a title, "the Deliverer." That indeed is how the same construction of the same word is rightly translated in Romans 11:26. The accurate rendering, then, is "to wait for His Son from heaven, Whom He raised from the dead, even Jesus, our Deliverer from the coming wrath." The wrath referred to is therefore not that which abides now on the unbeliever, as in John 3:36; nor can the phrase be taken to refer to the punishment of the lost in the other world. That the subject with which the apostle is dealing is that of waiting for the Son of God from heaven, is itself an indication that His coming will mean the deliverance of the church from the impending wrath. We know from the epistle itself that the church at Thessalonica had been instructed by Paul orally in matters relating to the Second Advent and the judgments destined to precede it (see ch. 5). The phrase, "the coming wrath," would therefore be familiar to them.

As to the question whether the church is to pass into the period of wrath and be delivered from the midst of it, light is thrown upon this as the epistle proceeds. A categorical statement is given in the fifth chapter. There the apostle says that "God appointed us not unto wrath, but unto the obtaining of salvation through our Lord Jesus Christ" (v. 9). Here again the subject is the Lord's coming. We who are "of the day" are to put on as a helmet "the hope of salvation," and for this reason, that "God appointed us not to wrath." The apostle shows that our deliverance is based on the death of Christ; it is not dependent upon our spiritual condition at the time. He "died for us, that whether we wake or sleep, we should live together with Him." The deliverance referred to is the completion of our salvation—"the redemption of our body."

In this passage, as in the first chapter, the wrath is obviously not that mentioned in John 3:36. Nor is the reference to what will take place in the other world. Even were it possible to conceive that there is any such reference, the statement is categorical, that the saints of the church are not appointed to wrath at any time, and that accordingly they are not appointed to the wrath to be poured out upon the world at the closing period of the present age. They are to obtain salvation when Christ comes to receive them unto Himself. That salvation will be the consummation of the present salvation which they enjoy through the redemptive work of the Cross.

This passage, with that in chapter 1:10, puts the subject in a clear light. The deliverance is not out of the midst of the wrath, but before it is poured out. This truth is confirmed in the second epistle, at the close of the second chapter, where the apostle says: "But we are bound to give thanks to God alway for you, brethren beloved of the Lord, for that God chose you from the beginning unto salvation" (v. 13). That "but" sets the deliverance of the saints in contrast to the state of the world just described in the same chapter as under the

*"This wrath is to be understood, then, of the calamities wherewith God will visit men upon the earth when the present period of grace is closed, and which will fall first upon the Jews, then upon the Gentiles (Rom. 2:2, 9). The calamities of the Jews are referred to in Jeremiah 4:7; Zechariah 14:2; Matthew 24:15–21, and those of the Gentiles in Zechariah 14:3; Matthew 24:30; Luke 21:25–29, among many passages. The believer is assured of deliverance from both through the Lord Jesus Christ (cp. 5:9; Rom. 5:9)." —From *"Notes on The Epistles to the Thessalonians,"* by C. F. Hogg and the Writer.

power of the Man of Sin, a state which meets with divine retribution.

While these epistles were addressed to the church at Thessalonica, it is necessary to bear in mind that they were indicted by the Spirit of God as part of the inspired Scriptures, and were therefore intended as permanent records for the instruction of churches everywhere. They were designed to abide as truth for the enlightenment and edification of the saints throughout this age. By this time by far the greater portion of the church, is already with the Lord. For those who remain on the earth, whether now, or subsequently, and so until the Rapture, these Scriptures are provided by God, that, inspired by their stimulating hope, the saints may be maintained in a spirit of expectancy, and that, like the Thessalonian saints of old, they may "wait for His Son from heaven."

In support of the view that part of the Church will be here during the Great Tribulation, it is urged that, while there is no penal suffering for believers, any disciplinary stroke on Israel or on the nations before Christ comes, has, in part at least, a corrective character, that it should lead to repentance, and that from this the last Tribulation, though of a very special kind, is not to be excepted. This line of teaching, however, does not adequately regard the fact that the Great Tribulation comes into a period distinctively marked as that of the wrath of God. It also fails to recognize the assurances given to the church in the passages we have just been considering.

The question is asked as to why a promise of deliverance from the wrath to come should be regarded as designed for the church, when there are other saints to whom the assurance has been given of preservation through the period of the Great Tribulation, and who would in that case themselves be present in the world in the period of wrath. In reply to this, Scripture makes a distinction which it is therefore necessary to observe. The promise given in the epistle to the Thessalonians shows that, for the church, deliverance from the wrath to come will be by means of the Rapture (an expression quite Scriptural; see 1 Thess. 4:17), by the power of the Lord, in the resurrection of those who have fallen asleep and the transformation of the living. That assurance is given to the church. Deliverance for the faithful who are preserved in the period that follows will come in a different manner. Theirs is an earthly destiny, and they are to be kept under God's protecting care in a special way. The Jewish nation, as such, is to be preserved for earthly peace and power in the millennium. Gentile peoples will also continue, for such are to enjoy millennial conditions. None of those who have worshiped the Beast and have received his mark will be so kept (Rev. 14:9–11). It follows that Jews and Gentiles who live through the Great Tribulation into the millennial reign of Christ are such as have not worshiped the Beast and have been preserved from death.

It is important, then, to distinguish between the teaching given, on the one hand, concerning the church, its character, its destiny, and its deliverance, and, on the other hand, concerning God's earthly people the Jews, a large number of which are assured of preservation, a residue of Gentiles also escaping death during the time of wrath, and sharing in the blessedness of Messiah's earthly reign.

As for those who are slain for their faithfulness, and will enjoy resurrection glory, God has His own way of dealing with people, and it is for us to accept what is written in the Scriptures, and to forego reasonings as to why certain people should be dealt with in one manner and certain others in another; why it should be the lot of some people to form part of the church and to be removed from the earth at the Rapture, other people afterwards having their lot with that part of the Jewish nation which is to be kept for millennial blessedness; and why certain people should experience the calamities of that time, and even suffer death, to enjoy resurrection life, apart from actual incorporation in the church. These things lie within the determining counsels of God. Deliverance for the church comes when the Lord comes into the air (1 Thess. 4:17); deliverance for the Jewish nation takes place when the Lord comes to the earth (Zech. 13:4, 11).

The Interval

The Scriptures already noticed indicate, apart from several similar considerations, that the period of "the wrath of God" marks an interval between the Rapture of the saints and the Second Advent of Christ to the earth for the overthrow of the foes of God and the deliverance of the Jewish nation from their time of trouble. The existence of such an interval is entirely consistent with the meaning of the word Parousia (lit., "being with"), which signifies not only a coming to, but a presence with. This point calls for further attention.

The teaching of the Word of God is always consistent. The plain significance of those Scriptures which we have been considering in the preceding pages is not contradicted by other passages. On the contrary, it is confirmed by them.

▪ CHAPTER TWO ▪

Objections Considered

We purpose now to notice some of the chief arguments advanced in favor of the view that the Lord will not remove the church until after the Tribulation.

(1) We are told that since Jehovah has said to Christ, "Sit Thou on My right hand, until I make Thine enemies Thy footstool" (Ps. 110:1; Matt. 22:44), **the Lord Jesus could not come to receive the saints to Himself, as in 1 Thessalonians 4:16, 17, until the time of the overthrow of His foes, which will not take place till after the Great Tribulation.**

This argument presupposes that when Christ comes to receive the church to Himself, He will cease to be at the right hand of God. That is an unwarranted inference. The Lord will not cease to occupy that position when He descends from heaven for the Rapture of the saints. The expression signifies a position of authority and power rather than a physical attitude. A king does not cease to occupy the throne of his country when he pays a visit elsewhere. His occupation of the throne does not depend upon his continuous session in the actual chair of state. Moreover, the martyr Stephen saw the Lord "standing on the right hand of God" (Acts 7:56), yet the Scripture was not broken which said, "Sit Thou on My right hand." An interval between the descent of Christ to the air for the Rapture of the saints and His Second Advent for the overthrow of His foes could not involve any change in His authority.

(2) The word *"apantēsis,"* "meet," in 1 Thessalonians 4:17, is said to signify that those who go to meet a person, return to their starting place with him, and that therefore when the Lord comes for the church He will come immediately with the church to the earth.

This idea forces a meaning into the word which it by no means invariably admits. It is true that the word usually suggests that those who go out to meet a person intend to return, in his company, to the place from whence they set out, but the return is not necessarily immediate. If a person leaves Liverpool for London, intending to meet a friend coming from Paris, and to go back with him to Liverpool, not immediately, but after a more or less prolonged stay with him in London, the word *apantēsis* would be quite applicable to describe the meeting, as much as if the return were immediate. Moreover, the form *apantaō,* "to meet," has a wide range of meaning. It is used of meeting a person in argument, and of kings meeting in battle. It is therefore unsafe to base a doctrine on one particular application of the word. We know that the saints are to be caught up to meet Christ, and are coming back with Him in His glory and power to deal with the kingdoms of the world, but to say that the latter event must immediately follow the former, because of a special significance of *apantēsis,* is untenable.

(3) The apostle Peter testified concerning Christ that the heavens must receive Him "until the times of restoration of all things" spoken of by the prophets (Acts 3:21). **The deduction is made from this that Christ cannot come until the Antichrist has run his course; could the rise and power of God's most awful opponent, it is asked, be "the times of restoration"?**

Before considering the phrase itself, it will be well to remark that we have not stated that Christ will come before even the rise of the Antichrist. Again, it is necessary to distinguish between the Rapture and the Second Advent. The Advent of Christ signifies His coming into the world. At His first Advent He was born in Bethlehem; at His Second Advent He will come to the Mount of Olives (Zech. 14:4). At "the Coming [or Parousia] of the Lord" (1 Thess. 4:15) for the Rapture of the saints He will descend to the air (v. 17). The Parousia is not the same as the Second Advent. Nowhere does Scripture state that the Rapture is immediately to be followed by the Second Advent.

As to "the times of restoration of all things," a significance attaches to the fact that it does not say "whom the heavens must receive until the restoration of all things spoken of by the prophets." "The times of the restoration" covers a period. The events which immediately precede the restoration are naturally included in the time relating to it. The wrath of God by which the world suffers retribution for its refusal of Christ and for its reception and worship of the Antichrist, and which will culminate in the destruction of the foes of God, is a necessary preliminary to the setting up of the Kingdom. That period of wrath, therefore, has its place in the times of restoration. In the restoration of a dilapidated building much rubbish has frequently to be cleared out of the way as the first act necessary to the purpose in view. The Rapture of the saints, coming previously to this period of wrath, would consistently be said to introduce "the times of the restoration."

Plainly no doctrine can be built upon this text, as that the Rapture of the saints must be followed in immediate succession by the Advent of the Lord with the saints and with His angels.

(4) It is stated that as the Man of Sin is to be destroyed by the "Coming" of the Lord, according to 2 Thessalonians 2:8, this indicates that His Coming at the Rapture and the destruction of the Man of Sin must be simultaneous.

A careful consideration of what is actually stated in this verse will show that the inference is without foundation. The rendering is as follows: "And then shall be revealed the lawless one, whom the Lord Jesus shall slay with the breath of His mouth, and bring to naught by the manifestation of His coming." The word rendered "manifestation" is *epiphaneia,* and is literally "a shining forth." The word rendered "coming" is *parousia,* and, as has already been pointed out, this (literally, "a being with") signifies the presence of a person with others. Its occurrence in Philippians 2:12, for instance, is a sufficient example, where Paul speaks of his *parousia,* his "presence" at Philippi, in contrast to his *apousia,* his absence from that city. *Parousia* always refers to a period of time, though some particular event in the period may be especially in view. What is here in view, then, is that event, connected with the *parousia* of the Lord with His saints, which will see the destruction of the lawless one. It is called the manifestation, or shining forth, of His *parousia* because, in company with His saints (who will previously have been with Him from the time of the Rapture when His *parousia* began), He will burst in upon the scene of the Man of Sin's activities, and will there and then bring the tyrant to naught, consuming him with the breath of His mouth. That will usher in the millennial reign of righteousness. "The manifestation of His *parousia*" strikingly confirms, then, the teaching that an interval will elapse between the Rapture and the Second Advent.

It will be well here to quote a paragraph or two on the subject of the Parousia, from notes on the epistle to the Thessalonians by C. F. Hogg and the writer. The note is taken from the commentary on the words in 1 Thessalonians 2:19, *"Are not even ye, before our Lord Jesus at* [lit., *in*] His coming?"

"*Parousia,* here rendered 'coming,' is a noun formed from the verb *pareimi*—to be present, as in Luke 13:1; John 11:28; Acts 10:33, etc., and hence 'a being present with.' In a papyrus document it is used of a royal visit to a certain district; in another a person states that the care of her property demands her 'presence' in a certain city . . . The usual translation is misleading, because coming is more appropriate to other words, such as *erchomai,* Luke 12:45; 19:23; *eleusis,* Acts 7:52; *eisodos,* 13:24; the difference being that, whereas these words fix the attention on the journey to, and the arrival at, a place, *parousia* fixes it on the stay which follows on the arrival there. It would be preferable, therefore, to transliterate the word rather than translate it, that is, to use 'parousia,' rather than 'coming,' wherever the reference is to the Lord Jesus.

"Where *parousia* is used of the Lord Jesus it refers to a defined period. Thus in 2 Peter 1:16 it describes, not the daily and general companying of the Lord with His disciples among the people, but that limited period during which He was transfigured before them, Matthew 17:1–8. Where it is used prophetically, *parousia* refers to a period beginning with the descent of the Lord from heaven, into the air, 1 Thessalonians 4:16, 17, and ending with His revelation and manifestation to the world.

"During the *parousia* of the Lord in the air with His people, Paul expected to give account of his stewardship before the Judgment Seat of Christ, 1 Corinthians 4:1–5; 2 Corinthians 5:10; the presence there of the Thessalonian converts and their commendation by the Lord, would mean reward to the evangelists who had been the means of their conversion and to the pastors and teachers who had labored among them. For a similar thought see 1 John 2:28, and cp. 1 Peter 5:4. There, too, all would be abundantly compensated for the afflictions they were enduring.

"The *parousia* of the Lord Jesus is thus a period with a beginning, a course, and a conclusion. The beginning is prominent in 4:15; 5:23; 2 Thessalonians 2:1, 1 Corinthians 15:23; James 5:7, 8; 2 Peter 3:4; the course, here and in 3:13; Matthew 24:2, 37, 39; 1 John 2:28; the conclusion, in 2 Thessalonians 2:8; Matthew 24:27."

Again, the passage in Matthew 24:37–39 clearly indicates a period. The Lord says that "as were the days of Noah so shall be the Parousia of the Son of Man." As the days of Noah ended with the coming of the Flood, so the coming period will terminate at the intervention of Christ, in the shining forth, or manifestation, of His Parousia, as in 2 Thessalonians 2:8. At that event He will be accompanied, not only by His angels, but by His saints. He is then coming "to be glorified in His saints, and to be marveled at in all them that believed" (2 Thess. 1:10). That His saints will then come with Him is confirmed by Revelation 19, which describes the same event, for the armies in heaven are seen following Him on white horses, "clothed in fine linen white and pure" (v. 14). The fine linen is defined in verse 8 as "the righteous acts of the saints." The marriage of the Lamb has by that time taken place in heaven, and His wife has made herself ready to come with Him.

As a further illustration of the fact that the Parousia is periodic, and not momentary, the passage in 2 Thessalonians 2 goes on to speak of the *parousia* of the Man of Sin himself. The *parousia* of this despot will be "according to the working of Satan with all power and signs and lying wonders, and with all deceit of unrighteousness." Obviously not merely the occasion of his rise to supremacy is intended by such a description, but his period of supremacy. These things will characterize his presence, his *parousia,* in the world.

Since the Parousia of Christ is a period, the idea that the outshining or manifestation of that Parousia, for the destruction of the Man of Sin, is the same thing as His descent into the air for His saints, is, to say the least, not proven.

(5) In his second epistle to the Thessalonians the apostle says "it is a righteous thing with God to recompense affliction to them that afflict you, and to you that are afflicted rest with us, at the revelation of the Lord Jesus from heaven with the angels of His power, in flaming fire, rendering vengeance to them that know not God, and to them that obey not the gospel of our Lord Jesus" (2 Thess. 1:6–8). It is concluded from this that the Church cannot obtain rest until Christ comes to render this vengeance, and therefore that the Rapture must immediately be followed by the Second Advent.

There is no valid ground in this passage for the inference that the Second Advent, or the coming of the Lord Jesus to render vengeance, is to be immediately preceded by the Rapture. The following note is from *Notes on the Epistle to the Thessalonians,* by C. F. Hogg and the writer.

"The subject immediately before the apostle's mind is not the rest of the saints, but the retribution of God on their persecutors. Hence the words, "and to you that are afflicted rest with us," are an incidental extension of the idea of recompense, and are to be read parenthetically, permitting the words that follow to be connected directly with the close of verse 6, thus: 'affliction to them that afflict you (and to you that are afflicted rest with us), at the revelation of the Lord Jesus.' The time indicated is not that at which the saints will be relieved of persecution, but that at which their persecutors will be punished. The time of relief for the saints had been stated in the earlier letter, 4:15–17; here a passing reference to a fact within the knowledge of the readers was all that was necessary. Such extensions of thought are not uncommon in epistolary writings; cp. v. 10, and 1 Thessalonians 1:6; 2:15, 16.

"Since, then, the rest of the saints begins with the Lord's descent into the air, which marks also the inauguration of the Parousia, the Parousia itself will intervene before the vengeance of God begins to be executed. Whether the period so termed is to be of longer duration—say, extending to years, or shorter—say, limited to hours or even to minutes, is not in question here."

(6) The Lord gave parting promise to the disciples that He would be with them "always [all the days] even unto the end of the world [age]." This is taken to indicate that the church must be here until the termination of the rule of the Antichrist and therefore also of the Great Tribulation.

The word rendered "end" is not *telos,* which might signify "a termination," but *sunteleia,* "a consummation"; so the R.V. margin accurately renders it. Not the actual termination, therefore, is in view, but the heading up of events which are destined to transpire at the close of the age. A period is connoted in all the five places in this Gospel where the word is found. Until whatsoever time the affairs of the world should arrive at such a consummation the Lord promised to be with His followers. Events might at any time be approaching such a crisis. The removal of the church would at once introduce it. This passage affords no proof that any part of the church must be here until the last day of the age. Other events to follow would be included in "the consummation." Moreover, the absence of the church would not render nugatory the presence of the Lord with any who become faithful during the following period.

(7) In the first epistle to the Corinthians the apostle states that the resurrection of the saints who have fallen asleep, and the transformation of the living saints, will take place "at the last trump" (1 Cor. 15:52). The suggestion is made that this is the last of the series of trumpets mentioned in Revelation 11:15, which introduces a closing scene before the setting up of the millennial kingdom.

The apostle Paul wrote to the church at Corinth long before the apostle John wrote the Apocalypse. The readers of the Corinthian epistle, being Greeks, were quite familiar with the metaphor of the last trumpet. To them it was a military metaphor, and simply indicated the signal given for an army to move. The phrase directed the mind not so much to the series of soundings, but to the fact that an army was to be set in motion. There is no valid reason for supposing a connection between Paul's use of the phrase and the series of trumpets described later in the book of Revelation. Moreover, there is no similarity between the event spoken of by Paul and the events introduced by the series of trumpets in the Apocalypse. The inference that Paul is referring to what was afterwards revealed to John is therefore quite unwarranted.

(8) The apostle states, in Romans 11:25, that "a hardening in part hath befallen Israel, until the fullness of the Gentiles be come in; and so all Israel shall be saved." On the supposition that "the fullness of the Gentiles" is the church, Israel, it is argued, will be saved immediately upon the completion of the church. The inference from this is that people will be brought into the church right up to the time when Israel is to be delivered, and that therefore some members of the church will be here during the Tribulation.

Even if "the fullness of the Gentiles" were coextensive with the church, it would not necessarily follow from the apostle's words that Israel's salvation will be immediately successive to the completion of the church. Certainly the one is conditional upon the accomplishment of the other; but the prediction would be amply fulfilled if there were an interval between the coming in of the fullness of the Gentiles and the deliverance of Israel. It is not necessary to the meaning of the apostle's words that, at the moment the fullness has come in, the hardening of Israel should cease. What he states is that one circumstance must precede the other, and that the latter cannot take place till the former is accomplished.

But it is a questionable interpretation which explains the coming in of the fullness of the Gentiles by the completion of the church. The apostle's subject here is not that of the church, but the dispensational dealings of God with

Jew and Gentile, His judicial severity toward the former and His goodness toward the latter. Paul has already used the word "fullness" to signify the promised blessing to the nation of Israel (v. 12), and has shown how God's mercy brought salvation to Gentiles. Again, in this chapter he distinguishes from Gentiles those Jews even who have accepted Christ, and thereby become part of the church; for the converted Jews, members of the church, constitute a spiritual Jewish "remnant" to which the apostle himself belongs (it being true also that in Christ there is neither Jew nor Gentile). The phrase, "the fullness of the Gentiles," would appear therefore to comprehend all Gentiles, as such, who will in any way receive deliverance and blessing previously to Israel's national restoration at the beginning of the Millennium.

(9) It is urged that the word *epiphaneia,* "appearing," signifies the manifestation of Christ in glory at His Second Advent for the overthrow of the ungodly and the establishment of His kingdom, and that, accordingly, the passages where this word occurs relatively to the subject cannot refer to a Rapture to take place some time beforehand.

Thus to limit the application of this word is an unfounded assumption. *Epiphaneia* was used among the Greeks in a variety of ways, as, for instance, of the appearance of an enemy to an army in the field, of one of the heathen gods to men, etc. In Scripture it is used of the manifestation of God's power in the help of His people Israel against the Canaanites (2 Sam. 7:23, LXX), and of the appearing of the people before Him (Amos 5:22). In the New Testament it is used of the Advent of the Savior at His incarnation (2 Tim. 1:10).

When the apostle exhorts Timothy to keep the commandment, "without spot, without reproach, until the appearing of our Lord Jesus Christ" (2 Tim. 6:14), it is an unwarrantable interpretation which makes it necessary to suppose that the reference is to His manifestation with His saints and angels in flaming fire. The context indicates that the reference is to the descent of the Lord Jesus into the air to the meeting with the saints, as in 1 Thessalonians 4:15–17. That event will certainly constitute an *epiphaneia,* an appearing, of Christ to His saints.

A similar passage is 2 Timothy 2:1, which is accurately rendered in the R.V., "I charge thee in the sight of God, and of Christ Jesus, who shall judge the quick and the dead, and by His appearing and His kingdom." (This has been wrongly rendered in the A.V., which reads as if the judgment of the living and the dead will be simultaneous.) What we have said above applies here, that there is no ground for the assumption which compels the idea that the appearing and the kingdom are simultaneous or immediately successive. "The appearing" is quite possibly at the descent of Christ for the Rapture of the saints, and "the Kingdom" the subsequent establishment of the earthly rule of Christ when He comes with His saints.

It is true that *"epiphaneia"* is used with reference to this latter event. This is clearly so in Matthew 24:27, which speaks of the shining forth of the glory of the Lord Jesus "as the lightning cometh forth from the east, and is seen even unto the west," but that is immediately consequent upon the unveiling *(apokalupsis)* of His Parousia with His saints. So again in 2 Thessalonians 2:8, the Man of Sin will be brought to naught "by the manifestation [*epiphaneia*] of His coming [*parousia*];" again in Titus 2:13, "looking for the blessed hope and appearing of the glory of our great God and Savior Jesus Christ." (Of this more presently.) But because *epiphaneia* is used, in these three passages, of the later event, that does not afford a ground for limiting every occurrence of the word respecting the future, to that event. Moreover this latter *epiphaneia,* or appearing, of Christ will be with the saints and not by way of His coming to call them to the air to meet Him.

It is necessary to guard against putting an undue limitation to the application of words in Scripture, especially when such words show a variety in their usage. The corresponding verb, *epiphainō,* is used of the stars (Acts 27:20), and of the grace, and kindness and love of God, made manifest in the coming of His Son for the salvation of men (Titus 2:11; 3:4).*

*See *The Epistles to the Thessalonians,* by C. F. Hogg and the writer.

What has been said above applies likewise to the word *apokalupsis*, an uncovering, unveiling. This is used in the New Testament with a number of different applications. As regards the future revelation of Christ, the very variety just referred to forbids its being restricted to one event. Clearly in 2 Thessalonians 1:7, which speaks of "the revelation of the Lord Jesus Christ from Heaven with the angels of His power, in flaming fire," the reference is to the Second Advent in judgment upon the world. But this does not justify the conclusion that the word refers to that event in every passage relating to the subject.

For instance, the apostle's commendation of the church at Corinth that they came behind in no gift, "waiting for the revelation of our Lord Jesus Christ" may well point to the time of the Rapture; for when the Lord comes to raise the dead saints and change the living, His act will certainly involve an unveiling of His person to them, and this is quite distinct from His revelation of Himself at His Second Advent, for the overthrow of His foes.

With regard to the trial of our faith, which is to be found "unto praise and glory and honor at the revelation of Jesus Christ," what is referred to here is by some associated with the time of the setting up of the earthly kingdom, by others to what the saints are to enjoy when the Lord comes to receive them unto Himself. So also in regard to their sufferings, in which they are to rejoice, as being partakers of Christ's sufferings, that "at the revelation of His glory also they may rejoice with exceeding joy" (4:13).

Even if the view is correct that this joy is fulfilled at the Second Advent, when the Lord comes to deal with the world in judgment and set up His kingdom, no ground whatever is thereby provided for deducing therefrom that a period does not intervene between the Rapture and the Second Advent, between the removal of His saints to meet the Lord in the air, and His coming with them. For as is pointed out, the latter event is the consummation of the hope of the saints, "the blessed hope," and this would be the time of "exceeding joy" and "praise, honor and glory."

The use of this word *apokalupsis* provides another instance of the need to avoid limiting the meaning and application of the phraseology of Scripture.

(10) From the parable of the tares the deduction is made that, since the tares and the wheat "grow together until the harvest," and the tares are bound in bundles to be burned, and the wheat is gathered into the barn, the church cannot be gathered in until the very end of the age, when the separation takes place, and the righteous shine forth in the kingdom.

This conclusion rests upon the assumption that the wheat represents, and is coextensive with, the church. The assumption will not, however, bear the test of the Scriptures which speak of the Rapture of the saints. Moreover, there is no direct intimation, either in this parable or in our Lord's interpretation of it, that He is speaking of the church in contradistinction to the ungodly. The parable and its interpretation show that the reapers are the angels, and that to them will be committed the work not only of binding the tares in bundles, but also of gathering the wheat into the barn (v. 30). Now there is no Scripture to show that the angels are agents in the Rapture of the saints. On the contrary, the passages which give details of that event state specifically that the Lord Jesus will accomplish the Rapture by His own power. "For the Lord Himself shall descend from heaven with a shout, with the voice of the archangel, and with the trump of God: and the dead in Christ shall rise first; then we that are alive, that are left, shall together with them be caught up on the clouds to meet the Lord in the air" (1 Thess. 4:16, 17). The details of this description, as given in the original, apply to Christ Himself. The article is absent both before "voice" and before "archangel," and this expresses the quality of the shout, its majesty and authority, characterizing it as being uttered by Christ Himself, and not as being the act of an archangel. In other words, the phrase is practically equivalent to "with an archangelic voice." This is confirmed by the preposition *en* (lit. "in," translated "with"), which indicates, not the accompaniment of another being, but the character of the shout itself. So with the phrase "with" (lit., "in") the trump of God. These considerations point to the threefold description as referring to one great signal.

Even if an archangel uttered his voice at

the time, there is nothing in this passage to correspond to the gathering in of the wheat by the angels, as mentioned in the parable, or to show that the angels take such a part in the Rapture.

On the other hand, if, as we have endeavored to show, Scripture elsewhere teaches that there is to be a period intervening between the Rapture of the saints and the Second Advent of Christ "with the angels of His power," then the act of the angels mentioned in the parable of the tares (which takes place at Christ's Second Advent to the earth) refers to the separation of the wicked from the multitude of righteous who during that period have dissociated themselves from the evil of the time and have waited for Messiah's return and kingdom.

There is another point in the parable, and its interpretation, suggesting a distinction between that event and what is said of the Rapture. The angel reapers are first to gather up the tares and bind them in bundles to burn them. The Lord interprets this as the gathering out of His Kingdom all things that cause stumbling and them that do iniquity, and the casting of them into the furnace of fire (vv. 41, 43). What happens immediately after that is the shining forth of the righteous as the sun in the kingdom of their Father (v. 43). So again, in the interpretation of the other parable of the net, "the angels shall come forth, and sever the wicked from among the righteous" (v. 49). At the Rapture the righteous will be severed from the wicked. There is nothing to show that the two events are similar or simultaneous. There is much to indicate the contrary.

(11) The argument is advanced that the apostles Peter and Paul expected events to take place before the Rapture; Paul knew that he must stand before Caesar (Acts 27:24), that he would suffer death (2 Tim. 4:6), that certain events must take place at Ephesus (Acts 20:29, 30), that "in later times some would fall away from the faith" (1 Tim. 4:1), and that the time would come when certain believers would not endure the sound doctrine and would turn from the truth (2 Tim. 4:3, 4); Peter knew that he would live to be old and would die for his Lord (John 21:18); again the church at Sardis knew that it was to have tribulation for ten days (Rev. 2:10); accordingly, in contrast to the view that Christ may return at any time, since certain events were destined to take place before that event, it is to be expected that the Rapture of the church will take place after the Great Tribulation.

Let it be noted, firstly, that nowhere have we expressed the view that any apostle expected the Lord to come during his lifetime, or that they taught the churches to anticipate the fulfillment of that event before those which they declared must take place in their lifetime or subsequently. Obviously they did not do so. All these things were long ago fulfilled. It is also true that the expectation of the occurrence of these circumstances did not weaken their hope. No view of the coming of Christ for the meeting of the saints with Him in the air has been expressed in these pages which is inconsistent with the expectation, by the apostles and the churches, of the events mentioned in connection with their lives.

What we have sought to point out from Scripture is that the Great Tribulation is appointed for the end of this age, that simultaneously with this there is to be a period of divine wrath upon the world, that from the wrath of God the church is to be delivered, that therefore no part of the church will be here during the Great Tribulation, and that this involves an interval between the Rapture and the Second Advent, which interval is called again and again in Scripture the Parousia of our Lord with His saints. Nothing concerning the events which were foretold as to take place during the apostle's lifetime and afterwards is contrary to this, nor can it be conceived how it could be so. What the Lord made known to an apostle or to a church, or what the apostles made known to churches, as certain to take place, does not in any way affect the teaching relating to the Rapture as destined to take place before the Great Tribulation. What is clear is that this latter event would not take place in the apostle's time, nor until after the events which the churches were to experience.

As to the apostle Paul's outlook, some have supposed that whereas he had formerly anticipated the Lord's return, in his closing days the knowledge of his impending death impaired that anticipation. On the contrary, his closing epistle, addressed to Timothy, makes clear that Paul was ready not only for death, but for the Rapture, and for winter as well (2 Tim. 4:6, 8, 21).

(12) It has been argued that, since the title "Antichrist" signifies "against Christ," and, further, since the Church which is His body is Christ mystical ("so also is Christ," 1 Cor. 12:12), therefore the title Antichrist must indicate an antagonism on his part against the church; and that as his persecutions take place during the Tribulation, the church (or part of it) must be here at the time.

Such an argument is a sort of special pleading. What is taught concerning the Antichrist shows that he denies the Father and the Son, and the truths relating to Him (1 John 2:22; 4:3), and that he will set himself against the cause of God and the kingdom of Christ (see Rev. 13, etc.). These facts are quite sufficient to account for his title "Antichrist." It is not at all necessary to suppose that his name involves the presence in the world of any part of the church during his satanic activities. There is no Scripture which shows it. If he is against the Father and the Son he is thereby against Christ.

An idea connected with this inference is that, since the apostle John taught his readers (members of the church) concerning the advent and activities of the Antichrist, this, being truth for the churches, indicates that churches will be here under those activities.

This, again, is a gratuitous and unfounded assumption. That an apostle predicted, in writing to a church, that a certain event was to take place, affords no ground for the supposition that churches are to be on the earth when it does take place. Peter, for instance, tells his readers that the heavens are to pass away with a great noise, and that the elements are to be dissolved with fervent heat, that the earth and its works are to be burnt up, and makes these events the basis of an exhortation to the saints to boldness and godliness of life, and to be "earnestly desiring" the coming of the day of God, in which these terrific events are to transpire. But that could not afford any ground for supposing that any part of the church will be here during those events. So neither can predictions concerning the Antichrist afford ground for the conclusion that saints of the Church will be here under his tyranny.

(13) Paul and Barnabas taught the churches that they must "through many tribulations enter into the Kingdom of God" (Acts 14:22). Since, then, the church was to pass through much tribulation, the conclusion is drawn that it will pass through "the Great Tribulation"; it has even been suggested that the "much tribulation" is practically the same thing as "the Great Tribulation."

This is confounding things that differ. Tribulation is indeed the characteristic lot of faithful followers of Christ in this life, but what is said of the Great Tribulation shows that it is of a distinctive and special character, that it affects the gentile nations as well as the Jewish nation, that it will come as a snare upon "all them that dwell on the face of all the earth" (Luke 21:35); it is to be "the time of Jacob's trouble," and it is to "try them that dwell upon the earth."

To suppose that the Lord's words, "Immediately after the tribulation of those days . . . shall appear the sign of the Son of man in heaven . . . and they shall see the Son of man coming . . . with power and great glory" (Matt. 24:29, 30), refers to the "much tribulation" through which Paul told the churches they must pass, is an utterly unfounded inference. For the Lord specifies the tribulation of which He was speaking, as appointed for a distinct period at the time of the end. It is a tribulation of unprecedented character, and the days will be such that, unless they were shortened, no flesh would be saved.

(14) It is stated that what the Lord Jesus addressed to His disciples on the Mount of Olives He addressed to them as members of His body, the church, and that accordingly members of the church will be here to see "the abomination of desolation," and will flee from Judaea to the mountains (Matt. 24:15, 16).

At the time of the Lord's discourse Peter, Andrew, James and John, and the rest, were simply His disciples, Jews who had become His followers. The building of the church, the body of Christ, was yet future. His words to them were, "I will build My Church" (Matt. 16:18). It is true that in foretelling the events of chapter 24 to the disciples He especially had regard to those to whom His utterances would be applicable in the age in which they would eventually be fulfilled. But to deduce that these who will then be living will be members of the church, is assuming what should be proved.

Taking the facts as they stand in the Gospel record, these disciples were at that time in the same position and category as godly Jews will be in the time to come, Jews who believe in Christ, and await the hope of His kingdom. As we have pointed out, the "ye" was addressed to them representatively in this way, just as the "ye" to Caiaphas and his associates was addressed to them as representatives of those who will actually see the Son of man coming in the clouds of heaven. The sequence of events, as mentioned in verses 21, 29, 30, marks a time at the end of the age and therefore not in the lifetime of the apostles.

(15) The Scriptures which speak of the Second Advent as the hope of the saints, are referred to as demonstrating that the Rapture must take place at the time of the Second Advent, and that therefore there could be no intervening period.

This view presupposes that the Rapture is held to be "the hope" of the saints. Now it is true that some who regard the Rapture as "the hope" argue that to expect the Great Tribulation first would weaken the power of the hope, and they are reasonably met with the answer that the knowledge that certain events must first take place has not had this weakening effect. How needful, then, to have regard to what Scripture states about the hope! While that which is to take place at the Rapture is indicated as a hope "set on Christ" (see 1 John 3:2, 3, R.V.), it is not the consummation of the hope. That will be fulfilled only when Christ comes with His saints in manifested glory, for the overthrow of the foes of God and the establishment of His kingdom. After the Rapture, which will be the initial act of the Parousia, the saints will still eagerly await the Second Advent. That will abide as their hope, until it is realized. Only when Christ is glorified where He was crucified, only when the world is the scene of His millennial glory, can "the hope" receive its complete fulfillment.

In such a hope there is nothing inconsistent or incompatible with the existence of a period between the Rapture and the Second Advent. In view of certain misunderstandings, therefore, it will be well to set this forth somewhat more fully.

When the apostle states that the grace of God has instructed us to live "soberly and righteously and godly in this present world: looking for the blessed hope and appearing of the glory of our great God and Savior Jesus Christ" (Titus 2:13), he is not referring to the Rapture. Believers hope indeed for the Rapture, but it is not "the blessed hope" of that passage. There is a single definite article before the two words "hope" and "appearing," and the *kai,* "and," which joins them makes the second explanatory of the first (as is frequently the case with *kai*). The *kai* is thus equivalent to our English phrase, "that is to say," or "namely." The meaning therefore is, "The blessed hope, namely, the appearing of the glory . . ."

As we have mentioned, the Rapture is also spoken of as a hope. "We know," says the apostle John, "that if He shall be manifested, we shall be like Him; for we shall see Him even as He is. And every one that hath this hope set on Him purifieth himself, even as He is pure" (1 John 3:2, 3). This manifestation is not that of Christ's Second Advent in glory, but His manifestation to His saints at the Rapture, and this is the event spoken of here as "this hope." When that has taken place, then "the blessed hope," the consummation of the hope of the saints will still await fulfillment.

The question as to whether the knowledge that certain events will take place weakens the hope does not therefore affect the subject thus viewed. We know of nothing now that must necessarily take place before the Rapture, but we know that certain events will take place before Christ appears in glory to deliver the Jews and set up His kingdom. This will continue, therefore, to be the hope during the period that intervenes between the Rapture and the Second Advent. There is nothing relating to the subject of the hope which compels the view, or must lead to the conclusion, that the Rapture is to take place after the Tribulation, and is to be followed immediately by the Second Advent. To say that "there is no hope set before the Church prior to the appearing of the Lord in the clouds of heaven" (i.e., when He comes in flaming fire) is a statement unwarranted by the teaching of Scripture.

(16) Upon the occasion of Christ's ascension the assurance was given to the disciples that He would "so come in like manner as they had beheld Him going into Heaven" (Acts 1:11). From the fact that "a cloud received Him out of their sight" (v. 10) the deduction is made that the coming of the Lord to the air for the Rapture of the church is to take place simultaneously with His coming in judgment for the setting up of His kingdom. For does not the prophecy of Daniel 7:13, say, "Behold, one like the Son of man came with the clouds of heaven . . . and there was given Him dominion, and glory, and a kingdom"? And did not Christ say, "They shall see the Son of man coming in the clouds of heaven with power and great glory" (Matt. 24:30)? Did He not testify the same thing to Caiaphas (Matt. 26:64)? And does not the Apocalypse say, "Behold, He cometh with clouds; and every eye shall see Him, and they also which pierced Him; and all the kindreds of the earth shall mourn over Him" (Rev. 1:7)? Moreover the saints of the church are to be caught up "in the clouds, to meet the Lord in the air" (1 Thess. 4:17).

Firstly, it is precarious to draw the conclusion that the two events are to be simultaneous from the fact that clouds are mentioned in connection with both; for clouds are associated with other similar events; see, for instance, Rev. 11:12. That He will come on the clouds at His Second Advent affords no ground for believing that He will not on a previous occasion come to the region of the clouds to receive the saints to Himself.

Secondly, there are several respects in which His Second Advent will differ from the Coming promised in Acts 1:11. At His Second Advent, for instance, He is coming "in flaming fire," coming "with the angels of His power." To conclude that the appearing of the sign of the Son of man in heaven, and the mourning of the tribes of the earth when they see "the Son of man coming on the clouds of heaven," was the expectation of which the apostles were again reminded when He had been taken up from them into heaven, is to put an unwarranted construction upon these Scriptures. It is an effort to enforce the idea of the coincidence of events for the distinction of which, and their separation in point of time, there is ample Scripture evidence.

Thirdly, in the Old Testament, the Gospels and the Acts, broad general statements of fact are made on the subject, which are differentiated in the epistles in point of circumstance. Due regard to this would prevent the confounding of things that differ.

(17) In Revelation 20:4, 5, we read of "the first resurrection." The passage is as follows: "And I saw thrones, and they sat upon them, and judgment was given unto them: and I saw the souls of them that had been beheaded for the testimony of Jesus, and for the Word of God, and such as worshiped not the Beast, neither his image, and received not the mark upon their forehead and upon their hand; and they lived, and reigned with Christ a thousand years. The rest of the dead lived not until the thousand years should be finished. This is the first resurrection." It is concluded from this that this is the time when the saints of the Church who have fallen asleep are to be raised, and that therefore this is the time of the Rapture. It has even been stated that "there can be no resurrection of the saints till then," and again, that "until the Beast and his persecution are destroyed together there can be no first resurrection" (Tregelles). Appeal in support of this is made to 1 Corinthians 15:22, 23, which states that "in Christ shall all be made alive. But each in his order: Christ the firstfruits, then they that are Christ's at His coming."

The statement, "This is the first resurrection," affords no ground for supposing that all the saints who have part in resurrection are to be raised at that time. For at the death of Christ "the tombs were opened; and many bodies of the saints that had fallen asleep were raised; and, coming forth out of the tombs after His resurrection, they entered into the holy city and appeared unto many" (Matt. 27:52, 53). It cannot be maintained, therefore, that "there can be no resurrection of the saints until the Second Advent."

Again, with regard to the statement, "This is the first resurrection," there is no verb in the original; this of itself suggests, what is borne out by other facts, that the first resurrection is not one summary event, but consists of different parts. It may be rightly understood as "This completes the first resurrection."

Further, the first resurrection began when Christ was raised, for, with reference to the resurrection of the saints, the apostle speaks of Christ as the "Firstfruits" (1 Cor. 15:23). The firstfruits is essentially a part of the first resurrection—"each in His own order; Christ the firstfruits." The clause which follows, "then they that are Christ's at His Parousia," refers to the act of the Lord at the Rapture, which introduces His Parousia with His saints, and not to the Second Advent. There is again, for instance, another resurrection unto life spoken of in the case of the two witnesses (Rev. 11:11).

It seems clear, then, that the first resurrection is made up of various events, beginning with the resurrection of Christ. No one passage describes the whole. Revelation 20:4, 5 gives the completion. The apostle John is there giving in detail, not the whole scene of the first resurrection, but the state of blessedness therein involved for those who, at that closing act, have part in the resurrection.

As regards the various companies mentioned in this passage, Revelation 20, they do not form the whole of the saints who are to enjoy resurrection and to share the reign of Christ, for there are a multitude of others of the saints who are already in glory who are to share the reign of Christ, and to whom the statements concerning the Beast and the image do not apply. Moreover, the undefined "they" at the beginning of the verse, in the statement, "And I saw thrones and they sat upon them," does not necessarily apply to the company of those mentioned at the end of the verse.

(18) "When this corruptible shall have put on incorruption, and this mortal shall have put on immortality, then shall come to pass the saying that is written, Death is swallowed up in victory" (1 Cor. 15:54). This is a quotation from Isaiah 25:8, and since that passage predicts the blessings of restored Israel (v. 7) and the reign of the Lord "in Mount Sion, and in Jerusalem and before his ancients gloriously" (24:23), it is argued that only at the time of Israel's restoration will the resurrection of those who are Christ's take place. For it is when He destroys "the face of the covering cast over all peoples and the veil that is spread over all nations," that death will be swallowed up in victory. Therefore, "There can be no coming of the Lord (much more no secret coming) until He appears for the accomplishment of His promises to His ancient people Israel" (Tregelles).

It should be noted that the Revised Version rendering is, "He hath swallowed up death." The accuracy of this past tense is confirmed by the quotation in the passage in 1 Corinthians. Again, it is a well-known principle in the apostle's method of quotation, that passages which in the Old Testament primarily refer to Israel are applied to the church, often with a slight variation of meaning. See, for example, Romans 10:6–11 and the Old Testament passages from which the quotations are taken. So with the passage in Isaiah 25:7, 8, when Israel has been restored and the veil is consequently taken away from the nations, death will have been swallowed in victory. The apostle's application of these words to the resurrection and transformation of the saints at the time of the Rapture, by no means implies that this event is to take place "at the time of Israel's restored blessing." To say that "any hope of a previous resurrection must be based, not on Scripture teaching, but upon some thought which has been formed in contradistinction to revealed truth," is quite beside the mark. Scripture does not, by the way, speak of a "secret Rapture."

(19) "After these things I saw, and behold, a great multitude, which no man could number, out of every nation, and of all tribes and peoples and tongues, standing before the throne and before the Lamb, arrayed in white robes, and palms in their hands; and they cry with a great voice, saying, Salvation unto our God which sitteth on the throne, and unto the Lamb. And all the angels were standing round about the throne, and about the elders and the four living creatures; and they fell before the throne on their faces, and worshiped God, saying, Amen: Blessing, and glory, and wisdom, and thanksgiving, and honor, and power, and might be unto our God forever and ever. Amen. And one of the elders answered, saying unto me, These which are arrayed in white robes, who are they, and whence came they? And I said unto him, My Lord, thou knowest. And he said to me, These are they which came out of the great tribulation, and they washed their robes, and made them white in the blood of the Lamb. Therefore are they before the throne of God; and they serve Him day and night in His temple: and He that sitteth on the throne shall spread His tabernacle over them. They shall hunger no more, neither thirst any more; neither shall the sun strike upon them, nor any heat: for the Lamb which is in the midst of the throne shall be their shepherd, and shall guide them unto fountains of water of life: and God shall wipe away every tear from their eyes" (Rev. 7:9–17).

It is stated that those who are thus described as coming out of the Great Tribulation form part of the church, and that therefore the Rapture must be after the Tribulation.

This interpretation is, again, a gratuitous assumption. There is no actual proof that this great multitude consists of people who have been resurrected. Whether this be so or no, their blessings are peculiarly millennial. Their service is "by day and by night" (not heavenly conditions). The closing promise is that "God shall wipe away every tear from their eyes." This is an earthly scene, judging from Isaiah 25:8. Again, the figurative description of the palm branches in their hands receives its interpretation from passages which speak of earthly gladness (cp. Lev. 23:40–42; Ezek. 40:16; 41:18; John 12:13).

Further, there is a distinct company, namely, "the elders," (always elsewhere in Scripture said of human beings), who with the angels and the living creatures are "round about the throne." These elders are themselves on thrones (5:4, not "seats," A.V.) are arrayed in white garments, and have crowns (*stephanoi*, crowns of reward) on their heads—three facts which indicate that they are not spirits. A spirit is not arrayed, nor crowned. Each detail is descriptive of reward. Here then is a company of human beings enjoying resurrection life in heaven, and quite distinct from the great gentile multitude who come out of the Great Tribulation (which, as we have noted, affects Gentiles as well as Jews). The former are blessed with Christ, the latter are blessed under Christ, Who "spreads His tabernacle over them" (7:15, R.V., which gives the accurate rendering; cp. Is. 4:5, 6).

Realizing what Scripture teaches as to the Rapture, and the fact that at that event Christ will be "our deliverer from the coming wrath," and, again, as to the Lord's Parousia with His saints after the Rapture, there is scriptural justification for the view that this great multitude consists of Gentiles who have refused the worship of the Beast during the interval. There is nothing to show that they form part of the church.

(20) Among other passages quoted in support of the view that the Rapture will take place after the Tribulation, are the following:

Believers are "kept by the power of God through faith unto a salvation ready to be revealed in the last time" (1 Pet. 1:4, 5). Meanwhile such suffer manifold temptations, that the trial of their faith "may be found unto praise and honor and glory at the revelation of Jesus Christ" (v. 7). They are to set their hope perfectly "on the grace that is to be brought unto them at the revelation of Jesus Christ" (v. 13). They are to rejoice in being partakers of Christ's sufferings, "that at the revelation of His glory"

they "may rejoice with exceeding joy" (4:12, 13). Again, the faithful elders are assured that "when the Chief Shepherd shall be manifested, they will receive the crown of glory that fadeth not away" (5:4).

Now none of these passages afford any evidence that there is to be no interval between the Rapture and the Second Advent. Even if the fact, that the salvation referred to in chapter 1:5 is "to be revealed in the last time," pointed to the occasion when the Lord comes in flaming fire, that would not show that the Rapture had not taken place at some time previously. For at the time when the Lord comes in judgment to set up His kingdom, the salvation, already enjoyed by the church in the Parousia of Christ, will be revealed in its consummated glory. Moreover, what has been already pointed out concerning the noun, *apokalupsis,* "a revelation," holds good for the corresponding verb. It could be used with reference to each of the two distinct events, the Rapture and the Second Advent. The coming of Christ for the meeting of the saints with Him in the air will be an *apokalupsis* (or "unveiling") to them, though not to the world; again, the coming of Christ with the angels of His power in flaming fire will be an *apokalupsis* to the world, each revelation having an entirely distinctive event associated with it, and separated the one from the other by an interval.

Verse 7 is understood by some to refer to the second of these events. If that is the meaning, it does not eliminate the occurrence of the interval separating it from the time of the Rapture. When the saints come in resurrection glory with Christ at His Second Advent, the trials experienced by them will certainly be found unto "praise, glory and honor." For Christ is then coming "to be glorified in His saints, and to be marveled at in all them that believed" (2 Thess. 1:10). So with verse 13. The same applies also to the "exceeding joy" in chapter 4:12, 13.

The passage which speaks of the reward of the crown of glory to be given when the Chief Shepherd appears *(phaneroō),* chapter 5:4 points to the judgment seat which follows upon the Rapture, and not to what will take place when the Lord is revealed in flaming fire, rendering vengeance to the foes of God.

(21) Appeal is made to the Authorized Version of 2 Thessalonians 2:2, 3, which makes the apostle say that the Day of Christ was not at hand, and would not come before the apostasy and the revelation of the Man of Sin.

The Authorized Version is untenable here. The Revised Version, "The Day of the Lord" is abundantly confirmed by manuscript evidence. The rendering, "is now present," is the accurate one. "The Day of the Lord" is a period distinct from the Day of Christ. That is clear from a consideration of all the passages where the phrases occur.

The Day of Christ begins with the Rapture. The Day of the Lord begins subsequently. What the apostle was teaching was that this latter period would not begin until after the apostasy and the revelation of the Man of Sin.*

The church at Thessalonica was being taught by errorists that the Day of the Lord had already begun. They might well be apprehensive about the fate of their departed loved ones. For the apostle had instructed them in his first epistle to expect the Rapture first. Now he writes to confirm his teaching and to correct the false doctrines to which they were listening. He makes his appeal "by [*huper,* "in the interests of"] the Parousia of our Lord Jesus Christ, and our gathering together unto Him" (v. 1). It was not to correct a mistake in his first epistle (as some who discredit the

*It has been recently stated that the New Testament "again and again changes 'the day of our Lord' for 'the day of the Lord Jesus' and for 'the day of Jesus Christ,'" and that therefore these varied names are blended into one; further, that "again and again Paul in particular seems to glory in changing the name"; also that when the apostle Peter says of Paul that "in all his epistles" he spoke of these things, he was referring "to the very same day of God" as Peter did.

Such inferences are entirely unfounded, and are contrary to that extreme precision of phraseology which is manifested in the God-breathed writings. The passages relating to "the day of the Lord" refer to that period which is introduced by the Second Advent of Christ, whereas the passages which contain the phrases in which the personal titles, Jesus, or Christ, or both, are found, are all used in quite a different connection and have to do with the circumstances of the Rapture of the saints, their presence with the Lord in His Parousia, and the judgment seat of Christ.

divine inspiration of Scripture affirm), it was to confirm what he had there written, that he appeals to his readers on the ground of the Rapture, the gathering to Christ, as distinct from and previous to, the Day of the Lord, which is to be ushered in by vengeance. They are still to wait for the Son of God from heaven, as they had done.

This passage, then, shows the Rapture to be a distinct event, prior to and separated from the revelation of Christ from heaven with His angels to render vengeance to the ungodly.

(22) In writing to the Thessalonian church the apostle says, "But concerning the times and the seasons brethren, ye have no need that aught be written unto you. For yourselves know perfectly that the day of the Lord so cometh as a thief in the night . . . But ye, brethren, are not in darkness that that day should overtake you as a thief" (1 Thess. 5:1, 2, 4). It has been inferred from this that the Day of the Lord will overtake the church, though not as a thief.

It is not necessary to suppose that the apostle's statement suggests that the Day of the Lord is to overtake the church as well as the world, and that the distinction is that it will not overtake the church as a thief. On the contrary, the order of the words and phraseology of the original, as well as the whole context of the passage, shows that the apostle is marking a sharp contrast between the circumstances relating to the Rapture of the saints (4:13–18) and those relating to the world, upon which the Day of the Lord will come with the personal intervention of Christ in judgment. The distinction, which is one in point both of time and character of event becomes clear when we put together the Scriptures which speak of the Day of the Lord. Here in verse 4 the stress which is placed upon the pronoun "ye" and "you" marks the contrast between the destiny of believers and the Day of the Lord which is to come upon the world. Taking the order of the original, the rendering is as follows: "But you, brethren, are not in darkness, that the day you as a thief should overtake." The word "you" is distinctive in its emphasis. The phrase "as a thief" goes closely with "overtake," and has no stress attached to it.

If there were any doubt as to the meaning, it would be necessary to understand the passage according to the teaching of other Scriptures, and this very epistle makes clear what the destiny of the church is.

What the apostle means is, not that the day will overtake the saints though not as a thief, but rather that, with regard to the saints, such is their character and destiny, that what will overtake the world as a thief will not come upon them at all. The saints are "sons of light" and "sons of day." When the Day of the Lord begins, those who have been caught up to meet Him will come with Him. The saints are not to be overtaken by the Rapture, they are to comfort one another in the prospect of it. The Day of the Lord, which will overtake the world as a thief, is entirely distinct from this.

This distinction in verse 4, which may not be clear to the reader of the English version, is confirmed, as we have said, by what the Scripture teaches in relation to the Day of the Lord, as well as in other ways which we have sought to point out. There are two Scriptures, for instance, which, if taken together, show that the Day of the Lord will begin when the Lord Jesus comes on the clouds of heaven, with great glory, for the overthrow of His foes, and the setting up of His kingdom, while Scripture further makes clear that at that Advent the saints will come in glory with Him. Joel's prophecy declares that the Day of the Lord will follow the turning of the sun into darkness and the moon into blood (Joel 2:30, 31). Christ declared that immediately after these calamities in the heavens He Himself would come with power and great glory, and all the tribes of the earth would mourn (Matt. 24:29, 30). The Day of the Lord is therefore to be ushered in by the coming of Christ in this manner.

The Second Advent is likewise described in Revelation 17:14, and in fuller detail in chapter 19:11–21. When Christ comes with power and great glory, as He foretold, He will overthrow the Beast and those who are gathered together under him. That is how the Day of the Lord will be ushered in. Now concerning those foes of God the passage says: "These shall war against the Lamb, and the Lamb shall overcome them, for He is Lord of lords, and King of kings; and they also shall overcome that are with Him, called, and chosen and faithful" (Rev. 17:14). Accordingly the saints are with Christ when He comes in glory, when the foes of God are overthrown and the Day of the Lord begins.

The Day of the Lord cannot have overtaken them as it will the world, for they are among the hosts of the Lord when it begins. It is the saints who are referred to in a similar passage in chapter 19:14, which says that "the armies which are in heaven followed Him upon white horses, clothed in fine linen, white and pure." It is not the angels which are clothed in fine linen. The fine linen belongs to the saints. The Day of the Lord will dispel and replace the world's night; the saints, in resurrection life and glory, are coming with Christ to share in the great event. They will have been previously caught up to meet Him before the Day of the Lord begins.

Conclusion

The consideration of these objections in the light of Scripture serves, then, to confirm what was set forth in the first chapter, namely, that the period in which the Great Tribulation will take place is to be likewise a period of the wrath of God in a series of retributive judgments; that from the wrath of God the church is assured of deliverance; and that this deliverance consists, not of preservation through the period of retribution, but of salvation from it at the Rapture.

V

The Roman Empire in the Light of Prophecy

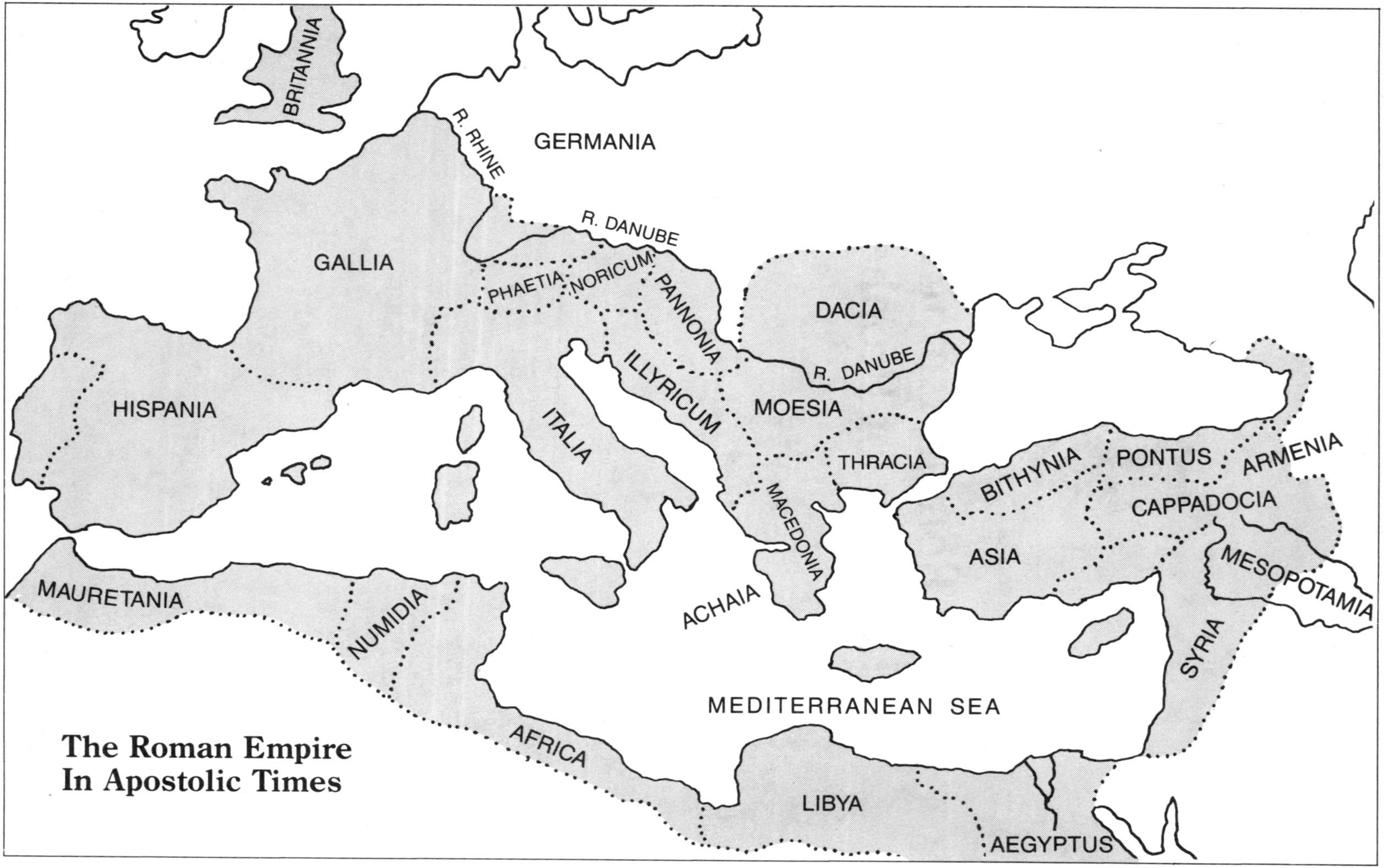
BRITANNIA
GERMANIA
R. RHINE
GALLIA
R. DANUBE
PHAETIA
NORICUM
PANNONIA
DACIA
R. DANUBE
HISPANIA
ILLYRICUM
MOESIA
ITALIA
THRACIA
BITHYNIA
PONTUS
ARMENIA
CAPPADOCIA
MACEDONIA
ASIA
MESOPOTAMIA
MAURETANIA
NUMIDIA
ACHAIA
SYRIA
MEDITERRANEAN SEA
AFRICA
LIBYA
AEGYPTUS
The Roman Empire
In Apostolic Times

▪ PREFACE ▪

The following pages are the outcome of several conversations with inquirers shortly after the outbreak of the great war, in 1914, and of requests for notes of the views expressed. The subject of these conversations had occupied the earnest if intermittent attention of the writer for over twenty years. The notes were expanded into a series of articles which appeared in *The Witness* during 1915. These have been revised and somewhat extended for the present volume, especially the last chapter, much of which was previously precluded by limitations of space.

In regard to past history, the outlines of events connected with the Roman and Turkish Empires are given with the hope that the records will prove helpful to those who read the history of nations in the light of Scripture.

In regard to the future, while there are many events which the Word of God has foretold with absolute clearness, and upon these we may speak unreservedly, yet there are many circumstances concerning which definite prediction has been designedly withheld, and upon which prophecy is therefore obscure. In such matters an effort has been made to avoid dogmatism. Prophecy was not given in order for us to prophesy.

On the other hand, the prophetic Scriptures are not to be neglected. Difficulty in understanding them is no reason for disregarding them. They are part of that Word, the whole of which is declared to be "profitable for doctrine, for reproof, for correction, for instruction in righteousness" (2 Tim. 3:16). They therefore demand prayerful and patient meditation.

For a speaker to refer to the study of the prophecies in a way which tends to minimize their importance in the minds of his hearers is to dishonor both the sacred Word and Him who inspired it. It is significant that the book of the Revelation opens with a promise of blessing to him who reads (the reference is especially to public reading) and to those who "hear the words of the prophecy, and keep the things which are written therein" (1:3), and at the close repeats the blessing for him who keeps its words (22:7).

The quotations in the present volume are from the Revised Version, the comparatively greater accuracy of its translations being important for a correct understanding of many of the passages considered.

While the book is published at the request of several friends, the author fulfills such re-

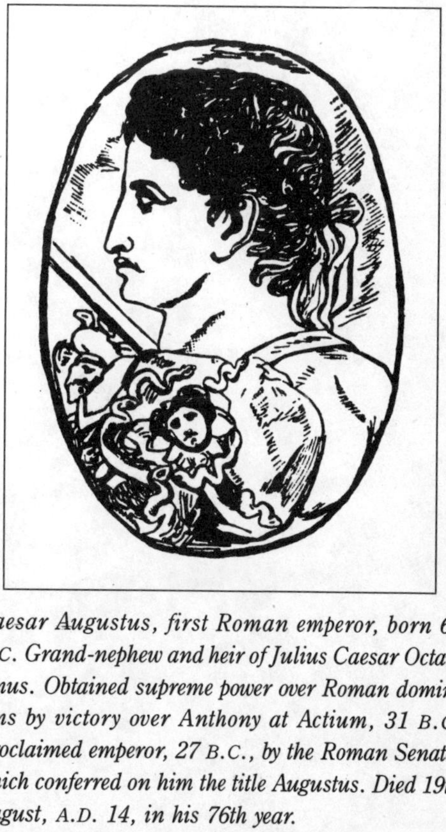

Caesar Augustus, first Roman emperor, born 63 B.C. Grand-nephew and heir of Julius Caesar Octavianus. Obtained supreme power over Roman dominions by victory over Anthony at Actium, 31 B.C. Proclaimed emperor, 27 B.C., by the Roman Senate, which conferred on him the title Augustus. Died 19th August, A.D. 14, in his 76th year.

quest with the earnest desire that in matters of doctrine that only may be accepted which can be confirmed from the Word of God itself, and that the Lord may graciously own what is in accordance with His mind for the glory of His name and the profit of the reader.

Bath, 1916 W. E. Vine

▪ CHAPTER ONE ▪

The Times of the Gentiles

The overthrow of the kingdom of Judah recorded in 2 Kings 24 and 25, and in the opening words of the book of Daniel, was a remarkable crisis in the history of the world. In judgment upon the people of God for their long-continued iniquity, sovereignty was removed from their hands, king and people were led into captivity, and Jerusalem was, in fulfillment of Jeremiah's words, given into the hand of Nebuchadnezzar, the king of Babylon (Jer. 21:10). The government of their land was thus committed to the Gentiles, and with the Gentiles it has remained from that day till now. These events took place in 606 and 587 B.C.

The Times of the Gentiles

But gentile control is not to continue indefinitely. This, which is plain from many Scriptures, was intimated by Christ to His disciples when He said of Jerusalem that the city would "be trodden down of the Gentiles until the times of the Gentiles be fulfilled" (Luke 21:24). The phrase, "the times of the Gentiles," calls for consideration, and especially as it has to do with Nebuchadnezzar's conquest just mentioned.

There are two words translated "times" in the New Testament; one is *chronoi,* which is invariably rendered "times"; the other is *kairoi,* which, when the two are found together, is rendered "seasons." Thus Paul, in writing to the Thessalonian church, says, "But concerning the times and the seasons, brethren, ye have no need that aught be written unto you" (1 Thess. 5:1, R.V.; cp. Acts 1:7). We may distinguish "seasons" from "times" in the following way: "times" denotes mere duration, lengths of time; "seasons" implies that these lengths of time have certain events or circumstances associated with them by which they are characterized. Thus the words almost exactly correspond to the terms "periods" and "epochs." Now the word *kairoi,* "seasons," is used in the phrase translated "the times of the Gentiles," which might accordingly be rendered "the seasons of the Gentiles." We look, then, for some special characteristic of the period or periods thus designated. We have observed that Nebuchadnezzar's overthrow of the kingdom of Judah involved the transference of its sovereignty from Jew to Gentile from that event onward. "The times of the Gentiles," accordingly, is that period, or succession of periods, during which dominion over the Jews and their land is committed to Gentile powers.

Nebuchadnezzar's Dream

Special significance attaches to the fact that no sooner had the times of the Gentiles begun than God made known the future course of their authority over His people, and the character and doom of that authority, and made it known to the first Gentile conqueror himself. It was in the second year of his reign that Nebuchadnezzar saw in a dream the great image by means of which the purposes of God were to be communicated to him. The description of this, given by Daniel to the troubled monarch, is as follows: "Thou, O king, sawest, and behold a great image. This image, which was mighty, and whose brightness was excellent, stood before thee; and the aspect thereof was terrible. As for this image, his head was of fine gold, his breast and his arms of silver, his belly and his thighs of brass, his legs of iron, his feet part of iron, and part of clay. Thou sawest till that a stone was cut out without hands, which smote the image upon his feet that were of iron and clay, and brake them in pieces. Then was the iron, the clay, the brass, the silver, and the gold, broken in pieces together, and became like the chaff of the summer threshingfloors: and the wind carried them away, that no place was found for them: and the stone that smote the image became a great mountain, and filled the whole earth" (Dan. 2:31-35).

Interpreting this vision, the prophet identified Nebuchadnezzar, the Chaldean monarch, with the head of gold, and foretold that his kingdom, or empire, would be followed in succession by three others, corresponding respectively to the different parts of the remainder of the image and to the nature of the metals composing them. Of the four kingdoms the last is to engage our chief attention in these papers. Passing from the first, the **Chaldean,** as specified in Daniel's words to the king, "Thou art this head of gold" (v. 38), we are shown that the second kingdom was that of the **Medes and Persians** by the prophet's record of the doom of Nebuchadnezzar's successor, Belshazzar: "In that night Belshazzar the Chaldean king was slain. And Darius the Mede received the kingdom" (Dan. 5:30, 31; cp. v. 28). That the third kingdom was the **Grecian** we find in the interpretation of part of a vision recorded in the eighth chapter: "The ram which thou sawest that had the two horns, they are the kings of Media and Persia. And the rough he-goat [who was seen to destroy the ram, v. 8] is the king of Greece" (vv. 20, 21; cp. chap. 10:20).

The Fourth Kingdom

The name of the fourth kingdom is not mentioned in the Old Testament, but the prediction given in the ninth chapter of Daniel's prophecies sufficiently identifies it. Messiah, it was said, would be cut off, and the people of a coming prince would destroy the city and the sanctuary. Now we know that the perpetrators of this were the Romans. We know, too, that by them the Grecian empire was conquered. The worldwide rule of the first **Roman** emperor is indicated in the words of Luke's introduction to his record of the birth of Christ: "Now it came to pass in those days, there went out a decree from Caesar Augustus, that all the world should be enrolled" (Luke 2:1).

It is important to note that this fourth kingdom will, in its final condition, be in worldwide authority at the close of the times of the Gentiles, that is, that the Roman power, though in a divided state, will not be finally destroyed until it meets its doom at the hands of the Son of God. This fact, which will receive fuller treatment later, and is borne out by several Scriptures, is plainly indicated in the passage which describes the last state of the fourth kingdom and its destruction. Immediately after showing that it would be a divided kingdom, and describing the nature of that division (vv. 41-43), the prophet says: "And in the days of those kings shall the God of Heaven set up a kingdom, which shall never be destroyed, nor shall the sovereignty thereof be left to another people; but it shall break in pieces and consume all these kingdoms, and it shall stand forever" (v. 44). Now this indestructible kingdom cannot be other than that of Christ, and by His kingdom the fourth is to be broken in pieces and consumed, thus involving the overthrow of all forms of gentile authority. Obviously no form of world government will exist between that of the fourth kingdom, in its condition described in verses 42, 43, and the kingdom of Christ which destroys it.

▪ CHAPTER TWO ▪

The Roman Dominion

An understanding of the Scriptures does not depend upon access to other books, or reference to historical records outside the limits of the Bible. The Word of God is its own interpreter, and all that is needed for our establishment in the faith is contained in its pages. On the other hand, the Bible throws light upon history not recorded therein, and it is with that in view that we give certain historical outlines in dealing with our subject.

The first part of the prophet's description of the fourth kingdom is as follows: "The fourth kingdom shall be strong as iron: forasmuch as iron breaketh in pieces and subdueth all things: and as iron that crusheth all these, shall it break in pieces and crush" (v. 40). A similar description is given in his account of a subsequent vision, in which he saw four great beasts coming up from the sea. In this vision the Roman kingdom again was undoubtedly symbolized by the fourth beast. This beast he describes as "terrible and powerful, and strong exceedingly; and it had great iron teeth: it devoured and brake in pieces, and stamped the residue with his feet" (7:7). So, again, in the words of the interpretation: "The fourth beast shall be a fourth kingdom upon earth, which shall be diverse from all the kingdoms, and shall devour the whole earth, and shall tread it down, and break it in pieces" (v. 23). Now all this exactly depicts the Roman power in its subjugation and control of the nations which eventually composed its empire. In the light, then, of these prophecies we give a brief sketch of its rise and conquests.

The Rise and Progress of the Roman Empire

The Romans, who early in the third century B.C. had become masters of all Italy, save in the extreme north, were drawn into a course of conquest beyond the limits of their own country by the rivalry of the rapidly advancing power of Carthage in North Africa. Carthage, a city founded some centuries earlier by Phoenician colonists from Tyre and Sidon, had at length become the capital of a great North African empire, stretching from Tripoli to the Atlantic Ocean, and embracing settlements elsewhere in countries and islands of the Mediterranean. These settlements included the greater part of Sicily, and that island, situated between the rival nations, became the first bone of contention between them. The precise cause of the struggle must not occupy us here, but the circumstances which decided the Roman government, in 264 B.C., upon an invasion of Sicily were of the deepest significance in the history of the world. By the year 242 Sicily was subdued. In the following year the island was ceded by Carthage, and the extension of Roman dominion beyond Italy was begun. The war continued intermittently, with many vicissitudes, for a century, but eventually the Carthagians were overwhelmingly defeated by land and sea. "Think you that Carthage or that Rome will be content, after the victory, with its own country and Sicily?" said a Greek orator, while the issues of the struggle in its earliest stage were yet in the balance. Rome's vast ambition, and her abundant means of gratifying it, justified the orator's fears. The islands of Sardinia and Corsica were shortly afterwards seized.

Defeated in Sicily, Carthage extended her dominions in Spain and made that country a base for marching through Gaul to attack the Romans from the north. Though their renowned leader Hannibal met with success, their effort was doomed to failure. Meanwhile Roman armies had pushed into Spain. After a fierce struggle of thirteen years the Carthagians were completely overcome there, and Spain soon became a Roman province. By the decisive battle of Zama, in North Africa, in 202, Carthage and its territories became tributary, and thus all the western Mediterranean passed under the supremacy of Rome. Eventually in 146, as a result of a final war, Carthage was razed to the ground, and its North African kingdom was constituted a Roman province under the name of Africa. War with the Celts in North Italy, commencing the next year, resulted in the extension of the boundary to the Alps, and countries beyond began to feel the terror of the Roman name.

Eastward Extension

The second century B.C. witnessed the spread of the iron rule eastward. The Grecian Empire of Alexander the Great, the third mentioned in Daniel's interpretation, had embraced all the countries surrounding the eastern half of the Mediterranean and had stretched far beyond the Euphrates. The disintegration of Alexander's empire after his death prepared the way for the Romans. Macedonia, the former seat of that empire, was their first great objective. A pretext for war was soon forthcoming, and war was actually declared in 200 B.C. A series of struggles ensued, and Macedonia was not finally subdued for over thirty years. Meanwhile matters had developed in Greece and Asia Minor. In the latter country Antiochus III, the Great, who had also conquered Syria and Palestine, was seeking to extend his dominions. Cities and states of Asia Minor, however, groaning under the tyranny of Antiochus, appealed to Rome for aid. The Romans declared war against him in 192 B.C. The first conflict occurred in Greece, which was largely under his influence. An early victory secured the submission of the Greek states. Antiochus retreated into Asia Minor, and was finally crushed at Magnesia in 190. The whole of Asia Minor was then surrendered to Rome. Actual possession was postponed and local government was largely granted both there and in Greece. But that policy proved impracticable, and the force of circumstances compelled a forward movement to universal empire. There was no such thing as the balance of power in the ancient world. Once a country became predominant there was nothing for it but the subjugation of its neighbors. The extension of Rome's dominions eastward was a fulfillment of a destiny beyond its own control. The reverent student of Scripture sees in the course of these events the unfolding of God's plans and the fulfillment of His Word.

The final campaign against the Macedonians was opened in 169 B.C., and in the next year they were overwhelmed at the decisive battle of Pydna. Macedonia and the adjacent state of Illyria became tributary, and eventually were reduced to Roman provinces.

The Romans then felt the necessity of definitely annexing Greece. Seventy towns in that country were plundered and 150,000 inhabitants were sold into slavery. Antiochus IV, Epiphanes, was now king of Syria and Palestine, and had possessed himself of almost the whole of Egypt. Such was the effect of the battle of Pydna, however, that he was at once compelled to hand over Egypt to the conquerors, and that country became a Roman protectorate. Syria passed under Roman control at the death of Antiochus Epiphanes, in 164, and by the end of a few decades all the states of Asia Minor had been incorporated.

Thus by the middle of this century the republic of Rome had gained ascendancy east and west. Its senate was recognized by the civilized world as "the supreme tribunal for kings and nations." Early in the next century Dalmatia and Thrace were subdued, and the latter was incorporated in the province of Macedonia. Wars with Mithradates, king of Pontus, Cappadocia and Armenia, resulted in the conquest of all his territories, and provinces were formed out of the states from thence westward to the Aegean sea.

Palestine Annexed

This century saw the actual interference of Rome in the affairs of Judaea. Syria had been made a province in 65 B.C. by the Roman general Pompey, and from thence he intervened in a strife which had for some time been raging amongst the leaders of the Jews. In 63 he marched an army into Judaea and took Jerusalem. At the final assault upon the temple 12,000 Jews perished. Judaea thus passed under the iron heel.

As a result of the wars of Caesar in northwestern Europe, in 58–51 B.C., what are now Switzerland, France, and Belgium were subdued and Britain was invaded. By Caesar also

Roman authority in Africa was consolidated across the entire length of the north of the continent. The conquests of Rome as a republic were complete. The Mediterranean had become a "Roman lake."

The Empire Completed

In 27 B.C. the purely republican form of constitution was abolished, and the government of the Roman world was concentrated in the hands of an emperor, the Caesar Augustus of Luke 2:1. In his reign were fulfilled the prophecies foretelling the birth of Christ. When the Prince of Peace was born in Bethlehem the din of strife was hushed throughout the empire, and Rome, under the restraining hand of God, ceased for a time its warring. By Augustus the northern territories of the empire were extended to practically the entire length of the Danube. The greater part of Britain became a province under Claudius. A later emperor, Trajan, added, at the beginning of the second century A.D., the province of Dacia, covering what are now Transylvania and most of Rumania. Under Marcus Aurelius (161–180) a large part of Mesopotamia was finally annexed.

This completes the actual conquests of the Romans. We will now note certain characteristics of their method of subjugation, viewed in the light of Daniel's prophecy concerning the fourth kingdom, that, like iron, it would "break in pieces and crush."

The Crushing of the Nations

The crushing process was evidenced in many ways, and especially by the establishment of a general system of slavery, which almost everywhere supplanted free labor. Slave-hunting and slave-dealing became a profession. To such an extent were they carried on at one period that certain provinces were well nigh depopulated. We are told that at the great slave-market in the island of Delos, off Greece, as many as ten thousand slaves were disembarked in the morning and bought up before the evening of the same day. Chained gangs worked under overseers and were confined in prison at night. To take an instance of the extreme rigor of the laws regulating the traffic, it is recorded by the historian Tacitus, that once, when the prefect of Rome had been killed by one of his slaves, of whom he owned a vast number, the whole of his slaves, many of them women and children, were executed together, in accordance with an ancient law. That event took place about the time, apparently, at which the apostle Paul arrived at Rome.

But not only were the nations ground down by slavery, the pages of Roman history abound in records of wholesale massacre and butchery. We may note, for instance, Luke's statement of Pilate's slaughter of Galileans while they were sacrificing (Luke 13:1). Records abound, too, of grossly burdensome taxation and financial exactions, in which the Romans outdid all tyrants that had preceded them. Usury flourished in the last century B.C. as it had never done before. Four percent per month was an ordinary exaction for a loan to a community. On one occasion a Roman banker, who had a claim on the municipality of Salamis, in Cyprus, kept its council blockaded until five of its members died of hunger.

By these methods the provinces of the empire were at one period reduced to a condition of unsurpassed misery. Nothing could more vividly describe the course of such a kingdom and the control exercised by it than the words of Daniel quoted above.

The Twofold Division

This fourth kingdom was destined to be divided; and in two respects, territorial and constitutional. The territorial division was indicated by the symbolism of the legs and feet of the image of Nebuchadnezzar's vision; the constitutional division was declared in Daniel's interpretation concerning the iron and clay (v. 40). The former of these divisions claims our consideration first. Territorially the kingdom would be first divided into two parts corresponding with the legs of the image. This actually took place in the fourth century of the present era.

The Roman Empire had continued in a more or less united condition for over three centuries after the accession of its first emperor, Augustus, in 27 B.C., though various signs of a coming division manifested themselves. It was not unusual, for instance, for an emperor to appoint an associate with himself in the imperial rank, and on one occasion Maximian, who thus became associated with Diocletian in A.D. 288, actually established his seat of government at Nicomedia, in Asia Minor. Constantine (323–337) united the empire under his sole rule, but paved the way for the final separation of east from west by founding, in 328, the city of Constantinople as a second Rome, after his own name, and establishing it as an eastern center of government with its own legislative institutions. This arrangement was favored by several conditions, national and otherwise, which characterized the countries of the eastern half as distinct from those of the western.

At the death of Constantine, in 337, his dominions were divided among his three sons, a division, however, which lasted but a brief time. The empire was in 353 again united under Constantius, the survivor of the three. The long impending division into two parts took place under Valentinian I, in the year of his accession, 364. Yielding to the wish of his soldiers that he should associate a colleague with himself, he placed his brother Valens in power in the east, with headquarters at Constantinople, he himself retaining control over the west.

The Tenfold Division

Prophetic Scriptures show that the Roman Empire would be further divided. Now while the ten toes of the image in Nebuchadnezzar's dream have not improperly been regarded as indicative of a tenfold division, the fact that the image had ten toes would be insufficient of itself to signify this, for the toes are naturally essential to a complete human figure. Moreover, the hands and their fingers, equally essential parts, have no territorial significance attached to them. The conclusion regarding the toes is, however, justified when we find the tenfold division abundantly confirmed by other Scriptures.

Thus the fourth beast in the vision in chapter 7, which, as we have seen, likewise symbolized the Roman kingdom, is described as having *ten horns* (v. 7). The interpretation clearly tells us what these are: "And as for the ten horns, out of the kingdom [the fourth] shall *ten kings* arise" (v. 24). The Apocalypse gives us further information regarding this division, unfolding with increasing clearness the details connected with it. In one of the visions given to the apostle John, he sees "a great red dragon, having seven heads and *ten horns*" (Rev. 12:3). The meaning of the ten horns is not there explained. We are told that the great dragon is "the old serpent, he that is called the Devil and Satan, the deceiver of the whole world" (v. 9). Turning now to the next chapter, we find another vision recorded, giving a fresh view of the same subject. A beast was seen "coming up out of the sea, having *ten horns* and seven heads, and on his horns ten diadems, and upon his heads names of blasphemy" (13:1). Again an explanation of the ten horns is withheld, but that they are identical with those of the twelfth chapter is undeniable. The apostle receives, however, a further vision, recorded in chapter 17: "I saw a woman sitting upon a scarlet-colored beast, full of names of blasphemy, having seven heads and *ten horns*" (17:3). And now the symbolism of the horns is explained: "the ten horns that thou sawest are *ten kings*, which have received no kingdom as yet; but they receive authority as kings, with the beast, for one hour. These have one mind, and they give their power and authority unto the beast" (vv. 12, 13).

We are now concerned, of course, solely with the tenfold division of the empire; other details of the visions just referred to remain for later consideration. We cannot fail to see that what is symbolized by the ten toes of the image, and by the ten horns of the fourth beast as revealed to Daniel, is identical with what is symbolized by the ten horns of the dragon and of the beast seen by John, namely, the Roman kingdom in its ultimately divided condition.

A Comparison of the Visions

The following points are noteworthy in comparing these visions relatively to the tenfold division. First, there is a parallelism in the order of the revelations given to the two seers, Daniel and John. A preliminary vision is given to each—more than one in the case of John—in which, in the matter of this territorial partition, symbols occur without explanation. Each then receives a further vision, in the interpretation of which the eventual division into ten kingdoms is plainly disclosed. To Daniel it is said: "As for the ten horns, out of the kingdom shall ten kings arise"; and to John: "The ten horns that thou sawest are ten kings, . . . which receive authority as kings with the beast for one hour."

Second, the ten kingdoms are seen to be contemporaneous, as is indicated by the coexistence of the ten horns of the beast, and further, by the fact that the ten kings mutually agree to a certain line of policy in handing over their authority to a supreme potentate (Rev. 17:12, 13).

Third, it is evident that the fourth kingdom is the last of the gentile world powers, and that it will exist in its tenfold state at the end of the times of the Gentiles. We observed this above in the case of the image, from the fact that the stone, symbolizing the kingdom of Christ, smote the image upon its toes. So now, in the vision of the four beasts, it is the fourth beast that is slain, his body destroyed, and given to be burned (Dan. 7:11). The personal agent of this destruction is here made known: "I saw in the night visions, and, behold, there came with the clouds of heaven One like unto a son of man, and He came even to the Ancient of Days, . . . and there was given Him dominion, and glory, and a kingdom, that all the peoples, nations, and languages should serve Him: His dominion is an everlasting dominion, which shall not pass away, and His kingdom that which shall not be destroyed" (vv. 13, 14). The finality of the fourth kingdom is clearer still from the interpretation given in the remainder of the chapter. The final world ruler is, of course, prominent in this vision; in his destruction is involved the destruction of his kingdom; his power and aggression are terminated when the Ancient of Days comes (v. 22); then it is that "the judgment shall sit, and they shall take away his dominion, to consume and to destroy it unto the end. And the kingdom and the dominion, and the greatness of the kingdoms under the whole heaven, shall be given to the people of the saints of the Most High: His kingdom is an everlasting kingdom, and all dominions shall serve and obey Him" (vv. 26, 27). Similarly, again, in Revelation 13 and 17, in the corresponding visions of the beast and its ten horns, the ten kings and their federal head, ruling at the time of the end, "shall war against the Lamb, and the Lamb shall overcome them, for He is Lord of lords, and King of kings; and they *also shall overcome* that are with Him, called and chosen and faithful" (Rev. 17:14).

The crushing of the image by the stone, the slaying of the fourth beast before the Ancient of Days, and the conquest of the ten kings and their chief by the Lamb, are therefore different views of the same event. The tenfold division of the fourth kingdom is obviously still future, and marks the condition of the world government at the close of the times of the Gentiles, and immediately prior to the kingdom of Christ.

The Testimony of Early Christian Writers

That the Roman Empire would in its final form be divided into ten kingdoms was held by Christian writers of the earliest postapostolic times. Their opinions are here given, not as forming any basis of exposition, but as expressions of early Christian conception of the Scriptures under consideration.

What is known as *The Epistle of Barnabas*, probably written early in the second century A.D., quotes from Daniel concerning the ten kingdoms to show that they would exist at the consummation of the present age. *Irenaeus* (circa A.D. 120–202), a disciple of Polycarp, who had been a companion of the apostle John, observes that "the ten toes are ten kings, among whom the kingdom will be divided." *Tertullian*, a contemporary of Irenaeus, remarks that "the disintegration and dispersion of the Roman state among the ten kings will produce Antichrist, and then shall be revealed that Wicked One, whom the Lord Jesus shall slay with the breath of His mouth and destroy by the brightness of His manifestation." *Hippolytus*, who was a follower of Irenaeus, and flourished in the first half of the third century, makes similar reference to the ultimate division. *Lactantius*, of the latter half of the third and the early part of the fourth centuries, writes as follows: "The empire will be subdivided, and the powers of government, after being frittered away and shared among many, will be undermined. Civil discords will then ensue, nor will there be respite from destructive wars, until ten kings arise at once, who will divide the world among themselves to consume rather than to govern it." *Cyril* (circa 315–386), who became bishop of Jerusalem in 350, quoting from Daniel, and speaking of the empire and its future division, implies that teaching on the subject was customary in the churches. *Jerome* (342–420) observes that "at the end of the world, when the kingdom of the Romans is to be destroyed, there will be ten kings to divide the Roman world among themselves." Similarly writes *Theodoret* in the fifth century, and others of that time make more or less direct reference to the subject. While the views of these writers differ considerably on other points of detail, all are unanimous as to the eventual division of the empire among ten contemporaneous potentates.

Processes at Work Since the Twofold Division

The medieval and modern history of the lands originally constituting the Roman Empire is a history of the formation of independent states in such a way as to point to the eventual revival of the empire in the tenfold division we have been considering. The process has been a long and involved one, for the counsels of God have had a far wider range than the mere shaping of national destiny. It has been the divine pleasure, for instance, that the gospel should be spread among all nations for the purpose of taking out from among them a people for the name of Christ, and for the formation thereby of His church. In contradistinction to this, and from the standpoint of the world itself, which, though under God's control, remains in alienation from Him, there has been a gradual development of the political, social, and religious principles which are ultimately to permeate the nations.

CHAPTER THREE

The Overthrow in the West: Germanic Invasions

In the interpretation of his vision of the beast, John is told of its rise, temporary removal, and reappearance: "The beast that thou sawest was, and is not; and is about to come up out of the abyss, and to go into perdition" (Rev. 17:8). Here the Roman world power, the imperial dominion, is in view. In verse 11 the final king himself is similarly described. The symbol of the beast is thus employed to describe first the dominion and then its imperial head. This symbolic association of locality and ruler is found elsewhere in Scripture, and is illustrated in this very chapter. The seven heads of the beast, for example, are interpreted in both ways: "The seven heads are seven mountains, . . . and they are seven kings" (v. 9, R.V.) The distinction between verses 8 and 11 may be observed in this way: in the first part of the chapter, verses 1–8, the beast is viewed as a whole, indicating worldwide government; in verse 11 the scope of the symbol is limited, the beast is a person, and is identified with one of the seven heads, or kings, he is "himself also an eighth, and is of the seven." With this individual we shall be occupied later.

A striking illustration of the symbolic use of the word "beast" to denote both a kingdom and the ruler over it is to be found in Daniel 7, where the following statements are made: "These great beasts, which are four, are four kings" (v. 17), and "The fourth beast shall be the fourth kingdom" (v. 23).

The statement of verse 8 seems, then, undoubtedly to refer to the empire; it did exist, it ceased to be, and it will reappear. The assertion that it "is not" must not be taken to mean that the beast had ceased to exist in John's time. The present tense is to be regarded as prophetic. The verb "to be" often has the force of continuance of existence. The whole statement implies a past existence, a discontinuance of that existence, a future reappearance. In the vision recorded in the thirteenth chapter, John saw one of the heads of the beast "as though it had been smitten unto death." If, as seems probable, this head is imperialism, then the overthrow of imperial Rome is likewise indicated in that passage.

In the light, then, of the words: "The beast that thou sawest was, and is not," we may now consider how the Roman Empire was overthrown.

Disintegration of the Western Half

We have seen that, at the accession of the Emperor Valentinian I in A.D. 364, the empire was divided into two parts. The succeeding century witnessed the disintegration of the western half. The cause was primarily from within. Augustus, the first emperor, had instituted a policy of settling colonies of "barbarians" from northern Europe within the frontiers of the empire. Later emperors adopted the policy more generally. The significance of this lies in the fact that by the barbarians who had already been thus established in the empire, the attacks were commenced which resulted in the dismemberment of its western provinces.

Alaric and the Goths

At the close of the fourth century hordes of Gothic tribes from northeastern and eastern Germany set out, under Alaric their chief, in quest of new lands. Settlements of these very Goths had already been established south of the Danube by the imperial government as allies of the Romans. After an excursion into Italy, in which they were temporarily checked, they poured, in 406, into defenseless Gaul.

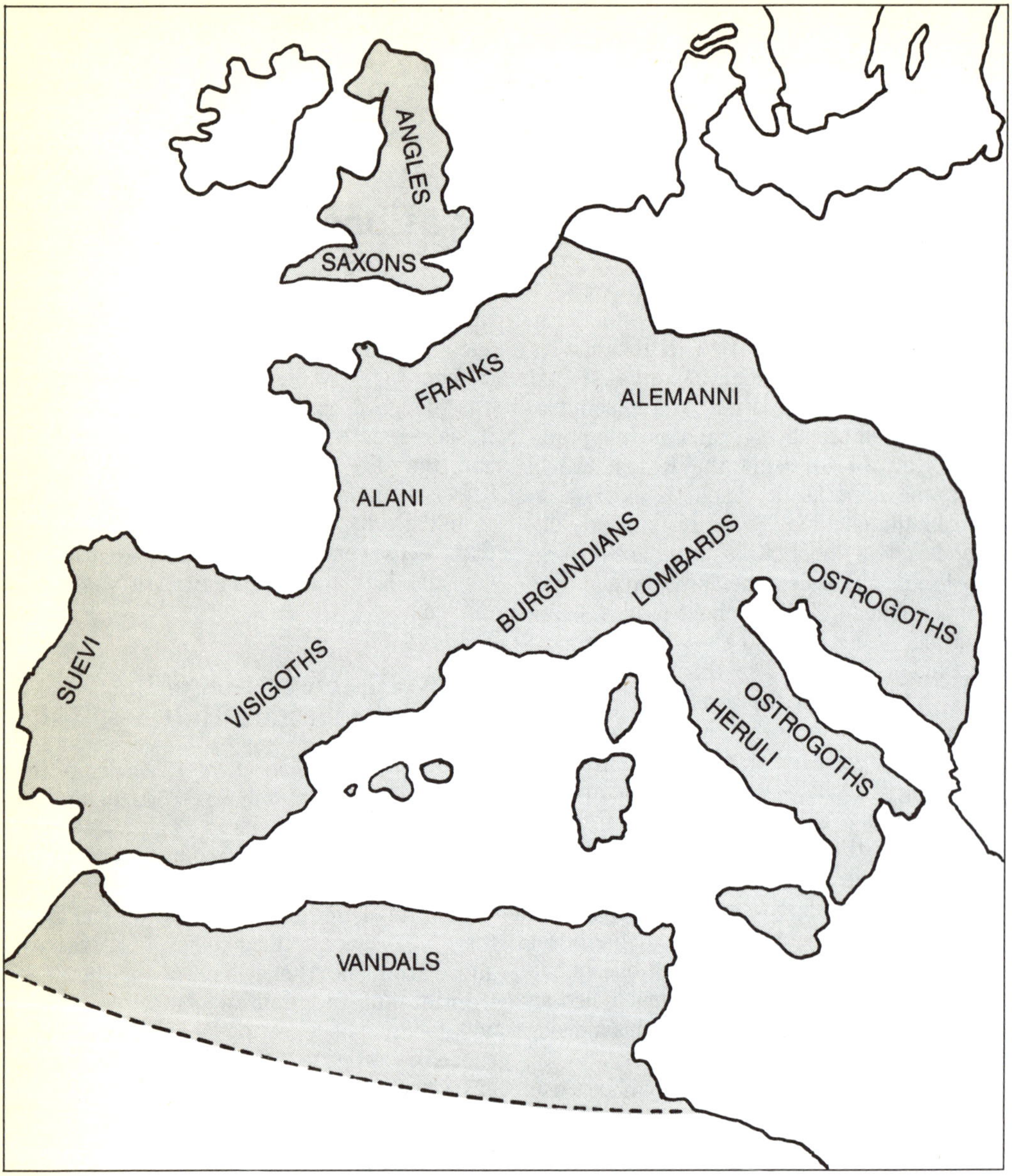

THE WESTERN ROMAN EMPIRE UNDER GERMANIC TRIBES

From thence Alaric returned to invade Italy, and three times in three years besieged Rome (408–410), eventually sacking the city. After his death, in 410, the Goths retired from Italy, entered Gaul, and permanently occupied the southern part of that country and a large part of Spain, where they were known as **Visigoths** (i.e., Western Goths).

Other Germanic tribes also streamed into Gaul. Of these, the **Franks** (whence the name France) issued from districts around the middle and lower Rhine and occupied northern Gaul; the **Suevi,** from north and northwest Germany, passed through into Spain; the **Alani,** formerly from eastern Europe, settled in west France and Spain; the **Burgundians,** from eastern Germany, seized that part of Gaul which eventually was named after them, Burgundy. The **Vandals,** from northern and central Germany, after being defeated by the

Franks, crossed into Spain under their leader Genseric, and from thence established themselves in the province of Africa, in 429. This occupation of Gaul and Spain was soon perforce recognized by the emperor at Rome. At the death of the emperor Honorius, in 423, Rome exercised little more than a nominal authority over the greater part of the west.

From Britain the Roman troops were withdrawn by Honorius, in 409, though the final abandonment of the island province did not take place till 436. Teutonic tribes from North Europe were soon engaged in invading this part of the empire. The **Jutes,** from Jutland, landed in 449, the **Saxons** in 477, and about the same time the **Angles.**

Attila and the Huns

Toward the close of the reign of Valentinian III (433–455), Gaul and Italy were invaded by the **Huns** under Attila. The Huns originally inhabited a large part of central and northern Asia. In the latter part of the fourth century they moved west into Scythia and Germany, driving the Goths before them. Attila's dominions thereafter extended over a vast area of eastern, central, and northern Europe, and he was regarded as of equal standing with the emperors at Constantinople and Rome. After a gigantic but futile incursion into Gaul, in 451, the Huns rushed into Italy, ravaging its northern plains. An embassy from Rome and an immense ransom saved the situation, Attila died in 453, and Italy was evacuated. The Huns eventually settled in southeastern Europe, and their dominion dwindled away. A trace of their name may be found in the word Hungary.

Genseric and the Vandals

In North Africa Genseric the Vandal established a powerful dominion, and set about preparing an invasion of Italy by sea. In 455 (the last year of the reign of Valentinian III) his army of Vandals and Moors attacked Rome, which was again given over to pillage. Its wealth and treasures were transported to Carthage, and with them the vessels of the temple at Jerusalem; these had been brought to Rome in A.D. 70 by Titus, the conqueror of Jerusalem. For twenty years after Genseric's achievement Roman emperors existed in little else than name, the real power being in the hands of a barbarian officer. In 476 the last emperor was deposed by Odoacer, the king of the **Heruli,** a tribe which, issuing from the shores of the Baltic, made successful inroads into Italy and occupied much of the country. Odoacer was, at the request of the Roman Senate, given the reins of government by the eastern Emperor Zeno, and news was dispatched to the court at Constantinople that no longer was there an emperor of the west. Subsequently, in 493, Odoacer was slain by Theodoric, the king of the **Ostrogoths,** who then became predominant in the Italian peninsula. The Ostrogoths (i.e., Eastern Goths) had broken off from the main body of their nation, and after settling south of the Danube moved into the province of Dalmatia.

Northern Limits of the Empire

Other Germanic tribes, in addition to those named above, firmly established themselves within the northern limits of the empire. Of these, two are worthy of mention, the **Alemanni,** who occupied most of what is now Switzerland and districts northward, and the **Lombards,** who settled in north Italy and the territory northeast of it.

The Ten Kingdoms Not Formed by the Germanic Invasions

There have been various attempts to identify with the ten prophetic kingdoms the states formed from the western half of the Roman Empire by the Germanic tribes from the north. Such attempts fail from the standpoints both of history and of prophecy. To group the tribes so as to make ten kingdoms out of them is, of course, possible in several ways, for there were at least eighteen such tribes. Accordingly lists put forward differ considerably. But such grouping is manifestly arbitrary. Again, since these invading nations occupied only the western half of the empire, the above allocation of the ten kingdoms necessarily leaves the eastern half out of consideration, and therefore excludes the land of Palestine from this stage of the prophetic forecast.

Now the prophecies concerning the times of the Gentiles are invariably focused upon the Jews and their land. The dealings of God with the Jews form the pivot of His dealings with other nations. Thus no scheme of prophetic exposition relative to this subject is to be regarded as scriptural which excludes Palestine from its scope. To endeavor to make the Word of God square with facts of history is to tamper with Scripture and to run the risk of obscuring its meaning and force.

The idea that the formation of the ten kingdoms took place in the fifth century fails to stand the test of Scripture in other respects. Of the ten kings prophecy foretells that "they receive authority as kings with the beast for one hour," that they "have one mind, and they give their power and authority unto the beast" (Rev. 17:13, 14). No such tenfold confederacy has existed in Europe; it certainly never existed among the chieftains of the Germanic tribes which invaded the west of the Roman Empire in the fifth century, neither is there any record of such an agreement among them. Nor, again, can it be said that they made war with the Lamb and were overcome by Him (v. 14). These prophecies still await fulfillment. Similar considerations apply to the passage in Daniel 7 in reference to the fourth kingdom. The ten kings, it is said, would arise out of that kingdom, and after them another king who would make war with the saints and prevail against them until the Ancient of Days came (vv. 21, 22, 24).

Again, since the persecution under the king who arises after the others continues until the Ancient of Days comes (v. 22), his war against the saints must have lasted from the fifth century until the present time, if he arose in that century. Moreover, as he was said to be going to subdue three kingdoms (v. 24), the seven kingdoms not so subdued must likewise have continued. This has obviously not been the case. From every point of view it is impossible to assign the tenfold division to any time in the past.

CHAPTER FOUR

The Overthrow in the East: the Turkish Empire

Having narrated the disintegration of the western half of the empire, we will now recount the events which involved the overthrow of the eastern half. The impoverishment of the imperial power at Rome, and the weakening effect of the Germanic attacks upon it, tended to enhance the power of the emperor at Constantinople. Indeed the eastern empire was soon regarded as the more important of the two, and for some time after the barbarian invasions in Italy the emperors at Constantinople claimed supremacy over the west.

Mohammed and the Khaliphs

The seventh century saw the ascendancy of Mohammed (born A.D. 570) in Arabia, to which country his personal power, temporal and religious, was limited. Upon his death, in 632, his followers determined on the invasion of Persia and the Asiatic dominions of the emperor at Constantinople. Mohammed's successor, Abubekr, the first of the Khaliphs (i.e., "representatives" of the prophet), at once waged war in both directions. Persia speedily succumbed; Syria and Palestine were subjugated after seven years by the Khaliph Omar. The reduction of Egypt followed, and during the remainder of this century the Saracens, the name by which the followers of Mohammed became termed in Christendom, extended their territory across the entire length of North Africa, and shortly afterwards even into Spain, where they overpowered the then disunited Visigoths.

The Saracen power in Western Asia was distracted during the next century by civil war, and was further weakened by unsuccessful wars against the Greeks. At length, in 750, the seat of government was moved from Damascus to Baghdad. From the eighth century onward, though the religion of Mohammed gained ground, and continues to do so today, the empire established by his followers dwindled rapidly, one province after another shaking off its allegiance until at the end of the tenth century its shattered dominions lay open to the nearest invader. The foe appeared in the shape of the formidable Turk.

Eastern Empire at End of 10th Century

In view of the entrance of this new enemy we may note the extent of the territory belonging at this time to the eastern branch of the old Roman world, the Byzantine Empire, as it is termed (from Byzantium, the ancient name of Constantinople). The Eastern emperors had recovered some of their lost ground in Asia, and at the close of the tenth century they held all Asia Minor, Armenia, a part of Syria, a considerable portion of Italy, and all the Balkan Peninsula.

The Appearance of the Turks

Beyond the northeastern border of the Saracen dominions lay the country of Turkestan, inhabited by the Turks, a branch of the warlike nation of the Tartars of Central Asia. With them the Saracens, after the establishment of their government at Bagdad, waged successful warfare for a time, taking numbers of Turks captive and dispersing them over the empire. This only facilitated the eventual downfall of the Saracen sovereignty. The Turks in Western Asia grew in influence, and at length the Turkish troops, breaking into open revolt, assumed control over the Khaliphate, deposing and nominating the Khaliphs at their will.

The Turks Embrace Mohammedanism

Early in the eleventh century the bulk of the Turkish nation, under its leader Tongrol Bek, moving out from Turkestan, swept down upon Persia. The Khaliphate at Bagdad was, however, permitted to remain, and not only so, but Tongrol Bek and all his tribes embraced the Mohammedan religion. The invaders then marched west in vast numbers to make an attack upon Christendom, and in the course of time subdued Armenia and most of Asia Minor. Europe became alarmed, and the Byzantine emperors eagerly sought the assistance of the nations of the west. Hence arose the Crusades, which had as their chief object the deliverance of Palestine from both Saracens and Turks, and which served to retard, though not to prevent, the advance of the Turkish power in Europe.

The Turks Enter Europe

Early in the thirteenth century a mighty movement of Mongols southwest from Central Asia, involving the immediate destruction of the Khaliphate at Bagdad, exerted an important influence upon the Turks, in driving those Turkish tribes which had remained east of Armenia westward into Asia Minor. This resulted in the establishment of various Turkish dynasties in that country. At the close of the thirteenth century the paramount power over these was exercised by Osman (or Othman, whence the name Ottoman), who seized all that remained of the ancient Roman world in Asia, and thus practically founded the Ottoman Empire. In the middle of the fourteenth century the way was opened for the Ottomans to advance into Europe. They were invited by one of the rival factions at Constantinople to undertake their cause. The Turks accordingly crossed the Hellespont and seized Gallipoli and the territory in the vicinity of the capital. Constantinople itself was left unattacked for the time. Under Murad I, the grandson of Osman, Rumania and several kingdoms south of the Danube, including Bulgaria, were subdued. The kings of Hungary, Bosnia and Serbia rose against the invader, but were severely defeated, and by the decisive victory of Kosovo, in 1389, Serbia and Bosnia were annexed.

Constantinople Taken

Constantinople was temporarily saved by another advance of the Mongol Tartars upon the Turkish dominions in Asia, where, in 1402, the Ottomans suffered a severe defeat. From

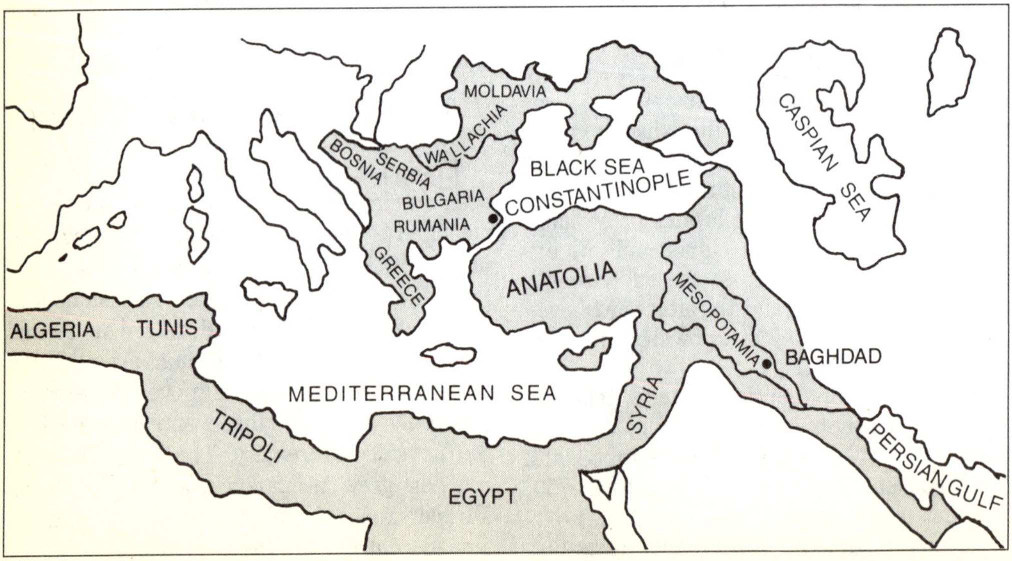

THE TURKISH EMPIRE IN THE 16TH CENTURY

this check they recovered, and during the first part of the fifteenth century were at war with the Hungarians and neighboring races, whom they eventually overthrew. In 1451 Mohammed II ascended the Ottoman throne, and in 1453 led an immense army against Constantinople. The city was taken by storm, the last of the Roman emperors of the east died fighting, and Mohammed II rode in triumph to the cathedral of St. Sophia, where he established the Moslem worship.

For over a hundred years after this the Turkish Empire continued to extend. Egypt was annexed in 1517, and in the middle of this century Tripoli and Algeria were added, as well as considerable districts in Europe and Asia. The Turks were now at the zenith of their power.

A Comparison of the Two Divisions

Recapitulating, we may compare the two divisions of the Roman Empire since their overthrow, from the *prophetic, religious* and *political* standpoints. From the *prophetic* point of view our interest in the west has thus far centered in the fact that the ten kingdoms were not formed by the fifth century invasions; our interest in the east centers chiefly in the land of Palestine, wrenched, as we have seen, from the eastern emperor by the Saracens, and then occupied by the Turks, who still possess it. From the *religious* standpoint, the Germanic tribes in the west accepted Roman Catholicism, hence its progress in that part of Europe; in the east the Turks had accepted Mohammedanism when invading the empire of the Khaliphs, hence the establishment of Islam throughout the Turkish dominions. *Politically,* the western invasion in the fifth century, and the consequent amalgamation of the Teutonic tribes with the peoples formerly under Roman control, led eventually to the formation of the various medieval monarchies of Western Europe which are today either kingdoms or republics. Affairs in the eastern half of the Roman world have moved more slowly in this respect, owing to the prolonged existence of the Ottoman Empire. The slow decay of the Turkish power from the middle of the sixteenth century onward has already resulted in the formation of some Eastern states, and the process still continues.

The Decline of the Turkish Empire

The decline of the power of the Turks set in during the latter half of the sixteenth century, when their dominions passed under incapable rulers. In the reign of Selim II (1566–1574) occurred the first conflict between the Turks and Russians, the former being driven back from Astrakkan. In 1593, during a war between Turkey and Austria, the provinces of Transylvania, Moldavia, and Wallachia rose in revolt. As the result of intermittent wars in the latter half of the seventeenth century Austria acquired almost the whole of *Hungary.* In 1770 Russia occupied *Moldavia* and *Wallachia,* which though nominally for a time under Turkey were practically Russian protectorates. During the next few years Russia regained the Crimea and all the neighboring district north of the Black Sea. At the commencement of the nineteenth century the Ottoman Empire was in a perilous condition. Napoleon had plans for its partition. Provincial governors were everywhere acting independently of the Sultan. In 1804 *Serbia* revolted, and after a few years of persistent struggle obtained its autonomy. *Greece* revolted in 1820, and, though subdued for a time, gained its independence in 1829 through the intervention of England, France, and Russia, and chiefly as the result of the naval battle of Navarino, in which the Turco-Egyptian fleet was annihilated. In the same year *Algeria* was annexed by the French. European rivalries prevented for a time any rapid diminution of the empire.

The Crimean War of 1854–5 had important consequences for the Balkan peoples. It gave them, under the slackening grasp of the Porte, twenty years of comparatively quiet national development. In 1860 Wallachia and Moldavia formed themselves into the single state of *Roumania.* In 1866 the Pasha of Egypt assumed the title of Khedive (i.e., king), thereby securing a measure of independence for the country. In 1875 the misrule of the Sultan led to the insurrection of Bosnia, Herzegovina, and Bulgaria. Serbia and Montenegro then took up arms. In 1877 a war with Russia saw Turkey without an ally. A complete Russian victory in 1878 issued in the treaties first of San Stefano and then of Berlin, by which Turkey yielded to Russia the state of *Bessarabia* and districts south of the Caucasus, the independence of *Serbia, Montenegro,* and *Roumania* were recognized by the Porte, *Bulgaria* was constituted an autonomous state, *Bosnia* and *Herzegovina* were ceded to Austria, *Thessaly* to Greece, and *Cyprus* to Britain. In 1885, as the result of a revolution, Eastern *Roumelia* became united to Bulgaria. Shortly after that date German influence began to gain ascendancy at the court of the Sultan, and, among other affairs, largely dominated the granting of railway concessions in Western Asia. The effects of that influence have been evidenced in the present war. In 1912 Italy annexed *Tripoli* after a brief war. In 1913 a short but sanguinary war with the Balkan States deprived Turkey of all her European dominions save for a small piece of territory in the vicinity of Constantinople. *Egypt,* which has been chiefly under British control for a considerable period, has in 1915 been practically annexed by Britain as a protectorate, the Khedive being deposed and a nominee of the British government being placed in authority. Britain has likewise annexed a district north of the Persian Gulf.

The Coming Overthrow

The continual decrease of the Turkish Empire, and more especially during the past hundred years, affords ground, apart from other considerations, for the expectation of its overthrow and the eventual cession of Palestine to the Jews, perhaps by a general agreement among the European powers, events which seem not far distant. National jealousies would not permit the permanent annexation of Palestine by any one of these powers, in whatever way the remaining Asiatic Turkish dominions may be divided. A proposal has already been put forward for its annexation to Egypt. Such an arrangement would in any case be merely temporary. To the Jews the land belongs, and by divine decree the Jews are to possess it again.

A Blank in Prophecy

It should be observed, in passing, that Scripture is apparently silent concerning the occupation of Palestine by the Saracens and Turks. Such silence is noticeable when we remember how definitely the occupation by the other gentile powers, the Chaldean, Medo-Persian, Greek, and Roman, and the order and character of their rule, were predicted. The cause of the silence is not difficult to ascertain.

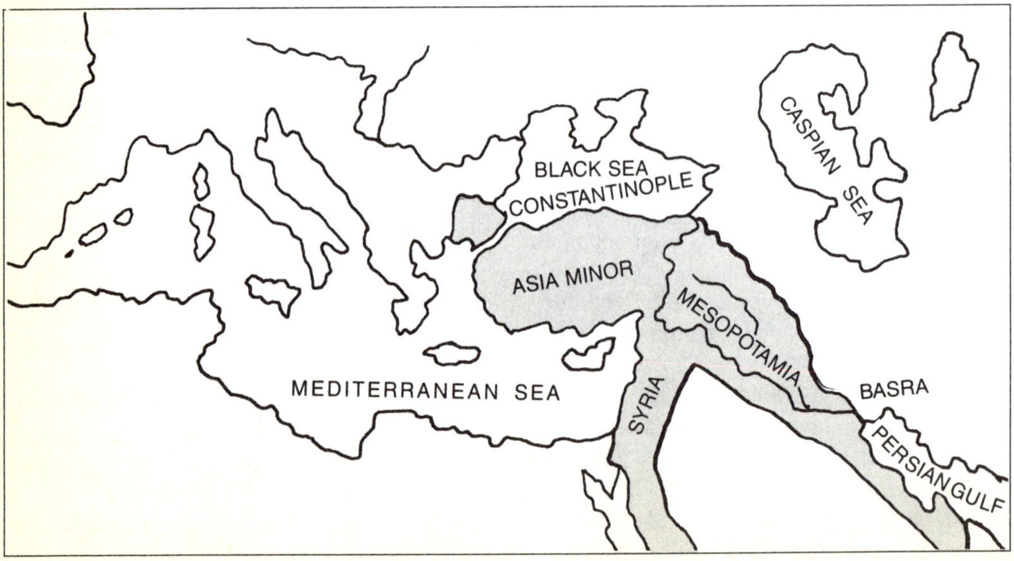

THE TURKISH EMPIRE IN 1914

The four gentile powers just mentioned had to do with the Jews as the recognized possessors of Palestine, either by way of removing them from their country or restoring them to it, or during such time as they were permitted to remain in it with liberty to continue their temple worship and sacrifice. The Chaldeans removed the Jews from the land, and the Medo-Persians repatriated them, the Greeks permitted their continuance in it, the Romans did so too until A.D. 70, when they crushed them. When, however, the Saracens and the Turks seized the land the Jews had been scattered, nor have they received national recognition while under them. Gentile occupation of Palestine during such times as the Jews remain in their present condition seems therefore to receive no direct notice in prophecy.

The restoration of Palestine to the Jews is closely connected with the revival of the Roman Empire in its tenfold form. Prior to considering the manner of this revival we must notice how during the period between the overthrow of that empire and its coming resuscitation, its dominions and their government have remained Roman in character, thus affording a further proof that the coming and final world power will not be entirely a new one, but will be a revival of the ancient Roman or fourth empire indicated in the prophecies of Daniel.

The Continuation of Roman Government and Influence

Such was the prestige of the Roman name and authority that the chieftains of the Germanic tribes which in the fifth century subdued the western half of the empire governed the conquered territories not so much as tribal chiefs, but as successors to, and in continuation of, the imperial rule; they introduced no radical changes in the provincial and municipal forms of government of their predecessors. Civil organization remained distinctly Roman, and has continued so; upon it are based some of the chief municipal institutions of modern life. Indeed Roman civil law still remains the foundation of modern jurisprudence.

In southeastern Europe, too, countries which were for centuries under the power of the Turk retained, in their municipal institutions and organization, the impress of Roman authority. It should be remembered that though the eastern or Byzantine portion of the ancient Roman Empire was distinct from the western, its emperors being designated as Grecian in contrast to the Roman, yet its legislative foundations were laid in the Roman Empire prior to the division of the east from the west. Byzantine imperialism was therefore really Roman under an eastern title. According as the states in the east have become freed from the Turkish yoke, so the character of their government and legislation has conformed in a large degree to those of the west. The further diminution of the Turkish Empire will doubtless see a corresponding revival of western conditions and methods.

Roman Imperialism Continued

It is important also to observe that notwithstanding the passing away of the Roman Empire as such, the principle of imperialism remained, and, amidst the vicissitudes of national government in Europe, has continued to the present time. The imperial power in the west was not abolished when in 476 the last Roman emperor was deposed. On the contrary, there was a kind of reunion imperially of the west with the east. For a considerable time the tribal kings of the west received recognition from the eastern emperors, and were regarded as their associates in imperial control. This was the case even with the Saxon kings in Britain, and on Saxon coins may be seen today the same title, *basileus* (i.e., king), as was borne by the emperors at Constantinople. Italy itself was wrested from the Teutons by the eastern Emperor Justinian in the sixth century, and remained under the Byzantine Caesars till 731.

Meanwhile the Roman senate continued to exercise its authority, and in 800 chose the Frankish king Charlemagne as their sovereign. He was already ruling over the greater part of Western Europe, and was now crowned as emperor at Rome by the pope. Though his empire fell to pieces after his death, his dominions retained, and have since retained, their Roman character.

Consideration of space forbids our tracing here the further continuance of imperialism as a factor in European politics. Recent history and present-day events indicate how rapidly we are approaching its final development at the close of the times of the Gentiles. The coming confederacy of European states will not result in the formation of a new empire, but will be the revival of the Roman in an altered form.

▪ CHAPTER FIVE ▪

The Coming Revival of the Roman Empire

1. The Geographical Standpoint

The coming revival of the Roman Empire will for our present purpose be best considered from the geographical, political, and religious standpoints.

Geographical Considerations

Any forecast of the exact delimitations of the ten kingdoms constituting the reconstructed empire must necessarily be largely conjectural. That their aggregate area will precisely conform to that of the ancient Roman Empire does not necessarily follow from the fact of its revival, and cannot be definitely concluded from Scripture. An extension of the territories of the empire in its resuscitated form would be quite consistent with the retention of its identity. Moreover, if Roman imperialism may be considered to have continued in the hands of Teutonic monarchs after the fall of the western part of the empire in 476, if, for instance, Charles the Great, of whom we have spoken in chapter four, ruled as a Roman emperor, despite the passing away of the actual empire itself, then the dominions which were under the rule of these later monarchs may yet be found incorporated in the empire, and so form parts of the ten kingdoms. In that case Germany and Holland would be included. Possibly, too, the empire will embrace all the territories which belonged to the three which preceded it, the Grecian, Medo-Persian, and Chaldean. Certainly when the stone fell on the toes of the image, the whole image, representing these former three as well as the fourth, was demolished. Suggestive also in this respect is the fact that the beast in the vision recorded in Revelation 13:2 was possessed of features of the leopard, the bear, and the lion, the same beasts which represented in Daniel's vision the Grecian, Medo-Persian, and Chaldean kingdoms (Dan. 7:4–6), the order in Revelation 13 being inverted. While political characteristics are doubtless chiefly in view in these symbols, there may at the same time be an indication of the eventual incorporation of the first three empires in the fourth. It must be remembered, too, that the authority of the federal head of the ten kingdoms is to be worldwide: "There was given to him authority over every tribe and people and tongue and nation" (Rev. 13:7). It is probable, therefore, that while the ten kingdoms will occupy a well-defined area, their dependencies and the countries which are allied with them will embrace practically the remainder of the world.

If, on the other hand, the Roman Empire is to be reconstructed in exact conformity territorially with its ancient boundaries—such a reconstruction is, of course, not inconceivable—we must consider what period of the conquests of the ancient empire to take, whether under the first emperor, Augustus, or during the apostolic age, or later. We may, perhaps, be helped by the facts already mentioned, that prophecy relating to gentile dominion is focused upon the Jews and Palestine, and has especially in view the presence of the nation in their land. Now, shortly after their overthow, in A.D. 70, their national recognition as possessors of the land ceased. This period, moreover, corresponds broadly to the close of the apostolic age. The dispersion of the Jews among the nations was completed by Adrian in the next century. He desolated the whole of Palestine, expelling all the remaining Jewish inhabitants.

A Review of the Ancient Territories

We will therefore now review the limits of the empire and of some of its provinces at that time, noticing certain circumstances of past and present history suggestive of future issues. In doing so we are not predicting that the boundaries of the revived empire will be those of the ancient.

Commencing with North Africa, it will be observed, on referring to the map, that practically the same strip of territory which belonged to the Roman Empire in the times of the apostles has passed directly under the government of countries which were themselves then within the empire. For Spain rules over Morocco, France over Algeria and Tunis, Italy recently seized Tripoli, and Britain has, since Turkey's entrance into the great war, virtually taken possession of Egypt. It seems not a little significant that no country which was outside the limits of the empire at the time under consideration has been permitted by God to annex these North African territories since the Saracens and the Turks were dispossessed of them.

Passing now to Asia, the territory in that continent which belonged to Rome in the first century is approximately what remained to Turkey immediately prior to the present war. Mesopotamia and most of Armenia were included. The war has already seen Turkey dispossessed of portions of these. The downfall of the Turkish Empire would almost certainly involve territorial rearrangements of deepest import in the light of prophecy, especially as regards Palestine.

Divisions of the Greek Empire: A Possible Renewal

The eighth chapter of Daniel apparently indicates that the Asiatic territories of the empire will be divided much as they were under the Greeks after the death of Alexander the Great. He was obviously symbolized by the great horn (v. 22). The four horns which came up in its place (v. 8) are clearly, too, the four generals who succeeded Alexander, and among whom his dominions were divided, Cassander ruling over Macedonia and Greece, Lysimachus over part of Asia Minor and Thrace (the extent of the latter province was almost exactly what now belongs to Turkey in Europe), Seleucus over most of Syria, Palestine, Mesopotamia, and the east, and Ptolemy over Egypt. Next follows a prediction carrying us to events which are evidently yet future. It is said, for instance, that these events will take place "in the latter time of their kingdom [not, it will be observed, in the time of the four kings themselves who succeeded Alexander, but of the kingdoms over which they ruled], when the transgressors are come to the full" (v. 23). The expressions in this chapter, "the time of the end" (v. 17), "the latter time of the indignation," "the appointed time of the end" (v. 19), and "the latter time of their kingdom" (v. 23), all point to a period still future, namely, to the close of the present age. Again, in reference to the "king of fierce countenance," while much of the prophecy can be applied to Antiochus Epiphanes in the second century B.C., yet no man has hitherto arisen whose character and acts have been precisely those related in verses 9–12 and 23–25. We may also compare what is said of "the transgression that maketh desolate" (v. 13) with the Lord's prophecy concerning the abomination of desolation (Matt. 24:15–22), a prophecy which also manifestly awaits fulfillment.

Possibly, therefore, these Asiatic territories will be similarly divided in the coming time. In regard to the first of the above-mentioned four divisions, the recent extension of Greece to include the ancient province of Macedonia is remarkable. This was an outcome of the Balkan War of 1912. The boundaries of Greece are now approximately what they were under Cassander in the time of the Grecian Empire, what they were also later as the provinces of Macedonia and Achaia in the Roman Empire. There has lately, therefore, been a significant reversion to ancient conditions in this respect.

Other European Territories

Coming now to the dual-monarchy of Austria-Hungary, reference to the map of the Roman Empire in the apostolic age will show that what are now Hungary, Transylvania, Bessarabia, and other states of the present monarchy were without the Roman boundaries, while Pannonia, or what is now Austria west of the Danube, was within; even when in the next century Dacia (now Transylvania, Bessarabia, etc.) was annexed, the two parts of the present dual kingdom were separate. The separation of Hungary from Austria has for a considerable time been a practical question of

European politics, and may be hastened by present events.

The northern and northeastern boundaries of Italy embraced the Trentino and the peninsula of Istria. Noticeable, therefore, are the present efforts of Italy to acquire these very districts, efforts which seem likely to achieve success. Roman states north of Italy covered what are now Baden, Wurtemberg, Luxemberg, and a large part of Bavaria. The possibility of an eventual severance of these from Prussian domination has been much discussed of late.

The Rhenish provinces of Alsace and Lorraine, originally portions of the Roman province of Gallia (now France), were snatched from France by Germany in the Franco-Prussian war of 1870–71. Their recovery is a supreme object of the efforts of the French in the present war, and not without hope of success.

The British Empire

As to Britain, at the time under consideration the greater part of the island was definitely included in the Roman Empire. Ireland and most of Scotland were never conquered by the Romans. Should Britain form one of the ten kingdoms, there is nothing to show that Ireland or any other part of the British Empire must of necessity be absolutely separated from it. Self-government may yet be possessed by those territories which have not yet received it, and it is significant that Ireland has now practically obtained it. That the lands which are linked with Britain as dependencies, or as in possession of self-government, should remain as integral parts of the empire is but consistent with the coming worldwide authority of the potentate who will be the federal head of the ten kingdoms. And that each state in the British Empire should have its own local government is, on the other hand, consistent with the establishment of a closer and complete confederacy of ten kingdoms, the area of which may correspond largely to that of the ancient Roman Empire. In contrast to the self-government of the other countries of the world at the coming period, the ten united kingdoms will eventually be absolutely under the control of the final emperor just mentioned, for the ten kings over these states, who receive authority as kings with him, will be of one mind to give their power and authority and their kingdom to him (Rev. 17:11, 13, 17).

What has been said of the British Empire may be true also of others of the ten kingdoms which have colonies or dependencies, and thus, while the ten kingdoms will themselves constitute an empire, their alliances and treaties with other countries of the world will apparently involve an extension of the authority of the controlling despot "over every tribe and people and tongue and nation" (Rev. 13:7). If, for instance, the United States of America were at that time in alliance with Britain (quite a possible contingency), their joint influence would probably extend to the whole of the American continents, which would thereby acknowledge his authority.

We may observe, too, the way in which the continent of Africa has come under certain European influences in modern times. The mention of this is simply suggestive. That the Scripture will be absolutely fulfilled is beyond doubt; the exact mode of its accomplishment is known to God.

2. The Political Standpoint

European Federation

Agencies are already at work for the establishment of a confederacy of European states—not the least significant of the many signs that the end of the age is approaching. The movement toward confederacy is doubtless receiving an impetus from the great upheaval in Europe. A circular issued in December, 1914, and distributed far and wide, announced the formation of a committee of influential men with the object of promoting a "European Federation." The circular says: "In sight of the present situation of ruin it ought to be the general opinion that a firmer economical and political tie is of utmost importance for all nations without exception, and that particularly for Europe the narrower bond of a federation, based on equality and interior independence of all partaking states, is of urgent necessity, which public opinion ought to demand."

A pamphlet published by the Committee recommends that the union of states shall be economical, political, and legal, with an international army as a common guarantee, and that European Federation should become the principal and most urgent political battle-cry for the masses of all European nations, and declares that "when the Governments are willing, when the public opinion of all peoples forces them to be willing, there is no doubt but that a reasonable and practical union of nations will prove to be as possible and natural as is at present a union of provinces, cantons, territories, whose populations often show more difference of race and character than those of nations now at hostilities." The committee calls upon the peoples of Europe to suffer the diplomatists no longer to dispose of them like slaves and by militarism to lash them to fury against each other. It calls upon them to see to it that never and nowhere should a member of any body or government be elected who is not an advocate of the federation, and that the trade union, society, or club to which any individual belongs should express sympathy with the movement in meetings and in votes. "The people," it is said, "have it now in their power, more than ever before, to control the Powers."

Two Possible Ways of Federation

The formation of ten federated states, covering at least the area of the ancient empire at the end of the first century of the present era, may be effected in two ways, either by the peaceful methods of arbitration and treaty, or as a result of strife and confusion. That the present European war will be succeeded by efforts for the creation of permanent international harmony and universal peace is probable, as is also some attempt at such a federation as is proposed by the above-mentioned committee. On the other hand, sinister indications abound today which point to industrial strife and revolution rather than peace. The condition of the industrial world presents a gloomy prospect indeed. There are ominous signs of keener conflict than ever between capital and labor. The forces of Socialism, Syndicalism, Communism, etc., are rapidly increasing in power and in international activity, and their avowed aims presage anything but peace in the near future. We may take, for example, the declared objects of "The Alliance of the Social Democracy"—now incorporated in the International Working Men's Association—"To destroy all States and all Churches with all their institutions and laws, religious, political, juridical, financial, magisterial, academical, economical, and social, and to establish in their place industrial cooperation and collective ownership of land and capital." All this sounds very pretentious, and would probably fail of complete accomplishment, but the agencies at work for it are strong. Attempts on a large scale would certainly lead to unprecedented disorder and chaos.

The Sea Symbolic of National Unrest

Not improbably the ten kingdoms of the reconstructed Roman Empire will arise as a result of political and social confusion. Thus it was in the case of the French Revolution and the consequent uprising of Napoleon. A repetition of such events on a far wider scale in the future is quite conceivable. In the prophetic vision given to the apostle John, the beast was seen "coming up out of the sea" (Rev. 13:1). Now the sea is in Scripture used figuratively of the nations, its characteristic restlessness symbolizing their commotion and strife. Compare the words of Isaiah: "Ah, the uproar of many peoples, which roar like the roaring of the seas; and the rushing of nations, that rush like the rushing of many waters! The nations shall rush like the rushing of many waters: but He shall rebuke them" (Is. 17:12, 13; see also Ps. 65:7; and Ezek. 26:3). To national unrest the Lord Jesus applied similar language when He foretold to the disciples that there would be "upon the earth distress of nations, in perplexity for the roaring of the sea and the billows; men fainting for fear, and for expectation of the things which are coming on the world" (Luke 21:25, 26). So also the waters which John had seen in his vision are described by the angel as "peoples, and multitudes, and nations, and tongues" (Rev. 17:15). Daniel, too, saw the four great beasts come up from the sea as a result of the breaking forth of the four winds of the heaven upon it, an undoubted representation of a condition of national disturbance (Dan. 7:2, 3). That the beast of Revelation 13:1 was seen coming up out of the sea points, therefore, to the probability that the ten kings who will have brief authority over the revived empire will be raised to their kingdom, not by constitutional methods, but as the result of revolutions and the collapse of present-day governments and institutions.

Revolutions and their Issues

Should any great measure of success attend the syndicalist and communist movements of the day, and especially if they are internationalized, the inevitable revolutions and disorder would almost certainly issue, as revolutions have so frequently issued, in despotism and autocracy, and perhaps in this way the ten kings would arise. The overthrow of the governments in the countries involved would remove what has certainly been the great restraint upon lawlessness* from the times of the apostles until now. Everything would be ripe for the appearance of a universal potentate. The cry would arise for "a man," a controlling organizer to bring order out of chaos. The unstable character of the rule of the ten kings, and the impoverishment of their kingdoms, would lead them, as a matter of diplomacy, to hand over their authority to him.

The Iron and the Clay

The political constitution of the successive empires during "the time of the Gentiles" was indicated in the image of Nebuchadnezzar's vision by the various substances of which the parts of the image were composed. While the regular deterioration in the relative value of these substances is noticeable, we are concerned now with those of the legs and feet. The legs were of iron, and the feet part of iron and part of potter's clay, not moist or miry clay, but "earthenware" (Dan. 2:41, R.V., margin), and consequently brittle (v. 42, margin).

That the iron symbolized militarism seems clear from what is said of the fourth kingdom, that "as iron breaketh in pieces and subdueth all things: and as iron that crusheth all these, shall it break in pieces and crush" (v. 40). Nations are broken and crushed by military power, and thus the nations were treated by the Romans. This was further signified by the iron teeth of the fourth beast, as is definitely stated in Daniel 7:19, 23: "And shall devour the whole earth, and shall tread it down, and break it in pieces."

The supposition that the clay represents democracy is gratuitous and arbitrary. The early Roman Empire, symbolized by the legs of the image, was built up under democratic rule. When republicanism was superseded by imperialism, democratic principles still prevailed. Democracy, therefore, played its part from the very commencement of the fourth kingdom, and had it been symbolized by the clay, not only the feet and toes but the legs themselves would have consisted of mingled iron and clay. Moreover, democracy in the generally accepted sense of the term has not always been found to be of an unstable or brittle character; witness the republicanism of the United States. Democracies, too, may be established on strictly constitutional principles.

Another explanation, therefore, of the symbolism of the clay must be sought, and it is not unlikely to be found in those revolutionary principles to which we have already referred, which were evidenced at the time of the French Revolution, and are finding expression, though in greater variety today, in such projects as those of the International Working Men's Association. Certainly the masses of the people of Europe are being permeated both by militarism and by the revolutionary doctrines of which we have spoken. Should these principles spread among the civil services and forces, everything would be in a complete state of preparedness for

Unprecedented Political and Social Upheaval

which would effect the overthrow of present forms of government. From the world's point of view the situation would require a consummate genius with powers of worldwide organization. Doubtless Satan's masterpiece of infidel ingenuity would be at hand for the occasion.

We are not predicting that this is to be the manner of the revival of the empire and of the advent of its imperial head. We have merely suggested possible circumstances in the light of Scripture and present-day movements. The

*See *The Epistles to the Thessalonians, with Notes Exegetical and Expository,* by C. F. Hogg and W. E. Vine.

actual circumstances attending the rise of the ten kings and their emperor must for the time remain conjectural. Certainly these kings will receive authority with him for one hour (Rev. 17:12), a phrase which may be translated "at the same time"; and certainly they will agree to give their power and authority to him (v. 13).

3. The Religious Standpoint

We will now note the religious conditions which are to prevail for a time upon the resuscitation of the empire. These are plainly indicated for us in Revelation 17. The apostle sees a woman sitting on the seven-headed and ten-horned beast. The woman is gorgeously arrayed, holds in her hand a golden cup full of abominations, and is drunken with the blood of the saints. Her name, written on her forehead, is

"Mystery, Babylon the Great,"

"the mother of the harlots and of the abominations of the earth" (vv. 3–6). The woman is symbolically described as the city of Rome (v. 18), and that leads on to a second mention of Babylon, in chapter eighteen, and a new description. Now to the description of the woman in chapter seventeen nothing more closely corresponds than the papacy. But if the Babylon of chapter seventeen is to be identified with that of chapter eighteen, the Papacy answers to the whole description only to a limited extent. While, however, there is much in common in the two descriptions in these chapters, yet the two Babylons are possibly to be distinguished. The Babylon of chapter seventeen is a "mystery," not so that of chapter eighteen. Again, the destruction of the one is different from that of the other. The first will be destroyed by the ten kings and their emperor (17:16), the second by the direct judgment of God (18:5, 8, 20); the first as the result of human antagonism, the second by famine, fire and earthquake. We are perhaps, therefore, justified in taking the more limited view in connection with the circumstances of chapter seventeen. Even so the woman may be regarded as representing the apostate sacerdotal systems which have sprung from the papacy as well as that system itself.

The position of the woman indicates an exercise of power which is voluntarily supported by the beast. That she sits upon the waters implies her religious dominion over the nations; that she is carried by the beast, who rules over the nations politically, implies that there will be a complete alliance between her and the ten kings with their chief, and that the sphere of her influence will be coextensive with the dominions of the beast.

The Papacy: Its Present Power

Now though the papacy lost its temporal power in 1870, it is far from having lost its political influence. Ecclesiastically, too, though it has received various setbacks, it is manifestly gaining power. This is especially observable, for example, in Britain, the overthrow of which as a Protestant power is undoubtedly the object of the persistent aggressiveness of Romanism. This aggressiveness is manifest in all the dominions of the British Empire, as well as in other lands.

Again, while certain governments have of late shaken off the ecclesiastical yoke, and infidelity has spread among the people of Roman Catholic lands, the number of Roman Catholics has increased with great rapidity. They were estimated at somewhat over 200,000,000 twenty years ago, they are now said to number about 300,000,000.

Indications are not wanting of a tendency toward

A Reunion of Christendom,

which would be facilitated by a willingness on the part of the papacy to adapt itself to the impulse of the time.

Present events, therefore, point to a great renewal of papal power involving the fulfillment of the prophecy relating to the woman and the beast that carries her. This renewed alliance between the political and the ecclesiastical powers will, however, be of brief duration. The successful efforts of governments in recent times to liberate themselves from papal authority, as in the case of France and Portugal, are but foreshadowings of the eventual entire destruction of ecclesiasticism and sacerdotalism under the revived Roman Empire. "The ten horns . . . and the beast, these shall hate the harlot, and shall make her desolate and naked, and shall eat her flesh, and shall burn her utterly with fire" (Rev. 17:16). Thus it would seem that, when at the very zenith of its power and ambition, the papacy, at the head of amalgamated Christendom, will suddenly meet its doom.

The Doom of Religious Babylon

Its accumulated wealth would probably be an incentive in determining the ten kings to take this step, owing possibly to the impoverishment of their kingdoms as a result of wars and political and social upheavals. An additional cause will doubtless be the widespread spirit of antagonism against all religion.

Submission to the papal yoke has invariably had an aftermath of infidelity; similarly the temporary subservience of the beast to the woman will issue in the casting off of all religious restraint and in the universal acknowledgment of the presumptuous claims of the world ruler.

Satanic Authority of the Emperor

The authority of this final emperor of the Roman kingdom will be satanic. "The dragon gave him his power, and his throne, and great authority" (Rev. 13:2); "the beast . . . was, and is not; and is about to come up out of the abyss, and to go into perdition" (Rev. 17:8). This implies that he has been on the earth in the past. The same thing is indicated in the interpretation of the seven heads. Topographically they are described as seven mountains, personally as seven kings (v. 9). Of these, five had fallen, the sixth was in power in John's time, the seventh had not then come (v. 10). The beast (clearly here symbolizing, not a kingdom, but a person) would be an eighth, and yet would be of the seven (v. 11). These heads have been regarded by some as forms of government, by others as empires, or again, as emperors. There seems to be no reason why they are not to be regarded as emperors, though doubtless their empires are in view, as being associated with them. Accordingly, the fact that the eighth is also one of the seven indicates his reappearance on the scene. Various suggestions have been made as to his identification, but this must remain uncertain until his advent. With him the ten kings for a time receive authority (v. 12), subsequently handing it over to him with their kingdom (v. 17), but not before they have together with him crushed the great religious system symbolized by the woman (v. 16). His stupendous power and brilliant abilities, the evidence of his superhuman origin, his phenomenal capacity for organization, and the consolidation of the empire under his absolute control will cause the whole world to marvel at him (Rev. 13:3; 17:8). To the world, in its divinely inflicted and therefore retributive delusion, he will appear like a god who has come to deliver from woe, and to introduce the long-looked-for age of peace and prosperity. Wonder will be succeeded by worship, both of the man and of Satan. "They worshiped the dragon, because he gave his authority unto the beast; and they worshiped the beast, saying, Who is like unto the beast? and who is able to war with him?" (13:4).

The world is now in course of rapid preparation for all this:

The "Superman"

has of late become a much-discussed topic in various classes of society and in the press, and the idea is supported by the theories of evolution which are receiving increasingly wide acceptance. A spirit of expectancy is being thus aroused which will undoubtedly facilitate the recognition of the man himself at his advent, and the acknowledgment of his claims to divine honor. But this will involve the worship of Satan, and to this end the effective agency of

Spiritism

has been long at work. Spiritism leads to devil worship. It must do so; its energizing power is Satan himself. Both spiritism and theosophy, and similar forms of error, all of which are rapidly on the increase today, are paving the way for worldwide worship of the dragon.

The imperial power and worship of this emperor will be promoted by another potentate similarly energized by Satan. This latter is the second beast, described in Revelation 13:11–end. Later on in the book he is called

The False Prophet

(Rev. 16:13; 19:20; 20:10), indicating that his activities are chiefly of a religious character, and perhaps that he will be more closely connected with Jewish affairs. He will make "the earth and them that dwell therein worship the beast," the emperor of the ten kingdoms (13:11), deceiving the world by supernatural signs wrought in the presence of the first beast (v. 12), and enforcing the worship of his image (v. 15), the abomination of desolation set up in the temple at Jerusalem (Matt. 24:15). With the worship of an image the times of the Gentiles began (Dan. 3:1), and with similar idolatry they will end. In the days of the early Roman emperors their deification was celebrated by the adoration of their images. Then, as formerly under Nebuchadnezzar, those who refused to worship suffered death. So will it be under the final emperor and his colleague.

Various opinions are held regarding these two beasts of Revelation 13, as to which is the Man of Sin spoken of by Paul in 2 Thessalonians 2, which the Antichrist mentioned in John's epistles, and which of the two is the willful king described in Daniel 11. Limitations of space preclude our entering into the subject in detail here. The present writer holds the view that all three are the same person, and that they are also the same as the horn in Daniel 7:8, 11, and as the first beast of Revelation 13, and that these are all different descriptions of the final head of the revived empire. The Old Testament passages somewhat briefly announce the arising of this worldwide ruler; the New Testament passages unfold and expand the preceding predictions concerning him, among the additional details given in the New Testament being the fact that he is to have a prophet who will assiduously support his claim to deity and his administration. It is the world emperor, and not his prophet, who is to be worshiped, and who therefore proclaims himself as God (2 Thess. 2:4). His prophet, the second beast of Revelation 13, in the exercise of all the power of the first, will cause the world to worship him (13:12). As his prophet and prime minister he would not himself endeavor to usurp the position of him whose avowed deity he seeks to support.

The similarity of the details in the above-mentioned passages indicates that the same person is in view in each case. His blasphemies, for instance, and his assumption of deity are mentioned in Daniel 7:25; 11:36, 37; 2 Thessalonians 2:3, 4, and Revelation 13:5, 6, and his war with the saints in Daniel 7:21, 25 and Revelation 13:7. Further, the blasphemous proclamation of himself as God is consistent with what is said in John's epistles concerning the Antichrist. For in his self-deification he is directly "antagonistic to Christ," he denies that Jesus is the Christ, and therefore denies the Father and the Son (1 John 2:22).

The two potentates will establish not only a universal religion, but also a

Universal System of Commerce

The second beast "causeth all, the small and the great, and the rich and the poor, and the free and the bond, that there be given them a mark on their hand, or upon their forehead; and that no man should be able to buy or to sell, save he that hath the mark, even the name of the beast or the number of his name" (Rev. 13:16, 17). This indicates a worldwide protectionist system, such a system as, for instance, might conceivably be established under some form of syndicalism. Undeniably, circumstances in the industrial world today manifest an increasing tendency in this direction. The principles previously mentioned, as now making for industrial and international revolution, and the present stupendous movements toward amalgamation, are clearly preparing for the fulfillment of this prophecy by facilitating the eventual establishment of the unrighteous commercial system of the reconstituted empire.

▪ CHAPTER SIX ▪

The Everlasting Kingdom

We have now to consider the dealings of the two beasts, the final Roman emperor and his false prophet, with

The Jews

With the Romans the Jews joined in the death of Christ, and with the rulers of this fourth empire they will be in agreement for a time at the close of their long course of apostasy. This was especially made known to Daniel in the prophecy of

The Seventy Weeks

(Dan. 9). These weeks (lit., *hebdomads,* or periods of seven, i.e., seven years each) had been divinely decreed (or "cut off," i.e., from the period of "the times of the Gentiles") upon his people and his city. From the going forth of the commandment to restore and to build Jerusalem unto the Anointed One (the Messiah), the Prince, would be seven weeks and threescore and two weeks. After this the Anointed One would be cut off, and would have nothing (Dan. 9:24–26). This period is 69 times 7, or 483 years, and to the very day this was the period commencing with the command of Artaxerxes Longimanus, King of Persia, for the restoration of Jerusalem (Neh. 2:1–9), and ending with the triumphal entry of Christ into the city (Matt. 21:1–11).* Four days later He was crucified, "the Anointed One was cut off and had nothing," i.e., He did not enter then upon His messianic kingdom. The prophecy predicted that the people of the prince (lit., "a prince") that would come would destroy the city and the sanctuary. That took place in A.D. 70, under Titus Vespasianus. But Titus is not "the prince that shall come." This, apart from other considerations, is clear from what follows: "And his [the prince's] end shall be with a flood [or rather, "in the overflowing," i.e., of the wrath of God]," a prediction at once inapplicable to Titus. The mention of

The Last "Week"

is deferred, indicating an interval between the sixty-ninth and the seventieth. Now the events predicted for the seventieth had no historical fulfillment immediately after the sixty-ninth. The one, therefore, did not follow the other consecutively. At the commencement of the intervening period the Jews were scattered from their land. At the seventieth they will have been restored, and the events of that week concern "the prince that shall come," the last world emperor, and his dealings with them. "He shall make a firm covenant with many [lit., "the many," i.e., the great majority of the nation] for one week" (v. 27). This covenant is described in Isaiah's prophecies as a "covenant with death" and an "agreement with Hell." The covenant, he says, "shall be disannulled," and the agreement "shall not stand; when the overflowing scourge shall pass through, then ye shall be trodden down by it" (Is. 28:18). That this refers to a time yet future and not to past Israelitic history may be gathered from verse 22, where the theme and the language are similar to those of the passage in Daniel now under consideration. Daniel tells us the mode of the disannulling. "In the midst of the week [R.V., margin] he shall cause the sacrifice and oblation to cease." Accordingly after three and a half years the Antichrist, manifesting his real character, will prove himself a traitor and break the covenant, and thus Isaiah's prediction will be fulfilled.

Apparently at the very time when he thus breaks his league with the Jews the Antichrist will determine upon his public deification and

*See *The Coming Prince,* by Sir Robert Anderson.

the establishment of his worship in the temple. For he it is who "opposeth and exalteth himself above all that is called God, or that is worshiped; so that he as God sitteth in the temple of God, showing himself that he is God" (2 Thess. 2:4). This, with the setting up of his image, will doubtless be the fulfillment of the prophecies recorded by Daniel, that "upon the wing [or pinnacle] of abominations shall come one that maketh desolate" (Dan. 9:27, cp. 11:31 and 12:11), and "they shall profane the sanctuary, even the fortress, and shall take away the continual burnt offering, and they shall set up the abomination that maketh desolate" (11:31, cp. 12:11); a fulfillment also of the Lord's prediction that "the abomination of desolation, which was spoken of by Daniel the prophet," will "stand in the holy place" (Matt. 24:15). In the establishment of this blasphemous worship of the emperor, the false prophet will play a prominent part, as we have seen from the latter part of Revelation 13.

The many references to the desolator and the desolations are indicative of the

Fierce Persecution

which will follow. This will be at first directed against "the remnant," the large numbers of Jews who will repudiate allegiance to the beast and to the false prophet, many doubtless having been converted to their coming Messiah through the testimony of two witnesses who will be sent from God to the nation. "They shall prophesy a thousand two hundred and three-score days, clothed in sackcloth" (Rev. 11:3-13). The success of their ministry will apparently arouse the bitter antagonism of Satan and his human instruments. The breaking of the covenant with the people as a whole indicates that an effort will also be made to crush the entire nation. Thus the latter half of the seventieth week will be the time of "Jacob's trouble," "a time of trouble, such as never was since there was a nation even to that same time" (Dan. 12:1), though the unprecedented tribulation will not be confined to the Jews only.

Armageddon and After

The bitter antagonism of the Man of Sin, and his colleague, the False Prophet, against God and His people will culminate in the gathering together of all the forces of the empire in Palestine in final conflict for the complete domination of the world. This tremendous event is thus indicated by the apostle John: "And I saw coming out of the mouth of the dragon, and out of the mouth of the beast, and out of the mouth of the false prophet, three unclean spirits, as it were frogs: for they are the spirits of devils [correctly, "demons"], working signs; which go forth unto the kings of the whole world, to gather them together unto the war of the great day of God, the Almighty" (Rev. 16:13, 14).

In reality the issue at stake will be the supremacy of Christ or of Satan in the earth. The objective will be neither territorial conquest nor naval supremacy, nor commercial predominance. The war of the beast and the ten kings under him is against the Lamb (Rev. 17:14). This the second Psalm had foretold: "Why do the nations rage, and the peoples imagine a vain thing? The kings of the earth set themselves, and the rulers take counsel together against the Lord, and against His Anointed, saying, let us break their bands asunder, and cast away their cords from us." The issue is not uncertain: "He that sitteth in the heavens shall laugh: the Lord shall have them in derision."

The Scene of the Conflict

in Har-Magedon, commonly known as Armageddon (Rev. 16:16). The name, which is associated with Megiddo, a locality famed in Old Testament history for its decisive battles (Judg. 5:19; 2 Kin. 23), doubtless stands here for a wider area, stretching, as we shall see, from the north to the south of the land.

The combatants, the conflict and its conclusion, are described by John in vivid language of terrible grandeur in Revelation 19:11-21: "And I saw the heaven opened: and behold, a white horse, and He that sat thereon, called Faithful and True; and in righteousness he doth judge and make war. And His eyes are a flame of fire, and upon his head are many diadems; and he hath a name written, which no one knoweth but He Himself. And He is arrayed in a garment sprinkled with blood: and His name is called the Word of God. And the armies which are in heaven followed Him upon white horses, clothed in fine linen, white and pure. And out of His mouth proceedeth a sharp sword, that with it he should smite the nations: and He shall rule them with a rod of iron: and He treadeth the winepress of the fierceness of the wrath of Almighty God. And he hath on His garment and on His thigh a name written, King of Kings, and Lord of Lords.

"And I saw an angel standing in the sun; and he cried with a loud voice, saying to all the birds that fly in mid heaven, Come and be gathered together unto the great supper of God; that ye may eat the flesh of kings, and the flesh of captains, and the flesh of mighty men, and the flesh of horses and of them that sit thereon, and the flesh of all men, both free and bond, and small and great.

"And I saw the beast, and the kings of the earth, and their armies, gathered together to make war against Him that sat upon the horse, and against His army. And the beast was taken, and with him the false prophet that wrought the signs in his sight, wherewith he deceived them that had received the mark of the beast, and them that worshiped his image: they twain were cast alive into the lake of fire that burneth with brimstone: and the rest were killed with the sword of Him that sat upon the horse, even the sword which came forth out of His mouth: and all the birds were filled with their flesh" (Rev. 19:11–21). Ezekiel similarly describes the scene in his prophecy in chapter 30:17–21.

Thus it is that the climax of the world's rebellion against God is to meet its doom. This is the manner of the overthrow of the ten-kingdomed empire, the fourth of Daniel's visions. Accordingly, what we have now read from Revelation 19 is identical with (1) the falling of the stone upon the feet of the image in Nebuchadnezzar's vision, the annihilation of all gentile government (Dan. 2:45); (2) the consuming of the dominion of the fourth beast in Daniel's subsequent vision (Dan. 7:26); (3) the pouring out of God's wrath upon the Antichrist, the desolator (Dan 9:27); and (4) the coming of the Son of man on the clouds of heaven with power and great glory (Matt. 24:30). The great emperor, the Man of Sin, is to be crushed by the Lord Jesus, "with the breath of His mouth," and brought to nought "by the manifestation of His coming" (2 Thess. 2:8).

Now this "manifestation of His coming" is, to transliterate the Greek words,

The Epiphany of His Parousia

An epiphany is, literally, the "shining forth" of that which has been hidden; and the word Parousia is, literally, "presence" (see margin of R.V. and Phil. 2:12). This latter word is used of the coming of Christ to the air for His saints, "to receive them unto Himself," and of their consequent presence with Him (1 Thess. 2:19). They are thus to be "ever with the Lord" (1 Thess. 4:17), and with Him they will come when He descends at His revelation "from heaven with the angels of His power in flaming fire, rendering vengeance to them that know not God, and to them that obey not the gospel of our Lord Jesus" (2 Thess. 1:7, 8). The sudden bursting forth of His glory thus "to execute judgment" (Jude 15) will be the "Epiphany, or shining forth, of His Parousia," and by it the Man of Sin is to be brought to nought and his empire demolished. He and his False Prophet will be "cast alive into the lake of fire," and his armies will perish (Rev. 19:20, 21).

This is to be the issue of the world's attempts to establish a millennium of its own by schemes of federation and amalgamation. This is the upshot of its fancied progress and improvement without God and His Christ.

We must now see what other Scriptures have to say concerning this scene. The instrument which the Lord uses for the destruction of His foes is a sword which proceeds *out of His mouth;* the destruction is described as the treading of the winepress.

The Voice of the Lord

First, as to the instrument. The sword is symbolic of the utterance of the Lord's voice. No material instrument is needed, a word is enough. This is clear from many passages. In the second Psalm the overthrow of the foe is thus described: "Then shall He *speak* unto them in His wrath, and vex them in His sore displeasure" (v. 5). Joel prophesies of the same event: "The sun and the moon are darkened, and the stars withdraw their shining: and the Lord *uttereth His voice* before His army; for His camp is very great; for He is strong that executeth His word: for the day of the Lord is great and very terrible; and who can abide it?" (Joel 2:10, 11; and see 3:16. With this compare Is. 11:4 and 30:30–33.) The same voice of judgment is implied in Paul's prediction of the doom of the lawless one, that "the Lord Jesus will slay him *with the breath of His mouth*" (2 Thess. 2:8). In the same connection we are doubtless to read Psalm 29, the psalm which describes the terrible majesty and effect of the *voice of the Lord.*

We must presently dwell more fully upon this psalm in order to observe its application to the circumstances under consideration, and its connection with the passages which describe the judgment of the foe as

The Treading of the Winepress

These passages are Isaiah 63:1–6; Joel 9:16; Revelation 14:17–20, and the one already quoted in Revelation 19. It is observable, too, that in the first of these the voice of the Lord is mentioned again, for the Deliverer describes Himself as "I that *speak in righteousness.*"

We shall first refer to Revelation 14:17–20. Two angels appear coming forth, the one from the temple in heaven with a sickle in his hand, the other from the altar. The latter calls to the one with the sickle to gather "the clusters of the vine of the earth," symbolic of the Man of Sin and his gathered armies. The angel then casts his sickle into the earth, gathers the vintage, and casts it into the winepress of the wrath of God. The winepress is "trodden without the city," and "there came out blood from the winepress, even unto the bridles of the horses, as far as a thousand and six hundred furlongs" (i.e., 200 miles). The great emperor and his prophet, and their vast forces, will thus be gathered in dense battle array throughout the length of Palestine, Jerusalem being their objective. Joel calls the scene of the battle "the Valley of Decision." "Come, tread ye," says the prophet, "for the winepress is full, the vats overflow; for their wickedness is great. Multitudes, multitudes in the valley of decision! for the day of the Lord is near in the valley of decision" (Joel 3:13, 14). The multitudes are the forces of the Man of Sin.

The first six verses of Isaiah 63 narrate in the form of a dialogue

The Overthrow of the Man of Sin

and his forces. The dialogue is between Messiah the Deliverer and the Jews. Having just overthrown the foe in the treading of the winepress, and the armies of the empire being destroyed throughout the battle line from the north of the land to the south, the Messiah, in the fruits of His victory, reveals Himself to His astonished earthly people. In wondering admiration they exclaim: "Who is this that cometh from Edom, with dyed garments from Bozrah? this that is glorious, marching in the greatness of His strength?" To this their Deliverer answers, "I that *speak in righteousness,* mighty to save." The significance of this is at once apparent to the reader who calls to mind the various passages mentioned above in reference to the voice of the Lord. "I that speak in righteousness"—this is the voice uttered before His army (Joel 2:10), "the sword that proceedeth out of His mouth" (Rev. 19:15); the "breath of His mouth," by which the Man of Sin is crushed (2 Thess. 2:8), and the "voice" of Psalm 29.

The people, struck by the appearance of the victor, next ask: "Wherefore art Thou red in Thine apparel, and Thy garments like him that treadeth in the winefat?" The language is doubtless symbolic. Messiah explains in reply how the threatening foes have been crushed: "I have trodden the winepress alone; and of the peoples there was no man with Me: yea, I trod them in Mine anger, and trampled them in My fury; and their lifeblood is sprinkled upon My garments, and I have stained all My raiment. For the day of vengeance was in Mine heart, and the year of My redeemed is come. And I looked, and there was none to help; and I wondered that there was none to uphold: therefore Mine own arm brought salvation unto Me; and My fury, it upheld Me. And I trod down the peoples in Mine anger, and made them drunk in My fury, and I poured out their lifeblood on the earth" (vv. 3–6). The words of a previous prophecy express the joyful recognition of the delivered nation: "And it shall be said in that day, Lo, this is our God; we have waited for Him, and He will save us: this is the Lord; we have waited for Him, we will be glad and rejoice in His salvation" (Is. 25:9).

Turning now to Psalm 29 we find

The Scene of Judgment

strikingly depicted; the very length of the battle line is indicated, in agreement with the later and clearer description in Revelation 20:14. Indeed, the passages which foretell the events of this coming terrible day afford a remarkable illustration of the progressive character of the revelations of Scripture. The psalm is divided into three parts: (1) The first three verses are a call to the saints in heaven, the "sons of the mighty," to worship the Lord in view of the judgment He is just about to execute for the deliverance of His people the Jews, their land and their city. (2) The second part, verses 3–9, describes the actual judgment by means of "the voice of the Lord." The psalmist was doubtless thinking of a thunderstorm. The Spirit of God was giving prophetic utterance concerning a more terrible scene, and the geographical limitations of the psalm are of prophetic import. The first place mentioned is Lebanon, in the north, with its mountainspur Sirion (vv. 5, 6). The last place is the wilderness of Kadesh, in the south, the center of which is Bozrah, in Edom (v. 8), a point of connection with Isaiah 63:1. Now the distance from Sirion to Bozrah, in the wilderness of Kadesh, is 200 miles, and this is the 1600 furlongs of Revelation 14:20. Here, then, in one fell stroke of divine wrath the Man of Sin and his forces are overthrown, and the Jews are delivered. The later revelations of Scripture thus enable us to pass from the natural and physical setting of the psalm to the veiled reality. Thus this portion of the psalm is to be read in connection with the passage from Revelation 19 quoted above. (3) The last two verses describe the results of the conquest.

The Jews in Their Extremity

were threatened with annihilation. But man's extremity is God's opportunity. The people now see their Deliverer in person, they "look on Him whom they pierced." They realize that their enemies were destroyed because "the Lord sat as King at the flood." And now "the Lord sitteth as King forever." He whose right it is to reign has come to Zion. Hence the psalmist can next say: "The Lord will give strength unto His people; the Lord will bless His people with peace." Armageddon is over, the winepress of God's wrath has been trodden, and the war against the Lamb is ended. Psalm 30 follows on with the people's song of praise for deliverance.

The judgments of God in the earth will be accompanied by

Seismic Disturbances,

including "a great earthquake such as was not since there were men upon the earth," the overthrow of the cities of the nations, and the displacement of islands and mountains (Rev. 16:18–21). Then doubtless will be fulfilled the prophecy of Zechariah, that in the day when the Lord goes forth to fight against the nations that are gathered against Jerusalem, His feet will stand upon the Mount of Olives, and the mountain will be divided, leaving a very great valley east of the city (Zech. 14:1–5).

The Everlasting Kingdom

In this tremendous intervention in the affairs of the world for the termination of gentile dominion the Son of God will be accompanied by all His saints. He will come "to be glorified in His saints, and to be marveled at in all them that believed" (2 Thess. 1:10). So from earliest times Enoch had prophesied: "Behold, the Lord came with His holy myriads, to execute judgment upon all" (Jude 14, 15, margin). And Zechariah: "The Lord my God shall come, and all the saints with Thee" (14:5). They are to take an active part in the inauguration of His kingdom, and in its government. For "the saints of the Most High shall receive the kingdom, and possess the kingdom forever, even forever and ever" (Dan. 7:18). "The kingdom and the dominion, and the greatness of the kingdoms under the whole heaven, shall be given to the people of the saints of the Most High" (v. 27).

Then shall the Lord "be King over all the

earth" (Zech. 14:9). God's claims will be vindicated. His Christ will reign as King of Righteousness, and King of Peace, the center of His government being the very place where once He was despised and rejected, and men cast Him out and crucified Him. Of the increase of His government and of peace there shall be no end, upon the throne of David, and upon His kingdom, to establish it, and to uphold it with judgment and with righteousness from henceforth even forever. The zeal of the Lord of hosts shall perform this (Is. 9:7). His saints "shall be priests of God and of Christ, and shall reign with Him a thousand years" (Rev. 20:6). Then will be fulfilled the words of the Lord, "I am returned unto Zion, and will dwell in the midst of Jerusalem: and Jerusalem shall be called the city of truth; and the mountain of the Lord of hosts the holy mountain" (Zech. 8:3). The days of Israel's mourning will be ended, the nation will be a "crown of beauty in the hand of the Lord, and a royal diadem in the hand of her God," and Jerusalem will be a praise in the earth (Is. 60:30; 62:3, 7). "The heavens shall rejoice and the earth be glad," and "the earth shall be full of the knowledge of the Lord, as the waters cover the sea" (Ps. 96:11; Is. 11:9). According to God's eternal counsel the despised Nazarene will yet be manifested and acknowledged by all as King of kings and Lord of lords.

"To Him be glory forever and ever, Amen."

V

The Four Women of the Apocalypse

▪ CHAPTER ONE ▪

Jezebel in Thyatira

Of the four women mentioned in the book of the Revelation two symbolize agencies that have spread corruption, while the other two are symbolic of the two great communities which God has formed to bear witness for Him, and to act as His instruments of government in the ages that are to come. The first woman is described in the letter to the church in Thyatira. She is the corruptress of the Lord's servants there, and the Lord remonstrates with that church for allowing her presence and influence. He says: "I have this against thee, that thou sufferest the woman Jezebel, which calleth herself a prophetess; and she teacheth and seduceth My servants to commit fornication, and to eat things sacrificed to idols" (2:20).

Thyatira Trade Guilds

Thyatira was situated northeast of Smyrna, in a fertile valley in the Province of Asia. Its inhabitants were possessed of considerable commercial advantages. At the same time they were grossly immoral. The citizens were formed into several trade guilds. Membership of these was essential to worldly success. Guild feasts were held at appointed times, and the proceedings on these occasions were characterized by the utmost licentiousness. "The bond which held a guild together lay always in the common religion in which all united, and in the common sacrificial meal of which all partook; the members ate and drank fellowship and brotherhood in virtue of the pagan deity whom they served. In the existing state of society it was impossible to dissociate membership of a guild from idolatry, and the idolatry was a kind that by its symbolism and its efficacy exerted great influence on its adherents, making them members of a unity which was essentially non-Christian and anti-Christian. In the second place, the common banquets were celebrated amid circumstances of revelry and enjoyment that were far from conducive to strict morality."*

"To hold aloof from the clubs was to set oneself down as a mean-spirited, grudging, ill-conditioned person, hostile to existing society, devoid of generous impulse and kindly neighborly feeling, an enemy of mankind."†

This shows the danger to which the converts in Thyatira were exposed. The woman spoken of as Jezebel, posing as a prophetess, as the advocate of broad-mindedness and enlightenment, would easily seduce the careless believer to go in for membership of a guild, or to return to it if it had been abandoned at conversion. The advantages would be great. Ridicule and persecution would be avoided. Prosperity in business would be practically ensured. Personal prestige in the city would be enhanced. And why not bring a healthy influence into society by joining the guild? These and other arguments, with which Christians who are tempted by the worldly minded are so familiar today, would be used to entice believers from their faithfulness to Christ.

Whether Jezebel was actually the woman's name or not, we may take it that there was such a woman in Thyatira, and that she inculcated doctrines in the church by which she successfully allured some of the believers to partake in the licentious and idolatrous practices referred to. Here, then, in the early days of church history antinomianism became rife, and immorality was practiced under the fair garb of the Christian faith; there was a form of godliness, but a denial of the power thereof.

---

*Prof. W. M. Ramsay, in the article "Thyatira" in *Hasting's Dictionary of the Bible.*

†Prof. W. M. Ramsay. *The Letters to the Seven Churches,* p. 348.

Jezebel and Ahab

We cannot dissociate this woman's name from the Jezebel of 1 Kings. She was the daughter of Ethbaal, a Sidonian. Her father was priest to Astarte, the vile goddess of the Syrians, the religion of whom was derived immediately from Babylon. Jezebel, whose name signifies a "dung heap," came into the midst of Israel as the wife of Ahab, and was the dominating influence amongst God's people. Her husband was practically her subordinate. The story of her pollution of the nation, her slaughter of the prophets of God, and her substitution for them of the prophets of Baal, is well-known. Through her instrumentality Ahab "did yet more to provoke the Lord, the God of Israel, to anger than all the kings of Israel that were before him." The gorgeous ritual of the worship of Astarte replaced that of Jehovah. Jezebel's baneful influence continued during the reigns of her two sons, Ahaziah and Jehoram, and, through the marriage of her daughter Athaliah to Jehoram, the son of Jehoshaphat, King of Judah, it extended to the tribe of Judah. Athaliah had a house of Baal erected in Jerusalem and her sons "broke up the house of God; and also all the dedicated things of the Lord did they bestow upon the Baalim" (2 Chr. 24:7).

The Seven Letters

In the letters to the seven churches there is every indication of a wider scope of teaching than what was immediately applicable to those churches. Clearly there is a great deal to be said for the view that the churches are, in the two chapters which contain the letters addressed to them, purposely arranged in an order which represents anticipatively the whole course of what is called Christendom during the present era. We notice, for instance, in connection with the subject we are considering, the immediate sequence of Thyatira after Pergamos. There were false teachers present in Pergamos but Thyatira suffered them. Pergamos was indifferent to the evil; Thyatira became associated with it. These two succeed Smyrna, which was appointed to endure persecution. Correspondingly in early church history, after the persecutions which took place in the period from the Emperor Domitian to Constantine, i.e., from about A.D. 170 to the beginning of the fourth century, the churches experienced a time of immunity from opposition and cruelty, and rapidly became possessed of worldly influence and authority. Departing from the path of simple allegiance to Christ, the church sought a power and affluence for which her founder had not destined her, and eventually placed herself under the ready patronage of the emperor. The weakening of paganism, and the self-aggrandizement of the churches, provided Constantine with an opportunity for acquiring supreme political power which his ability and energy were not slow to seize.

A Parallel

Under his prestige the union of the church with the world proceeded apace. The conditions represented by the letters to Pergamos and Thyatira rapidly took shape. As in the days of Israel under Ahab and Jezebel, the faithful ministers of God's Word, the true prophets of the Lord in the churches, were expelled, and pagan priests, advocates of the religion of the Egyptian goddess Isis, were brought into the house of God to act as the spiritual guides of His people. This diabolical amalgamation of Christianity with paganism was completed by Pope Damasus at the end of the fourth century. The apostate Church had become heathenized. Damasus was not only made the leading ecclesiastic in the church; he was also elected Pontifex Maximus, or Chief Pontiff, of the heathen world. Nothing could be more striking than the comparison between the idolatrous decadence of Israel under Jezebel and that of the church under the Roman prelacy. The corruptions which were spread by the symbolical Jezebel amidst the churches were of the same sort as those by which the pagan queen poisoned the life of God's earthly people Israel. Damasus vauntingly acted on the principle that the end justified the means. No matter how glaring the enormity, how unrighteous the deed, everything was justified so long as the cause of the church's religious and political power was advanced. The abominations of heathendom were admitted into the churches under the cloak of the Christian faith.

The Doom Pronounced

Thus what took place in the narrower sphere of Thyatira transpired subsequently in the broad realm of Christendom. Whether those who were guilty of yielding to Jezebel's seductions in Thyatira actually repented of their deeds, or whether the Lord's threat was carried out, we cannot definitely say. We may gather that it was so, however, from the fact that the Lord says, "I will kill her children with death; and all the churches shall know that I am He which searcheth the reins and the hearts: and I will give unto each one of you according to your works" (v. 23). Probably what took place in the slaughter of the children of Ahab and Jezebel in Israel (2 Kin. 10:11) had its counterpart in the case of Jezebel's children in the church in Thyatira. So, again, in the broader view of the subject, when the Babylonish ecclesiastical system of Christendom in its final form is hereafter overthrown by the anti-Christian federacy of nations (Rev. 17:16), then this threat against the evil in Thyatira will receive its fulfillment in the wider sphere of Christendom. This we are to consider more fully in our next chapter.

CHAPTER TWO

Mystery, Babylon the Great

The second of the two evil women described in the Apocalypse is the subject of a vision given to John and recorded in the seventeenth chapter. There came to him one of the seven angels that had the seven bowls of the wrath of God, and talked with him, saying, "Come hither, I will show thee the judgment of the great harlot that sitteth upon many waters; with whom the kings of the earth committed fornication,* and they that dwell in the earth were made drunken with the wine of her fornication."

The apostle was carried away in the spirit into a wilderness, a place suggestive of destitution and apparently symbolizing a condition barren of all that is fruitful for God, void of that which could delight His eye; a striking contrast, as we shall see, to the place from which the apostle was afterwards called to see the fair heavenly woman, the bride, the Lamb's wife. He now sees a woman "sitting upon a scarlet-colored beast, full of names of blasphemy, having seven heads and ten horns. And the woman was arrayed in purple and scarlet, and decked with gold and precious stones and pearls, having in her hand a golden cup full of abominations, even the unclean things of her fornication, and upon her forehead a name written, MYSTERY, BABYLON THE GREAT, THE MOTHER OF THE HARLOTS AND OF THE ABOMINATIONS OF THE EARTH."

Why "Mystery"?

That the woman is called "Babylon the Great" indicates her association with the ancient city of the East. That the word "Mystery" is annexed to the title implies that the appellation has a spiritual significance, that facts relating to the woman have something more than a mere geographical and historical connection with the city. A mystery in Scripture is not calculated to convey to the mind of the believer the obscurity attached to what is mysterious. It comprises facts which he is intended to understand, the truths relating to which are to shape his conduct according to the will of God, whether preventatively or formatively, and thus to direct his loyalty to Christ. A mystery lies outside the ken of the natural mind, for "the natural man understandeth not the things of the Spirit . . . they are spiritually discerned."

The last phrase of the woman's title, "the mother of the harlots and of the abominations of the earth," intimates that Babylon is the source both of unholy unions of the people of God with the world, whether in Israelitic history or in Christendom, for such associations are described in Scripture as spiritual fornication (Jer. 3:6, 8, 9; Ezek. 16:32, e.g.), and of all systematized idolatry in the world, for whatever is set before men as an object of worship other than God is, in the language of Scripture, an abomination. The language is also suggestive of the immorality and unchastity which accompanies idolatry.

Babylon the Source of Idolatry

Idolatry, in an organized form, originated with Babylon, under the rule of Nimrod, son of Cush. The name of the ancient god, Bacchus, denotes "Son of Cush," and is therefore to be identified with Nimrod, who was deified after his death. The most ancient pagan religions of the world, though varying in details, have certain features in common which are distinctly traceable to the primal system of idolatry known to have been established by Nimrod and

*The reason why these events are described as already having taken place, though they were actually future to the apostle's time, is because they are viewed from the time when the judgment is to be executed.

his queen Semiramis in Chaldea after Nimrod had made Babel the beginning of his kingdom (Gen. 10:10). The Baal and Astarte worship to which we have made reference in connection with Jezebel, sprang from the ancient Chaldean system. The nations had drunk of the wine of Babylon and had become intoxicated (Jer. 51:7). It was in this original Babel cult that the worship of a trinity of father, mother and son was initiated, the mother being regarded as the queen of heaven. That place she retained among the nations under such names as Astarte, among the Syrians; Diana, among the Ephesians; Aphrodite, among the Greeks; Venus, among the Romans; Isis, among the Egyptians. Israel itself was corrupted into worshiping the queen of heaven (Jer. 7:18; 44:17–25), and later the same Eastern source affected Christianity in the establishment of the worship of the Virgin Mary.

From Babylon to Rome

The Chaldean religion was transferred to Rome in the following way. After the capture of Babylon by the Medo-Persians, under Cyrus, in 539 B.C., the tonsured priests of the Chaldean cult, still unchanged in its character from the time of its inception in the days of Nimrod and Semiramis, were expelled. They fled to what is now Asia Minor, where they were welcomed by the Lydian king and established with all their ritual at his capital, Pergamos. Satan thus transferred thither the seat of his power ("Satan's throne," Rev. 2:13, R.V.). In 133 B.C., on the death of Attalus III, the last of the Lydian kings, his kingdom, and the Chaldean hierarchy with it, passed under the dominion the Romans. In the next century Julius Caesar removed the priests and all their ritualistic equipment to Rome, so as to enhance the glory of the office he already held as Pontifex Maximus, or "Chief Pontiff," of the pagan religion of Rome. Combining in himself political and religious authority, as both Imperator and Pontifex, he was now not only dictator of the republic, but also the recognized head of the Romanized oriental priesthood. Thus Rome became the seat of the Babylonish abominations. This was the satanic preparation for the corruption of the Christian religion when, having already declined from its apostolic purity, it found its ecclesiastical center in Rome. In this manner Rome became "Mystery Babylon." The vast political power of Rome had thus been mounted by the Babylonish woman before Christ appeared, and, at her instigation, the whole machinery of the empire was eventually set in motion to crush His true church.

What has been said above, then, provides the explanation of the fact that not only is the woman named "Mystery, Babylon the Great, the Mother of the Harlots and of the abominations of the earth," but also, in the interpretation at the end of the chapter, is identified with Rome, "the great city which reigneth over the kings of the earth" (v. 18).

Her Intoxication

The apostle saw the woman "drunken with the blood of the martyrs of Jesus" (v. 6). Everything that has been and is represented by mystic Babylon is chargeable with the slaughter of saints of God. The same spirit that leads men to the spiritual abominations of setting up any other object of worship than the true God, likewise instigates them to the persecution of His people. While the political rulers of the earth, allured by the woman's pomp and grandeur, are intoxicated by the wine of the cup of her abominations, she herself is intoxicated by the blood of the true followers of Christ.

The Woman and the Beast

Again, the woman was seen sitting on a scarlet-colored, seven-headed, tenhorned beast. It will be beyond the scope of our immediate subject to go fully into the details of the latter.*

In the interpretation the beast is indicated as the ultimate federal head of the ten-kingdomed league of nations. A comparison of the details of this seventeenth chapter with the thirteenth, and with Daniel 7, shows that the term "beast" is symbolic both of the monarch

*See "The Roman Empire in Prophecy," and "The Mysteries of Scripture," by the same writer.

and of his dominion (cp. Dan. 7, v. 17 with v. 23), and that his dominion will consist of the resuscitated Roman power in this altered form. That the woman is seen riding the beast clearly sets forth the domination of the ecclesiastical system centering in Rome over the political federation of nations. The ecclesiastical power has dominated the civil in separate kingdoms in past history, but at no time has it exercised its power over a league of federated nations. The fulfillment of the vision is yet future. It is true that the Romish religion has received severe checks and setbacks in the past, but it is nowhere decadent or dying today. Its converts are multiplying in almost every country, and its power is far from being on the wane. The woman will yet occupy, though only for a brief time, a position of religious and political domination over the nations comprised in what was the ancient empire. She not only rides the beast, she sits "upon many waters," which are interpreted as "peoples and multitudes and nations and tongues." That is to say, besides controlling the ten-kingdomed league with its rulers, she exercises her influence over the masses of the people.

Her Destruction

Her doom, however, is sealed. Her destruction is destined to take place at the hands of the very potentates who will have supported her. The change in the situation is dramatic. "The ten horns which thou sawest, and the beast [not "upon" the beast as in A.V.], these shall hate the harlot, and shall make her desolate and naked, and shall eat her flesh, and shall burn her utterly with fire" (v. 16). How this will actually transpire is made clear in the thirteenth chapter. The two beasts, the confederate world rulers there mentioned, will establish a religion coextensive with their universal dominion. Its creed will be simple but absolute. The emperor must be acknowledged as God. Refusal will be punished by death. "And he deceiveth them that dwell on the earth by reason of the signs which it was given him to do in the sight of the beast; saying to them that dwell on the earth, that they should make an image to the beast, who hath the stroke of the sword, and lived. And it was given unto him to give breath to it, even to the image of the beast, that the image of the beast should both speak, and cause that as many as should not worship the image of the beast should be killed" (Rev. 13:14, 15, R.V.). The power at the disposal of these two potentates will be sufficient for the enforcement of this worship. Every other religion must be crushed, Romanism included.

Various movements amidst humanity are today directly preparing for this. A striking illustration of the manner in which the woman is to be destroyed has taken place in Russia. Atheistic Communism is spreading its influence rapidly throughout the world. Its institutions are working in practically every nation. The idea of God and the Christian religion are to be overthrown. Man is to be his own savior and master. Within the pale of Christendom, in the congregations of those who dissent from Rome, rationalism and modernism are playing their part toward the same end. The issue of it all is clear from Scripture. The ruling potentates of the ten-kingdomed league, having committed their power to the Antichrist, will with him destroy popery and everything else that is associated with mystic Babylon. Its ecclesiastical possessions, with all its vast wealth and treasures, will be confiscated, its ritualistic paraphernalia given to destruction, its cathedrals, churches, and other idolatrous fanes demolished, and those who refuse to acknowledge the new worship slaughtered. The woman will be made "desolate," stripped of her wealth; "and naked," stripped of her finery; they will "eat her flesh," she will be deprived of her power; "and shall burn her utterly with fire," she will be reduced to utter social and political ruin. The divine decree has gone forth. The human instruments will be ready at the appointed time; "for God did put in their hearts to do His mind, and to come to one mind, and to give their kingdom unto the beast, until the words of God should be accomplished" (v. 17, R.V.).

CHAPTER THREE

The Woman Arrayed with the Sun

We are now to consider the two other women depicted in the Apocalypse. Their character is entirely different from those which have been before us in the preceding pages. The first is described in the twelfth chapter. This chapter really has its beginning in the last verse of chapter eleven. "The temple of God was opened in heaven, and the ark of His covenant was seen therein," details which, taken with the context, indicate that what follows has to do with the nation of Israel. Indeed the twelfth, thirteenth and fourteenth chapters are to be taken together, and carry us through affairs connected with that nation from the time of the birth of Christ till the end of the Great Tribulation and the overthrow of Antichrist by the Son of man.

The apostle was shown a great sign in heaven, "a woman arrayed with the sun, and the moon under her feet, and upon her head a crown of twelve stars; and she was with child, and she crieth out, travailing in birth, and in pain to be delivered. And there was seen another sign in heaven; and behold, a great red dragon, having seven heads and ten horns, and upon his head seven diadems. And his tail draweth the third part of the stars of heaven, and did cast them to the earth: and the dragon stood before the woman which was about to be delivered, that when she was delivered, he might devour her child. And she was delivered of a son, a man-child, who is to rule all the nations with a rod of iron: and her child was caught up unto God, and unto His throne" (Rev. 12:1–5, R.V.).

The Sun, Moon, and Stars

That she was arrayed with the sun, possibly points to the nation's being under the protecting power of God; that is directly set forth subsequently in the chapter. That the moon (an emblem of derived authority) is seen under her feet, indicates that the power she might have exercised under God has gone from her, and that at the time in view in the vision she is in a position of subjection to her foes. At the same time there is a suggestion that she is yet to be possessed of supreme authority on the earth. The first mention of the sun, moon and stars in the Bible is in connection with the government of the earth (Gen. 1:16). The crown of twelve stars indicates the glory and universality of the administration which God has determined for His chosen nation. He has said, "I will make . . . her that was cast far off a strong nation, and the Lord shall reign over them in Mount Zion from henceforth even forever, and thou, O tower of the flock, the hill of the daughter of Zion, unto thee shall it come; yea, the former dominion shall come, the kingdom of the daughter of Jerusalem" (Mic. 4:7, 8).

The Great Tribulation

Using the analogy of childbirth, Isaiah uttered a prediction concerning Israel which provides a key to the present passage. In connection with the birth of Christ in the nation, and the still future time of the Great Tribulation, "the time of Jacob's trouble," the prophet foretold that the historical order would be the reverse of the natural process of generation. Of Israel he says: "Before she travailed, she brought forth; before her pain came, she was delivered of a man-child. Who hath heard such a thing? Who hath seen such a thing?" Then as to the fact that a remnant of the nation will be preserved through the time of trouble and brought into millennial glory, he continues: "Shall a land be born in one day? Shall a nation be brought forth at once? For as soon as Zion travailed she brought forth her children. Shall I bring to the birth, and not cause to bring forth? saith the Lord. Shall I that cause to bring forth shut the womb? saith thy God." The Lord thus assures His people Israel that they shall be completely and suddenly delivered from their relentless foes, and that, though the nation will be largely depopulated, "a remnant shall be saved." That the time is millennial is clear from the joyous predictions that follow: "Rejoice ye with Jerusalem, and be glad for her, all ye that love her . . . rejoice for joy with her, all ye that mourn over her. . . . For thus saith the Lord, Behold I will extend peace to her like a river, and the glory of the nations like an overflowing stream . . . as one whom his mother comforteth, so will I comfort you, and ye shall be comforted in Jerusalem . . . and the hand of the Lord shall be known toward His servants, and He will have indignation against His enemies" (Is. 66:7–14).

The Man-Child

As to the man-child, the same prophet had given the divine assurance to the nation that it should give birth to the One who would break the yoke of its enemies and be its deliverer: "For unto us a Child is born, unto us a Son is given; and the government shall be upon His shoulder: and His name shall be called Wonderful, Counselor, Mighty God, Everlasting Father, the Prince of Peace. Of the increase of His government and peace there shall be no end, upon the throne of David, and upon His kingdom, to establish it, and to uphold it with judgment and with righteousness from henceforth and even forever. The zeal of the Lord of hosts shall perform this" (Is. 9:6, 7, R.V.). Micah speaks of the same events without referring to the inversion of the natural process in the analogy. He specifies the tribe into which the man-child would be born, and the place of His birth: "But thou, Bethlehem Ephratah, which art little to be among the thousands of Judah, unto thee shall One come forth unto me that is to be Ruler in Israel; Whose goings forth are from of old, from everlasting. Therefore will He give them up, until the time that she which travaileth hath brought forth: then the residue of His brethren shall return unto the children of Israel" (Mic. 5:2, 3).

The woman, then, seen in the vision given to the apostle, is Israel, and the man-child of whom she was delivered is Christ. So the apostle Paul, speaking of his own nation, says: "Of whom is Christ as concerning the flesh" (Rom. 9:5). He was not brought forth by the Church, be it noted, for the church springs from Him. The woman "was delivered of a Son, a Man-Child" (v. 5, R.V.), when Christ was born in Bethlehem—long anterior to the time of her travail, for that is yet to take place at the close of the present age. He it is who "is to rule all the nations with a rod of iron," as Jehovah had declared in the second Psalm: "Yet I have set My King upon My holy hill of Zion. I will tell of the decree: the Lord said unto Me, Thou art My Son; this day have I begotten Thee. Ask of Me, and I will give Thee the nations for Thine inheritance, and the uttermost parts of the earth for Thy possession. Thou shalt break them with a rod of iron; Thou shalt dash them in pieces like a potter's vessel" (Ps. 2:6–9).* The description given of Him as a "man-child" is suggestive of His perfect humanity, in virtue of which, or, to use His own words, "because He is the Son of man," "the Father gave Him authority to execute judgment" (John 5:27).

The Dragon

The vision next reveals the arch-adversary of God and His people. "And there was seen another sign in heaven; and behold, a great red dragon, having seven heads and ten horns, and upon his heads seven diadems. And his tail draweth the third part of the stars of heaven, and did cast them to the earth." These details are symbolic of his control over, and its effects upon, the Roman Empire, especially in its final and yet future phases, under the power of which, at his instigation, the Jewish nation is to suffer its last woes. The consideration of these details lies beyond our present subject.

"And the dragon stood before the woman

*Some would associate the church with Christ in the interpretation of the man-child. While several details are true of the church as well as of Christ, there is no direct indication that the symbolism refers here to more than Christ Himself.

which was about to be delivered, that when she was delivered, he might devour her child." The failure of his effort, intimated here by the absence of any further reference to it, is recorded in the Gospel of Matthew, in the account of the futile attempt of Herod to destroy the infant Christ. Instead, after all things concerning the days of His flesh and His resurrection were accomplished, "her child was caught up to God and unto His throne." This statement, actually fulfilled when Christ ascended, is reminiscent of His own words, "I also overcame, and sat down with My Father in His throne" (3:21).*

The Flight of the Woman

The vision now carries us, in point of time, from that event to the efforts of the devil against the Jewish people at the end of this age. He had been unable, in spite of numerous attempts, to prevent the Son of God from accomplishing his irremediable defeat at Calvary, and thereby, potentially, his everlasting destruction; his final premillennial effort will be against the nation, through the instrumentality of which Christ became the man-child.

"The woman fled into the wilderness, where she hath a place prepared of God, that there they may nourish her a thousand two hundred and threescore days" (v. 6). The subject of her flight and of the effort of the dragon against her is continued in verse 13. The parenthetic passage, from verses 7 to 12, indicates the time of these events. That passage describes the casting out of Satan the dragon from the heavenly places, a sphere in which his activities are as yet partly carried on (Eph. 6:12). Since his energies will then be confined to the earth, its godless inhabitants will be given over to the last premillennial woes, and a great voice in heaven declares that the time of the kingdom of God and the authority of His Christ has come. That proclamation is a time-indicator. The flight of the woman is to take place during the Great Tribulation. At that time, that which nationally corresponds to the symbolism of the woman will consist of the godly remnant of Israel, who are to be preserved alive through the time of extreme national distress and peril under the dragon's persecution. Then it is that the woman flees to the wilderness, as previously mentioned in verse 6. "There were given to her the two wings of the great eagle." God had borne His people "on eagle's wings" when they fled from Pharaoh into the wilderness of Sinai (Ex. 19:4; Deut. 32:12). So now the same metaphor describes His care in preserving them from the final fury of Satan. The eagle's wings are suggestive of swift escape and certain deliverance.

She is nourished "for a time, and times, and half a time," a period identical with the 1260 days of verse 6. For this period the Great Tribulation is destined to last (Dan. 7:25; 12:7). The time is the same as the latter part of the 70th week, or period of seven years, in Daniel 9. That the "times" are years is clear by comparison with Daniel 4:23. The one description views the period in its smaller divisions of days, the other in its broader divisions. God, who views things in their whole scope, takes into His view at the same time the minutest details.

The Place of Her Refuge

God has a place prepared as a temporary refuge for the Jewish remnant, "a shelter in the time of storm." That the locality is a wilderness suggests the absence of natural resources. Scripture has given intimation as to the region. East of Judaea, on the far side of Jordan and the Dead Sea, there lies a remarkable district occupied in ancient times by the nations of Edom, Moab and Ammon. The territory contains mountain fastnesses of an extraordinary character, hollowed out by gigantic gorges and chasms, occasionally broadening out into areas of considerable size, though still surrounded by lofty perpendicular cliffs. In some of these wide hollows lie the ruins of famous ancient cities, the most famous of which was Petra. Along the sides of the gorges there are caverns and tombs of enormous size, many of them artistically constructed, the whole of these gorges and recesses being sufficient altogether to provide accommodation for hundreds of thousands of inhabitants. The

*When the church is caught up it will not be to His Father's throne; see 1 Thessalonians 4:17.

ornamentation and sculpture give evidence of an attainment to a high degree of art, and suggest that the population, while secure from foes, lived in comparative ease and luxury. The nature of the locality is such that people could today take shelter there in immunity from the power of modern implements of war, safe even from the mightiest guns and the deadliest gases.

Now it is significant that the prophecies in the eleventh chapter of Daniel relating to the warfare of the end of the present age, the time of the Great Tribulation, predict that this very region is to be delivered from the attacks of the king of the north. "These shall be delivered out of his hand, even Edom and Moab, and the chief of the children of Ammon" (Dan. 11:41). Again, coincidentally with this, our Lord, foretelling events of the same period, and predicting the tyrannical acts of the Antichrist, gave warning that the people of Judaea should then flee to the same district. "When therefore," He says, "ye see the abomination of desolation, which was spoken of by Daniel the prophet, standing in the holy place (let him that readeth understand), then let them that are in Judaea flee unto the mountains" (Matt. 24:15, 16)—obviously the mountains lying to the east and southeast.

It has been pointed out that an army, attempting to cross from Judaea to this district, would have to traverse a sandy plain several miles wide, frequently the scene of sudden and terrific sandstorms of such violence as to render military movements impossible. It is not difficult to conceive how comparatively simple would be the fulfillment of that part of John's vision recorded in Revelation 12:15, 16, following upon the flight of the woman into the wilderness from the face of the serpent: "and the serpent cast out of his mouth after the woman water as a river, that he might cause her to be carried away by the stream. And the earth helped the woman, and the earth opened her mouth, and swallowed up the river which the dragon cast out of his mouth." The language is of course symbolic. The actual fulfillment, political and military, is known to God.

To whatever these details may actually refer, the godly remnant of the Jews, so frequently spoken of in the Psalms and the prophets, would be able to dwell in this region, under the care of Jehovah, literally, "in the secret place of the Most High," passing the night of the Great Tribulation "under the shadow of the Almighty" (Ps. 91:1). Their defense would be "the munitions of rocks." God's people would find here "a stronghold to the needy in his distress, a refuge from the storm, a shadow from the heat, when the blast of the terrible ones is as a storm against the wall" (Is. 25:4). The whole of this passage, from Isaiah 24:16 to the end of chapter 25, should be read in this connection. It speaks of the judgment which immediately precedes the Millennium and of the deliverance of God's people at that time.

There are numerous passages in the Old Testament which foretell, in language confirmatory of what we have been setting forth, the circumstances relating to God's protection of His people in the manner indicated. There may indeed be a prophetic import, relative to these events, in the fact that here David hid his father and mother while being pursued by King Saul (1 Sam. 22:3, 4). Cp. Isaiah 16:4, "Let Mine outcasts dwell with thee, Moab; be thou a covert to them from the face of the spoiler."

The Rest of the Jews

Baffled in his attempt to destroy the woman, the dragon, with increased wrath, goes away to make war "with the rest of her seed, which keep the commandments of God and hold the testimony of Jesus" (v. 17). Judging from the Lord's prophecies as recorded in Matthew 24:15–22, there will be a considerable number in the nation who are not included amongst those who flee to the mountains. Comparing this passage with what is set forth in Revelation 11 concerning the testimony of the two witnesses, we may gather that a multitude of Jews will by this time have turned to God as a result of their ministry and will be expectantly anticipating the appearing of Christ in glory. They would, therefore, properly be described as those "who keep the commandments of God and hold the testimony of Jesus," in contradistinction to those people who will own allegiance to, and obey the commands of, the Antichrist. The "testimony [or witness] of Jesus" is to be put into connection with verses 3–7 of the preceding chapter. It is especially a testimony given to the two witnesses there mentioned, of whom it is said that, when they had finished their testimony, "the beast that cometh up out of the abyss shall make war with them, and overcome them and kill them." We may reasonably conclude that these two witnesses are amongst "the rest of her seed" spoken of in chapter 12:17, and that the objects of Satan's malignity will be all God-fearing Jews in whatever part of the world they are found.

The vision passes. No more is seen of the woman. We do not even find in the remainder of the book of Revelation the definite mention of the establishment of the children of Israel in the land of Palestine, for it is not the specific object of the Apocalypse to describe this. The millennial blessedness of the nation as symbolized by the woman is there by implication. That God has determined to deliver His people Israel, and restore them to communion with Himself, with their Messiah reigning over them in peace and righteousness, and associating them with Himself in His sovereignty over the nations, is clearly foretold in many other Scriptures. Michael, who is spoken of in this twelfth chapter as defeating Satan and his angels, and driving them out of heaven (vv. 7–9), was described in the book of Daniel as "the great prince which standeth for the children of thy people" (Dan. 12:1), and the divine promise made to that prophet was "at that time [the time of unprecedented trouble, v. 1] thy people shall be delivered, every one that shall be found written in the book." The number of the children of Israel shall yet be "as the sand of the sea, which cannot be measured nor numbered; and it shall come to pass that, in the place where it was said unto them, Ye are not My people, it shall be said unto them, Ye are the sons of the Living God" (Hos. 1:10).

CHAPTER FOUR

The Bride the Lamb's Wife

We now turn to consider the last of the women mentioned in this book. The vision is one of undimmed glory. No adverse power is present. There is no dark background of suffering and persecution. Here we are brought to the closing presentation of one of the greatest subjects of Scripture. Previously it has been set forth in various ways, by illustration and type, by prophecy and doctrine; now it constitutes the final vision given to the beloved apostle. Here Christ is seen with His bride in all her beauty and glory. It is His glory that shines in her. His enemy who had assiduously sought to prevent her very existence and to thwart the divine purposes of Him who died to make her His own and hereafter to consummate her union with Himself, has been hurled to his doom. His subtlety and fierce antagonism have only served to enhance the glory and increase the blessedness of this union, and to show forth the power and grace of God who designed it.

A Change of Vision

It must have been a great relief to the apostle, after all that he had seen in prophetic vision, of upheaval and disaster, of fearful conflict and divine judgments, consequent upon the breaking of the Seven Seals, now to survey the scene of unclouded glory, which he describes in the latter part of chapter twenty-one and the beginning of chapter twenty-two. One of the seven angels who had taken his part in emptying the bowls of divine wrath at the last premillennial judgment on the foes of God, comes to give a message of joy and cheer to the wondering seer. It was one of those same angels that had shown him the vision of the other woman, the corruptress of the world (17:1-3). Then the invitation was, "Come hither, I will show thee the judgment of the great harlot"; now it is, "Come hither, I will show thee the bride, the wife of the Lamb" (21:9). Then the apostle was carried away in the Spirit into a wilderness, an appropriate locality for that vision of evil; now he is carried away to a great and high mountain, suggestive of strength, stability and permanency. We must mount to lofty heights to see the glory of God. It was when Moses and the elders of Israel had come up into the mount that they saw the glory of the Lord. The dazzling splendor of Christ's transfiguration was to be seen, not down on the plains of earth, but on the mountain's height. John was invited to behold the bride; the angel showed him a city, "that great city, the holy Jerusalem." How striking is the parallel to the vision of the evil woman! She, too, was presented as a city, "the great city which reigneth over the kings of the earth." That was Satan's anticipative imitation of the pure and virtuous woman, the bride of the Lamb, the heavenly city.

Concerning Christ and the Church

We have to go back to the beginnings of human history to see the first intimation of this combination of symbols. Let us see what the Genesis record states about the formation of Eve in this respect. In the Hebrew of Genesis 2:22, the word which means "to make" is purposely set aside and a word denoting "to build" is chosen instead: "the rib which the Lord God had taken from the man builded He into a woman, and brought her unto the man" (see R.V. margin). Here then is the application of the metaphor of building to the formation of her who was created to be a helpmeet for Adam, language anticipative of the words of Christ Himself long after: "I will build My Church" (Matt. 16:18). In the epistle which especially sets forth the union of the church with Christ, the same two figures are employed. The apostle Paul, in the epistle to the Ephesians, uses the metaphor of the city in reference to the church, in chapter 2:19, and then depicts it, in chapter 5, as the bride of Christ, the object of His love. For her He "gave Himself up . . . that He might present the Church to Himself a glorious Church, not having spot or wrinkle or any such thing." The apostle dwells upon the union of husband and wife (5:25–32) to complete his illustration of the union between Christ and the church.

Here then, in Revelation 21, the bride, the Lamb's wife, a symbolism suggestive of the closest relationship and the most intimate love, is also seen as "the Holy City, Jerusalem, coming down out of heaven from God, having the glory of God" (v. 10), an organized community, enjoying fellowship and association under the authority of the Lord. The next words have frequently been understood as if they referred directly to the light of the city; that is because the word *phōstēr,* which means "light-giver," has been translated "light." The margin of the Revised Version "luminary," gives the correct rendering. Christ Himself is in view. He it is who is described in the statement, "her Light [-giver] was like unto a Stone most precious, as it were a jasper stone, clear as crystal." He is the source of her light. The city owes all her glory to Him. He is the precious stone. The jasper sets forth the various traits of His character in their perfect combination.

The words "clear as crystal" represent one verb in the original, and may be translated more literally "crystallizing": that is to say, the stone is described not merely as clear as crystal itself, it has a crystallizing power. Christ imparts beauty to His redeemed, He makes His church resplendent with His own glory. In shining out upon creation she reflects His light, setting forth His character and attributes.

The Lamb and the Stone

The association of the figurative use of the Lamb and the stone, in reference to Christ, is frequent in Scripture. All that in His relationship to the church He is as the stone, emblematic of strength and stability as a foundation, as well as of ornamental splendor, is due to His sacrifice at Calvary as the Lamb of God. The reader will find profit in comparing in this respect the following Scriptures, which are but few among many: 1 Samuel 7:9, 12, which narrates how Samuel first took a sucking lamb for the whole burnt offering, as a preparation for victory over the Philistines, and then, after the conflict, a stone, to which he gave the name Ebenezer, as a celebration of victory accomplished; Psalm 118:22–27, where the psalmist sings both of the sacrifice to be bound to the altar and of the stone which is become the Head of the corner. So in 1 Peter 1:19, with 2:4–7, where the apostle first speaks of the value of the precious blood of Christ as of a Lamb without blemish and without spot, and then of His preciousness as the chief cornerstone. Again, the apostle Paul, in Ephesians 2:13, 30, speaks of the union of believers both Jew and Gentile in being made nigh together by the blood of Christ, and then represents them as being builded together upon the same foundation, "Christ Jesus Himself being the Chief Cornerstone."

The Wall and the Gates

The twelfth verse of Revelation 21 continues the description of the city, and the words, "having a wall great and high," are to be connected with the beginning of verse 11. The wall is emblematic of defense and security. There are twelve gates with twelve angels standing at them. The angels are associated with the church, though they never could form part of it. They have, for almost two thousand years, been learning by means of the church the wisdom and grace of God (Eph. 3:10 with 1 Cor. 11:10), and throughout the Millennium they will rejoice in witnessing the glories of the completed union between Christ and His bride.

On the gates are written the names of the twelve tribes of Israel. In Eastern cities the gate was the place where the elders sat to administer judgment. The name on the gate was not descriptive of the city itself, but of a locality outside it, suggesting that the said locality was under the influence of the city. Thus in the earthly Jerusalem, for example, there are the Jaffa Gate and the Damascus Gate. That the names of the tribes of Israel are on the gates of the heavenly city signifies that judgment over Israel will be administered by some who form part of the church. This is just what our Lord told His apostles. "When the Son of man," He said, "shall sit on the throne of His glory, ye also shall sit upon twelve thrones, judging the twelve tribes of Israel" (Matt. 19:28). The thrones of the apostles will not be literally and materially set up on the earth in the Millennium, for they themselves are part of the church. Their authority will therefore be exercised from the heavenlies.

There are three gates on each of the four sides of the city, for in the Millennium with Israel ruling over the whole world, the influence of the church will proceed in every direction. Again, the wall has twelve foundation stones, and on them are the names of the twelve apostles. This is not a matter of the administration of judgment, but of the foundation of the city itself, for the church is built upon the foundation of the apostles and prophets; that is to say, on the foundations of divine truth laid by them (Eph. 2:20). These foundations are adorned with all manner of precious stones, symbolic of the glories of the Lord Jesus and of the church in association with Him, as set forth in other Scriptures.

The adornment is not something additional to the foundation stones, as in the case of ordinary buildings, but forms an essential part of the foundation itself. The glories of the Lord, made known by the truths of Holy Scripture, will be revealed in perfection in the very church herself as well as through her instrumentality.

The Measurement

The city, the gates, and the wall were measured with a golden reed, indicative of a righteous and infallible judgment. But more than this, the very fact of the measurement indicates the preciousness to God of that which is measured. Compare chapter 11:1, which describes the measurement of the temple of God in Jerusalem, and the altar and the worshipers, all as being precious to God and set apart for His service and glory amidst the confusion of earth at that time. See again Psalm 16, where Christ, speaking of the saints as His "goodly heritage," says that "the measuring lines are fallen unto Him in pleasant places," a statement expressive of the infinite value to Him of His redeemed people (v. 6).

The angel measured the city "as far as twelve thousand furlongs." It is not necessary to understand by the preposition *epi,* "as far as," that the measurement is incomplete, though that may possibly be so, especially if the suggestion is that an angel cannot comprehend all the glories of the church. The preposition may, however, simply serve to emphasize the enormous dimensions of the city. The length and breadth and height of it are equal. Probably, in the vision given to John, the city was in the shape of a pyramid. In verse 17, which describes the height of the wall as 144 cubits, and this as being "the measure of a man, that is, of an angel," there is perhaps a suggestion that an angel can comprehend all that is conveyed by the wall, the protective outworks of the city, in contrast to the infinite wonders of God's grace as set forth in the structure of the city itself. A finite mind, whether of man or angel, can grasp the one, the other is comprehended only by God.

Its Temple

The city itself is "of pure gold, like unto pure glass" (v. 18, R.V.), while the street of the city is "like unto pure gold, as it were transparent glass." The gold exhibits the glory of divine righteousness. The city and the street are not only free from defilement, but therein are seen all the perfections of God's character as exhibited in Christ. There is no temple in the city, "for the Lord God Almighty and the Lamb are the temple thereof." There is no need to enter a sanctuary, for there God is publicly seen in Christ. For this reason no created light, as of the sun or moon, is required; the uncreated light of God irradiates the city. "The lamp thereof is the Lamb." That is to say, the light that shines does so as the outcome of the sacrifice of Calvary. The nations of earth will walk by the light of it (R.V., margin), and the kings of the earth will bring their glory into it. They cannot bring their material wealth into it, for it is heavenly, but they will acknowledge its glory, submit to its rule, and pay homage to Him whose city it is.

Entrance into It

All who have resurrection bodies, apart from those who constitute the church itself, will have free entry into the city; that is to say, there will be complete fellowship between those who symbolically constitute the city itself and those who have access to it. To use the somewhat imperfect illustration of an earthly city, there are those who, as its permanent residents, constitute its citizenship, and those who, as visitors, enjoy association with and the privileges of the citizens themselves. Those who have the right to enter into the heavenly city, that is to say, those who in resurrection life enjoy fellowship with the church, have their names written in the Lamb's Book of Life (v. 27).

The River and the Tree

It is a pity that a break was made by introducing chapter twenty-two here. The first five verses of the twenty-second chapter are a completion of the twenty-first. The apostle is now shown "a river of water of life, bright as crystal," which proceeds from the throne of God and of the Lamb. This is apparently symbolical of all the blessings that come from the Father and the Son by the Holy Spirit. Where God's throne is from thence flow streams of water, for He who is universally sovereign is the source of every blessing (see Ezek. 47:1; Joel 3:18; Zech. 14:8). "There is a river the streams whereof make glad the city of God, the Holy Place of the tabernacles of the Most High" (Ps. 46:4). Wherever the sovereignty of God is acknowledged, and wherever God Himself is worshiped, there His worshipers receive blessing. The river refreshes the city itself. Jesus said, "The water that I shall give him shall become in him a well of water springing up unto everlasting life" (John 4:14). The river also flows on to minister refreshment to others, and so it will be the joy of the church to be the channel of blessing to all the subjects of the wide kingdom of God.

On both sides of the river is the Tree of Life yielding fruit every month. All spiritual fruit comes from Christ. He is the Tree of Life. There will be no cherubim to guard the way. The tree will be of free access to all—it grows on either side of the river. The divine restrictions necessarily laid down in Eden, and the curse pronounced when man fell, will be forever removed. The fruit of the tree will impart delight and refreshment to all those who constitute the city, and to all who have access to it, for Christ will forever continue to minister of Himself to all His saints in glory. The leaves of the tree will be for the healing of the nations, so that from Christ Himself, through the instrumentality of the heavenly city, the nations of earth will not only receive their administration and their light, but also the undoing of the works of the devil and all the havoc he has wrought among them.

His Name in Their Foreheads

The servants of God and of the Lamb "shall do Him service and see His face, and His name shall be in their foreheads." Their capacity to serve then will depend upon their faithfulness now, and their sphere of service then will be determined by their rewards for service rendered now. There will be unbroken communion between Him and them, and they will unfailingly show forth His glory, presenting in perfection all the traits of His character. Those who look upon them will at once recognize Christ in them. Finally, those who constitute the city will reign with Christ forever and ever.

This beautiful city, then, with all that is set forth in the symbolism of this passage, is "the bride, the Lamb's wife." She it is who is to share His sovereign power. How striking the contrast in this closing prophecy of her reign with Him forever and ever, to what is set forth in the case of the woman in chapter seventeen, who sought to reign, and so successfully for a time, in her self-assumed pride and glory, over the kings and the inhabitants of the earth! May the wonders of our soon-to-be-realized glory in union with our blessed Lord and Redeemer, as set forth so vividly in this final vision of Holy Scripture, stimulate us the more earnestly to look for, and the more ardently to love, His appearing, and the more devotedly to present ourselves to Him for the service here of Him who loved us and gave Himself for us, that He might hereafter present us to Himself, "without spot or wrinkle, or any such thing."

The Sealed Book of the Apocalypse

▪ FOREWORD ▪

As the day draws near when we, like John, shall see in the hands of the one upon the throne the seven-sealed book, and hear the challenge to open it, which only one can accept—our Redeemer, the Lion of Judah, the Lamb once slain—and shall see Him opening those seals one by one and directing the unparalleled scenes of judgment portrayed for us in the Apocalypse, our hearts should surely be moved to make the utmost use of the little time that remains of the day of grace in which our lot is cast.

We may praise God that the book is still sealed, and in the meantime seek by His grace to judge the condition of things through which we are now passing, in the light of the judgment in which we find they are to end, and seek to be amongst those who "purify themselves and make themselves white and are refined."

We can also praise Him that when the seals are opened we shall be with Him who opens them, and be in full accord then with the judgments through which this poor world will pass ere creation is delivered from its bondage and corruption, and the kingdom of this world becomes "the kingdom of our Lord and His Christ."

W. R. Lewis

The Sealed Book of the Apocalypse

Scripture

"And I saw in the right hand of Him that sat on the throne a book written within and on the back, close sealed with seven seals. And I saw a strong angel proclaiming with a great voice, Who is worthy to open the book, and to loose the seals thereof; And no one in the heaven, or on the earth, was able to open the book, or to look thereon. And I wept much, because no one was found worthy to open the book, or to look thereon: and one of the elders saith unto me, Weep not: behold, the Lion that is of the tribe of Judah, the Root of David, hath overcome, to open the book and the seven seals thereof. And I saw in the midst of the throne and of the four living creatures, and in the midst of the elders, a Lamb standing as though it had been slain, having seven horns, and seven eyes, which are the seven Spirits of God, sent forth into all the earth. And He came, and He taketh it out of the right hand of him that sat on the throne. And when He had taken the book, the four living creatures and the four and twenty elders fell down before the Lamb, having each one a harp, and golden bowls full of incense, which are the prayers of the saints. And they sing a new song, saying, Worthy art Thou to take the book, and to open the seals thereof: for Thou wast slain, and didst purchase unto God with Thy blood men of every tribe, and tongue, and people, and nation, and madest them to be unto our God a kingdom and priests; and they reign upon the earth" (Rev. 5:1–10. R.V.).

The Judge and His Glory

The Gospel of John presents the Son of God as the world's Savior; the book of the Revelation presents Him as the universal Judge. The first chapter gives a description of Him in that capacity, depicting His perfect righteousness and the unerring character of His estimation. In the second and third chapters He is seen engaged in His work as the Judge of His saints. Judgment begins at the house of God, and consequently these preliminary chapters reveal Him discerning the ways of His servants in the churches with a view to the apportionment of rewards at His judgment seat.

The fourth chapter begins that portion of the book which deals with His judgment of the world. This is to be distinguished entirely from what has preceded. The fourth and fifth chapters describe a scene in heaven preparatory to the execution of judgment in the earth. The fourth presents a graphic and awe-inspiring description of the throne, its occupant, the symbols of the judgment about to issue from it, and the attendant worshipers and their worship. The fifth chapter, continuing the scene, brings Christ into view as the only person qualified to act as the judge of the world. At first, however, the book is seen in the right hand of God, close sealed with its seven seals, and there appears to be no possibility of the disclosure of its contents. The mention of the apparent absence of anyone worthy to open it prepares the way for the revelation of Him who alone is worthy. His glories are thrown into all the stronger light by the loud proclamation of the angel, "Who is worthy to open the book, and to loose the seals thereof"; and by the statement that no one in the wide universe was able to do so, or even to look on the book. The effect of this on the apostle was to fill him with grief. His sorrow, however, was soon turned to joy.

The Lion and the Lamb

It was one of the elders who said to him, "Weep not! behold, the Lion that is of the tribe of Judah, the Root of David, hath overcome, to open the book and the seven seals thereof." The elders are representative of those, both of this and former ages, who have a knowledge of the ways of God in Christ. That Christ is here called "the Lion that is of the tribe of Judah" and "the Root of David" indicates that the contents of the sealed book have to do particularly with the Jews, and this we find to be the case as we peruse the subsequent chapters. All that is mentioned of the affairs of the world centers in and around that nation and its city and temple.

The apostle beholds, in the midst of the throne, a Lamb. There is a solemn significance attaching to this title in view of the impending judgment. The sacrifice which was provided for the expiation of sins, and which forms the basis of the gospel of God's grace, must hereafter prove the doom of those who trample upon the blood of Christ. The gospel which proclaims the atoning character of His sacrifice is a savor of death unto death when it does not become a savor of life unto life. The combination of the figurative title, "Lion of Judah," with that of a lamb is very suggestive. The lamb is the emblem of meekness. The wrath of one who is meek is far more terrible than that of a passionate man. Now while Christ is essentially "meek and lowly," He is also essentially full of majesty and strength; He who is the Lamb is also the Lion. How fearful for His foes will be the exercise of His attribute in the latter respect, when divine justice demands that He carry out His "strange work"! The scene depicted in this chapter is a confirmation of the statement of Christ Himself in the days of His flesh, that the Father judgeth no man, but "He hath given all judgment unto the Son, and He gave Him authority to execute judgment, because He is the Son of man," (John 5:22, 27, R.V.).

The God-Man

We should notice that the Revisers have rightly put a comma after the word "overcome." In the original this verb is widely separated from the verb "to open." Emphasis is thus given to the victory of the Cross. There it was that Christ overcame. His Cross was the determining factor in the judgment of the world. "Now," He said, "is the judgment of this world; now shall the prince of this world be cast out" (John 12:31). The Lord stated, as the reason why the Father had committed all judgment into His hands, that He is the Son of man. He it is who through His incarnation combines in Himself the two natures of Godhead and manhood. He is thereby uniquely qualified to act as the judge. Being one in the Godhead with the Father, He has perfect knowledge of the character and the requirements of God; and being perfect man, having passed through human experiences, with all human temptations, sin apart, He has complete knowledge of man. On this account He alone could look on the book and open its seals. By Him and Him only the judgments contained therein can be executed.

His infinite knowledge and power, and all the glory and majesty of His being and position, are seen in the latter part of the fifth chapter to produce the worship not only of the heavenly host but of the whole creation. As the creation has been defiled by sin and brought thereby into the bondage of corruption, so it is to be delivered by the power of the Son of God, in virtue of His atoning work.

The Days of the Son of Man

The sixth chapter introduces the execution of the judgments contained in the sealed book. The period in which these events will transpire is the same as that described by the Lord as "the days of the Son of man" (Luke 17:22), the days, that is to say, when Christ will intervene in the affairs of the world, first by preliminary judgments and then in personal presence. "As it came to pass," He said, "in the days of Noah, even so shall it be also in the days of the Son of man. They ate, they drank, they married, they were given in marriage, until the day that Noah entered into the ark, and the flood came, and destroyed them all. Likewise even as it came to pass in the days of Lot; they ate, they drank, they bought, they sold, they planted, they builded; but in the day that Lot went out from Sodom it rained fire and brimstone from heaven and destroyed them all: after the same manner shall it be in the day that the Son of man is revealed" (vv. 26–30).

Note that He first speaks of "days of the Son of man" and then of "the day that the Son of man shall be revealed." "The days of the Son of man," corresponding to the days of Noah, form the period immediately preceding His appearing in glory, and therefore the time of the judgments spoken of in Revelation 6 and subsequent chapters.

The Church Removed

That the church will be removed prior to the execution of these judgments seems to be indicated by the following considerations:

1. The time referred to is that in which the world will be subject to the wrath of God. The period will therefore differ entirely in character from the present era, which is a time of unparalleled grace and the long-suffering of God. The Church is taught to wait for the Son of God from heaven as the one who "delivereth us from the wrath to come" (1 Thess. 1:10, R.V.). Again, "God hath not appointed us to wrath, but unto the obtaining of salvation through our Lord Jesus Christ" (5:10), a passage which also refers to the Lord's second coming. Further, "We shall be saved from the wrath of God through Him" (Rom. 5:9). These Scriptures clearly show that the church cannot be here during the time when the wrath of God is being executed upon the world in its rebellion under the Antichrist. There have been calamities during the present era which are recognizable as of a divinely retributive character. We must distinguish, however, between these occasional catastrophes and those recorded in the Apocalypse. The latter belong to a period characterized as a time of the wrath of God. The further the judgments proceed the more determined is man's resistance against God (see 9:20).

The Elders

2. In the fourth chapter those who are described as elders (the number 24 is undoubtedly symbolic) are clothed and crowned with crowns of reward *(stephanoi)*. They cannot therefore be in their present spirit-condition. Rewards for faithfulness have been assigned to them. They cannot then be merely the saints of Old Testament times, for the writer of the epistle to the Hebrews says that "apart from us [i.e., the saints of this age] they [the Old Testament saints] are not to be perfected" (Heb. 11:40). They would not therefore be clothed and crowned before those who belong to the church had similarly been clothed and crowned. We conclude accordingly that the fourth chapter describes a scene in which the church is present in the glory with the Lord, the saints who constitute it having received their rewards at the judgment seat of Christ.

Moreover, the company represented by the elders is seen in association with the Son of God in anticipation of the execution of His judgments and the establishment of His kingdom on earth. Their rewards having been given them, they now worship Him in view of His impending interference in the affairs of the world, and His personal intervention for the establishment of His kingdom. They will then come with Him in glory. They are to be identified as those who, in the description of the great event given in chapter nineteen, are seen accompanying Him "clothed in fine linen, white and pure," when He comes in His glorious Advent with the hosts of heaven (19:14). The same event is described by Paul when he says that the Lord Jesus will come "in flaming fire, rendering vengeance to them that know not God, and to them that obey not the gospel . . . when He shall come to be glorified in His saints, and to be marveled at in all them that believed" (2 Thess. 2:8, 10). They are seen "clothed in white raiment" both in chapter 4:4 and in chapter 19:14. They are around the throne in heaven in the former passage before the sealed book is opened, and they come forth with Him when the events recorded under the opening of the seals have transpired on earth. The church is therefore seen to be in heaven after the third chapter.

The Three Parts of the Apocalypse

3. That this is the position of the church in the fourth chapter is confirmed by the arrangement of the whole of the Apocalypse. When John was commissioned to pen the book he was told to write it in three parts "The things which thou sawest, and the things which are, and the things which shall come to pass hereafter [lit., "the things which shall come to pass after these things"]" (1:19).

(1) The things which he had seen he describes in the first chapter;

(2) Plainly, "the things which are" are given in the second chapter and the third. That they were not limited merely to the seven churches as existent in John's time is abundantly evident. The exhortation, "He that hath

an ear, let him hear what the Spirit saith to the churches," which accompanies each letter, is given to all believers. The message given to one of the churches is "Hold fast till I come" (3:25), and to another, "I come quickly: hold fast that which thou hast, that no one take thy crown" (3:11), words which apply to, and are needful for, all churches throughout this era. The return of the Lord, an event yet future, was the *terminus ad quem* to which the churches were directed, the consummating event which would bring to a close their present testimony and service on earth. "The things which are" must therefore relate to the earthly witness and experiences of churches throughout the whole of the era. There are other evidences of this in these two chapters, which we need not here enumerate.

(3) We get at the beginning of chapter four a clear indication of the third portion of the book, containing "the things that shall come to pass after these things." After the completion of the letters to the churches, John heard a voice saying, "Come up hither, and I will show thee *"the things which must come to pass after these things"*; the last clause is practically word for word the same as in chapter 1:19. "After these things," in chapter 4:1, repeated both at the beginning and at the end of the verse, undoubtedly refers to the things recorded in the second and third chapters. Church testimony on the earth has then ceased, and the next part of the book, from chapter four onward, relates to the subsequent affairs in the world.

Distinguishing Features of the Third Part

4. Again, there are several features which characterize the section of the Apocalypse beginning at chapter four, which distinguish it from Scriptures relating to the gospel and the church.

(a) The names of God are those by which He was known in ages previous to the gospel age, as in covenant relation with His earthly people. The title Father does not occur after chapter three, save in chapter 14:1, where it is "His Father"; nowhere is such a phrase found as "our Father," or "our God and Father." This is the more noticeable since to John was committed to unfold, in his gospel and epistles, the Father's name and character.

(b) The throne of God is seen in a very different light in these chapters from that elsewhere in the New Testament. It is not now a throne of grace to which believers draw near to obtain mercy. They are seen around it as worshipers. It is a throne of judgment exercised in vindication of the rights of the Son of God and against rebellious humanity. It is true that the throne has a rainbow around it, but that is a sign of God's covenant with the earth, and is indicative of ultimate mercy in the Millennium.

(c) The way in which Christ is spoken of as a Lamb differs from the way in which He is so represented elsewhere. Nowhere else do we read of "the wrath of the Lamb" (6:16). In chapter 17:14 the Lamb is seen overcoming His foes. The period indicated in these chapters, 4 to 19, must not be confounded with the present time of God's long-suffering mercy, and of gospel testimony by the church. The very word rendered Lamb in the Apocalypse is different from that used elsewhere of the sacrifice of Christ. In other passages it is *amnos,* here it is always *arnion;* this diminutive, expressive of the lowliness and humiliation of the Lord Jesus in His death, serves to set forth in greater contrast the statements of His majesty and power. It is when, as the Lamb, He takes the sealed book that He is also described as the Lion of Judah, and the opening of each seal is an act preparatory to judgment.

(d) This portion of the Apocalypse, since it relates to divine interposition in the affairs of the world, and since prophecy in this respect centers in the nation of Israel, is Jewish in its subject matter and its features. In the sixth chapter those who have been slain are heard crying for vengeance on their persecutors. This is entirely foreign to the attitude of the church, but is consistent with Old Testament history and prophecy relating to Israel and with the so-called imprecatory psalms. In the seventh chapter the 144,000 who are sealed are all of the nation of Israel. The prophecies which follow chapter ten are distinctly said to be "over [i.e., concerning] many peoples and nations, and tongues and kings" (10:11, R.V.), and Jerusalem and its temple immediately come into view, and the two witnesses who are to bear testimony in the Jewish nation during the close of this age. Chapter twelve presents Israel (not the church) under the symbol of a woman arrayed with the sun, and exhibits Satan's antagonism against the nation at the time of the end. The thirteenth chapter shows the human instruments of this satanic malignity, and the conditions of the world under them. Chapter fourteen predicts seven events relating, not to the church, but to the eschatological events of the same period respecting the faithful saints of the time, the nations of the world and the adherents of the Beast. The chapter begins with Mount Zion and ends with the city of Jerusalem. The fifteenth gives another scene in heaven preparatory to the final series of judgments in the earth. These are mentioned in chapters sixteen and nineteen, chapters seventeen and eighteen being parenthetic, relatively to the abominations of Babylon and the kings and leaders of the world. In all this any mention of the church as being on the earth is conspicuous by its absence. It has been rightly said that "the only place in which the church is seen from chapter 4:10 to chapter 19:4 is in heaven."

The Seventieth Week of Daniel 9

A comparison of the prophecies of the book of Daniel and this portion of the Apocalypse shows that what is predicted as about to take place under the breaking of the seven seals belongs to the same period as what is called "The Seventieth Week" of Daniel 9. That "week" is really a "hepdomad," or period of seven years, and is severed off (a literal rendering of the word translated "decreed"—or determined, A.V.—in Dan. 9:24) from the preceding sixty-nine. That prophecy has to do with the Jews and Jerusalem—"thy people and thy city"—and that which relates to the seventieth week is a brief outline beforehand of the events which will transpire under the rule of the Antichrist.

The outline is filled up by other Scriptures, and nowhere in greater detail than in the Apocalypse. A large proportion of the sacred volume concentrates upon the period under consideration, a fact which is suggestive of its extreme importance, as being the culmination of so much that has transpired in human history, and as immediately preceding the millennial reign of Christ. The week, or seven-years' period at the end, is marked by three outstanding events: (a) it begins with the covenant between the Antichrist and the Jews, after their complete political restoration, an agreement which Isaiah calls a "Covenant with Hell"; (b) halfway through the period the covenant will be broken by the Antichrist himself, and this will be followed by the Great Tribulation, a time spoken of in the Daniel 9 passage as one of desolation, and in Jeremiah 30:7 as the "time of Jacob's trouble," the policy of the world powers being the destruction of the Jewish race; (c) these efforts will issue in the overthrow of Antichrist and his colleague, and the forces under him, through the personal intervention of Christ for the deliverance of the nation and the establishment of His kingdom on earth. The prophetic scheme of Revelation 6 to 19 runs parallel to it.

The Opening of the First Seal

Turning now to the sixth chapter we notice that the period is ushered in by the opening of the first seal and the accompanying voice of one of the living ones, saying, "Come"—not "Come and see," as in the A.V.. The utterance is not an invitation to John, but a challenging command calling forth that which has been destined for the occasion. The immediate response is the appearance of a rider on a white horse.

We must distinguish this rider from the one in chapter 19:11. The rider in the latter case is Christ at His Second Advent. The one in chapter six is apparently a satanic anticipatory imitation of Christ, and represents the Antichrist at his accession to power. Whatever revolutionary upheavals or national wars may have given rise to his advent, he himself begins the period of his power in a different way. He wields not a sword, indicative of the carnage of warfare, but a bow, suggestive of conquest carried on at a distance and by the removal of individual opponents. He rides to power by an easily gained series of successes, and, as a satanically endued genius, he attains to leadership over the nations by his attractive personality and by his unprecedented powers of organization.

A Time of Strong Delusion

It would seem from other Scriptures that prior to his advent the world will be in a considerable amount of chaos and confusion owing to revolutions and social and international disturbances.* Gifted with capacities for the rectification of these troubles, he will introduce a brief period of peace, and men will be deceived into thinking that a golden age of permanent prosperity has begun. The days spoken of by the Lord, and referred to above as resembling those of Noah and the times of Lot, will have begun, and people will be planting, building, buying, selling, and marrying and given in marriage, in utter disregard of God. As a result of the covenant between Antichrist and the Jews, that nation, though in utter apostasy from God, will enjoy temporary affluence and power, and their position of completed political restoration will provide a key to international conditions in general.

We are told by the apostle Paul that the world will be given over by God to strong delusion (2 Thess. 2:11). The great potentate who is destined to control the affairs of the world for a brief time, through whom Satan will challenge the claims of the Son of God, will have power to deceive men into thinking that the age of universal peace and safety has been brought in at last. He might explain away even the Rapture of the church by some form of spiritist teaching. Whether or no, the fact that those who belong to the true Church have gone will only lead to the concentration of satanic efforts in the world. Even now the devil is persuading multitudes of religious people in Christendom into thinking that the Second Coming of Christ has already taken place, and that many of the prophecies of this part of the Apocalypse have been fulfilled.

The Other Three Horsemen

In this connection we may briefly refer to the other three horsemen, who appear on the opening of the second and third and fourth seals respectively. It is generally admitted that the significance of the appearance of the rider on the red horse, who wields a great sword, and takes peace from the earth, is that the world is plunged into war; and that the circumstances following the appearance of the rider on the black horse indicate conditions of famine: food is at famine prices, according to verse 6. The opening of the fourth seal, and the appearance of death as the rider on the pale horse, are followed by bloodshed, famine, pestilence, and destruction by wild beasts. All this reveals how, in a preliminary way, God will suddenly interfere with the state of peace and safety brought about by the advent of the Antichrist: "When they are saying peace and safety, then sudden destruction cometh upon them."

We are being told today that these events have already transpired; that the opening of the seals of the book has already begun; that the conditions referred to above have taken place in connection with the Great War, and are still in course of procedure. This is being taught with the aid of a widely advertised film entitled, *The Four Horsemen of the Apocalypse*. We need to be on our guard against this misapplication of Scripture, lest we be led away by the error of the evil one. By causing people to think that the judgments predicted for the coming period under the rule of the Man of Sin have already taken place, Satan is, as we have pointed out, preparing for the deception, the "strong delusion" referred to above.

Russellite Error

The teachings of the so-called International Bible Students' Association, which is another name for Millennial Dawn or Russellite teachings, are that Christ, who is blasphemously said to be only a Spirit, came in 1914, and that the calamities which have occurred, and are occurring, through the recent war and its effects, are the judgments which will issue in the Millennium. The time of universal regeneration is thus said to be near at hand, and therefore "millions now living will never die." There are other teachings by which an attempt is made to show that these prophecies in the

*See *The Roman Empire in the Light of Prophecy,* by the Author (written in 1915).

book of Revelation have had their fulfillment in past history. It is not our purpose to enter into these doctrines now, as they are not so insidious and dangerous as the Millennial Dawn teaching just mentioned.

How easy, when the Rapture of the church takes place, to persuade people that, as Christ (being a Spirit as Russellites say) is here, though unseen, so the thousands who have been suddenly removed are spirits, still here in the world! What an opportunity for Spiritists to advance their cause, and to persuade people that they can communicate through mediums with those who have been removed! Spiritism, Millennial Dawnism, and other forms of error will play their part in explaining the Rapture to satisfy their theories. The great event will seem far less startling to the world than we might at first suppose. Deny that Christ "cometh in the flesh" (see 2 John 7, R.V.), deny bodily resurrection, and the way is open for all sorts of satanic delusion.

Let Christians beware. The period of final judgments spoken of in Revelation 6 to 19 has not yet been ushered in. The time is undoubtedly near. But the disastrous events of the Great War, and the famines, pestilences, and earthquakes which have followed, are not the fulfillment itself. They are premonitory symptoms of what is impending.

The Fifth Seal Opened

After the breaking of the fifth seal the apostle sees underneath the altar the souls of them that had been slain for the Word of God and for the testimony which they held. They are heard crying out for vengeance. As we have mentioned this could not be applied to the church. When read in connection with other Scriptures relating to the period under Antichrist, we get a true view of what is here set forth. It would seem from the seventeenth chapter that the papal system will have acquired an unprecedented measure of world power by the time of the advent of Antichrist. The present indications of this are numerous. In the chapter referred to the woman is seen riding the beast until he and his ten-kingdomed confederacy overthrow and destroy her. The great ecclesiastical system, the travesty of the church of the living God, is doomed to destruction at the hands of combined anti-Christianity. Those mentioned after the opening of the fifth seal will have suffered death under one or other of those two systems, either during their association or after the overthrow of the ecclesiastical. The divine retribution upon the latter is to be meted out at the hands of man; Antichrist will be dealt with by the Son of God Himself.

The Sixth and Seventh Seals

The opening of the sixth seal introduces catastrophes of a still more terrible nature than those which have preceded. Some think that what is here mentioned at the close of the sixth chapter will transpire at the end of the whole period. This is possible. The opening of the seventh seal, however, introduces the events indicated under the blowing of the trumpets and the outpouring of the vials or bowls. The culmination of this is recorded in the nineteenth and twentieth chapters, after the parenthetic chapters seventeen and eighteen, which give the two aspects of Babylon, mystic and literal, and her judgments. The Son of God, invested with His own sovereign rights over the world, comes to overthrow the Beast and the False Prophet, and their assembled armies. Thus "the days of the Son of man," during which He has been acting in judgment from heaven, issue in "The Day." The Jews are delivered, the earth is rid of its anti-God tyrants. The usurper, Satan, whose instruments they were, is bound and shut down in the abyss, and the reign of the King of kings and Lord of lords begins.

The remaining contents of the sealed book disclose the final scene of the Millennium, when Satan is loosed for a season, and man is shown that not even the presence of Christ in sovereign power is sufficient to regenerate the heart; only repentance and faith and the efficacy of His sacrifice can effect that. The last and brief effort of mankind against God under the instigation of the evil one meets with immediate retribution. Satan is cast into the lake of fire. The earth and the heaven flee away. The tribunal of the great white throne is set, the dead are judged thereat, and the new heavens and earth, wherein dwelleth righteousness, are brought into being.

"Here, Babel and corruption,
  Man boasting in his shame;
But there, God's holy city
  His glory shall proclaim.

Here, those who follow Jesus,
  Reproach and shame must bear;
But there, enthroned, the meanest
  A diadem shall wear.

Here, down before his idol
  The heathen bends his knee;
But there, unveiled the glory
  Of God his eyes shall see.

The light of God shall cover
  The earth's wide fields, as spread
The tractless wastes of water
  O'er ocean's spacious bed.

O keep us, Holy Father,
  Keep us for that blest day,
When Jesus' royal scepter
  Holds undisputed sway.

Come, then, all-glorious Savior!
  Thy day bring swiftly nigh,
With foot that doth for fleetness
  The winds of Heaven defy.

Come! End the night of weeping,
  Bring in eternal day;
Come, Thou Bright Star of Morning!
  For this Thy people pray."

—J. BOYD

Special Issues

V

The Evolution Theory in the Light of Genesis

The Evolution Theory in the Light of Genesis

It has been advocated that we should regard the Genesis records of man's creation, innocence and fall as so much folklore, and that we should substitute for them the theory that man has derived his existence by evolutionary development from the apes. In a presidential address given before the British Association, the president declared that the Darwinian controversy had ended in the complete overthrow of the defenders of the biblical account, and in the triumph of Darwin. That was an unwarranted assumption. The president declared that even non-Darwinians were prepared to accept what he called "these facts" when full proofs were forthcoming. Surely that was an admission that something was lacking. The proof, if it is a proof at all, is at once to be acknowledged. As it is still purely theory, it lies in the realm of inference.

At least seven points of similarity were brought forward between the monkey and the man. All these are admitted, but when they are all put together, we are not left with the conclusion that because there are certain similarities the one is derived from the other. If we admit that there is a God who creates, it is as simple a thing for Him to create one hundred thousand species independently as it is to create protoplasm; and it is just as likely, and indeed, more than likely, that He would impart to different species similar elements in consideration of His determining will that they should have similar functions to discharge. Likeness is not to be taken for parentage; resemblance does not necessarily imply descent. Evolutionists have been searching, and are still searching, for a common fatherhood for man and the brute. What they have confronting them all the time is God's common makerhood of the various species.

The speaker at the British Association meeting said: "Our geological search has not produced so far final and conclusive evidence of man's anthropoid origin." So again we are left with inference. We turn from these inferences to ask one or two questions. When was life imparted to the lifeless? When did moral perception arise, and the power to adore the Creator and to bear His image? What has the ape been doing all these centuries? To the first two of these questions, the Genesis record supplies an answer. The statements of the first, second and third chapters have never been refuted. They are made naturally and reasonably, and they are confirmed by every branch of science. Chapter one gives the successive order of divine operations, and these, in that order, are confirmed by investigations in astronomy, geology, horticulture and zoology. Some of the most profound and learned scientists in the world have declared that the accounts given in these chapters of Genesis have corresponding to them that which has been discovered in nature.

The Bible was not written for scientists. It is not a record of man's researches. The Bible, from beginning to end, is the appeal of God to the souls of men. It does not trace for us by gradual unfoldings the idea of God. It presupposes God; it begins with the statement of the existence of God. When we come to this order and we find it stated, with regard to plants and animals, that the creative hand formed each after its own kind, then our conclusions as to the independent acts and formation of the different species are confirmed.

We learn in these chapters in Genesis (and if we were to give heed to the original language and the verbal forms there mentioned, we should see very clearly) that man derived his existence as a distinct and different being by a single act of Almighty God. That he derived his existence by a long continued process, through hundreds or thousands of years, is repugnant both to the language and teaching of Scripture. In the second chapter we find that what God had determined for man in chapter one is given to us in a beautiful setting. In chapter one, God had willed that man should have dominion over the realm of nature around him. In chapter two we see how he is situated in the possession of dominant authority. In chapter three we find how he fell from the place assigned to him by his Maker; and immediately there is a divine intimation as to the means which God would adopt for the redemption and the restoration of this His fallen creature.

The first three chapters form an essential introduction to the whole book. If these early chapters are counted as so much folklore, then discredit is cast upon the rest of the volume. These chapters form one complete section of divine revelation, which is a key to the whole book. Therein we learn the beginning of the scheme of redemption which is unfolded to us, and to which we are brought later on when we face the cross of Calvary. The book directs us in orderly unfoldings to the Redeemer at the Cross, to the life of the regenerate, and to their coming elevation to a position far higher than our first parents enjoyed, to a position of union in resurrection life with Christ Jesus.

But the question turns not merely upon those early chapters themselves, but upon the reference made by our Lord to them. The crux of the whole matter lies in the accuracy and veracity of Christ. The question was asked our Lord about the matter of divorce, and "He said to them, Have ye not read that He which made them at the beginning, made them male and female?" As to the order of the Greek sentence, it is necessary to associate the adverbial phrase, rendered "at the beginning," with what follows. There is no article in the phrase. It might well be translated, "He who created, initially male and female made He them." This is a plain and direct contradiction to evolutionary theories. Our Lord was not camouflaging scientific secrets. We need not the help of evolutionary theories to explain His language. He was asked a plain question, and He gave a plain answer. If the theory of protoplasm, with its nonsexual state, and similar other theories, are right, our Lord was wrong. His veracity, His accuracy are called in question.

Moreover, in regard to those chapters, Christ accepted and confirmed both the historicity of the early records of Genesis, and their Mosaic authorship. He was not adjusting His knowledge to the ignorance of His hearers. It is a dishonor to His name to conceive such an idea. He declared that He was "the truth." If He made the slightest mistake, then the whole scheme of redemption falls to the ground. If our Lord was inaccurate, then the work of the Cross is invalid for the sinner. There can be no atoning sacrifice, save on the part of a sinless Redeemer, and the sinlessness of Christ has been substantiated and confirmed by His most bitter enemies, and by His most ardent critics. Again and again the fall of man is put into association with the death of Christ. If the one is simply folklore, then there is no room for the other. What our Lord accepted and confirmed was similarly taught by His apostle Paul. It has established itself in the very hearts of millions of believers down through these centuries. We repudiate any theory that tends to discredit the honor of Christ. Let us beware of exchanging the truth of God for a lie.

Spiritism Unmasked

▪ PREFACE ▪

It is with much pleasure that I comply with the author's request that I should write a little foreword to his message on "Spiritism." Those of us who heard him give it in his recent lecture on the subject felt that it should if possible have a wider audience. It is true that there are already many such exposures in the field, but this one seems to me to cover ground not dealt with in the others I have read. Nor is this surprising. The cult is making such rapid developments, and its votaries are now to be found amongst so many of the professed religious leaders, that it is not to be wondered at that, waxing bolder by its successes, it more clearly manifests its origin. But be the manifestations what they may, the standard by which they are to be judged abides the same, and as the evil develops so it is met still at every turn by the unerring testimony of Scripture.

As the author shows, the relapse of Christendom to the practices hitherto associated with heathendom is a manifest and sure symptom of the gross darkness soon to set in and to end in judgment. As another has said, "It is shocking to find men amidst the darkness of heathenism practicing such customs; but to see men engaged therein where the name of Christ is known and where the living oracles of God are possessed, linking the name of Christ and the Scriptures therewith, is a thousandfold more so, and may be truly characterized as being appalling wickedness."

May this testimony for the truth be used of God to strengthen the faith of His children, and to unmask to many what is involved in Spiritism, and be the means in His hand of their deliverance from its solemn doom.

Bath, February 1920 W. R. Lewis

Spiritism Unmasked

The Claims of Spiritism

Spiritism is based on the assumption that the spirits of the departed can communicate with us, and accordingly it consists of efforts to enter into such communications. Spiritists claim to prove that life exists after death, and that the departed are able to render assistance to those still in the body. They also claim that the teachings of Spiritism conduce to the present comfort, the highest elevation, and the permanent blessing of humanity.

As to the first of these claims, the existence of life after death is one of the great foundation tenets of Christianity. The assistance of Spiritism, even if it were of bona fide value, would not be required to prove that. Nor is there anything new in the belief that "the spirit world manifests itself by producing effects in the physical world inexplicable by the laws of nature." That Spiritists do obtain communications with beings in the spirit world, has long been undeniable. There is, of course, much that passes for the real thing which is nothing but quackery and illusion. Making full allowance for this, however, the evidences produced by Spiritism, subjected, as they have been, to the severest tests, cannot be explained away. Psychical research yields an increasing volume of evidence corroborating the fact, acknowledged for ages past in human history, that certain powers of communication with spirit intelligences exist.

The Claims of Scripture

The question is as to the real character of the beings who are the source of the communications. Upon this the Bible provides abundant light. We are quite prepared for the repudiation of the Bible as a divine revelation. Yet for every argument advanced in disproof of it as a revelation from God, we can advance a hundred in proof of the validity of its claims as such. We will confine our attention to one in particular which bears directly upon our subject.

To the unprejudiced reader of Scripture the fact is undeniable that the prohibitions contained throughout this book had, as their underlying motive, the direct welfare of those to whom the prohibitions were given. They are the outcome of a wisdom which, acting for the best interests of men, has forbidden only what would prove detrimental to them. Now in all the passages which deal with the subject—and they are not only numerous, but are to be found in most of the books which constitute the volume—Spiritism, in any and every shape or form, is persistently and systematically prohibited. The fact is striking and significant that writers whose books were written at intervals during a period of fifteen hundred years, writers differing as widely as possible in status and calling, writing, too, in countries as far distant from one another as Italy from Chaldea, and without the possibility of arriving at the same conclusion either by mutual consultation or by mere imitation of their predecessors, adopt an identical attitude of condemnation of Spiritism, and bear an absolutely consistent testimony regarding it. This forms a link in a long chain of incontrovertible evidence that the book comes to us with divine authority and inspiration.

The Testimony of Scripture

Taking representative passages, we find in the Pentateuch the following:*

> "Turn ye not unto them that have familiar spirits, nor unto the wizards; seek not to be defiled by them: I am the Lord your God" (Lev. 19:31; see also 20:6 and 27).

> "There shall not be found with thee anyone . . . that useth divination, one that

*Quotations are from R.V. throughout.

> practiceth augury, or an enchanter, or a sorcerer, or a charmer, or a consulter with a familiar spirit, or a wizard, or a necromancer. For whosoever doeth these things is an abomination unto the Lord; and because of these abominations the Lord thy God doth drive them [the nations] out from before thee" (Deut. 18:10–12).

In the historical books it is said of King Saul, that he died, not only because he kept not the word of the Lord, but also because "he asked counsel of one that had a familiar spirit, to inquire thereby" (1 Chr. 10:13); and of Manasseh, that "he dealt with them that had familiar spirits, and with wizards: he wrought much evil in the sight of the Lord, to provoke Him to anger" (2 Kin. 21:6).

Turning to the prophetic books we find denunciation following remonstrance thus:

> "When they shall say unto you, Seek unto them that have familiar spirits, and unto the wizards that chirp and that mutter: should not a people seek unto their God? on behalf of the living should they seek unto the dead? To the law and to the testimony! If they speak not according to this Word, surely there is no mourning for them" (Is. 8:19, 20).

In the Acts of the apostles, the evil of sorcery is frequently exposed. In the epistles, the apostle Paul gives warning that those who practice it shall not inherit the kingdom of God (Gal. 5:20, 21). In the Apocalypse their doom is foretold as the second death, and exclusion from the city of God (Rev. 21:8; 22:14, 15).

The argument is raised in regard to the Leviticus passage, that the same book forbids the wearing of clothes of mingled materials, and that inasmuch as the latter prohibition is inapplicable to present-day life, so is that against dealing with familiar spirits. Such reasoning is almost too grotesque to deserve notice. Regulations made for the people of Israel regarding food and clothing were the outcome of the divine choice and care of the nation, and were intended for their welfare in the special circumstances under which that care was necessary. Certain prohibitions, in themselves of a salutary character for that people, were applicable solely to them under the Mosaic economy. The quotations just given suffice to show that the prohibitions against all forms of Spiritism are not confined to Israel but are of universal application.

Now the Bible has proved to be a means of enlightenment and advancement and a benefit in every way, wherever it has been received, whether in the life of the individual, or in the family, or in the nation; and this is the book which, forbidding only what is deleterious, absolutely and from beginning to end of its contents, prohibits Spiritism. Can it be conceived that God would term "an abomination to the Lord" that which carried with it the welfare of His creatures? On this showing alone Spiritism is injurious, and its humanitarian claims are invalid.

Concerning the Departed

But this is not the only kind of testimony provided in Scripture. There is instruction as to whether we are to look for the reappearance of the departed in spirit form, or to receive communications from them. In the first place, had this been so, we should have expected that a book which treats so constantly of communications from the other world, would have given frequent evidence of, and teaching concerning, such communications or appearances. This, however, is not the case. On the contrary, Job says, "When a few years are come, then I shall go the way, whence I shall not return" (Job 16:22), and David says of his dead child, "I shall go to him, but he shall not return to me" (2 Sam. 12:23). Significant also is the conversation in the spirit world between Abraham and the man who had spent his days in selfish ease. In seeking to persuade Abraham to send a messenger to his brethren still in the body, he argues that "if one go to them from the dead, they will repent." Abraham replies, "If they hear not Moses and the prophets, neither will they be persuaded if one rise from the dead." He thus discountenances the idea of one going in spirit form, and speaks only of the possibility that a messenger should be sent in the body by means of resurrection (Luke 16:27-31).*

Again, the Bible is a book which provides abundant comfort to those who are in trouble. But there is never a hint in it that comfort for the bereaved is to be derived from any sort of communication with spirits of the departed. When the apostle Paul imparts consolation to the bereaved concerning their departed, he does so as follows:

> "If we believe [and the "if" is not hypothetical: the implication is that we do believe] that Jesus died and rose again, even so them also that are fallen asleep in Jesus will God bring with Him. For this we say unto you by the word of the Lord, that we that are alive, that are left unto the coming of the Lord, shall in no wise precede them that are fallen asleep. For the Lord Himself shall descend from heaven, with a shout, with the voice of the archangel, and with the trump of God: and the dead in Christ shall rise first; then we that are alive, that are left, shall together with them be caught up in the clouds, to meet the Lord in the air: and so shall we ever be with the Lord. Wherefore comfort one another with these words" (1 Thess. 4:14-18).

If, as Spiritists say, "the early church was saturated with Spiritism"—an absolutely gratuitous assumption for which there is not a shred of evidence—here surely was the passage in which some reference might be expected to the comfort to be obtained from messages from the departed. The churches, however, were not so taught.

It is poor comfort that is not derived from sources absolutely reliable; and to seek to obtain comfort by disobedience to God is, to say the least, dangerous. There are unlawful means of procuring relief from sorrow, and Spiritism is one of these. True Christians—and by that term we mean those who by faith in the Son of God are in the enjoyment of vital union and communion with Him—have for nineteen centuries derived genuine and lasting comfort concerning their departed ones by the means thus graciously granted by God. They know that those who have died in the faith are "with Christ," that theirs is bliss unspeakable, undimmed and uninterrupted, and that there will be eternal reunion in resurrection glory at His Second Coming.

The Endor Medium

An appeal is made by Spiritists to the record in 1 Samuel 28, of King Saul's dealings with the woman at Endor, in order to show that Scripture testifies to the reality of mediumistic communications, and therefore to justify the practice. It is somewhat strange that any appeal should be made in this way to a book which invariably passes condemnation upon Spiritism. Yet it is easy to impose on those who are in comparative ignorance of the teachings of the Word of God. There is one thing that the narrative referred to makes quite clear, however, and that is that the Spiritism of modern times is identical in character with that described in the Bible.

The parallel is worthy of notice. In the modern seance, there is the applicant who seeks to obtain communication from a person who has departed this life; there is the medium who passes into temporary subconsciousness or unconsciousness in order to receive the communication; there is the "control," or the spirit-being whose special influence is regularly exercised over the medium; and there is, hypothetically, the spirit of the departed person from whom the message is desired. All this corresponds precisely with what took place as recorded in 1 Samuel 28. The applicant was Saul—who, by the way, would scarcely have had recourse to a practice which in his former days of well-doing he had endeavored to abolish from his kingdom, had this dealing with spirits been mere illusion and jugglery, and not actually a dark and evil reality. Then there was the woman, possessed of me-

*In the case of those who appeared with Christ at the Transfiguration, there is no evidence that they were in a disembodied state. The evidence rather points to the fact that they were "clothed upon with their house from heaven." We know that Elijah had been caught up without passing through death, and the presumption from Scripture evidence is that Moses had been raised from the dead. This narrative therefore affords no example of the return of the spirits of the departed. See Jude 5:9. Acts 26:23 is correctly rendered in the R.V. In 1 Corinthians 15:23, "Christ the firstfruits" is not to be taken as relating to priority of time in reference to the case of Moses.

diumistic powers. Thirdly there was the "familiar spirit," in present-day phraseology, "the control." Lastly, there was the departed prophet Samuel, from whom Saul hoped to receive a message. The modern and the ancient methods are the same. Present-day Spiritism is not a "new revelation," but an old sin. The indictments of Scripture therefore apply to the present practice. Moreover the identification of the two is confirmed by the fact that the Hebrew word frequently used to describe the practice signifies "one who consults the dead for information."

In that particular instance, however, the normal method of procedure was upset by God's interposition, and that in a way which consistently stamps the divine condemnation upon the practice. Without discussing here the much-discussed question as to whether Samuel himself was actually sent, the facts are that the machinery of the customary seance was entirely dislocated; the medium was terror-stricken by the unusual revelation, an alarm intensified by the disclosure of her applicant's identity; the message was not given through her mediumship at all, as was usual, but direct to Saul, and was a message, not of quiet information, but of stern denunciation. God Himself intervened to take things out of the hands of these Spiritists, and to communicate direct with the king. The whole narrative, with the comment in 1 Chronicles 10:13 above quoted, is condemnatory of the practice, and provides no ground of appeal whatever for the Spiritist, nor any justification for having recourse to such means of endeavoring to communicate with the departed. Nor, again, does the extraordinary event, with its divine intervention, provide any reason for supposing that the spirits of the departed come to the seance room or send messages at all.

The Truth About the Spirits

We turn now to another side of the evidence provided by Scripture. The book which has pronounced a ban on Spiritism makes known its true character. Those who practice Spiritism claim that the spirits with whom communication is held are those of human beings, but this has never been incontrovertibly demonstrated. It remains yet with Spiritists to prove that the controls, and the other spirits from whom their messages are derived, are human beings, and not those who, possessed of a considerable amount of knowledge of human circumstances, impersonate the departed with intent to deceive. This is of the utmost importance in view of the fact that the Scriptures warn us of the existence of evil spirits, and of their seductive activities. Satan, the archenemy of mankind, is called "the deceiver of the whole world" (Rev. 12:9). He is said to "fashion himself into an angel of light" (2 Cor. 11:14). Of the work of other evil spirits and their influence over mankind the Bible gives abundant evidence. It foretold that during the latter part of the present age there would be a falling away from the faith on the part of some, "through the power of seducing spirits and doctrines of demons" (1 Tim. 4:1), and that at the close of this dispensation the world would come under a specially organized activity of these beings (Rev. 16:13, 14).

The Hebrew and Greek words which describe these spirits have significant meanings. The Hebrew word is *shedim,* which denotes "mighty ones"; the Greek is *daimones* (or *daimonia*), i.e., "knowing ones." Their superhuman power is illustrated in the records of the Gospels and the Acts, and further in the physical condition of modern mediums and other subjects of Spiritist control. In regard to their knowledge, it is evident that demons have closely observed the ways and doings of men, and the dealings of God with humanity. They have thus been enabled to understand considerably the constitution of man and the conditions of his life. They can have little difficulty, therefore, in impersonating the departed, whose lives they have watched. Their knowledge of human affairs, coupled with the fact that they act under the guidance of Satan, enables them to predict the future to some extent. Further evidences of their superhuman knowledge abound in Scripture (see Matt. 8:29; Mark 1:24, 34; 5:7; Acts 16:17, etc.). They are shown to be not only deceptive, but cruel and, in many cases, unclean, and as seeking to control the bodies of men. They instigate men to rebel against God (Rev. 16:13, 14).

An Important Distinction

Demon-possession is not mere mental disease. For—

(a) Luke, himself a physician, distinguishes thus between the two. He speaks of a great number of people who came to be healed of their diseases, and, under a separate heading, of those who were troubled with unclean spirits (Luke 6:17, 18).

(b) Matthew's Gospel makes a similar distinction:

> "They brought unto Him all that were sick, holden with divers diseases and torments, possessed with demons, and epileptic (A.V. lunatic), and palsied" (Matt. 4:24).

Here again there is a clear differentiation between well-known mental affliction and demon-possession.

(c) Mark's Gospel bears the same testimony:

> "They brought unto Him all that were sick, and them that were possessed with demons . . . and He healed many that were sick with divers diseases, and cast out many demons" (Mark 1:32, 34).

(d) Demons are mentioned no less than seventy times in Scripture, and never once is the effect of their power referred to as a disease, but always as demon-possession. Persons so possessed lost the power of individual will, and their consciousness was yielded to the power of the demon. Hence the supernatural utterances and strength manifested, and the abnormal movements of the body while under such control; such indeed as are evidenced in the case of modern mediums.

(e) The Chinese have separate names for idiocy, insanity, epilepsy, hysteria and demon-possession. There are resemblances, of course, between the physical disease and the case of possession, but the differences are great and are not accountable by pathological diagnosis.

These differences are chiefly as follows:

(1) The person under the demon influence manifests an "automatic and methodical acting of a new personality"; he refers to himself not in the first person as in the case of a lunatic, but in the third person, as if speaking of another being. In insanity the assumed personality is obviously unreal. Not so, however, in the case of possession.

(2) A knowledge and power are evidenced, not possessed by the person affected when in his normal state, and inexplicable by pathology. There is today, for instance, the same recognition of, and hatred toward Christ, as in Scripture instances, such as the incident of the girl mentioned in Acts 16. This is especially the case in heathen lands, where aggressive mission work is carried on.

(3) There is a direct change in moral character; mediums frequently evidence antipathy to God, to Christ, to the Christian religion, and to prayer. The following admission was recently made by a Spiritist: "So long as you reply to our arguments with a text, we cannot teach you." The tendency to moral degeneracy is dealt with later on.

(4) Deliverance from the supernatural power comes when certain articles are abandoned or destroyed such as rings or books, or, in heathen lands, idols, shrines, etc.

The Reality of the Evil

These evidences are sufficient to give proof of the reality of demon-possession both in ancient and modern times. In all these respects the testimony of Scripture is corroborated by that from other sources. Those who try to explain the phenomena by pathology and psychology are constantly confronted with difficulties, which entirely disappear if the causes are attributable to demon-possession. Those who today are engaged in psychical research produce strong evidence that a distinct personality acts through the medium under control. A distinction must be made, in passing, between a demoniac and a demon-controlled medium. A demoniac is an involuntary victim, though he may, by yielding to sin, have brought the trouble on himself, his misdeeds opening the avenues of his being for demon aggression. A demon-controlled medium is a willing subject though deceived.

Mediumship is practiced in China in much the same way as in the West. Thus an applicant writes a charm for a medium. The latter takes an incense stick in his hand, and stands still, thereby notifying his willingness for the unseen being to take control. The charm is burned, the demon is worshiped and invoked. The medium announces what spirit has descended, and gives information. After returning to the normal state he often declares ignorance of what he had been stating during the process. Automatic writing is carried on in China in much the same manner. To a forked willow branch a pencil is attached, and a sanded platter placed beneath. The medium goes through the same process as just described. The pencil then traces characters on the sand, and so information is obtained.

Varying Methods

While this manifestation of demon power corresponds to what prevails in highly civilized lands, the activity of these powers of darkness is generally displayed in heathendom in the more openly repulsive forms. The reasons are not far to seek. Firstly, the true character and power of demons would naturally be shown in a more congenial atmosphere, such as that of heathen lands. Secondly, to adopt these methods largely where Christianity prevails, would hinder the purpose and influence of Satan, as the revelation of his character would prevent his work of deception. Thirdly, people of natural enlightenment, who are equally the objects of his delusions, would repudiate association with methods obviously debased. Accordingly in civilized communities the powers of darkness must adopt more subtle means of turning men away from God. The mode of activity is therefore adapted to varying conditions of time and locality. For people of refinement and education the method must be suitably alluring. In civilization, then, demon-control is dignified by plausible and euphemistic phraseology, and disguised by more specious methods.

Demons are capable not merely of dragging men into sensuality, but of persuading them to a life of asceticism, philanthropy, self-denial and morality—all excellent things in themselves—deceiving them all the while as to the path they are really treading, and blinding them as to the true character of sin in God's sight and the divinely appointed remedy. It is deplorable that leaders of thought and men and women of influence are today being thus beguiled, under the impression that they are merely engaging in psychical research for the benefit of their fellowmen.

Concerning Doctrines

The "doctrines of demons" are first directed against the honor of Christ, who is ever the object of satanic hostility. As long as the evil one has any degree of liberty he will use it in antagonism against the Son of God. With untiring effort, therefore, he and the hosts of darkness under him seek to undermine the Christian faith. In the first epistle of Timothy the apostle Paul, immediately after enumerating some of the great basic truths relating to the Son of God, says, "But the Spirit speaketh expressly, that in later times some shall fall away from the faith, giving heed to seducing spirits and doctrines of demons" (1 Tim. 3:16; 4:1). Special doctrines follow, which we must notice presently, but clearly the contrast is first with the truths in the preceding context relating to Christ.

When, therefore, we hear one of the leading present-day advocates of Spiritism proclaiming that the sacrifice of Christ was not vicarious, that He "came to place Himself before the tribunal of man's judgment," that He was simply a perfect medium, that He "occasionally lost His temper," that there is no resurrection and no hell, we have no difficulty in tracing such teachings to their satanic source, and in recognizing in them the outcome of the activities of these seducing spirits. Of similar origin are the statements of Mr. W. Stainton Moses, a noted medium of recent times, who repudiated the doctrines of redemption and atonement, and declared that "Far too much stress is laid on Christ's death," and that "It is no uncommon thing to die for an idea." "This idea," he says, "of a good God sacrificing His sinless Son as a propitiation for man, is repudiated as monstrous. Man is his own Savior." This, by the way, is not the language of Scripture, which says that Christ "offered Himself" (Heb. 9:14). The satanic source of the views of Mr. Stainton Moses—himself a renegade from the Christian faith, and eventually harassed by the spirit-beings under whose influence he had come—is suggested by his own confession. "All the information ever given me," he says, "in proof of the presence of the departed, might in harmony with my experience of the spirits, have been first obtained and then imparted by a false intelligence." The lamentable course of this man is a danger signal to those who are tempted to practice Spiritism.

A Spiritist Conference

The following identification of the teachings of Spiritism with those mentioned by the apostle Paul is remarkable. At a Spiritist conference recently held in Rhode Island, U.S.A., at which eighteen states were represented, the following four resolutions were passed:

1. That Sunday Schools should be discontinued;
2. That all Christian ordinances and worship should be abandoned;
3. That sexual tyranny should be denounced;
4. That abstinence from animal food should be affirmed.

The last two are precisely what the apostle predicted. The doctrines of demons would be as follows: "Forbidding to marry [or rather "hindering marriage"], and commanding to abstain from meats, which God created to be received with thanksgiving by them that believe and know the truth" (1 Tim. 4:3).

Admissions of Spiritists

That the spirit-controls of mediums are demons is confirmed by the testimony of Spiritists of the present times. It has often been confessed by mediums in the seance room that neither good angels nor the departed, but evil spirits, are in attendance. They acknowledge that they are frequently deceived and sometimes are in difficulty to determine whether they have been deceived or not. What a contrast is here presented to the teachings of Scripture! In the case of Spiritism there is acknowledged uncertainty; in the case of Scripture, irrefutable declarations! A Spiritist recently confessed that

> "most of the stories of returned friends are due to the work not of the latter but of other spirits."

Miles Grant, in "Spiritism Unveiled," says:

> "For seven years I held daily intercourse with what purported to be my mother's spirit. I am now firmly persuaded that it was nothing but an evil spirit, an infernal demon, who in that guise gained my soul's confidence, and led me to the very brink of ruin."

Madame de Morgan, in an address given before the Spiritualist Alliance, stated that

> "the resemblance [i.e., between the departed one and the spirit pretending identity with that of the departed] never seems to be perfect."

In a standard work explaining Spiritism, the writer says:

> "Communications from the spirit-world are not necessarily infallible truth."

A recent issue of *The Occult Review* contains the following statement:

> "Spiritists are well aware of the awful peril of obsession by evil spirits. Man has some very dangerous and powerful enemies behind the veil."

Lying Theories About the Other World

That spirits appeal to God is no proof of the validity of their claims. Unclean demons have confessed Christ. The cause of truth needs no assistance from means which God has condemned. Christ and His apostles repudiated such testimony (see Mark 3:11, 12; Acts 16:17, 18). Messages that come through automatic writing professing to describe worlds after death, the people who live therein, how friend meets friend, how youth and age are transformed, the various pursuits and occupations in the different spheres, etc.,* are all void of true proof as to their reality. The teaching of the Word of God shows that they are illusory, and not only so, but that they are part of a scheme of satanic deception to allure men away from God and the truth. And surely it is not difficult to grasp the fact that deceptive spirits, acting through automatic writing or through a medium in a state of subconsciousness, can present a view of after-death circumstances which are not substantiated by facts, but which, on the other hand, are merely blinds to keep the truth from the human heart!

> "The god of this world [Satan] hath blinded the minds of the unbelieving, that the light of the gospel of the glory of Christ, who is the image of God, should not dawn upon them" (2 Cor. 4:4).

It cannot be difficult to see that evil spirits, in order to allure men, make the teachings they inculcate conform to a certain extent to the doctrines of Christianity, omitting or repudiating at the same time those fundamental truths relating to Christ and His redemptive work which are absolutely essential for man's salvation.

An unclean spirit does not become pure because an applicant for information is reverent or intellectual. The character of the spirit remains the same though its tactics may be plausible. Not even the best motive—that for instance of seeking to get into touch with a departed relative—can purify an unholy intercourse, or can transform disobedience into righteousness. Whatever the means employed by the powers of darkness, their motives remain the same, namely to hinder the work of God and extend the domination of Satan. We are warned in the Word of God not to believe every spirit, but to prove the spirits whether they are of God (1 John 4:1). Spiritists appeal to this Scripture as a reason why people should attend seances and engage in the practice of Spiritism. That is an entire misapplication of the passage. It teaches, not that we are to tamper with Spiritism, but to test all teachings by the Scriptures, since false doctrines are the work of evil spirits acting through human teachers. To find oneself possessed of certain psychic powers and so to begin to dabble in automatic writings and other forms of Spiritism under the impression that this is only a means of natural and legitimate human development, is to throw oneself into the snare of Satan, and to invite the disastrous influence of the evil spirits who work under his direction.

Spiritists' Confessions of Evil Effects

We shall now employ some testimonies of Spiritists themselves to confirm this.

(1) Sir William Barrett, in his book on Necromancy (p. 15) speaks of "the steady downward course of mediums." Yet we are told now that Christ was a perfect medium. How absolutely void of the knowledge of the true Christ are those who offer such poor flattery to the Christian faith! How simple it is, after all, to create a Christ of one's vain imagination! How easy to suppose a being whose ways and deeds conform to the darkened thoughts of those who turn from the light of the truth!

(2) It has been publicly stated by one of the leading present-day exponents of Spiritism that "it has its dangerous element." Verily to put oneself under the power of evil spirits is dangerous. What a contrast to Christianity! Have the true followers of Christ ever found Christianity a dangerous practice? Does any danger lie there? We are told, forsooth, that Christianity has become effete! And yet there are hundreds of thousands, who, true to their Master, are ready today to lay down their lives for Him, and whose numbers are greater than in any preceding generation of the present era! Let a man accept Christ as his Lord and Savior and at once he becomes the dwelling place of the Spirit of God, and passes out of danger into safety.

(3) The celebrated medium D. D. Home, acknowledged that the spirits which controlled him were gaining entire mastery of his being. Imagine the spirits of departed friends doing this! The idea is preposterous. And as to those who died in faith in Christ, what an outrageous slur upon their character to suppose that they descend to the degradation that characterizes

*Cf. *The Weekly Dispatch,* Feb. 1st, 1920, and other issues.

many seances, or that they cooperate with mediums to the detriment of these latter persons, and in disobedience to the Word of God!

(4) Sir Oliver Lodge, an advocate of Spiritism from the standpoint of psychical research, has issued a warning, counseling "regulated moderation in the use of unusual power in the psychic direction." He advises anyone who has the power of receiving communications in any form "to see to it that he remains master of the situation." "To give up your own judgment," he says, "and depend solely on adventitious aid, is a grave blunder, and may in the long run have disastrous consequences."* Surely this piece of advice is sufficiently condemnatory in itself.

(5) Similar to the warning just quoted is that of Professor C. Flammarion, another exponent of Spiritism, who says:

> "It is prudent not to give oneself exclusively to occult subjects, for one might soon lose the independence of mind necessary to form an impartial judgment."

If that is true, what reliability can be placed upon the advice of those who are practicing Spiritism? Such testimonies only fall in line with the warnings of Scripture. To practice this sort of thing is to invite the disastrous control of a power which is purposively inimical to us.

(6) Sir William Barrett, again, says:

> "Spiritism is dangerous in proportion as it leads us to surrender our reason or our will to the dictates of an invisible and often lying being."

And again:

> "Granting the existence of the spirit-world, it is necessary to be on one's guard against the invasion of our will (when so surrendered) by a lower order of intelligence and morality."

How different from Christianity! Were such warnings ever called for in the case of Christians, to whom the injunction has been given "Yield yourselves unto God"?

*_Raymond_, by Sir Oliver Lodge, p. 235.

(7) The Spiritist, Mr. W. T. Stead, bore testimony to the immoral tendency of Spiritism and to the blasted lives of many who practice it. Mediums have again and again acknowledged that once the art of entering into spirit-communications has been acquired, the influence of the spirit-being becomes irresistible. The domination can scarcely be shaken off. In other words, when the power of communication between a medium and the control is established ("control," is, by the way, a highly suggestive term), the demon is unwilling to relinquish the relationship.

True Spiritualism

What a contrast, again, is presented to us between the foregoing testimonies and the teachings of the Bible concerning the power of the Spirit of God in relation to the Christian! What a contrast between the experiences of mediums and the experiences of those who are governed and guided by the Holy Spirit! For after all, there is a true means of intercommunication between God and the soul of the one who is born again of the Spirit of God and has received His Son.

> "When He, the Spirit of truth is come," saith the Lord, "He shall guide you into all the truth; for He shall not speak from Himself; but what things soever He shall hear, these shall He speak; and He shall declare unto you the things that are to come. He shall glorify Me: for He shall take of Mine, and shall declare it unto you" (John 16:13, 14).

This promise has been fulfilled in the experience of Christians ever since pentecost. Spiritism is a devilish counterfeit of this true Spiritualism, and a soul-destroying substitute for it. The Spirit of God is the one channel of communication between God Himself and the true Christian. Never was there any need of warning as to moderation in opening the avenues of our being to the benign influence of His Spirit. His control never works anything but the utmost good. To obey the divine command "Be filled with the Spirit" is to derive the highest benefit possible to a human being in this life. The believer who thus enjoys constant communion with his Redeemer, experiences that which produces true manliness and nobility and makes him a power for good to his fellowmen. The enlightenment which is granted him, and the leading of the Spirit of God, prove safeguards to him against attempting to follow the spurious, delusive, and damaging practices and teachings of Spiritism.

Independent Testimonies

Turning to another class of testimony, the following is the verdict of a doctor who for nearly half a century has been in contact with problems and cases relative to Spiritism. Speaking of those who have developed their powers as mediums, he says:

> "The tendency in such is ever downwards. The body physically seems, sooner or later, unable to bear the strain; the mind, in like manner, seems to lose its fiber, its concentration; the moral character markedly deteriorates; drunkenness and other vices prevail; and the whole condition becomes more or less deplorable."*

The same author quotes Professor Hudson as saying that the exercise of Spiritism

> "produces mental deterioration which keeps pace with physical decline; and which, no doubt, loosens all principles of morality and truth."

Yet this is the "science," or as Spiritists have decided to call it, the "religion," which claims to elevate humanity. In the disastrous practices associated with this so-called religion, men, women and young people are being encouraged to engage, under the pretext of the development of their latent powers.

The late Reader Harris, K.C., recorded the following:

> "The most remarkable case of mediumship I have met with was that of a young lady, who commenced with a little seemingly innocent table-turning at a children's party, and finished up by death in a madhouse."

The verdict of Mr. Birrell, at Bristol, is also worth recording. He said:

> "The records of Spiritism leave me unconvinced. They lack the things of morality, of grandeur, of emotion, in a word, of religion. They deal with petty things, mere prolonged egoism, as if the one thing we want to be assured of is continued existence and an endless capacity to exchange platitudes. A revelation of the life beyond the grave ought surely, if it is to do any good in the world, to be more stupendous than that—something of really first-class importance. Otherwise we are just as well without it."

These latter conditions are amply fulfilled in the teachings of the Bible, which, in contrast to the blighting effects of Spiritism, has wrought untold blessing in individual as well as national life. It has ennobled humanity, transformed the life, and beautified the character, giving to all who have accepted the Son of God as their Redeemer, a true and sufficient insight into the conditions of the other world.

Periodic Outbursts

The spread of Spiritism is so rapid and general today as to demand some account of its present significance. Seasons of approaching crisis in the world's history have almost invariably been accompanied by an outburst of Spiritist activity. The regularity of this in the records of the Bible is remarkable. There are abundant evidences from Scripture of the existence of the evil in the days prior to the Flood.†

Passing to the period of the exodus of Israel from Egypt, and their entry into Canaan, not only are records given us of the work of Spiritism in Egypt as an attempt to hinder the liberation of Israel (Ex. 7:10–22; 8:7), but in Palestine the iniquity of the Amorites and

*_Modern Spiritism_ by A. T. Schofield, M.D.; J. & A. Churchill.

†These are dealt with somewhat fully in Pember's _Earth's Earliest Ages_, and the conclusion to which he draws attention seems undeniable. The reader may also be referred to the book, _The Giant Cities of Bashan_, by Porter.

other Canaanite nations had reached a climax (see Gen. 15:16). That their sin was that of Spiritism is clear from the divine injunction given by Moses, already quoted:

> "When thou art come into the land . . . thou shalt not learn to do after the abominations of those nations. There shall not be found with thee . . . one that useth divination, one that practiceth augury, or an enchanter, or a sorcerer, or a charmer, or a consulter with a familiar spirit, or a wizard, or a necromancer. For whosoever doeth these things is an abomination unto the Lord: and because of these abominations the Lord thy God doth drive them out from before thee" (Deut. 18:9–12).

The next crisis, which occurred some five hundred years later, was that of the appointment of a king over Israel. That event set up the throne upon which ultimately the Messiah will sit, who is to wrest the world from the domination of Satan. The devil therefore attempted to blast the nation with the influence of Spiritism. That those who had "familiar spirits" (i.e., mediumistic controls) were numerous, is clear from the fact that King Saul had taken measures to purge the land from this evil, and that his drastic measures had not been entirely successful (see 1 Sam. 28:3, 7).

Another crisis, again five hundred years later, was the removal of the nation into captivity into Assyria and Chaldea. Spiritism had once more become rampant among the people. The records of this are given in 2 Kings 17:17 and 21:6. The widespread extent of the evil is evidenced in the already-quoted remonstrance of the prophet Isaiah against those who encouraged the people to make applications to mediums ("them that have familiar spirits"), Isaiah 8:19, 20. This national sin brought down the judgment of God upon them.

Again, some five hundred years after the captivity, at the period of the life, death and resurrection of Christ, and the time of pentecost, a tremendous manifestation of Spiritist activity took place. The records of the Gospels and the Acts show that sorcery and demon-possession abounded. The crisis of the coming of the Son of God and His redemptive work at Calvary, brought the satanic hosts again into evidence. Christ and His apostles were constantly confronted with the open hostility of demons. The agents of Spiritism were active in opposing the gospel (see Acts 8:7, 9–11; 13:8–12; 16:16–18; 19:13). Thus the personal intervention of God, in the coming of His Son and the gift of the Holy Spirit, was the occasion of one of the greatest displays of Spiritist activity up to that time.

The Modern Outburst

The obvious conclusion from the foregoing is that the worldwide Spiritist activities of recent times, portend another great crisis in the history of mankind. It seems necessary, therefore, to consider somewhat more closely the circumstances of the present-day manifestation of satanic power.

The modern outburst of Spiritism has been dated from 1847, when, owing to events in the United States, a widespread interest was aroused in mediumship. Thence it extended to Europe. In 1871 the number of Spiritists in U.S.A. was estimated at nine thousand. A recent estimate gives twenty million. The number of periodicals representing their teachings is numerous, and these are circulated in all the continents.

In the latter part of the last century a number of distinguished men became interested in the subject, and in 1891 the Society for Psychical Research was founded. The influence of this Society in the British Isles spread rapidly. In 1900 there were twenty-five Spiritist societies in the United States alone, and the mediums there numbered ten thousand. Spiritism assumed a more pronouncedly religious aspect; scores of churches were founded; Spiritist ministers were ordained, and Sunday schools and day schools were established. The institution of the Black Mass in Paris is well-known. The account of the prohibition of this abomination appeared in the *Daily Chronicle* of March 4th, 1907. The institution has, however, been recently revived.

The Religious Tendency

The tendency to regard Spiritism as a religion has become very marked. Mr. W. T. Stead represented it as the duty of all Christians to take up the study of Spirit-return and ministry as a religious duty. Evidences of the response to this are numerous. The following appeared in the *British Weekly* of November 4th, 1909:

> "Probably no more surprising address has been delivered in a theological college within our generation than that in which Dr. Amory Bradford urged the students of Hackney College to occupy themselves with occult and spiritualistic studies."

The *Guardian* of February 10th, 1916, contained an article boldly advocating intercourse with the dead. Again, in the *British Weekly,* of July 6th, 1917, we find the following:

> "Let science lead the way by all means. Borderland studies occupied thoughtful minds in England for a generation before the war, and the three years conflict has made us all Borderers."

The war, of course, has given a tremendous impetus to Spiritism. Multitudes who do not know the true and divinely appointed means of comfort in bereavement, have had recourse to mediums and other agencies, either in ignorance, or rejection, of God's condemnation of the practice. How deplorable it is that comfort should be sought by a means both contrary to divine command, and spurious and delusive, and not only so, but actually under the control of satanic power!

The Press—Religious and Secular

The tendency referred to above, to regard Spiritism as a religion rather than a science, is drawing a large number of ecclesiastics into the ranks of the Spiritists, and this is a further sign of the tremendous spread of the evil. In the February 1920 issue of *Nash's Magazine,* there appeared an article from the pen of a well-known bishop of the Church of England, discussing the attitude of the Christian church toward Spiritism. "Spiritualism," he says, "is in its nature the ally and not the enemy of Christianity." This is a surprising utterance from such a source. It is enough to refer to *The New Revelation,* a recent production by Sir Arthur Conan Doyle, which may fairly be said to represent the teachings of Spiritists today. The blasphemous statements of that book against the Son of God expose Spiritism as the deadliest enemy rather than the ally of the Christian faith. In addition to the disparagement of His person, the writer denies the value of His atoning work. He declares that inasmuch as "there never was any evidence of the fall of man," there is no justice in a vicarious sacrifice, nor in redemption from sin. This—and there is much more of the same sort—is quite in keeping with the tenets of Spiritists, who deny the essential and eternal deity of Christ, the efficacy of His atonement, and the truth of His resurrection. How can Spiritism be the ally of Christianity? The bishop further says that "Christians are naturally drawn toward Spiritism, and indeed toward Spiritual phenomena." They certainly have not derived any inclination thitherward from the teaching of Christ, nor from the Word of God. If any find themselves "naturally drawn," let them beware, lest they be found fighting against God, and against their own welfare! The bishop bases his arguments on the appearance of Christ to His disciples during the forty days immediately succeeding His resurrection, and on their recognition of Him and the converse they held with Him. It is scarcely consistent to use the great truth of the Lord's resurrection in order to support a heresy which denies it.

The following was a resolution recently moved in the house of Laymen:

> "That inquiry into psychical phenomena, undertaken in a reverent and scientific spirit, is consistent with the Christian faith, and may, under God's providence, be a means whereby doubting minds are confirmed in behalf of our twofold nature, and of the personal continuance after death of the spiritual part of our being."

If those who profess Christianity were satisfied with the Word of God, they would not need confirmation by such an inquiry. A lying spirit may say what is true as well as anyone else, but the motive nevertheless is to deceive. Part of the very deception of Spiritism is that it may teach an article of the Christian faith, such as the belief of the future life, but this does not constitute Spiritism an "ally of

Christianity." The apostle Paul did not regard as an ally the girl-medium at Philippi who cried out, "These men are servants of the most High God, which proclaim unto you the way of salvation" (Acts 16:16–18). That statement was true, but Paul repudiated a testimony derived from such a source. Spiritists boast that Spiritism will reestablish the fading belief in a future life. In the case of no true Christian is the belief fading. Moreover, the doctrine concerning the future life as taught by Spiritists is that of a future developed from the present by a process in advancing stages in various spheres. This is its "nobler gospel"! In reality it is no gospel at all. It is a delusive perversion of the teachings of Christianity.

An Ominous Increase

Such is the portentous advance of Spiritism that those who know that the crisis of the next great intervention of God is near, are not surprised to find a whole page of one of the most widely circulated newspapers of the day devoted to news concerning the records of messages received by a clergyman through automatic writing.* It is not surprising to see the subject of Spiritism taken up from time to time in the columns of almost every leading newspaper in the world's press. Nor is it surprising to find that seances are being held in churches as a regular part of the ecclesiastical routine.

A medium recently said, "I learn from spirits that a vast spiritual movement is working out a religious scheme." This is no mediumistic illusion. Evil spirits are doubtless thoroughly aware of future conditions. They know the Scriptures. Another medium lately gave information as from a control, that in a few years half the people in the world would be either Spiritists or would engage in some form of Spiritism.

The Approaching Crisis

The evil must be expected to continue making rapid strides. No careful student of Scripture will anticipate anything else. The Bible shows in what this so-called religion will culminate, and what is the character of the coming crisis, in which, as in similar circumstances in the past, the judgments of God will inevitably descend upon the earth. Our Lord foretold that the condition of the world just at the end of this age, prior to His return, would be similar to that which prevailed in the days of Noah, and again in the days of Lot's sojourn in Sodom and Gomorrah (Luke 17:22–30). The record concerning the former is that the earth was filled with corruption (Gen. 6:12). The prophecy uttered by Christ is confirmed in many other passages of the Word of God. Nowhere does the Bible teach that the latter part of this dispensation is to be characterized by the moral improvement of humanity. The apostle Paul pointed out that at this time men would give heed to seducing spirits and doctrines of demons (1 Tim. 4:1; see also 2 Tim. 3:1–5). The book of the Revelation shows that just before the establishment of the kingdom of God and the authority of Christ in the earth, by the execution of divine judgment upon the ungodly, the activity of Satan and his hosts of evil spirits will be greater than ever. The announcement of the impending inauguration of the kingdom in chapter twelve, verse 10, is accompanied by the following warning:

> "Woe for the earth and for the sea; because the devil has gone down unto you, having great wrath, knowing that he hath but a short time" (v. 12).

The next chapters speak of the two great world rulers, through whom Satan is to control human affairs for a short time at the close of this age. Under them the world will be in such a state as to necessitate the retributive intervention of God, as was the case in the days of Noah. The description given of the second of these two potentates suggests that they will exercise Spiritist powers (Rev. 13:11–18). This is made clear by the fact that they will act under the direction of Satan (v. 2), and from the statement in chapter sixteen, verses 13 and 14, that the spirits of demons speak through both of them. In this last passage the second ruler, again symbolized like the first by the term "beast," is also called "the false prophet." The evil spirits will use them to or-

*See the *Weekly Dispatch* of Jan. 18th, 1920, and subsequent issues.

ganize mankind in general rebellion against God.

For this state of things Spiritism is undoubtedly preparing the way. The spirits of demons, acting through the practices and teachings of Spiritists are, by the most seductive methods, leading multitudes in rejection of God's commands, and in denial of His Christ. The divine judgments must ere long descend upon this state of things. Disobedience to God brings first the retribution of delusion, and then judgments upon the iniquity. Of these we have a solemn instance in the words of Isaiah concerning Egypt of old:

> "The spirit of Egypt shall be made void in the midst of it; and I will destroy the counsel thereof: and they shall seek unto the idols, and to the charmers, and to them that have familiar spirits, and to the wizards; and I will give over the Egyptians into the hands of a cruel lord" (Is. 19:3, 4).

The circumstances of the crisis that is now approaching are given in considerable detail in the Word of God. By the personal intervention of Christ, the church, the true church, consisting of all who, having been born of the Spirit of God, are followers of Christ, will be removed from the earth (see 1 Thess. 4:15–17). The Lord Jesus will subsequently be revealed from heaven

> "with the angels of His power in flaming fire rendering vengeance to them that know not God, and to them that obey not the Gospel" (2 Thess. 7:8).

A Final Warning

Let Christians take heed against being drawn into tampering with Spiritism in any form. To play at planchette with the idea that it is an innocent toy, or to engage in thought-reading, table-turning, palmistry and clairvoyance, is to throw oneself into the devil's snare. Many a one has been allured into things of this sort at a social gathering, and has thereby entered on a course leading to results ruinous both to soul and to body. We should beware of counting trivial the character of that which we do not understand. Attempts to communicate with the other world through Spiritism are Satan's substitute for the work of the Holy Spirit, who leads us constantly into communion with God the Father and with His Son Jesus Christ.

Let us beware of what is called "The New Revelation." Spiritism is an ancient practice, by which for ages man has been allured to his destruction by Satan and his hosts of darkness. Let us never forget that

> "our wrestling is not against flesh and blood, but against the principalities, against the spiritual hosts of wickedness in the heavenly places." Let us "take the whole armor that we may be able to withstand in the evil day, and having done all, to stand."

The end of this age is drawing near. The "day of salvation" has already been lengthened out in the long-suffering of God. Satan knows his time is short, and is busier than ever alluring men to their doom by the false gospels of Spiritism, Theosophy, and other deceptions. Should the reader as yet know not the joy of God's pardoning mercy through the death of Christ, and the gift of eternal life in Him, this may be freely obtained. The divine conditions are simple. They are "repentance toward God and faith in our Lord Jesus Christ" (Acts 20:21). That those by whom this booklet is read—and who have not received the Lord Jesus Christ, the Son of God, by faith in Him, on the ground of His death for their sins—may be delivered from the blinding delusions of Satan and his hosts, and saved from coming doom, is the earnest prayer of the writer. "He that hath the Son hath the life; he that hath not the Son of God hath not the life" (1 John 5:12).

NEW TESTAMENT GREEK GRAMMAR

Course of Self-Help for the Layman

PREFACE

THE production of this Grammar is the outcome of a Class held many years ago in Exeter, for students desirous of acquiring a knowledge of the Greek Testament to avail themselves freely of a course of instruction in it. The method adopted was somewhat of a departure from the rigid order prevailing in the School Grammars. From the beginning use was made of the Greek New Testament, the simpler sentences and phrases being brought into use by way of exercises, with a gradual extension according as progress was made in the Grammar itself. The method proved both practicable and interesting.

More recently some of the Lessons in this volume appeared monthly in a Magazine, and it became evident that there is a fairly widespread desire to acquire the knowledge of the New Testament in the original tongue. The provision of Lessons in a Magazine involved their length being adjusted to circumstances of the space required for Magazine articles, and this meant a certain amount of overlapping (without repetition of subject matter from one Lesson to another), it not being possible to divide the subjects so as to put them completely into one Lesson. This, however, did not prove an interference in the course of the study. After some twenty-three lessons had been thus inserted, the Magazine was discontinued, and circumstances, over which the author had no control, have necessitated the publication of the Lessons according to the division previously adopted, but no hindrance to the study is thus presented.

Another result of Magazine work is the somewhat conversational style of guiding the studies and providing explanations, and this again is not without advantage. The student should study the Lessons patiently and thoroughly, and follow closely the advice given as to memorizing, and as to repeating certain parts of the Lessons. The Latin proverb *"Festina lente"* ("Hasten slowly") is of great importance in this respect, and though constant review is a laborious task, the ability to read certain parts of the Greek New Testament almost from the commencement of the studies provides interest for those who delight in the Word of God, and makes the task well worth while. The author is hopeful that, in spite of defects, some real contribution may have been made towards this important means of knowing the mind of the Lord.

W. E. VINE, M.A.

BATH

FOREWORD

THERE are many excellent translations of the New Testament from the original Greek into our English tongue, but it is admitted that the student of New Testament Greek has the advantage over the ordinary reader.

The author of this little text book has done a signal service to all who have the linguistic gift. Indeed under its guidance that talent will be discovered and improved. Mr. Vine has long experience in teaching this subject and his Grammar is no mere echo of other text books. His progressive method and the direct use of the Greek New Testament are his own. No better book can be put into the hands of those who have no previous knowledge of learning languages. It is worthy of a place in any "Teach Yourself" series, especially in this revised edition. Designed for the lay reader, it will also find a place in the equipment of others, who wish to feed first-hand upon the Word of God, and give themselves to its glorious ministry.

FRANCIS DAVIDSON

CONTENTS

INTRODUCTION

It has been well said that the Greek language is "the most subtle and powerful language that ever flowed from the tongue of man." Yet, comparatively speaking, it is easy, and particularly Biblical Greek. The language of the New Testament Greek was much simpler than what is known as Classical Greek, and is to be distinguished from the writings of men who aspire to literary fame. As the late Dr. J. H. Moulton wrote, "The New Testament writers had little idea that they were writing literature. The Holy Ghost spoke absolutely in the language of the people. . . . The very grammar and dictionary cry out against men who would allow the Scriptures to appear in any other form than that 'understanded of the people.'" The language spoken throughout the Roman Empire in the first century of this era was Hellenistic Greek, otherwise called the *Koinē,* or the common dialect of the people. How it came about that such a language became universal is described in the writer's manual "B.C. and A.D." or "How the world was prepared for the Gospel," one of the *Witness* manuals. The hand of God is strikingly seen in the national movements which eventually made it possible for the message of eternal life to be conveyed to all nations by means of the natural, yet powerful tongue which it is our privilege to study. The study indeed is important as it opens up the mind of God to us as no translation could ever do. Patience and perseverance are required, but the student who has a few hours to spare in the course of a month will soon make progress, and find that he is experiencing a new delight in the intelligent reading of the actual words by which "Men spake from God, being moved by the Holy Ghost" (2 Pet. 1:21).

▪ LESSON 1 ▪

The Alphabet

The student should familiarize himself with the alphabet, capital and small letters, and their names, and should observe carefully the notes given below. Learn the alphabet by heart; to know the order of the letters is useful for concordance work.

Capitals	Small	Name	Equivalent
Α	α	alpha	a
Β	β	beta	b
Γ	γ	gamma	g
Δ	δ	delta	d
Ε	ϵ	epsilon	e (short)
Ζ	ζ	zeta	z (dz)
Η	η	eta	e (long)
Θ	θ	theta	th
Ι	ι	iota	i
Κ	κ	kappa	k
Λ	λ	lambda	l
Μ	μ	mu	m
Ν	ν	nu	n
Ξ	ξ	xi	x
Ο	ο	omicron	o (short)
Π	π	pi	p
Ρ	ρ	rho	r
Σ	σ (ς)	sigma	s
Τ	τ	tau	t
Υ	υ	upsilon	u
Φ	φ	phi	ph
Χ	χ	chi	ch (hard)
Ψ	ψ	psi	ps
Ω	ω	omega	o (long)

Notes on the Alphabet

(1) There are two forms of the letter E, the short, *epsilon,* pronounced as in "met," the long, *eta,* pronounced as in "mate."

(2) Distinguish the shape of the small letter *eta* from the English "n"; the Greek letter has a long stroke on the right. On the other hand, distinguish the small letter *nu* (the English "n")

from the English letter "v." The "v" shape in English is a Greek small "n." The capital *eta* (English long "e") must be distinguished from the English capital H.

(3) There are two forms of the letter O, the short, *omicron,* as in "dot," the long, *omega,* as in "dote" (ŏ and ō).

(4) Distinguish the *xi* (English "x") from the *chi* (English "ch"), sounded hard, as in "Christ." The latter, though it looks like the English "x," combines the two letters c and h.

(5) Distinguish the Greek letter *rho* (English "r") from the English "p." The capital R in Greek is just like the English "P," and the small is somewhat similar. Familiarize the eye in looking at the Greek capital as an "R" not a "P."

(6) There are two forms of the letter "s." One is similar in shape to the English "s," but it is reserved for the end of a word and is never found elsewhere. Greek words, ending in the letter "s" must end with the "s" of that shape. Where "s" occurs in the part of a word other than the final letter the other form must be used. It is like an "o" with a horizontal stroke stretching from the top on the right hand side.

(7) There is no dot over the iota.

(8) In writing *upsilon* keep the letter curved, as if it is made like a "v" it will be confounded with the small *nu.*

(9) The small *gamma* must be distinguished from the English "y." The Greek *gamma* is always hard as in "go," not as in "gem."

(10) The student will observe that there is no "h," or rough breathing in the alphabet. Its place is taken by an inverted comma over a letter, thus— ὅς (who). The soft breathing is signified by a comma over the initial vowel, and denotes an absence of the h sound, thus— ἦν ("was"). Therefore the rough breathing or the soft comes over every vowel or diphthong that begins a word. Every word that begins with ρ (*rho*) must have the "h," or rough breathing, over it: thus ῥῆμα ("a word "). When a word begins with two vowels the breathings come over the second letter thus— υἱός ("a son," pronounced *hweos*) and αὐτός ("he," pronounced *owtos*). Double *rho* in the body of a word is written ῤῥ (the first with the smooth breathing, the second with the rough).

(11) Occasionally a vowel has a small iota underneath it, called the iota subscript. This iota is not pronounced but it is a very important mark to notice, as it often serves to distinguish different forms of the same word.

(12) The *omega* (signifying "great O") is the last letter in the alphabet. Thus when the Lord says "I am the Alpha and the Omega" (Rev. 22:13), our English equivalent (though we must not translate it so) would be "I am the A and the Z."

A Table of some Vowel Sounds

α = long and short, as in āh and făt.

ϵ = short only, as in sĕt.

η = long only, as in pain (or aim).

ο = short only, as in pŏt.

ω = long only, as in bōne.

ι = long and short, as in polīce and fĭt.

υ = long and short, as in trūe and pŭt.

The student should obtain *Nestle's Greek Testament* (small edition) published by the British and Foreign Bible Society, 146 Queen Victoria Street, London, E.C.4. That is the text which will be used in this course. [This edition of Vine's *New Testament Greek Grammar* uses the Fourth Revised Edition of the United Bible Societies' *The Greek New Testament,* which is available from the American Bible Society, Grand Central Station, New York, NY.]

▪ LESSON 2 ▪

The following three classes of consonants should be noted particularly,

(1) Labials: π, β, φ.

(2) Gutturals, or palatals: κ, γ, χ.

(3) Dentals: τ, δ, θ.

(*a*) A labial with s (πς, βς, φς) makes ψ.

(*b*) A guttural with s (κς, γς, χς) makes ξ.

(*c*) The dental with s is dropped, but in the case of δς, makes ζ.

(*d*) The letter ν becomes μ before labials; thus σύνφημι (lit. together to say, i.e., to agree) becomes σύμφημι. It becomes γ before gutturals; thus συνχαίρω (to rejoice with) becomes συγχαίρω. It is dropped before σ or ζ; thus συνστρατιώτης (fellow soldier) becomes συστρατιώτης; σύνζυγος (yokefellow) becomes σύζυγος. Before λ, μ, ρ, (which, with ν itself, are called liquids) ν is changed into the same letter; thus συνλαλέω (to talk with) becomes συλλαλέω; συνμαρτυρέω (to witness with) becomes συμμαρτυρέω.

Further Pronunciations

The guttural γ followed by another guttural, κ, γ, χ, is pronounced like the English "ng." Thus ἄγγελος (angel) is pronounced angelos (hard g, not as in the English word "angel," and ἄγκυρα (anchor) is pronounced ang-kura. In the following double vowels pronounce αυ as in "out"; ει as in "eight"; ου as in "boot", αι as in "by"; ευ as in "beauty."

Punctuation

There are four punctuation marks:— the comma (,); the semicolon or colon, expressed by a point above the line (·); the full stop or period, as in English; the note of interrogation (;). This latter is the same in form as the English semi-colon, but must be distinguished from it. The Greek ; is the English ?.

Exercise.—Write the following in Greek characters, without the aid of the Greek text, and correct the result from the text. A good deal of practice can be obtained this way. Avoid trying to learn the meanings of the words. The practice will facilitate progress afterwards. All the vowels are short unless marked long.

John 1:4–11— 4 en autō zōē ēn, kai hē zōē ēn to phōs tōn anthrōpōn; 5 kai to phōs en tē skotia phainei, kai hē skotia auto ou katelaben.

6 Egeneto anthrōpos, apestalmenos para theou, onoma autō Iōannēs; 7 houtos ēlthen eis marturian hina marturēsē peri tou phōtos, hina pantes pisteusōsin di' autou. 8 ouk ēn ekeinos to phōs, all' hina marturēsē peri tou phōtos. 9 Ēn to phōs to alēthinon, ho phōtizei panta anthrōpon, erchomenon eis ton kosmon. 10 en to kosmō ēn, kai ho kosmos di' autou egeneto, kai ho kosmos auton ouk egnō. 11 eis ta idia ēlthen, kai hoi idioi auton ou parelabon.

[Practice transcribing further from the Greek text into English letters and transcribing the latter back into the Greek text.]

INFLECTION signifies the change in the form of words to express variation in meaning. Declension is the system of change in the terminations of nouns, adjectives and pronouns to express different relations, as follows:—

GENDERS—There are three genders, Masculine, Feminine, Neuter. These are not determined as in English by conditions of sex. Names of inanimate objects are of different genders. The terminations of the words are a considerable guide.

NUMBERS—These are two, singular and plural. There is a dual (signifying two) in Greek but it does not occur m the Greek Testament.

CASES—There are five cases: (1) The Nominative, expressing the subject; (2) the Vocative, used in direct address; (3) the Genitive, which originally signified motion from and hence separation but afterwards came largely to denote possession. Accordingly it is convenient to associate the preposition "of" with it. Its range is very wide; (4), the Dative signifying the remote object; hence the preposition "to" is associated with it. It also has a large range of meaning, however, such as rest in, conjunction with, etc.; (5) the Accusative, expressing the object of a verb, and used after certain prepositions to express motion towards, etc.; These details will be considered later.

The Article

We are now in a position to consider the forms of the definite article "the" (there is no indefinite article "a").

The following must be learnt by heart, horizontally (masculine, feminine, neuter), and case by case in the order given. The forms largely provide a model to the endings of certain noun, adjective, and pronoun cases, as will be seen later.

Singular

	Masc.	Fem.	Neut.	
Nom.	ὁ	ἡ	τό	(the)
Gen.	τοῦ	τῆς	τοῦ	(of the)
Dat.	τῷ	τῇ	τῷ	(to the)
Acc.	τόν	τήν	τό	(the)

Plural

	Masc.	Fem.	Neut.	
Nom.	οἱ	αἱ	τά	(the)
Gen.	τῶν	τῶν	τῶν	(of the)
Dat.	τοῖς	ταῖς	τοῖς	(to the)
Acc.	τούς	τάς	τά	(the)

Note 1—The iota under the vowels in the dative singular must be observed carefully; it is very important. It is called iota subscript.

Note 2—The nominative and accusative are always the same in the neuter.

Note 3—The genitive plural always ends in ων.

Note 4—Masculine and neuter dative forms are always alike.

The First Declension

Nouns

There are three types of inflection of nouns. These are called the Three Declensions. The endings of the First, in the noun form first given, correspond with the feminine form of the article.

First Declension

(1) *Feminine nouns in* -η

πύλη, a gate

	Singular			Plural	
Nom.	πύλη	a gate.	Nom.	πύλαι	gates.
Voc.	πύλη	O gate!	Voc.	πύλαι	O gates!
Gen.	πύλης	of a gate.	Gen.	πυλῶν	of gates.
Dat.	πύλῃ	to a gate.	Dat.	πύλαις	to gates.
Acc.	πύλην	a gate.	Acc.	πύλας	gates.

(Learn the above paradigm by heart, putting the feminine of the article with each case, thus: ἡ πύλη, the gate; τὴν πύλην the gate; τῆς πύλης of the gate; etc.)

Declined like πύλη are the following, which should be learned by heart:

τιμή .... honor
φωνή .... a voice
ψυχή .... soul, or life
στολή .... garment
δίκη .... justice
σελήνη .... moon
ὀργή .... wrath, anger
εἰρήνη .... peace
ἐπιστολή .... letter
κεφαλή .... head
ἀδελφή .... sister
ἀρχή .... beginning, rule
νύμφη .... bride
βροχή .... rain
παιδίσκη . a damsel, maid, or bondwoman
ὀφειλή .... a debt
προσευχή .... prayer
ὑπακοή .... obedience
παρακοή .... disobedience
ἀγαθωσύνη .... goodness
ἁγιωσύνη .... holiness
καταλλαγή .... reconciliation
ὑπερβολή .... abundance, excellence
ὑπομονή .... patience

(Write a few of these out in full, on the model of πύλη.)

LESSON 3

First Declension Nouns in -α

(*These are feminine*)

Note 1—When a noun has the stem-ending -α preceded by a vowel or ρ, the singular retains α throughout, as follows:—

βασιλεία, a kingdom

	Singular	Plural
N. & V.	βασιλεία	βασιλεῖαι
Gen.	βασιλείας	βασιλειῶν
Dat.	βασιλείᾳ	βασιλείαις
Acc.	βασιλείαν	βασιλείας

On the model of this, write out in full ἡμέρα, a day

Note 2—When a noun has the stem-ending -α preceded by a consonant, the α becomes η in the genitive and dative singular (α being kept in the other cases), as follows:—

γλῶσσα, a tongue

	Singular	Plural
N. & V.	γλῶσσα	γλῶσσαι
Gen.	γλώσσης	γλωσσῶν
Dat.	γλώσσῃ	γλώσσαις
Acc.	γλῶσσαν	γλώσσας

Like βασιλεία and ἡμέρα, are the following, which should be committed to memory:—

ἀλήθεια .... truth
ἀδικία .... unrighteousness
ἄγνοια .... ignorance
ἀνομία .... iniquity (lit., lawlessness)
ἐργασία .... work, diligence, or gain
ἐριθεία .... contention, strife
ἐξουσία .... power, authority
μαρτυρία .... a witness
σκία .... a shadow
οἰκία .... a house
λυχνία .... a lampstand
σοφία .... wisdom
πέτρα .... a rock
θύρα .... a door

Like γλῶσσα are:—

δόξα .... glory
μέριμνα .... a care
θάλασσα .... a sea
ῥίζα .... a root

Write out in full, with their different cases and numbers, οἰκία, μέριμνα, and ῥίζα, putting the feminine article with its appropriate cases, singular and plural, before each, and giving the meanings of each case. Do this without referring to the printed lessons and correct your results therefrom: thus, ἡ οἰκία, the house; τὴν οἰκίαν, the house; τῆς οἰκίας, of the house, etc.

First Declension Nouns in -ης and -ας

(*These are masculine*)

Note 1—Masculine nouns of the first declension in -ης form the genitive singular in -ου and the vocative in -α. In the other cases they are declined just like πύλη (Lesson 2).

Note 2—Masculine nouns of the first declension in -ας also form the genitive singular in -ου and the vocative in -α. In other cases they are like βασιλεία (see above).

Note 3—The plural is the same throughout in all first declension nouns. Commit the following to memory:—

μαθητής, a disciple

	Singular	Plural
Nom.	μαθητής	μαθηταί
Voc.	μαθητά	μαθηταί
Gen.	μαθητοῦ	μαθητῶν
Dat.	μαθητῇ	μαθηταίς
Acc.	μαθητήν	μαθητάς

νεανίας, a young man

	Singular	Plural
Nom.	νεανίας	νεανίαι
Voc.	νεανία	νεανίαι
Gen.	νεανίου	νεανίῶν
Dat.	νεανίᾳ	νεανίαις
Acc.	νεανίαν	νεανίας

Write these out putting the masculine article ὁ, with its appropriate cases, singular and plural, before each, and the meanings. Correct the result from the above.

Like μαθητής are the following, which should be learned:

προφήτης . . . . a prophet
τελώνης . . . . a publican (tax collector)
κριτής . . . . a judge
ἐργάτης . . . . a laborer
ὀφειλέτης . . . . a debtor
ὑπρέτης . . . . an attendant, a servant

The Second Declension—Stem ending -o

Masculine nouns, and a few feminine, m this declension end in -ος. Neuter nouns end in -ον. Learn the following thoroughly. Write them out in full by memory, with the article ὁ for λόγος and τό for ἔργον and with the meanings.

λόγος, a word

	Singular		Plural	
Nom.	λόγος	a word	λόγοι	words
Voc.	λόγε	O word	λόγοι	O words
Gen.	λόγου	of a word	λόγων	of words
Dat.	λόγῳ	to a word	λόγους	to words
Acc.	λόγον	a word	λόγοις	words

ἔργον, a work

	Singular	Plural
Nom.	ἔργον	ἔργα
Voc.	ἔργον	ἔργα
Gen.	ἔργου	ἔργων
Dat.	ἔργῳ	ἔργοις
Acc.	ἔργον	ἔργα

Note 1—All neuter nouns have the same form in the nominative, vocative, and accusative.

Note 2—Observe the iota subscript under the dative singular.

Note 3—The masculine article ὁ must go with masculine nouns when "the" comes before, and the neuter τό with neuter nouns.

With the help of a few extra words, some forms, and some simple principles, we shall be able at once to read some sentences from the New Testament. The third declension will be reserved till later.

Memorize the following:—

The present tense of the verb "to be"

	Singular	
1st person	εἰμί	I am
2nd person	εἶ	thou art
3rd person	ἐστί(ν)	he (she, it, or there) is

	Plural	
1st person	ἐσμέν	we are
2nd person	ἐστέ	ye are
3rd person	εἰσί(ν)	they (or there) are

Note—In English, "thou" is singular and "ye" is plural.

Note—The ν at the end of the 3rd person is used before a vowel, or at the end of a sentence.

Imperfect Tense

	Singular	
1st person	ἦν	I was
2nd person	ἦσθα	thou wast
3rd person	ἦν	he (she, it, or there) was

	Plural	
1st person	ἦμεν	we were
2nd person	ἦτε	ye were
3rd person	ἦσαν	they (or there) were

Note—The personal pronouns are included in the verb forms; they are expressed by separate words only when the pronouns require emphasis. These will be given later. When there is another subject of the verb the pronoun is, of course, omitted; thus, ἦν ὁ λόγος is "was the Word."

Learn the following words:— ἐν, in (this preposition is always followed by the dative case; thus ἐν ἀρχῇ, "in (the) beginning"—the omission of the Greek article here will be explained later, it must be rendered in English in this phrase; πρός, towards or with (this is followed by the accusative thus, πρὸς τὸν θεόν, "with God," the article is often used with proper names, but must not be rendered in English); ἐκ, of, or out of; καί, and; οὗτος, this (masculine); αὕτη, this (feminine); τοῦτο, this (neuter); οὐ, not (οὐ has two other forms, οὐκ and οὐχ; οὐκ is used when the next word begins with a vowel, and some consonants; οὐχ when the next word begins with an aspirate ʽ); δέ, but, or and.

υἱός	a son	ἄμπελος	a vine (fem.)
ἄνθρωπος	a man	κόσμος	a world
ὁδός	a way (fem.)	καθώς	even as
ἐγώ	I	οὗτος	this (masc.)
σύ	thou	αὕτη	this (fem.)

Translate into English without referring to the texts (these are supplied to enable students to make their own corrections from the Testament). For the meaning of the words see above.

Ἐν ἀρχῇ ἦν ὁ λόγος, καὶ ὁ λόγος ἦν πρὸς τὸν θεόν, καὶ θεὸς ἦν ὁ λόγος. οὗτος ἦν ἐν ἀρχῇ πρὸς τὸν θεόν. (John 1:1–2).

Καὶ αὕτη ἐστὶν ἡ μαρτυρία τοῦ Ἰωάννου (John 1:19).

οὗτός ἐστιν ὁ υἱὸς τοῦ θεοῦ (John 1:34).

σὺ εἶ ὁ υἱὸς τοῦ θεοῦ (John 1:49).

Ἦν δὲ ἄνθρωπος ἐκ τῶν Φαρισαίων (John 3:1).

Ἐγώ εἰμι ἡ ὁδὸς καὶ ἡ ἀλήθεια καὶ ἡ ζωή (John 14:6).

ἐγώ εἰμι ἡ ἄμπελος (John 15:5).

ἐκ τοῦ κόσμου οὐκ εἰσὶν καθὼς ἐγὼ οὐκ εἰμὶ ἐκ τοῦ κόσμου (John 17:16).

Οὗτός ἐστιν ὁ μαθητής (John 21:24).

After writing out the English correctly, retranslate the above sentences into Greek, correcting your results from the texts.

LESSON 4

Adjectives and Pronouns Corresponding to the First and Second Declensions

Note—The masculine and neuter endings correspond to the nouns of the second declension (see λόγος and ἔργον, Lesson 3); the feminine endings correspond to nouns of the first declension (see πύλη, Lesson 2). If the noun forms have been learned thoroughly the adjectives are easily committed to memory.

First Form

ἀγαθός, good

Singular

	Masc.	Fem.	Neut.
Nom.	ἀγαθός	ἀγαθή	ἀγαθόν
Voc.	ἀγαθέ	ἀγαθή	ἀγαθόν
Gen.	ἀγαθοῦ	ἀγαθῆς	ἀγαθοῦ
Dat.	ἀγαθῷ	ἀγαθῇ	ἀγαθῷ
Acc.	ἀγαθόν	ἀγαθήν	ἀγαθόν

Plural

	Masc.	Fem.	Neut.
N. & V.	ἀγαθοί	ἀγαθαί	ἀγαθά
Gen.	ἀγαθῶν	ἀγαθῶν	ἀγαθῶν
Dat.	ἀγαθοῖς	ἀγαθαῖς	ἀγαθοῖς
Acc.	ἀγαθοῦς	ἀγαθάς	ἀγαθά

As with the nouns, if the -ος of the masculine preceded by a vowel or ρ the feminine ends -α instead of -η and retains it throughout (see βασιλεία, Lesson 3). Thus:—

Second Form

ἅγιος, holy

Singular

	Masc.	Fem.	Neut.
Nom.	ἅγιος	ἁγία	ἅγιον
Voc.	ἅγιε	ἁγία	ἅγιον
Gen.	ἁγίου	ἁγίας	ἁγίου
Dat.	ἁγίῳ	ἁγίᾳ	ἁγίῳ
Acc.	ἅγιον	ἅγιον	ἅγιον

The plural is like that of ἀγαθός

Write out from memory μικρός, μικρά, μικπόν, "little," remembering the rule about the feminine ending -α after ρ, and correct the result from ἅγιος, ἁγία, ἅγιον above.

Rule—An adjective agrees with the noun which it qualifies in number, gender and case.

Write out in full, from memory, all the cases and genders, singular and plural, with the meanings, of ὁ δίκαιος ἄνθρωπος, "the just man," and correct the results from the paradigms above. Do the same with ἡ καλὴ ἀγγελία, "the good message," and τὸ καλὸν ἔργον, "the beautiful work."

Demonstrative Adjectives and Pronouns

οὗτος, "this"; ἐκεῖνος, "that."

Note 1—The endings, masculine, feminine, and neuter, are practically the same as those of the article, ὁ, ἡ, τό.

Note 2—It is important to observe the aspirate over the second vowel in the nominative of the masculine and feminine, singular and plural.

Note 3— -αυ- runs through the feminine *except in the genitive plural, which has* -ου-; the neuter plural has -αυ- in the nominative and accusative.

Singular: "this"

	Masc.	Fem.	Neut.
Nom.	οὗτος	αὕτη	τοῦτο
Gen.	τούτου	ταύτης	τούτου
Dat.	τούτῳ	ταύτῃ	τούτῳ
Acc.	τοῦτον	ταύτην	τοῦτο

Plural: "these"

	Masc.	Fem.	Neut.
Nom.	οὗτοι	αὗται	τοῦτα
Gen.	τούτων	τούτων	τούτων
Dat.	τούτοις	ταύταις	τούτοις
Acc.	τούτους	ταύτας	ταῦτα

Singular: "that"

Nom.	ἐκεῖνος	ἐκείνη	ἐκεῖνο

(*Remaining case endings as above*)

Plural: "those"

Nom.	ἐκεῖνοι	ἐκεῖναι	ἐκεῖνα

(*and so on as above*)

Rule 1—οὗτος and ἐκεῖνος agree, in number, gender, case, with the noun which they qualify, and the noun always has the article, which, however, is not translated. Thus οὗτος ὁ ἄνθρωπος is "this man"; οὗτος ὁ υἱος "this Son"; ταύτην τὴν ἐντολήν "this commandment"; ἐν ἐκεινῃ τῇ ὥρᾳ "in that hour."

Rule 2—The noun with its article may come first and the adjective οὗτος or ἐκεῖνος after it, without altering the meaning. Thus: either ἡ φωνὴ αὕτη or αὕτη ἡ φωνή is "this voice" ("this sound"). "This Scripture" is either ἡ γραφὴ αὕτη or αὕτη ἡ γραφή. "That disciple" is either ἐκεῖνος ὁ μαθητής or ὁ μαθητὴς ἐκεῖνος.

Rule 3—When οὗτος and ἐκεῖνος stand alone, without a noun, they are demonstrative pronouns. Thus οὗτος means "this man," αὕτη "this woman," τοῦτο "this thing," ταῦτα "these things," ἐκεῖνος "that man," ἐκεῖνη "that woman," ἐκεῖνο "that thing."

Or again they may simply denote "this," "that," "these," "those," when they stand, for instance, as the subject or object of a verb. Thus οὗτός ἐστιν ὁ μαθητής is "this is the disciple" (John 21:24); καὶ αὕτη ἐστὶν ἡ μαρτυρία is "And this is the witness" (John 1:19).

Learn this vocabulary before doing the exercise, and revise the verb εἰμί (p. 20).

ὥρα .... an hour
ζωή .... life
ἄνθρωπος .... a man
δικαιοσύνη .... righteousness
κριτής .... a judge
ἐκ from (is followed by the genitive case)
εἰς unto or among (takes the accusative case)
ἡμέρα .... a day
ἐντολή .... a commandment
δοῦλος .... a servant
δίκαιος .... righteous
στέφανος .... a crown
ἐν .... in (takes the dative case)

Exercise—Translate the following sentences, without referring to the Testament, unless necessary. When the English has been written out, translate it back into Greek, correcting the result from the Greek Testament.

Σῶσόν (save) με (me) ἐκ (from) τῆς ὥρας ταύτης . . . ἦλθον (I came) εἰς (unto) τὴν ὥραν ταύτην (John 12:27).

αὕτη ἐστὶν ὑμῶν (your) ἡ ὥρα (Luke 22:53).

ἐν ταῖς ἡμέραις ταύταις (Luke 24:18).

ἐξῆλθεν (went forth) οὖν (therefore) οὗτος ὁ λόγος εἰς (among) τοὺς ἀδελφοὺς ὅτι (that) ὁ μαθητὴς ἐκεῖνος οὐκ (not) ἀποθνήσκει (dies) (John 21:23).

Οἴδαμεν (we know) ὅτι (that) οὗτός ἐστιν ὁ υἱὸς ἡμῶν (our) (John 9:20).

αὕτη δέ ἐστιν ἡ αἰώνιος (eternal) ζωή (John 17:3), αἰώνιος has the same form in the feminine as the masculine.

ἐν ἐκείνῃ τῇ ἡμέρᾳ (John 14:20).

Οὐχ οὗτός ἐστιν Ἰησοῦς ὁ υἱὸς Ἰωσήφ; [note the question mark] (John 6:42).

Οὗτοι οἱ λόγοι πιστοὶ καὶ ἀληθινοί (Rev. 22:6, the verb εἰσίν "are" is omitted).

Οὗτοι οἱ λόγοι ἀληθινοὶ τοῦ θεοῦ εἰσιν (Rev. 19:9).

καὶ αὕτη ἐστὶν ἡ ἐντολὴ αὐτοῦ (His) (1 John 3:32).

ἐν τούτῳ ἡ ἀγάπη τοῦ θεοῦ τετελείωται (has been perfected) (1 John 2:5).

Οὗτοι οἱ ἄνθρωποι δοῦλοι τοῦ θεοῦ τοῦ ὑψίστου (Most High) εἰσίν (Acts 16:17).

ὁ τῆς* δικαιοσύνης στέφανος, ὃν (which) ἀποδώσει (shall give) μοι (to me) ὁ κύριος ἐν ἐκείνῃ τῇ ἡμέρᾳ (2 Tim. 4:8).

*This article is not to be translated, as it occurs with an abstract noun. The order, "the of righteousness crown" is common in Greek. Note that the subject of a verb (here ὁ κύριος) often comes after it. This has the effect of stressing the subject.

LESSON 5

Demonstrative Pronouns (*Continued*)

There is another demonstrative pronoun, the meaning of which is similar to that of οὗτος (Lesson 4). It is ὅδε, ἥδε, τόδε "this" (this one here). It consists simply of the article ὁ, ἡ, τό with -δε added.

The following demonstrative pronouns should also be noted, all declined like οὗτος:—

(*a*) of quality: τοιοῦτος, τοιαύτη, τοιοῦτο, "such."

(*b*) of quantity: τοσοῦτος, τοσαύτη, τοσοῦτο, "so great."

(*c*) of number: τοσοῦτοι etc., "so many." This is simply the plural of (*b*).

(*d*) of degree: τηλικοῦτος etc., "so very great." This occurs only in 2 Cor. 1:10; Heb. 2:3; Jas. 3:4; Rev. 16:18.

The Personal Pronoun, Third Person

For the third person, "he, she, it," the Greeks used the adjectival pronoun αὐτός, αὐτή, αὐτό. This is given here because its endings are those of the 1st and 2nd declensions. The student should become thoroughly familiar with the meanings.

Singular

	Masc.		Fem.		Neut.	
N.	αὐτός	he	αὐτή	she	αὐτό	it
G.	αὐτοῦ	of him (or his)	αὐτῆς	of her (or hers)	αὐτοῦ	of it (or its)
D.	αὐτῷ	to him	αὐτῇ	to her	αὐτῷ	to it
A.	αὐτόν	him	αὐτήν	her	αὐτό	it

Plural

N.	αὐτοί	they	αὐταί	they	αὐτα̣	them
G.	αὐτῶν	of them (their)	αὐτῶν	of them (their)	αὐτῶν	of them (their)
D.	αὐτοῖς	to them	αὐταῖς	to them	αὐτοῖς	to them
A.	αὐτούς	them	αὐτάς	them	αὐτά	of them

Note—Distinguish between αὕτη, this (fem.) and αὐτή, she; between αὗται, these (fem.) and αὐταί, they (fem.).

Rule—When αὐτός in all its cases is connected with a noun, it becomes a reflexive pronoun and denotes "himself, herself, itself." Thus, Ἰησοῦς αὐτὸς οὐκ ἐβάπτιζεν, "Jesus Himself baptized not."

Rule—When preceded by the article, αὐτό·, in all its cases, means "the same." Thus, ἐν τῇ αὐτῇ γνώμῃ is "in the same judgment" (1 Cor. 1:10); τὸ αὐτό means "the same thing."

Note—We must carefully note the order in which αὐτός occurs with a noun and article, and distinguish the two meanings of the pronoun as for example, in the two rules just mentioned: αὐτὸ τὸ πνεῦμα is "the Spirit Himself," but τὸ αὐτὸ πνεῦμα is "the same Spirit." When αὐτός comes after the article it denotes "the same."

Before doing the exercise below, learn the following vocabulary and review all preceding vocabularies. Also review the verb "to be" (Lesson 3).

χάρις . . . . thanks or grace
σπουδή . . . . zeal
καρδία . . . . heart
οὐρανός . . . . heaven
πόθεν . . . . whence
ἐρημία . . . . wilderness
ἄρτος . . . . loaf
οὖν . . . . therefore
ἄλλος . . . . other
ἔσω . . . . within
ὑπό . . . . by (takes the genitive)
γάρ for (never begins a sentence; usually the second word)
μετά with (takes the genitive; it is shortened to μετ' before a vowel)
δέ but (never comes first word in the sentence)

Exercise—Translate the following, with the help of the meaning given. Correct your result from the English Testament. Then rewrite your corrected rendering back into Greek, without looking at the Exercise, and correct your Greek from the Exercise afterwards.

εἶπον (they said) οὖν αὐτῷ, Μὴ (not) καὶ (also) σὺ (thou) ἐκ τῶν μαθητῶν αὐτοῦ εἶ; (John 18:25).

ἔλεγον (said) οὖν αὐτῷ οἱ ἄλλοι μαθηταί (John 20:25).

ἦσαν ἔσω οἱ μαθηταὶ αὐτοῦ καὶ Θωμᾶς (Thomas) μετ' αὐτῶν (John 20:26) (this word is not "of them" here, but "them," after the preposition μετά. as it takes the genitive).

Σίμων καὶ (also) αὐτὸς ἐπίστευσεν (believed) (Acts 8:13).

Δημητρίῳ (to Demetrius) μεμαρτύρηται (it hath been witnessed) ὑπὸ πάντων (all) καὶ ὑπὸ αὐτῆς τῆς ἀληθείας (3 John 12).

καὶ (both) κύριον αὐτὸν καὶ Χριστὸν ἐποίησεν (hath made) ὁ θεός, τοῦτον τὸν Ἰησοῦν (Jesus), for the two preceding words see Rule 1 under οὗτος, Lesson 4; note that the subject of this sentence is ὁ θεός (Acts 2:36)

Χάρις δὲ τῷ θεῷ τῷ δόντι (the One giving, or putting) τὴν αὐτὴν σπουδὴν . . . ἐν τῇ καρδίᾳ Τίτου (2 Cor. 8:16)

τῶν γὰρ τοιούτων ἐστὶν ἡ βασιλεία τῶν οὐρανῶν (Matt. 19:14)

οἱ γὰρ τοιοῦτοι τῷ κυρίῳ ἡμῶν (our) Χριστῷ οὐ δουλεύουσιν (serve—takes the dative) (Rom. 16:18)

καὶ λέγουσιν (say) αὐτῷ οἱ μαθηταί, Πόθεν ἡμῖν (to us) ἐν ἐρημίᾳ ἄρτοι τοσοῦτοι . . . ; (Matt. 15:33).

The Relative Pronoun

Note 1—The relative pronoun ὅς, ἥ, ὅ, "who. which," has the same form as the endings of οὗτος, αὕτη, τοῦτο, (see last Lesson) and therefore as those of the 1st and 2nd declensions.

Note 2—Each form has the rough breathing.

Note 3—There are certain forms of this pronoun which look exactly like those of the article ὁ, ἡ, τό, but which always have an accent (turning to the left in the text, though turning to the right when put by themselves as below); these must be distinguished; the forms are as follows:—in the singular, the nom., fem. and neut., and the acc. neut.; in the plural, the nom., masc. and fem. For example, ὁ is "the" but ὅ is "which."

Singular

	Masc.		Fem.		Neut.	
N.	ὅς	who or that	ἥ	ditto	ὅ	which
G.	οὗ	of whom, or whose	ἧς	"	οὗ	of which
D.	ᾧ	to whom	ᾗ	"	ᾧ	to which
A.	ὅν	whom or that	ἥν	"	ὅ	which

Plural
(*Meanings are the same as in the singular*)

N.	οἵ	ἥ	ὅ
G.	ὧν	ὧν	ὧν
D.	οἷς	αἷς	οἷς
A.	οὕς	ἅς	ἅ

Rule 1—The Relative Pronoun refers back to some noun or pronoun in another clause, and this latter noun or pronoun is called its antecedent. Thus in οὐδεὶς (no one) γὰρ (for) δύναται (is able) ταῦτα τὰ σημεῖα (these signs) ποιεῖν (to do) ἅ (which) σὺ (thou) ποιεῖς (doest) (John 3:2), ἅ, the relative, refers back to σημεῖα, the antecedent.

Rule 2—Relative pronouns agree with their antecedents in number and usually in gender, but not in case. Thus in ὁ ἀστὴρ (the star) ὃν εἶδον (which they saw) . . . προῆγεν (went before) αὐτοὺς (them) (Matt. 2:9), ὅν is singular and masculine, in agreement with the antecedent ἀστήρ, but the case differs.

Rule 3—The case of a relative pronoun depends (with certain exceptions) upon the part it plays in the clause in which it stands. Thus in the following:—λειτουργὸς (a minister) . . . τῆς σκηνῆς (of the tabernacle) τῆς ἀληθινῆς (the true) ἥν (which) ἔτηξεν (pitched) ὁ κύριος (the Lord) (Heb. 8:2), ἥν is in the accusative case because it is the object of the verb ἔπηξεν. Again, in παντὶ (to everyone,) . . . ᾧ (to whom) ἐδόθη (has been given) πολύ (much) (Luke 12:48), ᾧ is necessarily in the dative.

▪ LESSON 6 ▪

POSSESSIVE PRONOUNS

These are declined just like adjectives of the first and second declensions (see ἀγαθός, Lesson 4). They are :—

	Masc.	Fem.	Neut.	
1st Pers.	ἐμός	ἐμή	ἐμόν	my
	ἡμέτερος	ἡμετέρα	ἡμέτερον	our
2nd Pers.	σός	σή	σόν	thy
	ὑμέτερος	ὑμετέρα	ὑμέτερον	your

For the third person, his, hers, its, theirs, the genitive case (sing. and plur.) of αὐτός, αὐτή, αὐτό, he, she, it, is used (see Lesson 5), or the genitive case of the reflexive pronoun ἑαυτοῦ, (see below), which signifies "his own," "her own," etc. As to the former, αὐτοῦ ("of him") is "his," and so with the feminine and neuter. Thus "on his shoulders" is ἐπὶ τοὺς ὤμους αὐτοῦ, lit. "on the shoulders of him" (ὦμος, a shoulder).

Rule—When a noun is qualified by a possessive pronoun or the genitive of a personal pronoun, it has the article. The pronoun αὐτοῦ, αὐτῆς, αὐτοῦ (his, hers, its), or αὐτῶν (their), comes either before the article and noun or after them. Thus "his son" would be either ὁ υἱός αὐτοῦ or αὐτοῦ ὁ υἱός. With other possessive pronouns the article may be repeated (see sentences 4 and 5, in the exercise below).

Vocabulary

νεκρός, -ά, -όν . . . . dead
πρεσβύτερος . . . . elder
ἀγρός . . . . a field
ὀφθαλμός . . . . an eye
καρδία . . . . a heart
ἕτοιμος, -η, -ον . . . . ready
καιρός . . . . a time
οὔπω . . . . not yet
πάντοτε . . . . always

Exercise

Translate the following sentences after learning the vocabulary. Correct the result from the English Version (preferably the Revised [or the New Revised Standard or New King James]). Then retranslate from the English into Greek, without referring to the Greek unless necessary, and correct your result from it afterwards.

(1) ὅτι (for) οὗτος ὁ υἱός μου νεκρὸς ἦν (Luke 15:24).

(2) Ἦν δὲ (but, or now) ὁ υἱὸς αὐτοῦ ὁ πρεσβύτερος ἐν ἀγρῷ (Luke 15:25. Note that this sentence begins with the verb "was," the subject "his son" coming after).

(3) Τετύφλωκεν (He hath blinded) αὐτῶν τοὺς ὀφθαλμοὺς καὶ ἐπώρωσεν (He hath hardened) αὐτῶν τὴν καρδίαν (John 12:40).

(4) καὶ ἡ κοινωνία (fellowship) δὲ (indeed) ἡ ἡμετέρα . . . μετὰ (with—takes the genitive) τοῦ υἱοῦ αὐτοῦ Ἰησοῦ Χριστοῦ ("is" is omitted) (1 John 1:3).

(5) λέγει (saith) οὖν (therefore) αὐτοῖς ὁ Ἰησοῦς, Ὁ καιρὸς ὁ ἐμὸς οὔπω πάρεστιν (is come), ὁ δὲ καιρὸς ὁ ὑμέτερος πάντοτέ ἐστιν ἕτοιμος (John 7:6).

The Regular Verb

Before taking the third declension nouns, adjectives and pronouns, we shall study the simpler parts of the Regular Verb. A few introductory notes will serve here.

Note 1—There are in Greek three *Voices*—(1) *the Active Voice* (as in English), signifying that a person, or thing, does something; e.g., λύω, I loose: (2) *the Middle Voice* (not used in English, signifying that a person, or thing, does something for or upon himself, or itself (i.e., in self-interest); e.g., λύομαι, I loose for myself: (3) *the Passive Voice* (as in English), signifying that an action is done upon a person, or thing; e.g., λύομαι, I am loosed. This form is the same as the middle in many respects.

Note 2—There are five *Moods* (1) *the Indicative,* which is used to make an assertion, absolutely, e.g., "I loose": (2) *the Imperative,* which is used to make a command, e.g., "loose thou": (3) *the Subjunctive,* which asserts a supposition or condition, e.g., "I may loose": (4) *the Optative,* used in expressing wishes, and in other ways to be explained later: (5) *the Infinitive,* expressing an act or state, usually rendered by the preposition "to," e.g., "to loose," but often used as a verbal noun, e.g., "the act of loosing."

Note 3—There is also a set of verbal adjectives called *Participles.* These are also used as nouns. They will be treated separately.

Note 4—There are six *Tenses* in the Active Voice, signifying the present, past, or future. Most of these six run through all the Moods and Participles. In the Indicative Mood the tenses run as follows:—

1 *Present,*	λύω, I loose, or I am loosing
2 *Future,*	λύσω, I shall loose
3 *Imperfect,*	ἔλυον, I was loosing
4 *Aorist,*	ἔλυσα, I loosed
5 *Perfect,*	λέλυκα, I have loosed
6 *Pluperfect,*	ἐλελύκειν, I had loosed

Note 5—There are two sorts of verbs, which come under the heading of *Conjugations.* We shall for some time be occupied only with the First Conjugation, the verbs of which end in x, and we shall take the Indicative Mood, completing the others after studying the remaining class of nouns and pronouns. The purpose of this order is to enable the student the more readily to read certain passages of Scripture.

Conjugation of the Verb in -ω-
Active Voice

Indicative Mood

Introductory Notes

(1) The endings after the stem λυ- should be written out separately and memorized. Then memorize the whole form of the specimen verb.

(2) The characteristic letter of the future tense is the -σ- before the endings, which otherwise are the same as those of the present tense.

(3) The vowel ἐ- which precedes the imperfect, first aorist and pluperfect forms is called the *Augment* and characterizes these tenses as past, or historic.

(4) The initial syllable λε- which begins the perfect and pluperfect forms is called a *reduplication,* i.e., a doubling of the syllable.

(5) Note the -σ- in the first aorist, and the characteristic vowel -α- except in the 3rd person singular.

(6) Note the -κ- in the perfect and pluperfect. The endings of the perfect are the same as those of the first aorist.

Present Tense

Singular		Plural	
λύω	I loose	λύομεν	we loose
λύεις	thou loosest	λύετε	ye loose
λύει	he looses	λύουσι	they loose

Future Tense

λύσω	I shall loose	λύσομεν	we shall loose
λύσεις	thou wilt loose	λύσετε	ye will loose
λύσει	he will loose	λύσουσι	they will loose

Imperfect Tense

ἔλυον	I was loosing	ἐλύομεν	we were loosing
ἔλυες	thou wast loosing	ἐλύετε	ye were loosing
ἔλυε	he was loosing	ἔλυον	they were loosing

First Aorist Tense

ἔλυσα	I loosed	ἐλύσαμεν	we loosed
ἔλυσας	thou loosedst	ἐλύσατε	ye loosed
ἔλυσε	he loosed	ἔλυσαν	they loosed

Perfect Tense

λέλυκα	I have loosed	λελύκαμεν	we have loosed
λέλυκας	thou hast loosed	λελύκατε	ye have loosed
λέλυκε	he has loosed	λελύκασι	they have loosed

Pluperfect Tense

ἐλελύκειν	I had loosed	ἐλελύκειμεν	we had loosed
ἐλελύκεις	thou hadst loosed	ἐλελύκειτε	ye had loosed
ἐλελύκει	he had loosed	ἐλελύκεσαν	they had loosed

Additional Notes

Note 1—Some verbs have a second aorist tense, with tense-endings like those of the imperfect. The meaning is the same as the first aorist.

Note 2—As we have observed in ἐστί (or ἐστιν), the letter -ν is added to the 3rd person singular when the word comes last in a sentence, or when the next word begins with a vowel. This -ν is likewise added to the 3rd person plural when it ends in -σι.

LESSON 7

INDICATIVE MOOD (*Continued*)

Like λύω are πιστεύω, to believe; δουλεύω, to serve; προφητεύω, to prophesy, νηστεύω, to fast, κελεύω, to command; βασιλεύω, to reign; παύω, to cause to cease; κλείω, to shut, and others.

The student, who should have learnt the indicative mood of λύω by heart, should write out all *the tenses* of that mood of "I believe" in English, in all the persons, singular and plural, and put the Greek against them from memory, so as to become thoroughly familiar with the forms; this thoroughness will make progress easy. As an example of what to do we will give the present and 1st aorist:—

Present Indicative

I believe	πιστεύω	We believe	πιστεύομεν
Thou believest	πιστεύεις	You believe	πιστεύετε
He believes	πιστεύει	They believe	πιστεύουσι

First Aorist Indicative

I believed	ἐπίστευσα	We believed	ἐπιστεύσαμεν
Thou believedst	ἐπίστευσας	Ye believed	ἐπιστεύσατε
He believed	ἐπίστευσε	They believed	ἐπίστευσαν

(*Write out the whole mood this way, in the right order of the Tenses*)

The following verbs consist of λύω combined with a preposition:— ἀπολύω to loose, release, put away; καταλύω to destroy. In forming the augment ἐ- for the imperfect, aorist and pluperfect tenses of such compound verbs, the final vowel of the preposition is simply changed to -ε-. Thus the imperfect of ἀπολύω is ἀπέλυον and the aorist is ἀπέλυσα.

Before doing the exercise below, memorize the following vocabulary, and the verbs above at the beginning of this Lesson.

Vocabulary

κύριος	a lord	μέχρι	until
δοῦλος	a servant	θάνατος	death
νῦν	now	ἀλλά	but
ναός	a temple	ἀπό	from
μαθητής	a disciple		

Exercise—Write out a translation of the following without reference to the English Version. Correct your results from the English Testament. Rewrite the sentences from the English back into the Greek, without referring to the Greek. Correct your results from the exercise now given.

(1) ὁ κύριος τοῦ δούλου ἐκείνου (see Lesson 4, Rule 1) ἀπέλυσεν (1st aorist) αὐτόν (Matt. 18:27).

(2) Νῦν ἀπολύεις τὸν δοῦλόν σου (Luke 2:29).

(3) Ἐγὼ καταλύσω τὸν ναὸν τοῦτον (Mark 14:58).

(4) ἐπίστευσαν εἰς (on) αὐτὸν οἱ μαθηταὶ αὐτοῦ (John 2:11).

(5) πεπιστεύκατε ὅτι (that) ἐγὼ παρὰ (from) τοῦ θεοῦ ἐξῆλθον (came out) (John 16:27).

(6) ἐγὼ πεπίστευκα (perfect tense, as in R.V.) ὅτι σὺ εἶ (see verb "to be") ὁ Χριστὸς ὁ υἱὸς τοῦ θεοῦ (John 11:27).

(7) ἀλλὰ ἐβασίλευσεν ὁ θάνατος ἀπὸ Ἀδὰμ μέχρι Μωϋσέως (Moses) (Rom. 5:14)—(the article before θάνατος must not be translated; an abstract noun often has the article).

(8) καὶ ἐβασίλευσαν μετὰ (with) τοῦ Χριστοῦ (Rev. 20:4) (the subject of the sentence is "they" and is included in the verb).

(9) βασιλεύσουσιν (future) μετ' αὐτοῦ (Rev. 20:6).

Before proceeding further with, the other moods of the verb, we shall make easiest headway in the reading of the Testament by taking the remainder of the nouns, adjectives and pronouns.

Previously to learning these the student should thoroughly review the nouns of the first and second declensions, πύλη *(Lesson 2),* βασιλεία, γλῶσσα, μαθητής, νεανίας, λόγος *and* ἔργον *(Lesson 3), the adjectives* ἀγαθός *and* ἅγιος *(Lesson 4), and the pronouns* οὗτος, ἐκεῖνος, αὐτός *(Lesson 4), memorizing all that may have been forgotten. This is necessary in order to keep distinct in the mind the forms that follow, and especially the third declension.*

Contracted Nouns and Adjectives of the Second Declension

Note—Contraction means the combining of two distinct vowels to form one vowel sound. There are very few contracted nouns and adjectives, but they must be noted.

Rule 1—When the vowel ο-, in the final syllable, is preceded by ε or ο in the stem, the two vowels generally contract, forming one vowel sound -ου (to be pronounced as in "boot "). Thus νόος (νό-ος), the mind, becomes νοῦς; ὀστέον a bone, becomes ὀστοῦν.

Rule 2—When Omega is preceded by ε or ο, they combine to form simply -ω. Thus νόῳ becomes νῷ.

Rule 3—The vowels -εη combine to form -η, and the vowels -εα combine to form -η or -α. These are illustrated in the adjectives below.

νοῦς, mind

	Singular		Plural	
Nom.	(νόος)	νοῦς	(νόοι)	νοῖ
Voc.	(νόε)	νοῦ	(νόοι)	νοῖ
Gen.	(νόου)	νοῦ	(νόων)	νῶν
Dat.	(νόῳ)	νῷ	(νόοις)	νοῖς
Acc.	(νόον)	νοῦν	(νόους)	νοῦς

Note—This contraction does not by any means invariably take place. Thus, while ὀστοῦν, a bone, is contracted thus from ὀστέον in John 19:36, we find ὀστέων instead of ὀστῶν in Heb. 11:22. (There is no need to learn the neuter paradigm ὀστοῦν).

Contracted Adjectives

χρύσεος, χρυσέα, χρύσεον, golden, becomes χρυσοῦς, χρυσῆ, χρυσοῦν, etc., according to the rules above.

	Singular			Plural		
	M.	F.	N.	M.	F.	N.
N.	χρυσοῦς	χρυσῆ	χρυσοῦν	χρυσοῖ	-αῖ	-ᾶ
[V.	χρύσεε	χρυσῆ	χρυσοῦν]	[χρυσοῖ	-αῖ	-ᾶ]
G.	χρυσοῦ	χρυσῆς	χρυσοῦ	χρυσῶν	-ῶν	-ῶν
D.	χρυσῷ	χρυσῇ	χρυσῷ	χρυσοῖς	-αῖς	-οῖς
A.	χρυσοῦν	χρυσῆν	χρυσοῦν	χρυσοῦς	-ᾶς	-ᾶ

Two Irregular Adjectives

Note—The following adjectives are important, as they are of very frequent occurrence; they should be committed to memory. They are irregular only in the masculine and neuter singular, which present shortened forms.

μέγας, great

Singular

	Masc.	Fem.	Neut.
Nom.	μέγα	μεγάλη	μέγα
Gen.	μεγάλου	μεγάλης	μεγάλου
Dat.	μεγάλῳ	μεγάλῃ	μεγάλῳ
Acc.	μέγαν	μεγάλην	μέγα

Plural

The plural is regular, as if from μεγάλος, and runs μεγάλοι, μεγάλαι, μεγάλα, etc.

πολύς, many

Singular

	Masc.	Fem.	Neut.
Nom.	πολύς	πολλή	πολύ
Gen.	πολλοῦ	πολλῆς	πολλοῦ
Dat.	πολλῷ	πολλῇ	πολλῷ
Acc.	πολύν	πολλήν	πολύ

Plural

The plural is regular as if from πολλός, and runs πολλοί, πολλαί, πολλά, etc.

The Third Declension

Introductory Note—Nouns in this declension are of all three genders. There is a considerable variety and hence a number of paradigms are necessary, but all follow a simple form which presents little or no difficulty.

The essential thing is to know the *stem,* i.e., the elementary part of the word apart from the endings, or inflections. The stem can always be found from the genitive singular by taking away the inflection ending. Note that the genitive singular in the third declension usually ends in -ος. Take away the -ος and you have the stem. The stem will be a guide to the nominative case.

We will begin with two simple forms, one of a masculine noun (the feminine would be the same) and one of a neuter noun. When these are learned, the rest will follow easily.

αἰών, an age (masc.)
stem, αἰών-

	Singular		Plural	
N.	αἰών	an age	αἰῶνες	ages
V.	αἰών	O age	αἰῶνες	ages
G.	αἰῶνος	of an age	αἰώνων	of ages
D.	αἰῶνι	to an age	αἰῶσι(ν)	to ages
A.	αἰῶνα	an age	αἰῶνας	ages

ῥῆμα, a word (neut.)
stem, ῥηματ-

	Singular	Plural
Nom.	ῥῆμα	ῥήματα
Voc.	ῥῆμα	ῥήματα
Gen.	ῥήματος	ῥημάτων
Dat.	ῥήματι	ῥήμασι(ν)
Acc.	ῥῆμα	ῥήματα

Notes

(1) The nominative and vocative are alike, and in the neuter the accusative also, as in the first and second declensions.

(2) The accusative singular ending -α was originally -ν, as in the other declensions, and the -ν is retained in several third declension nouns, the stems of which end in a vowel. These will be illustrated later. The -α ending should, however, be regarded as normal.

(3) The genitive singular ending is -ος, added to the stem.

(4) The dative singular ending is -ι, added to the stem.

(5) The nominative plural, in masculine and feminine nouns, ends in -ες, added to the stem. Neuter plurals always end in -α in the nominative, vocative, and accusative.

(6) The accusative plural masculine ends in -ας.

(7) The genitive plural ends in -ων, added to the stem. All genitive plurals end -ων.

(8) The dative plural ends in -σι, added to the stem, with various modifications. The -ν in brackets in the dative plural does not belong to the word; it is added at the close of a sentence, or when the next word begins with a vowel; this is simply for the sake of the sound.

▪ LESSON 8 ▪

Third Declension (*Continued*)

Rule 1—The usual ending of the nominative singular is ς, added to the stem. The nominative endings provide a considerable variety and present a difference in form from that of the stem seen in the other cases. There are certain principles which govern the formation of the nominative, but these need not be learned. They simply serve to show that the variety of the third declension nouns is based on one form of case ending. The student should become familiar with the actual examples given and should keep in memory the other case endings, namely, -α, -ος, -ι, of the singular, and -ας, -ων, -σι, of the plural, as already learned in the noun αἰών.

We will first take the noun κῆρυξ, a herald. The paradigm is as follows:—

	Singular	Plural
Nom.	κῆρυξ	κήρυκες
Voc.	κῆρυξ	κήρυκες
Gen.	κήρυκος	κηρύκων
Dat.	κήρυκι	κῆρυξι
Acc.	κήρυκα	κήρυκας

The question arises as to why the nominative, vocative singular, and dative plural have an ξ, whereas the rest of the cases have a κ. The explanation is as follows:—

When the stem (here κήρυκ-) ends in κ, or γ, or χ (which letters are called *gutturals*), the addition of the ς to the stem produces the letter ξ in the nominative and vocative singular and the dative plural. Thus κῆρυκ with ς, makes not κῆρυκς but κῆρυξ. The other cases retain the κ-.

Take another noun with a guttural stem:—

In Heb. 1:8 the student will see the word φλογός. This is a genitive case. Take away the -ος and the stem is φλογ-. The Concordance shows that the nominative is φλόξ. The ξ is due to the combination of the letters γ and ς. So νυκτός (Mark 5:5) is the genitive of νύξ "night." Write out in full, on the model of κῆρυξ above, φλόξ, φλόγα, etc. (dat. plur. φλοξί) and νύξ, νύκτα, etc.

We will next take the noun Ἄραψ, an Arab. The paradigm is as follows:—

	Singular	Plural
Nom.	Ἄραψ	Ἄραβες
Voc.	Ἄραψ	Ἄραβες
Gen.	Ἄραβος	Ἄραβων
Dat.	Ἄραβι	Ἄραψι
Acc.	Ἄραβα	Ἄραβας

The stem is seen to be Ἄραβ-. When a stem ends in π, or β, or φ (which letters are called *labials*) the addition of the ς to the stem produces the letter ψ. Thus Ἄραβ- with ς makes, not Ἄραβς, but Ἄραψ.

Now for a third specimen:—In Acts 4:25, the word παιδός occurs (a genitive case). The

Concordance shows that the nominative is παῖς. Take away the -ος and we get the stem παιδ-. The paradigm is as follows:—

	Singular	Plural
Nom.	παῖς	παῖδες
Voc.	παῖς	παῖδες
Gen.	παιδός	παίδων
Dat.	παιδί	παισί
Acc.	παῖδα	παῖδας

We observe that the stem is παιδ-. Now whenever a stem ends in τ, or δ, or θ (which letters are called *dentals*) the addition of ς causes the dropping of the τ, δ, or θ. Hence παιδς becomes παῖς and παιδσι becomes παισί. Similarly ἐλπιδ- is the stem of ἐλπίς, hope. The student should write out ἐλπίς in all its cases from memory, on the model of παῖς.

Note—Nouns in the third declension whose nominative ends in -ις, -υς, -αυς, *and* -ους *usually have, in the accusative singular, a shortened form, ending in* -ν. *Thus while the stem of* χάρις, *grace (or thanks) is* χαριτ-, *and hence the genitive is* χάριτος, *and the dative* χάριτι, *the accusative is* χάριν, *but* χάριτα *exceptionally in Acts 24:27.*

To take a fourth variety, ἰχθύος is "of a fish." Take away the -ος and we get the stem ἰχθυ-. This stem ends, then, in a vowel. When a stem ends in a vowel the nominative is formed by simply adding the ς; "a fish" is ἰχθύς.

Bearing in mind the note just given, that the accusative of nouns ending in -υς etc. end, not in -α, but in -ν, we have the following paradigm for ἰχθύς:—

	Singular	Plural
Nom.	ἰχθύς	ἰχθύες
Voc.	ἰχθύς	ἰχθύες
Gen.	ἰχθύος	ἰχθύων
Dat.	ἰχθύϊ	ἰχθυσί
Acc.	ἰχθύν	ἰχθῦς

Rule 2 (not to be committed to memory)—When a stem ends in -ν, or -ντ, or -ς the nominative is formed by lengthening the preceding vowel. The same is usually the case with a stem ending in -ρ.

Take for example, ποιμεν-, the stem of the word for "a shepherd." The nominative is ποιμήν (note the η instead of ε); the accusative is ποιμένα, the genitive ποιμένος, etc. Note that the dative plural is ποιμέσι (not ποιμένσι—the ν was dropped before ς); again, λέων a lion (stem λεοντ-) has accusative λέοντα, genitive λέοντος, etc. The dative plural is λέουσι not λέοντσι—a combination too awkward for Greek ears; note the ω in the nominative instead of ο. So again with ῥήτωρ, an orator (stem ῥήτορ-), it has accus. ῥήτορα, etc. The dative plural is ῥήτορσι.

Write out the declension of ποιμήν, λέων, and ῥήτωρ in full.

Note—One or two nouns ending in ρ are a little irregular. The two following must be memorized:—

πατήρ, a father

	Singular	Plural
Nom.	πατήρ	πατέρες
Voc.	πάτερ*	πατέρες
Gen.	πατρός	πατέρων
Dat.	πατρί	πατράσι
Acc.	πατέρα	πατέρας

* (*Note short* ε)

Note—μήτηρ, a mother, and θυγάτηρ, a daughter, are declined in the same way. Write them out in full from memory, not forgetting the shortened form in the gen. and dat. sing., and the gen. plur., and the α in the dat. plural.

ἀνήρ, a man

	Singular	Plural
Nom.	ἀνήρ	ἄνδρες
Voc.	ἄνερ	ἄνδρες
Gen.	ἀνδρός	ἀνδρῶν
Dat.	ἀνδρί	ἀνδράσι
Acc.	ἄνδρα	ἄνδρας

Note—ἀστῆρ, a star, keeps the ε throughout (e.g., gen. ἀστέρος), except that the dative plural is ἀστράσι.

Exercise

Learn the following vocabulary before doing the exercise, and review the indicative mood of λύω.

λέγω .... I say
τηρέω .... I keep
ποιέω .... I do
πιστεύω .... I believe
φανερόω .... I manifest
κόσμος .... world
ἐπιθυμία .... lust
σάρξ .... flesh (gen. σαρκός)
διάκονος .... a servant
καλός, -ή, -όν .... good
οἶνος .... wine
ἕως .... until
ἄρτι .... now
ἑπτά .... seven
ἀστήρ .... star
ὀφθαλμός .... eye
βίος .... life
ἀρχή .... beginning
σημεῖον .... sign
δόξα .... glory
μαθητής .... disciple
νύξ .... night
φυλακή .... a guard, or watch
λυχνία .... lampstand
ἀλαζονεία .... vainglory

Translate, correcting the result from the English Bible, and then re-translate into the Greek:

(1) λέγει ἡ μήτηρ αὐτοῦ τοῖς διακόνοις (John 2:5).

(2) σὺ τετήρηκας (see τηρέω in the vocabulary above. What tense is indicated by the reduplicating syllable τε- ?) τὸν καλὸν οἶνον ἕως ἄρτι. Ταύτην ἐποίησεν (1st aorist of ποιέω—note the augment ἐ-) ἀρχὴν τῶν σημείων ὁ Ἰησοῦς ἐν Κανὰ τῆς Γαλιλαίας καὶ ἐφανέρωσεν (1st aorist of φανερόω) τὴν δόξαν αὐτοῦ καὶ ἐπίστευσαν εἰς (on) αὐτὸν οἱ μαθηταὶ αὐτοῦ (John 2: end of verse 10 and 11).

(3) τετάρτῃ ("at the fourth") δὲ φυλακῇ (this is a dative of time—hence the whole phrase is "at [not "to"] the fourth watch") τῆς νυκτὸς ἦλθεν (He came) πρὸς (to) αὐτοὺς (Matt. 14:25).

(4) οἱ ἑπτὰ ἀστέρες ἄγγελοι τῶν ἑπτὰ ἐκκλησιῶν εἰσιν καὶ αἱ λυχνίαι αἱ ἑπτὰ ἑπτὰ ἐκκλησίαι εἰσίν (Rev. 1:20, end, R.V.).

(5) πεπιστεύκαμεν τὴν ἀγάπην ἣν ἔχει ὁ θεὸς ἐν ἡμῖν (us) (1 John 4:16).

(6) ὅτι πᾶν τὸ ἐν τῷ κόσμῳ, ἡ ἐπιθυμία τῆς σαρκὸς καὶ ἡ ἐπιθυμία τῶν ὀφθαλμῶν καὶ ἡ ἀλαζονεία τοῦ βίου, οὐκ ἔστιν ἐκ τοῦ πατρὸς ἀλλ' ἐκ τοῦ κόσμου ἐστίν. (1 John 2:16) Bear in mind that ὅτι is "for"; πᾶν τό is "all the," i.e., "all that is."

(7) Πέτρος δὲ καὶ Ἰωάννης ἀνέβαινον εἰς τὸ ἱερὸν ἐπὶ τὴν ὥραν τῆς προσευχῆς τὴν ἐνάτην. (Acts 3:1) ἀνέβαινον is the 3rd person plural, imperfect tense of ἀναβαίνω, I go up: the augment is formed by changing the final vowel of the preposition ἀνα "up" to -ε: βαίνω is "I go"; the augment must come immediately before it. This is always the case where a preposition is combined with a verb. ἱερόν, "temple"; ἐπί, "at"; προσευχή, prayer; ἐνάτος, "ninth."

(8) εὑρίσκει Φίλιππος τὸν Ναθαναὴλ καὶ λέγει αὐτῷ, Ὃν ἔγραψεν Μωϋσῆς ἐν τῷ νόμῳ καὶ οἱ προφῆται εὑρήκαμεν, Ἰησοῦν υἱὸν τοῦ Ἰωσὴφ τὸν ἀπὸ Ναζαρέτ. (John 1:45) ἔγραψεν is the 3rd pers. sing. 1st aorist of γράφω, "I write"; εὑρήκαμεν is the 1st pers. plur. of the perfect of εὑρίσκω, "I find."

LESSON 9

The Third Declension (*Continued*)

Rule 3—Some nouns ending in -ις and -ευς have a genitive ending with -εως instead of -ος. The two following should be memorized:—

πόλις, a city (feminine)
(stem πολι-)

	Singular	Plural	
Nom.	πόλις	πόλεις	(for πόλεες)
Voc.	πόλι	πόλεις	(")
Gen.	πόλεως	πόλεων	
Dat.	πόλει	πόλεσι	
Acc.	πόλιν	πόλεις	(for πόλεας)

(*Note the accusative in* -ιν; *see note in Lesson 8*)

Like πόλις are δύναμις, power; κρίσις, judgment; ὄφις, a serpent, and others.

βασιλεύς, a king

	Singular	Plural	
Nom.	βασιλεύς	βασιλεῖς	(for βασιλέες)
Voc.	βασιλεῦ	βασιλεῖς	(")
Gen.	βασιλέως	βασιλέων	
Dat.	βασιλεῖ	βασιλεῦσι	
Acc.	βασιλέα	βασιλεῖς	(for βασιλέας)

Note (1) the ordinary accusative ending -εα, (2) the nom., voc. and acc. plural in -εες and -εες; contract these double vowels to ει (for the sake of sound).

Like βασιλεύς are γραμματεύς, a scribe; γονεύς, a parent.

Neuter Nouns of the Third Declension

These are important, and are of two chief kinds. Remember that all neuters have the same form for the nominative, vocative and accusative cases.

(1) Most conform to the example ῥῆμα on p. 48.

Learn the following :—

αἷμα .... blood
γράμμα .... a letter
θέλημα .... a will
κρίμα .... a judgment
ὄνομα .... a name
πνεῦμα .... a spirit
στόμα .... a mouth
σῶμα .... a body

There are a few words not ending in -μα which are neuter and come here, such as πῦρ, fire (genitive πυρός); φῶς, light (genitive: φωτός); τέρας, a wonder (genitive τέρατος).

(2) Other neuters ending in -ος have some contracted endings. The following model must be memorized:—

γένος, a race, generation

	Singular		Plural	
Nom.	γένος		(γένεα)	γένη
Voc.	γένος		(γένεα)	γένη
Gen.	(γένεος)	γένους	(γενέων)	γενῶν
Dat.	γένει			γένεσι
Acc.	γένος		(γένεα)	γένη

Note 1—The genitive singular γένεος contracts to γένους; the nominative, vocative and accusative γένεα contract to γένη; the genitive plural γενέων to γενῶν.

Note 2—These neuters in -ος, must be distinguished from second declension masculine nouns ending in -ος like λόγος (Lesson 3).

The student will soon become accustomed to the two varieties as found in the New Testament.

Note 3—These neuter plurals in -η (for -εα) must be distinguished from first declension feminines ending in -η, like πύλη (Lesson 2). The context generally helps to distinguish.

Adjectives Containing Third Declension Forms

These are of two kinds: (1) Those which contain endings of the first declension as well as the third. (2) Those which have the same form in the masculine and feminine.

(*I*) These adjectives are of great importance; the verbal adjectives, called participles, are formed on these models. As the participles run parallel to the adjectives now to be learned we shall take them together.

Adjectives

Form I: ἑκών, -οῦσα, -όν willing

Singular

	Masculine	Feminine	Neuter
Nom.	ἑκών	ἑκοῦσα	ἑκόν
Voc.	ἑκών	ἑκοῦσα	ἑκόν
Gen.	ἑκόντος	ἑκούσης	ἑκόντος
Dat.	ἑκόντι	ἑκούσῃ	ἑκόντι
Acc.	ἑκόντα	ἑκοῦσαν	ἑκόν

Plural

	Masculine	Feminine	Neuter
Nom.	ἑκόντες	ἑκοῦσαι	ἑκόντα
Voc.	ἑκόντες	ἑκοῦσαι	ἑκόντα
Gen.	ἑκόντων	ἑκουσῶν	ἑκόντων
Dat.	ἑκοῦσι	ἑκούσαις	ἑκοῦσι
Acc.	ἑκόντας	ἑκούσας	ἑκόντα

Note—The feminine conforms to the first declension (see γλῶσσα, Lesson 3), the masculine and neuter to the third declension.

Form II: πᾶς, πᾶσα, πᾶν, all, every

	Singular			Plural		
	M.	F.	N.	M.	F.	N.
Nom.	πᾶς	πᾶσα	πᾶν	πάντες	πᾶσαι	πάντα
Voc.	πᾶς	πᾶσα	πᾶν	πάντες	πᾶσαι	πάντα
Gen.	παντός	πάσης	παντός	πάντων	πασῶν	πάντων
Dat.	παντί	πάσῃ	παντί	πᾶσι	πάσαις	πᾶσι
Acc.	πάντα	πᾶσαν	πᾶν	πάντας	πάσας	πάντα

Participles

Present Participles

Present participles of the active voice of the verb are formed exactly like the above. They are verbal adjectives, and qualify nouns just as adjectives do. In Greek the present participle of εἰμί (see Lesson 3) is, in its three genders, ὤν, οὖσα, ὄν. Notice that, if we take away the ἐκ- of ἑκών above, we have the participial forms in full. Thus ὤν, "being," is declined as follows:—

	Singular			Plural		
	M.	F.	N.	M.	F.	N.
Nom.	ὤν	οὖσα	ὄν	ὄντες	οὖσαι	ὄντα
Voc.	ὤν	οὖσα	ὄν	ὄντες	οὖσαι	ὄντα
Gen.	ὄντος	οὔσης	ὄντος	ὄντων	οὐσῶν	ὄντων
Dat.	ὄντι	οὔσῃ	ὄντι	οὖσι	οὔσαις	οὖσι
Acc.	ὄντα	οὖσαν	ὄν	ὄντας	οὔσας	ὄντα

Coming now again to the verb λύω, the present participle is λύων, λύουσα, λῦον, and signifies "loosing." These various forms may qualify some noun or pronoun or may simply qualify the definite article. In every case there is agreement in case, number and gender. Thus in Heb. 1:7, ὁ ποιῶν is literally "The (One) making," translated "Who maketh." Again, in 1 Cor. 15:57, τῷ δὲ θεῷ χάρις τῷ διδόντι literally is "But to God thanks, the (One) giving" ἡμῖν, to us, ὁ νῖκος, the victory (for νῖκος see γένος, above); in Jas. 1:5, παρὰ τοῦ διδόντος θεοῦ is "from the giving

God." In the following sentence note the feminine participle λέγουσαν "saying," in agreement with the fem. φωνήν, "a voice": ἤκουσεν (he heard, 1st aorist of ἀκούω, I hear) φωνὴν λέγουσαν αὐτῷ, Σαοὺλ Σαούλ, (Saul, Saul), τί (why) με διώκεις; "persecutest thou" (Acts 9:4).

Exercise

Translate the following (after learning the vocabulary), correcting your result from the English version. Then retranslate into Greek, correcting your result from the Greek text.

Ἴδε	Behold
ἀμνός	a lamb
αἴρω	I bear, take away
ποιέω	I do
διάβολος	Devil
ἀπ' ἀρχῆς	from (the) beginning
ἔχω	I have
ἁμαρτάνω	I sin
ἀγάπη	love
μένω	I abide
μαρτυρία	witness
μή	not
αἰώνιος, -ος, -ον	eternal

(1) Τῇ ἐπαύριον βλέπει τὸν Ἰησοῦν ἐρχόμενον πρὸς αὐτόν καὶ λέγει, Ἴδε ὁ ἀμνὸς τοῦ θεοῦ ὁ αἴρων τὴν ἁμαρτίαν τοῦ κόσμου. (John 1:29)—note the article ὁ and the participle αἴρων agreeing with it; this is literally "the (One) bearing."

(2) ὁ ποιῶν τὴν ἁμαρτίαν ἐκ τοῦ διαβόλου ἐστίν, ὅτι ἀπ' ἀρχῆς ὁ διάβολος ἁμαρτάνει. (1 John 3:8a).

(3) Ὁ θεὸς ἀγάπη ἐστίν, καὶ ὁ μένων ἐν τῇ ἀγάπῃ ἐν τῷ θεῷ μένει καὶ ὁ θεὸς ἐν αὐτῷ μένει. (1 John 4:16b).

(4) ὁ πιστεύων εἰς τὸν υἱὸν τοῦ θεοῦ ἔχει τὴν μαρτυρίαν ἐν ἑαυτῷ (in himself), (1 John 5:10a).

(5) 11 καὶ αὕτη ἐστὶν ἡ μαρτυρία, ὅτι ζωὴν αἰώνιον ἔδωκεν ἡμῖν ὁ θεός, καὶ αὕτη ἡ ζωὴ ἐν τῷ υἱῷ αὐτοῦ ἐστιν. 12 ὁ ἔχων τὸν υἱὸν ἔχει τὴν ζωήν· ὁ μὴ ἔχων τὸν υἱὸν τοῦ θεοῦ τὴν ζωὴν οὐκ ἔχει. (1 John 5:11-12)—note that αἰώνιος has the same form in the feminine as the masculine—hence αἰώνιον is feminine agreeing with ζωήν, though the form looks like a masculine.

ἔδωκεν is "gave"; its subject is ὁ θεός.

▪ LESSON 10 ▪

The Participles of the Active Voice (*Continued*)

As the present participle, ending in -ων, -ουσα, -ον (e.g., λύων, "loosing ") corresponds to the present tense, indicative (λύω, "I loose") and is really an adjective (see last Lesson), so *the future participle* (e.g., λύσων, "being about to loose") corresponds to the future tense, indicative (λύσω, "I will loose"; see the verb λύω, Lesson 6). This future participle is declined in exactly the same way as the present participle in all cases, numbers and genders. Hence this participle of λύω is λύσων, λύσουσα, λῦσον (Review the present participle in Lesson 9 and form this on the model with the added σ in the middle of the word). The use of the future participle is rare.

There is no participle corresponding to the imperfect tense indicative (ἔλυον, Lesson 6).

The *first aorist participle* ends in -ας, -ασα, -αν and is declined exactly like the adjective πᾶς, πᾶσα, πᾶν (see Lesson 9). This participle corresponds to the first aorist indicative (e.g., ἔλυσα, "I loosed," see Lesson 6). Thus the aorist participle of λύω is λύσας, λύσασα, λῦσαν (three genders). Notice that the augment, ἐ- (in ἔλυσα) is dropped; that is to say, the participle is not ἔλυσας but λύσας. There is no augment outside the indicative mood.

The student should write out the singular and plural, in all genders and cases, of λύσας, λύσασα, λῦσαν, from memory, on the model of πᾶς, πᾶσα, πᾶν.

The first aorist participle is very common. Study the following passages:—

(*a*) ὁ πέμψας με is "The (One) having sent me": πέμψας is the nom. sing. masc., first aorist participle of πέμπω, "I send" (future πέμψω, "I will send," i.e., for πέμπσω, -πσ becoming ψ): it agrees in case, number and gender with the article ὁ.

(*b*) ἵνα ("in order that") ἀπόκρισιν ("an answer"—accusative of ἀπόκρισις) δῶμεν ("we may give") τοῖς ("to the [ones]") πέμψασιν ("having sent") ἡμᾶς ("us"). Note that πέμψασιν is the dative plural masc., in agreement with τοῖς. This use of the participle in agreement with the article is very frequent.

Corresponding to the perfect indicative (e.g., λέλυκα "I have loosed," see Lesson 6) is *the perfect participle*, which ends in -ως, -υια, -ος. Thus, the perfect participle of λύω is λελυκώς, λελυκυῖα, λελυκός (three genders). The accusative is λελυκότα, λελυκυῖαν, λελυκός; the masculine and neuter have third declension endings, and the feminine has first declension endings, with -α- throughout, because the preceding letter is a vowel, -ι-, and not a consonant (see Lesson 3, Note 1). The indicative mood tenses and participles thus far learned may be set out as follows:—

	Indicative Mood (1*st Person*)		*Participles* (*Nominative*)	
Present	λύω	λύων	λύουσα	λῦον
Imperfect	ἔλυον		none	
Future	λύσω	λύσων	λύσουσα	λῦσον
First Aorist	ἔλυσα	λύσας	λύσασα	λῦσαν
Perfect	λέλυκα	λελυκώς	λελυκυῖα	λελυκός
Pluperfect	ἐλελύκειν		none	

Exercise—The student who has gone carefully through the Lessons up to this point will now be able, with a vocabulary and the translation of a few words here and there (to be explained later), to render considerable portions of the New Testament. We will take the first seven lines (1:1-3a) of the Epistle to the Hebrews. Learn the meanings given in brackets and refer to the various places in the past Lessons as mentioned. Study the passage again and again. Retranslate it. If time permits learn it by heart.

Πολυμερῶς (an adverb meaning "by many portions") καὶ πολυτρόπως ("in many ways") πάλαι ("formerly" or "of old") ὁ θεὸς λαλήσας (1st aorist participle of λαλέω, I speak—see λύσας above—"having spoken") τοῖς πατράσιν (dative plural of πατήρ—see Lesson 8) ἐν ("by"—ἐν often has this meaning instead of "in") τοῖς προφήταις (see under μαθητής, Note 3, Lesson 3), ἐπ' (for ἐπί, a preposition which, when followed by the genitive case, means "at": the ι is omitted before the ἐ- of the next word) ἐσχάτου (ἔσχατος, -η, -ον, "last" "the" is understood: "at the last" or "at the end") τῶν ἡμερῶν τούτων (ἡμέρα, "a day": for τούτων see Lesson 4, and Rule 2; note that the order here is the same as in ἡ φωνὴ αὕτη, i.e., article noun, demonstrative adjective) ἐλάλησεν (3rd person singular 1st aorist of λαλέω) ἡμῖν (to us) ἐν υἱῷ, ὃν (Lesson V, here accusative as the object of ἔθηκεν) ἔθηκεν ("He appointed") κληρονόμον ("heir"—accus. sing., agreeing in case and gender with ὅν) πάντων, ("of all things"—gen. plur. neut. of πᾶς—lit. "of all") δι' (for διά, which, when followed by the genitive, means "by") οὗ (see Lesson 5—genitive case "whom") καὶ ("also") ἐποίησεν (1st aorist of ποιέω, I make) τοὺς αἰῶνας· (Lesson 7) ὃς ὢν (present participle of εἰμί—"being") ἀπαύγασμα (an effulgence, or shining forth—the article "the" is not here expressed in Greek, but must be inserted in English) τῆς δόξης (Lesson 3, Note 2, and Vocab.—here the article signifies "the glory (of Him)," i.e., "His glory") καὶ χαρακτὴρ ("impress or "very image"—our word "character" is a transliteration of it, but not here a translation) τῆς ὑποστάσεως (ὑπόστασις "substance"—like πόλις, Lesson 9) αὐτοῦ, (lit. "of Him," i.e., His—see αὐτός, Lesson 5), φέρων (pres. participle of φέρω, I bear, uphold) τε ("and"—always comes second in the clause) τὰ πάντα ("all things"—acc. plur. neut.—the article τά is not to be translated) τῷ ("by the"—the dative case here expresses the instrument, and is called the instrumental dative; hence we must translate by "by") ῥήματι (dative of ῥῆμα, see Lesson 7, page 48) τῆς δυνάμεως (gen. case of δύναμις, power, like πόλις) αὐτοῦ, ("His"):

Translate verses 7 and 8 of the same chapter, with the help of the following vocabulary:—

εὐθύτης	uprightness	ῥάβδος	a scepter
πῦρ	fire	πρός	to
φλόξ	a flame	μέν	indeed
λειτουργός	a minister	λέγω	I say

Hebrews 1:7 καὶ πρὸς μὲν τοὺς ἀγγέλους λέγει, Ὁ ποιῶν τοὺς ἀγγέλους αὐτοῦ πνεύματα καὶ τοὺς λειτουργοὺς αὐτοῦ πυρὸς φλόγα, 8 πρὸς δὲ τὸν υἱόν, Ὁ θρόνος σου ὁ θεός εἰς τὸν αἰῶνα τοῦ αἰῶνος, καὶ ἡ ῥάβδος τῆς εὐθύτητος ῥάβδος τῆς βασιλείας σου.

Note that ὁ ποιῶν is "the (One) making" (present participle—we must render by "who maketh"): ὁ θεός is "O God": the next phrase is literally "unto the age of the age," but its English equivalent is "for ever and ever" and it must be so translated.

Third Declension Adjectives of Two Terminations

These have no separate form for the feminine. There are two kinds. The first kind consists of a simple form ending in -ων, with stem ending -ον, and therefore with genitive ending in -ονος, etc. This must be distinguished from the adjectives ending in -ων (with genitive ending -οντος) which have three forms for the three genders (see ἑκών, ἑκοῦσα, ἑκόν, Lesson 9).

The following is an example:—

σώφρων, sober minded (stem, σωφρον-)

	Singular		Plural	
	M. & F.	Neut.	M. & F.	Neut.
Nom.	σώφρων	σῶφρον	σώφρονες	σώφρονα
Voc.	σῶφρον	σῶφρον	σώφρονες	σώφρονα
Gen.	σώφρονος	σώφρονος	σωφρόνων	σωφρόνων
Dat.	σώφρονι	σώφρονι	σώφροσι	σώφροσι
Acc.	σώφρονα	σῶφρον	σώφρονας	σώφρονα

The second kind ends in -ης (neut. -ες). It contracts double vowels into a single sound. *This is a large and important class of adjective.* The contracted forms in the following paradigm must be memorized thoroughly (the uncontracted forms in brackets are quite regular and the endings will already be known).

ἀληθής, -ές, true

Singular

	Masc. & Fem.		Neut.
Nom.		ἀληθής	ἀληθές
Voc.		ἀληθές	ἀληθές
Gen.	(ἀληθέος)	ἀληθούς	ἀληθούς
Dat.	(ἀληθέϊ)	ἀληθεῖ	ἀληθεῖ
Acc.	(ἀληθέα)	ἀληθῆ	ἀληθές

Plural

	Masc. & Fem.		Neut.	
Nom.	(ἀληθέες)	ἀληθεῖς	(ἀληθέα)	ἀληθῆ
Voc.	(")	ἀληθεῖς	(")	ἀληθῆ
Gen.	(ἀληθέων)	ἀληθῶν	(ἀληθέων)	ἀληθῶν
Dat.		ἀληθέσι		ἀληθέσι
Acc.	(ἀληθέας)	ἀληθεῖς	(")	ἀληθῆ

LESSON 11

Personal Pronouns

Commit the following to memory:—

First Person

	Singular		Plural	
Nom.	ἐγώ	I	ἡμεῖς	we
Gen.	ἐμοῦ or μου	of me	ἡμῶν	of us
Dat.	ἐμοί or μοι	to me	ἡμῖν	to us
Acc.	ἐμέ or με	me	ἡμᾶς	us

Second Person

	Singular		Plural	
Nom.	σύ	thou	ὑμεῖς	you or ye
Gen.	σοῦ	of thee	ὑμῶν	of you
Dat.	σοί	to thee	ὑμῖν	to you
Acc.	σέ	thee	ὑμᾶς	you

For the *Third Person,* "he, she, it," αὐτός, αὐτή, αὐτό, see Lesson 5.

Reflexive Pronouns

In English these end in "-self," "-selves." They are used when the object of a sentence or clause refers to the same person or thing as the subject.

Forms occurring in the New Testament include the following:—

ἐμαυτόν	myself	ἑαυτῶν	of yourselves, of themselves
σεαυτοῦ	of thyself		
σεαυτόν	thyself	ἑαυτοῖς	to yourselves
ἑαυτόν (or αὑτόν)	himself	ἑαυταῖς	same (fem.)
ἑαυτήν (or αὑτήν)	herself	ἑαυτούς, ἑαυτάς, etc.	

Note 1—When αὐτός, -ή, -ό immediately follows a noun or pronoun with which it is connected it means "self." Thus ὁ ἄνθρωπος αὐτός is "the man himself"; ὁ αὐτός ἄνθρωπος is "the same man."

Note 2—This use of αὐτός as a reflexive must carefully be distinguished from the personal use "he." When used in the nominative for the third person, it is always emphatic: e.g., αὐτὸς ἐγὼ . . . δουλεύω, I myself serve (Rom. 7:25): αὐτοὶ γὰρ ὑμεῖς θεοδίδακτοί ἐστε, for ye yourselves are taught of God (lit. God-taught) (1 Thess. 4:9).

Note 3—The ε- of ἑαυτόν, etc., is often dropped and the word contracted to αὑτόν, etc. In that case αὑτός, "himself," and the other forms must be distinguished from αὐτός, "he," etc.

Note 4—This third person reflexive pronoun is also used for the first and second persons, when there would be no ambiguity. Thus ἑαυτοῖς is "in ourselves," (Rom. 8:23) instead of ἐν ἡμῖν αὐτοῖς. Again, τῆν ἑαυτῶν σωτηρίαν is "your own salvation," lit., "the salvation of yourselves" (Phil. 2:12) instead of τῆν ὑμῶν αὐτῶν σωτηρίαν.

Other examples are: βλέπετε δὲ ὑμεῖς ἑαυτούς, "But take ye heed to yourselves" (Mark 13:9; cp. 2 John 8); προσέχετε ἑαυτοῖς "take heed to yourselves" (Luke 12:1).

(*Review the demonstrative pronouns, Lesson 4, and the personal and relative pronouns, Lesson 5*)

Indefinite Pronouns

The pronoun τις (masc. and fem.), τι (neut.) one, means "someone," "anyone," "a certain," "some," "any." It is declined as follows, the masculine and feminine being the same, and the endings those of the third declension:—

	Singular		Plural	
	M. & F.	Neut.	M. & F.	Neut.
Nom.	τις	τι	τινες	τινα
Gen.	τινος	τινος	τινων	τινων
Dat.	τινι	τινι	τισι	τισι
Acc.	τινα	τι	τινας	τινα

Examples—εἰσίν τινες ὧδε there are some here (Mark 9:1); Ἑκατοντάρχου δέ τινος (and of a certain centurion) δοῦλος (a servant), (Luke 7:2); Ἄνθρωπός τις ἦν πλούσιος, "(there) was a certain rich man," lit., "a certain man was rich" (Luke 16:1); οὔτε (nor) ὕψωμα (height) οὔτε (nor) βάθος (depth) οὔτε (nor) τις (any) κτίσις (creature) ἑτέρα (other) (Rom. 8:39).

Note 1—The indefinite pronoun τις never stands first in a sentence.

Note 2—If used with a noun it generally follows the noun.

Note 3—Other indefinite pronouns are οὔτις and μήτις, each of which means "no one." They are formed by the addition of τις to the negatives οὐ and μή, "not."

Interrogative Pronouns

The simple interrogative pronoun is τίς, τί, who? what? In form it is exactly like the indefinite pronoun τις, τι, the only difference being that it has an accent pointing from left to right. The two must be carefully distinguished.

Examples—Τίς ἐστιν ἡ μήτηρ μου καὶ τίνες εἰσὶν οἱ ἀδελφοί μου; Who is My mother, and who are My brethren? (Matt. 12:48); τίνα σεαυτὸν ποιεῖς; Whom makest Thou Thyself? (John 8:53).

There is an adjectival use of τίς in agreement with a noun, e.g., Τί σημεῖον (What sign) δεικνύεις (showest Thou) ἡμῖν (to us); (John 2:18).

The following interrogative pronouns should also be memorized; they correspond to the relative pronouns οἷος and ὅσος given below. They are all of 1st and 2nd declension endings.

Qualitative, ποῖος, -α, -ον, of what kind?

Quantitative, πόσος, -η, -ον, how great?

The plural πόσοι, -αι, -α signifies "how many?"

There is a relative pronoun, ὁποῖος, "of what kind," corresponding to ποῖος, and occurring five times in the New Testament. In Acts 26:29, it is rendered "such as"; in 1 Cor. 3, 13 "of what sort"; in Gal. 2:6 "whatsoever"; in 1 Thess. 1:9 and Jas. 1:24 "what manner of."

An indefinite relative, "whoever," "whatever," is formed by combining τις, τι, with ὅς, ἥ, ὅ, both parts being declined as follows:—

Singular

	Masc.	Fem.	Neut.
Nom.	ὅστις	ἥτις	ὅ,τι
Gen.	οὗτινος	ἧστινος	οὗτινος
Dat.	ᾧτινι	ᾗτινι	ᾧτινι
Acc.	ὅντινα	ἥντινα	ὅ,τι

Plural

	Masc.	Fem.	Neut.
Nom.	οἵτινες	αἵτινες	ἅτινα
Gen.	ὧντινων	ὧντινων	ὧντινων
Dat.	οἷστισι	αἷστισι	οἷστισι
Acc.	οὕστινας	ἅστινας	ἅτινα

Note—The genitive singular masculine is shortened to ὅτου in the phrase ἕως ὅτου "as long as," "until," lit., "until whatever (time)" (See Matt. 5:25).

Other relative pronouns are as follows:—

Qualitative, οἷος, -α, -ον, such as.

Quantitative, ὅσος, -η, -ον, so great as, and its plural ὅσοι, -αι, α, so many as.

Compare the interrogatives above, ποῖος and πόσος.

The following table will sum up the chief pronouns which correspond to one another:—

Demonstrative οὗτος (this)	Relative ὅς (who)	Interrogative τίς (who?)	Indefinite τις (someone)
τοιοῦτος (such an one)	οἷος (such as)	ποῖος (of what sort?)	——
τοσοῦτος (so great)	ὅσος (so great as)	πόσος (how great?)	——
τοσοῦτοι (so many)	ὅσοι (so many as)	πόσοι (how many?)	——

Distributive Pronouns

(1) ἄλλος, ἄλλη, ἄλλο, another (i.e., another of the same sort, of like kind). The plural of this denotes "others." It is declined like ὅς, ἥ, ὅ.

(2) ἕτερος, ἑτέρα, ἕτερον, another (i.e., another of a different kind).

(3) ἀλλήλων, ἀλλήλοις, ἀλλήλους, of each other, to each other, each other; this is used only in the genitive, dative, and accusative plural.

(4) ἕκαστος, -η, -ον, each; this is used only in the singular.

Vocabulary and Exercise

Learn the following words and translate the passages below, correcting your rendering from the English Revised Version; retranslate the English into the Greek without referring to the exercise, and correct your Greek from the exercise.

οἰκοδομέω . . . I build	δέ . . . but
οἰκία . . . a house	κύριος . . . lord
πέτρα . . . a rock	φυτεύω . . . I plant
πρός . . . to (followed by the accusative)	ποτίζω . . . I water
ἀληθινός . . . true	οὖν . . . therefore
σπείρω . . . I sow	διάκονος . . . a minister
θερίζω . . . I reap	ὡς . . . as
ποῦ . . . where?	ὥστε . . . so then, or so that
γογγυσμός . . . a murmuring	ποιέω . . . I do
περί . . . concerning	ἀκούω . . . I hear
ὄχλος . . . a multitude	οὔτε . . . neither, nor
μέν . . . indeed	φρόνιμος . . . prudent

Translate with the help of the accompanying notes:—

(1) Ἐγὼ μέν εἰμι Παύλου, ἕτερος δέ, Ἐγὼ Ἀπολλῶ, οὐκ ἄνθρωποί ἐστε; 5 τί οὖν ἐστιν Ἀπολλῶς; τί δέ ἐστιν Παῦλος; διάκονοι δι' ὧν ἐπιστεύσατε, καὶ ἑκάστῳ ὡς ὁ κύριος ἔδωκεν. 6 ἐγὼ ἐφύτευσα, Ἀπολλῶς ἐπότισεν, ἀλλὰ ὁ θεὸς ηὔξανεν· 7 ὥστε οὔτε ὁ φυτεύων ἐστίν τι οὔτε ὁ ποτίζων ἀλλ' ὁ αὐξάνων θεός. 8 ὁ φυτεύων δὲ καὶ ὁ ποτίζων ἕν εἰσιν, (1 Cor. 3:4b-8a): Note the special significance of ἕτερος, "another" of a different character, not another of the same sort (ἄλλος): δι' is for διά, which with the genitive (ὧν) denotes "by means of": ἐπιστεύσατε, 2nd pers. plural, 1st aor. of πιστεύω: ἔδωκεν "gave" (to be explained later): note that τί is "what" (neut. of τίς—so in R.V., not "who" as in A.V.), but τι, without the accent in verse 7, is "anything." What is the ἐ- in ἐφύτευσα, and in ἐπότισεν [see Lesson 6, Note 3]? Verbs like ποτίζω ending in -ίζω in the present tense change the ζ to σ in the 1st aorist: ηὔξανεν is the imperfect tense of αὐξάνω "was giving the increase": note that ἀ- makes the augment ἠ- not ἐα-: ἕν is "one," it is the neuter of εἷς, μία, ἕν (masc., fem., neut.) and is to be distinguished from ἐν, "in." It might be rendered "one thing." Note the four occurrences of the article ὁ with the present participle, (lit., "the one planting," etc.), this must be rendered by "he that planteth," etc.

(2) Πᾶς οὖν ὅστις ἀκούει μου τοὺς λόγους τούτους καὶ ποιεῖ αὐτούς, ὁμοιωθήσεται ἀνδρὶ φρονίμῳ, ὅστις ᾠκοδόμησεν αὐτοῦ τὴν οἰκίαν ἐπὶ τὴν πέτραν· (Matt. 7:24): Πᾶς is "every one", for μου see beginning of this Lesson. For τούτους see Lesson 4, Rule 2, ὁμοιωθήσεται "shall be likened." ᾠκοδόμησεν is the 3rd pers. sing. of the 1st aorist of οἰκοδομέω; note that the augment of verbs beginning in οἰ is formed by turning the οἰ- into ᾠ- with the iota underneath. The future of verbs ending in -έω ends in -ήσω, and the 1st aorist in -ησα.

(3) ἦσαν δέ τινες ἐξ αὐτῶν ἄνδρες Κύπριοι καὶ Κυρηναῖοι, οἵτινες ἐλθόντες εἰς Ἀντιόχειαν ἐλάλουν καὶ πρὸς τοὺς Ἑλληνιστάς εὐαγγελιζόμενοι τὸν κύριον Ἰησοῦν (Acts 11:20). Translate ἦσαν "there were"; ἐξ is for ἐκ "of" or "out of"; Κύπριοι Cyprians; ἐλθόντες "having come" (see later); ἐλάλουν is the 3rd pers. plur. imperf. tense of λαλέω, "I speak"—the -ουν is for -εον; εὐαγγελιζόμενοι "preaching" (see later).

(4) ἐν γὰρ τούτῳ ὁ λόγος ἐστὶν ἀληθινὸς ὅτι Ἄλλος ἐστὶν ὁ σπείρων καὶ ἄλλος ὁ θερίζων (John 4:37), Ἄλλος . . . ἄλλος is "one . . . another."

(5) καὶ γογγυσμὸς περὶ αὐτοῦ ἦν πολὺς ἐν τοῖς ὄχλοις· οἱ μὲν ἔλεγον ὅτι Ἀγαθός ἐστιν, ἄλλοι [δὲ] ἔλεγον, Οὔ, ἀλλὰ πλανᾷ τὸν ὄχλον. John 7:12, οἱ μέν is "some indeed"—the "indeed" should be omitted in translating; Οὔ is "No"; πλανᾷ "He deceiveth."

▪ LESSON 12 ▪

THE VERB (*Continued*)

THE IMPERATIVE MOOD

Having learned the Indicative Mood (which makes assertions) and the Participles (or Verbal Adjectives), which correspond to the tenses of Indicative, we have now to consider the Imperative Mood (which makes commands).

There are only three tenses, the Present, which gives a command indicating continuous action, or repeated action (e.g., λῦε, "loose thou, and continue to do so"), the First Aorist, which gives a command without reference to its continuance or frequency (e.g., λῦσον, "loose thou"—a single act) and the Perfect, λέλυκε, "do thou have had loosed, and let it remain so"; this last is rarely used. There is no Future Imperative. There are two persons, the second and the third.

The following specimen should be committed to memory and then should be written out in a column parallel to the tenses of the Indicative Mood, tense against tense where they correspond.

Present Tense (*continuous actions*)

	Singular	
2nd pers.	λῦε	loose thou
3rd pers.	λυέτω	let him loosen
	Plural	
2nd pers.	λύετε	loose ye
3rd pers.	λυέτωσαν or λυόντων	let them loosen

First Aorist (*momentary action*)

	Singular	
2nd pers.	λῦσον	loose thou
3rd pers.	λυσάτω	let him loosen
	Plural	
2nd pers.	λύσατε	loose ye
3rd pers.	λυσάτωσαν or λυσάντων	let them loosen

Perfect

	Singular	Plural
2nd pers.	λέλυκε	λελύκετε
3rd pers.	λελυκέτω	λελυκέτωσαν or λελυκόντων

(the meanings are "do thou have had loosed," "let him have had loosed," "do ye have had loosed," "let them have had loosed.")

Note 1—There is no augment (ἐ-) in the 1st Aorist of the Imperative, nor indeed does the augment occur outside the Indicative Mood.

Note 2—Observe the characteristic -σ- of the 1st Aorist, and the characteristic reduplication λε- of the Perfect, as in the Indicative Mood.

Note 3—The Aorist Imperative is very frequent in the New Testament and must be carefully noted.

The following vocabulary will be a guide to the exercise below. The student should learn the list, if time permits, at all events the verbs. Then translate the six passages given in the exercise, correcting the result from the English version. Retranslate from the English into Greek, correcting from the Greek version.

ναός . . . . a temple
ἀπολύω . . . . I let go
ἐκεῖνος . . . .(see Lesson 4, plural "these")

ὅθεν . . . . wherefore
ἅγιος, -α, -ον . . . . holy
κλῆσις . . . . a calling (gen. κλήσεως)
ἐπουράνιος, -α, -ον . . . . heavenly
μέτοχος . . . . a partaker
κατανοέω . . . . I consider
'Αρχιερεύς . . . High Priest (see Lesson 9)
πιστός, -ή, -όν . . . . faithful
ὅλος, -η, -ον . . . . all
οἶκος . . . . a house

γεμίζω . . . . I fill (the future is γεμίσω)
ὑδρία . . . . a water pot
ὕδωρ . . . . water (gen. ὕδατος—to be explained later)
ἕως . . . . up to
ἄνω . . . . the brim
ἀντλέω . I draw out, (used of water etc.—future ἀντλήσω)
φέρω . . . . I bear
ἀρχιτρίκλινος . . . . . . a governor of a feast

μή . . . . not (always used instead of οὐ with the Imperative)
θησαυρίζω . . . . I lay up treasure
θησαυρός . . . . a treasure
ἐπί . . . . upon (when used with a genitive)
γή . . . . earth
ὅπου . . . . where
σής . . . . a moth
βρῶσις . . . . rust
ἀφανίζω . . . . I corrupt
κλέπτης . . . . a thief
διορύσσω . . . . I break through
κλέπτω . . . . I steal
καρδία . . . . a heart

Exercise on the Imperative Mood

Translate:—

(1) Λύσατε (λύω here means "to destroy") τὸν ναὸν τοῦτον (John 2:19). Note the 1st Aorist, 2nd person plur., "destroy ye."

(2) 'Απόλυσον τοὺς ἀνθρώπους ἐκείνους (Acts 16:35).

(3) 'Υμεῖς (ye) οὖν (therefore) ἀκούσατε τὴν παραβολὴν (Matt. 13:18—the 'Υμεῖς is emphatic).

(4) "Οθεν, ἀδελφοὶ ἅγιοι, κλήσεως ἐπουρανίου μέτοχοι, κατανοήσατε τὸν ἀπόστολον καὶ ἀρχιερέα τῆς ὁμολογίας ἡμῶν 'Ιησοῦν, 2 πιστὸν ὄντα τῷ ποιήσαντι αὐτὸν ὡς καὶ Μωϋσῆς ἐν ὅλῳ τῷ οἴκῳ αὐτοῦ (Heb. 3:1, 2, with the aid of the vocab). *Note 1*—κατανοήσατε is the 1st Aorist Imperative, 2nd person plural of κατανοέω—verbs ending in -έω make the future end in

-ήσω, lengthening the ε to η and so in the 1st Aorist: so ποιέω makes the future ποιήσω; *2*—ὄντα is accus. sing. masc. pres. participle of εἰμί: *3*—ποιήσαντι is dat. sing. 1st Aorist Participle of ποιέω, I make.

(5) λέγει αὐτοῖς ὁ Ἰησοῦς, Γεμίσατε τὰς ὑδρίας ὕδατος. καὶ ἐγέμισαν αὐτὰς ἕως ἄνω. 8 καὶ λέγει αὐτοῖς, Ἀντλήσατε νῦν καὶ φέρετε τῷ ἀρχιτρικλίνῳ (John 2:7, 8a). The genitive ὕδατος here signifies "with water" (the genitive must be rendered "with," after a verb denoting "to fill"). Note carefully the difference in the tenses of the Imperative Mood verbs in this verse: Γεμίσατε and Ἀντλήσατε are 1st aorists "fill ye up," "draw out," a single act in each instance; but φέρετε is a present tense, "be carrying" (there is, in this change of tense, a peculiarly delicate suggestion of politeness with regard to the recognition of the place of honor held by the governor of the feast).

(6) Μὴ θησαυρίζετε ὑμῖν θησαυροὺς ἐπὶ τῆς γῆς, ὅπου σὴς καὶ βρῶσις ἀφανίζει καὶ ὅπου κλέπται διορύσσουσιν καὶ κλέπτουσιν· 20 θησαυρίζετε δὲ ὑμῖν θησαυροὺς ἐν οὐρανῷ, ὅπου οὔτε σὴς οὔτε βρῶσις ἀφανίζει καὶ ὅπου κλέπται οὐ διορύσσουσιν οὐδὲ κλέπτουσιν· 21 ὅπου γάρ ἐστιν ὁ θησαυρός σου, ἐκεῖ ἔσται καὶ ἡ καρδία σου (Matt. 6:19-21). *Note 1*—ὑμῖν (dative plural) "for yourselves," lit., "for you"; the dative signifies "for" as well as "to," and the personal pronoun here stands for the reflexive pronoun, which in full would be ὑμῖν αὐτοῖς (see Lesson 11, Note 4): *2*—ἀφανίζει is singular number "doth corrupt," although it has two subjects "moth and rust," the two being regarded as one subject: *3*—for κλέπται compare μαθητής (Lesson 3): *4*—σου (verse 21) is lit. "of thee," i.e., "thy": *5*—ἔσται is "shall be," this will be learned later.

The Subjunctive Mood

In English the Subjunctive Mood expresses supposition, doubt or uncertainty, and follows the conjunctions if, lest, though, etc. In Greek the scope of the Subjunctive is much wider.

There is no future or imperfect tense and no perfect in the Active Voice save in one irregular verb. Accordingly the following are the only two Subjunctive tenses in the verb λύω and similar verbs. Note the *iota subscript* (i.e., written under) in the 2nd and 3rd persons singular, and the long vowels η or ω in all the persons.

Present Subjunctive

λύω	I may loose	λύωμεν	we may loose
λύῃς	thou mayest loose	λύητε	ye may loose
λύῃ	he may loose	λύωσι	they may loose

First Aorist Subjunctive

The meaning is either "I may loose" or "I may have loosed," etc.

λύσω	λύσωμεν
λύσῃς	λύσητε
λύσῃ	λύσωσι

Note 1—The endings are the same in each tense, save for the characteristic σ in the First Aorist.

Note 2—There is a Second Aorist in some verbs, with the same meaning as the First. This will be noticed later.

First Aorist Participles in the Active Voice have terminations corresponding to these. See the paragraphs dealing with the Aorist Participle in Lesson 10.

▪ LESSON 13 ▪

THE SUBJUNCTIVE MOOD (*Continued*)

The following is the present tense of the Subjunctive Mood of εἰμί, the verb "to be," of which it is the only Subjunctive tense. The student will observe that the words are precisely the same as the endings of the present Subjunctive of λύω (Lesson 12).

	Singular	Plural	
ὦ	I may be	ὦμεν	we may be
ᾖς	thou mayst be	ἦτε	you may be
ᾖ	he may be	ὦσι(ν)	they may be

The following are the principal uses of the Subjunctive Mood in the New Testament:—

I—It is used in *clauses expressing purpose.* These are known as *Final Clauses* (i.e., as having an end or object in view). They are introduced by such conjunctions as ἵνα and ὅπως, each of which means "in order that," or simply "that," and negatively by ἵνα μή or ὅπως μή, "in order that not" or "lest," or even by μή alone, which when so used means the same thing.

Examples

The following sentences give examples of purpose expressed positively:—

John 10:10b, ἐγὼ (I) ἦλθον (came) ἵνα (in order that) ζωὴν (life—the accusative of the object of the verb following) ἔχωσιν (they may have 3rd person plural, pres. subjunctive of ἔχω, I have) καὶ (and) περισσὸν (abundance) ἔχωσιν (they may have).

Matt. 6:4, ὅπως (in order that) ᾖ (may be) σου ἡ ἐλεημοσύνη (thine alms—lit., of thee the alms) ἐν τῷ κρυπτῷ (in secret—τῷ not to be translated).

In the following sentence note that the tenses are *1st Aorist Subjunctive:* John 1:7, οὗτος (This one, i.e., He) ἦλθεν (came) εἰς (for or unto) μαρτυρίαν (a witness), ἵνα (that) μαρτυρήσῃ (he might bear witness—3rd pers. sing. 1st aor. subjunc. of μαρτυρέω, I bear, witness—the future is μαρτυρήσω, I shall bear witness, the -ε- of the present ending being lengthened to -η-) περὶ (concerning) τοῦ φωτός (the light genitive of φῶς—the preposition περί takes the genitive), ἵνα (that) πάντες (all) πιστεύσωσιν (might believe—3rd pers. plur., 1st aor. subjunc.) δι' (by means of—short for διά, is followed by the genitive) αὐτοῦ (him).

Translate the 8th verse and note the emphatic ἐκεῖνος, "he" ("that one"): οὐκ ἦν ἐκεῖνος τὸ φῶς, ἀλλ' ἵνα μαρτυρήσῃ περὶ τοῦ φωτός.

The question arises What is the difference in meaning between the present subjunctive and the 1st aorist, seeing that both are rendered by "may, etc."? The answer is that the present signifies continuous or repeated action (as, for example, ἔχωσιν in John 10:10 above): the aorist signifies either single action or action undefined in point of time. Thus in the last instance μαρτυρήσῃ speaks of John's witness without reference to its continuity, and πιστεύσωσιν points to the single act of faith in believing.

Exercise

Translate, with the help of the accompanying notes, 1 Cor. 1:10:—Παρακαλῶ δὲ ὑμᾶς, ἀδελφοί, διὰ τοῦ ὀνόματος τοῦ κυρίου ἡμῶν Ἰησοῦ Χριστοῦ, ἵνα τὸ αὐτὸ λέγητε πάντες καὶ μὴ ᾖ ἐν ὑμῖν σχίσματα, ἦτε δὲ κατηρτισμένοι ἐν τῷ αὐτῷ νοῒ καὶ ἐν τῇ αὐτῇ γνώμῃ.

Παρακαλῶ, "I exhort": διὰ, "by": ὀνόματος (genitive of ὄνομα, a name—genitive after διά): τὸ αὐτὸ, "the same [thing]" (see Lesson 5)—this is the accusative, as object of λέγητε (pres. subjunctive of λέγω, "I speak," subjunctive after ἵνα): μὴ ᾖ, "[there] may not be"—note the negative μή (not οὐ) with the subjunctive: ἐν, "among" (takes the dative): σχίσματα, "schisms" (note that in Greek a neuter plural subject of a verb takes the verb in the singular; thus σχίσματα is the subject of ᾖ [singular] "schisms may not be"): ἦτε (subjunc. of εἰμί—-see above): κατηρτισμένοι, "joined" (explained later): νοΐ, dative of νοῦς, "mind" (see Lesson 7): γνώμῃ, "judgment."

(*After becoming thoroughly familiarized with this verse, retranslate it, correcting your result.*)

II—The subjunctive is used in certain *Conditional Clauses* (these are introduced in English by "if"), which imply either possibility or uncertainty with the prospect of decision. In these cases ἐάν ("if") is used to introduce the subjunctive. Where the supposition assumes a fact, εἰ (which also means "if") is used followed by the *indicative.* See also p. 113.

Examples

Thus in Matt. 4:3, Εἰ υἱὸς εἶ τοῦ θεοῦ, "if Thou art (the) Son of God," does not express uncertainty or possibility, but signifies "assuming that Thou art the Son of God" (εἶ, "thou art," is the 2nd pers. sing. of the pres. indic. of εἰμί—see Lesson 3). But in Matt. 17:20, ἐὰν ἔχητε πίστιν ὡς κόκκον σινάπεως, "if ye have faith as a grain of mustard seed" (ἔχητε being the pres. *subjunctive* of ἔχω, I have) does not assume that they have faith, but suggests an uncertainty with the prospect of fulfillment, hence the subjunctive is used.

Note: ἐάν is really εἰ ἄν and the ἄν determines the use of the subjunctive.

Exercise

Translate with the help of notes and, after thoroughly learning the texts, retranslate from the English into Greek.

(1) ἐὰν οὖν θεωρῆτε τὸν υἱὸν τοῦ ἀνθρώπου ἀναβαίνοντα ὅπου ἦν τὸ πρότερον; (John 6:62) The "what then" is not expressed in Greek, it is understood; the Greek sentence simply begins with "if": θεωρῆτε is pres. subjunc. of θεωρέω, I behold; ἀναβαίνοντα is acc. sing. masc. of pres. participle of ἀναβαίνω, I ascend; τὸ πρότερον, lit. "the former," is an adverbial phrase meaning "before."

(2) ἐὰν τὰς ἐντολάς μου τηρήσητε, μενεῖτε ἐν τῇ ἀγάπῃ μου, καθὼς ἐγὼ τὰς ἐντολὰς τοῦ πατρός μου τετήρηκα καὶ μένω αὐτοῦ ἐν τῇ ἀγάπῃ. (John 15:10) ἐντολάς is acc. plur. of ἐντολή, a commandment, and is the object of the verb τηρήσητε, which is the 1st aor. subj. of τηρέω, I keep: μενεῖτε is the future indic. 2nd pers. plur. of μένω, I abide, and will be explained later. Note the reduplication in τετήρηκα (what tense is this? See λέλυκα, Lesson 6).

(3) περιτομὴ μὲν γὰρ ὠφελεῖ ἐὰν νόμον πράσσῃς· ἐὰν δὲ παραβάτης νόμου ᾖς, ἡ περιτομή σου ἀκροβυστία γέγονεν. (Rom 2:25) περιτομὴ, circumcision: μὲν, indeed: ὠφελεῖ "profiteth"—3rd pers. sing. pres. indic. of ὠφελέω, I profit: νόμον, "the Law"—the object of πράσσῃς, "thou doest" (pres. subjunc. of πράσσω: δὲ, but: παραβάτης, a transgressor: ᾖς, "thou art"—pres. subjunc. of εἰμί (see above); ἀκροβυστία, uncircumcision: γέγονεν, "has become" (to be explained later).

III—The subjunctive is used in *clauses beginning with a relative pronoun or adverb, like* "whoever," "whenever," or "wherever," *which do not refer to a definite person or thing;* in other words, when the word "ever" can be used after the relative.

Note that ἄν or ἐάν follows the relative. This ἄν is not translatable, it simply has a generalizing effect in these clauses. The ἄν is joined to ὅτε "when," making ὅταν "whenever." Two other relatives to be memorized are ὅπου, "where," and ἕως, "until."

Examples

(1) Matt. 18:6: Ὃς δ' ἂν ("but whosoever"—the relative pronoun ὅς with ἄν makes "whosoever": δ' is for δέ, "but"; it never comes first in the sentence) σκανδαλίσῃ (shall cause to stumble—3rd pers. sing. 1st aorist, subjunc. of σκανδαλίζω—ζ in the present tense becomes σ in the future and 1st aorist) ἕνα ("one" accus. masc. of εἷς—the numerals will be given later) τῶν μικρῶν τούτων (of these little [ones]) τῶν πιστευόντων (the [ones] believing) εἰς ἐμέ (on Me).

(2) John 2:5: Ὅ τι ἂν (ὅστις is "whosoever" and the neuter ὅτι is written separately, ὅ τι, or with a comma between, ὅ, τι) λέγῃ (He saith—pres. subjunc.) ὑμῖν (to you) ποιήσατε (do ye—2nd pers. plur. 1st aorist imperative of ποιέω).

(3) Matt. 6:2: Ὅταν (whensoever—a relative adverb, for ὅτε ἄν) οὖν (therefore) ποιῇς (thou doest —pres. subjunc.) ἐλεημοσύνην (alms), μὴ σαλπίσῃς (do not sound a trumpet—1st aor. subjunc. of σαλπίζω—μή with the 1st aor. subjunc. stands for the imperative) ἔμπροσθέν (before—takes the genitive) σου (thee).

Translate: ὅταν ἐν τῷ κόσμῳ ὦ, φῶς εἰμι τοῦ κόσμου. (John 9:5) ὅταν, "when" (see R.V.): ὦ, "I am" (pres. subjunc. of εἰμί, see above).

IV—The Subjunctive is used in *Deliberative Questions*, i.e., when persons are deliberating as to what is to be done. This is known as the Deliberate Subjunctive. Thus, "Shall we continue in sin?" is ἐπιμένωμεν τῇ ἁμαρτίᾳ; (Rom. 6:1): ἐπιμένωμεν (note the long ω) is 1st pers. plur. pres. subjunc. of ἐπιμένω, a compound of ἐπί and μένω, "I abide"; the article τῇ is not to be translated, as it is used with abstract nouns such as ἁμαρτία, i.e., when it denotes sin in general. The dative case must here be translated "in sin." The dative case has several significances, which must be rendered appropriately in English according to the word which governs the noun. This will be explained later.

V—The Subjunctive is used in *certain forms of exhortation.* This is called *the Hortatory Subjunctive.* In English it is introduced by "let." Thus 1 Thess. 5:6, γρηγορῶμεν καὶ νήφωμεν is "let us watch and let us be sober"; note the long ω in distinction from the pres. indicative; the first verb is the present subjunctive, first person plural of γρηγορέω, "I watch," and the second verb is the same tense and person of νήφω, "I am sober."

The student should become thoroughly familiar with the whole of this lesson before taking up the next. The use of the Subjunctive is very important. The examples given should be read again and again until the student can easily retranslate them from English into Greek For further treatment of the Subjunctive see the additional rules of Syntax.

▪ LESSON 14 ▪

Extra Note on Negative Commands or Prohibitions

For these the Imperative Mood is used, or in certain instances the Subjunctive. The student should review the Imperative Mood of λύω (Lesson 12) and learn now the Imperative of εἰμί, which is as follows:—

ἴσθι	be thou	ἔστε	be ye
ἔσθω or ἤτω	let him (or her, or it) be, or let there be	ἔστωσαν	let them be

Note—The negative in prohibitions is always μή.

I—The *Present Imperative* with μή most frequently denotes a command to cease to do something, or not to do what is already being done. Thus μὴ κλαίετε is "do not weep," and in Matt. 6:19, μὴ θησαυρίζετε is "do not treasure" ὑμῖν (for yourselves) θησαυροὺς ἐπὶ τῆς γῆς (on the earth).

II—When a command is given not to do something at all, not to begin to do something, μή with the *Aorist Subjunctive* is used. As an example study again the sentence in *III*, (3), Lesson 13 from Matt. 6:2, noticing the latter part of the verse:—Ὅταν οὖν ποιῇς ἐλεημοσύνην, μὴ σαλπίσῃς (do not sound a trumpet—σαλπίσῃς is the 2nd pers. sing. 1st Aorist Subjunctive). Here the command is not to begin that practice.

Exercise

(1) The student should now be able to translate the whole of Matt. 6:19-23. Some of this has already been given. Write out a translation with the help of the following vocabulary. If any noun is forgotten, turn to the English Version (preferably the R.V. [NRSV or NKJV]), but try to translate without doing this. Retranslate the passage into Greek.

ἀφανιζω	I consume
διορύσσω	I dig through
κλέπτω	I steal
ἐκεῖ	there
ἔσται	3rd sing. fut. of εἰμί
καί	also (verse 21)
καρδία	heart
λύχνος	lamp
σῶμα	body
ὀφθαλμός	eye
ἁπλοῦς	single
ὅλος, -η, -ον	all or (the) whole
φωτεινός, -ή, -όν	full of light
πονηρός	evil
σκοτεινός	full of darkness
πόσος	how great

6:19 Μὴ θησαυρίζετε ὑμῖν θησαυροὺς ἐπὶ τῆς γῆς, ὅπου σὴς καὶ βρῶσις ἀφανίζει καὶ ὅπου
κλέπται διορύσσουσιν καὶ κλέπτουσιν· 20 θησαυρίζετε δὲ ὑμῖν θησαυροὺς ἐν οὐρανῷ, ὅπου
οὔτε σὴς οὔτε βρῶσις ἀφανίζει καὶ ὅπου κλέπται οὐ διορύσσουσιν οὐδὲ κλέπτουσιν· 21 ὅπου
γάρ ἐστιν ὁ θησαυρός σου, ἐκεῖ ἔσται καὶ ἡ καρδία σου. 22 Ὁ λύχνος τοῦ σώματός ἐστιν ὁ
ὀφθαλμός. ἐὰν οὖν ᾖ ὁ ὀφθαλμός σου ἁπλοῦς, ὅλον τὸ σῶμά σου φωτεινὸν ἔσται· 23 ἐὰν δὲ ὁ
ὀφθαλμός σου πονηρὸς ᾖ, ὅλον τὸ σῶμά σου σκοτεινὸν ἔσται. εἰ οὖν τὸ φῶς τὸ ἐν σοὶ σκότος
ἐστίν, τὸ σκότος πόσον. (Matt. 6:19-23)

(2) ἡ πίστις (faith) σου (of thee—i.e., "thy faith") σέσωκέν (perf. of σώζω I save) σε· ὕπαγε (go) εἰς εἰρήνην (peace) καὶ ἴσθι (see Imperative of εἰμί above) ὑγιὴς (whole) ἀπὸ (from, with genitive) τῆς μάστιγός σου (μάστιξ, a scourge, plague—genitive μάστιγος), Mark 5:34.

(3) ἔστω (let be) δὲ ὁ λόγος (speech) ὑμῶν ναὶ (yea) ναί, οὒ οὔ. For ἔστω see Imperative of εἰμί above, Matt. 5:37a.

(4) Jas. 5:12b (middle of verse)—μὴ ὀμνύετε (ὀμνύω, I swear) . . . ἤτω ("let be"—see the Imperative of εἰμί) δὲ ὑμῶν τὸ Ναὶ (lit., "the nay of you") ναὶ καὶ τὸ Οὒ οὔ.

The Optative Mood

This Mood is used either (*a*) in expressing wishes or (*b*) in what are called dependent questions, or (*c*) in deliberative questions. Further details are given later. The use of the Optative is not frequent in New Testament.

Memorize the following:—

The Optative Mood of εἰμί
"I might be," etc.

Singular	Plural
εἴην	εἴημεν or εἶμεν
εἴης	εἴητε or εἶτε
εἴη	εἴησαν or εἶεν

The Optative Mood of λύω.

Present
(*The precise meaning is determined by the context.*)
"I might loose," etc.

Singular	Plural
λύοιμι	λύοιμεν
λύοις	λύοιτε
λύοι	λύοιεν

Future
"I should loose," etc.

Singular	Plural
λύσοιμι	λύσοιμεν
λύσοις	λύσοιτε
λύσοι	λύσοιεν

First Aorist
"I might loose," etc. (according to context)

Singular	Plural
λύσαιμι	λύσαιμεν
λύσαις	λύσαιτε
λύσαι or λέσειε	λύσαιεν or λύσειαν

Examples of the Optative Mood

(*a*) The following are examples of the expression of a wish:—

(1) Τὸ ἀργύριόν σου σὺν σοὶ εἴη εἰς ἀπώλειαν (Acts 8:20). This is literally "Thy money with thee be unto destruction" (εἴη, 3rd sing. opt. of εἰμί, here simply means '"be," i.e., "may [it] be").

(2) 1 Thess. 3:12: ὑμᾶς ("you"—the accus. object of the two succeeding verbs) δὲ ὁ κύριος (the Lord) πλεονάσαι (make to increase—3rd sing. 1st aor. opt. of πλεονάζω, i.e., may He make to increase) καὶ περισσεύσαι (make to abound—same tense of περισσεύω) τῇ ἀγάπῃ (in love—dative of the point in which the verb is applied: hence we must translate by "in" though there is no preposition in the Greek: the article is used because the noun is abstract) εἰς ἀλλήλους (to one another).

(*b*) The following are examples of dependent questions, i.e., questions which are not asked directly, but depend upon some preceding statement:—

(1) Ὡς (as, or while) δὲ ἐν ἑαυτῷ (in himself) διηπόρει (was doubting—3rd pers. sing. imperf. indic. of διαπορέω—for διηπόρεε, the -εε contracting to -ει—the change from α to η is due to the fact that when a preposition, here διά, is joined to a verb, here ἀπορέω the augment, which must come before the verb, joins with the vowel of the preposition, α and η combining to form η thus, not διαηπόρει but διηπόρει) ὁ Πέτρος (Peter—the article is used with proper names) τί (what) ἂν εἴη (might be—the ἄν is not translated) τὸ ὅραμα (the vision). Note that εἴη is in the optative as the question is not asked directly "What is the vision?" but indirectly, depending on the statement "Peter doubted in himself" (Acts 10:17).

(2) ἀνακρίνοντες (searching—pres. participle, nom. plur. of ἀνακρίνω, I search) τὰς γραφὰς (the Scriptures) εἰ ἔχοι ταῦτα οὕτως (literally, if these [things] had thus—ταῦτα is the neuter plur. "these [things]" and is the subject of ἔχοι—*neuter plurals take the verb in the singular*—ἔχοι is the optative of ἔχω, I have, and the optative is used because instead of the direct question "Are these things so?" it is put in an indirect way, "searching if these things were so." The use of ἔχω is idiomatic. That is, whereas the Greek is "if these things had so," we must say "if these things were so" (Acts 17:11).

(c) The following is an example of a deliberative question, i.e., a direct question asked not simply for the sake of information but in a rhetorical way:—

καί τινες ἔλεγον (and some were saying), Τί ἂν θέλοι (What would—optative of θέλω, I will, I wish) ὁ σπερμολόγος οὗτος (this babbler) λέγειν (say—infinitive mood, see below), Acts 17:18.

Exercise

Translate, with the help of the accompanying notes:—

(1) Ὁ δὲ κύριος κατευθύναι ὑμῶν τὰς καρδίας εἰς τὴν ἀγάπην τοῦ θεοῦ καὶ εἰς τὴν ὑπομονὴν τοῦ Χριστοῦ. (2 Thess. 3:5) κατευθύναι is the 1st aorist, optative of κατευθύνω, I direct (the omission of the -σ-, which marks the future and 1st aorist tenses, will be explained later): καρδία heart: ὑπομονή patience (note "the patience of Christ"—not as in the A.V.).

(2) Ἐπηρώτων δὲ αὐτὸν οἱ μαθηταὶ αὐτοῦ τίς αὕτη εἴη ἡ παραβολή. (Luke 8:9) Ἐπηρώτων is "were asking" (for this form see later): μαθητής, a disciple: τίς,"what" (feminine, agreeing with παραβολή a parable), this is the subject of εἴη (optative, "might be").

(3) ζητεῖν τὸν θεὸν, εἰ ἄρα γε ψηλαφήσειαν αὐτὸν: (Acts 17:27a) ζητεῖν to seek (infin.—translated in our Version "that-they-should-seek"): ἄρα γε, to be translated together "haply": ψηλαφήσειαν is 3rd pers. plur. 1st aor. optative of ψηλαφάω, I feel after.

▪ LESSON 15 ▪

The Infinitive Mood

The Infinitive (in English expressed by "to," e.g., "to be," "to loose ") is a verbal noun, that is to say, it partakes of the nature both of a verb and a noun.

It has no different forms for cases and persons and is therefore indeclinable.

It is always neuter, and as a noun it may be used with different cases of the neuter article.

As a noun it may stand as the subject or as the object of another verb or be governed by a preposition.

As a verb it may itself have a subject or an object. All these points are illustrated below.

Memorize the following:

Infinitive Mood of εἰμί

Present Infinitive	εἶναι	to be.
Future Infinitive	ἔσεσθαι	to be about to be.

Infinitive Mood, Active, of λύω

Present Infinitive	λύειν	to loose.
Future Infinitive	λύσειν	to be about to loose.
1st Aor. Infinitive	λῦσαι	to loose at once.
Perfect Infinitive	λελυκέναι	to have loosed.

Some Examples of The Infinitive Mood

(1) Where the Infinitive, as a noun, is the subject of another verb:

καλὸν ἀνθρώπῳ τὸ οὕτως εἶναι, "(it is) good for a man thus to be" (1 Cor. 7:26). In this sentence the verb ἐστί, "it is," is understood; i.e., καλόν ἐστι "it is good." Now the subject of this is τὸ οὕτως εἶναι lit., "the thus to be," i.e., "the thus to be is good": ἀνθρώπῳ is "for a man."

The article may be omitted: e.g., αἰσχρὸν γάρ ἐστιν (for it is shameful) γυναικὶ (for a woman) λαλεῖν (to speak) ἐν ἐκκλησίᾳ (in church), 1 Cor. 14:35.

Rule—In such instances, when the Infinitive has a subject, the subject, if expressed, is put in the accusative Case.

Thus, in Matt. 17:4, καλόν ἐστιν (it is good) ἡμᾶς (us) ὧδε (here) εἶναι (to be), i.e. "it is good that we should be here" ἡμᾶς is the accusative subject of the Infinitive.

But if the subject of the Infinitive is the same person or thing as the subject of the preceding verb, the subject of the Infinitive is generally omitted, and any words qualifying the omitted subject are put in the nominative. Thus in Rom. 1:22, φάσκοντες εἶναι σοφοί, "professing (themselves) to be wise"; if this were fully expressed it would be φάσκοντες (professing) ἑαυτοὺς εἶναι σοφοί, (themselves to be wise); but the same persons are the subject both of "professing" and "to be"; accordingly ἑαυτοὺς is omitted and σοφοί is put in the nominative.

Note the omission of the subject in the following, from Jas. 2:14: ἐὰν πίστιν λέγῃ τις ἔχειν, lit., "if anyone saith to have faith," i.e., saith he hath faith. Here τις, "anyone," is the subject of λέγῃ (pres. subjunc. after ἐάν, if), and the same person is the unexpressed subject of ἔχειν "(himself) to have." If it were expressed in full it would have to be ἐὰν πίστιν λέγῃ τις ἑαυτὸν ἔχειν ("himself to have")—(not αὐτὸν ἔχειν ["him to have," which would mean some other person]). Because the person is the same subject for both verbs λέγῃ and ἔχειν, the accusative subject of ἔχειν is omitted. We must, however, insert it in English and say "If anyone saith he hath" (πίστιν is the accus. object of ἔχειν).

(2) The following is an example of the Infinitive as the object of the verb:—

2 Cor. 8:11, νυνὶ δὲ (but now) καὶ (also) τὸ ποιῆσαι (the doing) ἐπιτελέσατε (complete). What tense of the Infinitive of ποιέω, I do, is ποιῆσαι? Note its noun character with the article; τὸ ποιῆσαι form together the object of the verb ἐπιτελέσατε: this is the 2nd pers. plur., 1st Aorist Imperative of ἐπιτελέω, I complete or fulfill. What is the force of the Aorist Imperative as distinct from the present? (See Lesson 12, 2nd paragraph).

(3) In the following instances the Infinitive is governed by a preposition:—

Matt. 13:5a, 6b: διὰ τὸ μὴ ἔχειν βάθος γῆς . . . διὰ τὸ μὴ ἔχειν ῥίζαν "on-account-of the not having (lit., to have) depth . . . on-account-of the not having root." In each clause ἔχειν (the pres. Infinitive of ἔχω) is a verbal noun, used with the article τὸ. In English the verbal noun is "having"; so τὸ ἔχειν is "the having." When the preposition διά means "on account of" the noun governed by it is in the accusative case. Hence τὸ ἔχειν here is accusative. But ἔχειν is not only a noun, it is also a verb, and as such it governs its object βάθος in the accusative case (for the neuter noun βάθος see γένος, Lesson 9). The negative with the Infinitive is μή (not οὐ).

So also in the second clause, διά governs τὸ ἔχειν as a noun in the accusative case, and τὸ ἔχειν as a verb governs its object ῥίζαν, "a root," in the accusative case.

Matt. 20:19: εἰς τὸ ἐμπαῖξαι καὶ μαστιγῶσαι καὶ σταυρῶσαι, "to mock and scourge and crucify. The three verbs are, respectively, the first aorist Infinitive (see λῦσαι above) of ἐμπαίζω (future ἐμπαίξω), I mock, μαστιγόω (fut. μαστιγώσω), I scourge, and σταυρόω (fut. σταυρώσω), I crucify. The article τό goes with all three, and the article and the three infinitives are all governed in the accusative case by the preposition εἰς: literally "unto the to mock and to scourge and to crucify." The εἰς really signifies "with a view to," or "with the object of (mocking, etc.)."

(Other uses of the Infinitive will be explained later. The above are sufficient to illustrate the force of this Mood.)

The student should go over very thoroughly the above examples of the Infinitive. After studying the notes, write out the English translations in a list, and then translate them back into the Greek text. This will help to overcome the difficulties of the Infinitive.

Exercise

Translate the following, with the help of the accompanying notes, learning first the words and their meanings.

(1) νυνὶ δὲ καὶ τὸ ποιῆσαι ἐπιτελέσατε, ὅπως καθάπερ ἡ προθυμία τοῦ θέλειν, οὕτως καὶ τὸ ἐπιτελέσαι ἐκ τοῦ ἔχειν. (2 Cor. 8:11) νυνί, now: ὅπως, in order that: καθάπερ, just as: προθυμία, readiness: θέλω, I will.

Notes—τοῦ θέλειν is lit. "of the to will," i.e., "of the being willing": this follows προθυμία and so the translation is "readiness to will," the genitive of the Infinitive signifying intention or purpose.

(2) πλὴν τοὺς ἐχθρούς μου τούτους τοὺς μὴ θελήσαντάς με βασιλεῦσαι ἐπ' αὐτοὺς ἀγάγετε ὧδε καὶ κατασφάξατε αὐτοὺς ἔμπροσθέν μου. (Luke 19:27) πλὴν, howbeit: ἐχθρός, an enemy: θελήσαντάς, accus. plur. masc., 1st aorist participle of θέλω, I wish, am willing, lit. "having been willing":—accus. in agreement with ἐχθρούς: βασιλεῦσαι, 1st aorist Infin. of βασιλεύω, I reign, lit. "me to reign": ἐπ' for ἐπί over: ἀγάγετε, 2nd pers. plur. Imperative of a 2nd aor. (see later) doubled syllable form of ἄγω, I bring: ὧδε, hither: κατασφάξατε 1st aor. Imperative of κατασφάζω, I slay: ἔμπροσθέν, before (takes the genitive case).

(3) οἷς ἠθέλησεν ὁ θεὸς γνωρίσαι τί τὸ πλοῦτος τῆς δόξης τοῦ μυστηρίου τούτου ἐν τοῖς ἔθνεσιν, ὅ ἐστιν Χριστὸς ἐν ὑμῖν, ἡ ἐλπὶς τῆς δόξης· 28 ὃν ἡμεῖς καταγγέλλομεν νουθετοῦντες πάντα ἄνθρωπον καὶ διδάσκοντες πάντα ἄνθρωπον ἐν πάσῃ σοφίᾳ, ἵνα παραστήσωμεν πάντα ἄνθρωπον τέλειον ἐν Χριστῷ: (Col. 1:27, 28) ἠθέλησεν, 3rd pers. sing., 1st aor. Indic. of θέλω, I am willing, I am pleased (this verb takes η for augment instead of ε): γνωρίσαι, 1st aor. Infin. of γνωρίζω, I make known: πλοῦτος, wealth, riches (a neut. noun like γένος): ἔθνεσιν, (dat. plur. of ἔθνος, a nation—here "Gentiles" another neut. noun like γένος—dative case after ἐν): ἐλπὶς, hope (genit. ἐλπίδος): καταγγέλλομεν, I proclaim (pronounced *katangello*): νουθετοῦντες, nom. plur. masc. pres. participle of νουθετέω, I admonish—the ending -ουντες is contracted for -εοντες (see later): διδάσκω, I teach: παραστήσωμεν, "we may present," subjunctive (for the form see later): τέλειος, perfect.

(4) ὁ δὲ θεὸς τῆς ἐλπίδος πληρώσαι ὑμᾶς πάσης χαρᾶς καὶ εἰρήνης ἐν τῷ πιστεύειν, εἰς τὸ περισσεύειν ὑμᾶς ἐν τῇ ἐλπίδι ἐν δυνάμει πνεύματος ἁγίου. (Rom. 15:13) ἐλπίδος [see under (3)]: πληρώσαι, 3rd pers. sing. 1st aor. optative of πληρόω, I fill (the optative of a wish): χαρᾶς, genit. of χαρά, joy (genitive is used after words of filling to signify "with"): πιστεύειν, Infin. as verbal noun, dative after ἐν—"in believing" (τῷ not to be translated): περισσεύειν, to abound—accus. of the Infin. verbal noun governed by εἰς: ὑμᾶς is the accus. subject of the Infin. (lit. "unto the you to abound"—i.e., "that ye may abound"): δύναμις, power: ἅγιος, holy.

Retranslate the above four passages from English into Greek, correcting your result from the original.

The Second Aorist Active

Some verbs have a Second Aorist tense. Its meaning is the same as the First Aorist: it differs only in form. Very few verbs have both a First and Second Aorist: λύω has only the first. We shall therefore take as an example the verb τύπτω, I strike.

Note 1—The endings of the Second Aorist Indicative are the same as those of the Imperfect, and as it is a past tense the augment is used. There is this difference in form, however, that the endings are added to the simple stem (see below).

Note 2—In the other moods the endings are the same as those of the present tenses. Here again, the endings are added to the simple stem.

If the Present and Imperfect tenses have been thoroughly learned there is no need to write out the Second Aorist forms in all the persons, save for the sake of practice. Remember that there is no augment except in the Indicative mood.

Second Aorist of τύπτω, I strike

Indicative, ἔτυπον, I struck
(etc., see the Imperfect endings)
Imperative, τύπε, strike thou
(etc., see the Present endings)
Subjunctive, τύπω, I (may) strike
(etc., see the Present endings)
Optative, τύποιμι, I (might) strike
(etc., see the Present endings)
Infinitive, τυπεῖν, to strike
Participle, τυπών, -οῦσα, -όν, having struck

It will be observed that the stem of the Present tense of τύπτω is τυπτ- but the stem of the second Aorist is τυπ-.

The Second Perfect

This tense is rare. It occurs only in the Active Voice and is simply a modified form of the Perfect. Thus, whereas the Perfect of τύπτω is τέτυφα, the 2nd Perfect is τέτυπα. Note the reduplication τε-, characteristic of all Perfect tenses.

LESSON 16

Note for Review—A complete paradigm of the Active Voice should be drawn up by the student from preceding Lessons, putting the Moods as headings of parallel columns, in the following order: Indicative, Imperative, Subjunctive, Optative, Infinitive, Participles: and the names of the tenses down the left side—Present, Imperfect, Future, 1st Aorist, Perfect, Pluperfect, 2nd Aorist, remembering that the Imperfect and Pluperfect Tenses are found only in the Indicative Mood, and that there is no Future in the Imperative and Subjunctive.

The Passive Voice of the Verb

Whereas a verb is in the Active Voice when its subject is spoken of as acting or doing something, the Passive Voice signifies that the subject is acted upon. In English the Passive is formed by the use of the verb "to be" with the Passive Participle. Thus the Passive of "I loose" is "I am loosed" (always to be distinguished from the continuous tense of the Active Voice, formed by the verb "to be" with the Present Participle active, e.g., "I am loosing"). In Greek the Passive is formed (save in certain Perfect Tenses) simply by the addition of a different set of endings to the stem from those in the Active Voice.

The following are the Indicative Mood Tenses of the Passive Voice of λύω. The student must memorize them; but only after being thoroughly familiar with the Active Voice forms.

The Passive Voice of λύω

Indicative Mood

Present Tense: "I am being loosed"

Singular

1st p.	λύομαι	(I am, etc.)
2nd p.	λύῃ or λύει	(thou art, etc.)
3rd p.	λύεται	(he is, etc.)

Plural

1st p.	λυόμεθα	(we are, etc.)
2nd p.	λύεσθε	(ye are, etc.)
3rd p.	λύονται	(they are, etc.)

Note the iota in the 2nd pers. sing. This form, λύῃ, is the same as the 3rd pers. sing., pres. subjunctive active. There is no difficulty in distinguishing them as to the meaning. The context makes that clear. The Active is "he may loose," the Passive "thou art being loosed."

Note that λυ- is the stem. The endings should be learned apart from the stem.

Imperfect Tense: "I was being loosed," etc.

	Singular	Plural
1st p.	ἐλυόμην	ἐλυόμεθα
2nd p.	ἐλύου	ἐλύεσθε
3rd p.	ἐλύετο	ἐλύοντο

Future Tense: "I shall be loosed"

	Singular	Plural
1st p.	λυθήσομαι	λυθησόμεθα
2nd p.	λυθήσῃ	λυθήσεσθε
3rd p.	λυθήσεται	λυθήσονται

First Aorist: "I was loosed"

	Singular	Plural
1st p.	ἐλύθή	ἐλύθημεν
2nd p.	ἐλύθης	ἐλύθητε
3rd p.	ἐλύθη	ἐλύθησαν

(Note—The endings of the First Aorist Passive resemble the Imperfect of εἰμί *except in the 2nd and 3rd pers. sing.—see Lesson 3. Observe the -θ- characteristic of the Passive Voice, and the Augment)*

Perfect Tense "I have been loosed"

	Singular	Plural
1st p.	λέλυμαι	λελύμεθα
2nd p.	λέλυσαι	λέλυσθε
3rd p.	λέλυται	λέλυνται

Pluperfect Tense: "I had been loosed"

	Singular	Plural
1st p.	ἐλελύμην	ἐλελύμεθα
2nd p.	ἐλέλυσο	ἐλέλυσθε
3rd p.	ἐλέλυτο	ἐλέλυντο

Exercise on the Indicative Mood of the Passive Voice

Translate the following sentences and passages, after learning the vocabulary. Correct your rendering from the R.V. [or NRSV or NKJV] text and retranslate from the English into Greek.

Vocabulary

μαρτύριον .... witness
ἄνομος .... lawless
τότε .... then
σάρξ (gen. σαρκός) .... flesh
ἐντολή .... commandment
μακάριος, -α, -ον .... blessed
πτωχός, -ή, -όν .... poor
οὐρανός .... heaven
πραΰς .... meek
δικαιοσύνη .... righteousness
ἐλεήμων (neut. -ον) .... merciful

(1) ὅτι (because) ἐπιστεύθη (1st aor. indic. passive of πιστεύω, I believe) τὸ μαρτύριον ἡμῶν ἐφ' ὑμᾶς (2 Thess. 1:10). The subject of the verb is τὸ μαρτύριον ἡμῶν. Note that ἐφ' is for ἐφί, "unto" (not "among," as A.V.): the ι is dropped before the υ of ὑμᾶς and then the π becomes φ because of the rough breathing, the ʽ. To say ἐπ' ὑμᾶς would be awkward: hence the π becomes aspirated to φ.

(2) καὶ τότε ἀποκαλυφθήσεται (future passive of ἀποκαλύπτω, I reveal) ὁ ἄνομος (2 Thess. 2:8).

(3) οἳ οὐκ ἐξ αἱμάτων οὐδὲ ἐκ θελήματος σαρκὸς οὐδὲ ἐκ θελήματος ἀνδρὸς ἀλλ' ἐκ θεοῦ ἐγεννήθησαν. (John 1:13) ἐξ is for ἐκ, "of," the κ becoming ξ before the αἱ of αἱμάτων). Note this gen. plur., lit., "bloods": αἷμα and θέλημα are declined like πνεῦμα (Lesson 9). For ἀνδρὸς see Lesson 8. ἐγεννήθησαν is 3rd plur. 1st aor. pass. of γεννάω, I beget (passive "am born"). The change from α in γεννάω to η will be explained later.

(4) ὁ ἔχων τὰς ἐντολάς μου καὶ τηρῶν αὐτὰς ἐκεῖνός ἐστιν ὁ ἀγαπῶν με· ὁ δὲ ἀγαπῶν με ἀγαπηθήσεται ὑπὸ τοῦ πατρός μου, κἀγὼ ἀγαπήσω αὐτὸν καὶ ἐμφανίσω αὐτῷ ἐμαυτόν. (John 14:21) Note the pres. participles of ἔχω, I have, τηρέω, I keep, ἀγαπάω, I love. Note the difference between the future passive ἀγαπηθήσεται (3rd pers.) and the future active ἀγαπήσω (1st pers.): ὑπό is "by"—it takes the genitive: κἀγὼ is short for καὶ ἐγώ : ἐμφανίσω is the future of ἐμφανίζω, I manifest. It would be well to commit this verse to memory.

(5) Μακάριοι οἱ πτωχοὶ τῷ πνεύματι, ὅτι αὐτῶν ἐστιν ἡ βασιλεία τῶν οὐρανῶν. 4 μακάριοι οἱ πενθοῦντες, ὅτι αὐτοὶ παρακληθήσονται. 5 μακάριοι οἱ πραεῖς, ὅτι αὐτοὶ κληρονομήσουσιν τὴν γῆν. 6 μακάριοι οἱ πεινῶντες καὶ διψῶντες τὴν δικαιοσύνην, ὅτι αὐτοὶ χορτασθήσονται. 7 μακάριοι οἱ ἐλεήμονες, ὅτι αὐτοὶ ἐλεηθήσονται. (Matt. 5:3-7) Study carefully the following notes. The verb "to be" is often omitted; εἰσίν, "are," is to be understood after μακάριοι: τῷ πνεύματι is dative of the point in which an adjective (here πτωχοί, poor) is applied; hence we must say "poor in spirit" (the article must not be translated): αὐτῶν, "of them," i.e., "theirs", πενθοῦντες is the pres. participle, nom. plur. masc. of πενθέω, I mourn, for πενθέοντες, the εο contracting to ου: παρακληθήσονται is 3rd pers. plur., future, indic. passive of παρακαλέω, I comfort: κληρονομήσουσιν is the fut. active of κληρονομέω, I inherit: πεινῶντες is the nom. plur., masc., pres. participle of πεινάω, I hunger, for πεινάοντες the αο contracting to ω: so διψῶντες is from διψάω, I thirst: χορτασθήσονται is 3rd plur. fut. passive of χορτάζω, I fill, satisfy (verbs in -ζω take σ in fut. and 1st aor.): ἐλεηθήσονται is fut. passive of ἐλεέω, I show mercy.

Imperative Mood, Passive Voice

Present Tense

	Singular		Plural	
2nd p.	λύου	be thou loosed	λύεσθε	be ye loosed
3rd p.	λυέσθω	let him (her, it) be loosed	λυέσθωσαν or λυέσθων	let them be loosed

Aorist Tense: "Be thou loosed (at once)"

	Singular	Plural
2nd p.	λύθητι	λύθητε
3rd p.	λυθήτω	λυθήτωσαν

Perfect Tense
(expressing continuance of a past act)

	Singular	Plural
2nd p.	λέλυσο	λέλυσθε
3rd p.	λελύσθω	λελύσθωσαν or λελύσθων

Students should now obtain a copy of the little Greek-English Lexicon to the New Testament, by A. Souter. This is published by The Clarendon Press, Oxford. It is one of the best books of reference published in connection with Greek Testament study, and forms a good companion to Nestle's Text. Being small in size it is handy for taking about. In the course of the next few lessons this book will be substituted for the vocabularies given in the exercises. [More up to date and informative is the *Shorter Lexicon of the Greek New Testament* by Gingrich and Danker, available from Zondervan Publishing House and the University of Chicago Press.]

▪ LESSON 17 ▪

Exercise on the Imperative Mood

Learn the following vocabulary. Then translate the passages with the help of the notes. Re-translate into the Greek, correcting your result.

Vocabulary

κόκκος . . . . grain	θάλασσα . . . . sea
σίναπι . . . . (gen. -εως) mustard (declined like πόλις, Lesson 9)	καρδία . . . . heart
	περισσῶς . . . . exceedingly

(1) εἶπεν δὲ ὁ κύριος, Εἰ ἔχετε πίστιν ὡς κόκκον σινάπεως, ἐλέγετε ἂν τῇ συκαμίνῳ [ταύτῃ], Ἐκριζώθητι καὶ φυτεύθητι ἐν τῇ θαλάσσῃ· καὶ ὑπήκουσεν ἂν ὑμῖν. (Luke 17:6) ἔχετε is 2nd pers., plur., pres. indic. of ἔχω: ἐλέγετε ἂν is "ye would say" (this construction of the imperfect with ἄν is explained later): Ἐκριζώθητι 2nd per., sing., 1st aor. imperative passive of ἐκριζόω I root up; φυτεύθητι, the same form from φυτεύω, I plant: ὑπήκουσεν ἄν, "it would obey"—1st aor. active of ὑπακούω, note that the augment is formed by the change of the α of ἀκούω into η, ὑπ being for ὑπό, a preposition compounded with the verb ἀκούω. The preposition does not augment, the main verb does. Note the datives in this verse, one after λέγω, the other after ἐν.

(2) Μὴ ταρασσέσθω ὑμῶν ἡ καρδία· πιστεύετε εἰς τὸν θεόν καὶ εἰς ἐμὲ πιστεύετε. (John 14:1) ταρασσέσθω is 3rd pers., sing., pres. imperative, passive of ταράσσω, I trouble: πιστεύετε may be 2nd pers. plur. of either the pres. indic. active or the pres. imperative active of πιστεύω, i.e., either "believe ye" or "ye believe."

(3) λέγουσιν πάντες, Σταυρωθήτω. This verb is the 1st aor. imperative of σταυρόω, I crucify, i.e., "let Him be crucified" (see λυθήτω, above). This sentence is from Matt. 27:22 (end of verse); translate verse 23: ὁ δὲ ἔφη, Τί γὰρ κακὸν ἐποίησεν; οἱ δὲ περισσῶς ἔκραζον λέγοντες, Σταυρωθήτω. ὁ δὲ is "but he," ἔφη, "said." What tense of ποιέω is ἐποίησεν? ἔκραζον is 3rd pers., plur., imperf. indic. active of κράζω, I cry out, "they kept on crying out."

(4) εἰ γὰρ οὐ κατακαλύπτεται γυνή, καὶ κειράσθω· εἰ δὲ αἰσχρὸν γυναικὶ τὸ κείρασθαι ἢ ξυρᾶσθαι, κατακαλυπτέσθω. 7 ἀνὴρ μὲν γὰρ οὐκ ὀφείλει κατακαλύπτεσθαι τὴν κεφαλήν εἰκὼν καὶ δόξα θεοῦ ὑπάρχων· ἡ γυνὴ δὲ δόξα ἀνδρός ἐστιν. 8 οὐ γάρ ἐστιν ἀνὴρ ἐκ γυναικός ἀλλὰ γυνὴ ἐξ ἀνδρός. (1 Cor. 11:6-8) κατακαλύπτεται 3rd pers., sing., pres. indic., passive of κατακαλύπτω, I cover up, veil (for the form see λύομαι): γυνή, "a woman," an irregular noun of the 3rd declension (its gen., dat., acc., sing. are γυναικός, γυναικί, γυναῖκα, and the plural cases are γυναῖκες, γυναικῶν, γυναιξί, γυναῖκας): κειράσθω, 3rd pers., sing., aor. imperative, middle, of κείρω, I shear, "let her be shorn."

The Subjunctive Mood, Passive Voice

Present Tense: "I may be loosed" (a process)

1st p.	λύωμαι	λυώμεθα
2nd p.	λύῃ	λύησθε
3rd p.	λύηται	λύωνται

Note the long vowel, characteristic of the subjunctive present, etc. Also the iota subscript in the 2nd pers. sing.

First Aorist: "I may be loosed" (a definite act)

1st p.	λυθῶ	λυθῶμεν
2nd p.	λυθῇς	λυθῆτε
3rd p.	λυθῇ	λυθῶσι(ν)

Note the endings, like the subjunctive of εἰμί; *see Lesson 13.*

Perfect Tense: "I may have been loosed."

This tense is formed by the perfect participle (see later), with the subjunctive of the verb εἰμί; *thus the literal meaning would be "(that) I may be having been loosed," but the literal meaning must not be pressed.*

1st p.	λελυμένος ὦ	λελυμένοι ὦμεν
2nd p.	λελυμένος ᾖς	λελυμένοι ἦτε
3rd p.	λελυμένος ᾖ	λελυμένοι ὦσι(ν)

Note—The λελυμένος, being a participle, is also an adjective, and therefore must agree in gender and number with the subject: λελυμένος, -η, -ον is declined like a 2nd declension adjective. Note, e.g., the -οι of the plural. This would be -αι if women were spoken of.

Exercise on the Subjunctive Mood of the Passive Voice.

Before doing this exercise it will be necessary for the student to review the five principal uses of the Subjunctive mood as given in Lesson 13.

Translate the passages with the help of the notes, learning the meanings of new words. Retranslate into the Greek and correct from the Text.

I—Containing instances of the Subjunctive, Passive, in clauses of *Purpose* (see Lesson 13, *I*).

(1) ἔπεμψα δὲ τοὺς ἀδελφούς, ἵνα μὴ τὸ καύχημα ἡμῶν τὸ ὑπὲρ ὑμῶν κενωθῇ ἐν τῷ μέρει τούτῳ, ἵνα καθὼς ἔλεγον παρεσκευασμένοι ἦτε. (2 Cor. 9:3) ἔπεμψα, 1st aor. indic., active of πέμπω, I send: ἵνα μή, "in order that . . . not": τὸ καύχημα ἡμῶν τὸ ὑπὲρ ὑμῶν, lit., "the boasting of us (i.e., our boasting) the (i.e., the [boasting]) on behalf of you"; we may render by "our boasting, that, namely, on your behalf": κενωθῇ (1st aor. subjunc., passive of κενόω, I make void), "may (not) be made void": ἔλεγον (1st per. sing., imperf. indic., active of λέγω) "I was saying": παρεσκευασμένοι ἦτε, 2nd pers., plur., perf. subjunc., passive, of παρασκευάζω, I prepare; this is composed of the preposition παρά and the verb σκευάζω; verbs beginning with two consonants (except a mute and a liquid) reduplicate by a simple ε; hence παρα becomes παρε- as with the ordinary augment when a preposition is prefixed to a verb.

(2) ὅπως ἂν ἀποκαλυφθῶσιν ἐκ πολλῶν καρδιῶν διαλογισμοί. (Luke 2:35b) ὅπως, "in order that"; ἄν not to be translated; ἀποκαλυφθῶσιν, 3rd pers., plur., 1st aor. subjunc., passive of

ἀποκαλύπτω, I reveal, agreeing with its subject διαλογισμοί, thoughts; ἐκ can simply be rendered "of"; it takes the genitive, πολλῶν (see Lesson 7).

II—Containing instances of the Subjunctive Passive in *Conditional Clauses* (see Lesson 13, *II*).

(1) 31 νῦν κρίσις ἐστὶν τοῦ κόσμου τούτου, νῦν ὁ ἄρχων τοῦ κόσμου τούτου ἐκβληθήσεται ἔξω· 32 κἀγὼ ἐὰν ὑψωθῶ ἐκ τῆς γῆς, πάντας ἑλκύσω πρὸς ἐμαυτόν. (John 12:31-32) κρίσις, judgment; κόσμος, world; ἄρχων, prince, ruler; ἐκβληθήσεται, 3rd pers., sing., fut. indic., passive of ἐκβάλλω, I cast out (an irregular verb); ἔξω, out (an adverb); κἀγώ for καὶ ἐγώ; ὑψωθῶ 1st aor. subjunc., passive of ὑψόω, I lift up; ἕλκω, I draw; πρός, to.

(2) Οἴδαμεν γὰρ ὅτι ἐὰν ἡ ἐπίγειος ἡμῶν οἰκία τοῦ σκήνους καταλυθῇ, οἰκοδομὴν ἐκ θεοῦ ἔχομεν, οἰκίαν ἀχειροποίητον αἰώνιον ἐν τοῖς οὐρανοῖς. (2 Cor. 5:1) οἴδαμεν, we know (irregular): ἐπίγειος, -α, -ον, earthly; οἰκία, house; σκήνος, tabernacle, tent (3rd declension, neut. like γένος, genit. -ους): καταλυθῇ, 1st aor. subjunc., pass. of καταλύω, I loosen down, take down (of a tent), dissolve; οἰκοδομή, a building; ἀχειροποίητος, not-hand-made (the prefix ἀ- signifies a negative; χείρ, the hand; ποιητός, a verbal adjective, "made"—hence "not made with hands").

III—Containing an instance of the Subjunctive Passive in *Relative Clauses* (see Lesson 13, *III*).

ἀμὴν δὲ λέγω ὑμῖν, ὅπου ἐὰν κηρυχθῇ τὸ εὐαγγέλιον εἰς ὅλον τὸν κόσμον, καὶ ὃ ἐποίησεν αὕτη λαληθήσεται εἰς μνημόσυνον αὐτῆς. (Mark 14:9) ὅπου, "where"—ὅπου ἐάν together make "wherever," introducing an indefinite relative clause, i.e., a relative clause expressing indefiniteness—the ἐάν must not be translated here by "if," it simply adds the idea of indefinite locality to ὅπου; κηρυχθῇ, 3rd pers. sing., 1st aor. subjunc., passive of κηρύσσω, I preach—translate by "is preached" (not "was preached"; the aorist in the subjunctive mood is not necessarily a past tense, here it points to the preaching as a precise announcement)—note the subjunctive in a relative clause with ἐάν, "wherever the gospel is preached": καί, also; λαληθήσεται fut. indic., passive of λαλέω, I speak; εἰς, "unto" or "for"; μνημόσυνον, a memorial.

IV—Containing an instance of the *Deliberative Subjunctive* (see Lesson 13, *IV*).

πῶς οὖν πληρωθῶσιν αἱ γραφαὶ ὅτι οὕτως δεῖ γενέσθαι. (Matt. 26:54) πῶς, how; οὖν, therefore; πληρωθῶσιν, 3rd pers. plur., 1st aor. subjunc., passive of πληρόω, I fulfill, agreeing with its subject γραφαί: γραφή, a writing, scripture; οὕτως, thus; δεῖ, it is necessary; γενέσθαι, "to become" (an irregular verb—see later).

V—The use of the Subjunctive Passive in *Exhortations* is very rare (see Lesson 13, *V*)

LESSON 18

Optative Mood, Passive Voice

Present Tense: "I might be loosed," etc.

	Singular	Plural
1st p.	λυοίμην	λυοίμεθα
2nd p.	λύοιο	λύοισθε
3rd p.	λύοιτο	λύοιντο

Future Tense: "I should be loosed"

	Singular	Plural
1st p.	λυθησοίμην	λυθησοίμεθα
2nd p.	λυθήσοιο	λυθήσοισθε
3rd p.	λυθήσοιτο	λυθήσοιντο

First Aorist: "I might be (or am to be) loosed"

	Singular	Plural
1st p.	λυθείην	λυθείημεν
2nd p.	λυθείης	λυθείητε
3rd p.	λυθείη	λυθεῖεν

Perfect: "I might have been loosed"

	Singular	Plural
1st p.	λελυμένος εἴην	λελυμένοι εἴημεν
2nd p.	λελυμένος εἴης	λελυμένοι εἴητε
3rd p.	λελυμένος εἴη	λελυμένοι εἴησαν

The Optative Passive is very rare. No exercise therefore will be given upon it.

The Infinitive Mood, Passive Voice

Pres. Infin.	λύεσθαι, to be loosed
Future	λυθήσεσθαι, to be about to be loosed
First Aor.	λυθῆναι, to be loosed (at once)
Perfect	λελύσθαι, to have been loosed

Exercise on the Infinitive Passive

Before doing this exercise review the Notes on the Infinitive Mood at the end of Lesson 14. Study the accompanying notes, and learn the meanings of new words; after translating, retranslate as usual.

(1) πιστὸς δὲ ὁ θεός, ὃς οὐκ ἐάσει ὑμᾶς πειρασθῆναι ὑπὲρ ὃ δύνασθε ἀλλὰ ποιήσει σὺν τῷ πειρασμῷ καὶ τὴν ἔκβασιν. (1 Cor. 10:13b) πιστός, faithful; ἐάσει, 3rd pers. sing., fut. indic., of ἐάω, I permit, allow; πειρασθῆναι, 1st aor. infin., passive, of πειράζω, I tempt; ὑπέρ, above; ὅ, acc., neut., sing., of ὅς; δύνασθε, ye are able; πειρασμός, a temptation; ἔκβασις, a way of escape.

(2) ἀλλὰ μετὰ τὸ ἐγερθῆναί με προάξω ὑμᾶς εἰς τὴν Γαλιλαίαν. (Mark 14:28) Note particularly the phrase μετὰ τὸ ἐγερθῆναί με—the preposition μετά is "after," it governs the whole of the rest of the phrase in the accusative case; the article τό describes the phrase ἐγερθῆναί με, which, literally, is "me to be raised," the verb being the 1st aor. infin., passive, of ἐγείρω, I raise. These two words form the construction known as the Accusative with the Infinitive, which will be explained later. Accordingly τὸ ἐγερθῆναί με is "the me to be raised." Literally, then, the whole phrase is "after the Me to be raised," i.e., "after the [event] that I am raised," and hence we must translate by "after I am raised," for that is the corresponding idiom in English; προάξω fut. of προάγω, I go before.

(3) ὁ δὲ Ἰωάννης διεκώλυεν αὐτὸν λέγων, Ἐγὼ χρείαν ἔχω ὑπὸ σοῦ βαπτισθῆναι, καὶ σὺ ἔρχῃ πρός με; (Matt. 3:14) διεκώλυεν, 3rd pers. sing., imperf. indic., of διακωλύω, I hinder—"he was hindering" (note the augment, the compounded preposition διά changing to διε); βαπτισθῆναι, 1st aor., infin. passive of βαπτίζω; ἔρχῃ, comest (an irregular verb).

(4) οὗτος ἤκουσεν τοῦ Παύλου λαλοῦντος· ὃς ἀτενίσας αὐτῷ καὶ ἰδὼν ὅτι ἔχει πίστιν τοῦ σωθῆναι. (Acts 14:9) ἤκουσεν, imperfect of ἀκούω, I hear, which takes the genitive case (τοῦ Παύλου)—note that ἀ- make augment ἡ-. The τοῦ is not to be translated; the article often goes with a proper name; λαλοῦντος, gen., sing., masc., pres. participle of λαλέω, I speak—for λαλέοντος (εο becomes ου); ἀτενίσας, nom., sing., masc., 1st aor. partic. of ἀτενίζω, I look steadfastly; ἰδών, seeing (explained later); σωθῆναι, 1st aor. infin., pass. of σώζω, I save: the τοῦ is not to be translated—τοῦ σωθῆναι is a genitive construction after πίστιν, faith, lit., "faith of the to be saved," i.e., "faith to be saved."

The Participles of the Passive Voice

Note—These are verbal adjectives, like those of the active voice. They are declined like adjectives, the particular form agreeing in case, number and gender with the noun or pronoun to which the participle refers.

Present Participle: "being loosed"

Masc. λυόμενος Fem. λυομένη Neut. λυόμενον

This is declined, singular and plural, like ἀγαθός (see Lesson 4).

Future Participle: "about to be loosed"

Masc. λυθησόμενος Fem. λυθησομένη Neut. λυθησόμενον

First Aorist Participle: "having been loosed"

Masc. λυθείς Fem. λυθεῖσα Neut. λυθέν

This is declined like ἑκών, ἑκοῦσα, ἑκόν (Lesson 9), -ε- taking the place of -ο- in the masc. and neut. in all cases except the nom. sing. masc., and dat. plur., and -ει- taking the place of -ου- in the fem. and in all genders in the dat. plural.

Thus the genitive singular is λυθέντος, λυθείσης, λυθέντος, the accusative singular is λυθέντα, λυθεῖσαν, λυθέν, and the dat. plural is λυθεῖσι, λυθείσαις, λυθεῖσι.

Perfect Participle: "having been loosened"

Masc. λελυμένος Fem. λελυμένη Neut. λελυμένον

Exercise

Translate the following passages, with the help of the accompanying notes, learning the meaning of new words and retranslating into the Greek.

(1) τῇ γὰρ ἐλπίδι ἐσώθημεν· ἐλπὶς δὲ βλεπομένη οὐκ ἔστιν ἐλπίς· ὃ γὰρ βλέπει τίς ἐλπίζει; (Rom. 8:24) τῇ . . . ἐλπίδι is dat. of instrument, "by hope"; ἐσώθημεν, 1st pers. plur., 1st aor., indic. passive, of σώζω, I save; βλεπομένη, nom., sing., fem., pres. partic., passive, of βλέπω, I see, "being seen"; ὅ neut. of ὅς; τις, anyone.

(2) καὶ ἐπέθηκαν ἐπάνω τῆς κεφαλῆς αὐτοῦ τὴν αἰτίαν αὐτοῦ γεγραμμένην· Οὗτός ἐστιν Ἰησοῦς ὁ βασιλεὺς τῶν Ἰουδαίων. (Matt. 27:37) ἐπέθηκαν, they put up (a form explained later); ἐπάνω, above (a preposition taking the genitive); κεφαλή, a head; αἰτία, an accusation (here the accus. object of the verb ἐπέθηκαν); γεγραμμένην, acc., sing., fem., perf. partic., passive, of γράφω, I write, "having been written," or simply "written" (the root of γράφω is γραπ-, and γεγραπμένην becomes γεγραμμένην, the π assimilating to the μ for the sake of sound).

(3) καὶ γὰρ ἐγὼ ἄνθρωπός εἰμι ὑπὸ ἐξουσίαν τασσόμενος ἔχων ὑπ᾽ ἐμαυτὸν στρατιώτας. (Luke 7:8a) καί, also; ὑπό, under; ἐξουσία, authority; τασσόμενος, nom., sing., masc., pres. partic., passive, of τάσσω, I set, "being set"; στρατιώτης, a soldier (like μαθητής, Lesson 3).

(4) 14 ὁ δὲ ἐγερθεὶς παρέλαβεν τὸ παιδίον καὶ τὴν μητέρα αὐτοῦ νυκτὸς καὶ ἀνεχώρησεν εἰς Αἴγυπτον, 15 καὶ ἦν ἐκεῖ ἕως τῆς τελευτῆς Ἡρῴδου· ἵνα πληρωθῇ τὸ ῥηθὲν ὑπὸ κυρίου διὰ τοῦ προφήτου λέγοντος, Ἐξ Αἰγύπτου ἐκάλεσα τὸν υἱόν μου. (Matt. 2:14-15) ὁ δέ, but he; ἐγερθείς, nom., sing., masc., 1st aor., partic. passive, of ἐγείρω, I arouse, awake, lit., "having been aroused," παρέλαβεν "took" (an irregular verb); παιδίον, a little child; νυκτός, by night, genitive of νύξ (genitive of time); ἀνεχώρησεν, 3rd pers. sing., 1st aor. indic., active, of ἀναχωρέω, I depart (note the augment -ε- in the preposition ἀνε); ἐκεῖ, there; ἕως, until; τελευτή, an end, or death; πληρωθῇ, 3rd pers. sing., 1st aor. subj., passive, of πληρόω, I fulfill; ῥηθέν, nom., sing., neut., 1st aor. partic., passive, of ρέω, I utter, speak (see λυθείς, λυθεῖσα, λυθέν, above); διά, by means of (takes the genitive).

THE SECOND AORIST PASSIVE

The tense endings are the same as those of the first aorist throughout the moods (save in one ending) but the ending is added to the simple root and without the -θ-. Thus, whereas the first aorist indic. passive of τύπτω, I strike, is ἐτύφθην, etc., the second aorist is ἐτύπην, etc. The only exception is in the 2nd pers. sing., imperative, where -θι is found instead of -τι.

The following will be sufficient. The student who has learned the first aorist tenses will readily supply the full second aorist from memory. They should at all events be written out in full. The meanings are the same.

Indicative	ἐτύπην
Imperative	τύπηθι (3rd p. s. τυπήτω)
Subjunctive	τύπω
Optative	τυπείην
Infinitive	τυπῆναι
Participle	τυπείς, -εῖσα, έν

The Middle Voice

Whereas in English there are only two voices, active and passive, the Greek language has three. The Middle Voice chiefly signifies that a person has a special interest in the effects of his action, that he is acting either upon, or for, himself, or that when he is acting for others he has a personal interest in their condition or welfare. Sometimes, however, it is scarcely possible to distinguish in meaning between the middle and the active. Examples are given below.

In four tenses of the middle voice the forms are the same as those of the passive. These are the present, imperfect, perfect and pluperfect. Accordingly for the paradigm of these the student is referred to the passive voice (Lesson 16). The future and aorist tenses are different.

Middle Voice—Indicative Mood

For the four following tenses see the passive voice: *Present*, λύομαι, etc., "I am loosing myself (or, for myself)"; *Imperfect*, ἐλυόμην, etc., "I was loosing myself (or for myself)"; *Perfect*, λέλυμαι, etc., "I have loosed myself (or for myself)"; *Pluperfect*, ἐλελύμην, etc., "I had, etc."

Future: "I will loose myself (or for, etc.)"

	Singular	Plural
1st p.	λύσομαι	λυσόμεθα
2nd p.	λύσῃ	λύσεσθε
3rd p.	λύσεται	λύσονται

First Aorist: "I loosed myself (or for, etc.)"

	Singular	Plural
1st p.	ἐλυσάμην	ἐλυσάμεθα
2nd p.	ἐλύσω	ἐλύσασθε
3rd p.	ἐλύσατο	ἐλύσοντο

Imperative Mood

For the two following tenses see the Passive Voice: *Present,* λύου, etc., "loose thyself (or for thyself)"; *Perfect,* λέλυσο, etc., "have loosed thyself (or for thyself)," etc. There is no imperfect or pluperfect outside the indicative, nor any future in the imperative and subjunctive.

First Aorist: "loose thyself (or for thyself)

	Singular	Plural
2nd p.	λῦσαι	λύσασθε
3rd p.	λυσάσθω	λυσασθωσαν or λυσάσθων

Subjunctive Mood

For the two following tenses see the Passive Voice: *Present,* λύωμαι, etc., "I may loose myself (or for myself)"; *Perfect,* λελυμένος ὦ, etc., "I may have loosed myself (or for myself)."

First Aorist: "I may loose myself (or for myself)"

	Singular	Plural
1st p.	λύσωμαι	λυσώμεθα
2nd p.	λύσῃ	λύσησθε
3rd p.	λύσηται	λύσωνται

▪ LESSON 19 ▪

Middle Voice—Optative Mood

For the two following tenses see the Passive Voice: Present, λυοίμην, etc., "I might loose myself (or for myself)"; Perfect λελυμένος εἴην, etc., "I might have loosed myself (or for myself)."

Future: "I should loose myself (or for myself)"

	Singular	Plural
1st p.	λυσοίμην	λυσοίμεθα
2nd p.	λύσοιο	λύσοισθε
3rd p.	λύσοιτο	λύσοιντο

First Aorist: "I might loose myself (or for myself)"

	Singular	Plural
1st p.	λυσαίμην	λυσαίμεθα
2nd p.	λύσαιο	λύσαισθε
3rd p.	λύσαιτο	λύσαιντο

Infinitive Mood

Present (like the Passive), λύεσθαι, "to loose oneself (or for oneself)"; *Perfect* (like the Passive), λελύσθαι, "to have loosed oneself (or for oneself)."

Future, λύσεσθαι, "to be about to loose oneself (or for oneself)."

First Aorist, λύσασθαι, "to loose oneself (or for oneself) immediately."

Participles

Present (like the Passive), λυόμενος, -η, -ον, etc., "loosing oneself (or for oneself)"; *Perfect* (like the Passive) λελυμένος, -η, -ον, etc., "having loosed oneself (or for oneself)." *Future,* λυσόμενος, -η, -ον, "being about to loose oneself (etc.)." *First Aorist,* λυσάμενος, -η, -ον, "having loosed oneself (or for oneself) immediately."

The student should compare and contrast the above Futures and First Aorists in the various Moods with those of the Passive Voice, noting carefully the differences. They should be written out in parallel columns from memory.

Exercise on the Middle Voice

Translate the following passages with the help of the accompanying notes, learning new words and retranslating into Greek.

(1) αἰτεῖτε καὶ οὐ λαμβάνετε διότι κακῶς αἰτεῖσθε, ἵνα ἐν ταῖς ἡδοναῖς ὑμῶν δαπανήσητε.

(Jas. 4:3) αἰτεῖτε, 2nd pers. plur., pres. indic., active of αἰτέω, I ask (for αἰτέετε: -εε- contracts to -ει-); λαμβάνω, I receive; διότι, because; κακῶς, evilly, amiss; αἰτεῖσθε, (for αἰτέεσθε), same person, number, tense and mood as αἰτεῖτε, but middle voice, "ye ask for yourselves" (note the purposive change, stressing the selfishness); ἡδονή, pleasure; δαπανήσητε, 1st aor. subjunc., of δαπανάω, I spend.

(2) καὶ νῦν τί μέλλεις; ἀναστὰς βάπτισαι καὶ ἀπόλουσαι τὰς ἁμαρτίας σου ἐπικαλεσάμενος τὸ ὄνομα αὐτοῦ. (Acts 22:16) τί, why? μέλλεις, 2nd sing., pres. indic., of μέλλω, I delay, tarry; ἀναστάς, "having arisen" (an aor. partic., explained later); βάπτισαι, 2nd pers. sing., 1st aor., imperative, middle, of βαπτίζω, lit., "get thyself baptized"; ἀπόλουσαι, same tense and voice of ἀπολούω, I wash away, "get (thy sins) washed away"; ἐπικαλεσάμενος, 1st aor. participle, middle, of ἐπικαλέω, I call upon, "calling for thyself upon . . ." Note the force of all these aorists, implying decisive and immediate action, the middle voice signifying, in the first two instances, that Saul was to arrange for the thing to be done.

(3) οἱ γὰρ Φαρισαῖοι καὶ πάντες οἱ Ἰουδαῖοι ἐὰν μὴ πυγμῇ νίψωνται τὰς χεῖρας οὐκ ἐσθίουσιν, κρατοῦντες τὴν παράδοσιν τῶν πρεσβυτέρων, 4 καὶ ἀπ' ἀγορᾶς ἐὰν μὴ βαπτίσωνται [in earlier editions of Nestle: ῥαντίσωνται] οὐκ ἐσθίουσιν, καὶ ἄλλα πολλά ἐστιν ἃ παρέλαβον κρατεῖν, βαπτισμοὺς ποτηρίων καὶ ξεστῶν καὶ χαλκίων [καὶ κλινῶν]. (Mark 7:3, 4) πυγμή, a fist (the dative here signifies "with the fist," an idiom used of washing; to wash with the fist was to wash "diligently"); νίψωνται, 3rd pers. plur., 1st aor. subjunc., middle, of νίπτω, I wash—conditional subjunctive after ἐὰν μή, "if not," i.e., unless; χείρ, a hand (fem.); ἐσθίω, I eat; κρατοῦντες, for κρατέοντες, nom., plur., masc., pres. partic., of κρατέω, I hold fast; παράδοσις, a tradition (declined like πόλις); πρεσβύτερος, an elder; ἀπ', for ἀπό (with genit.); ἀγορά, a market place; ῥαντίσωνται, 1st aor. subjunc., middle, of ῥαντίζω, I sprinkle (note the force of the middle voice in each case, intimating zealous self-interest in washing and sprinkling), ἄλλα, neut. plur., of ἄλλος, other, "other things" (distinguish this from ἀλλά, "but"); ἐστιν though singular, must be translated "are," owing to the rule that *when the subject of a verb is in the neuter plural the verb is put in the singular*. Here we must render by "there are"; παρέλαβον, "they received" (an irregular verb); κρατεῖν, pres. infin.; for ποτήριον, ξέστης and χαλκίον see Souter's or another lexicon.

(4) Ὁμοία γάρ ἐστιν ἡ βασιλεία τῶν οὐρανῶν ἀνθρώπῳ οἰκοδεσπότῃ, ὅστις ἐξῆλθεν ἅμα πρωῒ μισθώσασθαι ἐργάτας εἰς τὸν ἀμπελῶνα αὐτοῦ. (Matt. 20:1) ὅμοιος, -α, -ον, like; for βασιλεία and οἰκοδεσπότης, see Souter; ὅστις, who; ἐξῆλθεν, "went out" (an irregular verb); ἅμα πρωΐ, lit. "together early," i.e., "early in the morning", μισθώσασθαι, 1st aor. infin., middle, of μισθόω, I hire (infinitive of purpose), "to hire for himself."

(5) Ἐν σοφίᾳ περιπατεῖτε πρὸς τοὺς ἔξω τὸν καιρὸν ἐξαγοραζόμενοι. (Col. 4:5) περιπατεῖτε, (for περιπατέετε), 2nd pers. plur., pres. imperative, active of περιπατέω, I walk; ἔξω, without; ἐξαγοραζόμενοι, nom., plur., masc., pres. participle, middle, of ἐξαγοράζω, I buy up, "buying up for yourselves."

(6) καὶ ἐξάπινα περιβλεψάμενοι οὐκέτι οὐδένα εἶδον ἀλλὰ τὸν Ἰησοῦν μόνον μεθ' ἑαυτῶν. (Mark 9:8) ἐξάπινα, suddenly, περιβλεψάμενοι, 1st aor. participle, middle, of περιβλέπω, I look around (περί, around, βλέπω, I look)—"having looked around"—the middle voice expresses, in a way that cannot well be brought out in English, their deep interest: οὐκέτι, no longer; οὐδένα, accus. of οὐδείς, nobody; εἶδον, "they saw" (an irregular verb); μόνον, alone; μεθ' for μετά (when this preposition takes the genitive it denotes "with").

Note—The student should become familiar with the whole of the regular verb λύω *in the three voices, Active, Middle and Passive. This will greatly facilitate the reading of the Greek Testament. To help towards the thorough acquisition of the regular verb it will be well to write out in full from memory (correcting the result if necessary) the various tense endings of the following regular verb on the model of* λύω:—βουλεύω, *I advise (the meaning of this in the middle voice is "to advise oneself," that is, "to deliberate").*

Deponent Verbs

These are the verbs which have no active voice, but are either middle or passive in form, though they are active in meaning. They were called Deponent from the Latin verb "*deponere*," to lay aside, as they are considered to lay aside passive meanings.

The following are very common and should be committed to memory, especially the various irregular forms of the tenses mentioned.

βούλομαι, I will, wish, purpose; imperf. ἐβουλόμην; 1st aor. ἐβουλήθην.

ἀποκρίνομαι, I answer; for the past tense "I answered," either the 1st aor. passive, ἀπεκρίθην, is used (and this is the usual form), or the 1st aor. middle, ἀπεκρινάμην. Thus "he answered" is usually ἀπεκρίθη, but in seven places we find ἀπεκρίνατο.

γίνομαι, I become; imperf. ἐγινόμην; fut. γενήσομαι; 1st aor. (passive in form) ἐγενήθην; perfect γεγένημαι. There is a perfect with an active form, γέγονα, and with the same meaning, "I have become"; there is also a 2nd aor., ἐγενόμην, "I became," with the same endings as in the imperfect. This 2nd aor. is common in the 3rd pers. sing., optative, γένοιτο, in the phrase μὴ γένοιτο, "let it not be," translated "God forbid."

δέχομαι, I receive; 1st aor. ἐδεξάμην; perf. δέδεγμαι.

λογίζομαι, I reckon; 1st aor. ἐλογισάμην, I reckoned; 1st aor. pass ἐλογίσθην, I was reckoned.

ἄρχομαι, I begin; fut. ἄρξομαι; 1st aor. ἠρξάμην.

ἔρχομαι, I come; imperf. ἠρχόμην; other forms are irregular, as follows:—future ἐλεύσομαι; perfect ἐλήλυθα; 2nd aor. ἦλθον.

Exercise on the Deponent Verbs

(1) Translate: Ἐν ἀρχῇ ἦν ὁ λόγος, καὶ ὁ λόγος ἦν πρὸς τὸν θεόν, καὶ θεὸς ἦν ὁ λόγος.
2 οὗτος ἦν ἐν ἀρχῇ πρὸς τὸν θεόν. 3 πάντα δι' αὐτοῦ ἐγένετο, καὶ χωρὶς αὐτοῦ ἐγένετο οὐδὲ
ἕν. ὃ γέγονεν 4 ἐν αὐτῷ ζωὴ ἦν, καὶ ἡ ζωὴ ἦν τὸ φῶς τῶν ἀνθρώπων· 5 καὶ τὸ φῶς ἐν τῇ σκο-
τίᾳ φαίνει, καὶ ἡ σκοτία αὐτὸ οὐ κατέλαβεν. 6 Ἐγένετο ἄνθρωπος ἀπεσταλμένος παρὰ θεοῦ,
ὄνομα αὐτῷ Ἰωάννης· 7 οὗτος ἦλθεν εἰς μαρτυρίαν, ἵνα μαρτυρήσῃ περὶ τοῦ φωτός, ἵνα
πάντες πιστεύσωσιν δι' αὐτοῦ. 8 οὐκ ἦν ἐκεῖνος τὸ φῶς, ἀλλ' ἵνα μαρτυρήσῃ περὶ τοῦ φωτός.
9 Ἦν τὸ φῶς τὸ ἀληθινόν, ὃ φωτίζει πάντα ἄνθρωπον, ἐρχόμενον εἰς τὸν κόσμον. (John 1:1-9)
In ver. 3, δι' is for διά, by; ἐγένετο is 3rd pers. sing., 2nd aor. of γίνομαι (see list above), and, though plural in meaning is singular, as it has a neuter plural subject πάντα, all things—"all things became (or came to be)." The next ἐγένετο is singular in agreement with ἕν, one thing (ἕν is the neut. of the numeral εἷς, μία, ἕν, masc., fem., neut., "one"); οὐδέ is not even."—ἐγένετο οὐδὲ ἕν, "not even one thing came to be" (distinguish the numeral ἕν from the preposition ἐν, in); ὅ, neut. of the rel. pron. ὅς, which; γέγονεν 3rd pers. sing., perf., of γίνομαι, hath come to be; in ver. 5 κατέλαβεν, comprehended, is an irregular verb, to be learned later. In ver. 6 translate Ἐγένετο by "there was"; ἀπεσταλμένος, sent (for this perfect participle see later); παρά with genit., "from." In ver. 7 ἦλθεν is 3rd pers. sing., 2nd aor. of ἔρχομαι (see above); εἰς, unto (i.e., "for "); μαρτυρήσῃ, 1st aor. subjunc. of μαρτυρέω; περὶ, concerning; πιστεύσωσιν, 1st aor. subj. In ver. 9 πάντα is acc., sing., masc., "every"; ἐρχόμενον, nom., sing., neut., pres. partic., "coming" this agrees and goes with φῶς (neut.), not with ἄνθρωπον.

(2) Translate: εἶδεν ὁ Ἰησοῦς τὸν Ναθαναὴλ ἐρχόμενον πρὸς αὐτὸν καὶ λέγει περὶ αὐτοῦ,
Ἴδε ἀληθῶς Ἰσραηλίτης ἐν ᾧ δόλος οὐκ ἔστιν. 48 λέγει αὐτῷ Ναθαναήλ, Πόθεν με γινώσκεις;
ἀπεκρίθη Ἰησοῦς καὶ εἶπεν αὐτῷ, Πρὸ τοῦ σε **Φίλιππον** φωνῆσαι ὄντα ὑπὸ τὴν συκῆν εἶδόν
σε. 49 ἀπεκρίθη αὐτῷ Ναθαναήλ, Ῥαββί, σὺ εἶ ὁ υἱὸς τοῦ θεοῦ, σὺ βασιλεὺς εἶ τοῦ Ἰσραήλ.
(John 1:47-49) εἶδεν, saw—an irregular 2nd aorist (see later), Ἴδε, behold; ἀληθῶς, truly; Πόθεν, whence? γινώσκεις, 2nd pers. sing., pres. indic. of γινώσκω, I know; ἀπεκρίθη, 3rd pers.

sing., 1st aor. indic. (passive in form) of ἀποκρίνομαι (see list above); this takes the dative "(answered) to him." Study carefully the phrase Πρὸ τοῦ σε Φίλιππον φωνῆσαι with the help of the following remarks, and see notes on the Infinitive, Lesson 15—πρό, before (a preposition taking the genitive); τοῦ (this article, genitive case after πρό, is not to be translated; it qualifies the whole phrase that follows); σε, thee, is the object of φωνῆσαι ("called thee"); φωνῆσαι is the 1st aor., infin. of φωνέω, I call, lit. "to have called"; the subject of the infinitive is Φίλιππον (for this construction of the accus. with the infin. see Lesson 18, p. 123); this phrase σε φωνῆσαι Φίλιππον is, lit., "Philip to have called thee"; this whole phrase, with its article τοῦ, is governed by πρό; literally, therefore, we have "Before Philip to have called thee." The only way to translate this concise idiomatic phrase is "Before Philip called thee"; ὄντα is acc. sing., masc., of ὤν the pres. partic. of εἰμί (see Lesson 9) "being" (i.e., "when thou wast"); ὑπό, under; εἶδον, I saw. In ver. 49 the τοῦ before Ἰσραήλ is not to be translated, as the article is generally used with a proper noun.

▪ LESSON 20 ▪

VERBS WITH CONTRACTED VOWEL ENDINGS

Note—Contractions take place only in the present and imperfect tenses. All other tenses, since they have no two vowels coming together, are formed regularly, taking, however, a long vowel in the last syllable but one (see below).

When α, ϵ, ο precede a vowel, whether long or short, it is generally contracted into one syllable. This has been illustrated in nouns and adjectives with contracted vowels (see Lesson 7). There are three forms of verbs, those with α— stems, e.g., τιμάω (τιμῶ), stem τιμα–, I honor; those with ϵ— stems, e.g., φιλέω (φιλῶ), stem φιλϵ– I love; those with ο— stems, e.g., ϵ—δηλόω (δηλῶ), stem δηλο– I manifest.

In the following paradigms the uncontracted forms are given in brackets. The contracted forms should be memorized.

(τιμάω) τιμῶ, I honor

CONTRACTED VERBS WITH –ϵ– STEMS
ACTIVE VOICE
INDICATIVE MOOD

Present Tense

1st p.	(τιμάω)	τιμῶ	(τιμάομϵν)	τιμῶμϵν
2nd p.	(τιμάϵις)	τιμᾷς	(τιμάϵτϵ)	τιμᾶτϵ
3rd p.	(τιμάϵι)	τιμᾷ	(τιμάουσι)	τιμῶσι

Imperfect Tense

1st p.	(ἐτίμαον)	ἐτίμων	(——ομϵν)	ἐτιμῶμϵν
2nd p.	(——ϵς)	ἐτίμας	(——ϵτϵ)	ἐτιμᾶτϵ
3rd p.	(——ϵ)	ἐτίμα	(——ον)	ἐτίμων

IMPERATIVE MOOD

Present Tense

2nd p.	(τίμαϵ)	τίμα	(τιμάϵτϵ)	τιμᾶτϵ
3rd p.	(——έτω)	τιμάτω	(——έτωσαν)	τιμάτωσαν

SUBJUNCTIVE MOOD

The present tense is exactly like the indicative present, owing to the contractions.

OPTATIVE MOOD

Present Tense

1st p.	(τιμάοιμι)	τιμῷμι	(——οιμϵν)	τιμῷμϵν
2nd p.	(——οις)	τιμῷς	(——οιτϵ)	τιμῷτϵ
3rd p.	(——οι)	τιμῷ	(——οιϵν)	τιμῷϵν

Note that the iota becomes subscript in each person. There is an alternative and more usual form for this tense, as follows:—

1st p.	τιμῴμην	——ημεν
2nd p.	——ης	——ητε
3rd p.	——η	——ησαν

Infinitive Mood (*Present*)

(τιμάειν) τιμᾷν

Participle (*Present*)

Masc.	Fem.	Neut.
(τιμάων) τιμῶν	(τιμάουσα) τιμῶσα	(τιμάον) τιμῶν

Passive and Middle Voices
Indicative Mood

Present Tense

1st p.	(τιμάομαι)	τιμῶμαι	(——όμεθα)	τιμώμεθα
2nd p.	(——ῃ)	τιμᾷ	(——εσθε)	τιμᾶσθε
3rd p.	(——εται)	τιμᾶται	(——ονται)	τιμῶνται

Imperfect Tense

1st p.	(ἐτιμάομην)	ἐτιμώμην	(——όμεθα)	ἐτιμώμεθα
2nd p.	(——ου)	ἐτιμῶ	(——εσθε)	ἐτιμᾶσθε
3rd p.	(——ετο)	ἐτιμᾶτω	(——ονται)	ἐτιμῶντο

Imperative Mood

Present Tense

2nd p.	(τιμάου)	τιμῶ	(——εσθε)	τιμᾶσθε
3rd p.	(——έσθε)	τιμάσθω	(——έσθωσαν)	τιμάσθωσαν
			(or —έσθων)	τιμάσθων

Subjunctive Mood

Like the Indicative

Optative Mood

Present Tense

1st p.	(τιμαοίμην)	τιμῴμην	(——οίμεθα)	τιμῴμεθα
2nd p.	(——οιο)	τιμῷο	(——οισθε)	τιμῷσθε
3rd p.	(——οιτο)	τιμῷτο	(——ονται)	τιμῷντο

Infinitive Mood

Present Tense

(τιμάεσθαι) τιμᾶσθαι

Participle

Masc.	Fem.	Neut.
(τιμαόμενος) τιμώμενος	(—ομένη) τιμωμένη	(—όμενον) τιμώμενον

Exercise on Contracted Verbs in -αω

Translate and retranslate, as in previous exercises:

(1) ἐγὼ δὲ λέγω ὑμῖν, ἀγαπᾶτε τοὺς ἐχθροὺς ὑμῶν καὶ προσεύχεσθε ὑπὲρ τῶν διωκόντων ὑμᾶς. (Matt. 5:44) ἀγαπᾶτε, pres., imperative active of ἀγαπάω; προσεύχεσθε pres., imperative of προσεύχομαι (see Deponent Verbs, last Lesson); ὑπέρ, for, on behalf of (takes the genitive); διωκόντων, gen., plur., pres. partic. of διώκω.

(2) καὶ τὸ ἀγαπᾶν αὐτὸν ἐξ ὅλης τῆς καρδίας καὶ ἐξ ὅλης τῆς συνέσεως καὶ ἐξ ὅλης τῆς ἰσχύος καὶ τὸ ἀγαπᾶν τὸν πλησίον ὡς ἑαυτὸν περισσότερόν ἐστιν πάντων τῶν ὁλοκαυτωμάτων καὶ θυσιῶν. (Mark 12:33) ἀγαπᾶν, pres. infinitive—the article is not translatable, it indicates the noun character of the infinitive verb, and thus τὸ ἀγαπᾶν are together the subject of ἐστιν; ἐξ (i.e., ἐκ) "out of" (or "with"); συνέσεως, genit. of συνέσις; περισσότερον, a comparative degree, "more." The comparative, which in English is followed by the word "than," is in Greek simply followed by the genitive case. Thus περισσότερον πάντων is not "more of all" but "more than all"; θυσιῶν, gen., plur. of θυσία.

(3) 15 Ὅτε οὖν ἠρίστησαν λέγει τῷ Σίμωνι Πέτρῳ ὁ Ἰησοῦς, Σίμων Ἰωάννου, ἀγαπᾷς με πλέον τούτων; λέγει αὐτῷ, Ναί, κύριε, σὺ οἶδας ὅτι φιλῶ σε. λέγει αὐτῷ, Βόσκε τὰ ἀρνία μου. 16 λέγει αὐτῷ πάλιν δεύτερον, Σίμων Ἰωάννου, ἀγαπᾷς με; λέγει αὐτῷ, Ναί, κύριε, σὺ οἶδας ὅτι φιλῶ σε. λέγει αὐτῷ, Ποίμαινε τὰ πρόβατά μου. ἠρίστησαν, 3rd pers. plur., 1st aorist active, of ἀριστέω; (John 21:15-16) Σίμων Ἰωάννου, "Simon, son of John"; the word υἱός, son, was omitted in this phrase; πλέον, more, a comparative followed by the genitive, i.e., "more than these," see above in (2); σύ, note the emphasis on this pronoun; οἶδας, knowest (an irregular verb).

(4) μακάριοι οἱ πεινῶντες καὶ διψῶντες τὴν δικαιοσύνην, ὅτι αὐτοὶ χορτασθήσονται. (Matt. 5:6) πεινῶντες and διψῶντες (for πεινάοντες and διψάοντες), nom., plur., pres. partic. of, πεινάω and διψάω; χορτασθήσονται, 3rd pers. plur., fut. indic., passive, of χορτάζω.

Contracted Verbs With –ε– Stems

These present little difficulty. The -ε- drops out before a long vowel, or vowel combination like -οι- or -ου-. Besides this, -εε- becomes -ει-, and -εο- becomes -ου-. A few tenses will be sufficient to illustrate this. The student should write out the whole of the verb φιλέω in the same way as τιμάω, observing the contractions now mentioned.

(φιλέω), φιλῶ, I love (stem φιλε-)

Indicative Mood, Active

Present Tense

1st p.	(φιλάω)	φιλῶ	(——έομεν)	φιλοῦμεν
2nd p.	(——έεις)	φιλεῖς	(——έετε)	φιλεῖτε
3rd p.	(——έει)	φιλεῖ	(——έουσι)	φιλοῦσι

Imperfect Tense

1st p.	(ἐφίλεον)	ἐφίλουν	(——έομεν)	ἐφιλοῦμεν
2nd p.	(——εες)	ἐφίλεις	(——έετε)	ἐφιλεῖτε
3rd p.	(——εε)	ἐφίλει	(——εον)	ἐφίλουν

The remainder of the active and the middle and passive tenses can be formed easily. Here the present participle active contracts as follows:

(φιλέων) φιλῶν (φιλέουσα) φιλοῦσα (φιλέον) φιλοῦν.

The infinitive passive is φιλεῖσθαι (for φιλέεσθαι)

Contracted Verbs in —οω.

In this third class the following rules should be noted:—

ο followed by a long vowel becomes ω.

ο followed by a short vowel becomes ου.

ο followed by a vowel combination containing ι becomes οι (except in the pres. infin. active, where —οειν becomes —-ουν).

(δηλόω) δηλῶ, I manifest (stem δηλο—)

Active Voice
Indicative Mood

Present Tense

1st p.	(δηλόω)	δηλῶ	(δηλόομεν)	δηλοῦμεν
2nd p.	(—όεις)	—οῖς	(—όετε)	—οῦτε
3rd p.	(—όει)	—οῖ	(—όουσι)	—οῦσι(ν)

Imperfect Tense

This has —ου— throughout: ἐδήλουν (for ἐδήλοον), —ους, —ου, —οῦμεν, etc.

Imperative Mood

Present Tense

This has —ου— throughout: δήλου (for δηνλοε), δηλούτω, etc.

Subjunctive Mood

Present Tense

1st p.	(δηλόω)	δηλῶ	(δηλόωμεν)	δηλῶμεν
2nd p.	(—όῃς)	—οῖς	(—όητε)	—ῶτε
3rd p.	(—όῃ)	—οῖ	(—όωσι)	—ῶσι(ν)

Optative Mood

Present Tense

This has —οειν throughout and is like φιλοίμι.

Infinitive—*Present:* (δηλόειν) δηλοῦν

Participle—*Present:* δηλῶν, δηλοῦσα, δηλοῦν

Passvie and Middle Voices
Indicative Mood

Present Tense

δηλοῦμαι, —οῖ, —οῦται (the plur. has —ου— in all persons)

Imperfect Tense

ἐδηλούμην, etc. (—ου— throughout)

Imperative Mood

Present Tense

δηλοῦ, —ούσθω, etc. (—ου— throughout)

Subjunctive Mood

Present Tense

δηλῶμαι, δηλοῖ, δηλῶται, etc. (—ω— in plural)

Optative Mood

Present Tense

δηλοίμην, etc. (—οι— throughout)

Infinitive—*Present:*—δηλοῦσθαι

Participle—*Present:*—δηλούμενος, —η, —ον

Note—The future active of the three contracted verbs is τιμήσω, φιλήσω, δηλώσω; the perfect is τετίμηκα, πεφίληκα, δεδήλωκα; the first aorist passive, ἐτιμήθην, ἐφιλήθην, ἐδηλώθην; the perfect middle and passive, τετίμημαι, πεφίλημαι, δεδήλωμαι.

Exercise on Contracted Verbs in —εω and —οω

Translate and retranslate the following:—

(1) Ὁ φιλῶν πατέρα ἢ μητέρα ὑπὲρ ἐμὲ οὐκ ἔστιν μου ἄξιος, καὶ ὁ φιλῶν υἱὸν ἢ θυγατέρα ὑπὲρ ἐμὲ οὐκ ἔστιν μου ἄξιος· 38 καὶ ὃς οὐ λαμβάνει τὸν σταυρὸν αὐτοῦ καὶ ἀκολουθεῖ ὀπίσω μου, οὐκ ἔστιν μου ἄξιος. (Matt. 10:37-38: 37) Ὁ φιλῶν is lit. "the one loving" (pres. partic.), i.e., "he that loveth", ὑπὲρ, above, i.e., "more than"; θυγατέρα acc. of θυγάτηρ.

(2) 16 λέγει αὐτῷ πάλιν δεύτερον, Σίμων Ἰωάννου, ἀγαπᾷς με; λέγει αὐτῷ, Ναί, κύριε, σὺ οἶδας ὅτι φιλῶ σε. λέγει αὐτῷ, Ποίμαινε τὰ πρόβατά μου. 17 λέγει αὐτῷ τὸ τρίτον, Σίμων Ἰωάννου, φιλεῖς με; ἐλυπήθη ὁ Πέτρος ὅτι εἶπεν αὐτῷ τὸ τρίτον, Φιλεῖς με; καὶ λέγει αὐτῷ, Κύριε, πάντα σὺ οἶδας, σὺ γινώσκεις ὅτι φιλῶ σε. λέγει αὐτῷ [ὁ Ἰησοῦς], Βόσκε τὰ πρόβατά μου. (John 21:16-17) οἶδας, thou knowest (an irregular verb): Ποίμαινε pres. imperative; τὸ τρίτον, the third time; ἐλυπήθη, 3rd pers. sing., 1st aorist passive of λυπέω; εἶπεν, 3rd pers. sing., of an irregular 2nd aor. form of λέγω, he said.

(3) ἐραυνῶντες εἰς τίνα ἢ ποῖον καιρὸν ἐδήλου τὸ ἐν αὐτοῖς πνεῦμα Χριστοῦ προμαρτυρόμενον τὰ εἰς Χριστὸν παθήματα καὶ τὰς μετὰ ταῦτα δόξας. (1 Pet. 1:11) ἐραυνῶντες, nom. plur., pres. participle, active, of ἐραυνάω; εἰς τίνα ἢ ποῖον, "unto what or what sort of"; ἐδήλου, 3rd pers. sing., imperf., indic., of δηλόω; προμαρτυρόμενον, nom. sing., neut., pres. partic. of a deponent verb, agreeing with πνεῦμα (neuter simply in grammatical gender); μετὰ ταῦτα, after these things.

(4) Κατὰ δὲ ἑορτὴν ἀπέλυεν αὐτοῖς ἕνα δέσμιον ὃν παρῃτοῦντο. (Mark 15:6) Κατὰ, at; ἀπέλυεν, 3rd pers. sing., imperf. indic. of ἀπολύω (the imperfect signifying a custom "he used to," etc.—note the augment at the end of the prefixed preposition ἀπε–; ἕνα, one; παρῃτοῦντο, 3rd pers. plur., imperf. indic. of the deponent contracted verb παραιτέομαι (a verb with several meanings, here "to ask").

Note—Among the contracted verbs, the verb ζάω, I live, which is a little irregular, is important. The present indicative is ζῶ (or ζάω), ζῇς, ζῇ, ζῶμεν, ζῆτε, ζῶσι; future, ζήσω, or ζήσομαι; 1st aor. ἔζησα. The present participle ζῶν, ζῶσα, ζῶν, (genitive, ζῶντος, ζώσης, ζῶντος) is very frequent in the New Testament and is found in most of its cases.

Exercise

Translate and retranslate: ἐγώ εἰμι ὁ ἄρτος ὁ ζῶν ὁ ἐκ τοῦ οὐρανοῦ καταβάς· ἐάν τις φάγῃ ἐκ τούτου τοῦ ἄρτου ζήσει εἰς τὸν αἰῶνα, καὶ ὁ ἄρτος δὲ ὃν ἐγὼ δώσω ἡ σάρξ μού ἐστιν ὑπὲρ τῆς τοῦ κόσμου ζωῆς. (John 6:51) καταβάς, 1st aor. partic. of καταβαίνω, "having come down": φάγῃ, 2nd aor. subjunc. of an irregular verb ἐσθίω, "I eat" (2nd aor., ἔφαγον—formed from another root); εἰς τὸν αἰῶνα, lit. "unto the age," signifies "for ever," and must be so translated; δώσω, I will give (see later).

▪ LESSON 21 ▪

Verbs With Stem Ending in λ, μ, ν, ρ

Since the consonants λ, μ, ν, ρ are known as liquids, verbs with stems ending in these letters are called Liquid Verbs. The personal endings are regular throughout, but certain simple changes occur in the preceding syllable or stem ending, as follows:—

(1) While the future tense keeps the verbal stem, which has a short vowel, the present tense stem usually has a long vowel, or, in the case of stems ending in λ the λ is doubled. Originally the future ended in -σω, as in the regular verb, but the σ dropped.

Thus the stem of the verb αἴρω, I raise, or take up, is ἀρ-, and the future is ἀρῶ. The stem of ἀποκτείνω, I kill, is ἀποκτεν-, and the future is ἀποκτενῶ. Again the stem of ἀγγέλλω (pronounced angellō), I renounce, is ἀγγελ-, and the future is ἀγγελῶ.

Note that the future, active and middle, of liquid verbs is declined like the present of contracted verbs in -εω.

(2) The first aorist, active and middle, omits the σ like the future, but lengthens the vowel in the preceding syllable by way of compensation.

Thus φαίνω (stem φαν-), I shine, has fut. φανῶ and 1st aor. ἔφηνα; ἀγγέλλω has 1st aor. ἤγγειλα (note the long -ει-).

(3) In the perfect, μ and ν cannot come before κ. One or the other is dropped. So we get κρίνω, I judge, perfect κέκρικα (not κέκρινκα); while, φαίνω has perfect πέφηνα (not πέφηνκα) and μένω and has μεμένηκα, lengthening the vowel.

(4) In the perfect passive ν is changed into σ or into μ before the ending -μαι, or else is dropped. Thus φαίνω makes πέφασμαι instead of πέφανμαι; κρίνω makes κέκριμαι instead of κέκρινμαι.

Exercise on Liquid Verbs

Translate and retranslate the following passages:—

(1) Μετὰ δέ τινας ἡμέρας εἶπεν πρὸς Βαρναβᾶν Παῦλος, Ἐπιστρέψαντες δὴ ἐπισκεψώμεθα τοὺς ἀδελφοὺς κατὰ πόλιν πᾶσαν ἐν αἷς κατηγγείλαμεν τὸν λόγον τοῦ κυρίου πῶς ἔχουσιν. (Acts 15:36) Μετὰ, after; εἶπεν, said (an irregular aorist of λέγω); Ἐπιστρέψαντες, nom., plur., masc., 1st aorist participle of ἐπιστρέφω, I return (future -ψω) lit. "returning" (the aorist indicating decisive and immediate action); ἐπισκεψώμεθα, 1st pers. plur., 1st aor. subjunc. of the deponent verb ἐπισκέπτομαι, I visit, "let us visit" (the 1st pers. plur. of the subjunc. present and 1st aor. is often used in a hortatory way, "let us," etc., κατὰ, throughout; κατηγγείλαμεν, 1st pers. plur., 1st aor., indic. of καταγγέλλω, I preach (note the position of the augment η, and the long vowel combination a lengthened from ε after the dropping of the σ in the liquid verb); πῶς ἔχουσιν, how they do (lit. "how they have," i.e., "how they are getting on").

(2) πολλοὶ μὲν οὖν ἐξ αὐτῶν ἐπίστευσαν καὶ τῶν Ἑλληνίδων γυναικῶν τῶν εὐσχημόνων καὶ ἀνδρῶν οὐκ ὀλίγοι. 13 Ὡς δὲ ἔγνωσαν οἱ ἀπὸ τῆς Θεσσαλονίκης Ἰουδαῖοι ὅτι καὶ ἐν τῇ Βεροίᾳ κατηγγέλη ὑπὸ τοῦ Παύλου ὁ λόγος τοῦ θεοῦ, ἦλθον κἀκεῖ σαλεύοντες καὶ ταράσσοντες τοὺς ὄχλους. 14 εὐθέως δὲ τότε τὸν Παῦλον ἐξαπέστειλαν οἱ ἀδελφοὶ πορεύεσθαι ἕως ἐπὶ τὴν θάλασσαν, ὑπέμεινάν τε ὅ τε Σιλᾶς καὶ ὁ Τιμόθεος ἐκεῖ. (Acts 17:12-14) γυναικῶν, gen. plur. of γυνή (irregular); ἔγνωσαν, 3rd pers. plur., 2nd aor. of γινώσκω, "I know" (irregular);

κατηγγέλη, 3rd pers. sing., 2nd aor. passive of καταγγέλλω, "was preached," agreeing with its subject λόγος (the 1st aor. passive is κατηγγέλθην—the 2nd aor. is simply an alternative form); ἦλθον, 3rd pers. plur., 2nd aor. of ἔρχομαι, I come (see Lesson 19); κἀκεῖ, for καὶ ἐκεῖ, also there; ἐξαπέστειλαν, 3rd pers. plur., 1st aor. indic. active of ἐχαποστέλλω, "I send away" (note the augment ε after the second preposition ἀπο, and the long ει before the single λ); πορεύεσθαι, pres. infin. of πορεύομαι (deponent); ἕως, as far as, ἐπὶ, to; ὑπέμειναν, 3rd pers. plur., 1st aor. of ὑπομένω.

(3) Ὅταν δὲ νηστεύητε, μὴ γίνεσθε ὡς οἱ ὑποκριταὶ σκυθρωποί, ἀφανίζουσιν γὰρ τὰ πρόσωπα αὐτῶν ὅπως φανῶσιν τοῖς ἀνθρώποις νηστεύοντες· ἀμὴν λέγω ὑμῖν, ἀπέχουσιν τὸν μισθὸν αὐτῶν. 17 σὺ δὲ νηστεύων ἄλειψαί σου τὴν κεφαλὴν καὶ τὸ πρόσωπόν σου νίψαι, 18 ὅπως μὴ φανῇς τοῖς ἀνθρώποις νηστεύων ἀλλὰ τῷ πατρί σου τῷ ἐν τῷ κρυφαίῳ· καὶ ὁ πατήρ σου ὁ βλέπων ἐν τῷ κρυφαίῳ ἀποδώσει σοι. (Matt. 6:16-18) νηστεύητε, pres. subjunc., after the indefinite Ὅταν, whenever; γίνεσθε, 2nd pers. plur., pres. imperat. of γίνομαι (deponent); φανῶσιν, 1st aor. subjunc. of φαίνω, I appear (subjunc. of purpose after ὅπως); νηστεύων, pres. partic.; ἄλειψαι, 2nd pers. sing., 1st aor. imperat., middle of ἀλείφω, "anoint for thyself"; νίψαι, ditto of νίπτω; ἀποδώσει, shall reward (see later).

The Second Conjugation, or Verbs in -μι

The student should thoroughly review the First Conjugation verb before learning the following. The endings of the second conjugation differ from the first only in the present and imperfect tenses, and, in several verbs, in the second aorist active and middle. The other tenses are like those of the First Conjugation, with certain exceptions.

There are two classes, (I) those that double the stem, the reduplication being especially by means of the vowel ι. Thus in δίδωμι, I give, the stem, δο-, is doubled by the prefix δι-; in τίθημι, I put, the stem, θε-, is doubled by τι-; in ἵστημι I place, or stand, the stem, στα-, makes ἱ (for σι): (II) those that add the syllable -νυ- or -ννυ- to the stem, before the person endings. Thus in δείκνυμι, I show, the stem is δεικ- and -νυ- is inserted before the ending -μι; in κεράννυμι, I mix (stem κερα-), -ννυ- is inserted.

Second Conjugation, Class I

There are three regular forms, viz., with stems ending in α-, ε-, ω-. The following model paradigms should be memorized, the persons, I, thou, he (she, it), we, you, they, being borne in mind.

ἵστημι, I stand	τίθημι, I put	δίδωμι, I give
(stem στα-)	(stem θε-)	(stem δο-)

Note—The following important details must be remembered as to the meanings of the tenses of ἵστημι:—

(1) The present, imperfect, future and 1st aorist of the active voices are transitive, and signify "I cause to stand," "I place," etc.

(2) The perfect and pluperfect are intransitive and are used in a present and imperfect sense, signifying "I stand," "I take my stand," "I was standing." That is to say, these are not to be rendered by "I have stood," "I had stood." These two tenses have a continuous significance and hence we must render by present and imperfect meanings.

(3) The 2nd aorist is also intransitive, and means "I stood."

Active Voice
Indicative Mood

Present Tense

Sing.			
	ἵστημι	τίθημι	δίδωμι
	ἵστης	τίθης	δίδως
	ἵστησι(ν)	τίθησι(ν)	δίδωσι(ν)
Plur.			
	ἵσταμεν	τίθεμεν	δίδομεν
	ἵστατε	τίθετε	δίδοτε
	ἱστᾶσι(ν)	τιθέασι(ν)	διδόασι(ν)

Imperfect Tense
I was standing, putting, giving, etc.

Sing.			
	ἵστην	ἐτίθην	ἐδίδουν
	ἵστης	ἐτίθεις	ἐδίδους
	ἵστη	ἐτίθει	ἐδίδου
Plur.			
	ἵσταμεν	ἐτίθεμεν	ἐδίδομεν
	ἵστατε	ἐτίθετε	ἐδίδοτε
	ἵστασαν	ἐτίθεσαν	ἐδίδοσαν

2nd Aorist

	I stood		
Sing.		No Singular	
	ἔστην		
	ἔστης		
	ἔστη		
Plur.			
			(*we gave*)
	ἔστημεν	ἔθεμεν	ἔδομεν
	ἔστητε	ἔθετε	ἔδετε
	ἔστησαν	ἔθεσαν	ἔδοσαν

Note—The place of the singular in the *two* last tenses is taken by the 1st aorist ἔδωκα, —κας, —κε.

Imperative Mood

Present Tense (continuous action)
stand thou, put thou, etc.

Sing.			
	ἵστη	τίθει	δίδου
	ἱστάτω	τιθέτω	διδότω

Plur.

	ἵστατε	τίθετε	δίδοτε
	ἱστάτωσαν	τιθέτωσαν	διδότωσαν

2nd Aorist (*immediate action*)
(*same meaning, but decisive*)

Sing.			
	στῆθι or στα*	θές	δός
	στήτω	θέτω	δότω
Plur.			
	στῆτε	θέτε	δότε
	στήτωσαν	θέτωσαν	δότωσαν

* *Note*—στα is used only in compound verbs, as ἀνάστα (Acts 12:7: Eph. 5:14).

Subjunctive Mood

Present Tense
That I, etc., may stand, put, give

Sing.			
	ἱστῶ	τιθῶ	διδῶ
	ἱστῇς	τιθῇς	διδῷς
	ἱστῇ	τιθῇ	διδῷ
Plur.			
	ἱστῶμεν	τιθῶμεν	διδῶμεν
	ἱστῆτε	τιθῆτε	διδῶτε
	ἱστῶσι(ν)	τιθῶσι(ν)	διδῶσι(ν)

2nd Aorist

στῶ	θῶ	δῶ
etc.	etc.	etc.

(*Like the present in each verb*)

Optative Mood

Present Tense
that I, etc., might stand, put, give

Sing.			
	ἱσταίην	τιθείην	διδοίην
	ἱσταίης	τιθείης	διδοίης
	ἱσταίη	τιθείη	διδοίη
Plur.			
	ἱσταῖμεν	τιθεῖμεν	διδοῖμεν
	ἱσταῖτε	τιθεῖτε	διδοῖτε
	ἱσταῖεν	τιθεῖεν	διδοῖεν

2nd Aorist
(same meaning, but decisive)

Sing.			
	σταίην	θείην	δοίην (δῴην)
	σταίης	θείης	δοίης (δῴης)
	σταίη	θείη	δοίη (δῴη)
Plur.			
	σταίημεν	θείημεν	δοίημεν
	σταίητε	θείητε	δοίητε
	σταῖεν	θεῖεν	δοῖεν

Infinitive Mood

		to stand, to put, to give	
Present	ἱστάναι	τιθέναι	διδόναι
2nd Aor.	στῆναι	θεῖναι	δοῦναι

Participles

Present Tense
standing, putting, giving

ἱστάς, -ᾶσα, -άν τιθείς, -εῖσα, -έν διδούς, -οῦσα, -όν

2nd Aorist
standing, putting, giving

στάς, -ᾶσα, -άν θείς, -εῖσα, -έν δούς, -οῦσα, -όν

Exercise on the above Tenses of the Active Voice of Verbs in -μι

Translate and retranslate:—

(1) αὐτὸς δὲ ᾔδει τοὺς διαλογισμοὺς αὐτῶν, εἶπεν δὲ τῷ ἀνδρὶ τῷ ξηρὰν ἔχοντι τὴν χεῖρα, Ἔγειρε καὶ στῆθι εἰς τὸ μέσον· καὶ ἀναστὰς ἔστη. (Luke 6:8) ᾔδει, knew (see later); εἶπεν, he said; ἔχοντι dat., sing., masc., pres. partic. of ἔχω, agreeing with ἀνδρὶ (dat. of ἀνήρ); στῆθι 2nd aor. imperative; ἀναστὰς, 2nd aor. partic. of ἀνίστημι, I arise, "having arisen"; ἔστη, 2nd aor. indic. of ἵστημι.

(2) Βλέπετε, ἀδελφοί, μήποτε ἔσται ἔν τινι ὑμῶν καρδία πονηρὰ ἀπιστίας ἐν τῷ ἀποστῆναι ἀπὸ θεοῦ ζῶντος. (Heb. 3:12) Βλέπετε, 2nd pers. plur., pres. imperat.; μήποτε lest at any time; ἔσται fut. of εἰμί; ἐν τῷ ἀποστῆναι, lit., "in the to depart from," the verb is the 2nd aor. infin. of ἀφίστημι (a compound of ἀπό and ἵστημι); the infinitive is a verbal noun, and is governed by the preposition ἐν, which takes the dative; hence we must translate by "in departing," the article τῷ not being translated.

(3) οὐδὲ καίουσιν λύχνον καὶ τιθέασιν αὐτὸν ὑπὸ τὸν μόδιον ἀλλ' ἐπὶ τὴν λυχνίαν, καὶ λάμπει πᾶσιν τοῖς ἐν τῇ οἰκίᾳ. (Matt. 5:15) τιθέασιν, see the pres. indic. of τίθημι; πᾶσιν, dat. plur. of πᾶς, dative after λάμπει, "it giveth light to."

(4) τίς δὲ ἐξ ὑμῶν μεριμνῶν δύναται ἐπὶ τὴν ἡλικίαν αὐτοῦ προσθεῖναι πῆχυν; (Luke 12:25) μεριμνῶν, nom. sing., masc., pres. partic. of μεριμνάω, "I am anxious"; δύναται, 3rd pers. sing., pres. indic. of δύναμαι, (a deponent verb); ἐπί, to; προσθεῖναι, 2nd aor. infin. of προστίθημι, I put to (πρός and τίθημι).

(5) Αἰτεῖτε καὶ δοθήσεται ὑμῖν, ζητεῖτε καὶ εὑρήσετε, κρούετε καὶ ἀνοιγήσεται ὑμῖν· 8 πᾶς γὰρ ὁ αἰτῶν λαμβάνει καὶ ὁ ζητῶν εὑρίσκει καὶ τῷ κρούοντι ἀνοιγήσεται. 9 ἢ τίς ἐστιν ἐξ ὑμῶν ἄνθρωπος, ὃν αἰτήσει ὁ υἱὸς αὐτοῦ ἄρτον, μὴ λίθον ἐπιδώσει αὐτῷ; 10 ἢ καὶ ἰχθὺν αἰτήσει, μὴ ὄφιν ἐπιδώσει αὐτῷ; 11 εἰ οὖν ὑμεῖς πονηροὶ ὄντες οἴδατε δόματα ἀγαθὰ διδόναι τοῖς τέκνοις ὑμῶν, πόσῳ μᾶλλον ὁ πατὴρ ὑμῶν ὁ ἐν τοῖς οὐρανοῖς δώσει ἀγαθὰ τοῖς αἰτοῦσιν αὐτόν. (Matt. 7:7-11) Αἰτεῖτε, 2nd pers. plur., pres. imperat. of the contracted verb αἰτέω; δοθήσεται, it shall be given (passive of δίδωμι, see later); εὑρήσετε, fut. of εὑρίσκω; ἀνοιγήσεται, fut. passive of ἀνοίγω; πᾶς ὁ αἰτῶν lit., "everyone the (one) asking," to be rendered "everyone that asketh"; αἰτήσει, fut., lit., "whom his son shall ask a loaf"; μή, this is not to be translated, it simply indicates that a negative answer to the question is expected: ἐπιδώσει fut. of ἐπιδίδωμι; οἴδατε, know (see later); διδόναι, pres. infin.; πόσῳ, how much, dat. of degree, "by how much"; αἰτοῦσιν, dat., plur., pres. participle, lit., "to the (ones) asking."

LESSON 22

Passive and Middle Voices of Verbs in —μι

Note 1—The Passive, Indicative, Present of the verb ἵστημι has the meaning of "I am caused to stand," "I am placed," etc., and hence it simply denotes "I stand," etc. Almost the only passive tense used in the New Testament is the 1st aorist.

Indicative Mood (Passive and Middle)

I take my stand; am put; am given

Sing.			
	ἵσταμαι	τίθεμαι	δίδομαι
	—σαι	—σαι (or τιθῇ)	—σαι
	—ται	—ται	—ται
Plur.			
	—μεθα	—μεθα	—μεθα
	—σθε	—σθε	—σθε
	—νται	—νται	—νται

Imperfect

I was taking my stand; was putting; was giving

Sing.			
	ἱστάμην	ἐτίθεμην	ἐδιδόμην
	—σο	—σο (or ἐτίθου)	—σο (or ἐδίδου)
	—το	—το	—το
Plur.			
	—μεθα	—μεθα	—μεθα
	—σθε	—σθε	—σθε
	—ντο	—ντο	—ντο

2nd Aorist (Middle only)

Sing.			
		I put	*I gave*
	(None)	ἐθέμην	ἐδόμην
		ἔθου	ἔδου
		—ετο	—ετο
Plur.			
		—έμεθα	—όμεθα
		—εσθε	—οσθε
		—εντο	—οντο

Imperative Mood (Passive and Middle)

Present Tense: be stood, or stand; be put, or put; be given, or give

Sing.			
	ἵστασο, or ἵστω	τίθεσο, or τίθου	δίδοσο, or δίδου
	ἱστάσθω	τιθέσθω	διδόσθω
Plur.			
	ἵστασθε	τίθεσθε	δίδοσθε
	ἱστάσθωσαν	τιθέσθωσαν	διδόσθωσαν

2nd Aorist (Middle only)

Sing.			
		put thou	*give thou*
	(None)	θοῦ	δοῦ
		θέσθω	δόσθω
Plur.			
		θέσθε	δόσθε
		θέσθωσαν	δόσθωσαν

Subjunctive Mood (Passive and Middle)

that I might be stood, stand, etc.

Sing.			
	ἱστῶμαι	τιθῶμαι	διδῶμαι
	——ῇ	——ῇ	——ῷ
	——ῆται	——ῆται	——ῶται
Plur.			
	——ώμεθα	——ώμεθα	——ώμεθα
	——ῆσθε	——ῆσθε	——ῶσθε
	——ῶνται	——ῶνται	——ῶνται

2nd Aorist (Middle only)

Sing.	(None)	θῶμαι	δῶμαι
		θῇ	δῷ
		θῆται	δῶται
Plur.			
		θώμεθα	δώμεθα
		θῆσθε	δῶσθε
		θῶνται	δῶνται

Optative Mood (Passive and Middle)

Present Tense: that I might be stood, stand, etc.

Sing.			
	ἱσαίμην	τιθείμην	διοίμην
	—αῖο	—εῖο	—οῖο
	—αῖτο	—εῖτο	—οῖτο

Plur.

—αίμεθα	—είμεθα	—οίμεθα
—αῖσθε	—εῖσθε	—οῖσθε
—αῖντο	—εῖντο	—οῖντο

2nd Aorist (Middle only)

Sing.

(None)	θείμην	δοίμην
	θεῖο	δοῖο
	θεῖτο	δοῖτο

Plur.

	θείμεθα	δοίμεθα
	θεῖσθε	δοῖσθε
	θεῖντο	δοῖντο

Infinitive Mood (Passive and Middle)

Present Tense

to be stood, to stand (for oneself), etc.

ἵστασθαι	τίθεσθαι	δίδοσθαι

2nd Aorist (Middle only)

to put for oneself, etc.

(None)	θέσθαι	δόσθαι

Participles (Passive and Middle)

Present Tense

being stood, or standing for oneself, etc.

ἱστάμενος, -η, -ον	τιθέμενος, -η, -ον	διδόμενος, -η, -ον

2nd Aorist (Middle only)

having been stood or having stood for oneself, etc.

(None)	θέμενος, -η, -ον	δόμενος, -η, -ον

Perfect: ἑστάμενος, τεθείμενος, δεδομένος

Exercise on the above Tenses of the Passive and Middle Voices in Verbs in -μι

(1) καὶ ἡ γλῶσσα πῦρ· ὁ κόσμος τῆς ἀδικίας ἡ γλῶσσα καθίσταται ἐν τοῖς μέλεσιν ἡμῶν, ἡ σπιλοῦσα ὅλον τὸ σῶμα καὶ φλογίζουσα τὸν τροχὸν τῆς γενέσεως καὶ φλογιζομένη ὑπὸ τῆς γεέννης. (Jas. 3:6) ἐστίν is to be understood in the first clause; the verb "to be" is often omitted; τῆς, not to be translated, being simply the article with an abstract noun; καθίσταται, is set, pres. indic. pass. of καθίστημι; σπιλοῦσα, nom., sing., fem., pres. partic. of σπιλέω, lit. "the (one) defiling"; φλογίζουσα, pres. partic. pass.; ὑπό, by (takes the genit.).

(2) ἔδοξεν γὰρ τῷ πνεύματι τῷ ἁγίῳ καὶ ἡμῖν μηδὲν πλέον ἐπιτίθεσθαι ὑμῖν βάρος πλὴν τούτων τῶν ἐπάναγκες. (Acts 15:28) ἔδοξεν, 3rd pers. sing., 1st aor. of δοκέω, "it seemed good"; from μηδὲν to βάρος *is the accusative with the infinitive construction*, lit. "no greater burden to be put upon, etc."; πλέον, acc. neut. of πλέων; ἐπιτίθεσθαι, pres. infin. pass.; βάρος, acc. case (as βάρος is a neut. noun, μηδέν is neut. to agree with it); πλήν, except (takes the genit.); ἐπάναγκες (here only in New Testament).

(3) Διαιρέσεις δὲ χαρισμάτων εἰσίν, τὸ δὲ αὐτὸ πνεῦμα· 5 καὶ διαιρέσεις διακονιῶν εἰσιν,
καὶ ὁ αὐτὸς κύριος· 6 καὶ διαιρέσεις ἐνεργημάτων εἰσίν, ὁ δὲ αὐτὸς θεός ὁ ἐνεργῶν τὰ πάν-
τα ἐν πᾶσιν. 7 ἑκάστῳ δὲ δίδοται ἡ φανέρωσις τοῦ πνεύματος πρὸς τὸ συμφέρον. 8 ᾧ μὲν γὰρ
διὰ τοῦ πνεύματος δίδοται λόγος σοφίας, ἄλλῳ δὲ λόγος γνώσεως κατὰ τὸ αὐτὸ πνεῦμα,
9 ἑτέρῳ πίστις ἐν τῷ αὐτῷ πνεύματι, ἄλλῳ δὲ χαρίσματα ἰαμάτων ἐν τῷ ἑνὶ πνεύματι,
10 ἄλλῳ δὲ ἐνεργήματα δυνάμεων, ἄλλῳ [δὲ] προφητεία, ἄλλῳ [δὲ] διακρίσεις πνευμάτων,
ἑτέρῳ γένη γλωσσῶν, ἄλλῳ δὲ ἑρμηνεία γλωσσῶν. (1 Cor. 12:4-10) τὸ αὐτό (see Lesson 5); ὁ ἐνεργῶν, the (one) energizing (working in), i.e., "who worketh in"; πᾶσιν, dat. plur., masc.; δι-'δοται, pres. passive (pres. of constant action "is given"); πρὸς, with a view to; συμφέρον, acc., neut., pres. partic. of συμφέρω, lit. "profiting" (i.e., "with a view to the profiting"); ᾧ, to the one (this is the meaning of the relative pronoun ὅς when followed by ἄλλος, another, in the next clause); κατὰ, according to; ἑτέρῳ, to another; ἑνί, dat. of εἷς, "one."

Note—The other tenses, active, passive and middle, of these three verb forms of the 2nd conjugation are formed like those of the 1st conjugation. The indicative mood and the 1st person of the tenses are given; the other moods and tenses can be formed on the model of λύω. The meanings are regular, save in ἵστημι (see below). Forms not given are not in New Testament.

Other Tenses of Verbs in –μι

Fut. Active		
στήσω	θήσω	δώσω
(I shall cause to stand)	(I shall put)	(I shall give)
1st Aor. Act.		
ἔστησα	ἔθηκα	ἔδωκα
(I caused to stand)	(I put)	(I gave)
Perf. Act.		
ἕστηκα	τέθεικα	δέδωκα
(I stand)	(I have put)	(I have given)
Pluperf.		
ἱστήκειν or εἱστήκειν	——	——
(I was standing)		
Fut. Passive		
σταθήσομαι	τεθήσομαι	δοθήσομαι
(I shall stand)	(I shall be put)	etc.
1st Aor. Pass.		
ἐστάθην	ἐτέθην	ἐδόθην
(I stood)	(I was put)	etc.
Fut. Mid.		
στήσομαι	θήσομαι	δώσομαι
(I shall stand)	(I shall put)	etc.
Perf. Mid. or Pass.		
——	τέθειμαι	δέδομαι

Note the rough breathings on the perf. and pluperf. of ἵστημι. There are two forms of the perf. partic. act., ἑστηκώς and ἑστώς.

Note that the ending of the 1st aor. active of τίθημι and δίδωμι is -κα and not -σα as in λύω.

Exercise on the above Tenses of the Three Verbs

Translate and retranslate:—

(1) εἱστήκεισαν δὲ οἱ δοῦλοι καὶ οἱ ὑπηρέται ἀνθρακιὰν πεποιηκότες, ὅτι ψῦχος ἦν, καὶ ἐθερμαίνοντο· ἦν δὲ καὶ ὁ Πέτρος μετ᾽ αὐτῶν ἑστὼς καὶ θερμαινόμενος. (John 18:18) εἱστήκεισαν, pluperf. tense, "they were standing" (not "they had stood," as in ordinary pluperfects); πεποιηκότες, nom., plur., masc., perf. partic. act. of ποιέω, "having made"; ἐθερμαίνοντο, imperf. middle, "were warming themselves"; ἑστώς, perf. partic., "standing."

(2) ὁ ἔχων τὴν νύμφην νυμφίος ἐστίν· ὁ δὲ φίλος τοῦ νυμφίου ὁ ἑστηκὼς καὶ ἀκούων αὐτοῦ χαρᾷ χαίρει διὰ τὴν φωνὴν τοῦ νυμφίου. αὕτη οὖν ἡ χαρὰ ἡ ἐμὴ πεπλήρωται. (John 3:29) ὁ ἔχων the (one) having, i.e., "he that hath"; ὁ ἑστηκώς, perf. partic. with present meaning, "the (one) standing," i.e., "who standeth"; ἀκούω takes the genit.; χαρᾷ, this dative has the meaning "with joy"; διά, because of; αὕτη ἡ χαρά (see Lesson 5, *Personal Pronoun*).

(3) 41 ἦν δὲ ἐν τῷ τόπῳ ὅπου ἐσταυρώθη κῆπος, καὶ ἐν τῷ κήπῳ μνημεῖον καινὸν ἐν ᾧ οὐδέπω οὐδεὶς ἦν τεθειμένος· 42 ἐκεῖ οὖν διὰ τὴν παρασκευὴν τῶν Ἰουδαίων, ὅτι ἐγγὺς ἦν τὸ μνημεῖον, ἔθηκαν τὸν Ἰησοῦν. (John 19:41-42) ἐσταυρώθη, 1st aor. passive of σταυρόω; οὐδέπω οὐδείς, lit. "not yet no one," but we must translate by "no one yet"; in Greek two negatives do not, as in English, make a positive, hence the οὐδέπω ("not yet") must be rendered by "yet"; τεθειμένος, perf. partic. passive; ἔθηκαν, 3rd pers. plur., 1st aor. indic.

(4) 31 οἱ πατέρες ἡμῶν τὸ μάννα ἔφαγον ἐν τῇ ἐρήμῳ, καθώς ἐστιν γεγραμμένον, Ἄρτον ἐκ τοῦ οὐρανοῦ ἔδωκεν αὐτοῖς φαγεῖν. 32 εἶπεν οὖν αὐτοῖς ὁ Ἰησοῦς, Ἀμὴν ἀμὴν λέγω ὑμῖν, οὐ Μωϋσῆς δέδωκεν ὑμῖν τὸν ἄρτον ἐκ τοῦ οὐρανοῦ, ἀλλ᾽ ὁ πατήρ μου δίδωσιν ὑμῖν τὸν ἄρτον ἐκ τοῦ οὐρανοῦ τὸν ἀληθινόν· 33 ὁ γὰρ ἄρτος τοῦ θεοῦ ἐστιν ὁ καταβαίνων ἐκ τοῦ οὐρανοῦ καὶ ζωὴν διδοὺς τῷ κόσμῳ. 34 Εἶπον οὖν πρὸς αὐτόν, Κύριε, πάντοτε δὸς ἡμῖν τὸν ἄρτον τοῦτον. 35 εἶπεν αὐτοῖς ὁ Ἰησοῦς, Ἐγώ εἰμι ὁ ἄρτος τῆς ζωῆς· ὁ ἐρχόμενος πρός ἐμὲ οὐ μὴ πεινάσῃ, καὶ ὁ πιστεύων εἰς ἐμὲ οὐ μὴ διψήσει πώποτε. 36 ἀλλ᾽ εἶπον ὑμῖν ὅτι καὶ ἑωράκατέ [με] καὶ οὐ πιστεύετε. 37 Πᾶν ὃ δίδωσίν μοι ὁ πατὴρ πρὸς ἐμὲ ἥξει, καὶ τὸν ἐρχόμενον πρὸς ἐμὲ οὐ μὴ ἐκβάλω ἔξω, 38 ὅτι καταβέβηκα ἀπὸ τοῦ οὐρανοῦ οὐχ ἵνα ποιῶ τὸ θέλημα τὸ ἐμὸν ἀλλὰ τὸ θέλημα τοῦ πέμψαντός με. 39 τοῦτο δέ ἐστιν τὸ θέλημα τοῦ πέμψαντός με, ἵνα πᾶν ὃ δέδωκέν μοι μὴ ἀπολέσω ἐξ αὐτοῦ, ἀλλὰ ἀναστήσω αὐτὸ [ἐν] τῇ ἐσχάτῃ ἡμέρᾳ. (John 6:31-39) ἔφαγον, 3rd pers. plur., 2nd aor. of ἐσθίω (irregular, see later); γεγραμμένον, perf. partic. passive of γράφω; note the different tenses of δίδωμι here, διδούς is pres. part., δός is 2nd aor. imperat.; in verse 35 ὁ ἐρχόμενος (pres. partic. of ἔρχομαι) is "he that cometh" (lit. "the (one) coming"—deponent); οὐ μὴ πεινάσῃ, *this 1st aor. subjunc. with* οὐ μὴ *is an idiomatic construction used to express a strong negative assurance, "shall by no means," etc. Here again, the two negatives make a strong negative; the construction of* οὐ μὴ *with 1st aor. subjunc. is very important, and is a curious instance of the use of the 1st aor. with a future meaning;* οὐ μὴ διψήσει (fut. of διψάω) has the same negative assurance, only now the fut. indic. is used, which is according to the usual meaning of that tense; εἶπον I said (2nd aor. of λέγω irregular); ἑωράκατε 2nd pers. plur., perf. indic. of ὁράω (irregular); in ver. 37 note ὃ with the accent, neut. of ὅς, which; ἥξει, fut. of ἥκω, I come (a different verb from ἔρχομαι); οὐ μὴ ἐκβάλω, another instance of οὐ μή with the fut. (see above, and for ἐκβάλω see on Liquid Verbs, Lesson 21); καταβέβηκα perf. of καταβαίνω; ποιῶ, subjunc. of purpose after ἵνα; πέμψαντος, gen., sing., 1st aor. partic. of πέμπω, "of the (one) having sent"; ἀπολέσω 1st aor. subjunc. of ἀπόλλυμι "I loose," subjunc. of purpose after ἵνα; ἐξ αὐτοῦ, of it (ἐξ is for ἐκ, out of); ἀναστήσω fut. of ἀνίστημι.

▪ LESSON 23 ▪

SPECIAL VERBS BELONGING TO CLASS I OF -μι CONJUGATION

The following are conjugated like ἵστημι:—

ὀνίνημι, I benefit, once only in New Testament, in Phil. 20, where ὀναίμην is 2nd aor. optat., middle, "may I benefit."

πίμπρημι, I burn, once only in New Testament, Acts 28:6, where πίμπρασθαι is pres. infin. passive.

φημί, I say; besides this 1st pers., only the following are in New Testament—3rd pers. sing., φησί(ν); 3rd pers. plur., φασί, they say; 3rd pers. sing., imperfect, ἔφη, said he (very frequent).

Deponent Verbs:—

δύναμαι, I am able, -σαι, -ται, etc., as in ἵσταμαι; imper. ἐδυνάμην or ἠδυνάμην; infin. δύνασθαι; partic. δυνάμενος; fut. δυνήσομαι; 1st aor. ἐδυνήθην (or ἠδυνήθην)

ἐπίσταμαι, I know, feel sure (only in present tenses in New Testament).

καθῆμαι, I sit; 2nd pers. sing. καθῇ (for καθῆσαι); imperf. ἐκαθήμην; imperat. κάθου; infin. καθῆσθαι; partic. καθήμενος.

κεῖμαι, I lie down (this and the preceding verb are really perfects).

ἀφίημι, *I send away, let go, forgive*

This is a compound of ἀπό (from) and ἵημι (I send) only used in New Testament compounded with a preposition. The forms below (many of which are irregular) are those most frequent in New Testament and should be memorized.

Present Indicative

1st p.	ἀφιημι	ἀθίεμεν (or -ομεν)
2nd p.	ἀφεῖς	ἀφίετε
3rd p.	ἀφίησι	ἀφιοῦσι

Imperf. 3rd pers. sing., ἤφιε: note that, contrary to the rule for the augment (that in a verb compounded with a preposition the verb itself receives the augment and not the preposition) the preposition is augmented here (see Mark 1:34; 11:16). Pres. imperat. 3rd pers. sing., ἀφιέτω; pres. infin. ἀφιέναι; fut. indic. ἀφήσω (regular); 1st aor. ἀφηκα; 2nd aor. imperat., 2nd pers. sing., ἄφες; 2nd pers. plur. ἄφετε; 2nd aor. subjunc. ἀφῶ, etc.; 2nd aor. partic. ἀφείς, ἀφεῖσα, ἀφέν; pres. indic. pass., 3rd pers. plur. ἀφίενται; perf. ἀφέωνται; fut. indic. pass. ἀφεθήσομαι (chiefly in 3rd sing. ἀπεθήσεται); 1st aor. pass. ἀφέθην.

Exercise on special verbs in Class I

Translate and re-translate:—

(1) καὶ ὁ Κορνήλιος ἔφη, Ἀπὸ τετάρτης ἡμέρας μέχρι ταύτης τῆς ὥρας ἤμην τὴν ἐνάτην προσευχόμενος ἐν τῷ οἴκῳ μου, καὶ ἰδοὺ ἀνὴρ ἔστη ἐνώπιόν μου ἐν ἐσθῆτι λαμπρᾷ 31 καὶ φησίν, Κορνήλιε, εἰσηκούσθη σου ἡ προσευχὴ καὶ αἱ ἐλεημοσύναι σου ἐμνήσθησαν ἐνώπιον τοῦ θεοῦ. (Acts 10:30-31) ἔφη, (see under φημί); Ἀπὸ, from (takes the genit.); μέχρι, until (takes the genit.); ἤμην, an alternative form of ἦν, I was (imperf. of εἰμί); τὴν ἐνάτην, the ninth (ὥραν, "hour" understood), accusative of time, "at the ninth hour", προσευχόμενος, pres. partic. (deponent): ἔστη, (see ἵστημι); ἐνώπιον before (takes the genit.); φησίν, (see φημί); εἰσηκούσθη 3rd pers. sing., 1st aor. pass. of εἰσακούω; ἐμνήσθησαν 3rd pers. plur., 1st aor. pass. of μιμνήσκομαι.

(2) Καὶ ἔρχεται εἰς οἶκον· καὶ συνέρχεται πάλιν [ὁ] ὄχλος, ὥστε μὴ δύνασθαι αὐτοὺς μηδὲ

ἄρτον φαγεῖν. 21 καὶ ἀκούσαντες οἱ παρ' αὐτοῦ ἐξῆλθον κρατῆσαι αὐτόν· ἔλεγον γὰρ ὅτι ἐξέστη. 22 καὶ οἱ γραμματεῖς οἱ ἀπὸ Ἱεροσολύμων καταβάντες ἔλεγον ὅτι Βεελζεβοὺλ ἔχει καὶ ὅτι ἐν τῷ ἄρχοντι τῶν δαιμονίων ἐκβάλλει τὰ δαιμόνια. 23 καὶ προσκαλεσάμενος αὐτοὺς ἐν παραβολαῖς ἔλεγεν αὐτοῖς, Πῶς δύναται Σατανᾶς Σατανᾶν ἐκβάλλειν; 24 καὶ ἐὰν βασιλεία ἐφ' ἑαυτὴν μερισθῇ, οὐ δύναται σταθῆναι ἡ βασιλεία ἐκείνη· 25 καὶ ἐὰν οἰκία ἐφ' ἑαυτὴν μερισθῇ, οὐ δυνήσεται ἡ οἰκία ἐκείνη σταθῆναι [in earlier editions of Nestle: στῆναι]. (Mark 3:20-25) Notice the construction ὥστε μὴ δύνασθαι αὐτούς; *the particle* ὥστε, *so that, is followed by the accusative with the infinitive to express result;* here αὐτούς is the accusative subject of δύνασθαι, lit., "them to be able," the whole clause being, lit., "so that them not to be able," i.e., "so that they were not able" (cp. ὥστε, etc., in Matt. 8:24, and in Matt. 13:32, where ἐλθεῖν is 2nd aor. infin. of ἔρχομαι); ἄρτον is the object of φαγεῖν, which is 2nd aor. infin. of ἐσθίω (irreg.). In ver. 21 οἱ παρ' αὐτοῦ is "the (ones) beside Him," translated freely in A.V., "His friends"; ἀκούσαντες, 1st aor. partic., "having heard"; ἐξῆλθον, 3rd pers. plur. 2nd aor. of ἐξέρχομαι; κρατῆσαι, 1st aor. indic. of κρατέω, to lay hold (decisively); ἐξέστη, 2nd aor. indic. of ἐξίστημι, lit., "I stand out," and hence "am insane"; καταβάντες, nom., plur., masc., 2nd aor. partic. of καταβαίνω (a liquid verb, see Lesson 21); ἔλεγον, imperf. "were saying"; ἐν, by; προσκαλεσάμενος, 1st aor. partic. of the deponent προσκαλέομαι, "I call to myself." In verse 24 ἐφ' is for ἐπί, against; μερισθῇ, 1st aor. subjunc. pass. of μερίζω; σταθῆναι, 1st aor. infin. pass. of ἵστημι, to stand (not "to be stood"); στῆναι, 2nd aor. infin. active (here equivalent to the passive in meaning).

(3) Ἐὰν γὰρ ἀφῆτε τοῖς ἀνθρώποις τὰ παραπτώματα αὐτῶν, ἀφήσει καὶ ὑμῖν ὁ πατὴρ ὑμῶν ὁ οὐράνιος· 15 ἐὰν δὲ μὴ ἀφῆτε τοῖς ἀνθρώποις, οὐδὲ ὁ πατὴρ ὑμῶν ἀφήσει τὰ παραπτώματα ὑμῶν. (Matt. 6:14-15) ἀφῆτε, 2nd pers. plur., 2nd aor. subj. of ἀφίημι (the aor. expressing completeness and decision); ἀφήσει, fut. indic.

The Second Class of Verbs in -μι

Verbs in -νυμι or -ννυμι

Note—Most of these have a second form in the present and imperfect like λύω. Thus δείκνυμι, I show, has another form δεικνύω, and ζώννυμι, I gird, has ζωννύω. All other tenses are formed without the -νυ- and follow the endings of the regular verb.

δείκνυμι, *I show*

Act. indic. pres.	δείκνυμι, -νυς, -νυσι (etc. throughout)
or	δεικνύω, -εις, -ει (like λύω)
Act. indic. imperf.	ἐδείκνυν, -νυς, -νυ, etc.
Act. imperat. pres.	δείκνυ (or -νυε), -νύτω, etc.
Act. subj. pres.	δεικνύω, -ῃς, ῃ, etc.
Act. opt. pres.	δεικνύοιμι, etc.
Act. infin. pres.	δεικνύναι
Act. partic. pres.	δεικνύς, -νῦσα, -νύν (or -νύων, etc.)
Pass. & Mid. indic. pres.	δείκνυμαι, etc.
Pass. & Mid. indic. imperf.	ἐδεικνύμην, etc.
Pass. & Mid. imperat.	δείκνυσο, etc.
Pass. & Mid. subjunc.	δεικνύωμαι, etc.
Pass. & Mid. opt.	δεικνυοίμην, etc.
Pass. & Mid. infin.	δείκνυσθαι (or -νύεσθαι)
Pass. & Mid. partic.	δεικνύμενος, etc.

Other tenses: Act fut. δείξω; perf. δέδειχα; pass. and mid. perf. δέδειγμαι, etc.

Note that the stem of δείκνυμι ends in a consonant, δεικ-; the stem of ζώννυμι ends in a vowel, ζω-. This determines the fut. and 1st aor. endings, the vowel stems simply taking -σ-; e.g., ζώσω, ἔζωσα, etc.

VERBS LIKE δείκνυμι

μίγνυμι, I mix; 1st aor. ἔμιξα; perf. past pass. μεμίγμενος.

ἀπόλλυμι, I destroy (ἀπό and ὄλλυμι, the simple verb not being in New Testament); fut. ἀπολέσω (or ἀπολῶ); 1st aor. ἀπώλεσα (note the ω augment); perfect, with intransitive meaning "I perish," ἀπολώλα; partic. ἀπολώλως; pres. partic. mid. ἀπολλύμενος (plur. "the perishing"); fut. mid. ἀπολοῦμαι (for -έσομαι, liquid verb); 2nd aor. ἀπωλόμην.

ὀμνύω (or ὄμνυμι), I swear; 1st aor. ὤμοσα; 1st aor. infin. ὀμόσαι.

ῥήγνυμι, I tear (also ῥήσσω); fut. ῥήξω; 1st aor. ἔρρηξα.

ἀμφιέννυμι, I clothe; perf. partic. ἠμφιεσμένον (Matt. 11:8: Luke 7:25).

σβέννυμι, I quench; fut. σβέσω; fut. pass. σβεσθήσομαι.

στρώννυμι, or στρωννύω, I strew, spread; 1st aor. ἔστρωσα; perf. partic. pass. ἐστρωμένος.

For κεράννυμι, I mix, κορέννυμι, I satisfy, ῥώννυμι, I strengthen, see the Lexicon.

Exercise on 2nd Class of Verbs in -μι

Translate and re-translate:—

(1) Ἄνδρες Ἰσραηλῖται, ἀκούσατε τοὺς λόγους τούτους· Ἰησοῦν τὸν Ναζωραῖον, ἄνδρα ἀποδεδειγμένον ἀπὸ τοῦ θεοῦ εἰς ὑμᾶς δυνάμεσι καὶ τέρασι καὶ σημείοις οἷς ἐποίησεν δι' αὐτοῦ ὁ θεὸς ἐν μέσῳ ὑμῶν καθὼς αὐτοὶ οἴδατε. (Acts 2:22) ἀκούσατε, 1st aor. imperat.; ἀποδεδειγμένον, perf. partic. pass. of ἀποδείκνυμι (see δείκνυμι above); δυνάμεσι, dat. plur. of δύναμις; οἷς, note that this dative plural is attracted to the case of the preceding dative nouns; the strict grammatical construction would be ἅ, acc. plur. as the direct object of ἐποίησεν ("which He did"), but the ἅ becomes οἷς by attraction of the relative pronoun to the preceding noun.

(2) Τίς ἄνθρωπος ἐξ ὑμῶν ἔχων ἑκατὸν πρόβατα καὶ ἀπολέσας ἐξ αὐτῶν ἓν οὐ καταλείπει τὰ ἐνενήκοντα ἐννέα ἐν τῇ ἐρήμῳ καὶ πορεύεται ἐπὶ τὸ ἀπολωλὸς ἕως εὕρῃ αὐτό; (Luke 15:4) ἑκατὸν, a hundred, is indeclinable; ἀπολέσας, 1st aor. partic. of ἀπόλλυμι (see above), having lost; ἐπὶ, after; ἀπολωλὸς, acc. sing., neut., perf. partic. (see above); εὕρῃ, 2nd aor. subjunc. of εὑρίσκω.

(3) Καὶ καθ' ὅσον οὐ χωρὶς ὁρκωμοσίας· οἱ μὲν γὰρ χωρὶς ὁρκωμοσίας εἰσὶν ἱερεῖς γεγονότες, 21 ὁ δὲ μετὰ ὁρκωμοσίας διὰ τοῦ λέγοντος πρὸς αὐτόν· Ὤμοσεν κύριος, καὶ οὐ μεταμεληθήσεται· Σὺ ἱερεὺς εἰς τὸν αἰῶνα. (Heb. 7:20, 21) καθ' ὅσον, according as, χωρὶς, apart from (takes genit.); οἱ μὲν, they indeed (note this use of the article alone, as a personal pronoun, so ὁ δὲ, but He, in the next clause); γεγονότες, nom., plur., masc., perf. partic. of γίνομαι, I become (see later) with εἰσίν this means "they have become"; μετὰ, with; λέγοντος, gen. sing., masc., pres. partic.; Ὤμοσεν, 1st aor. of ὄμνυμι; μεταμεληθήσεται, fut. of the deponent verb μεταμέλομαι, "I repent."

(4) κἀκεῖνος ὑμῖν δείξει ἀνάγαιον μέγα ἐστρωμένον· ἐκεῖ ἑτοιμάσατε. (Luke 22:12) δείξει, (see δείκνυμι); ἐστρωμένον, perf. partic. of στρώννυμι; ἑτοιμάσατε, 2nd pers. plur., 1st aor. imperat. of ἑτοιμάζω.

▪ LESSON 24 ▪

Irregular and Defective Verbs

(1) Some Irregular Futures and 1st Aorists

(*a*) Whereas verbs in -εω make future in -ήσω, the following have -έσω:—ἀρκέω I suffice; ἐπαινέω, I praise (1st aor. ἐπῄνεσα); καλέω, I call; τελέω, I finish; φορέω, I carry. The following makes future and 1st aor. in -ευ-:—πνέω, I blow, 1st aor. ἔπνευσα. So καίω, I burn, makes καύσω, and κλαίω, I weep, makes κλαύσω.

(*b*) Some verbs in -ίζω make fut. in -ιῶ instead of -ίσω:—ἀφορίζω, I separate; ἐλπίζω, I hope; κομίζω, carry. In these the first aorist resumes the -σ, e.g., ἀφώρισα.

(*c*) Several active verbs have their future in middle form. The following are common and should be memorized:—

ἀκούω	I hear,	fut.	ἀκούσομαι
ζάω	I live,	"	ζήσομαι
λαμβάνω	I take,	"	λήμψομαι
φεύγω	I flee,	"	φεύξομαι
πίνω	I drink,	"	πίομαι

(*d*) Some liquid verbs in λ transpose the vowel and the λ in the fut., 1st aor. and perf. passive:—βάλλω, I throw, has fut. pass. βληθήσομαι; 1st aor. ἐβλήθην; perf. βέβλημαι: καλέω, I call, has κληθήσομαι, ἐκλήθην, κέκλημαι.

(2) Some Irregular Perfects and Pluperfects

(*a*) Some verbs, instead of reduplicating by the consonant, like λέλυκα, do so by the vowel ε, where the consonant would not sound well: thus ξηραίνω, I wither, has perf. pass. ἐξήραμμαι.

(*b*) Some have a double reduplication, i.e., by both the consonant and a vowel:—ἀκούω, I hear, has perf. ἀκήκοα; ἔρχομαι, I come, has perf. ἐλήλυθα.

(*c*) Verbs beginning with θ reduplicate by τ, sometimes changing the vowel:—τρέφω, I nourish, makes perf. τέτροφα, and perf. pass. τέθραμμαι; θραύω, I crush, makes perf. pass. τέθραυσμαι (inserting a σ, see Luke 4:18).

Irregular and Defective Verbs

(*continued*)

The following list of irregular verbs should memorized thoroughly. Only the first person singular of the irregular tenses, Indicative, is given; the other person endings are according to the regular verb. If the following are committed to memory the irregular forms, with which the reader constantly meets in the New Testament, provide no difficulty.

Note—The verbs marked with a dagger are those which derive their forms from different verbal stems. The tenses are thus made up of different verb roots with the same meaning.

Principle Parts of Irregular Verbs

Present	*Future*	*1st Aorist*	*Perfect*	*2nd Aorist*	*1st Aorist Passive*
ἄγω (lead)	ἄξω	ἦξα		ἤγαγον	
† αἱρέω (take)	αἱρήσω		ᾕρηκα	εἷλον	ᾑρέθην
ἀποθνήσκω (die)	ἀποθανοῦμαι			ἀπέθανον	
ἀναβαίνω (go up)	ἀναβήσομαι		ἀναβέβηκα	ἀνέβην	
γινώσκω (know)	γνώσομαι		ἔγνωκα	ἔγνων	ἐγνώσθην
γίνομαι (become) or γίγνομαι	γενήσομαι		γέγονα passive γεγένημαι	ἐγενόμην	ἐγενήθην
ἐγείρω (arouse)	ἐγερῶ	ἤγειρα	ἐγήγερκα		ἠγέρθην
† ἔρχομαι (come)	ἐλεύσομαι		ἐλήλυθα	ἦλθον	
† ἐσθίω (eat)	φάγομαι			ἔφαγον	
ἔχω (have)	ἕξω		ἔσχηκα	ἔσχον	
λαμβάνω (receive)	λή(μ)ψομαι		εἴληφα passive εἴλημμαι	ἔλαβον	ἐλήφθην
† λέγω (say)	λέξω or ἐρῶ	ἔλεξα	passive λέλεγμαι εἴρηκα εἴρημαι	εἶπον	ἐλέχθην or ἐρρέθην or ἐρρήθην
μανθάνω (learn)	μαθήσομαι		μεμάθηκα	ἔμαθον	
† ὁράω (see)	ὄψομαι		ἑώρακα	* εἶδον	ὤφθην
πάσχω (suffer)			πέπονθα	ἔπαθον	
πίπτω (fall)	πεσοῦμαι		πέπτωκα	ἔπεσον	
† τρέχω (run)	δραμοῦμαι			ἔδραμον	
τυγχάνω (happen)	τεύξομαι			ἔτυχον	
† φέρω (bear)	οἴσω	ἤνεγκα	ἐνήνοχα	ἤνεγκον	ἠνέχθην

* *Note*—οἶδα, I know, is a perfect with a present meaning; it is connected with εἶδον, I saw; the pluperfect is ᾔδειν, I knew; the 2nd aorist infin. is ἰδεῖν and the 2nd perfect infin. εἰδέναι.

Exercise on Irregular Verbs

Translate and retranslate:—

(1) τί με ἐρωτᾷς; ἐρώτησον τοὺς ἀκηκοότας τί ἐλάλησα αὐτοῖς· ἴδε οὗτοι οἴδασιν ἃ εἶπον ἐγώ. 22 ταῦτα δὲ αὐτοῦ εἰπόντος εἷς παρεστηκὼς τῶν ὑπηρετῶν ἔδωκεν ῥάπισμα τῷ Ἰησοῦ εἰπών, Οὕτως ἀποκρίνῃ τῷ ἀρχιερεῖ; (John 18:21, 22) τί, why?; ἐρωτᾷς, 2nd pers. sing., pres. indic. of ἐρωτάω; ἐρώτησον, 1st aor. imperat.; ἀκηκοότας, acc., plur., masc. of ἀκηκοώς, -υῖα, -ός (gen. -οοτος), perf. partic. of ἀκούω (for the declension of the participle see Lesson 10); τί, what; οἴδασιν, 3rd pers. plur. (see note at foot of above list); εἶπον, (see λέγω above); note the emphatic position of ἐγώ. In ver. 22 note αὐτοῦ εἰπόντος; *these genitives (i.e., a pronoun or noun,*

with the participle of a verb each in the genitive case) form what is known as the genitive absolute construction; it cannot be put literally in English; the actual English equivalent is "he having said", it is best rendered by "when he had said"; this construction is sometimes used when the main sentence has a different subject (*here* εἷς, *one*); παρεστηκώς, perf. partic. of παρίστημι, I stand by ("one standing by of the attendants"); ἔδωκεν, 1st aor. ("gave"); εἰπών, 2nd aor. partic. of λέγω ("saying"); ἀποκρίνῃ, 2nd pers. sing., pres. indic. (takes the dative).

(2) Μετὰ ταῦτα ἀπῆλθεν ὁ Ἰησοῦς πέραν τῆς θαλάσσης τῆς Γαλιλαίας τῆς Τιβεριάδος. 2 ἠκολούθει δὲ αὐτῷ ὄχλος πολύς, ὅτι ἐθεώρουν [In earlier editions of Nestle: ἑώρων] τὰ σημεῖα ἃ ἐποίει ἐπὶ τῶν ἀσθενούντων. (John 6:1, 2) Μετὰ, after; ἀπῆλθεν 2nd aor. of ἀπέρχομαι (see list); ἠκολούθει, 3rd pers. sing., imperf. of ἀκολουθέω (takes dat.); ἑώρων, 3rd pers. plur., imperf. of ὁράω; ἐπὶ upon (with gen.); ἀσθενούντων, gen., plur., pres. partic. of ἀσθενέω.

(3) καὶ εὐθὺς ἀποστείλας ὁ βασιλεὺς σπεκουλάτορα ἐπέταξεν ἐνέγκαι τὴν κεφαλὴν αὐτοῦ. καὶ ἀπελθὼν ἀπεκεφάλισεν αὐτὸν ἐν τῇ φυλακῇ 28 καὶ ἤνεγκεν τὴν κεφαλὴν αὐτοῦ ἐπὶ πίνακι καὶ ἔδωκεν αὐτὴν τῷ κορασίῳ, καὶ τὸ κοράσιον ἔδωκεν αὐτὴν τῇ μητρὶ αὐτῆς. (Mark 6:27, 28) ἀποστείλας, 1st aor. partic. of ἀποστέλλω; ἐπέταξεν, 3rd pers. sing., 1st aor. of ἐπιτάσσω; ἐνέγκαι, 1st aor. infin. of φέρω (see list); ἀπελθών, 2nd aor. partic. of ἀπέρχομαι; ἀπεκεφάλισεν, 1st aor. of ἀποκεφαλίζω; ἤνεγκεν (see φέρω).

(4) καὶ ἰδοὺ εἷς τῶν μετὰ Ἰησοῦ ἐκτείνας τὴν χεῖρα ἀπέσπασεν τὴν μάχαιραν αὐτοῦ καὶ πατάξας τὸν δοῦλον τοῦ ἀρχιερέως ἀφεῖλεν αὐτοῦ τὸ ὠτίον. (Matt. 26:51) τῶν μετὰ, of the (ones) with; ἐκτείνας, 1st aor. partic. of ἐκτείνω, "having stretched out"; ἀπέσπασεν, 1st aor. of ἀποσπάω; πατάξας, 1st aor. partic. of πατάσσω; ἀφεῖλεν, 2nd aor. of ἀφαιρέω (see αἱρέω).

(5) ἐγὼ ἐλήλυθα ἐν τῷ ὀνόματι τοῦ πατρός μου, καὶ οὐ λαμβάνετέ με· ἐὰν ἄλλος ἔλθῃ ἐν τῷ ὀνόματι τῷ ἰδίῳ, ἐκεῖνον λήμψεσθε. (John 5:43) ἐλήλυθα (see ἔρχομαι, above); ἔλθῃ, 2nd aor. subjunc. of the same; τῷ ἰδίῳ, his own; λήμψεσθε, fut. of λαμβάνω.

(6) πειρασμὸς ὑμᾶς οὐκ εἴληφεν εἰ μὴ ἀνθρώπινος· πιστὸς δὲ ὁ θεός, ὃς οὐκ ἐάσει ὑμᾶς πειρασθῆναι ὑπὲρ ὃ δύνασθε ἀλλὰ ποιήσει σὺν τῷ πειρασμῷ καὶ τὴν ἔκβασιν τοῦ δύνασθαι ὑπενεγκεῖν. (1 Cor. 10:13) εἴληφεν, 3rd pers. sing., perf. of λαμβάνω; εἰ μὴ, except (lit. "if not"). In the next sentence ἐστί is purposely omitted; ἐάσει, fut. of ἐάω; πειρασθῆναι, 1st aor. infin. pass. of πειράζω; τοῦ δύνασθαι, *this construction of the genit. of the article with the infinitive is used to signify purpose,* lit., "(in order to) the being able"; ὑπενεγκεῖν, 2nd aor. infin. of ὑποφέρω (see above).

(7) ἀπελθόντες δὲ εὗρον καθὼς εἰρήκει αὐτοῖς καὶ ἡτοίμασαν τὸ πάσχα. (Luke 22:13) ἀπελθόντες, 2nd aor. partic. of ἀπέρχομαι, "having gone away"; εὗρον, 3rd pers. plur., 2nd aor. indic. of εὑρίσκω; εἰρήκει, 3rd pers. sing., plupf. of λέγω, "He had said"; ἡτοίμασαν, 1st aor. indic. of ἑτοιμάζω.

Impersonal Verbs

These are used only in the 3rd pers. sing., and in English are translated with the pronoun "it."

The chief impersonal verbs are:—

δεῖ, it is necessary, one ought; imperf. ἔδει; subjunc. δέῃ; infin. δεῖν.

δοκεῖ, it seems (from δοκέω).

μέλει, it is a care.

πρέπει, it becomes; imperf. ἔπρεπε; pres. partic. πρέπον, becoming.

χρή, it is expedient, fitting (only in Jas. 3:10).

Exercise on Impersonal Verbs

Translate and retranslate:—

(1) τὸ γεγεννημένον ἐκ τῆς σαρκὸς σάρξ ἐστιν, καὶ τὸ γεγεννημένον ἐκ τοῦ πνεύματος πνεῦμά ἐστιν. 7 μὴ θαυμάσῃς ὅτι εἶπόν σοι, Δεῖ ὑμᾶς γεννηθῆναι ἄνωθεν. (John 3:6,7) γεγεννημένον, nom., sing., neut., perf. partic. pass. of γεννάω. With the article, τὸ, this, lit., is "the (thing) having been born," i.e., "that which has been born"; θαυμάσῃς, 2nd pers. sing., 1st aor. subjunc. of θαυμάζω; *this tense of the subjunc. with* μή *is used to express a negative command and this is a substitute for the imperative mood*— "do not marvel"; Δεῖ, it is necessary, is followed by the accusative with the infinitive construction, ὑμᾶς (the accusative) with γεννηθῆναι, 1st aor. infin. passive of γεννάω, lit. "you to be born"; accordingly the whole phrase "it is necessary you to be born" is to be rendered by "ye must be born." See the same construction in verse 30, "it is necessary Him to increase, but me decrease" (ἐλαττοῦσθαι, contracted for —όεσθαι, is pres. infin. of ἐλαττόμαι). See again 4:4, where ἔδει is imperfect, "it was necessary"; διέρχεσθαι, to go through (διά and ἔρχομαι compounded), "it was necessary Him to go through" is "He must needs go through."

(2) δεῖ γὰρ τὸν ἐπίσκοπον ἀνέγκλητον εἶναι ὡς θεοῦ οἰκονόμον, μὴ αὐθάδη, μὴ ὀργίλον, μὴ πάροινον, μὴ πλήκτην, μὴ αἰσχροκερδῆ, 8 ἀλλὰ φιλόξενον φιλάγαθον σώφρονα δίκαιον ὅσιον ἐγκρατῆ, 9 ἀντεχόμενον τοῦ κατὰ τὴν διδαχὴν πιστοῦ λόγου, ἵνα δυνατὸς ᾖ καὶ παρακαλεῖν ἐν τῇ διδασκαλίᾳ τῇ ὑγιαινούσῃ καὶ τοὺς ἀντιλέγοντας ἐλέγχειν. (Tit. 1:7-9) This accus. with the infin. after δεῖ should be clear, and the rest of the verse can be translated with the help of the Lexicon; note that αὐθάδη is accus., sing., masc. of αὐθάδης, -ης, -ες (see ἀλήθης Lesson 10); ἀντεχόμενον, is pres. partic. of the deponent verb ἀντέχομαι (it takes the genit.); καί . . . καί, both . . . and; ἀντιλέγοντας, acc., plur., pres. partic.

(3) λέγει, Ναί. καὶ ἐλθόντα εἰς τὴν οἰκίαν προέφθασεν αὐτὸν ὁ Ἰησοῦς λέγων, Τί σοι δοκεῖ, Σίμων; οἱ βασιλεῖς τῆς γῆς ἀπὸ τίνων λαμβάνουσιν τέλη ἢ κῆνσον; ἀπὸ τῶν υἱῶν αὐτῶν ἢ ἀπὸ τῶν ἀλλοτρίων; (Matt. 17:25) ἐλθόντα, acc., sing., 2nd aor. partic. of ἔρχομαι, agreeing with αὐτόν, "him coming. Jesus anticipated" (προέφθασεν, 1st aor. of προφθάνω, rendered "prevented" in A.V. and "spake first" in R.V.); Τί σοι δοκεῖ, what seems it to thee? (impersonal).

▪ LESSON 25 ▪

Notes on the Cases

The Genitive

(1) The genitive is used (*a*) *with several verbs expressive of sense* or *mental affections,* e.g., ἀκούω, I hear; γεύομαι, I taste; θιγγάνω, I touch; ἐπιθυμέω, I desire; μνημονεύω, I remember; λανθάνω, I forget; (*b*) *with verbs of accusing, and condemning, etc.,* whether of the person accused or of the charge. See, e.g., ἐγκαλέω in Acts 19:40, and κατηγορέω in John 5:45; (*c*) *with verbs and adjectives of filling, lacking, etc.,* e.g., ἐμπίπλημι in Luke 1:53, γεμίζω in John 2:7, ὑστερέω in Rom. 3:23, and λείπω in Jas. 1:5; (*d*) *with verbs of separations, difference, hindrance,* e.g., μεθίστημι in Luke 16:4, κωλύω in Acts 27:43, παύω in 1 Pet. 4:1, ἀπαλλοτριοῦμαι in Eph. 2:12, ἀστοχέω in 1 Tim. 1:6, διαφέρω in 1 Cor. 15:41, and in Matt. 10:31, where the meaning is "to be superior"; (*e*) *with verbs of ruling,* e.g., ἄρχειν, etc., in Mark 10:42.

(2) For the genitive after adjectives in the *comparative degree* see later.

(3) *Adverbs of time* take the genitive, e.g., ὀψέ, late (Matt 28:1) λίαν πρωΐ, very early, τῆς μιᾶς σαββάτων, an idiom for "the first day of the week" (Mark 16:2); ἅπαξ, once (Heb. 9:7).

(4) The following *genitive phrases* are used instead of prepositions with a noun: νυκτός, by night (Matt. 2:14); ἡμέρας, by day (Luke 18:7); τοῦ λοιποῦ, for the rest (Gal. 6:17); ποίας (ὁδοῦ), by what (way) (Luke 5:19).

(5) The *objective genitive* expresses the object of a feeling or action, and must be distinguished from the ordinary subjective genitive expressing possession. Thus προσευχῇ τοῦ θεοῦ in Luke 6:12, is "prayer to God" (the preceding article is not to be translated); in Rom. 10:2, ζῆλον θεοῦ is "zeal towards God"; in 2 Cor. 10:5, τοῦ Χριστοῦ is "to Christ"; so with εἰδώλου in 1 Cor. 8:7; and τοῦ υἱοῦ in Gal. 2:20, "in the Son."

(6) The genitive is used in expressing *price, penalty, equivalent, etc.,* ἀσσαρίου in Matt. 10:29, is "for a farthing"; cp. τοσούτου, for so much (Acts 5:8), and δηναρίου, for a penny (Rev. 6:6).

(7) *The genitive absolute.* The genitive of a noun in agreement with a participle is frequently used in a subordinate sentence without being dependent on any other words, and the genitive refers to some other person or thing than subject of the principal sentence. In translation this construction is rendered in various ways, e.g., Matt. 17:9, καταβαινόντων αὐτῶν is, lit., "they descending (from the mountain)," i.e., "as they were coming down, etc." The principal sentence has another subject, viz., ὁ Ἰησοῦς. The construction is called "absolute," because it is disconnected from the main sentence. Thus, again, in Matt. 9:33, ἐκβληθέντος τοῦ δαιμονίου is "the demon having being cast out" (gen. of 1st aor. pass. of ἐκβάλλω), and the main sentence is ἐλάλησεν ὁ κωφός, the dumb man spake.

Exercise

Translate and re-translate:—

(1) Ἐγένετο δέ μοι ὑποστρέψαντι εἰς Ἰερουσαλὴμ καὶ προσευχομένου μου ἐν τῷ ἱερῷ γενέσθαι με ἐν ἐκστάσει. 18 καὶ ἰδεῖν αὐτὸν λέγοντά μοι. (Acts 22:17, 18a) Ἐγένετο, it came to pass; προσευχομένου μου, gen. absolute, "while I was praying"; γενέσθαι με, acc. with the infin., lit., "me to become," i.e., "that I became" or "that I fell"; so ἰδεῖν, lit., "(me) to see," i.e., "that I saw." This acc. with infin. construction follows the impersonal verb "it came to pass" (see later).

(2) ζητούντων τε αὐτὸν ἀποκτεῖναι ἀνέβη φάσις τῷ χιλιάρχῳ τῆς σπείρης ὅτι ὅλη συγχύνεται Ἰερουσαλήμ. (Acts 21:31) ζητούντων is the gen. absolute with the pronoun αὐτῶν not expressed but understood, lit., "(they) seeking (to kill him)," i.e., "as they were seeking to kill him"; ἀνέβη, 2nd aor. of ἀναβαίνω; συγχύνεται is present tense but in English must be rendered by the past, "was in an uproar" (for this construction see Lesson 32).

(3) καὶ ὑμεῖς ὅμοιοι ἀνθρώποις προσδεχομένοις τὸν κύριον ἑαυτῶν πότε ἀναλύσῃ ἐκ τῶν γάμων, ἵνα ἐλθόντος καὶ κρούσαντος εὐθέως ἀνοίξωσιν αὐτῷ. (Luke 12:36) ἐλθόντος and κρούσαντος are gen. absolute participles agreeing with αὐτοῦ, understood, lit. "he coming and knocking"; ἀνοίξωσιν, 1st aor. subjunc. of ἀνοίγω, subjunc. of purpose after ἵνα.

(4) Ἀναχωρησάντων δὲ αὐτῶν ἰδοὺ ἄγγελος κυρίου φαίνεται κατ' ὄναρ τῷ Ἰωσὴφ λέγων, Ἐγερθεὶς παράλαβε τὸ παιδίον καὶ τὴν μητέρα αὐτοῦ καὶ φεῦγε εἰς Αἴγυπτον καὶ ἴσθι ἐκεῖ ἕως ἂν εἴπω σοι· μέλλει γὰρ Ἡρῴδης ζητεῖν τὸ παιδίον τοῦ ἀπολέσαι αὐτό. (Matt. 2:13) Note the opening gen. absolute phrase, lit., "they having departed"; Ἐγερθεὶς, nom., sing., masc., 1st aor. partic. pass. of ἐγείρω; παράλαβε, 2nd aor. imperat. of παραλαμβάνω; εἴπω, 2nd aor. subjunc. of λέγω (the ἂν expresses indefiniteness, but is not to be translated); τοῦ ἀπολέσαι, 1st aor. infin. of ἀπόλλυμι, with the article, a phrase of purpose, "to destroy," the infin. being a noun in the genitive case, gen. of intention.

The Dative

(1) Verbs denoting *intercourse, companionship, etc.,* take the dative. See the dative after ἀκολουθέω in Matt. 9:9; after κολλάω in Luke 15:15; after ὁμιλέω in Acts 24:26.

(2) After the verbs "to be," "to become," the dative often denotes *possession.* Thus in Matt. 18:12, ἐὰν γένηταί τινι ἀνθρώπῳ is lit. "if there be to any man," i.e., "if any man have."

(3) Verbs denoting *assistance* take the dative. See Matt. 4:11 (διηκόνουν, "they were ministering αὐτῷ, to Him"); also 15:25.

(4) Also verbs expressing *mental affections;* e.g., ὀργίζομαι, I am angry (Matt. 5:22); ἀρέσκω, I please (Gal. 1:10); πιστεύω, I believe (Matt. 21:25); πείθομαι and ὑπακούω, I obey (Acts 5:36-37; Rom. 10:16); προσκυνέω I worship (Matt. 2:2).

(5) The dative expresses *the mode of an action, or the circumstance attending it.* See, e.g., τῇ προθέσει (Acts 11:23); χάριτι (1 Cor. 10:30); παντὶ τρόπῳ, in every way, etc. (Phil. 1:18); προσωυχῇ, with prayer (James 5:17).

(6) The dative expresses *cause or motive.* See, e.g., τῇ ἀπιστίᾳ, through unbelief, and τῇ πίστει, through faith (Rom. 4:20).

(7) The dative expresses *instrument.* See, e.g., πυρί, with fire (Matt. 3:12); ἀδικίᾳ, etc., by (all) iniquity, etc. (Rom. 1:29); χάριτι, by grace, (Eph. 2:5-8); ἰδίᾳ δόξῃ καὶ ἀρετῇ, by His own glory and virtue (2 Pet. 1:3). So χράομαι, I use, takes this dative; see παρρησίᾳ (2 Cor. 3:12).

(8) The dative sometimes is used to express *the agent.* Note αὐτῷ, by Him (Luke 23:15); ὑμῖν, by you (2 Cor. 12, 20); αὐτοῖς, by them (Luke 24:35).

(9) The dative expresses *the sphere in which a quality exists.* See τῷ πνεύματι, in spirit (Matt. 5:3); τοῖς ποσίν, in his feet (Acts 14:8); φύσει, in nature (Eph. 2:3).

(10) The dative is used in some expressions of time, either a period or a point. For the period see ἔτεσι, for (about 450) years (Acts 13:20); for the point see τοῖς γενεσίοις αὐτοῦ, on his birthday (Mark 6:21); τῇ τρίτῃ ἡμέρᾳ, on the third day (Matt. 20:19).

The Accusative

(1) A verb sometimes takes a noun in the accus. case which is akin to it in meaning, and so the meaning of the verb is extended. This is known as the *cognate accusative* Thus in Matt. 2:10, ἐχάρησαν χαρὰν μεγάλην is, lit., "they rejoiced a great joy," i.e., "they rejoiced exceedingly."

So in Luke 2:8, φυλάσσοντες φυλακάς, "watching watches," is "keeping watch." In Col. 2:19, αὔξει τὴν αὔξησιν is "with the increase."

(2) An accusative sometimes defines the verb more closely; this is called *the accusative of closer definition.* It must be rendered in English by a prepositional phrase. Thus in John 6:10, τὸν ἀριθμόν is "in number"; in Phil. 1:11, καρπὸν is "with the fruit."

(3) *Relations of time and space* are frequently expressed by the accusative, e.g., Luke 22:41, λίθου βολήν, a stone's throw; so σταδίους in John 6:19; in Rev. 3:3, ποίαν ὥραν, what hour, is acc. of time; see ἔτη, years (acc., plur., neut.) in Luke 15:29.

(4) The accusative is sometimes *irregular,* some word or phrase being understood to complete the sense. See, e.g., ὁδὸν in Matt. 4:15; γνώστην in Acts 26:3; τὸ ἀδύνατον, the impossibility, in Rom. 8:3.

Exercise

Translate and retranslate:—

(1) Ταπεινώθητε οὖν ὑπὸ τὴν κραταιὰν χεῖρα τοῦ θεοῦ, ἵνα ὑμᾶς ὑψώσῃ ἐν καιρῷ, 7 πᾶσαν τὴν μέριμναν ὑμῶν ἐπιρίψαντες ἐπ' αὐτόν, ὅτι αὐτῷ μέλει περὶ ὑμῶν. 8 Νήψατε, γρηγορήσατε. ὁ ἀντίδικος ὑμῶν διάβολος ὡς λέων ὠρυόμενος περιπατεῖ ζητῶν [τινα] καταπιεῖν· 9 ᾧ ἀντίστητε στερεοὶ τῇ πίστει εἰδότες τὰ αὐτὰ τῶν παθημάτων τῇ ἐν [τῷ] κόσμῳ ὑμῶν ἀδελφότητι ἐπιτελεῖσθαι. (1 Pet. 5:6-9) αὐτῷ μέλει, lit., "it-is-a-care to Him" (the verb is impersonal), i.e., "He careth"; ἀντίστητε, 2nd aor. imperat. of ἀνθίστημι, , governing the dative ᾧ; τὰ αὐτὰ . . . ἐπιτελεῖσθαι, accus. with the infin., after εἰδότες, "knowing the same things to be accomplished"; τῇ . . . ἀδελφότητι, in the brotherhood (see Rule 9 under the Dative).

(2) πᾶσα γὰρ φύσις θηρίων τε καὶ πετεινῶν, ἑρπετῶν τε καὶ ἐναλίων δαμάζεται καὶ δεδάμασται τῇ φύσει τῇ ἀνθρωπίνῃ, 8 τὴν δὲ γλῶσσαν οὐδεὶς δαμάσαι δύναται ἀνθρώπων, ἀκατάστατον κακόν, μεστὴ ἰοῦ θανατηφόρου. 9 ἐν αὐτῇ εὐλογοῦμεν τὸν κύριον καὶ πατέρα καὶ ἐν αὐτῇ καταρώμεθα τοὺς ἀνθρώπους τοὺς καθ' ὁμοίωσιν θεοῦ γεγονότας, 10 ἐκ τοῦ αὐτοῦ στόματος ἐξέρχεται εὐλογία καὶ κατάρα. οὐ χρή, ἀδελφοί μου, ταῦτα οὕτως γίνεσθαι. (James 3:7-10) τῇ φύσει, etc., dat. of the agent (see Rule 8) "by human nature."

(3) Μὴ οὖν τις ὑμᾶς κρινέτω ἐν βρώσει καὶ ἐν πόσει ἢ ἐν μέρει ἑορτῆς ἢ νεομηνίας ἢ σαββάτων· 17 ἅ ἐστιν σκιὰ τῶν μελλόντων, τὸ δὲ σῶμα τοῦ Χριστοῦ. 18 μηδεὶς ὑμᾶς καταβραβευέτω θέλων ἐν ταπεινοφροσύνῃ καὶ θρησκείᾳ τῶν ἀγγέλων, ἃ ἑόρακεν ἐμβατεύων, εἰκῇ φυσιούμενος ὑπὸ τοῦ νοὸς τῆς σαρκὸς αὐτοῦ, 19 καὶ οὐ κρατῶν τὴν κεφαλήν, ἐξ οὗ πᾶν τὸ σῶμα διὰ τῶν ἁφῶν καὶ συνδέσμων ἐπιχορηγούμενον καὶ συμβιβαζόμενον αὔξει τὴν αὔξησιν τοῦ θεοῦ. (Col. 2:16-19) κρινέτω and καταβραβευέτω are 3rd pers. sing., pres. imperat.; ἑόρακεν, 3rd pers. sing., perf. indic. of ὁράω.

▪ LESSON 26 ▪

The Comparison of Adjectives

There are three degrees of comparison—Positive, Comparative, Superlative.

The regular method of forming the comparative and superlative degrees is by adding -τερος and -τατος to the stem of adjectives of the 2nd declension in -ος, and to the stem of those of the 3rd declension in -ης.

Examples

ἰσχυρός, -ά, -όν, strong (stem ἰσχυρο-); ἰσχυρότερος, -α, -ον, stronger; ἰσχυρότατος, -η, -ον, strongest.

ἀληθής, -ής, -ές, true (stem ἀληθεσ-); ἀληθέστερος, -α, -ον, truer; ἀληθέστατος, -η, -ον, truest.

Note—When the last vowel but one of the adjective is short the final ο of the stem is lengthened to -ω. Thus σοφός, wise, σοφώτερος, σοφώτατος; νέος, new, νεώτερος, νεώτατος.

The following form their degrees of comparison irregularly:—

Positive	*Comparative*	*Superlative*
ἀγαθός, good	κρείσσων, (or -ττων), better	κράτιστος, best
κακός, bad	χείρων, or ἥσσων, or ἥττων, worse	χείριστος, worst
πολύς, much or many	πλείων, or πλέων, more	πλεῖστος, most
μικρός, little	μικρότερος or ἐλάσσων, less	ἐλάχιστος, least
μέγας, great	μείζων, greater	μέγιστος, greatest

Note 1—These comparatives in -ων are declined like σώφρων (acc. -ονα, gen. -ονος, etc., see Lesson 10); μείζων has an alternative acc. sing. μείζω (i.e., besides μείζονα), and alternative nom. and acc. plural forms, masc. and fem. μείζους (instead of μείζονες and -ονας), neut. μείζω (instead of μείζονα).

Note 2—Adjectives and adverbs in the comparative degree are followed in one or two ways, either (*a*) by ἤ, than, and a noun or pronoun in the same case as the noun or pronoun with which the adjective agrees, or (*b*) simply by the noun or pronoun in the genitive case without ἤ.

Thus (a) John 3:19, μᾶλλον τὸ σκότος ἢ τὸ φῶς, rather the darkness than the light.

(b) John 1:50: μείζω ("greater things," neut. plur. for μείζονα) τούτων ("than these," gen. of comparison) ὄψῃ ("thou shalt see," fut. of ὁράω).

Exercise on the Comparison of Adjectives

Translate and retranslate:

(1) ἐγὼ δὲ ἔχω τὴν μαρτυρίαν μείζω τοῦ Ἰωάννου· τὰ γὰρ ἔργα ἃ δέδωκέν μοι ὁ πατὴρ ἵνα τελειώσω αὐτά, αὐτὰ τὰ ἔργα ἃ ποιῶ μαρτυρεῖ περὶ ἐμοῦ ὅτι ὁ πατήρ με ἀπέσταλκεν· (John 5:36) μείζω, acc., sing., fem.; τελειώσω 1st aor. subjunc. after ἵνα; μαρτυρεῖ, sing. after a neut. plur. subject αὐτὰ τὰ ἔργα, "the very works"; ἀπέσταλκεν, perf. of ἀποστέλλω.

(2) αὐτοῖς δὲ τοῖς κλητοῖς, Ἰουδαίοις τε καὶ Ἕλλησιν, Χριστὸν θεοῦ δύναμιν καὶ θεοῦ σοφίαν. (1 Cor. 1:24)

(3) Καὶ ἔλεγεν, Πῶς ὁμοιώσωμεν τὴν βασιλείαν τοῦ θεοῦ ἢ ἐν τίνι αὐτὴν παραβολῇ θῶμεν; 31 ὡς κόκκῳ σινάπεως, ὃς ὅταν σπαρῇ ἐπὶ τῆς γῆς, μικρότερον ὂν πάντων τῶν σπερμάτων τῶν ἐπὶ τῆς γῆς, 32 καὶ ὅταν σπαρῇ, ἀναβαίνει καὶ γίνεται μεῖζον πάντων τῶν λαχάνων καὶ ποιεῖ κλάδους μεγάλους, ὥστε δύνασθαι ὑπὸ τὴν σκιὰν αὐτοῦ τὰ πετεινὰ τοῦ οὐρανοῦ κατασκηνοῦν. (Mark 4:30-32) ὁμοιώσωμεν, 1st aor. subjunc. (the deliberative subjunctive, "how are we to liken"); θῶμεν, 2nd aor. subjunc. of τίθημι; σπαρῇ, 3rd pers. sing., 1st aor. subjunc. pass. of σπείρω, "I sow" (a liquid verb, see Lesson 21); ὄν, nom., sing., neut., pres. partic. of εἰμί, "being"; ὥστε δύνασθαι . . . τὰ πετεινὰ, *the acc. with the infin. after* ὥστε, *"so that," expresses result,* lit., "so that the birds to be able," i.e., "so that the birds are able"; κατασκηνοῦν, pres. infin.

(4) τοσούτῳ κρείττων γενόμενος τῶν ἀγγέλων ὅσῳ διαφορώτερον παρ' αὐτοὺς κεκληρονόμηκεν ὄνομα. (Heb. 1:4) τοσούτῳ, by so much (dat. of degree); γενόμενος, 2nd aor. partic. of γίνομαι; ὅσῳ, by how much; παρ' αὐτοὺς, "in-comparison-with them."

(5) τότε πορεύεται καὶ παραλαμβάνει μεθ' ἑαυτοῦ ἑπτὰ ἕτερα πνεύματα πονηρότερα ἑαυτοῦ καὶ εἰσελθόντα κατοικεῖ ἐκεῖ· καὶ γίνεται τὰ ἔσχατα τοῦ ἀνθρώπου ἐκείνου χείρονα τῶν πρώτων. οὕτως ἔσται καὶ τῇ γενεᾷ ταύτῃ τῇ πονηρᾷ. (Matt. 12:45) εἰσελθόντα, nom., plur., neut., 2nd aor. partic. of εἰσέρχομαι, "having entered" (note the verb in the sing. following); τὰ ἔσχατα, the last things, i.e., "the last state"; with this the neut. plur. χείρονα agrees.

▪ LESSON 27 ▪

ADVERBS

Adverbs are formed from adjectives by changing the ν of the gen. plur. masc. to ς. Thus the gen. plur. of ἀληθής, true, is ἀληθῶν, and the adverb is ἀληθῶς, truly, verily.

The comparative and superlative degrees of adverbs are formed by using the neut. sing. of the comparative degree of the adjective and the neut. plur. of the superlative of the adjective respectively.

Thus ταχέως is "quickly"; τάχιον, more quickly; τάχιστα, most quickly (Acts 17:15). Note ὡς with the superlative is idiomatic—ὡς τάχιστα is "as quickly as possible," lit., "as most quickly."

The comparative adverb περισσοτέρως, more abundantly, is formed in the same way as in the positive degree, and not by the neut. sing. (2 Cor. 11:23).

Note the adverb ὄντως, truly; it is formed from the pres. partic. of εἰμί.

The following irregular comparisons should be memorized:—

Positive	*Comparative*	*Superlative*
εὖ, well	βέλτιον or κρεῖσσον, better	
καλῶς, well	κάλλιον, better	
κακῶς, badly	ἧσσον (or -ττον), worse	
πολύ, much	μᾶλλον, more	μάλιστα, most
	πλεῖον or πλέον, more	

Forms omitted in the above are not found in the New Testament.

Exercise on Adverbs

Translate and retranslate:—

(1) Διὰ τοῦτο δεῖ περισσοτέρως προσέχειν ἡμᾶς τοῖς ἀκουσθεῖσιν, μήποτε παραρυῶμεν. (Heb. 2:1) δεῖ, impersonal, "it is necessary"; this is followed by the acc. with the infin. προσέχειν ἡμᾶς lit., "us to give heed," i.e., "that we should give heed", περισσοτέρως, more abundantly, i.e., "more earnestly"; ἀκουσθεῖσιν, dat., plur., neut., 1st aor. partic. pass. "to the (things) having been heard."

(2) δῴη αὐτῷ ὁ κύριος εὑρεῖν ἔλεος παρὰ κυρίου ἐν ἐκείνῃ τῇ ἡμέρᾳ. καὶ ὅσα ἐν Ἐφέσῳ διηκόνησεν, βέλτιον σὺ γινώσκεις. (2 Tim. 1:18) δῴη, 3rd pers. sing., 2nd aor. subjunc. of δίδωμι, the subjunc. of a wish, "may He give"; εὑρεῖν, 2nd aor. infin. of εὑρίσκω; βέλτιον, lit. "better," the comparative being here equivalent to the superlative "very well."

(3) ἔτρεχον δὲ οἱ δύο ὁμοῦ· καὶ ὁ ἄλλος μαθητὴς προέδραμεν τάχιον τοῦ Πέτρου καὶ ἦλθεν πρῶτος εἰς τὸ μνημεῖον. (John 20:4) ἔτρεχον, imperf.; προέδραμεν, 2nd aor. of προτρέχω, "I run before."

(4) Καὶ διὰ τοῦτο καὶ ἡμεῖς εὐχαριστοῦμεν τῷ θεῷ ἀδιαλείπτως, ὅτι παραλαβόντες λόγον ἀκοῆς παρ' ἡμῶν τοῦ θεοῦ ἐδέξασθε οὐ λόγον ἀνθρώπων ἀλλὰ καθώς ἐστιν ἀληθῶς λόγον θεοῦ, ὃς καὶ ἐνεργεῖται ἐν ὑμῖν τοῖς πιστεύουσιν. (1 Thess. 2:13) παραλαβόντες, 2nd aor. partic. of παραλαμβάνω; ἐδέξασθε, 1st aor. of δέχομαι.

Note to Students—The Lesson on "Some Additional Rules of Syntax" may be taken next, the intervening Lessons being postponed.

▪ LESSON 28 ▪

Prepositions (Part 1)

The special significance of the cases in nouns, etc., was pointed out in Lesson 2. The relations broadly stated there, and a variety of others, are expressed also by means of prepositions. Thus, while the accusative itself chiefly signifies motion towards, this relation may be expressed by such a preposition as πρός, with the accusative of the following noun. Again, one of the meanings of the genitive case is motion from, and this is likewise conveyed by ἀπό, with that case of the following noun. The dative may signify rest in a place, or the instrument of an action, etc., and each of these is expressed, e.g., by ἐν with the dative of the noun; a useful example of ἐν in this way is ἐν μαχαίρᾳ, with a sword (Luke 22:49).

Sometimes the use of the preposition is merely emphatic. The case of the noun alone would have expressed the same meaning, but with less force. In most instances, however, the preposition denotes a relation which the noun itself would be insufficient to indicate.

Some prepositions govern one case only; others govern two cases with different meanings; a few are used with three cases, the meanings differing in each case.

Again, the same preposition may have a considerable variety of meanings, and the actual sense must be gathered largely from the context.

Certain prepositions are closely allied in some of their meanings. They express much the same relationship but from different points of view. In English, for instance, we use the prepositions "by" and "through" to signify the same transaction, yet there is a real distinction. We say that something is done by a person, or through him. These prepositions are not, however, synonymous or interchangeable, and in Greek it is specially necessary to observe the distinction.

It is important for the student to become thoroughly acquainted with all the prepositions. The list should be committed to memory.

(*a*) Prepositions Governing One Case Only

(1) *Those used with the accusative only*

ἀνά and εἰς

ἀνά, up. This is frequently compounded with verbs. Separately with a noun it has a special meaning, as ἀνὰ μέσον, in the midst of (Mark 7:31; Rev. 7:17); ἀνὰ μέρος, by turn (1 Cor. 14:27); with numerals, ἀνὰ δύο, two by two (Luke 10:1); with measures, signifying "apiece," ἀνὰ δηνάριον, a denarius, apiece (Matt. 20:9,10); ἀνὰ μετρητάς, measures apiece (John 2:6); in Rev. 21:21 ἀνὰ εἷς ἕκαστος is each one separately.

εἰς, to, unto, into, towards. This is used (*a*) of place, and the proper meaning is to be gathered from the context; (*b*) of persons, "towards" or "with reference to," as in Rom. 12:16; Acts 2:25, or "over against," as in Luke 12:10; εἰς Χριστόν is "unto Christ" (Rom. 6:3); (*c*) "of purpose," "with a view to," "in order to," "for"; εἰς τὸ σταυρωθῆναι, lit. "unto the to-be-crucified," i.e., "in order to be crucified" (Matt. 26:2); cp. 1 Cor. 11:24; (*d*) to express equivalence (Rom. 4:3); (*e*) with the meaning of ἐν, e.g., εἰς τὸν ἀγρόν in the field (Mark 13:16), cp. Acts 8:40: 21:13.

(2) *Those used with the genitive only*

ἀντί, ἀπό, ἐκ, πρό

ἀντί, over against, instead of, for; the idea is that of an equivalent, often with the sense of opposition. Note the phrase ἀνθ' ὧν, lit. "in return for which things," i.e., "because," Luke 1:20; 12:3; 19:44; 2 Thess. 2:10.

ἀπό, from (from the exterior); sometimes this is equivalent to "on account of," as in Matt. 18:7.

Note the phrases with adverbs ἀπὸ τότε, from then (Matt. 4:17); ἀπ' ἄρτι, henceforth, (Matt. 23:39); ἀπὸ τοῦ νῦν, from now (Luke 1:48, etc.), and others.

ἐκ or ἐξ, from (the interior); this is used of place, origin, source, cause. Note the use signifying belonging to a class, e.g., ὁ ὢν ἐκ τῆς ἀληθείας, he who is of the truth, cp. Rom. 2:8; 4:12-14; Gal. 3:9; also those referring to time, e.g., ἐκ τούτου, from this time (John 6:66); ἐξ ἐτῶν ὀκτώ, for eight years (Acts 9:33).

πρό, before, used of time or place, and in the phrase πρὸ πάντων, before all things, of superiority.

(3) *Those used with the dative only*

ἐν and σύν

ἐν, in, used of time or place. Like ἐκ, this may be used to denote "on," as in ἐν τῷ θρόνῳ μου (Rev. 3:21); cp. Heb. 1:3. It signifies "among" in Matt. 2:6; Acts 2:29; 1 Pet. 5:1-2, and with numbers, e.g., ἐν δέκα χιλιάσιν, among ten thousands.

It is also used to denote *accompaniment*, or even *instrument*, 1 Tim. 1:18; Heb. 9:25; Eph. 6:2; Luke 22:49; Matt. 5:34: 9:34.

Note its use with a noun adverbially, e.g., ἐν τάχει, speedily (Rev. 1:1).

Also its use with the infinitive as a noun, where it signifies "while." Thus in Matt. 13:4, ἐν τῷ σπείρειν αὐτόν, lit., "in the him to sow," i.e., "while he was sowing" (an acc. with the infin., both with the article, and all governed by the preposition). With relative pronouns it denotes "while" see ἐν ᾧ, in Mark 2:19; so ἐν οἷς in Luke 12:1 is "while."

σύν, together with. Occasionally this denotes "besides." Thus in Luke 24:21, ἀλλά γε καὶ (lit. "but indeed also," i.e., "moreover") σὺν πᾶσιν τούτοις, beside all this (lit. "these things").

Exercise

Translate and retranslate:—

(1) καὶ αὐτὸ τοῦτο δὲ σπουδὴν πᾶσαν παρεισενέγκαντες ἐπιχορηγήσατε ἐν τῇ πίστει ὑμῶν τὴν ἀρετήν, ἐν δὲ τῇ ἀρετῇ τὴν γνῶσιν, 6 ἐν δὲ τῇ γνώσει τὴν ἐγκράτειαν, ἐν δὲ τῇ ἐγκρατείᾳ τὴν ὑπομονήν, ἐν δὲ τῇ ὑπομονῇ τὴν εὐσέβειαν, 7 ἐν δὲ τῇ εὐσεβείᾳ τὴν φιλαδελφίαν, ἐν δὲ τῇ φιλαδελφίᾳ τὴν ἀγάπην. 8 ταῦτα γὰρ ὑμῖν ὑπάρχοντα καὶ πλεονάζοντα οὐκ ἀργοὺς οὐδὲ ἀκάρπους καθίστησιν εἰς τὴν τοῦ κυρίου ἡμῶν Ἰησοῦ Χριστοῦ ἐπίγνωσιν. (2 Pet. 1:5-8) αὐτὸ τοῦτο, this phrase, lit., "itself this," is an adverbial accusative and must be translated "for this very (cause)"; παρεισενέγκαντες, nom., plur., 1st aor. partic. of παρεισφέρω (see φέρω in list of irregular verbs, Lesson 24); καθίστησιν, note this 3rd pers. sing. after the neut. plur. subject ταῦτα.

(2) Εὐλογητὸς ὁ θεὸς καὶ πατὴρ τοῦ κυρίου ἡμῶν Ἰησοῦ Χριστοῦ, ὁ εὐλογήσας ἡμᾶς ἐν πάσῃ εὐλογίᾳ πνευματικῇ ἐν τοῖς ἐπουρανίοις ἐν Χριστῷ, 4 καθὼς ἐξελέξατο ἡμᾶς ἐν αὐτῷ

πρὸ καταβολῆς κόσμου εἶναι ἡμᾶς ἁγίους καὶ ἀμώμους κατενώπιον αὐτοῦ ἐν ἀγάπῃ, 5 προορίσας ἡμᾶς εἰς υἱοθεσίαν διὰ Ἰησοῦ Χριστοῦ εἰς αὐτόν, κατὰ τὴν εὐδοκίαν τοῦ θελήματος αὐτοῦ, 6 εἰς ἔπαινον δόξης τῆς χάριτος αὐτοῦ ἧς ἐχαρίτωσεν ἡμᾶς ἐν τῷ ἠγαπημένῳ. 7 ἐν ᾧ ἔχομεν τὴν ἀπολύτρωσιν διὰ τοῦ αἵματος αὐτοῦ, τὴν ἄφεσιν τῶν παραπτωμάτων, κατὰ τὸ πλοῦτος τῆς χάριτος αὐτοῦ 8 ἧς ἐπερίσσευσεν εἰς ἡμᾶς, ἐν πάσῃ σοφίᾳ καὶ φρονήσει. (Eph. 1:3-8) ἐξελέξατο 1st aor. mid. ἐκλέγω; ἧς in verse 6 is an example of attraction from the acc., as the object of following verb, to the genitive of the word but one, χάριτος; we must not translate "of which" but by "which"; "freely-bestowed" is one word.

▪ LESSON 29 ▪

Prepositions (Part 1)

Prepositions Used With the Accusative and Genitive Cases

διά, κατά, μετά, περί, ὑπέρ, ὑπό

διά with the accusative means "on account of," "because of."

διά with the genitive has three chief meanings:—

(1) of *place,* signifying "through" (John 4:4; 1 Cor. 13:12).

(2) of *instrument,* signifying "by means of," "through" (2 Thess. 2: 2).

(3) of *time,* signifying (*a*) "during" (Heb. 2:15; διὰ νυκτός is "by night" (i.e., during, without reference to a particular time), Acts 5:19; (*b*) "after" (Matt. 26:61).

κατά with the accusative means:—

(1) of *place,* either (*a*) "throughout" (Luke 8:39), or (*b*) "before" (Luke 2:31), or distributively, e.g., διώδευεν ("He was journeying"—impf. of διοδεύω) κατὰ πόλιν, from city to city (Luke 8:1).

(2) of *time,* (*a*) "in" or "at" (Matt. 1:20), (*b*) distributively, κατ' ἔτος, year by year (Luke 2:41), καθ' ἡμέραν, daily (Matt. 26:55); καθ' εἷς (or καθεἷς), one by one (John 8:9).

(3) of *comparison,* "according to." Note κατὰ πίστιν, according to faith (Heb. 11:13); also the idioms κατ' ἰδίαν, alone (Matt. 14:13), καθ' ἑαυτόν, by himself (Acts 28:16).

κατά with the genitive means either (*a*) "down" (Matt. 8:32) or (*b*) "against" (Mark 11:25) or (*c*) "throughout" (Luke 4:14).

μετά with the accusative means "after" (Matt. 26:2); in Luke 22:20, μετὰ τὸ δειπνῆσαι is "after supper" (the verb in the aor. infin. being equivalent to a noun).

μετά with the genitive means "with" (Matt. 1:23).

περί with the accusative means (1) of *place,* "around" (Matt. 8:18); (2) of *time,* "about" (Matt. 20: 3); (3) of *an object of thought,* "about" (Luke 10: 40) or "with reference to" (1 Tim. 1:19).

περί with the genitive means "about" or "concerning" (Acts 8:12), sometimes almost like ὑπέρ, for (Rom. 8:3; 1 Thess. 5:25).

ὑπέρ with the accusative means "above" and is used in comparison (Matt. 10:24); note the use after a comparative adjective for the sake of emphasis where the meaning is "than" (Luke 16: 8; Heb. 4:12).

ὑπέρ with the genitive means "on behalf of," "for" (1 Cor. 15:3; 2 Cor. 5:14-15).

ὑπό with the accusative means "under" (Matt. 5:15); note the phrase in Acts 5:21, ὑπὸ τὸν ὄρθρον, under (i.e., close upon) the dawn, i.e., very early in the morning.

ὑπό with the genitive means "by" (Matt. 4:1).

Prepositions Used With the Accusative, Genitive and Dative

ἐπί, παρά, πρός

ἐπί with the accusative has the following meanings:—

(1) of *place,* "upon," with the idea of motion (Matt. 5:15); note the use after the verb "to

hope" (1 Tim. 5:5, and ch. 4:10, where the preposition is used with the dative, "upon" of rest rather than motion—see below).

(2) of *authority,* "over" (Luke 1:33).

(3) of *intention,* "for" or "against" (Matt. 3:7: 26:55).

(4) of *direction,* "towards," "with regard to" (Luke 6:35; Mark 9:12).

(5) of *quantity,* "up to," e.g., ἐπὶ πλεῖον, to a further point, i.e., any further (Acts 4:17). Note the phrase ἐφ' ὅσον, inasmuch as, also used of time, "as long as" (Matt. 9:15).

(6) of *time,* "during," "for" (Luke 10:35; 18:4). Note the phrase ἐπὶ τὸ αὐτό, at the same place, or at the same time, i.e., together (Luke 17:35; Acts 2:1, etc.).

ἐπί with the genitive has the following meanings:—

(1) of *place,* "upon" (Matt. 6:10) so figuratively (John 6:2); or "before" (1 Tim. 5:19), or "on the basis of," e.g., ἐπ' ἀληθείας, in truth (Mark 12:14); cp. 2 Cor. 13:1.

(2) of *authority,* "over" (Acts 6:3).

(3) of *time,* "in the time of" (Luke 3:2; Rom. 1:10; Heb. 1, 2).

ἐπί with the dative has the following meanings:—

(1) of *place,* "upon," with rest implied (Luke 21:6).

(2) of *superintendence,* "over" (Luke 12:44).

(3) of *condition, ground, etc.,* "on" or "at" (Matt. 4:4; Mark 9:37; Acts 11:19). Note the phrase ἐφ' ᾧ, on condition that, wherefore, because (Rom. 5:1.2, etc.).

(4) of *quantity,* "beside," "in addition to" (Luke 3:20).

παρά with the accusative has the following meanings:—

(1) of *place,* "by," "near" (Matt. 13:4; Acts 10: 6).

(2) of *contradistinction,* "contrary to," "rather than" (Rom. 1:25-26: 4:18).

(3) of *comparison,* "above," "than" (Luke 13: 2; Heb. 9:23).

Note the phrase παρὰ τοῦτο, therefore, in 1 Cor. 12:15-16, where the idea is that of consequence through comparison.

παρά with the genitive means "from" (beside and proceeding from); it is used of persons (Matt. 2:4; John 16:27). Note the phrase οἱ παρ' αὐτοῦ, lit., "those from Him," i.e., "His friends."

παρά with the dative means "with," whether of *nearness,* as in John 14:17; 19:25; Acts 10:6; or of *estimation* or *ability,* as in Matt. 19:26; Rom. 2:13. Note the phrase παρ' ἑαυτοῖς, lit., "with yourselves," i.e., "in your own conceits."

πρός with the accusative has the following meanings:—

(1) of *direction,* "to" (1 Cor. 13:12): δεῦτε πρός με is "hither to me" (Matt. 11:28)

(2) of *company* with the thought of attitude towards, "with" (John 1:1; Matt. 13:56).

(3) of *mental direction,* either "towards" or "against" (Luke 23:12; Acts 6:1). Note the meaning "in regard to" in Heb. 1:7.

(4) of *estimation,* "in consideration of" (Matt. 19:8; Luke 12:47; Rom. 8:18).

(5) of *purpose,* "for," "in order to" (Matt. 6: 1; 1 Cor. 10:11).

πρός with the genitive occurs once only in New Testament in Acts 27:34, where the idea is "belonging to" or "for."

πρός with the dative means "near," "at," or "about" (Luke 19:37; John 20:12).

Exercise

Translate and retranslate:—

(1) οὐ γὰρ εἰς χειροποίητα εἰσῆλθεν ἅγια Χριστός, ἀντίτυπα τῶν ἀληθινῶν, ἀλλ' εἰς αὐτὸν τὸν οὐρανόν, νῦν ἐμφανισθῆναι τῷ προσώπῳ τοῦ θεοῦ ὑπὲρ ἡμῶν· 25 οὐδ' ἵνα πολλάκις προσφέρῃ ἑαυτόν, ὥσπερ ὁ ἀρχιερεὺς εἰσέρχεται εἰς τὰ ἅγια κατ' ἐνιαυτὸν ἐν αἵματι ἀλλοτρίῳ, 26 ἐπεὶ ἔδει αὐτὸν πολλάκις παθεῖν ἀπὸ καταβολῆς κόσμου· νυνὶ δὲ ἅπαξ ἐπὶ συντελείᾳ τῶν αἰώνων εἰς ἀθέτησιν [τῆς] ἁμαρτίας διὰ τῆς θυσίας αὐτοῦ πεφανέρωται. 27 καὶ καθ' ὅσον ἀπόκειται τοῖς ἀνθρώποις ἅπαξ ἀποθανεῖν, μετὰ δὲ τοῦτο κρίσις. (Heb. 9:24-27) Note κατ' ἐνιαυτὸν, "year by year" (verse 25); in verse 26 note the acc. with the infin. αὐτὸν . . . παθεῖν (from πάσχω), after the impersonal ἔδει, it was necessary Him to suffer; in verse 27 καθ' ὅσον is "according as" (lit., "according to how much").

(2) καὶ ἐπὶ τὴν αὔριον ἐκβαλὼν ἔδωκεν δύο δηνάρια τῷ πανδοχεῖ καὶ εἶπεν, Ἐπιμελήθητι αὐτοῦ, καὶ ὅ τι ἂν προσδαπανήσῃς ἐγὼ ἐν τῷ ἐπανέρχεσθαί με ἀποδώσω σοι. 36 τίς τούτων τῶν τριῶν πλησίον δοκεῖ σοι γεγονέναι τοῦ ἐμπεσόντος εἰς τοὺς λῃστάς; 37 ὁ δὲ εἶπεν, Ὁ ποιήσας τὸ ἔλεος μετ' αὐτοῦ. εἶπεν δὲ αὐτῷ ὁ Ἰησοῦς, Πορεύου καὶ σὺ ποίει ὁμοίως. (Luke 10:35-37) Note the acc. and infin. after ἐν τῷ . . ., lit., "in the me to come back," where the phrase "me to come back" is a noun clause agreeing with τῷ, the whole governed by ἐν; δοκεῖ σοι, does it seem to thee; ἐμπεσόντος, gen. of 2nd aor. partic. of ἐμπίπτω; μετ' αὐτοῦ, lit., "with him."

LESSON 30

Interrogative Particles and Numerals

(*a*) Sometimes εἰ, if, is used elliptically, i.e., without any preceding clause such as "Tell us" or "Say." Thus in Matt. 12:10 εἰ ἔξεστι is "is it lawful?" In Acts 19:2 εἰ . . . ἐλάβετε is "did ye receive" (for "tell me if ye received"). See also Acts 7:1: 21:37: 22:25.

(*b*) ἤ is occasionally used to introduce a question; in this case, too, a former clause is to be understood. See Rom. 3:29: 6:3: 7:1.

(*c*) ἆρα introduces a question in three places, Luke 18:8; Acts 8:30; Gal. 2:17. It is not to be translated. It is to be distinguished from ἄρα with the acute accent, which means "then" or "accordingly," as in Gal. 2:21.

Exercise on the Particles

Translate and retranslate:—

(1) καὶ ἀτενίσαντες εἰς αὐτὸν πάντες οἱ καθεζόμενοι ἐν τῷ συνεδρίῳ εἶδον τὸ πρόσωπον αὐτοῦ ὡσεὶ πρόσωπον ἀγγέλου. 1 Εἶπεν δὲ ὁ ἀρχιερεύς, Εἰ ταῦτα οὕτως ἔχει; (Acts 6:15–7:1) Εἰ is not to be translated; οὕτως ἔχει, is, lit., "have thus" (sing. verb after neut. plur. subject), i.e., "have these things thus," is "are these things so?"

(2) ἢ ἀγνοεῖτε ὅτι, ὅσοι ἐβαπτίσθημεν εἰς Χριστὸν Ἰησοῦν, εἰς τὸν θάνατον αὐτοῦ ἐβαπτίσθημεν; 4 συνετάφημεν οὖν αὐτῷ διὰ τοῦ βαπτίσματος εἰς τὸν θάνατον, ἵνα ὥσπερ ἠγέρθη Χριστὸς ἐκ νεκρῶν διὰ τῆς δόξης τοῦ πατρός, οὕτως καὶ ἡμεῖς ἐν καινότητι ζωῆς περιπατήσωμεν. (Rom. 6:3-4) ὅσοι followed by the 1st pers. plur. of the verb is "as many (of us) as were, etc.," i.e., "all we who were . . ."; συνετάφημεν, 1st pers. plur., 2nd aor. indic., passive of συνθάπτω (note the irregular formation and the regular augment after the preposition).

(3) Ἢ ἀγνοεῖτε, ἀδελφοί, γινώσκουσιν γὰρ νόμον λαλῶ, ὅτι ὁ νόμος κυριεύει τοῦ ἀνθρώπου ἐφ' ὅσον χρόνον ζῇ; (Rom. 7:1) γινώσκουσιν, dat., plur., masc., pres. partic. (not 3rd pers. plur., pres. indic.), lit., "to the (ones) knowing," i.e., "to them that know."

(4) εἰ δὲ ζητοῦντες δικαιωθῆναι ἐν Χριστῷ εὑρέθημεν καὶ αὐτοὶ ἁμαρτωλοί, ἆρα Χριστὸς ἁμαρτίας διάκονος; μὴ γένοιτο. (Gal. 2:17) εὑρέθημεν, 2nd aor. indic. pass.; in the sentence beginning with ἆρα, the verb ἐστί is understood. The verb "to be" is frequently omitted.

Numerals

The Cardinal Numerals

The numbers εἷς, one; δύο, two; τρεῖς, three, τέσσαρες, four, are declined as follows:—

	Masc.	*Fem.*	*Neut.*
Nom.	εἷς	μία	ἕν
Gen.	ἑνί	μιᾷ	ἑνί
Acc.	ἕνα	μίαν	ἕν

Nom., Gen., Acc., δύο; Dat., δυσί(ν).

Nom. and Acc., Masc. and Fem., τρεῖς, Neut., τρία.
Gen. in all three genders, τριῶν.
Dat. in all three genders, τρισί.
Nom. and Acc. Masc. and Fem., τέσσαρες, Neut., τέσσαρα.
Gen. in all three genders, τεσσάρων.
Dat. in all three genders, τέσσαρσι(ν).

Like εἷς are declined its negative compounds οὐδείς and μηδείς, no one.

The rest of the cardinal numerals in New Testament are to be found in the Lexicon.

The signs for numerals are not numbers but letters with an accent: 1 is α´; 2 is β´; the letters after θ´ go in tens: ι´ is 20; κ´ is 30; but this goes only to π´, 80; after this the letters go in hundreds: ρ´ is 100; χ´ is 600. Thus 666 is χξς´ (Rev. 13:18). ς´ is 6; ϙ´ is 90; ϡ´ is 900.

The Ordinal Numerals

For "first" the superlative πρῶτος is used. Succeeding numbers are formed from the stems of their cardinal numbers and are declined like adjectives of the first two declensions—in -ος, etc. Cardinal numbers are sometimes used instead of ordinals in reckoning the days of the week.

Distributive Numerals

These are formed either by repeating the number or by a preposition with the number. Thus, "two and two" is either δύο δύο (Mark 6:7) or ἀνὰ δύο (Luke 10:1). "One by one" is εἷς καθ' εἷς in Mark 14:19 and John 8:9.

LESSON 31

Some Additional Rules of Syntax

Several rules of Syntax have been noted in the exercises. A few of the most important are given here.

(*a*) Negative Questions

(1) When οὐ is used in a negative question an affirmative reply is expected. See, e.g., 1 Cor. 9:1.

(2) When μή is used a negative answer is expected, but the μή is not to be translated. Thus μὴ ἀδικία παρὰ τῷ θεῷ, Is there unrighteousness with God? (Rom. 9:14). The negative may be brought out in this way, "There is not unrighteousness with God, is there?" But that is not a translation.

(3) μήτι more strongly suggests a negative answer. See Matt. 7:16; 26:22, 25.

(*b*) Some Uses of the Subjunctive Mood

(1) In *exhortations* in the 1st person (the negative is always μή). Thus in John 19:24, μὴ σχίσωμεν, "let us not rend," the verb is 1st aor. subjunc. of σχίζω, and λάχωμεν, "let us cast lots," is the 2nd aor. subjunc. of λαγχάνω.

(2) In *prohibitions* the subjunctive aorist is used with μή, as an alternative to the imperative. See ἐνδύσησθε in Matt. 6:25, and note the imperative μεριμνᾶτε preceding.

(3) Similarly in *requests*. See εἰσενέγκῃς in Matt. 6:13, the 1st aor. subjunc. of εἰσφέρω.

(4) In *deliberative questions* or those expressing doubt. In 1 Cor. 11:22, εἴπω is 2nd aor. subjunc. of λέγω, and ἐπαινέσω is 1st aor. subjunc. of ἐπαινέω.

(5) *Strong denials* take the aorist subjunctive with the double negative οὐ μή. See Matt. 5:18-20; 24:2; 24:35; Luke 6:37; John 6:37; 8:51; 10:28; 13:8; Heb. 13:5; where ἀνῶ is 2nd aor. subjunc. of ἀνίημι.

Exercise

Translate and re-translate:—

(1) διόπερ εἰ βρῶμα σκανδαλίζει τὸν ἀδελφόν μου, οὐ μὴ φάγω κρέα εἰς τὸν αἰῶνα, ἵνα μὴ τὸν ἀδελφόν μου σκανδαλίσω. (1 Cor. 8:13)

(2) Τοῦτο γὰρ ὑμῖν λέγομεν ἐν λόγῳ κυρίου, ὅτι ἡμεῖς οἱ ζῶντες οἱ περιλειπόμενοι εἰς τὴν παρουσίαν τοῦ κυρίου οὐ μὴ φθάσωμεν τοὺς κοιμηθέντας. (1 Thess. 4:15) φθάσωμεν, 1st aor. subjunc. of φθάνω.

(3) ἄρα οὖν μὴ καθεύδωμεν ὡς οἱ λοιποί ἀλλὰ γρηγορῶμεν καὶ νήφωμεν. (1 Thess. 5:6)

(4) ἢ δοκεῖς ὅτι οὐ δύναμαι παρακαλέσαι τὸν πατέρα μου, καὶ παραστήσει μοι ἄρτι πλείω δώδεκα λεγιῶνας ἀγγέλων; 54 πῶς οὖν πληρωθῶσιν αἱ γραφαὶ ὅτι οὕτως δεῖ γενέσθαι; (Matt. 26:53, 54)

(*c*) The Optative Mood

(1) This expresses wishes. See, e.g., 1 Thess. 3:11-12, where all the optatives are 1st aorists. The negative is μή. See, e.g., Mark 11:14; φάγοι is 2nd aor. opt. of ἐσθίω.

(2) With ἄν there is a potential sense, expressing possibility; ἄν is never translatable. See, e.g., Acts 8:31.

Exercise

Translate and retranslate:—

(1) Πέτρος δὲ εἶπεν πρὸς αὐτόν, Τὸ ἀργύριόν σου σὺν σοὶ εἴη εἰς ἀπώλειαν ὅτι τὴν δωρεὰν τοῦ θεοῦ ἐνόμισας διὰ χρημάτων κτᾶσθαι. (Acts 8:20) εἴη εἰς ἀπώλειαν is "may it be unto destruction," i.e., "may it perish."

(2) Ὁ δὲ κύριος κατευθύναι ὑμῶν τὰς καρδίας εἰς τὴν ἀγάπην τοῦ θεοῦ καὶ εἰς τὴν ὑπομονὴν τοῦ Χριστοῦ. (2 Thess. 3:5)

(3) ὁ δὲ Παῦλος, Εὐξαίμην ἂν τῷ θεῷ καὶ ἐν ὀλίγῳ καὶ ἐν μεγάλῳ οὐ μόνον σὲ ἀλλὰ καὶ πάντας τοὺς ἀκούοντάς μου σήμερον γενέσθαι τοιούτους ὁποῖος καὶ ἐγώ εἰμι παρεκτὸς τῶν δεσμῶν τούτων. (Acts 26:29)

▪ LESSON 32 ▪

Rules of Syntax (*Continued*)

(*d*) Dependent Clauses

Note—Sentences containing dependent clauses consist of a principal clause containing the main subject and its predicate or verb, and one or more subordinate or dependent clauses. These latter may be formed in a variety of ways, as follows:—

(I) Object Clauses. Here the subordinate clause is itself the object of the verb in the principal clause. Thus in Matt. 9:28, Πιστεύετε ὅτι δύναμαι τοῦτο ποιῆσαι, the clause from ὅτι to ποιῆσαι is the object of Πιστεύετε.

(*a*) If the verb in the principal clause is in the past tense the verb in the dependent clause is usually in the present indicative (sometimes the optative), but must be translated in English by the past tense. Thus in John 11:13, ἐκεῖνοι δὲ ἔδοξαν ὅτι . . . λέγει is, lit, "but they thought that He is speaking." We must render by "that He was speaking." Cp. John 20:14; Mark 5:29.

(*b*) Sometimes ὅτι serves to introduce a *quotation:* it is not to be translated in that case. See, e.g., Matt. 7:23; Luke 8:49.

(*c*) *In indirect questions* the verb in the object clause. is found either in the indicative, or the subjunctive or the optative.

The indicative intimates that the object of inquiry concerns a matter of fact. See, e.g., Luke 23:6, ἐπηρώτησεν εἰ . . . ἐστιν, "he asked if he were..." (here also the verb in the dependent clause goes into the present tense); cp. Acts 10:18.

The subjunctive expresses future possibility. See, e.g., Matt. 6:25, and Luke 19:48, where ποιήσωσιν is 1st aor. subjunc.

The optative expresses the possibility of what may be thought to exist or to have existed. See, e.g., Luke 1:29; Acts 17:11; 17:27 (εὕροιεν is 2nd aor. opt.). See both indic. and opt. in Acts 21:33.

(II) Conditional Clauses. The dependent clause begins with "if." There are four kinds of supposition:—

(*a*) The supposition of a fact. Here the dependent or εἰ clause has the indicative. See, e.g., Matt. 4:3; Rom. 4:2.

(*b*) The supposition of a possibility, or uncertainty with the prospect of decision. Here ἐάν (i.e., εἰ ἄν) is used with the subjunctive (rarely εἰ). See, e.g., Matt. 17:20; John 3:3-5; 2 Tim. 2:5.

(*c*) The supposition of an uncertainty. Here the optative is used, and always with εἰ. See, e.g., 1 Pet. 3:14: Acts 24:19.

(*d*) The supposition of an unfulfilled condition. Here the indicative is used with εἰ in the dependent clause, and the main clause takes ἄν. Two tenses are chiefly used in this main clause, the imperfect and the aorist.

When the imperfect is used with ἄν, present time is indicated, e.g., "If this were so (which is not the case), something else would be taking place (but it is not so)." Thus in John 8:42, Εἰ ὁ θεὸς πατὴρ ὑμῶν ἦν ἠγαπᾶτε ἂν ἐμέ, If God were your Father (which is not the case), ye would love Me (but ye do not). Note the imperfect tense with ἄν. See, e.g., Luke 7:39; John 5:46; Heb. 4:8.

When the aorist is used with ἄν, past time is indicated, e.g., "If this had been so (which was not the case) something else would have occurred (but it did not)." Thus, in 1 Cor. 2:8, εἰ γὰρ ἔγνωσαν, οὐκ ἂν . . . ἐσταύρωσαν, For if they had known (which was not the case) they would not have crucified . . . (but they did so). See, e.g., John 14:28; Luke 12:39 (where ἀφῆκεν is 1st aor. of ἀφίημι). Sometimes the pluperfect is used with ἄν. See John 11:21; 14:7.

Exercise on Object and Conditional Clauses

Translate and re-translate:—

(1) εἷς δὲ ἐξ αὐτῶν, ἰδὼν ὅτι ἰάθη, ὑπέστρεψεν μετὰ φωνῆς μεγάλης δοξάζων τὸν θεόν. (Luke 17:15) ἰάθη, 1st aor. indic. pass. of ἰάομαι; ὑπέστρεψεν 1st aor. of ὑποστρέφω.

(2) ὁ δὲ Πιλᾶτος ἐθαύμασεν εἰ ἤδη τέθνηκεν καὶ προσκαλεσάμενος τὸν κεντυρίωνα ἐπηρώτησεν αὐτὸν εἰ πάλαι ἀπέθανεν. (Mark 15:44) τέθνηκεν, perf. of θνήσκω; προσκαλεσάμενος, 1st aor. partic. middle; ἀπέθανεν, 2nd aor. of ἀποθνήσκω.

(3) καὶ εἰ μὲν ἐκείνης ἐμνημόνευον ἀφ' ἧς ἐξέβησαν, εἶχον ἂν καιρὸν ἀνακάμψαι. (Heb. 11:15) ἐξέβησαν, 1st aor. of ἐκβαίνω (note the change of κ to ξ before the ε augment); εἶχον, imperf. of ἔχω; ἀνακάμψαι, 1st aor. infin. of ἀνακάμπτω.

(4) καὶ εἰ μὴ ἐκολόβωσεν κύριος τὰς ἡμέρας, οὐκ ἂν ἐσώθη πᾶσα σάρξ· ἀλλὰ διὰ τοὺς ἐκλεκτοὺς οὓς ἐξελέξατο ἐκολόβωσεν τὰς ἡμέρας. (Mark 13:20) ἐκολόβωσεν, 1st aor. of κολοβόω; ἐξελέξατο, 1st aor. mid. of ἐκλέγω.

(5) καὶ λέγετε, Εἰ ἤμεθα ἐν ταῖς ἡμέραις τῶν πατέρων ἡμῶν, οὐκ ἂν ἤμεθα αὐτῶν κοινωνοὶ ἐν τῷ αἵματι τῶν προφητῶν. (Matt. 23:30)

(III) Final Clauses or Clauses of Purpose. These are introduced either by ἵνα, to the end that (with stress on the result) or ὅπως (with stress on the method) or μή (signifying "lest" or "that . . . not"). See also Lesson 13.

(*a*) The verb in the dependent clause is usually in the subjunctive. See, e.g., Matt. 2:8: 6:16; Luke 6:34. The negative is always μή. See, e.g., Matt. 18:10; Heb. 12:15,16. After verbs of fearing μή is rendered by "lest" or "that." See, e.g., 2 Cor. 12:20-21.

(*b*) Sometimes the future indicative is used, but never after ὅπως. Thus ἔσται in Heb. 3:12. Other tenses of the indicative are occasionally found.

Exercise on Final or Purpose Clauses

Translate and retranslate:—

(1) Τότε προσηνέχθησαν αὐτῷ παιδία ἵνα τὰς χεῖρας ἐπιθῇ αὐτοῖς καὶ προσεύξηται· οἱ δὲ μαθηταὶ ἐπετίμησαν αὐτοῖς. (Matt. 19:13) προσηνέχθησαν, 1st aor. pass. of προσφέρω; ἐπιθῇ, 2nd aor. subjunc. of ἐπιτίθημι; προσεύξηται, 1st aor. subjunc. of προσεύχομαι.

(2) Ταῦτα ἐλάλησεν Ἰησοῦς, καὶ ἐπάρας τοὺς ὀφθαλμοὺς αὐτοῦ εἰς τὸν οὐρανὸν εἶπεν, Πάτερ, ἐλήλυθεν ἡ ὥρα· δόξασόν σου τὸν υἱόν, ἵνα ὁ υἱὸς δοξάσῃ σέ, 2 καθὼς ἔδωκας αὐτῷ ἐξουσίαν πάσης σαρκός, ἵνα πᾶν ὃ δέδωκας αὐτῷ δώσῃ αὐτοῖς ζωὴν αἰώνιον. 3 αὕτη δέ ἐστιν ἡ αἰώνιος ζωὴ ἵνα γινώσκωσιν σὲ τὸν μόνον ἀληθινὸν θεὸν καὶ ὃν ἀπέστειλας Ἰησοῦν Χριστόν. 4 ἐγώ σε ἐδόξασα ἐπὶ τῆς γῆς τὸ ἔργον τελειώσας ὃ δέδωκάς μοι ἵνα ποιήσω. (John 17:1-4) For ἐλήλυθεν see ἔρχομαι. In all cases after ἵνα here the 1st aor. subjunc. is used.

(3) Ταῦτα δέ, ἀδελφοί, μετεσχημάτισα εἰς ἐμαυτὸν καὶ Ἀπολλῶν δι' ὑμᾶς, ἵνα ἐν ἡμῖν μάθητε τὸ Μὴ ὑπὲρ ἃ γέγραπται, ἵνα μὴ εἷς ὑπὲρ τοῦ ἑνὸς φυσιοῦσθε κατὰ τοῦ ἑτέρου. (1 Cor. 4:6) While μάθητε is 2nd aor. subjunc. (of μανθάνω) yet φυσιοῦσθε is pres. indic.

▪ LESSON 33 ▪

SOME RULES OF SYNTAX (*Continued*)

(*e*) THE INFINITIVE MOOD

This mood partakes of the character of both verb and noun. Hence it may itself be a subject or an object of another verb, or may have a subject or an object. See Lesson 15.

(1) For an example of the infinitive as the subject of a verb see Rom. 7:18.

(2) For an example of the infinitive as an object see Phil. 2:6, where εἶναι is used as a noun with the article τό, both being the object of ἡγήσατο.

(3) *When the subject of the infinitive is expressed it is always in the accusative case.* The English rendering is usually by a clause beginning with "that." Thus, in Acts 14:19, νομίζοντες αὐτὸν τεθνηκέναι is, lit., "thinking him to have died," i.e., "thinking that he had died." In Luke 24:23, λέγουσιν αὐτὸν ζῆν is, lit., "who say Him to live," i.e., "who say that He is alive."

But when the subject of the infinitive is the same as that of the preceding verb it is not expressed, except for emphasis, and any words in agreement with it are put in the nominative. Thus in Rom. 15:24, ἐλπίζω γὰρ διαπορευόμενος θεάσασθαι ὑμᾶς, I hope passing through to see you, if the subject of θεάσασθαι were expressed it would be με, but the same person is the subject of both verbs, and hence it is omitted and the participle agreeing is in the nominative. Cp. Rom. 1:22.

(4) The infinitive may be in various cases. For the genitive see Luke 10:19, where τοῦ πατεῖν is, lit.,"(power) of treading," i.e., "power to tread." So in Acts 27:20, where ἡμᾶς is the acc. subject. In 2 Cor. 1:8, there is an example both of the acc. with the infin., and of the genit. of the infin. The genitive often expresses purpose (Matt. 2:13; 3:13; 21:32), or even result (Acts 7:19).

For the dative see 2 Cor. 2:13. Here τῷ . . . εὑρεῖν is dative of cause "through (my not) finding"; με is the acc. subject; Τίτον is the object.

(5) These cases of the infinitive often come after prepositions. See Matt. 13:5,6, where each διά governs all that follows. In Matt. 24:12, note that τὴν ἀνομίαν is the subject of the infin. Cp. Mark 5:4. In Matt. 13:25, the acc. with the infinitive is governed by ἐν; in 26:32, the article with the acc. and infin. are all governed by μετά. In Matt. 6:1, αὐτοῖς is "by them."

(6) ὥστε with the infin., or with the acc. and infin., expresses result. See Luke 9:52, and Matt. 24:13, 32; Acts 16:26.

(7) The infinitive is occasionally used as an imperative (Phil. 3:16, στοιχεῖν; Rom. 12:15).

(8) The negative with the infinitive may be either οὐ or μή; οὐ denies as a matter of fact; in all other cases and generally speaking μή is used. Note οὐδ' (not μηδ') in John 21:25: οἶμαι is "I suppose," but the οὐ intimates the certainty that the world would not contain, etc.

Exercise on the Infinitive

Translate and retranslate:—

(1) δέομαι δὲ τὸ μὴ παρὼν θαρρῆσαι τῇ πεποιθήσει ᾗ λογίζομαι τολμῆσαι ἐπί τινας τοὺς λογιζομένους ἡμᾶς ὡς κατὰ σάρκα περιπατοῦντας. (2 Cor. 10:2) τὸ μὴ . . . θαρρῆσαι, lit., "the not . . . to be bold" is the object of δέομαι; παρών, is nom. pres. partic. of πάρειμι.

(2) ἐν δὲ τῷ πορεύεσθαι ἐγένετο αὐτὸν ἐγγίζειν τῇ Δαμασκῷ, ἐξαίφνης τε αὐτὸν περιήστραψεν φῶς ἐκ τοῦ οὐρανοῦ 4 καὶ πεσὼν ἐπὶ τὴν γῆν ἤκουσεν φωνὴν λέγουσαν αὐτῷ, Σαοὺλ Σαούλ, τί με διώκεις; (Acts 9:3-4) ἐγένετο is "it came to pass" (see γίνομαι); this is followed by the acc. with the infin.; πεσὼν aor. partic. of πίπτω.

(3) Ἔλεγεν δὲ παραβολὴν αὐτοῖς πρὸς τὸ δεῖν πάντοτε προσεύχεσθαι αὐτοὺς καὶ μὴ ἐγκακεῖν. (Luke 18:1) πρὸς τὸ δεῖν, lit., "unto the to be necessary"; then follows the acc. with the infin., "them to pray," i.e., "that they ought always to pray."

(4) λέγει αὐτῷ Ναθαναήλ, Πόθεν με γινώσκεις; ἀπεκρίθη Ἰησοῦς καὶ εἶπεν αὐτῷ, Πρὸ τοῦ σε **Φίλιππον** φωνῆσαι ὄντα ὑπὸ τὴν συκῆν εἶδόν σε. (John 1:48) φωνῆσαι, 1st aor. infin. with **Φίλιππον** as subject and σε as object.

(5) νυνὶ δὲ καὶ τὸ ποιῆσαι ἐπιτελέσατε, ὅπως καθάπερ ἡ προθυμία τοῦ θέλειν, οὕτως καὶ τὸ ἐπιτελέσαι ἐκ τοῦ ἔχειν. (2 Cor. 8:11) ποιῆσαι, 1st aor. infin.; ἐκ τοῦ ἔχειν, lit., "out of the having."

(6) πάντα ὑπέταξας ὑποκάτω τῶν ποδῶν αὐτοῦ. ἐν τῷ γὰρ ὑποτάξαι [αὐτῷ] τὰ πάντα οὐδὲν ἀφῆκεν αὐτῷ ἀνυπότακτον. νῦν δὲ οὔπω ὁρῶμεν αὐτῷ τὰ πάντα ὑποτεταγμένα. . . . 15 καὶ ἀπαλλάξῃ τούτους, ὅσοι φόβῳ θανάτου διὰ παντὸς τοῦ ζῆν ἔνοχοι ἦσαν δουλείας. (Heb. 2:8, 15)

(*f*) Participles

These are verbal adjectives. Hence they agree with nouns expressed or understood.

(1) The present and perfect participles are often used with the verb "to be," making compound tense forms. See καιομένη ἦν, was burning, in Luke 24:32; also Gal. 4:24, "are allegorized." Literalism must not be pressed. Thus in Matt. 18:20, εἰσιν . . . συνηγμένοι is not "are having been gathered together," but "are gathered together." In Luke 3:23, ἦν . . . ἀρχόμενος is "was beginning (His ministry)," not "began to be (about thirty)."

(2) A participle may simply be an adjective as in τῇ ἐχομένῃ ἡμέρᾳ (Acts 21:26), on the next day, where the verb is a partic. middle of ἔχω. So in 1 Tim. 1:10, ὑφιαινούσῃ is "healthful," but is a present participle.

(3) The participle with the article is often equivalent to a noun: in 1 Thess. 1:10, τὸν ῥυόμενον ἡμᾶς, lit. "the (One) delivering us," is "Our Deliverer." In Mark 4:14, ὁ σπείρων is "the sower."

(4) The participle is frequently explanatory. Thus in Phil. 2:7, λαβών explains the sentence "He emptied Himself"; in verse 8 γενόμενος explains "He humbled Himself." In Rom. 12:9, etc., the participles show how the command in verse 8 is to be carried out. So in 1 Pet. 2:8, and in 3:1 and 7, the participles show the mode of the fulfillment of the commands in verse 17.

Exercise in Participles

Translate and retranslate:—

(1) Ἀλλὰ τότε μὲν οὐκ εἰδότες θεὸν ἐδουλεύσατε τοῖς φύσει μὴ οὖσιν θεοῖς· 9 νῦν δὲ γνόντες θεόν, μᾶλλον δὲ γνωσθέντες ὑπὸ θεοῦ, πῶς ἐπιστρέφετε πάλιν ἐπὶ τὰ ἀσθενῆ καὶ πτωχὰ στοιχεῖα οἷς πάλιν ἄνωθεν δουλεύειν θέλετε; (Gal. 4:8-9) εἰδότες (see οἶδα); οὖσιν, dat., plur., masc., pres. partic. of εἰμί, to (those) not being gods.

(2) οὐχὶ μένον σοὶ ἔμενεν καὶ πραθὲν ἐν τῇ σῇ ἐξουσίᾳ ὑπῆρχεν; τί ὅτι ἔθου ἐν τῇ καρδίᾳ σου τὸ πρᾶγμα τοῦτο; οὐκ ἐψεύσω ἀνθρώποις ἀλλὰ τῷ θεῷ. (Acts 5:4) μένον, nom., sing., neut., pres. partic. of μένω, lit., "remaining (did it not remain to thee)?"; πραθὲν, nom., sing., neut., 2nd aor. partic. pass. of πιπράσκω.

(3) ὑμεῖς γὰρ μιμηταὶ ἐγενήθητε, ἀδελφοί, τῶν ἐκκλησιῶν τοῦ θεοῦ τῶν οὐσῶν ἐν τῇ

Ἰουδαίᾳ ἐν Χριστῷ Ἰησοῦ, ὅτι τὰ αὐτὰ ἐπάθετε καὶ ὑμεῖς ὑπὸ τῶν ἰδίων συμφυλετῶν καθὼς καὶ αὐτοὶ ὑπὸ τῶν Ἰουδαίων, 15 τῶν καὶ τὸν κύριον ἀποκτεινάντων Ἰησοῦν καὶ τοὺς προφήτας καὶ ἡμᾶς ἐκδιωξάντων καὶ θεῷ μὴ ἀρεσκόντων καὶ πᾶσιν ἀνθρώποις ἐναντίων, 16 κωλυόντων ἡμᾶς τοῖς ἔθνεσιν λαλῆσαι ἵνα σωθῶσιν, εἰς τὸ ἀναπληρῶσαι αὐτῶν τὰς ἁμαρτίας πάντοτε. ἔφθασεν δὲ ἐπ' αὐτοὺς ἡ ὀργὴ εἰς τέλος. (1 Thess. 2:14-16) ἐπάθετε, 2nd aor. of πάσχω; ἔφθασεν, 1st aor. of φθάνω.

LESSON 34

Accents

(1) The accents were used originally to give the correct pitch or tone to a syllable. There are three—the acute (´), the grave (`), the circumflex (ˆ). The acute stands only on one of the last three syllables of a word, the circumflex only on one of the last two, the grave only on the last. An accent is marked only on vowels; in diphthongs on the second vowel, as in οὕτως, οὖν.The acute and the grave are put after the aspirate or breathing, whether the rough breathing (῾), as in ἕξω, or the soft breathing (᾿), as in ἔχω. The circumflex is put over the breathing, as in οὗτος.

(2) A word that has the acute on the last syllable, as in βασιλεύς, is called *oxytone* (sharp-toned). When the acute is on the last syllable but one (the penult), as in οὕτως, it is called *paroxytone.* When the acute is on the last but two (the ante-penult), as in ἄνθρωπος, it is called *proparoxytone.* The antepenult, if accented, always has the acute.

(3) If the last syllable of a word contains a long vowel, the acute accent must be on the last or last but one, the circumflex on the last only. If, therefore, the last syllable of a proparoxytone is lengthened by declension the accent is thrown forward, so that the word becomes paroxytone, e.g., ἄνθρωπος, but ἀνθρώπων.

(4) When the circumflex comes on the last syllable, as in αὐτοῦ, it is called *perispomenon:* when on the penult, as in οὗτος, it is called *properispomenon.* This pronoun provides an example of the fact that a penult has the circumflex when it is long by *nature,* when the last syllable is short by nature. Otherwise, it takes the acute, e.g., λόγος. A syllable is long by *nature* when it has a long vowel, e.g., τιμή, or a diphthong, e.g., κτείνω; it is long by *position* when it is followed by two consonants, e.g., ἵσταντες, or by one of the double consonants, ζ (δ and σ), ξ (κ and σ), ψ (π and σ), e.g., ἰσόψυχος.

(5) Final αι and οι are regarded as short in determining the accent, as in ἄνθρωποι, νῆποι, but as long in the optative; thus ποιήσοι (not ποίησοι).

(6) Genitives in εως and εων from nouns in -ις and -υς of the third declension have the acute on the antepenult, e.g., πόλεως (genitive of πόλις), but βασιλέως (gen. of βασιλεύς). So with all in -εύς.

(7) An oxytone changes its acute to a grave accent before other words in the sentence, e.g., θεὸς ἦν.

Contracted syllables

(8) A contracted syllable is accented if either of the original syllables had an accent. A contracted penult or antepenult is accented regularly. A contracted final syllable is circumflexed, e.g., τιμῶ, from τιμάω. But if the original word was oxytone the acute is retained, e.g., βεβώς, from βεβαώς. If neither of the original syllables had an accent the contracted form is accented without regard to the contraction. Thus τίμαε becomes τίμα.

Accents Regarding Enclitics and Proclitics

(9) An enclitic is a word which loses its accent and is pronounced as part of the preceding word. The following are enclitics:—(*a*) the indefinite pronoun τις in all its forms; (*b*) the personal pronouns μοῦ, μοί, μέ, σοῦ, σοί, σέ; (*c*) the pres. indic. of εἰμί (except the 2nd sing. εἶ);

(*d*) φημί, φησίν, φασίν; (*e*) the particles γε, τε, and the inseparable δε in ὅδε, etc.; (*f*) the indefinite adverbs ποτέ, που, περ, πω, πως.

If a word is proparoxytone it receives from the enclitic an acute on the last syllable as a second accent, e.g., ἄνθρωπός τις, and so if a word is properispomenon, e.g., δεῖξόν μοι.

(10) Enclitics lose their accent when the preceding word is (*a*) oxytone, e.g., αὐτόν τινας (Mark 12:13); (*b*) paroxytone, e.g., Ἰουδαίων τε (Acts 14:1); (*c*) perispomenon, e.g., ἀγαπῶν με (John 14:21).

(11) Enclitics retain their accent (*a*) if they begin or end a sentence, e.g., φησίν in John 18:29; (*b*) if they are dissyllables after a paroxytone (to avoid three successive unaccented syllables), e.g., λόγου ἐστίν (Jas. 1:23); (*c*) when the preceding syllable is elided, e.g., δι' ἐμοῦ, John 14:6; (*d*) if a dissyllable after a proclitic (see below), e.g., οὐκ εἰμί, John 3:28; (*e*) the personal pronouns μοῦ, μοί, etc., keep their accent after an accented preposition, e.g., περὶ ἐμοὺ, John 15:26 (except after πρός in πρός με, John 6:65).

(12) Ἐστί (ἐστίν) at the beginning of a sentence retains its accent, and after οὐκ, μή, εἰ, καί, ἀλλά and τοῦτο, or a paroxytone syllable, e.g., Ἰουδαίων ἐστίν (John 4:22), or in mild emphasis, e.g., νῦν ἐστίν (John 4:23). Again, ἔστι, denoting existence or possibility, retains its accent, e.g., ἅγιον ἔστιν (Acts 19:2).

(13) Some monosyllables have no accent, and are closely attached to the following word. They lose their accent in it. These are called *proclitics.* Such are the articles ὁ, ἡ, οἱ, αἱ, the prepositions εἰς, ἐξ (ἐκ), ἐν, the conjunctions εἰ and ὡς and the negative οὐ (οὐκ, οὐχ). But οὐ takes the acute when it stands alone, as οὔ, no! A proclitic followed by an enclitic is oxytoned, as οὔτις (which may be written as one word).

(14) Examples of change of words by accents: ἡ, the (fem.), ἤ, or, than, ἥ, who (fem.); τίς, who? τις, someone; οὐ, not, οὗ, where; ποῦ, where?, που, somewhere; αὐται, they (fem. plur.), αὗται, these (fem.).

▪ ENGLISH INDEX ▪

GREEK INDEX

NOTE.—*This list is limited to certain particles, prepositions, pronouns, adjectives, etc., and a few irregular verbs, all of frequent use and which receive special notice*

INDICES

Scripture Index

Subject Index

Greek Index